SUCCESSFUL STEP BY STEP DIY

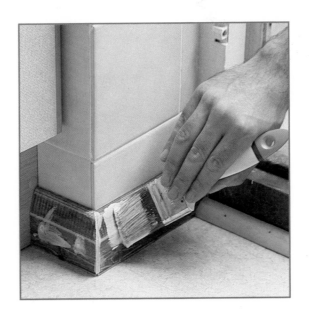

CLB 2654
This edition published 1993 by Colour Library Books Ltd.
Godalming, Surrey, England.
Copyright © Eaglemoss Publications Ltd 1993
All rights reserved.
0 86283 819 3
Printed in Portugal

SUCCESSFUL DIY
STEP BY STEP
DIY

Colour Library Books

CONTENTS

1 POWER TOOLS

2 DECORATING

3 BUILDING

4 CARPENTRY

5 STORAGE

6 PLUMBING

7 ELECTRICS

INTRODUCTION

Each chapter of Successful Step-by-Step DIY includes:

■ Guidance in basic skills you'll need to use again and again

■ Practical advice on buying materials

■ Information about the special tools you're likely to need

The first chapter gives advice on choosing **power tools** and accessories.

Decorating is full of practical guidance on the basics – painting and hanging wallpaper – as well as jobs like fixing tiles and laying floorcoverings. There are lots of tips on how to make light work of preparation, the key to a really good-looking finish.

Building tells you how to look after the structure of your home – from installing insulation and putting in double glazing, to repairing damp patches and dealing with rotten woodwork.

Carpentry begins by examining the different types of wood and man-made board which you can buy. It teaches you all the basic skills you need to give you confidence when tackling repair jobs on windows, doors and interior woodwork.

The chapter on **storage** is packed with suggestions on how to exploit wood's versatility as a material for shelves, fitted wardrobes and built-in cupboards.

Plumbing includes everything you need to know to deal with your home's water system, plus ideas on how to repair, modernize and improve your plumbing.

Electrics explains how your home's electrical system works – mains electricity is not something to tamper with unless you know exactly what you're doing. There are also clear instructions for plenty of jobs which the amateur can tackle safely.

1

POWER TOOLS

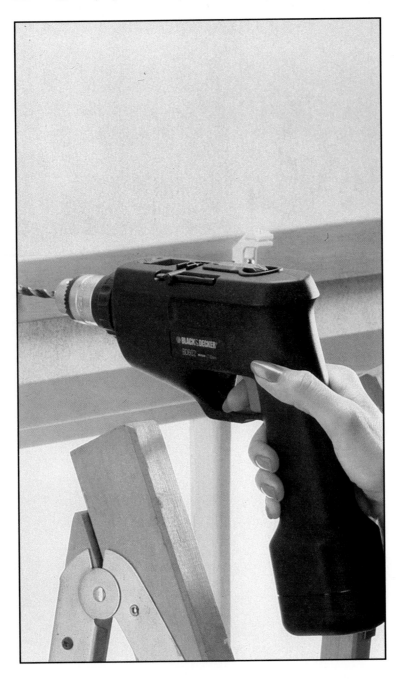

CHOOSING A POWER DRILL

Of all DIY tools, a power drill is probably the most essential – and certainly the most versatile. Modern drills have come a long way from the early low-powered, fixed-speed models, and can be used for all kinds of jobs.

Knowing what you want

Any drill will make small screw holes in wood or brick, but more powerful models are capable of drilling pipe-sized holes through solid masonry, or cutting large holes in metal. To be sure of getting the right drill at the right price, make sure you know:
■ What the manufacturer's technical specifications really mean.
■ Which features you need for the sort of jobs you plan to tackle.

You might also want to consider what accessories are available for your chosen make of drill, and which are likely to prove a good investment. Choosing accessories is covered on pages 13-18.

WHAT THE JARGON MEANS

The manufacturer's specifications commonly include a number of details about a drill's operating performance:

No load speed is the speed at which the drill runs on its own, when not drilling into anything or powering an attachment. It will run slower in use, depending on the job it is doing.

No load impact rate is the speed of the hammer action when a hammer drill runs on its own, without drilling into anything.

Torque is the turning force exerted by the drill. The higher the torque, the tougher the jobs it can tackle, and the less easily it will jam.

Drilling capacity is the maximum diameter of hole which can be

drilled. This varies according to the material, but should only matter if you need to drill large holes in masonry or metal.

Power input and output are the amount of power the drill draws in use without overheating, and the amount turned into useful work. Most manufacturers quote the input power of the drill but not the output power, which is usually much less. Generally, output is about 50% of input, but more expensive tools tend to have better input/output ratios.

Double insulated (or a ▣ symbol) means that all electrically live parts are protected and that the casing of the drill itself is made of an insulating material. No earth connection is needed at the plug, so the flex only has two wires.

ANATOMY OF A DRILL

Before buying a drill, think about what you are going to use it for. The drill shown here has all the features you are ever likely to need for DIY work, but not all of them are essential. If you aren't sure what features you want, cover the points below and you won't go far wrong.

Speed A two-speed drill is absolutely essential unless you are only going to do light work. The minimal extra cost is far outweighed by the increased versatility.

It's best if the speed is adjusted by a mechanical gearbox rather than electronically. A variable speed facility – controlled electronically or by an acceleration trigger – is a bonus but not essential.

Power A 500–600W motor will happily cope with the vast majority of DIY jobs. If you are in doubt, go for the drill with the most powerful motor you can afford.

Capacity A 13mm (½″) chuck is more versatile than a 10mm (⅜″) one unless you only ever intend to drill small holes.

Maximum hole size depends mainly on what you're drilling. For example, the largest bit that can be used for drilling mild steel is roughly the same size as the chuck jaws; in hard masonry around one and a half times its size; and in soft materials about twice the chuck size. Hole-drilling capacity is also affected by the drill's power output.

Comfort The most powerful, multi-feature drills can be very heavy and are much larger than simple models. If you need to work in tight corners, this can be a handicap.

Handle styles vary. It's best to try out a range of drills in the shop to see which sort of grip and balance feels comfortable.

Important features

Some features are important for virtually all DIY jobs including:

■ Hammer action, which comes as standard on most drills. Making holes in concrete is difficult, if not impossible, without it.

■ Removable chuck – essential for running many larger accessories (see pages 16-17), which are connected directly to the drill's spindle.

■ Low speed setting – essential for running a screwdriving attachment (see page 15); get a reversing model if you want to be able to remove screws too. A low speed setting is also useful for drilling into crumbly materials like plaster, for very hard masonry, and for making large holes in wood.

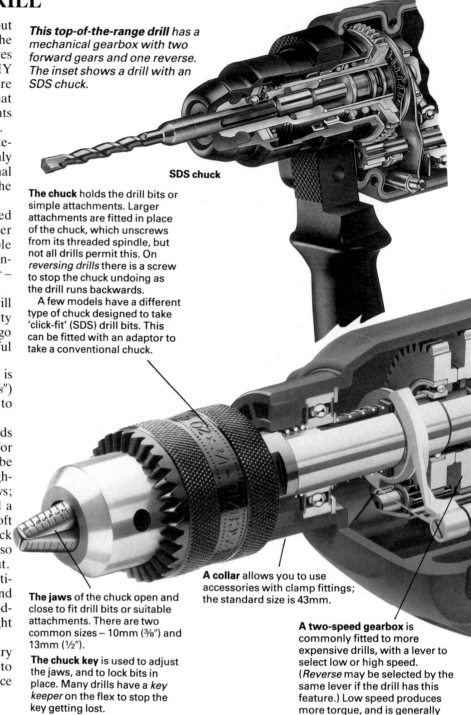

This top-of-the-range drill has a mechanical gearbox with two forward gears and one reverse. The inset shows a drill with an SDS chuck.

SDS chuck

The chuck holds the drill bits or simple attachments. Larger attachments are fitted in place of the chuck, which unscrews from its threaded spindle, but not all drills permit this. On *reversing drills* there is a screw to stop the chuck undoing as the drill runs backwards.

A few models have a different type of chuck designed to take 'click-fit' (SDS) drill bits. This can be fitted with an adaptor to take a conventional chuck.

The jaws of the chuck open and close to fit drill bits or suitable attachments. There are two common sizes – 10mm (⅜″) and 13mm (½″).

The chuck key is used to adjust the jaws, and to lock bits in place. Many drills have a *key keeper* on the flex to stop the key getting lost.

A collar allows you to use accessories with clamp fittings; the standard size is 43mm.

A two-speed gearbox is commonly fitted to more expensive drills, with a lever to select low or high speed. (*Reverse* may be selected by the same lever if the drill has this feature.) Low speed produces more torque, and is generally for materials which are hard to drill.

Trade tip

Better to hire?

  ❝ It really isn't worth buying a power tool or costly attachment that's only going to be used once or twice. Most hire shop ranges include all the popular tools (and they're usually heavy-duty models so they'll do the job better too!).

This could even apply to the drill itself; if you only have occasional need for a powerful drill, it may be better to buy a light duty model that's easy to handle, then hire a bigger one when you need it. ❞

Hammer action vibrates the chuck backwards and forwards as well as rotating it – especially useful for smashing particles of masonry, but only when used with special tungsten-carbide tipped bits. Don't use hammer on wood or metal.

There are different systems, including a 'pneumatic' type which cuts down vibration for the user.

Variable torque control is used when screwdriving. If the pre-selected torque is reached, the drill automatically shuts down to prevent overtightening. Anti-jamming devices are similar.

The motor is rated in watts (W). Motor sizes for domestic drills vary from around 350W to 700W. The higher the rating, the more powerful the drill.

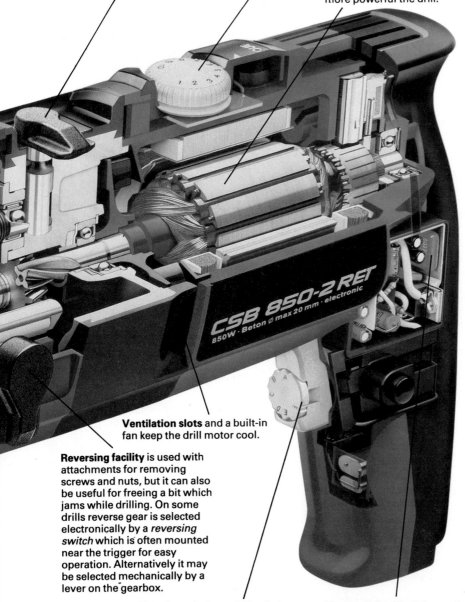

Ventilation slots and a built-in fan keep the drill motor cool.

Reversing facility is used with attachments for removing screws and nuts, but it can also be useful for freeing a bit which jams while drilling. On some drills reverse gear is selected electronically by a *reversing switch* which is often mounted near the trigger for easy operation. Alternatively it may be selected mechanically by a lever on the gearbox.

The trigger is the on/off switch. On variable speed drills it may be called an *acceleration trigger* because the drill speed is varied according to the amount of pressure applied. This is useful, since it allows you to start drilling slowly then accelerate up to full speed once the drill bit 'bites'.

Some models have an adjustable *speed selector* controlled by a wheel which limits the amount the trigger can be pulled in.

The trigger lock button is pressed in to hold the trigger down – avoiding the need to apply constant finger pressure.

Electronic feedback keeps the drill speed constant, even when the load on it increases.

The alternative to a two-speed gearbox is an **electronic speed selector** which gives you a choice of low or high speeds. It is not as useful, since it produces *less* torque at low speeds rather than more.

CORDLESS DRILLS

Cordless drills are designed for situations where it's difficult or impossible to plug into a mains supply. They don't give the same sort of performance as mains-powered models – the maximum speed may be as low as 400rpm, compared with the 2,000–3,000rpm of the conventional type – but they are perfectly adequate for drilling screw holes in wood and masonry, and excellent for low-speed jobs like screwdriving.

For drilling larger holes and working with materials like steel, where greater twisting force (torque) is needed, it's best to have a drill with two gears rather than electronic speed control.

Most cordless drills have a reverse action switch, and the more powerful ones have a hammer action. Because it is relatively easy to overload the motor, a protective cut-out may be fitted. The chuck size is generally not as big as the larger mains-powered models – 10mm (3/8") is normal.

Power is provided by a rechargeable battery pack which is usually built into the handle. A mains-fed charger is supplied with the drill to top up the batteries, and some battery packs are removable so that a spare can be used while the first one is being recharged. With other models, the whole drill has to be plugged in to the charger.

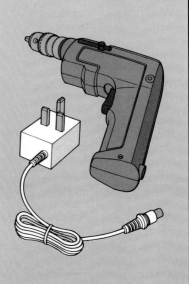

Most cordless drills come with a mains charger to recharge the built-in batteries.

DRILL SAFETY

General safety: electrical
■ Choose a double-insulated drill with a plastic non-conducting body.
■ Protect the flex from oil, abrasive sharp edges and heat, and keep it out of the way of the bit or attachment in use. Never lift a drill by the flex, and use a purpose-made extension lead if it is too short.
■ If possible, keep the drill in a stand or wall bracket rather than letting it lie on the floor or work-bench between use.
■ Have the drill serviced regularly.

General safety: physical
Keep small children away whenever you use a drill.
■ Check that the drill is not switched on before plugging it in. It's safest to unplug the drill before changing bits – and always remove the chuck key before plugging it back in.
■ Don't wear loose clothing, and tie back long hair.
■ Wear safety glasses and other protective clothing – especially when drilling masonry or hard materials.

When drilling walls:
■ Locate the position of electric cables and water pipes before you start – they should run in a straight line to the fittings they serve, but the safest way to trace them is with a metal detector.

When working outdoors:
■ Protect the drill and its leads from damp. A plug-in circuit breaker will safeguard against shocks.
■ It's better to wear rubber soled shoes when working outdoors.

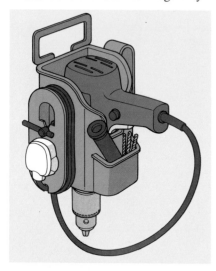

A drill tidy keeps a drill ready for instant action, and guards against accidental damage.

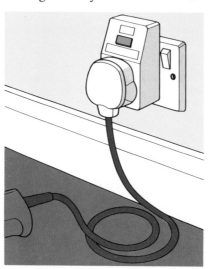

Fit an RCB (residual current device) to guard against shocks if the lead gets damaged.

Use a metal detector to check for hidden cables and water pipes before drilling a wall.

▌PROBLEM SOLVER▐

Avoiding breakdowns
The main cause of breakdowns is that the drill has been overstressed by using it on tougher materials than it was designed for. A light-duty DIY hammer drill, for instance, is fine for drilling screw holes in brick or masonry; but if you try to drill a large, deep hole in concrete with it, you could well burn out the motor.

If you think there is a risk of overheating the motor, stop at intervals to let the drill cool off. If you let it run for a short while with no load, the fan will help it to cool – but only if the ventilation slots on the drill's outer casing are free from oil and grime.

Use a slim screwdriver to clean out any accumulated bits that have blocked the ventilation slots – don't let any fall into the casing or it may damage the motor. Don't forget to unplug first.

Stop frequently when drilling tough materials, to give the drill a chance to cool down.

Clean out the ventilation slots at regular intervals to prevent the drill from overheating.

Servicing and repairs
Although spares for common models are sometimes available, it's inadvisable to repair a drill yourself unless you know what you are doing; you could make the drill dangerous, as well as invalidating any service warranty which may be in force.

Instead, get the drill serviced by the maker's agents. Most popular makes have regional service centres listed in their instruction leaflets. Otherwise, take the drill to a specialist shop which stocks that make.

Ask for an estimate before committing yourself; a faulty trigger action (a common reason for failure) is quite cheap to repair. If the motor has burnt out on an expensive drill, it is probably worth having it replaced, but on a simple drill the cost of replacement may not be much less than the price of a brand new one.

CHOOSING DRILL ACCESSORIES

Accessories extend the scope of the average power drill way beyond drilling, transforming it into an all-purpose tool with countless uses around the home.

The range, which is enormous, broadly divides into three groups:

Drill stands and guides make drilling easier or more accurate. They may be custom-built to suit a particular make, but many fit any drill.

Chuck-mounted accessories use the motor as a power source for jobs other than drilling. They have a spindle small enough to use with both 10mm (⅜″) and 13mm (½″) chucks, and fit most drills.

Drill-powered attachments convert the drill into some other type of power tool, which usually entails removing the chuck. They tend to be custom-made for a particular model.

Below and overleaf is a group-by-group accessory guide and the chart on page 18 summarizes their uses and points out any special details.

STANDS AND GUIDES

Controlling a power drill with complete precision takes more practice than many people imagine. Drill stands and guides are designed to hold or align the drill so that accurate work is virtually guaranteed.

Horizontal drill stands (also called *bench stands*) hold the drill on a workbench so that your hands are left free to work. Their main use is with wire brushes, polishing mops or grinding wheels. Some types clamp on the edge of a workbench and swivel through 90° for extra versatility.

Vertical drill stands, sometimes called *drill presses*, are useful if you do a lot of very accurate drilling (for instance in furniture making when drilling dowel joints). The drill is clamped in a sliding cage which moves up and down the stand when a hand lever is pulled; there should also be a depth stop allowing holes of the same depth to be drilled repeatedly. They may be custom-made or universal to fit any drill with a 43mm collar.

Drilling guides ensure that holes are drilled squarely or to a set depth. Many drills have a depth stop built in (usually as part of the side handle), but a drilling guide helps to keep the drill square on to the work face.

Guides are particularly useful for making holes in boards that are too big to fit under a vertical stand, and for drilling accurate holes into walls.

Clip-on spirit levels fit to any drill with a 43mm collar and help to ensure that the drill is lined up accurately when drilling vertically or horizontally.

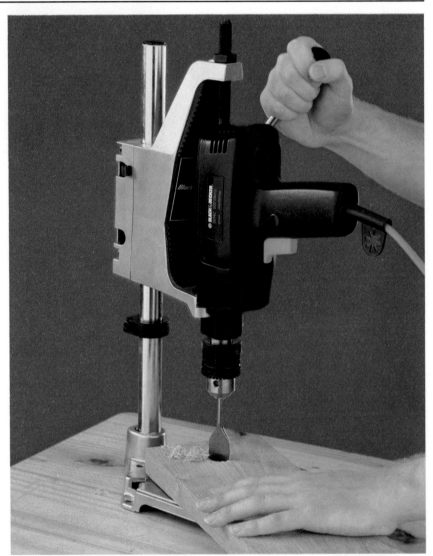

A vertical drill stand makes drilling more accurate.

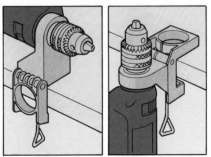

Some horizontal stands can be swivelled through 90°.

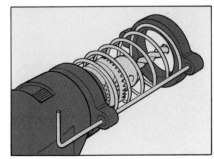

Drill guides keep the drill straight and level.

CHUCK-MOUNTED ACCESSORIES

Smaller drill accessories which fit in the chuck jaws are often excellent value, and make light work of laborious jobs such as sanding, rust-cleaning and polishing.

Accessories normally have a drive spindle small enough to fit both 10mm (⅜″) and 13mm (½″) chucks. If you need the larger chuck size for large drills and your existing chuck is removable, you should be able to buy a 13mm replacement.

Standard accessories can't be used with a click-fit SDS chuck, but a converter chuck is available for drills with this feature.

Trade tip

Neat 'n tidy

❝ Keep your drill, drill bits and other accessories neatly together in a **drill tidy** (see right). Made of impact-resistant plastic, most types have a built-in carrying handle, and some can be hung on the wall when not in use. ❞

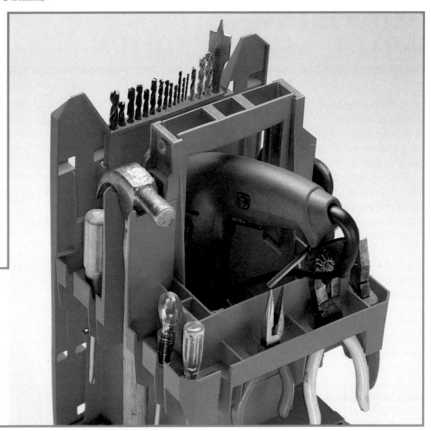

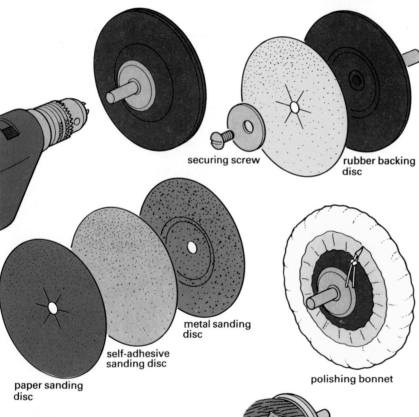

securing screw

rubber backing disc

metal sanding disc

self-adhesive sanding disc

paper sanding disc

polishing bonnet

flapwheel

drum sander

cup wire brush

disc wire brush

A rubber backing pad is used as the base for a number of useful accessories, the most common of which are paper or metal *sanding discs*. Some designs hold the discs with a central screw; others are for use with self-adhesive discs. Sanding discs are good for rough work, but tend to gouge the surface. A more sophisticated version that cuts down on gouging has the backing pad fitted with a universal joint. This allows the disc to remain flat on the work even if the drill is tilted.

Polishing bonnets slip over the backing pad.

Flapwheels are made from strips of abrasive paper (in a choice of grades) mounted on a shaft. They are very good at stripping paint and rust and won't clog in use.

Drum sanders aren't as fierce as disc sanders but are still quite coarse in action. They work best on flat or gently curved surfaces.

Wire brushes come in a variety of shapes and sizes to cover virtually any job. The two main types are *discs*, which brush at right angles to the drill shaft, and *cups*, which brush in line with it. Some discs have their own shank for fitting into the drill chuck; others must be mounted on an *arbor*.

Grinding wheels and stones can be used for sharpening tools or finishing metal. **Rotary rasps** are used for wood shaping.

A drill arbor is a multi-purpose shaft on which you can mount other accessories such as *grinding wheels, disc wire brushes* and *polishing mops*. These accessories are often used in conjunction with a *horizontal drill stand*.

Special cutters include: *Hole saws* for cutting large holes. Different types are used for wood or metal. *Tank cutters* are made for cutting metal only. Both these accessories need a drill with a low-speed setting. *Cone cutters* are used in thin wood or metal. The tapered cutting edge opens out a drilled hole to the size you want.

Screwdriver bits have hexagonal heads which fit in the chuck (the drill must have a low speed setting). They make fast work of jobs using a lot of screws, and with a reverse-action drill they allow you to remove screws too. Sets of bits containing flat, cross-head and Allen key patterns are available.

You can also get a *magnetic bit adaptor* which fits between the chuck and the screwdriver bit to make changing bits easier.

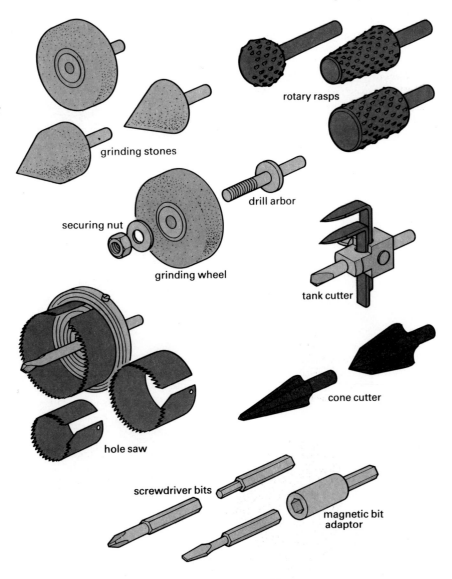

rotary rasps

grinding stones

securing nut

drill arbor

grinding wheel

tank cutter

cone cutter

hole saw

screwdriver bits

magnetic bit adaptor

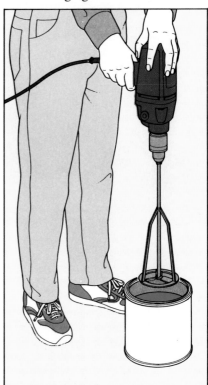

Mix paint or plaster with a powered stirrer.

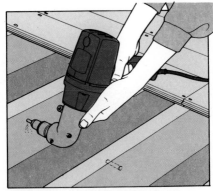

Drill holes at right-angles to the drill with an angle drive.

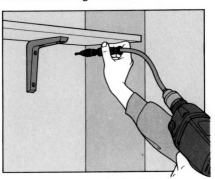

In tight spaces use a flexible drive shaft – but only for light drilling.

Paint stirrers/mixers provide a fast method of thoroughly mixing paint and the more robust versions will mix plaster or textured finish paints such as Artex.

Angle drives make it possible to drill holes at right angles to the drill – useful where room is tight. However, this accessory is expensive unless you anticipate doing a lot of work with it.

Flexible drive shafts allow you to extend the reach of a drill into even tighter spaces: one end fits into the drill chuck, while the other has a miniature chuck.

Flexible drives aren't designed for heavy drilling, but are good for powering small accessories such as polishers. When buying, check the maximum safe speed of the shaft – it may be less than the drill's.

DRILL-POWERED ATTACHMENTS

Think carefully before investing in one of the larger drill attachments. If you don't use power tools very often, they may be a good buy.

However, some attachments – notably power saws and orbital sanders – can, if abused, strain the drill beyond its design limits and shorten the life of the motor. Also, because they are designed as attachments, they are limited by the speed of the drill. This means they may not perform so well as the equivalent self-powered tool which runs at a higher speed.

 Safety wear

Safety equipment must be worn when drilling, grinding or sanding.

■ To protect your eyes wear *safety spectacles* or better still *goggles*.

 ■ A *dust mask* with replaceable cotton or foam *filters* protects against dust and/ or grit.

■ Heavy-duty *leather gloves* must be worn with accessories like saws or grinders.

■ Grinding metal produces a lot of sparks, so use a *full-face helmet*.

■ Wear *ear defenders* when working with noisy tools.

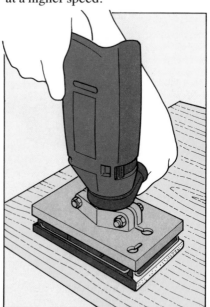

An orbital sander *gives a fine finish on large flat areas.*

Use a jigsaw *for freehand sawing and around curves.*

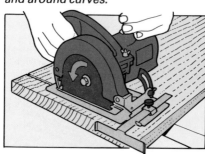

A circular saw *makes cutting lengths of timber easy.*

Jigsaws are driven from the drill by an adaptor fitted in place of the chuck. They are custom-made to fit particular models of drill.

Circular saws, like jigsaws, have a drive adaptor and are custom-made. Take great care when using one – wear protective gloves.

Orbital sanders have an operating speed much lower than the 10,000rpm of a self-powered sander, so they cannot be considered as effective.

Bench sander/grinders may be chuck- or adaptor-driven and clamp on to the side of the workbench. The sander is used for wood (see below), the grinder for metal. Wear eye protection when using one.

Milling machine/shapers are driven from the chuck. There is wide range of cutting bits available for making slots and grooves or matching up the profile of mouldings.

Dovetailers are driven from the chuck and make cutting dovetail joints very easy. The main frame clamps to the wood and the drill-mounted cutter slots into it.

Drill sharpeners are powered from the chuck. They are worth buying if you do a lot of drilling or use expensive, large diameter bits. You can also get chisel/plane sharpeners.

Drill-powered pumps are useful for emptying tanks or fishponds or for mopping up after an accidental flood.

Lathes are used to turn wood (right). Some are driven straight from the chuck while on other designs, the chuck is replaced by a drive adaptor.

Although lathe attachments are less efficient than proper self-powered lathes, they are much cheaper.

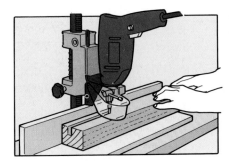

Cutting slots in wood with a milling machine.

A dovetailer helps to make drawer construction easy.

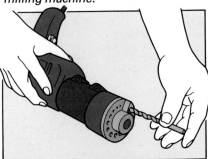

Drill sharpeners will even deal with masonry bits.

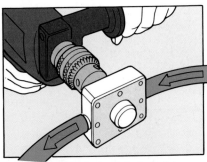

Pumping out large tanks is quick and easy with a drill pump.

FITTING ATTACHMENTS

Before fitting any attachment, check the hammer action is off and unplug the drill.
Chuck-mounted accessories Fit the spindle into the chuck jaws and lock with the chuck key. Check that the accessory runs true by hand-rotating the chuck.
Larger attachments Remove the chuck first, supporting the drill carefully. On non-reversing drills the chuck simply unscrews after jarring it with the key as shown; reversing drills have an extra locking screw which **must** be removed first.

Afterwards, fit the spindle adaptor and clamp the tool in place on the collar by tightening the clamping screws – this may require an Allen key.

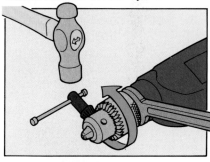

On an ordinary drill, lock the spindle with an open-ended spanner, then fit the chuck key and tap it sharply in an anticlockwise direction . . .

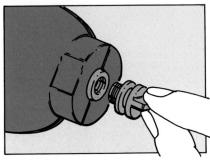

. . . then unscrew the chuck and replace it with the spindle adaptor nut. Slide the attachment on to the collar and tighten the clamping screws.

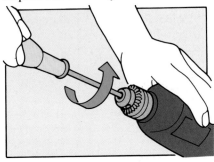

On reversing drills, the chuck is locked by an extra screw. Open the chuck jaws fully to get at it, then remove the chuck in the normal way.

17

WHAT TO USE A DRILL FOR

JOB	DRILL	BIT TYPE OR ATTACHMENT	DRILL SPEED	HAMMER ACTION	NOTES
DRILLING Small holes in wood (up to 10mm – ⅜")	Any drill	Twist drill or wood bit	1,800-2,000rpm	Off	
Large holes in wood (over 10mm – ⅜")	Any drill	Flat bit; hole saw for boards	600-1,500rpm	Off	
Small holes in metal (up to 10mm – ⅜")	Any drill	High-speed steel (HSS) twist drill	900-1,500rpm	Off	Lubricate with light oil to keep the drill bit cool
Large holes in metal (over 10mm – ⅜")	Any drill	High-speed steel (HSS) twist drill; hole saw	900-1,000rpm	Off	Lubricate with light oil to keep the drill or hole saw cool
Small holes in plaster or masonry (eg wallplugs)	Any drill with hammer action	Masonry drill	1,800rpm	On	
Medium holes in plaster and masonry (eg water pipes)	For soft materials, see above; for tough materials, see below	Masonry drill	1,400rpm	On	
Small/medium holes in concrete	Powerful (500W min) drill with 13mm (½") chuck and hammer action	Masonry drill	900-1,200rpm	On	
	Electro-pneumatic drill	Masonry drill	900-1,200rpm	On	Hire only
Large holes in masonry (eg drainpipes)	Heavy duty rotary percussion drill	Masonry drill or core drill	900-1,200rpm	On	Hire only
Driving screws	Drill with low-speed, acceleration trigger and reversing action	Screwdriving bits or attachment	Lowest speed on drill	Off	A magnetic bit holder is very useful
DECORATING Sanding small areas	Any drill	Sanding discs; flapwheels	Top speed on drill	Off	Sanding discs may gouge the surface
Sanding large areas	Most drills with removable chuck	Orbital sanding attachment	Top speed on drill	Off	Less efficient than an integral machine.
Stripping paint	Any drill	Sanding discs; flapwheels; wire brushes	Top speed on drill	Off	Care needed to avoid damaging the workpiece
Stirring paint	Any drill	Paint stirrer attachment	Top speed on drill	Off	Insert into paint before switching on
De-rusting metal	Any drill	Flapwheels; Wire brushes; sanding discs	Top speed on drill	Off	Wear goggles and dust mask
Grinding metal	Any drill	Grinding wheel	Top speed on drill	Off	Use with care – wear safety equipment
Polishing	Any drill	Polishing bonnet; polishing mop; polishing sponge	Low speed	Off	Avoid hard polishing – it's very easy to go right through the surface finish
WOODWORKING Sawing wood freehand	Drill must be compatible with attachment	Jigsaw attachment	Top speed on drill	Off	Less efficient than an integral tool
Sawing wood	Drill must be compatible with attachment	Circular saw attachment	Top speed on drill	Off	Less efficient than an integral tool

Other special-purpose woodworking attachments are relatively expensive and in most cases are custom-made to fit particular makes of drill. Instructions will vary from make to make.

WORKING WITH POWER TOOLS

An electric drill is an essential part of any DIY toolkit; it provides a versatile power source which can be fitted with a wide range of attachments. But this shouldn't rule out using integral power tools for more specialized tasks. Being designed for the job, they tend to be more powerful, more efficient and easier to handle than their drill attachment equivalents.

The main question to answer before buying an integral power tool is whether you can justify the cost (see panel below). If you are only likely to use it a couple of times a year, you may be better off buying an attachment – and then spending a bit more on a really good quality drill with a powerful motor.

Alternatively, most integral tools can be hired as and when they are needed. This has an advantage in that hire tools are invariably heavy duty models, so there should be no risk of overloading them on domestic jobs – unlike attachments.

ARE THEY WORTH BUYING?

Specialized integral tools make light work of many jobs, but before buying you need to weigh up whether the use they will get justifies their cost.

POWER SANDERS

Orbital sander – a good buy if you do a lot of woodwork or decorating. An attachment is adequate for light work, otherwise hire when needed.

Belt sander – only worth buying if you are a keen woodworker and will use it a lot, otherwise hire. There is no attachment that does exactly this job.

Power file – a fairly useful tool to have, but few will use it a lot. Not available for hire or as an attachment.

POWER SAWS

Jigsaw – worth buying if you expect to do a lot of woodwork, otherwise hire when you need it. Attachments can be used for light duties.

Sabre saw – worth buying if you cut up a lot of logs or heavy timbers, otherwise don't bother. Can be hired; there are no similar attachments.

Circular saw – worth buying if you expect to cut up a lot of heavy sheet material, otherwise hire when you need it. Attachments are often rather underpowered.

GENERAL PURPOSE TOOLS

Hot air stripper – a versatile tool and worth buying. No equivalent attachment.

Glue gun – not essential, but can be useful if you do a lot of repetitive glueing of almost any material. No equivalent attachment.

Electric screwdriver – not really worth the expense unless you do a lot of repetitive screwdriving. A low-speed reversing drill can be used instead.

Angle grinder – won't be needed often, so better to hire than buy.

WOODWORKING TOOLS

Power plane – only keen woodworkers will need one often, so better to hire. No equivalent attachment.

Router – for keen woodworkers only. There is no identical attachment, but there are plenty of gadgets for carrying out some of its functions.

SANDERS AND SAWS

POWER SANDERS

Orbital sanders

These work best on large flat areas and are better for finishing than for coarse work. They get their name because the abrasive paper is attached to a rubber sole plate which moves with an orbital motion.

Most accept a third of a standard abrasive sheet, although some take half sheets, which means a larger area is sanded in a given time. Check how the paper is changed; it's easier on some machines than others.

The more powerful the motor, the harder you will be able to use the tool. The orbiting speed of the sole plate is also important – faster speeds give a better finish. Most operate at 10,000 orbits per minute, although some are as low as 4,000 or as high as 25,000. Variable speed models are also available; slower speeds can be used with coarse abrasive for initial rough work, followed by faster sanding with finer abrasives.

Sanding produces a lot of fine dust, often simply blown out of an extraction port. Better models have a dust bag, or connections for a vacuum cleaner.

When using an orbital sander, don't press down too hard – let the weight of the tool do the work, or you may find you interfere with the orbital motion.

Disc sanders

These resemble sanding disc attachments, but rotate with an eccentric motion to avoid scouring a single spot. They can also be used for polishing.

Like orbital sanders, disc sanders produce a lot of fine dust. Dust bags are a common feature, and you may come across special discs with holes that allow the dust to be extracted through them. Disc sanders can also be used for polishing.

Belt sanders

Orbital and disc sanders are far from ideal for jobs like varnishing as they

circular saws

belt sander

orbital sanders

belt sander

disc sander

leave fine scratches which show through the finish. The alternative is to use a belt sander, following the grain of the wood.

Belt sanders have two rollers over which a special 'endless' belt of abrasive paper is fitted. One roller, usually the back, is driven by the motor, while the other is used to tension the belt. A flat rubber or steel plate then presses the belt flat against the workpiece.

Again, belt speed is important: the higher the speed, the better the finish. Likewise, the more powerful the motor, the more punishment it will take.

Like orbital sanders, belt sanders are really only suitable for flat surfaces. On the plus side they give a better finish, and remove waste material much more efficiently.

Against this, they are more difficult to use and generally more expensive. Running out of belts can also be a problem, so always have replacements to hand.

Power files

A power file is like a narrow belt sander – 6 or 13mm (¼ or ½") wide – for filing and shaping wood and other materials. The belt is carried on an arm in front of the tool, allowing you to work in confined spaces.

A variable control adjusts the belt speed to suit the job and material. As with a belt sander, you need to keep a supply of sanding belts to hand; different types are needed for different materials.

Accessories may include a cranked arm for work on curved surfaces. Dust bags are common.

POWER SAWS

Jigsaws

Although a jigsaw can be used for making straight cuts in wood up to 50mm (2″) thick, its main purpose is for making curved and short straight cuts in wood, metal or plastic laminates. It has a short, thin, replaceable blade that plunges up and down at the front of the tool. Most models also have a tilting sole plate that allows you to make bevel cuts of up to 45°.

The blade moves up and down at about 3000 times per minute, although two-speed and variable-speed models are available. Slower speeds are better for cutting plastics and metals. Variable-speed models allow you to tailor the speed of cutting to suit the job, and to start slowly for greater accuracy.

Useful features on some models include electronic feedback to maintain the cutting speed if the resistance of the workpiece varies; a blower to keep sawdust away from your cutting line; and a scrolling facility that permits the blade to be turned to follow sharp curves.

Many jigsaws also come with a side fence for making long, straight cuts, but this may not be strong enough to hold the blade steady. A better method is to clamp a straight length of wood to the workpiece so that the edge of the tool's sole plate can be held against it.

Sabre saws

The power tool equivalent of a panel saw, the sabre saw has a powerful motor and a coarse tooth blade that moves backwards and forwards. The blade may be as much as 300mm (1′) long and is suitable for rough cutting wood up to 150mm (6″) thick, or steel up to 12mm (½″) thick. Different blades are available for each material.

As well as a pistol-grip handle containing the on-off trigger, an extension of the body provides a second hand-hold for steadying the saw. In use, mark the cut on the workpiece, hold the blade just above it and operate the trigger. Then bring the blade into contact with the mark and allow the saw to cut its way through. Don't apply a lot of pressure, otherwise you may overload the motor.

Circular saws

Intended for long, straight cuts in wood, man-made boards, plastic laminates, thin metals, bricks, building blocks and ceramic tiles, the circular saw is a versatile tool, but needs handling with care.

Blades and cutting discs for different materials are made in 125, 150 and 184mm (5, 6 and 7½″) diameters. The larger the blade, the thicker the material that can be cut, and tools made to take large blades have more powerful motors than the smaller versions. (You can of course increase the cutting depths by sawing from both sides.) Blades must be fitted the correct way round, the direction is marked on them.

The blade should have a 360° guard, with a spring loaded lower half that swings out of the way as you begin a cut. Most types have a lever for retracting the guard if you want to begin a cut in the middle of the workpiece.

A side fence is normally part of a circular saw's standard equipment, but may not be strong or long enough. Overcome this either by fixing a long batten to the fence with woodscrews, or by clamping a batten to the workpiece so that the sole plate can be held against it.

jig saws

sabre saw

power file

Sanders and saws are more powerful than the equivalent drill attachments and easier to handle. A jigsaw and an orbital or disc sander are probably the most versatile for general DIY.

To use a circular saw safely, adjust the depth of cut so that the blade will just cut through the workpiece. Rest the soleplate on the edge of the work.

Switch on and allow to reach full speed before you move forward and begin cutting; the guard will be pushed clear. Don't force the saw forward – let it cut its own way.

Power saw safety

- Never wear loose-fitting clothing.
- Always unplug the tool to change saw blades.
- Keep hands clear of the blade at all times.
- Release the trigger lock after each cut and switch off at the plug if not making another immediately.
- Keep flex away from the blade.
- Keep away from children.
- Never use outdoors in the wet.

GENERAL PURPOSE TOOLS

HOT AIR GUNS

The main use of hot air guns is for stripping paint and varnish, where they are far less likely to char the wood than a blowtorch. However, they have many other uses too, including thawing frozen pipes, drying glue or damp surfaces, warming plastic pipes to allow them to be bent, and soft soldering.

Basically, the gun is like a powerful hair dryer, with heating elements and a fan. Most offer two temperature settings (usually around 300° and 550°C), although it is possible to buy a model that provides for variable temperature settings from 100 to 560°C.

Accessories include a range of nozzles that direct the blast of hot air away from anything which might be damaged by the extreme heat. One is fan shaped, for stripping thin mouldings and window frames. Another is designed for pipe soldering and heats around the joint.

Hot air gun safety
- Never place your hand in front of the nozzle in use.
- Unplug when not in use.
- Allow the gun to cool before putting away.
- Keep away from children.

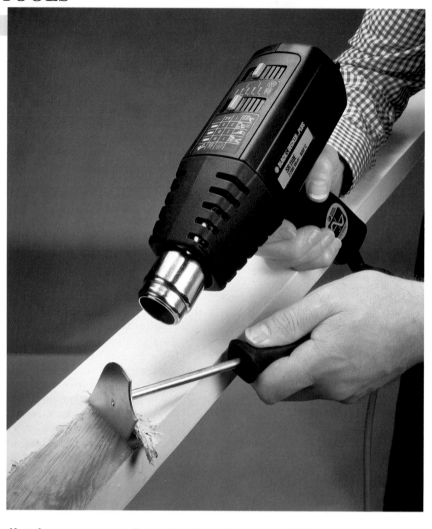

Hot air guns are versatile tools with a wide range of DIY uses, from stripping paint to soldering pipe joints. They come with several different nozzles, allowing them to be adapted to suit the job in hand.

Glue guns come with a range of glue sticks to suit different materials. These are fed in from the back, then melted and forced out of the nozzle as a rapidly drying glue.

Glue gun safety
- Rest the gun on scrap wood, cardboard or metal when heating up or when not in use.
- Never touch the hot glue.
- Unplug when finished and allow to cool before putting away.
- Keep away from children.

GLUE GUNS

Although sometimes considered a gimmick, a glue gun provides a convenient and effective method of sticking a wide range of materials, including wood, metal and plastic. Shaped like a pistol, the gun contains heating elements that melt a special glue stick fed in from the rear. With some guns, the glue stick is simply pushed in with your thumb, while the more sophisticated versions have a trigger control. The fine nozzle at the front allows the melted glue to be applied just where you want it, even in tight corners.

A major advantage of glue guns is that the glue sets very quickly: parts need only be held together for a short time, and hand pressure is usually enough to ensure a good bond. Some guns also offer a wall-plugging facility, using a special glue, so that holes of any size in brick or concrete can be plugged to accept screws – an ideal solution on old bricks.

ELECTRIC SCREWDRIVER

Cordless rechargeable screwdrivers are designed to save effort on repetitive screwing jobs, though it's questionable whether they are any more effective than conventional spiral ratchet screwdrivers (which cost far less), and they may be too bulky for use in tight corners.

Another drawback is that most models only come with a single screwdriver bit. Although this is double ended to take slotted or cross-head screws, it restricts the tool's uses by limiting you to screws of a certain size.

Most cordless screwdrivers come with a wall mounting bracket and trickle charger so that they are always ready for use. All feature forward and reverse action, allowing screws to be driven in and removed, and most have a spindle lock that allows final tightening by hand. Some models also have variable torque settings to adjust the turning force applied to the screw.

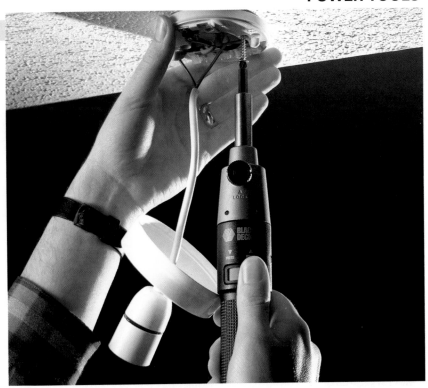

Electric screwdrivers have rechargeable batteries for cordless operation, but may be bulkier and more awkward than a conventional screwdriver.

Angle grinders are powerful, versatile grinding and cutting tools. DIY models are costly and less powerful than industrial versions so you may be better off hiring one when you need it.

⚠ Angle grinder safety
Angle grinders are among the most dangerous of all tools.
■ Never wear loose-fitting clothes.
■ Wear a full-face mask, heavy leather gloves and boots.
■ Always start the grinder and allow it to reach full speed before touching it to the work.
■ Always unplug to change discs.
■ Switch off after use, and unplug if not using again immediately.
■ Do not use outside in wet conditions.
■ Keep flex away from disc.
■ Keep away from children.

ANGLE GRINDERS

Angle grinders can be used to cut and grind all types of metal, to remove rust, and – when fitted with the correct type of disc – for cutting brick, stone and concrete. DIY angle grinders come with two basic sizes of grinding or cutting disc: 112mm (4″) and 225mm (9″). The larger size is better for heavy work.

Because of the work they do, the motor should be powerful; on a small machine it is commonly 600W, while on a larger one it may be as much as 1800W. Other points to look for are the ease with which the discs can be changed – some have a spindle lock to prevent the tool rotating while you do this – and whether the side handle position is adjustable. All types should have a guard around the disc which is spring loaded to prevent it contacting the disc.

In addition to being supplied with a cutting disc, the machine should have a rubber backing pad for sanding discs – much like that used with an electric drill. Usually, you have to remove the disc guard in order to use this.

When grinding, hold the machine with the disc at an angle of about 30° to the work for roughing, or 15° for finishing. Cuts can be made with the disc edge-on to the workpiece.

23

WOODWORKING TOOLS

POWER PLANES

A power plane takes the effort out of smoothing rough-sawn wood and sizing timber accurately. It has a rotating cutter which may turn at speeds of anywhere between 14,500 and 19,000 rpm.

The faster the speed, the smoother the finish is likely to be. The power of the motor is also important, since this affects the maximum depth of cut – which can range up to 3.5mm (⅛″).

Better power planes also provide chamfering and rebating facilities. The maximum depth of these is important; some may offer a rebate depth of as much as 22mm (⅞″).

When buying, check if spare blades are provided and see whether they can be changed easily. Check, too, how easy it is to adjust the depth of cut, and if the machine has a side fence as standard or as an optional extra.

Ideally, a power plane should

Power planes are capable of high-speed finishing and rebating.

have two handles so that you can guide it easily, plus a guard to protect the cutters when it is not in use. Some models are provided with a shavings collection bag – useful, as all types produce plenty of waste.

> ### ⚠ Planer safety
> ■ Never wear loose-fitting clothing.
> ■ Unplug when removing blades.
> ■ Release the trigger lock at the end of each cut, and switch off at the socket unless making another immediately.
> ■ Retract blade when not in use.
> ■ Keep away from children.

ROUTERS

Routers are simple tools, but have a wide range of uses in specialist woodworking, including cutting decorative chamfers and mouldings, and making rebates, grooves or traditional joints such as dovetails or box joints.

A router is basically an electric motor that slides up and down in guides attached to a baseplate. A specially shaped revolving cutter fitted to the motor spindle then carves out the desired shape as the machine is slid across the workpiece.

When buying, look for a high power motor and high spindle rpm, since the two combined will prevent the cutter from juddering and produce a cleaner cut. The machine should also be sturdily constructed, with a finely calibrated depth stop so that you can adjust the depth of cut accurately. And check how easily the cutters are changed – on some models it is quite tricky.

To use, begin by setting the cut and plunge depth, then rest the sole plate on the workpiece and switch on the motor. Press down until the cutter bites into the wood by the desired amount, and slide the machine along the cutting line. Then, when you reach the end of the cut, allow the motor to rise on its springs so that it clears the workpiece before switching off.

> ### ⚠ Router safety
> ■ Never wear loose fitting clothes.
> ■ Always unplug when changing cutters.
> ■ Switch off at the end of each cut, and switch off at the plug if not making another immediately.
> ■ Keep hands clear of the cutter.
> ■ Keep flex clear of the cutter.
> ■ Keep away from children.

Routers can be fitted with a wide range of cutters for creating grooves, rebates and mouldings.

2

DECORATING

TOOLS FOR PREPARATION

Preparing surfaces for decorating is a lot easier if you use the right tools, but there's no sense in buying more than you need.

A basic kit might consist of a stripping knife, filling knife, hot air stripper, pointing trowel, combination shavehook, sanding block and wire brush. But if your house contains a lot of mouldings, you'd be wise to add more scrapers. It's also worth 'doubling up' on some tools if two of you are working at the same time.

As a general rule, buy the best tools you can afford. Providing you look after them (ie clean them after every session), they work out cheaper than 'bargains' which don't last. Quality tools perform better too.

Hot air strippers (right) make light work of paint stripping.

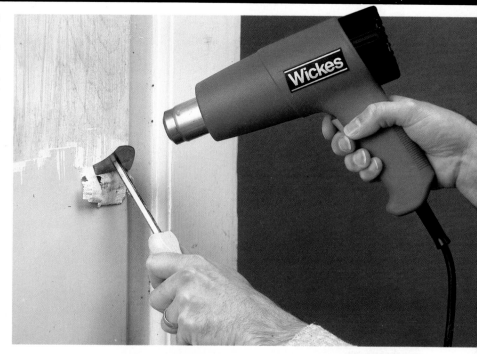

TOOLS FOR SCRAPING

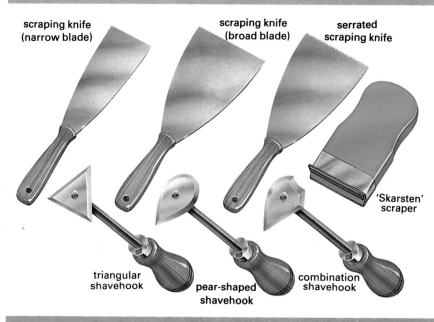

scraping knife (narrow blade)

scraping knife (broad blade)

serrated scraping knife

'Skarsten' scraper

triangular shavehook

pear-shaped shavehook

combination shavehook

Scraping knives are for scraping off wallpaper and large areas of paint. They resemble filling knives, but their broad steel blades are hardened so that they don't flex out of shape.
Serrated scraping knives have a toothed edge for piercing the surface of plastic-coated washable papers.
Shavehooks are for scraping paint or other finishes from frames, mouldings and similar awkward areas. Three head patterns are commonly available – *triangular*, *pear-shaped* and *combination*. A combination head is most useful, so long as you have a stripping knife for flat surfaces.
Hook ('Skarsten') scrapers are particularly good for removing thin surface coatings such as flaking varnish; the guarded blade reduces the risk of gouging the underlying surface.

TOOLS FOR FILLING

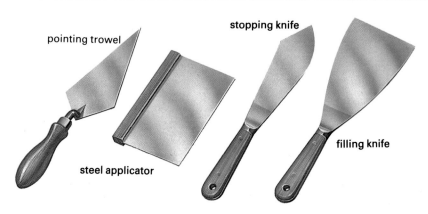

pointing trowel

stopping knife

steel applicator

filling knife

Filling knives look like stripping knives but have a thin, flexible blade. They are only useful as long as the blade remains clean and rust-free.
Stopping knives have shaped blades designed for applying putty and filler to intricately shaped mouldings.
Applicators have a broad flexible steel or plastic blade for 'feathering' layers of filler flush with surrounding surface. They are particularly useful for finishing joints in plasterboard.
A pointing trowel is invaluable for applying heavier fillers such as sand and cement mortar.

TOOLS FOR APPLYING HEAT

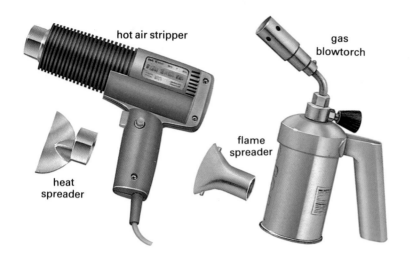

hot air stripper

gas blowtorch

flame spreader

heat spreader

Electric hot air strippers are among the handiest of all power tools. As well as stripping paint with only a minimal risk of scorching, they make light work of loosening vinyl tiles and old adhesives. Basic models have a simple heat on/off trigger; more sophisticated versions allow you to vary the air flow too, for greater control. Operating temperature is around 500°C – enough to melt solder.

Gas blowtorches are safer and more reliable than they used to be, and have the advantage of portability.

Both hot-air strippers and blowtorches generally come with fan-shaped nozzle attachments which concentrate the heat for dealing with awkward corners.

TOOLS FOR SANDING

cork sanding block

wire brush

abrasive block

disc sanding attachment

orbital sander

Sanding blocks are sold in wood, cork and resilient foam with an abrasive covering. Wood blocks have a screw-tightened slot for holding the paper. Cork blocks are cheaper, and can be more comfortable to hold. Abrasive blocks tend to clog, and can work out expensive on large jobs, though you can use them like plain blocks instead.

A wire brush is useful for cleaning masonry, or scratching a surface prior to repainting. Alternatively, use a *wire brush* drill attachment.

Disc sander drill attachments are cheap and versatile, but too harsh for sanding large surfaces – it's virtually impossible to get an even finish. *Flap wheel* attachments are gentler, and good for sanding mouldings.

Orbital sanders make light work of sanding large surfaces, and are one of the best power tool buys. You can also get orbital sander drill attachments.

ABRASIVES GUIDE		
TYPE OF ABRASIVE	**RANGE AVAILABLE**	**WHERE TO USE**
Sandpaper (glasspaper) Traditional type; glass particles bonded to paper backing. Red *garnet paper* is similar and lasts longer, but is more expensive.	Nine grades: 3, 2½, S2 (coarse); M2, F2 (medium); and 1½, 1, 0, 00 (fine). Garnet paper grades run from 2 (coarse) to 8/0 (very fine).	Wood, man-made boards, filler, light sanding or paintwork.
Aluminium oxide paper Generally green or black. Its high resilience makes it the preferred material for power sanding eqipment.	Grades (grit numbers) run from 3 (grit 24) which is coarse, to 9/0 (grit 320) which is very fine.	Wood, paintwork, filler, plaster, old decorated surfaces.
Silicon carbide (wet-and-dry) paper Resilient and washable. Gentler action than other types, especially when wet; finest grades are very fine.	Generally graded by grit No. Grit Nos 60-120 are fairly coarse, Nos 150-280 are medium to fine, and Nos 320-500 are fine to extra fine.	Paintwork, (wash to prevent clogging), varnish, bare woodwork, metal (use dry).
Steel wool Often overlooked as a sanding material. Comfortable and convenient for fine finishing.	Generally available in six grades: 2, 1 (coarse to medium); 0, 00 (medium to fine); and 000, 0000 (very fine).	Paint topcoats (prior to repainting), intermediate varnish coats, old polished surfaces.

PREPARING TO REDECORATE

Redecorating an entire room the way you want it is among the most rewarding of all DIY jobs. It's also one of the most cost-effective, because in this case time, not skill, is what you pay a professional for.

The following pages of this chapter take you step by step through every stage of redecorating a room, from removing old finishes and preparing the surfaces, to wallpapering and repainting. But in most rooms in need of a major overhaul, there are things which need doing long be-fore you pick up a scraper or paint-brush. And if you rush straight in, the chances are you'll get held up by problems you hadn't bargained for.

The answer is to treat decorating a room like any other major struc-tural project, working to a sequence and planning it through in advance.

Start at the beginning

The place to start planning for redecoration is not your local paint and paper store, but the room you're about to transform.

Before you go any further, carry out a thorough survey based on the plan overleaf so that you can antici-pate the kind of structural and cleaning problems that might other-wise disrupt work later.

Then work out your own rede-coration programme, balancing what needs to be done against your own time and resources.

Trade tip

Be prepared

6 Decorating a room fully can involve a huge array of tools and materials, as the picture shows. Some you'll have to buy, some you may have already, and some you can borrow or hire.

Start by making a checklist so that you get everything to hand before you start – this should save disasters like running out of brush cleaner when the shops are closed and all your brushes are covered in paint.

Also, think now about where you're going to store and clean your equipment, while still keeping everything readily to hand. Decorating can work out expensive if you have to keep replacing things that have been lost around the house. 9

Decorating even a small room calls for a surprising number of tools.
For preparation: Scrapers, stripping compounds, hot-air stripper, fillers, wood putty, filling knife, sandpaper and block, dust sheets.
For painting: Brushes, rollers and trays, brush cleaner.
For papering: Stepladder, shears, spirit level, pasting table.

WHAT ORDER TO DO THINGS IN

The following list highlights the major stages in a full redecoration programme. Use it to pick out the relevant points and plan your own programme.

1 Check for structural problems
- Carry out a thorough survey of room (see opposite).
- Make yourself a checklist of essential repairs.

2 Organize tools and materials
- Choose decorative options.
- Make checklist of materials and tools.
- Buy materials and buy or borrow tools.

3 Clear room and cover up
- Remove as much furniture as possible.
- Mask or remove fitted furniture and wall fittings (see *Surveying the room* opposite). Cover up floor.

4 Preliminary clean
- Remove strip foam insulation from windows/doors.
- Clean condensation mould off windows.
- Vacuum clean all surfaces.

5 Remove old decorations
- Remove unwanted panelling/cladding.
- Strip old ceiling paint/coverings.
- Strip wallcoverings and woodwork.

6 Carry out modifications
- Unblock or rebuild fireplace.
- Install wiring for wall lights and new sockets.
- Move ceiling light fittings.
- Fit new decorative mouldings.

7 Carry out repairs
- Repair damaged plasterwork and make good.
- Patch damaged wood; sand stripped woodwork.

8 Final cleaning
- Wash down walls and ceilings with sugar soap.
- Wipe over woodwork with sugar soap; vacuum floor.

9 Redecorate ceiling

10 Redecorate walls
(but if papering, do paintwork first.)

11 Redecorate paintwork

12 Refit fixtures and refurnish

Trade tip

Covering up

❝ Experts are forever disagreeing about the best way to cover things up – here are my own favourite methods:

☐ Use cloth dust sheets in preference to plastic ones on floors – plastic sheets are cheap and easy to lay, but they can get extremely slippery when wet. Anything that's spilt tends to run straight off the surface on to what you're trying to protect.

☐ Plastic sheets come into their own when covering soft furnishings. Use them under cloth sheets to provide a waterproof layer.

☐ You can hire proper dust sheets, but old sheets, curtains or blankets will do just as well.

☐ When laying dust sheets, shake them outdoors beforehand and allow plenty of overlap – they always get scuffed up. Shake them outdoors again to remove dust before painting.

☐ Tape or pin dust sheets to the skirtings where possible, then mask by hand when you paint the woodwork.

☐ Always use masking tape for fiddly bits, and don't leave it in place for too long – it will stick fast. ❞

Survey a room (above) before you decorate, so that you can pinpoint problems which might otherwise hold up work.

Cover up thoroughly (left). **A**. Tape or pin the edges of dust sheets to the skirtings. **B**. Cover small fixtures using plastic bags held on with masking tape.
   Move any remaining furniture to the middle of the room and protect with a double layer of plastic and cloth dust sheets.

SURVEYING THE ROOM

Ceilings Check for leaks (brown staining), and for cracking or loose plasterboard (shown by blistering along the joints).
Texture painted ceilings may hide defective lath and plaster: if possible, check from above.
Check for old distemper or other unstable finishes; if the finish comes off on your fingers, it must be removed completely.

Decorative mouldings Check for loose or damaged mouldings such as covings, picture rails, skirtings and architraves. Fix or replace before decorating.
Tops of mouldings gather hidden dust and dirt; make a note to clean.

Walls Check for dampness, especially around and under windows. Embossed or woodchip paper may disguise defective plaster; panelling could hide damp walls or poor plaster.
If necessary, book free damp survey to investigate suspect areas.
Remove or mask off fittings screwed to the wall. Pull out old wallplugs. If plugs are to be reused, mark their positions with pins.

Services Let down radiators if possible (see overleaf). Remove lampshades and mask fittings.
Decide whether to remove light fittings/sockets or install additional power points.
Ideally, get an electrician to remove wall lights and isolate supply.

Windows Remove old foam strip insulation.
Clean off condensation mould around frames.
Sticking windows may need removing and overhauling, disturbing the surrounding walls.
Remove all window dressings and tracks/poles.

Doors Remove old foam strip insulation/draught excluders. Sticking doors may need trimming.
Remove door furniture if at all possible.

Fireplace With open fires, have the chimney swept. Cover fire surround unless painting.
Decide whether to unblock fireplace or build in new surround.

Furniture Remove as much furniture as possible.
Move remaining furniture to middle of room and cover with plastic dust sheets (cotton ones may let through spillages).
Cover or mask built-in furniture which can't be taken down.

Floorcoverings Aim to lift fitted carpets if possible (see overleaf). Protect and cover remaining floorcoverings.

Floors Check wooden floors for loose boards and nail or screw down.
Check solid floors for signs of damp: tape a piece of glass over the bare surface and leave for a day – moisture on the underside indicates dampness.

LOWERING A RADIATOR

There's usually enough 'give' in the pipework for you to lift a radiator off its brackets and lower it to the floor without having to drain the system and disconnect it. Beware, though, of radiators with staining around the pipes or valves; this indicates weeping joints, which may fall apart if you interfere with them. And if the radiator doesn't give easily, don't try to force it.

Refitting is the exact reverse of dismantling. Make sure you open the lockshield valve the exact number of turns it took to close it, and bleed the radiator afterwards.

1 Turn off the heating. Close the radiator on/off valve, then lift off or unscrew the cover of the lockshield valve fitted to the pipe on the other side.

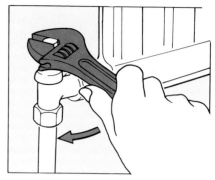

2 Use an adjustable wrench or spanner to close the valve, turning the movable head fully clockwise. Make a note of how many turns it takes to do this.

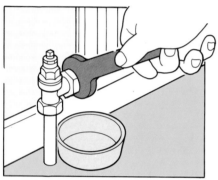

3 Place bowls under both valves and use your adjustable wrench to loosen off the connector nuts **one full turn only**. At this stage, water will start to drip.

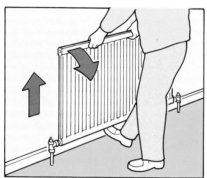

4 Lift the radiator upwards, using your foot as a lever, until you feel it disengage from its wall brackets. Then lower it gently towards you.

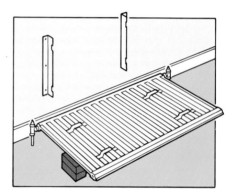

5 Support the radiator at both ends to take the strain off the pipework. Retighten the connector nuts temporarily to stop the water leaking.

REMOVING A CARPET

Foam-backed fitted carpets are stuck down with double-sided tape, and are difficult to lift successfully without the backing disintegrating.

Protect them instead with layers of first plastic and then cloth dust sheets. Fix the edges of the sheets to the skirtings with masking tape (available from car accessory shops) or drawing pins, then hand-mask when you come to paint the woodwork.

Hessian-backed fitted carpets with a separate underlay are secured by gripper strips around the edge of the room, and by cover strips at doorways. You may also find tacks holding down awkward areas.

Removing a carpet like this requires a carpet fitter's bolster and knee-kicker, both of which you can hire cheaply from tool hire shops.

Once you have freed the carpet, roll it up tightly across the shortest dimension. Either store it in another room, or turn it round so that it is clear of the walls and cover with a dust sheet.

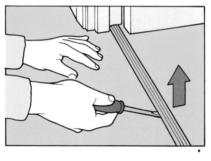

1 At doorways, prise off cover strips. If there is no carpet on the other side, the strip will fit over the edge and may need to be levered up gently.

2 Pull out any tacks you can find, using a tack lifter or pliers. When you're fairly sure only the grippers are holding the carpet, start to free it.

3 Kneel facing the edge and push the teeth of the knee-kicker into the carpet ahead of you. Jolt it forward and pull upwards to free the grippers.

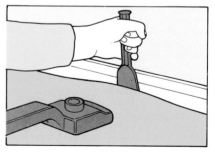

4 If you find it difficult to free the edge, use a bolster to prise it up as you kick. Carry on along the edges until you have freed the whole carpet.

HOW TO STRIP WALLPAPER

Any papered wall that is to be recovered with wallpaper must be stripped first. Many home-owners face the additional problem of stripping painted walls that have been lined with ugly or poorly applied textured papers.

There are two basic methods, depending on the type of paper, so check the panel on the right and make sure you know what you're dealing with before you start.

Soak and strip is the cheapest and still the most effective method for most wallpapers.

Soaking the paper loosens the paste, causing it to peel away – a process which you can speed up by adding washing up liquid or wallpaper stripper to the water. Another trick is to score the paper first, helping the water to penetrate the outer surface.

Steam stripping using a hired steam stripper is faster and more effective on heavy and painted-over papers, but it does have some disadvantages (see overleaf), and the hire cost mounts up if you don't tackle the work in one go.

Stripping tools

A decent stripping knife is essential. Spend a little more on one with a rigid blade which won't flex and dig into the plaster; don't be tempted to economize by using a filling knife instead.

There's also a patented scraper with a roller on the base which keeps the blade at the correct angle for stripping. These are useful for fragile surfaces such as plasterboard, where it's easy to slip and gouge the surface.

KNOW YOUR WALLPAPER

WALLPAPER TYPE	STRIPPING METHOD
Uncoated – plain, non-washable paper.	Soak and scrape. Ready pasted types peel off easily if left to soak. Other types need scraping as well, depending on thickness.
Coated – washable paper coated with thin film of PVC.	Score, soak and strip. Water must be given time to penetrate outer water resistant coating.
Vinyl – plastic washable coating on thin paper backing.	Peel off. Vinyl layer separates easily from backing and can be peeled off in whole lengths. If necessary, strip backing by soaking and scraping.
Plain lining paper – usually emulsion painted, but may be found under surface paper.	Score, soak and strip. Water must be given time to penetrate behind paint. Paint may have penetrated paper, requiring heavy scraping.
Woodchip – textured lining paper in which wood pulp is sandwiched between heavy backing and light facing paper; usually painted.	Score and steam strip. Try to avoid layers separating. Avoid prolonged steaming if plaster underneath is in poor condition.
Embossed – textured relief paper containing plaster and other additives. Two types: medium (ie Anaglypta) and heavy (ie Supaglypta). May be printed or emulsion painted.	Score and steam strip. Let steam soften paint coating before attempting to scrape. Older embossed papers are very hard work to remove.

Wallpaper stripping requires plenty of energy, but little in the way of equipment. A wire brush provides a gentle means of scoring the surface of light paper; for heavier ones use a home-made scorer.

washing up bowl

wallpaper stripper

home-made scoring tool

stripping tool with roller

heavy cloth

stripping knife.

wire brush

33

STRIPPING BY HAND

Stripping wallpaper is a messy business, so cover up the floor even if you've cleared the room. The debris will be sticky and wet, so if you're using cloth dust sheets, place a plastic sheet or an opened-out bin liner directly·underneath the patch you're working on. (Don't cover the whole floor in plastic sheets – they become slippery and unsafe.)

With so much water around, it's a good idea to turn off the electricity at the mains. Don't let the room get too warm, or the soaked paper may dry out before you get round to stripping it.

Avoid a flood

❛ When you're soaking a really stubborn paper, water tends to slosh all over the place instead of soaking into the surface.

A trick I use is to add a small handful of ordinary wallpaper paste to the water first. Not surprisingly this makes it slightly sticky, helping it adhere to the wall instead of running down it and over the floor. ❜

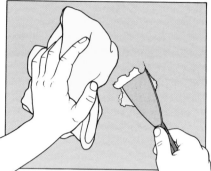

1 Soak the paper thoroughly with a sponge or old floor cloth, leave a couple of minutes, then test to see if it has loosened. If not, you must score it.

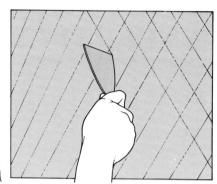

2 One way of scoring is to use the corner of your stripping knife, held as shown to stop it gouging the plaster. Score in a diamond pattern.

3 Alternatively, knock some nails through a block of wood so the heads just show through. Run this lightly across the paper in criss-cross bands.

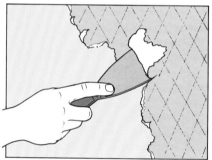

4 Keep the blade angle shallow as you remove the paper, so you don't cut into the wall. Stubborn patches may need an extra soaking before they shift.

STEAM STRIPPING

Nearly all papers that need steam stripping benefit from being scored thoroughly first. The art of using a steam stripper is to work two-handed, holding the plate against ·the paper just long enough to soften it, then scraping off the debris before it dries out. It takes a while to judge this correctly, so don't overdo the steam to start with or you risk damaging the wall.

On textured papers, wait until the steam has penetrated right through before scraping – stripping a layer at a time is much harder.

Protect the ceiling

❛ Steam strippers are notorious for softening what they're not supposed to, and ceiling lining papers are the most vulnerable – the steam rises and condenses, soaking into the paper and leaving gravity to do the rest.

I stop this happening by taping cheap plastic dust sheets to the part of the ceiling I'm working under (in a small room cover the whole ceiling). ❜

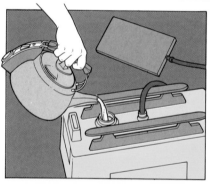

1 Fill the water tank up to the level indicator, then lay down the plate vent side up and switch on. When steam begins to emerge, the machine is ready for use.

2 Hold the plate against the surface for 15 seconds, then check with your knife to see if the steam has penetrated every layer. Repeat if necessary.

3 As the paper gives way, move the plate on to the next sector and push away the debris with your knife. Angle the plate upwards to stop it dripping .

4 Remove stubborn nibs after you've cleared the bulk of the paper. Apply the steam in 10-second bursts, scraping down immediately.

PREPARING WALLS AND CEILINGS

Although it's possible to give walls and ceilings a quick facelift if the surface is in good condition, on most redecorating jobs there is no substitute for preparation. Modern paints and wallpapers are a great deal more efficient than they used to be, but if the underlying surface is poor, then no amount of hastily applied finish will disguise it.

At the very least, you should make sure that the surface is clean and dry. But walls and ceilings which have been repaired, stripped, or cleared of stick-on decorations may need more extensive treatment. For example, after filling all the obvious blemishes, the surface may still be uneven enough to warrant lining with paper before painting or wallpapering. Or it may need sealing prior to finishing.

Assuming that you have already made any necessary repairs, and that the room is cleared ready for action, check the chart below to find out what surfaces need what treatment.

.... Shopping List ....

General cleaning: bucket or bowl, sugar soap, clean cloths, dust sheets, access equipment.
Filling: filler, filling knife, wire brush, sanding equipment.
Priming/sizing: large wall brush, primer/sealer, plaster stabilizer, spirit based sealer, thinned emulsion, size or thinned paste.
Lining with paper: papering tools, paste, lining paper (see overleaf).

PREPARATION GUIDE

SURFACE	BEFORE PAINTING . . .	BEFORE WALLPAPERING . . .
Emulsion paint (sound)	■ Sand down bumps and nibs of paint ■ Fill depressions ■ Wash down	■ Fill large holes ■ Sand smooth ■ Coat with size
Emulsion paint (cracked/flaking)	■ Sand back to sound edge ■ Fill depressions with fine surface filler ■ If area is large, hang lining paper	■ Sand back to sound edge ■ Fill large holes ■ Coat with size
Emulsion paint (over lining paper)	■ Check surface is dry ■ Stick down peeling edges ■ Wash *lightly*	■ Strip unless completely sound; otherwise treat as emulsion
Gloss paint (sound)	■ Sand with wet and dry paper to key surface for new coat ■ Fill depressions and wash down	■ Fill large holes ■ Sand smooth ■ Coat with size
Gloss paint (cracked/bubbling)	■ Sand back to sound edge ■ Cover depressions with fine surface filler	■ Sand back to sound edge ■ Fill large holes ■ Coat with size
New plaster	■ Leave in bare state for at least a month ■ Brush off salt deposits ■ Use emulsion paint *only*; do not decorate again for 6 months	■ Leave for 6 months ■ Coat with size
Old plaster	■ Fill holes/cracks ■ Sand smooth ■ Wash off last traces of old decorations ■ Coat repairs and unprepared patches with primer/sealer or stabilizer ■ If heavily patched, hang lining paper	■ Fill large holes ■ Sand smooth and size filled areas ■ Ideally, hang lining paper
Bare plasterboard	■ Fill holes/dents ■ If new, 'spot' nail heads with primer ■ Cover cracked joints between boards with scrim tape and plaster (on ceiling, fill with flexible sealant) ■ Sand smooth ■ Wash lightly	■ Fill holes/dents ■ Sand smooth ■ Coat with size
Bare brick	■ Remove dirt/powdery deposits with stiff or wire brush ■ Coat with primer/sealer	

WASHING DOWN

The one step you can't avoid when repainting an existing painted surface is washing down. Even though it's often hardly noticeable, the dirt and grease that accumulates on old paint can discolour the new coat or stop it from drying. In extreme cases it may even cause the finish to lift off or crack.

Use sugar soap, or a similar cleaner, mixed with water according to the maker's instructions. Ordinary detergent foams too much and leaves soapy residues that are hard to rinse off. Sugar soap bites into the paint – you don't need to rub hard – and leaves no deposits.

On plasterboard, and on heavy lining papers (ie woodchip, Anaglypta) which are already painted, take care not to let the washing water soak into the surface. Work on small areas at a time and sponge off frequently.

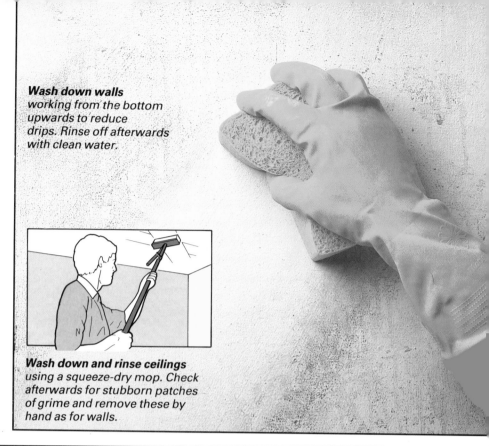

Wash down walls working from the bottom upwards to reduce drips. Rinse off afterwards with clean water.

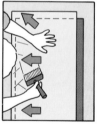

Wash down and rinse ceilings using a squeeze-dry mop. Check afterwards for stubborn patches of grime and remove these by hand as for walls.

HANGING LINING PAPER

Hanging lining paper is a simple way to smooth a wall that's been stripped or heavily repaired. Wallpaper manufacturers also recommend it before hanging delicate printed wallpapers and unbacked fabrics. If you are painting over lining paper, hang it vertically like ordinary wallpaper. If it is to be papered over, hang the strips horizontally – called *cross-lining*.

Lining paper comes in three grades: *heavy* (for poor surfaces), *medium* (for most jobs) and *light* (for smooth surfaces that require lining anyway). The rolls measure 555mm × 11m (22″×36′), so measure the area being covered to work out how many you need and add one extra for wastage.

Using lining paper

Lining paper is easier to hang than wallpaper – there's no pattern to worry about, no need to soak it, and the paper sticks readily using standard wallpaper paste.

Sand down any nibs and bumps beforehand, but don't worry about the hollows – these can be filled, along with any other imperfections, once the paper is up. Leave the paper to dry for 24 hours.

Vertical hanging

Treat the paper like ordinary wallpaper. Align the first strip on each wall against a vertical guideline just under a roll's width from the corner, butt the next strip against it

(don't overlap), and so on down the wall as far as you can go.

At corners (which are never square), paper in towards the corner from one side leaving an overlap. Then paper back in from the other side to cover the overlap left by the first strip.

Trim off the excess at the top and bottom of the wall, and at corners, using a sharp knife held against the blade of a stripping knife.

1 **For vertical hanging,** use a spirit level to draw a guideline on each wall slightly less than a roll's width from the nearest corner.

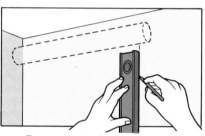

2 Cut a length of paper 100mm (4″) longer than the height of the wall. Paste in a criss-cross pattern out towards the edges to avoid getting paste on the table.

3 Align the pasted length with the guideline, leaving a 50mm (2″) overlap top and bottom. Smooth out with a dry cloth, then trim off the excess.

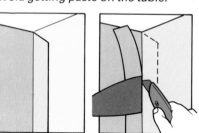

4 At internal corners, turn the first length around the corner then hang the second over it. Trim off the excess, using a stripping knife as a guide.

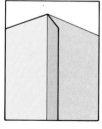

5 Follow the same sequence for external corners: turn the first length round, hang the length on the return side over it, then trim the overlap.

PREPARING BARE PLASTER

What you do with bare plaster depends on its age and condition.

New plaster must be left to dry for at least a month. If salt crystals (efflorescence) appear during this time, brush them off.

Old plaster needs to be made good. Coat patches with general purpose primer/sealer; if crumbly, apply plaster stabilizer. Damp plaster may indicate a problem area. If not, leave to dry out before decorating.

Sealing the surface

Dry plaster tends to suck the moisture out of paint or wallpaper paste before these can bond properly. The answer is to apply a sealing coat first – often called *sizing*.

Before painting, seal with primer/sealer or a thinned coat of the paint you are using. Mix emulsion paint with one quarter of its volume of water. Use *alkali-resisting* primer

before applying oil paint.

Before papering/lining, size with purpose-made size or a coat of wallpaper paste. Use a fungicidal paste or size to prevent mould growth – especially under vinyl papers.

Seal the surface of bare plaster with primer or paint if painting, size if papering. Stabilizing solution will help to bind crumbling old plaster.

Brush off efflorescence on the surface of new plaster. It is caused by salts crystallizing as the plaster dries. Continue at intervals until no more appears.

Cross-lining

Work out beforehand how many widths it takes to cover the wall, allowing an extra 50mm (2″) top and bottom for trimming. Then draw a horizontal guideline right around the room, to align the first strip on each wall.

Fold the strips concertina-fashion after pasting, then unfold them on the wall, smoothing as you go. As they're so narrow, you can run them straight round corners.

1 **To cross-line the walls,** start by drawing a horizontal guideline right around the room, just under a roll's width from where the ceiling and walls meet.

2 As you paste each strip, fold it concertina-fashion into an easily manageable length. Grip it between your fingers and thumbs, keeping the folds intact.

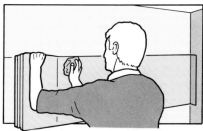

3 Begin in a corner. Align the top edge of the first strip with the guideline, leaving a small overlap. Then unfold along the wall, smoothing as you go.

4 The lengths are narrow enough to be continued around corners without falling out of alignment. After completing the wall, trim off top and bottom.

Trade tip

Don't spare the paste!

❝ Lining paper is quite porous, so there's no need to leave pasted lengths to soak, as you have to with some wallpapers. Even so, make sure the lengths are thoroughly wet before you hang them, or the paper will dry and shrink unevenly, leaving unsightly gaps at the joints. ❞

Where narrow strips join, leave an overlap and let the paper dry, then tear off . . .

. . . to leave a barely visible 'feathered' edge which you can then fill to hide it completely.

PREPARING CEILINGS

Although by and large you can treat ceilings as you would walls, they have special problems of their own.

If the ceiling has been lined and painted over, it's worth doing your best to keep the lining paper intact. Wash down gently, using as little water as possible, and carry out any minor repairs as shown.

Relining a ceiling is much more difficult. Not only is there the problem of access, but for the lining to be effective you'll probably need to use a heavyweight covering such as Anaglypta (which is more difficult to hang). Papering ceilings is covered on pages 77-80.

Cracks in ceilings may not respond to normal filling treatment if they are caused by movement in the floor above – the filler simply shakes loose. In this case fill with flexible sealant instead, allowing a few days for a skin to form before you paint over it.

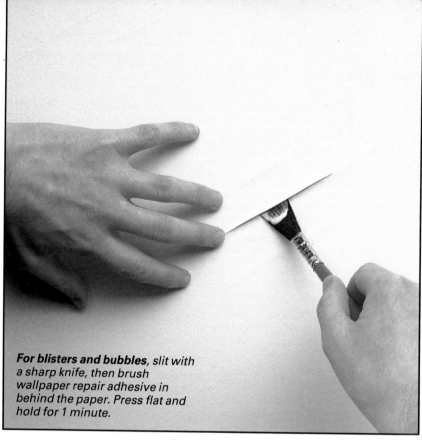

For blisters and bubbles, slit with a sharp knife, then brush wallpaper repair adhesive in behind the paper. Press flat and hold for 1 minute.

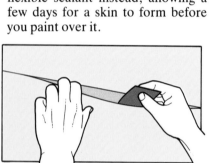

1 *To fix peeling edges in lining paper, start by sanding behind them to remove all traces of dust and old paste. Clean afterwards with a damp cloth.*

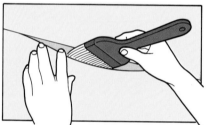

2 *Brush wallpaper repair adhesive behind the edges and press flat. If they curl, secure with sticking putty (eg Blu-Tak) while the adhesive dries.*

If part of the paper is missing, but the rest is largely sound, cover the area with ready mixed skimming plaster. Smooth level with the surrounding edges.

▌PROBLEM SOLVER▐

Dealing with blemishes

On painted surfaces, you may come across blemishes which no amount of washing down will remove. These include:
- Stains such as nicotine.
- Water marks left on a ceiling after a leak.
- Mould patches

Stains must be sealed before repainting, otherwise there's a risk that they will bleed through the new finish. Use spray-on stain blocking compound – a relatively new innovation – or traditional spirit-based sealer (which is thinned with methylated spirits).

Kill mould patches by washing with bleach solution or a proprietary mould remover.

If the blemish has ruined the surface of lining paper, cut out the damaged area and paste on a patch as shown.

Spray indelible stains with aerosol stain blocking compound. Alternatively, paint with spirit-based primer/sealer, feathering the edges of the patch.

Treat black mould with a solution of one part bleach to three parts water. Apply with a sponge-type scourer, working it well into the surface of the paint.

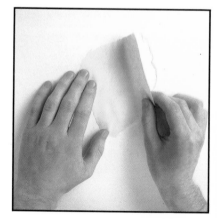

Patch damaged lining paper by tearing a new piece roughly to fit so that it has thin, feathered edges. Paste in place, then cover the edges with filler.

PREPARING WOODWORK AND FITTINGS

As with everything else in decorating, getting a good finish on skirtings, doors and window frames depends on good preparation. On sound surfaces, this may be as simple as giving the paint a quick rub-down and clean. But if there is any damage to the surface, or faults in the original finish, make sure these get dealt with at the same time.

Bare wood should only need a light rub-down with glasspaper to remove any roughness or sharp edges. Fill the end grain and any other blemishes, then apply knotting compound and a coat of primer.

Painted wood in good condition should be lightly rubbed down and then cleaned. Minor imperfections can be filled or sanded as appropriate; prime any spots where you have rubbed through to bare wood.

If the paint surface is very poor, it's often wiser to strip it completely and start again from bare wood (see pages 43-46). Serious damage or rot in the underlying timber must be treated and then replaced with a new section, cut and shaped to fit (see page 42).

Metal fittings need thorough cleaning, and all traces of corrosion must be removed. Afterwards, coat with primer or a one-coat paint.

Depending on the job, you may need a wide range of materials for cleaning and preparation:

Cleaners include sugar soap and white spirit (useful for degreasing metal surfaces or old, dirty paintwork). A supply of clean cloths is essential.

Abrasives include glasspaper or garnet paper for sanding woodwork, and wet and dry or aluminium oxide paper for rubbing down metal. Wet and dry paper used wet gives a finer finish on painted wood, but is messy. Steel wool is a handy alternative for cleaning metal, and gives a smooth finish to bare wood.

Flap wheel and rotary wire brush drill attachments make light work of metal fittings in need of extensive rubbing down.

Fillers include general purpose acrylic or cellulose filler for larger cracks and dents, plus fine surface filler for dents shallower than 3mm (1/8") and patches where the grain has become raised.

Fibreglass resin and epoxy fillers are better for repairing areas subject to heavy wear and tear. They are quick setting and very strong, with a non-absorbent surface which takes a good finish – but they are expensive. Use flexible or aerosol foam filler for joints with adjoining surfaces which are likely to move.

Sealers and primers include *knotting compound* to stop resin oozing out of knots, *general purpose primer* for bare wood, *aluminium primer* for patches which have been heat stripped, and *metal primer* for fittings. Rusty metal is best treated with chemical *rust remover/neutralizer*.

You also need scrapers and filling tools, an electric drill, and woodworking tools if you have any patching to do.

Preparation materials can cover a surprising number of different products: assess the job before you start and lay on supplies of everything needed.

knotting compound

metal primer

general purpose primer

rust remover

general purpose filler (ready mixed)

white spirit

flexible filler

fine surface filler

resin filler (flexible)

resin filler (rigid)

flap wheel attachment

wire brush attachments

scrapers

wet and dry paper

glasspaper

39

PREPARING WOODWORK

PREPARING SOUND PAINTWORK

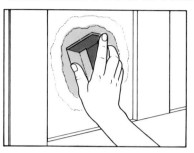

1 Rub down blemishes and runs with medium grade glasspaper and a sanding block, feathering the edges into the surrounding surface. Rub down the whole surface with fine glasspaper or steel wool to 'key' it.

2 After sanding, wash down the surface with a solution of sugar soap to remove the dust and clean off any grease (which might contaminate the new paint). Pay special attention to awkward areas such as mouldings.

MINOR DAMAGE AND GAPS

Splits, dents and cracked joints should be filled and sanded to blend into the surrounding surface. Use whatever filler suits the situation.

Splits and dents can be repaired with general purpose filler – either powder or ready mixed. But for small irregularities, ready mixed fine surface filler bonds more readily and gives a smoother finish.

Vulnerable edges which have received knocks are likely to be knocked again. Use resin or epoxy filler (both of which are stronger than the wood itself) to fill these areas.

Cracked joints are often subject to movement, so use a flexible filler. If the movement is due to looseness rather than shrinkage, strengthen the joint first with screws or nails.

Gaps along adjoining surfaces may also be prone to movement. Pack with pieces of polystyrene or cardboard packing material, then fill with flexible sealant or foam filler. Let sealant form a skin before painting. Foam filler can be shaped once dry.

Sand painted surfaces so that the filler can get a grip. Rake out and scrape any loose material from cracks back to a sound edge using the corner of a scraper.

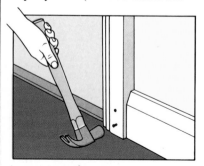

Check whether cracks in joints are due to shrinkage or looseness. Strengthen loose joints with extra screws or nails to prevent further movement.

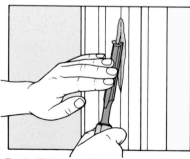

Resin filler must be mixed with hardener and cures quickly. After hardening, shape it with woodworking tools and smooth with wet and dry paper.

Pack the gaps along adjoining surfaces with pieces of polystyrene or cardboard. Then fill with flexible sealant or aerosol foam filler.

DEFECTIVE PAINTWORK

Where large patches of the existing paintwork are badly blistered or flaking, it's best to strip it back to bare wood and start again. Choose between the three methods below, depending on the situation.

Heat from a hot air gun or blowlamp is cheap, efficient and fairly easy. But on a window you risk cracking the glass, and blowlamps can char woodwork.

Abrasives or scrapers are hard work, but convenient for small areas. On mouldings, however, it is easy to damage the details – especially if using power tools.

Chemicals are expensive and messy, but they don't damage the wood, and are ideal for fiddly areas and mouldings. Make sure any residue is neutralised and cleaned off, or it may affect the paint. For removable items like doors, professional dipping is a possible, but costly, option.

Use a hot air gun together with a stripping knife, working it under the blistered paint. Keep a container handy to hold the scrapings.

Powered sanders and drill attachments help when removing paint with abrasives, but avoid using on mouldings – these should be tackled by hand.

Scraping on its own works best on curves. Check constantly that the blade doesn't dig in: if it does, alter the angle in case you are catching the grain.

Chemical stripper removes several coats in one go – providing you give it time to penetrate. Clean thoroughly after scraping up the softened residue.

Trade tip

Spot checks

6 Discolouring and marks on a painted surface suggest that it wasn't prepared properly first time around. Treat them now, or they'll work their way through the new topcoat too.

Knots show up as oily looking rings in the paint. The cure is to sand a small area back to bare wood, and apply knotting compound. Follow with coats of primer and undercoat, then sand to blend into the surface.

Rust marks caused by nail or screw heads also need sanding back. Apply metal primer to seal the head and fill if necessary, then refinish as above. 9

PREPARING METAL FITTINGS

Most corrosion-free metal fittings only need degreasing and a very light rub down. The simplest method is to use fine wire wool dipped in white spirit; for areas which need smoothing as well, rub with wet and dry paper first. Wash down, rinse and dry thoroughly before priming.

Dealing with corrosion

Whether the metal is bare or painted, all traces of corrosion must be removed before painting.

Rusty patches on steel or cast iron need a thorough wire brushing to remove loose flakes. Afterwards, either sand them back to bare, sound metal using aluminium oxide paper or a flap wheel, or treat them with chemical rust remover/ neutralizer (as used for car repairs).

There are several types of rust remover, but most contain acids and can be dangerous: follow the maker's instructions, and be sure to wear gloves and goggles.

After treatment, wash down and rinse in clean water to remove all traces. Dry, then prime quickly to prevent corrosion recurring.

Metal windows may need rust-treating inside and out – even if you leave the exterior painting until later. Use a separate container to dip the brush in, so you don't contaminate the rest of the fluid.

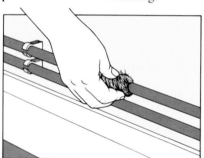

Aluminium, copper and brass need only a light clean using fine steel wool soaked in white spirit. Use wet and dry paper to rub down pitted areas.

A rotary wire brush attachment is less tiring than brushing by hand where you're faced with a large area of rusty, flaking steel or cast iron.

Chemical rust cures often contain strong acids – apply with care using an old brush. Afterwards, wash down and rinse to neutralize the residue, then leave to dry.

◣ PROBLEM SOLVER

Dealing with rot

Any localized patches of rot in the woodwork must be repaired – and the cause investigated – before preparation.

Small patches are usually *wet rot*, which you can deal with yourself: either cut back the affected timber to sound wood and join in a new section, or cut out the rot and patch it with a kit containing anti-rot fungicidal pellets.

Call in a specialist surveyor if you suspect *dry rot*, which is much more serious and must be treated professionally.

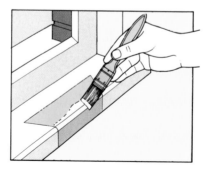

Large patches of wet rot must be sawn or chiselled out, and new timber glued and nailed in their place. Coat the repair with preservative before priming.

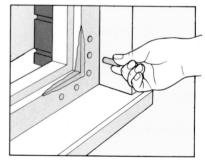

Small areas can be patched with a repair kit. Brush on hardener and apply the resin filler, then insert fungicidal pellets to kill any remaining rot spores.

STRIPPING WOODWORK

Whether you are decorating the house or renovating furniture, it's sometimes necessary to give woodwork more than just a light rub down.

There are several reasons for stripping back to bare wood:
■ If you want to show off the grain, any paint must be removed before staining and/or varnishing it.
■ Thick paint may have obscured the detail of mouldings or carving. Stripping should restore the original form, before refinishing.
■ Paint or varnish which was faulty (or which was badly applied) may have peeled and lifted. Removing it will avoid further problems.

How to strip
There are three main ways to remove paint and varnish from wood. In every case, start by removing fittings, handles, catches and so on. The options are:
Heat stripping, using a blowtorch or hot air gun to soften and blister the paint so it will scrape off.
Chemical stripping, applying a liquid, gel or paste to the surface, then leaving it to soften the paint or varnish before scraping it off.
Sanding or scraping with hand or power tools. This may be all you need, but must be done in any case after heat or chemical stripping.

The chart overleaf shows the pros and cons of each method. The final choice often depends on the nature of the surface and whether you are applying varnish or paint afterwards. The first thing to know is what you are dealing with.

What finish do you have?
Paint is obvious, but test clear finishes by dabbing an inconspicuous spot – first with white spirit then methylated spirit – on a clean white cloth and seeing if any comes off.
■ White spirit removes oiled and waxed finishes. Both are easier to restore than to remove.
■ Methylated spirit removes French polish, and high-gloss finish traditionally used for pianos and fine furniture. Similar (but cheaper) shellac polish responds to the same treatment.

All these finishes require special treatment (see page 245). Most other clear finishes respond to chemical or heat stripping, with the following exceptions:
■ Plastic resin coating (a modern finish found mainly on floors and furniture) only responds to heat.
■ Stained wood may be a 'skin-deep' varnish/stain which comes away easily. If the wood has been dyed before varnishing, the colour will be hard to shift and you may have to resort to bleaching the wood.

WORTH STRIPPING?
Thick paint may conceal a surface which is not what you expected. Interior joinery such as doors may have been patched with filler, and it was once common to improve the surface of furniture by filling the grain with plaster of Paris. If possible, test a concealed patch first to see whether the paint comes off easily, and to get an idea of the condition of the wood underneath.

If you plan to renovate an old piece of furniture, there are several points to note;
■ Before stripping *any* old piece, check that it is not valuable. Sometimes even a rough original finish is more highly valued than a modern, hardwearing version.
■ Beware of stripping veneered furniture. Most methods which remove the finish tend to lift the veneer as well.

STRIPPING PAINT AND VARNISH

METHOD	BEST USED FOR	RELATIVE COST	TOOLS REQUIRED
Blowtorch	Large areas, but not under clear finishes as the wood may scorch. Do not use near glass, as there is a danger of cracking it.	Low. Gas canisters are fairly cheap and small ones last up to 3 hours (large ones 5 hours).	Paraffin or spare gas canisters for large jobs; selection of scrapers and shave hooks. Nozzles.
Hot air stripper	Large areas, including simple mouldings. Use with care near glass. Needs mains power nearby.	Fairly low. Stripper costs slightly more to run than blowtorch.	Scrapers and shave hook according to work in hand. Extension cable for use outdoors. Nozzles.
Liquid and gel stripper	Carved shapes, such as wooden mouldings and banisters. Furniture.	Fairly high, particularly if you have to neutralize it with white spirit afterwards.	Old paintbrush, tough rubber gloves, selection of scrapers and shave hooks, cloth and solvent.
Paste stripper	Small, intricately shaped areas.	High. Leave paste in place for a long time to avoid a second application.	Old knife or spatula, cloth, rubber gloves, polythene, scrapers and shave hooks.
Dipping	Large items, eg doors, which do not require a fine finish. Dipping loosens glued joints and can dry out the wood.	Fairly high – there may be transport charges as well if you don't have a large car or van.	Tools to remove and re-fit doors.
Power sander	Large, flat areas, particularly where there is only a thin coat of paint.	Apart from the cost of the power tools, abrasive paper will be the main expense.	Plenty of abrasive paper in a range of grades, face mask.
Scraping	Flat areas, convex curves and simple mouldings, particularly if the finish is brittle. Also use after heat or chemical stripping.	Economical, but you may find you can only use scrapers in conjunction with other techniques.	Scrapers and shave hooks, Skarsten scraper (with interchangeable blades for mouldings), goggles.
Hand sanding	Rarely used for stripping, but essential for finishing, particularly if the grain has been raised.	Economical. Tougher aluminium oxide paper lasts longer on large areas but costs more.	Sanding block; plenty of abrasive sheets in a range of grades, or an abrasive block.

HEAT STRIPPING

The choice is between a gas blow-torch (or new-style gas-heated gun), and an electric hot air gun.

■ Protect the area below with plenty of layers of damp newspaper.

■ With a blowtorch it is important to keep moving, to avoid scorching the wood – hot air guns are less likely to cause this problem.

■ As the paint bubbles under the heat, use a scraper to lift it off. Use shaped shave hooks to remove paint from mouldings. The amount of heat you need to apply depends on the age and thickness of the paint.

■ Directional nozzles can be fitted to torches and guns to concentrate the heat into awkward areas.

 Fire hazards

Remember that both the shreds of paint and the protective newspaper are flammable. Keep an eye open for over-heated paint dropping on to the paper. Handle blowtorches with care and only point them at the work.

With a blowtorch play the flame over the paintwork, from side to side. Keep the flame moving over the surface as it starts to bubble, to prevent scorching.

Use a stripping knife to scrape away the softened paint, working with the grain. Make sure the shreds do not fall on you – they may still be hot enough to burn.

With an electric hot air stripper the technique is much the same. Although scorching is less likely, do not hold it on one spot or the gun may overheat.

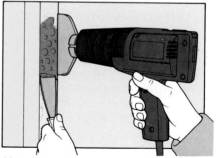
Use a directional nozzle if you have to work near to glass. Turn it round so that it deflects the heat away from the glass to stop it cracking.

CHEMICAL STRIPPING

Chemical strippers are easy to use but must be handled with care. Lay dust sheets in case of spills and cover the area with thick paper to collect the debris.

Types of stripper

First decide whether to use a liquid, gel or paste stripper:

■ Pastes tend to be more efficient, but cost more. Some types must be wrapped to prevent them drying out while they are softening the paint. Several layers of paint should peel away with the wrapping, which saves scraping and damaging the surface.

■ Liquids can only be used where they are unlikely to run off the surface. For vertical surfaces and mouldings, use a gel or paste.

Cleaning solvents

Next check how the surface should be cleaned. Some strippers are water-soluble while others are solvent-based and must be cleaned off with white spirit.

■ Water-soluble strippers are cheaper (you do not need extra solvent) but the water tends to raise the grain of the wood. They are best used for joinery which does not require a fine finish – or where you are intending to bleach the surface, since this process will raise the grain anyway.

■ Solvent-based strippers may need large quantities of white spirit for thorough cleaning, but do not raise the grain of the wood.

■ Water-soluble strippers can be used to strip paint from metal fittings (but dry iron and steel thoroughly to prevent rust – a hairdryer will help). Solvent-based strippers do not promote rust.

DIP AND STRIP

The easy alternative to painting on a chemical stripper and scraping away the softened finish is to use a commercial dipping service. These are reasonably cheap and effective but there are several limitations:

■ You can only strip movable joinery or items of furniture.

■ The strong chemicals remove the paint easily, but also extract the natural oils, often leaving the wood looking lifeless and dull.

■ The treatment is likely to raise the grain, which then needs sanding smooth.

■ Dipping may also cause glued joints to loosen.

Trade tip

Stripping fittings

❝Remove metal fittings and tie together with a piece of string. Dunk in a glass jar of stripper and leave for several minutes. Remove and clean thoroughly. ❞

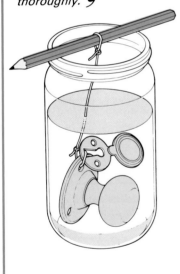

△ **Chemical safety**
Be careful how you handle chemical strippers – wear rubber gloves and rinse off splashes immediately. Don't be tempted to decant them into plastic containers while you are working, or you may find the stripper eats through the plastic and leaves you without a bottom to the container.

1 *Apply gel or liquid stripper with an old paintbrush, leaving it for a few minutes to soften the paint. Cover no more than 1sq m (1sq yd) at a time. When the paint bubbles up, use a scraper to lift it off, ensuring surrounding surfaces are well protected.*

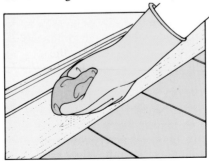

2 *Repeat until all paint has been lifted, then wash down with water or white spirit using a cloth or old paintbrush to neutralize the chemicals.*

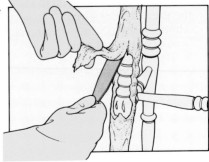

Apply paste stripper with a broad spatula, then wrap if recommended. Leave for several hours before lifting the blanket or scraping off, then neutralize.

SANDING AND SCRAPING

Some sanding or scraping is always needed after using heat or chemicals, and in some circumstances may be enough by itself. The main points to think about are:

■ Always work along the grain.

■ Work in slow stages as it is easy to damage the surface – especially with thin veneer or fine mouldings.

■ Wear suitable protective gear – goggles when scraping brittle paint, a face mask when power sanding.

■ When stripping old paintwork, take particular care not to inhale the dust in case it contains lead. Vacuum it up as soon as possible.

Scraping Whatever other method you use it pays to start by using a scraper to remove loose paint or varnish. You may find that as you scrape the flakes, more comes away. Use a flat scraper to finish large areas, shaped ones for mouldings.

Sanding With varnish and thin paint a power sander (see below) will strip and finish the surface at the same time, but can only be used on totally smooth, flat surfaces. Most work needs to be finished by hand, with abrasive paper or steel wool.

Use a Skarsten scraper along the grain of the wood, with the handle at about 45° to the surface. Shaped blades are available for mouldings.

Use a shave hook in a suitable shape for the surface: a combination hook is the most useful, since it has several different profiles.

Finish roughened surfaces and smooth away raised grain by hand sanding, particularly in areas where you cannot use a power sander.

Steel wool and water or white spirit can be used to neutralize and smooth in one go. This is good for mouldings, where it is impossible to sand evenly.

PROBLEM SOLVER

Difficult surfaces

Some surfaces may be damaged by attempting to strip them in the same way as wood:

Aluminium (eg window frames) may react with chemical stripper, so be careful when stripping wooden subframes round metal windows.

Cast iron fireplaces and **steel window frames** are difficult to strip with a blowtorch or hot air blower, since the metal conducts the heat away before the paint has softened. Chemical strippers should be used.

Marble fire surrounds which have been painted over may be indistinguishable from wood. They cannot easily be heat-stripped and although chemicals work well, they destroy the surface polish – plan to have the marble professionally refinished.

Plastics cannot be stripped with either heat or chemicals, which will damage them. Some types of paints chemically combine with plastics so that they are impossible to strip. If the paint is flaking, you can peel it off, but well bonded paint must be painted over.

POWER SANDERS

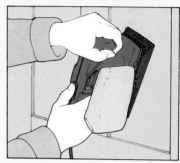

Orbital sanders have a large, flat surface, which moves in a circular, polishing motion – good for fine work. Most have a dust bag.

Disc sanders can be fitted to power drills: always hold at a slight angle as shown, and keep the surface moving along the wood to prevent scouring.

Drum sanders which can be attached to power drills have very limited use along edges and convex curves.

Eccentric sanders are like an integral version of the disc sander, designed to avoid the problem of scouring.

INDOOR PAINT FINISHES 1: WALLS AND CEILINGS

Although emulsion is the most popular choice for walls and ceilings, it is also worth thinking about oil-based eggshell, gloss, and specialized paints for problem areas.

Emulsion paint

All emulsion paints are water-based, so they dry quickly by evaporation, with little smell. Most contain vinyl to give a tough surface, but they come in a variety of finishes.

Matt emulsion is non-reflective and good at hiding lumps and hollows.

Silk emulsion has a soft sheen and is slightly less opaque.

Satin emulsion has even more of a shine and is resistant to steamy atmospheres. (Confusingly, the word satin is also used to describe some eggshells – see below). Marks wipe off all emulsions, but silk and satin are easiest to clean.

Emulsion paint is made in different consistencies, which affects how it is applied.

Liquid paint is usually the least expensive and can be applied with brush or roller, but tends to spatter.

Non-drip paint clings in jelly-like lumps but flows smoothly when applied with a brush or roller.

'Solid' ('roller') paint is even thicker and comes in a tray. It is particularly good for ceilings since spattering is kept to a minimum.

Eggshell paint

Eggshell (sometimes misleadingly called 'satin') is based on an oil solvent rather than water. It takes longer to dry and smells more than emulsion paint, and requires white spirit or brush cleaner for cleaning tools and mopping up.

Eggshell can normally be applied direct to walls and ceilings, and gives a tough, easy-clean surface with a soft sheen. It can also be used on wood and metal, but may need a primer or undercoat first.

Other options

Problem areas and special finishes may mean choosing an alternative type of paint.

Gloss paints used on walls are hardwearing and damp-resistant but tend to show up faults. Available in both liquid and non-drip form, most glosses are oil-based, but there are water-based types too. All are covered on pages 49-50.

Texture paints are thick, water-based coatings which give a textured or patterned surface. They are good at covering faults and cracks but hard to remove if you fancy a change. There are two types: *ready mixed* texture paint is like a thick emulsion; *powder* texture paint comes in bags for mixing with water.

Masonry paints contain tough reinforcing additives and can be used on exposed brickwork and utility areas such as cellars and outhouses.

Damp-resistant and cellar paints are another choice for problem areas.

Trade tip

Colour limitations

6 *Emulsion paint is sold in a wide range of colours in both liquid and non-drip form. But shades which have to be mixed aren't available in non-drip. 'Solid' emulsions have a limited range of colours – brilliant white and a few pastel shades.*

Eggshell and gloss have a comprehensive colour range, but special-purpose paints (like cellar paints) are often limited to a few shades.

Texture paints can be tinted by adding pigment or overpainted with a coloured topcoat. 9

Choosing the right sort of paint depends both on the look you want and on the type of surface you are covering (see overleaf).

WHICH PAINT TO USE WHERE

TYPE OF SURFACE	SUITABLE PAINTS	APPLICATION NOTES
Old paint	Any topcoat should be suitable if the old paint is sound. Major colour changes may need extra coats. Eggshell is good at hiding colours.	Clean with sugar soap. Sand down old gloss so new paint sticks. Clean off distemper and treat the surface with stabilizing primer.
Lining paper/textured papers	Use matt or silk finish emulsion – the latter looks particularly good over lining paper. Only use eggshell if you prime first.	Emulsion paint is applied direct with no special treatment. Prime with emulsion or acrylic primer before coating with eggshell.
Bare plaster/absorbent surfaces	Use any type of emulsion or eggshell, but in all cases prime surface first so it won't absorb moisture from paint too rapidly and cause flaking.	If using matt emulsion, a first coat of three parts paint to one of water will effectively seal the surface. Use general-purpose primer on very absorbent surfaces.
Walls subject to condensation	Use eggshell, gloss or satin vinyl – the shiny surface resists moisture. Avoid matt emulsion which lets moisture penetrate the plaster.	Ensure the wall is thoroughly dry and any mould is treated with diluted bleach or mould killer. Protect from condensation until the paint is dry.
New plaster	Use matt emulsion *only* as this allows the wall to breathe – essential until the plaster is completely dry.	Seal with a first coat of three parts emulsion to one of water.
Irregular surfaces	Use emulsion or eggshell – shiny finishes tend to show the faults more. Texture paint can be used to conceal cracks and hollows, but is difficult to remove. Consider using ready mixed skim plaster instead.	Fill and sand before painting unless using texture paint. Heavy patches of new filler may need more coats of paint than the rest of the wall.
Plasterboard	Paint with any type of emulsion or use eggshell.	Seal with thinned emulsion or primer before using eggshell.
Bare brick	Paint with emulsion or exterior masonry paint.	Seal with alkali-resisting primer/sealer.
Powdery/loose plaster	Paint with emulsion or eggshell after sealing the surface.	Seal with alkali-resisting primer/sealer after brushing off debris.
Cellar walls	If dry, use emulsion or masonry paint. If slightly prone to damp, waterproofing or 'cellar paint' may help – but not if the water penetration is severe.	Brush down any powdery residues and make good any damaged mortar pointing. Apply special waterproofing paints according to the maker's instructions.

PAINT COVERAGE

The figures below are a guide to the amount of paint needed on a sound, normally absorbent surface. The range given allows for variations between makes, surfaces and techniques, but note these points:
■ Very absorbent surfaces and heavy textures may need more.
■ A major colour change may require extra coats.

■ Paint tends to go on thicker when it is warm and dry than when it is cold or damp.
■ Non-drip paint may cover less but should require fewer coats.
　Don't buy too little paint. If you have to buy a second batch, you may find it difficult to get a good colour match – especially if the colour is non-standard and has to be mixed specially.

Area covered per litre of paint

Matt emulsion	12.5-16 sq m	14.5-19 sq yd
Silk emulsion	11-16 sq m	13-19 sq yd
Eggshell	15-16 sq m	17.5-19 sq yd

Texture paint sold dry in bags covers about 1.5-2.0 sq m (or sq yd) per kg.

DRYING TIME

The figures below give typical times taken for paint to form a skin which is dry to the touch – and if you are applying another coat, a guide to how long it should be left to harden properly. But note that drying times are affected by the weather and conditions in the room being painted. Warm, dry air speeds up drying; cold, wet conditions slow it. Don't try to speed up the drying time artificially, as this may affect the paint's stability.

	Touch dry	Re-coatable
Emulsion	2 hrs	4 hrs
Eggshell	4-6 hrs	16 hrs

INDOOR PAINT FINISHES 2: WOODWORK AND FITTINGS

Interior woodwork and fittings present you with a wide range of different surfaces. Most can be painted quite easily, but some need special paints or preparation. The most common general purpose finish is gloss paint, while eggshell can be used for a soft sheen.

Gloss paint

This comes in several formulas, each with advantages and disadvantages. For metal, use only oil-based paints.

Liquid gloss is normally oil-based which delays the drying time and gives it a lingering smell. It dries to a tough shine which some say is still the best looking gloss. Brushes and splashes must be washed with white spirit or brush cleaner.

Non-drip gloss doesn't spatter so easily. It usually has a synthetic base such as polyurethane, and with some types brushes and splashes can be cleaned with a strong solution of detergent and warm water. Non-drip normally covers in one coat but tends not to go so far as liquid gloss and some painters find it harder to get a really good finish without marks.

Acrylic gloss paints are water-based. They dry quickly with very little smell and you can apply a second coat the same day. You can also use them on wood which has been washed or rained on without having to wait for it to dry thoroughly (useful if you are painting outdoors as well). Brushes and splashes clean up with water.

Microporous coatings are gloss finishes for outdoor use which flex

and allow wood to 'breathe'. They should not be necessary indoors.

Undercoats are formulated to match the gloss they are used with. They are not always needed, but provide a sound base for the topcoat, and help to mask any base colour.

Eggshell

This paint has a soft sheen, and may be described as an oil-based 'satin'. It is used on walls with no undercoat, but an undercoat may be needed on wood and metal.

Enamel paint

Enamels are mainly used for small jobs as they are rather expensive. They have good covering power because they contain large amounts of fine colouring material.

Rust resistant enamel also contains rust preventing agents. Primer and undercoat are not needed, and many enamels are very quick drying. The solvent varies – check the instructions for cleaning brushes and splashes in case you need a special cleaner. Some solvents may react with certain types of old paint and plastics. If in doubt, check compatibility on a concealed area.

Spray paints for household use are normally a type of enamel. Car touch-up cans are also useful, but check compatibility.

Special purpose paints

Radiator and heat resisting enamels – not essential for heating pipes and so on, but may last longer.

Bath and porcelain enamels for repairing or refinishing fittings.

Primers

Primers needed for various surfaces are listed in the table overleaf.

Lead in paints

Paint for children's rooms and toys must be lead-free. Almost all new paint is – the greatest risk is from existing coats of very old paint. But as some paints may still contain lead, don't use any paint unless it says LEAD-FREE on the can.

Different surfaces require a variety of paints.

WHICH PAINT TO USE WHERE

TYPE OF SURFACE	SUITABLE PAINTS	APPLICATION NOTES
Bare softwood/man-made boards	One or two coats of gloss paint or eggshell after preparation.	Fill, sand, seal knots with knotting. Apply primer, then undercoat, or use a primer/undercoat.
Bare hardwood	Most hardwood looks good varnished rather than painted. If you do choose paint, treat as softwood.	Oily woods like teak may affect the paint's ability to bond. Wipe with white spirit to remove the oil.
Sound old paint	Apply one or two coats of gloss or eggshell. Enamel is an option on small items but check compatibility with existing paint.	Wash with sugar soap or rub down lightly so paint can grip the surface. Use undercoat if changing colour radically.
Unsound old paint on wood	One or two coats of gloss or eggshell. Use fine surface filler and undercoat if surface is patchy after preparation.	If mainly sound, sand patches and treat as bare wood. If not, strip and repaint. Use aluminium primer if wood is charred by heat stripping.
Varnished/stained wood	Use gloss paint or eggshell after preparation.	Strip thoroughly with varnish remover. Treat as bare wood.
Aluminium/alloys (eg door furniture/windows)	Paint is unnecessary. Use gloss, or enamel without primer. Rust resistant enamel may be unsuitable.	Rub down lightly with fine steel wool and white spirit. Prime with zinc chromate before applying gloss.
Stainless steel/chrome plate (eg pipes/bathroom fittings)	Paint is unnecessary, but you can use enamel or gloss without primer.	Degrease with white spirit. Do not rub down unless pitted.
Copper and brass (eg pipework)	Paint with gloss, eggshell or enamel. No primer or undercoat is needed.	Rub down lightly with fine steel wool and white spirit. Wipe clean and dry.
Sound cast iron/steel	Use gloss, eggshell or enamel. Rust resistant enamel is an option in areas where it may get damp.	Degrease with white spirit, wash and dry. Prime at once with zinc phosphate primer.
Rusty cast iron/steel	Use rust resistant enamel without primer. Otherwise use gloss, eggshell or enamel after priming.	Remove rust and fill with epoxy putty. Treat at once with zinc phosphate primer.
Galvanized steel (eg older metal window frames)	Use gloss or eggshell after priming. Some enamels are unsuitable.	DON'T sand unless rusty. Wash and prime with calcium plumbate (LEAD).
Plastics	Rigid plastic: use enamel or gloss direct – check compatibility. Flexible plastic: don't paint.	Degrease with white spirit. Rub down lightly with wet and dry paper or wire wool to key the surface.
Baths/basins	Use bath enamel/repair paint or have resurfaced professionally.	Rub down with wet and dry paper. May need special undercoat.
Childrens' furniture/toys	Enamel or gloss – MUST be lead-free. If in doubt, don't use it.	Strip any old paint (especially primer) that might contain lead.
Radiators and hot pipes	Gloss, eggshell, radiator enamel or heat resisting enamel.	Rub down lightly and degrease with white spirit.

PAINT COVERAGE AND DRYING TIME

For notes on these charts see page 48.

Area covered per litre of paint

Eggshell	15-16 sq m	18-19 sq yd
Gloss	10-17 sq m	12-20 sq yd
(Non-drip)	10-12 sq m	12-14 sq yd
Undercoat	12-14 sq m	14-17 sq yd
Enamel	—	—

Drying times

	Oil-based gloss	Water-based gloss	Eggshell	Enamel
Touch dry:	4-6 hrs	1-2 hrs	4-6 hrs	1-2 hrs*
Re-coatable	16 hrs	2-6 hrs	16 hrs	6 hrs**

* Some enamels dry even more rapidly.
** Some types can be given a second coat within minutes, but if this is not done, the paint must be left to harden thoroughly.

CHOOSING PRIMERS AND SEALERS

With few exceptions, most types of bare surface need special treatment before you can apply a topcoat of paint. In most cases, you use a primer, often followed by a suitable undercoat. On problem surfaces you may also need to apply a sealer before priming.

Primers provide a sound base for the decorative finish, and protect the underlying surface from deterioration due to weathering or chemical attack.

By themselves, most primers only offer a limited amount of weather protection to the surface underneath, so for outside work apply undercoat and topcoat as soon as possible. However, two coats of primer alone provide useful protection for the hidden surfaces of any woodwork (such as a window frame) which is fixed against masonry.

Applying a primer is much like using any other type of paint. A brush is normally the best tool – there is no need to use a top quality one – but on large areas a roller is often quicker. Depending on the type of surface, you may need to vary your painting technique.

Sealers may be needed before applying a primer to masonry or woodwork. They are designed either to bind a weak or loose surface, or to prevent chemicals in the surface from working their way through the paint.

Sealers aren't necessary when painting iron and steel, but you may need to apply a rust remover or neutralizer to prevent corrosion from continuing under the paint surface.

Preparation and application

Smooth surfaces should be clean and dry. Prepare by filling and rubbing down the irregularities. Apply one coat of primer, making sure that the surface is well covered, and allow to dry thoroughly. Then rub down lightly to remove any roughness (caused by the surface absorbing moisture), dust or impurities in the finish.

Uneven surfaces such as pitted metal or rough masonry should be brushed down to remove loose particles, and you may need to treat or seal the surface before priming. The irregularities make it difficult to apply any coating evenly, so if necessary use a combination of brushing and stippling techniques – it's important that the entire surface gets covered. There is no need to rub down the primer.

If you have a large area to do, it could be worth hiring a spray gun, while for small areas – metal in particular – an aerosol may be the simplest option.

Specialized primers (below) are designed to deal with the problems posed by painting a variety of different surfaces.

TYPES OF PRIMER AND SEALER

WOOD PRIMERS/ SEALERS

Acrylic primer water-based general purpose wood primer; dries in about 2 hours. Normally white.

Aluminium wood primer oil-based; dries in 16–24 hours. Silver-grey.

Knotting spirit-based knot sealer; can be overpainted after 1 hour. Pale brown in colour.

Sanding sealer Normally spirit-based; used on bare wood to seal the pores and fibres prior to sanding, or to stop topcoats from bleeding through.

Wood primer oil-based; dries in about 12 hours. White or pink.

WARNING: Although most versions are non-toxic, a few types contain lead. These are not suitable for children's rooms, toys or furnishings.

MASONRY PRIMERS/ SEALERS

Alkali-resisting primer oil-based; for use under oil-based paints on masonry surfaces containing cement/lime, or which are affected by efflorescence. Dry after 16–24 hours. Normally off-white.

Primer sealer oil-based; used for sealing porous or crumbly surfaces – but add thinners if surface is highly absorbent. Dries in 24 hours. Normally off-white in colour.

Stabilizing primer Off-white primer used to bind masonry surfaces which have become powdery. Provides a colour base for painting.

Stabilizing solution Clear fluid for binding masonry surfaces which have become powdery. Does not colour the surface.

Stain blocker Off-white spray sealer for small stains which may bleed through emulsion painted finish (not suitable under gloss or eggshell). Dries in 10 minutes.

METAL PRIMERS/ RUST TREATMENTS

Calcium plumbate Use on new, untreated galvanized iron, such as traditional metal window frames. CONTAINS LEAD. Not suitable for children's rooms, toys or furnishings. Dries in 16–24 hours.

Etch primer Specialist coating (care needed in use) with excellent bonding to clean metals; used as preparation under metal primer. Dries in 1–4 hours.

Zinc chromate Suitable for most metals, including aluminium, iron and steel; dries in 1–2 hours. Often yellow in colour, but may be tinted dark red. Normally sold in large tins only.

Zinc phosphate Buff or light grey non-toxic primer suitable for most metals including aluminium, iron and steel; dries in 2–3 hours. Normally only available in large tins.

Red oxide primer Used on mild steel; dries in 1–2 hours. Dark red.

Red lead primer Used on iron and steel; has excellent corrosion resistance. CONTAINS LEAD. Not suitable for children's rooms, toys or furnishings. Dries in 24 hours.

Rust converter/neutralizer Chemically combines with rust to form a stable compound (usually a black phosphate), works in 15 minutes.

Rust remover Usually a form of acid which dissolves rust on iron and steel in around 15 minutes.

Rust resisting primer Quick-drying primer with rust inhibitors to prevent corrosion. Normally dark brown or black in colour.

GENERAL-PURPOSE PRIMERS

Acrylic primer/undercoat White, water-based coating suitable for woodwork, plasterboard and masonry, but not bare metal. (Nail heads in wood or plasterboard should be spot-treated with metal primer.) Dries in half an hour.

Universal (all-purpose) primer Oil-based coating suitable for most materials including metal – though not necessarily as effective as specialized primers. White or off-white. Dries in about 6 hours.

WHAT TO USE WHERE

TYPE OF SURFACE	PREFERRED TREATMENT	OTHER OPTIONS
WOODWORK		
Softwood/man-made boards	Seal knots with knotting and apply wood primer or primer/undercoat.	Aluminium primer (resinous/charred wood); calcium plumbate (around metal frames).
Hardwood	Aluminium wood primer (thin slightly).	Wood primer or acrylic primer/undercoat.
Hardboard	Do not use wood primer – use thinned emulsion paint or acrylic primer/undercoat.	Aluminium wood primer.
Before varnishing	Seal with a first coat of thinned varish.	Sanding sealer.
MASONRY		
Bare plaster/absorbent walls	Before emulsion, seal with a first coat thinned with one quarter water.	General-purpose primer (on very absorbent surfaces) or acrylic primer/undercoat.
Bare brick	Seal with thinned alkali-resisting primer/sealer.	Stabilizing solution.
Powdery/loose plaster	Brush down and seal with alkali-resisting primer/sealer.	Stabilizing primer. Stabilizing solution.
Crumbling render	Brush down and seal with stabilizing solution.	Stabilizing primer.
METALS		
Aluminium/alloys	Zinc chromate. Do not use rust treatments.	Etch primer, general purpose primer.
Sound cast iron/steel	Degrease and dry. Apply zinc phosphate or red oxide primer.	General purpose primer.
Rusty cast iron/steel	Remove/neutralize rust and fill with epoxy putty. Prime at once with zinc phosphate.	Rust resisting primer.
Galvanized steel	Do NOT sand unless rusted. Wash, then prime with calcium plumbate.	General-purpose primer (allow new galvanized steel to dull first).

CHOOSING PAINTING TOOLS

Choosing the right painting tool can make any decorating job simpler and quicker. It also helps to get a good finish, whatever type of paint you want to apply and whatever surface you are decorating.

Painting walls and ceilings

For large areas, a roller is usually quicker and less tiring to use than a brush, and the paint tends to go on thinner and more evenly. Because of this, using a roller gives a good 10% more coverage in most cases.

The drawbacks are that you may get more spatter when using liquid paint, and some people dislike the 'orange peel' texture which can be left by a roller. Also, you still need a small brush or pad to finish off edges and corners, and cleaning up the sleeve afterwards can waste time, cleaner and paint. On small jobs, it's likely to be less trouble to use a brush.

You can use a roller for any type of paint providing you fit the right sort of sleeve (see overleaf). For textured papers or texture paint, use one with a pile which is long enough to cope with bumps and dips without skipping over the surface.

If you prefer to use a brush, pick one at least 100mm (4″) wide – commonly called a *wall brush*. Most people find this the most comfortable size – larger brushes are heavy when loaded with paint and can be hard on the wrists. Alternatively, you can use a large paint pad. In both cases, you still need a smaller brush or pad for edging. When painting masonry, choose a brush designed for the job – rough walls are hard on brushes.

An option which gives very even coverage and a good finish is to use a spray gun. These can be hired, but may work out very expensive unless you have a large area to do. It also takes a long time to mask the areas you don't want painted.

Painting woodwork and fittings

Use brushes or pads as you prefer. Narrow rollers can also be used for large wood panels. Pads allow a more even coverage than brushes, but can be tricky in corners. They are also harder to clean properly – especially when using oil-based paint – so you may prefer to use the disposable type.

A 50mm (2″) brush for large areas plus a 25mm (1″) one for smaller ones will cope with most

jobs – although you may want another, smaller brush for awkward areas. The equivalent pad sizes are normally around 60×50mm (2½×2″) and 100×50mm (4×2″).

Varnishing

Varnish is best applied with brushes, and you need the same sizes as for paint. But it's a good idea to keep a set of brushes just for varnishing – there is always a risk of discolouring the finish if the bristles are not completely clean.

Painting problem areas

Some areas require special tools.

Edging and glazing bars are easier to paint with a cutting-in brush, or edging, sash or crevice pad. A hand-held paint shield helps guard areas you don't want to paint.

Radiators are hard to paint behind – although you only have to worry about the areas you can see. Either let the radiator down from the wall (see page 32), or use a radiator brush or roller.

Pipes and railings are difficult to paint evenly. If you have a lot to do, you can use a special pipe roller or sheepskin paint mitten.

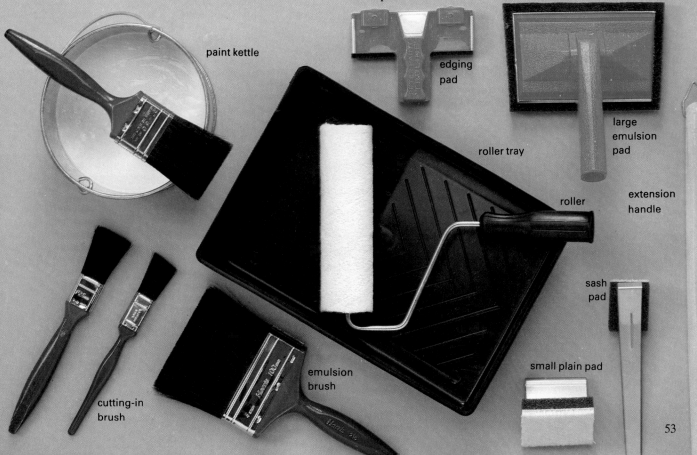

paint kettle

edging pad

large emulsion pad

roller tray

roller

extension handle

sash pad

cutting-in brush

emulsion brush

small plain pad

BRUSHES

emulsion brush

paint kettle

Paint brushes commonly range in width from 12mm (½″) to 150mm (6″). The most useful widths are 25mm (1″) for windows, 50mm (2″) for large areas of woodwork and 100mm (4″) for walls.

Cheap brushes are best for rough work and things like bitumen paint (which is hard to clean off) because they can be thrown away. Where finish is important, medium priced brushes work just as well as expensive ones (which take hours of use before they're 'broken in').

Look for a thick filling of fairly long bristles – tapered evenly at the ends and split to aid the paint flow. Brushes for masonry paint have tougher bristles than those for indoor work. All new brushes lose some bristles; flick backwards and forwards across your fingers to tease them out, and don't use a new brush for top coats straight away.

Use brushes with a metal or plastic **paint kettle** rather than painting from the tin. It helps to control the amount you get on the bristles.

ROLLERS

standard roller

roller tray

narrow roller

Standard rollers are usually either 190mm (7½″) or 225mm (9″) wide, but larger rollers 305mm (12″) and 380mm (15″) wide are also made. You need a roller tray to fit the roller unless using 'solid' roller paint which comes with its own.

Rollers have a metal or plastic frame with a removable sleeve. The sleeve can be made from foam, synthetic fibre, mohair or sheepskin. The pile varies in length. Sheepskin is expensive but holds the most paint. It must not be used with

gloss. Fibre and mohair are cheaper and can be used with gloss. Foam is cheap but spatters badly and gives a poor finish in most cases.

Narrow rollers about 50mm (2″) wide are for large areas of woodwork.

Ceiling rollers have a long handle and a tray to hold the paint. Ordinary rollers can be used by fitting an extension handle. More expensive types have a telescopic handle; simpler ones have a hollow in the handle into which a broom stick can be jammed.

PAINT PADS

pad tray

large emulsion pad

small plain pad

Paint pads are made from rectangles of mohair or synthetic pile about 6mm (¼″) thick, backed with foam and clipped into a frame in a metal or plastic handle. There are various sizes ranging from about 60×50mm (2½×2″) to 225×100mm (9×4″). In general, the large ones are for walls, the small ones for awkward areas and woodwork.

For the best results, it's important only to load the pile with paint – if paint clogs the foam and hardens, the pile will not brush the surface evenly. Paint pad 'kits' often include a tray with a built-in roller to make loading easier. Some makes feature clip-on replacement pads, others must be discarded complete if worn or clogged.

SPECIAL PURPOSE PAINTING TOOLS

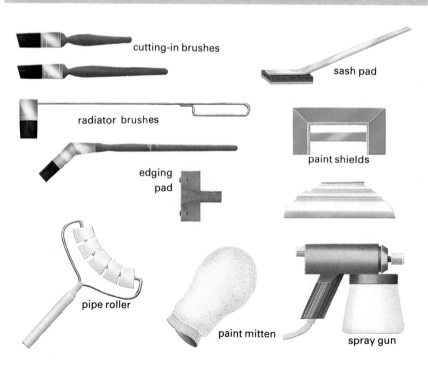

cutting-in brushes

sash pad

radiator brushes

edging pad

paint shields

pipe roller

paint mitten

spray gun

Cutting-in brushes have their bristles set to finish at a slant. This makes it easier to run down an edge when painting round windows or where two colours join in a corner.

Edging, sash and crevice pads are for awkward areas and corners. They cover a smaller area than ordinary pads, and edging pads have guide wheels to help them follow a line accurately.

Paint shields are held against a surface you don't want to paint.

Radiator brushes have long handles and an angled head to reach down into the narrow gap behind a radiator.

Pipe rollers or curved rollers are for painting plumbing fittings – they are spring loaded to mould themselves to awkward shapes.

Paint mittens are for very awkward areas like railings.

Sprays are expensive but can be hired. They make quick work of large areas of paintwork, but you must mask the area thoroughly. Aerosols can be used for small jobs.

PAINTING WALLS AND CEILINGS

Aside from good preparation, there are three rules for achieving a successful finish when painting walls and ceilings.

■ Choose the right tools for the job.

■ Paint in the right order so that you don't smudge previously painted areas, or find yourself having to stop at an inconvenient place.

■ Arrange proper access so that you're always painting from a comfortable position.

Before you start, gather together a supply of newspaper, old rags and plastic bin liners, plus a cloth for wiping drips. If you're using oil-based gloss or eggshell, make sure you have plenty of brush cleaner.

Arranging access

Two stepladders – one about 1.8m (6') high and one about 1.2m (4') – are your most useful pieces of equipment. On ceilings, place a scaffold board between them to create a platform stretching across a comfortable working area. On walls, two of you can use a stepladder each to reach the high spots.

Make sure the top steps are wide enough to take a roller tray. (You can also buy bolt-on roller tray attachments for stepladders.)

Scaffold boards can be hired from hire shops and builder's merchants, but you could consider buying one since they have many other uses.

Position your working platform so that you can paint the walls comfortably between chest and shoulder height. Painting at full stretch is tiring, and makes tools hard to control.

WHAT ORDER TO PAINT IN

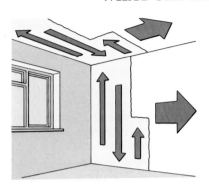

■ As a general rule, paint the ceiling first, then the walls. If the room has coving and this is to be the same colour as the ceiling, paint it at the same time.

Otherwise, leave it until you've painted the walls.

■ Always start at the window end of a room and paint away from the light; this makes it easier to see where you've just painted. If there is more than one window, choose the largest. On other walls, start on the right if you are right-handed, on the left if you are left-handed.

■ Aim to complete whole walls (or ceilings) in one go – stopping part-way through could leave unsightly drying marks. If there are two of you, work on separate areas and complete them both in the same session.

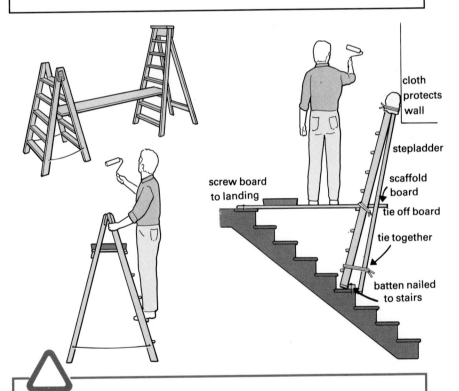

cloth protects wall

stepladder

scaffold board

screw board to landing

tie off board

tie together

batten nailed to stairs

Avoiding mess

❛ ■ *Keep paint tins together and make a point of replacing the lids straight away.*

■ *Never leave painting tools, kettles or trays on the floor.*

■ *Discard paint-soaked newspaper and rags immediately into a plastic bin liner.*

■ *Keep a damp (or solvent-soaked) rag close by to mop up splashes as soon as they occur.*

■ *Keep your hands and tools as clean as possible at all times.* ❜

On stairwells you may have to improvise a working platform. For safety, nail a batten to the staircase to hold the larger pair of stepladder legs steady.

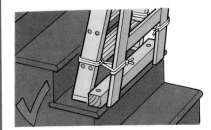

Avoid using chairs as supports, as they are rarely strong enough. Old tea chests, a portable workbench, or steps laid on their side are good alternatives.

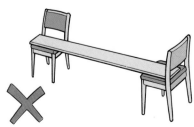

PREPARING THE PAINT

Decant the paint into a clean container before you start. If you're using a wall brush, it's worth buying a plastic or metal **paint kettle**; otherwise use a roller tray.

If the paint is old and a skin has formed on the surface, you may be able to 'rescue' it by straining it into the container through a pair of old tights. Lift the skin carefully from one side so as not to break it up. However, it's wiser to discard the paint, as partial drying may have changed its consistency.

Unless the tin specifically says otherwise, stir the paint thoroughly using a clean stick.

A paint kettle gives you room to dip in a brush without getting paint on the ferrule (the metal part). It's also lighter to carry than a large paint tin.

Tie a length of string taut between the handle pivots and use it to scrape off excess paint as you withdraw the brush. You can also use it as a brush rest.

BRUSH TECHNIQUES

Even if you use a roller or paint pad to cover the main area, you still need a brush to fill in around the edges; the ideal size is 50mm (2″).

On a small area, or one containing lots of awkward corners, it's often simpler to use a 75–100mm (3–4″) brush for the whole job.

Some people also find brushes handier for applying resin-based paints, as they are easier to clean than roller and pad equipment.

Always brush away from a wet edge rather than into it so that the paint thins out (called 'feathering'). This stops unsightly lines forming between areas of paint.

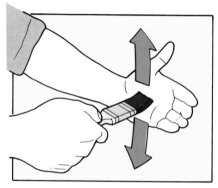

Flick the brush across your hand to 'tease' out any loose bristles. Then load it about a third of the way up to avoid getting paint on the ferrule.

When painting narrow strips, hold the brush between finger and thumb. Cover with loose strokes, draw off at right angles, then smooth with one continuous stroke.

To paint a clean edge, bend the bristles so that a bead of paint forms. Twist the brush so the bristles thin out and draw the bead along the edge.

On larger areas, apply the paint in broad vertical bands, gripping the brush as shown. Continue brushing until the bristles show signs of emptying . . .

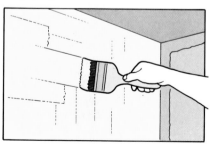

. . . then, without reloading, brush across the bands using much gentler stokes to even out the paint. Finish with light vertical strokes to remove the brushmarks.

ROLLER PAINTING

Choose your roller according to the surface and type of paint. Use a short pile for smooth surfaces, a long pile if the surface is uneven or textured. Cheap foam rollers are really only suitable for emulsion, while for gloss or eggshell, a short pile synthetic or mohair roller is the best choice.

When loading a roller, take care not to dip it too far into the tray; roll on the ramp several times to spread the paint and avoid drips.

Trade tip

Which direction?

6 With emulsions, it's easiest to work across the wall in bands. Start at the top, working from a platform or stepladder, then remove the platform and do the lower half.

With resin-based paints, it's wiser to work up and down the wall so that drips and roller lines can be rolled out as soon as they occur. 9

Paint in zig-zag or criss-cross strokes until the roller begins to empty. Then run back across the area with parallel strokes to remove the streaks.

TECHNIQUES FOR CEILINGS

Cover a ceiling in bands about a metre (or yard) wide, working away from the main light source. Keeping the roller just in front of you helps avoid drips.

An extension roller can be used instead of a platform on low ceilings, but is less easy to control. You still need to brush-paint around the edges first.

When brush painting, slip paper plate or piece of card over the handle to catch drips. Paint small areas at a time, and take care not to overload the brush.

USING PAINT PADS

1 Load the pad from a roller tray or paint pad tray (these have built-in rollers to make loading easier). Try not to get paint on the backing or handle.

2 Do the edges first, using a small pad or edging pad. Rest the wheels of an edging pad against the wall and run along it in a single continuous stroke.

3 Cover an area of about a square metre (or square yard) working across the surface in short, random strokes. Then go back and sweep over any marks.

CLEANING EQUIPMENT

Even cheap throw-away tools must be cleaned thoroughly between sessions: flecks of partly dried paint on bristles and rollers are guaranteed to ruin the finish. With rollers, it's helpful to blot the excess paint in a sheet of newspaper before slipping the sleeve off its frame.

Emulsion can be washed off in the sink using warm water and washing up liquid. Work your fingers through the bristles of brushes and the fibres of rollers or pads to shift any paint that's already partly dried. Then rinse under a cold tap until the water runs clear and pat dry between sheets of newspaper.

Water washable eggshells and glosses are easier to clean if you work neat washing up liquid into the bristles prior to washing in warm water. Rinse and pat dry.

Solvent clean eggshells and glosses must be dissolved first using white spirit or brush cleaner. Pour the solvent into a jar and do the brushes first, working the bristles vigorously. Then pour the contents of the jar into a kettle or paint tray to clean rollers or pads. Afterwards, wash the tools in warm water and washing up liquid, rinse in cold water, then pat dry.

Wrap painting tools in cling film or plastic bags if you have to take a quick break.

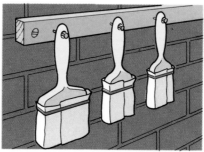

Store brushes with the bristles wrapped in newspaper held on with elastic bands.

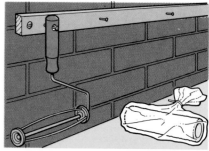

Seal rollers in plastic bags – but make sure they're dry first. Store handles separately.

◢ PROBLEM SOLVER

What went wrong?

With paint faults, prevention is better than cure: most can only be put right by stripping or rubbing down the faulty coat and starting again.

The following precautions will also guard against faults:
- If in doubt about the compatibility of paint surfaces, test on a hidden area first.
- Don't use old paint.
- Make sure previously stored tools are clean and dry.

Staining may be due to contaminated paint, or to substances in the wall becoming 'activated' by solvents in the paint.
To cure: leave to dry, then treat with aerosol stain block or spirit-based sealer before repainting.

Poor coverage of an underlying colour cannot be cured simply by applying the paint more thickly, which leads to tears and runs. Either switch to a 'one coat' topcoat (these contain denser pigments for increased covering power), or apply one thin coat and another when dry.

Blistering is common when painting over lining paper, but most of the bubbles will disappear as the paint dries. Slit any that remain with a trimming knife and slip a little wallpaper repair adhesive behind. Retouch when dry. Blistering of paint surfaces could be due to incompatibility. Cure as for crazing.

Crazing indicates that the topcoat is incompatible with the underlying paint.
To cure: leave to dry, then rub down and apply a coat of primer/sealer.

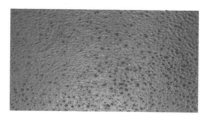

'Orange peel' is an effect produced by cheap foam rollers. If it's not to your liking, repaint using good quality synthetic pile or lambswool.

Partially dried runs and tears are easy to miss when painting walls and ceilings. Don't attempt to brush out.
To cure: leave to dry, then rub down and repaint, 'feathering' the edges.

Flaking occurs when the topcoat fails to grip the underlying surface. This could be because the surface hasn't been properly prepared, or (rarely) because the paint itself is faulty.
To cure: rub down when dry and apply a coat of primer/sealer.

Wrinkling is a sign that the underlying paint surface hasn't dried properly. It usually appears within a few minutes.
To cure: stop immediately and wipe off the blistered topcoat with a clean rag. Leave to dry out thoroughly, then rub down and repaint.

PAINTING WOODWORK AND FITTINGS

Assuming you've prepared the surfaces properly, getting a good finish on woodwork and metal is as much about painting in the right order as it is about skill with a brush. The secret is not to rush, and to plan things so that you always work out from an edge which is still wet: brushmarks and ridges are nearly always the result of painting over previously painted areas after these have begun to dry.

Within any one room, aim to paint the movable joinery – doors and windows – early in the day so that they'll be dry enough to close by nightfall. Paint the rest of the fixtures working from the highest point downwards: this way, any dust that's disturbed will fall on to unpainted areas.

Tools and equipment

Brushes are still the best painting tools for woodwork and metal. Normally, you can get by with just two: a 50mm (2″) brush for flat areas, and a 25mm (1″) brush for mouldings and rebates. For very large areas, a 75mm (3″) brush will

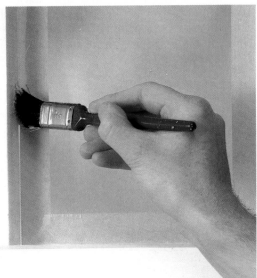

do the job quicker but not necessarily better. And a 19–25mm (¾–1″) cutting-in brush is a good buy if you have a lot of glazing to paint.

Other requirements will depend on the areas being painted (see overleaf), but may include:
■ Access equipment.
■ A paint kettle, plus jars for storing and cleaning brushes.

Use masking tape to get a clean edge when painting window frames.

■ Cleaning rags and appropriate solvent for the paint being used.
■ Screwdrivers and other tools for removing door/window furniture.
■ A paint shield and masking tape.
■ Fine and medium abrasive papers or steel wool, for rubbing down.

BRUSH TECHNIQUES

Tease out loose bristles on the flat of your hand. If you spot flecks of old paint, soak in brush restorer or paint stripper and flush clean under a cold tap.

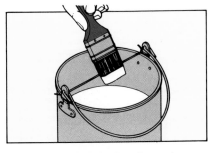

Always use a paint kettle, and don't dip the bristles more than a third of the way in. Scrape off excess paint – the prime cause of runs – against a piece of string.

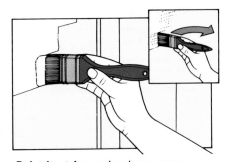

Paint in strips, using long, even strokes running with the grain. Continue until the brush empties, then 'lay off' with reduced pressure and shorter strokes.

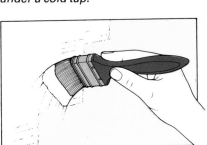

After reloading, blend the next series of strokes with the first by fanning the bristles slightly. Always work to a wet edge, so you don't overpaint partly dried areas.

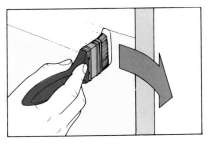

Always paint towards an edge and brush off it, or the paint will 'catch' and run. Where necessary, paint the end grain first using short, dabbing strokes.

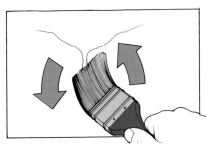

Deal with runs as they appear by working the paint over the surface before it can dry. Where there's a choice, it helps if you start at the top and work down.

PAINTING WINDOWS

Windows must be painted in a strict order (see below), depending on whether they are sashes or casements. Before you start, remove the stays, catches, locks and any other fittings. If the screws are clogged with old paint, dab on a little paint stripper to clear the slots and then remove the fittings.

Sealing the glass

Carry the paint about 3mm (⅛″) on to the panes so that it forms a weather seal between the glass and the frame. There are two ways to ensure you get a clean edge:

Paint the frame direct using a cutting in brush or a paint shield (see below). Both methods take practice, but are convenient if you are doing a lot of painting.

Mask the frame first using masking tape. This is effective, but costly and time-consuming. Make sure the contact edge of the tape is stuck down throughout its length – not forgetting the 3mm (⅛″) for the weather seal – or paint may creep underneath. Remove the tape before the paint dries hard.

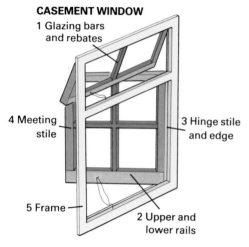

CASEMENT WINDOW

1 Glazing bars and rebates
4 Meeting stile
3 Hinge stile and edge
5 Frame
2 Upper and lower rails

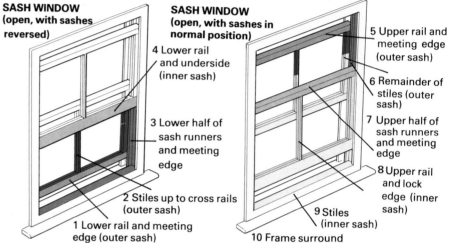

SASH WINDOW (open, with sashes reversed)

4 Lower rail and underside (inner sash)
3 Lower half of sash runners and meeting edge
2 Stiles up to cross rails (outer sash)
1 Lower rail and meeting edge (outer sash)

SASH WINDOW (open, with sashes in normal position)

5 Upper rail and meeting edge (outer sash)
6 Remainder of stiles (outer sash)
7 Upper half of sash runners and meeting edge
8 Upper rail and lock edge (inner sash)
9 Stiles (inner sash)
10 Frame surround

Painting order – casement window. Hold the casement open with coathanger wire while you paint it. Drive a small nail into the bottom rail, hook the wire over it, then hook the other end in one of the vacant screw holes in the frame.

Painting order – sash window. Sashes must be painted in two sessions, starting with the sashes reversed. Take extra care with the runners – paint them as thinly as you can get away with, and adjust the sashes slightly as soon as the paint is touch-dry to release any stuck areas. After completing the full sequence, touch up any missed areas.

STAIRS, SKIRTINGS AND MOULDINGS

When painting any type of fixed joinery, the golden rules are:

■ Apply the paint thinly – even if this means you need two coats.

■ Use the right size brushes – a 25mm (1″) brush for rebates, mouldings and rounds (ie balusters), and a 50mm (2″) brush for the larger areas.

Plan the work so that you aren't rushed and don't have to finish at anything other than a definite edge. Stairs may have to be painted in two sessions: do all the risers and alternate treads in one, then paint the remaining treads in the other.

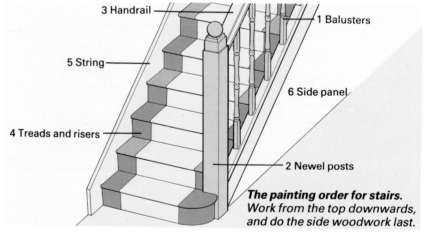

3 Handrail
1 Balusters
5 String
6 Side panel
4 Treads and risers
2 Newel posts

The painting order for stairs. Work from the top downwards, and do the side woodwork last.

Trade tip

Keep it clean

❛ No matter how clean the surfaces are after preparation, dust is bound to settle on them – so wipe everything down again just before you paint it. Some DIY stores sell sticky tack rags precisely for this purpose. Otherwise use a just-damp lint-free cloth – an old linen handkerchief is ideal. ❜

Use a paint shield on skirtings – even where you have rolled back the carpet – otherwise the paint brush will pick up dust from the gap below.

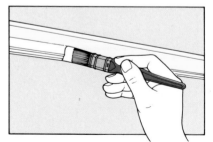

On picture rails and other mouldings, define the edges with a small brush, then switch to a larger brush to cover the remaining area.

PAINTING DOORS AND FRAMES

Like windows, there is a set sequence for painting doors depending on whether they are flush-panelled, glass or full-panelled.

Again, it's advisable to remove as much of the furniture – handles, lock covers, fingerplates – as possible before you start. Wedge the door partway open so that you can get at the edges and avoid being locked in (but keep the handle with you in the room just in case).

As a general rule, on each section work down from the top (so that you catch any drips), and from the centre towards the edges. Apply the paint sparingly to avoid runs.

On panelled and glazed doors, paint the moulding areas in thin coats using a 25mm (1″) brush.

Trade tip

Painting in two colours

❛ If you are painting a door different colours either side, paint the side on which the door opens first. Then paint the lock edge, the meeting edges of the door stops and the hinge side of the architrave the same colour.

Switch to the second colour and paint the reverse side of the door, followed by the hinge edge, and the architrave up to and including the door stops. ❜

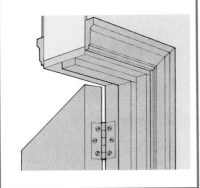

Treat a glass door or French window as you would a casement window.

Paint a panel door starting with the panels and mouldings. The door can be left at this point if you need to take a break before completing the rails and stiles.

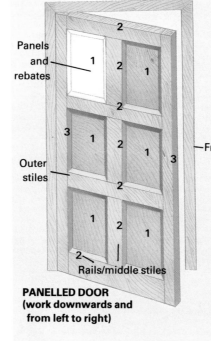

PANELLED DOOR
(work downwards and from left to right)

Paint a flush door in one session, working quickly so that the edges stay wet. Keep your strokes long, but light, and don't overbrush.

GLASS DOOR
(work downwards and from left to right)

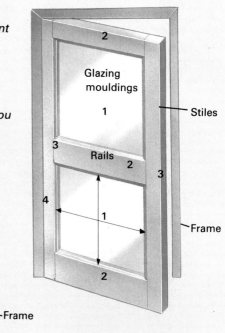

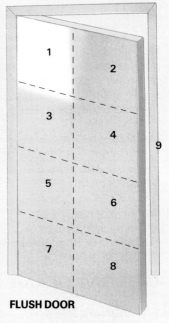

FLUSH DOOR

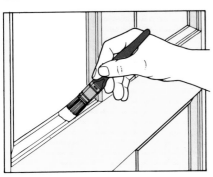

Paint the moulded rebates on a panelled door as if they were separate pieces of wood, using a small brush. This will help to avoid drips on the panels.

Take extra care at the edges: paint with light strokes, angled outwards as shown, so that there is no danger of the paint catching and forming runs.

Trade tip

Undercoat or not?

❛ Think of undercoat as a very thin filler – for disguising pits in the surface, hiding an old colour, or building up the 'body' of the paint film so that it looks smooth and hard. Like filler, too, undercoat is made to be sanded before overpainting.

Normally, it's only necessary to undercoat bare wood. But if a painted surface is heavily sanded and patched, undercoat helps draw the patches together. ❜

PAINTING METAL FITTINGS

As long as the surface is properly prepared, there should be no need to apply a layer of undercoat to metal fittings.

Intricate decorative metalwork is best removed and spray painted.

Radiators should be painted cold, though if you turn them on after about an hour you'll speed the drying process. Work from the centre outwards with a 50mm (2") brush, taking extra care not to catch paint on the sharp edges. Avoid getting paint near the valves.

Pipes should be painted with a 25mm (1") brush. Apply the paint as thinly as possible, and on vertical sections work down from the top.

Windows must also be painted thinly or they won't fit (the tolerances are closer on metal frames). If the paint build-up is already heavy, it may be better to strip it first using chemical stripper.

When painting, follow the same sequence as for wooden casements.

Using enamel

Painting metal with hard-curing enamel calls for a slightly different technique to gloss or eggshell:
- Use the larger of your two brushes wherever possible.
- Apply the paint thinly, using minimal pressure and long, steady strokes.
- Work quickly. On a flat surface, it's easier to pour on the paint straight from the can, then use the brush to spread it evenly.

When using enamel paint, work quickly with long, light strokes and keep the paint coat thin. Use a large brush wherever possible.

1 Use pieces of cardboard to protect other surfaces when painting around the back of pipes. Apply the paint thinly, to avoid runs.

2 Take extra care when painting radiators not to let the paint 'catch' on the sharp edges. Avoid getting paint on the control valves or their connections.

PROBLEM SOLVER

Runs and blemishes

If you discover a run or other blemish after the paint has started to dry, don't attempt to brush it out.

Leave the paint to dry fully, then rub down with fine grade glasspaper and touch in with fresh paint.

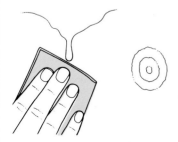

Stuck sashes

If sashes are sticking due to the new paint, you should be able to release them with an old kitchen knife.

Once you've got the sashes moving again, tape a piece of medium grade wet and dry paper over the blade and use this to smooth down the previously stuck edges. Where necessary, touch in any patches that show with a very thin coat of paint.

TOOLS FOR HANGING WALLCOVERINGS

Although most wallpapering tools are quite specialized, you can't really do without them. Measured against the cost of calling in a professional, they are relatively inexpensive, and if you have a full set (see panel) you'll find the job goes a lot more smoothly.

Access equipment

Before considering hand tools, spare a thought for access. A single stepladder should allow you to reach everywhere you need to, but check first. If you are tall, you may find a home-made hop-up or low folding steps more convenient.

Papering ceilings and stairwells raise special access difficulties. These are discussed in the relevant chapters.

A BASIC TOOLKIT

For measuring and marking:
- Plumbline and chalk

or
- Spirit level and straightedge
- Tape measure

For pasting and hanging:
- Pasting table
- Pasting brush
- Plastic buckets (2–3)
- Smoothing brush
- Seam roller

For cutting and trimming:
- Special wallpaper scissors
- Pair of ordinary scissors
- Sharp trimming knife

Wallpapering tools tend to be used one after the other in quick succession, and it's easy to mislay them when the room is covered in trimmings. The answer is to use a decorator's apron with a wide front pocket, so that everything stays close to hand.

MARKING AND MEASURING TOOLS

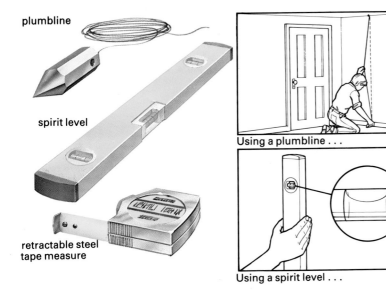

plumbline

spirit level

retractable steel tape measure

Using a plumbline . . .

Using a spirit level . . .

A plumbline is the most convenient tool for marking vertical lines on walls (which ensure that drops are hung straight). Consisting of a long, thin cord with a weight attached to the end, you pin it at the top of the wall, rub the cord with chalk, then snap it against the wall to leave a mark once the weight has stopped moving.

Professional plumblines have the weight shaped to a point for accuracy; but for wallpapering, you can easily make your own from a length of thin garden twine and a heavy steel bolt.

Alternatively, use a **spirit level and straightedge** and mark the lines in pencil.

A retractable steel tape measure – ideally the 3m (10′) size – is the best tool for measuring long drops.

TOOLS FOR CUTTING AND TRIMMING

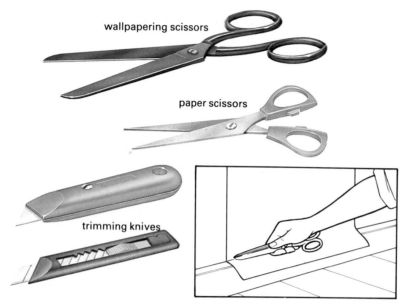

wallpapering scissors

paper scissors

trimming knives

Marking with scissors

Wallpaper scissors (sometimes called *shears*) are absolutely essential, both for cutting drops to size, and for trimming them once they are on the wall. The ideal overall length is 250–300mm (10–12″), which helps give clean, straight cuts.

The backs of wallpaper scissor blades are specially designed for creasing the paper so that you know where to trim. However, in confined spaces and around awkward shapes you may find ordinary **paper scissors** easier to handle.

A sharp trimming knife should never be used for cutting drops to size, or for trimming – the paste-soaked paper will simply tear. But with vinyl coverings, you'll find one useful for trimming through the overlaps at corners.

There are also a number of patented cutting gadgets on sale. These may be useful, but if possible you should see how they suit you before buying.

TOOLS FOR PASTING AND HANGING

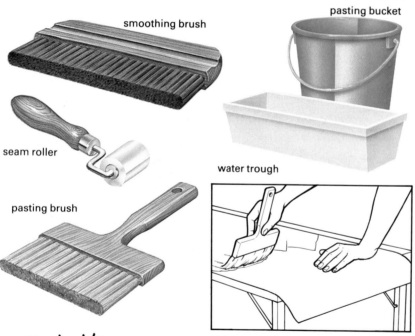

smoothing brush

pasting bucket

seam roller

water trough

pasting brush

Using a pasting table

A pasting table provides the ideal flat surface on which to paste wallpaper, and is a better investment than you might think. (If you're really trying to economize, you could use a flush door or a sheet of man-made board propped on chairs or trestles.)

Purpose-made pasting tables are made of hardboard with a softwood frame and fold flat for easy storage. Choose one measuring around 2m (6′6″) long by about 600mm (2′) wide – just wider than a roll of wallpaper.

Plastic buckets come in handy for mixing paste and cleaning tools. If you have a lot of papering to do, mix the paste in two buckets so that one batch can be left to stand while you use the other. A piece of string tied across the top of the bucket provides an easy way to wipe excess paste off the brush.

Pasting brushes are available, but an ordinary paintbrush will do just as well – 100mm (4″) is the ideal size.

A water trough is essential for most ready-pasted papers (though with some, you brush water on the drops as if you were pasting). You can buy plastic troughs complete, or a flat-packed cardboard kit which you fold together.

A smoothing brush is a wide brush with soft, good-quality bristles and no handle, used to smooth out the paper on the wall. You may find a **dry sponge** easier to use with vinyls, and for high quality, hand-printed papers, a special **felt roller** is recommended.

Seam rollers are for pressing down the joints between drops to ensure the edges don't lift. They are more efficient than using a soft cloth and won't damage the paper.

For most types of paper, use a **wooden seam roller**; for relief wallcoverings, which are easy to crush, use a wide, **foam-covered roller** instead.

Trade tip

The versatile dowel

❛I keep a piece of 12mm (½″) diameter wooden dowel, slightly longer than the width of a roll of wallpaper (about 600mm – 2′) in with my decorating kit. This has several uses:
■ Use it to hold back the rolled end of a drop during pasting.
■ Tape it between two chairs and use it to hang drops after pasting and folding.
■ When papering a ceiling, use it to hold a concertina-folded drop as you carry it to the ceiling, and to support the drop as you smooth it out. ❜

CHOOSING PAPER AND PASTE

Wallcoverings come in a huge range of designs and materials, which means that for most jobs you'll be spoilt for choice. The various types are described in detail overleaf, but to make choosing easier, start by asking yourself these questions:

When do you plan to start? Some wallcoverings have to be ordered days or weeks in advance; if you want to start hanging straight away, this immediately limits you to designs stocked by the shop.

Is this your first attempt at papering? If it is, you should avoid cheap papers (which tend to stretch), expensive papers (which must be kept free of paste on the right side) and speciality coverings such as flocks and foils (which are difficult to handle).

What is the condition of the wall? Lumps and bumps will show up even more if you choose a very thin wallcovering, or one with a glossy finish or regularly striped pattern. Textured wallcoverings, however, help to disguise uneven walls.

Are the walls irregularly shaped, with awkward obstacles? This makes pattern matching difficult. If possible, choose papers with a random pattern match so that you don't have to spend ages trying to match motifs between lengths.

Are you papering a ceiling? Look out for patterns specially designed for ceilings. These have small or subdued patterns and do not have a 'right way up'.

Is there a lot of direct sunlight on various parts of the room at differ-

Clever choice of wallcoverings adds a designer touch to any room.

ent times of the day? Look out for colour-fast papers which won't fade (see symbols box below).

Is the room prone to condensation? Spongy vinyls have a slight insulating effect, helping to reduce condensation. They are also easy to clean, which makes them a good choice for kitchens and bathrooms.

How much wear and tear will the covering have to withstand? In hallways, kitchens and children's rooms, it may be a good idea to use a covering with a spongeable – or even scrubbable – finish (see be-

low). Strong textures and patterns can also help to disguise marks.

What type of wallcovering are you using? If you are hanging a delicate printed paper you may be advised to put up lining paper first. This involves much more work, so be sure to check the maker's label.

Will you want to re-decorate soon? If so, you may want to choose strippable or peelable papers which make re-decoration easy.

WALLCOVERING SYMBOLS

Whatever a wallcovering is made of, standardized symbols on the manufacturer's label will give clues to the surface finish and any other special features. These symbols can often be found in wallpaper pattern books as well. The most common symbols are shown on the right, so if you're looking for a specific quality (eg good light fastness) be sure to check before buying.

There may also be special instructions for hanging (and stripping) the wallcovering – either on the label, or in a separate leaflet. Read these before buying any equipment.

Symbol	Meaning	Symbol	Meaning	Symbol	Meaning
~	Spongeable	☀	Good light fastness	⊢•⊣	Straight match
≈	Washable	⌐	Strippable	⊢•⊣	Offset match
≋	Super-washable	⌐	Peelable	$\frac{50}{25}$ cm	Design repeat Distance offset
▦	Scrubbable	⊔	Ready pasted	≋	Co-ordinated fabric available
☀	Moderate light fastness	⊫	Paste-the-wall	↑	Direction of hanging
		•⊢∘	Free match	↓↑	Reverse alternate lengths

TYPES OF WALLCOVERING

WALLPAPERS

This group covers a wide range of wallcoverings from the cheapest to the most expensive. Different types of paper have their own limitations.

■ Cheaper lightweight papers tend to crease or tear and may stretch.

■ Expensive printed papers are often unwieldy and may be ruined if you get paste on the right side.

Coated papers are wipeable and easy to handle.

Embossed wallpapers have a relief pattern stamped into them. They are recommended for use on bumpy walls, but are easily crushed and may be difficult to stick. (See *Relief wallcoverings* right.)

RELIEF WALLCOVERINGS

This term covers a range of plain white wallcoverings which have a deeply embossed or relief pattern. All help to disguise bumps and other surface defects, and most are designed to be painted.

Woodchip is an economical covering made of wood chippings sandwiched between layers of paper.

Anaglypta is a brand name for a heavy-duty embossed wallpaper, with the pattern stamped on the surface. The range includes copies of original Victorian designs.

Relief vinyls have a deeply embossed pattern and flat paper backing, making them easier to handle.

Blown vinyl relief coverings come in pastel shades as well as white, which don't need painting.

Lincrusta is a top-of-the-range covering made (like linoleum) from oxidized linseed oil and fillers. It comes in rolls or panels, for use below chair rails (dados), in halls and areas receiving heavy wear.

DECORATIVE BORDERS

Decorative borders have become quite common over the last few years. You can use them to contrast or co-ordinate with a wallcovering, or to decorate a plain painted wall. Some types are pasted like conventional wallpaper; others are ready-pasted for soaking and sticking, or are self-adhesive with a protective, peel-off backing, which makes them easier to stick to vinyls. They are not suitable for use with high relief wallcoverings.

VINYLS

Vinyls divide broadly into *plain* and *textured* types. There are several different methods of manufacture, but look for ones with a *flat back* (paper-backed), as this gives an even, absorbent surface for pasting and makes the covering easy to strip. Many vinyls come ready-pasted; if not, make sure you use a paste containing fungicide.

Plain vinyls may be smooth or have a very slight surface texture. They are easy to hang and are available in a wide range of patterns, often with co-ordinating fabrics. Some types have a light-reflective finish which gives the wall a soft sheen; not recommended for bumpy surfaces.

Textured vinyls undergo various heat treatments during manufacture to produce a random or regular relief pattern, combined with an embossed colour pattern. *Blown vinyl* has a flat back and a puffy texture. *Sculptured vinyl* is a heavier duty version with a deeply textured spongy layer – often imitating wall tiles. It is flat-backed, crush-resistant, and suitable for use on uneven walls.

Textured vinyls are also well suited to condensation-prone rooms, where they provide a waterproof, insulating layer.

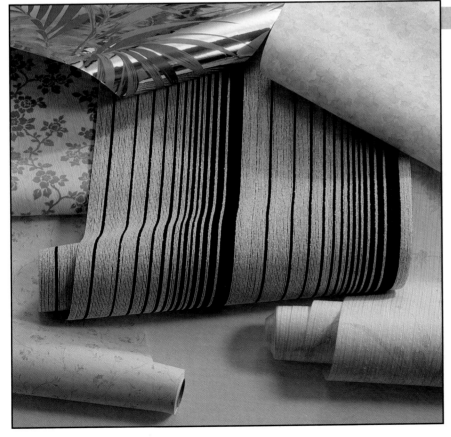

SPECIALITY COVERINGS

The wallcoverings in this group are distinguished by their unusual surface, or by the way they're hung.

Novamura is a polyethylene covering with a soft feel, almost like felt. It is very light, easy to hang and a good choice for ceilings. You paste the wall, not the covering.

Metal foil coverings have shiny patterns. They are unsuitable for poor surfaces – the shine highlights blemishes. Again, paste the wall.

Paper-backed fabrics include hessians and grasscloths. The thicker types can be unwieldy to hang, and with all types you need to take great care not to get paste on the right side.

Unbacked fabrics are generally expensive and need skill to hang – you have to paste the wall, and use special trimming techniques. They are covered elsewhere.

Flocks have a velvety pile on a paper backing. Vinyl flocks are easier to hang and clean.

WALLPAPER PASTES

Modern wallpaper pastes come in two forms – as a **powder** to mix with cold water, and **ready mixed** in tubs.

Starch-based pastes stay workable the longest and have good adhesion, but they are susceptible to mould growth and are not a good choice where there is damp or condensation.

Cellulose-based pastes give slightly less adhesion, but resist mould growth and are less likely to stain the face of the wallcovering.

PVA-based pastes aren't really pastes but adhesives. They usually come ready mixed in special formulas for hanging speciality coverings such as Lincrusta or fabrics.

Some makes use a combination of the above bases. But whatever the base, look for a paste marked 'with fungicide' if you plan to hang vinyl wallcoverings.

What strength?

Pastes range in strength from 'regular', through 'all purpose', to 'heavy duty'. The labelling varies between brands, so check the instructions or ask your supplier's advice when buying the wallcovering. Generally, the heavier the covering, the stronger the paste, but it's always worth using stronger-than-usual paste on gloss-painted walls and areas subject to heat.

How much?

Coverage for ready-mixed types varies, but should be specified on the tub. With powder types much depends on the absorbency of the covering and the porosity of the wall, but as a rule of thumb 2.5 litres (½ gal) will cover 3-4 rolls.

Other products

Overlap/repair/border adhesive is formulated for sticking paper backing to a vinyl surface. It is usually sold in tubes or tubs.

Size is sold in powder form for sealing absorbent surfaces prior to pasting. Unless the surface is very poor, you can make your own size by diluting ordinary wallpaper paste to half its normal strength.

Always check the manufacturer's instructions to ensure the paste suits the wallcovering and the surface you are hanging it on.

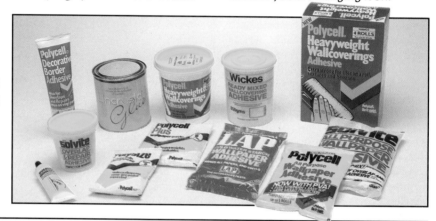

BUYING WALLCOVERINGS

Standard wallpaper rolls measure 10.05m×530mm (33'×21"), although many manufacturers make their rolls slightly smaller, 10m×520mm (33'×20½"). In either case, use the chart below to find out how many rolls you will need.

■ Measure the height of the walls.

■ Measure the total distance around the room. Include ordinary doors and windows, but exclude any large areas (eg fitted cupboards) that don't need papering.

■ Read off on the chart the number of rolls needed for the height and distance around the room.

If the room size does not correspond with the sizes given on the chart, or the rolls are a non-standard size, either consult the manufacturer's own coverage chart or use the following method:

■ Measure the height of the wall being papered – the drop length.

■ Where appropriate, round up the drop length to take in an exact number of pattern repeats.

■ Divide the length of the roll by the drop length, to find how many drops you can cut from each roll.

■ Measure around the room to see how many drops you need. Round up to the nearest whole number.

■ Divide the total number of drops by the number of drops per roll, to give the total number of rolls.

Trade tip

Check the colour

❝ Although wallpaper colours can vary even within the same batch, there may be quite startling variations between one batch and another.

Avoid the problems this creates by checking that all your rolls are from the same batch – the batch number should be given on the manufacturer's label. It's also worth estimating on the generous side: it's safer to buy a bit extra than go back for more rolls from a different batch. ❞

NUMBER OF ROLLS REQUIRED

WALLS Distance around room	9m 30'	10m 34'	12m 38'	13m 42'	14m 46'	15m 50'	16m 54'	17m 58'	19m 62'	20m 66'	21m 70'	22m 74'	23m 78'	25m 82'	26m 86'	27m 90'	28m 94'	30m 98'
Height																		
2.15-2.30m 7'-7'6"	4	5	5	6	6	7	7	8	8	9	9	10	10	11	12	12	13	13
2.30-2.45m 7'6"-8'	5	5	6	6	7	7	8	8	9	9	10	10	11	11	12	13	13	14
2.45-2.60m 8'-8'6"	5	5	6	7	7	8	9	9	10	10	11	12	12	13	14	14	15	15
2.60-2.75m 8'6"-9'	5	5	6	7	7	8	9	9	10	10	11	12	12	13	14	14	15	15
2.75-2.90m 9'-9'6"	6	6	7	7	8	9	9	10	10	11	12	12	13	14	14	15	15	16
2.90-3.05m 9'6"-10'	6	6	7	8	8	9	10	10	11	12	12	13	14	14	15	16	16	17
3.05-3.20m 10'-10'6"	6	7	8	8	9	10	10	11	12	13	13	14	15	16	16	17	18	19

Ceilings: to calculate the number of rolls required, work out the area in square metres and divide by five.

HANGING WALLPAPER

Although it's true to say that wall-papering isn't as easy as the professionals make it look, it isn't that difficult either. Much depends on doing things in the right order so that you avoid problems rather than create them. There are also several things you can do to make life easier before you start.

If you're new to wallpapering:
■ Choose a medium sized, regularly shaped room for your first attempt. (More difficult jobs such as papering ceilings and stairwells are covered on pages 77-82.)
■ Choose a vinyl or good-quality medium weight paper that won't stretch during hanging. That way, you are less likely to run into any serious problems on your first attempt at hanging wallpaper.

And even if you consider yourself an 'old hand' at papering:
■ Check the paper manufacturer's label for advice on which paste/adhesive to use and any special preparation or hanging instructions.
■ Make sure you have the essential tools: pasting table, bucket, pasting brush, plumbline or spirit level, papering scissors, tape measure, smoothing brush and seam roller.

Preparing the walls
As with all decorating, there is no substitute for proper preparation.
■ Existing wallcoverings must be stripped, and the wall cleaned down and made good. How much time you spend on this depends on the thickness of the new covering, but generally the more the better – even thick lining papers like woodchip show up bumps and hollows.
■ If the old covering is a 'peelable' vinyl on a paper backing, check that the backing is firmly stuck – if not, strip it.
■ Rub down gloss-painted walls with coarse abrasive paper or steel wool to help the paste grip.
Lining paper may be recommended by the paper manufacturer. If not, the choice is yours – lining is more work, but gives superior results. It also makes the wallcovering easier

to hang, which cuts down the risk of blemishes. **Sealing** ('sizing') is essential if the wall is bare plaster, advisable in other cases. Otherwise, the paste soaks too quickly into the wall and the paper bubbles or peels.
■ On old, very porous plaster it's best to use a purpose-made wall-paper size unless you've already sealed the surface with stabilizer.
■ On painted walls, use your chosen wallpaper paste diluted with around three to four parts water.
■ On new plaster, you should delay hanging any wallcoverings until the surface has dried out – which could take up to six months. In the meantime, give the plaster a coat of emulsion thinned with four parts paint to one part water: this will make it more liveable with, and provide a good surface for pasting at a later date.

Fixtures and fittings
Anything fixed to the walls with wallplugs is best removed – the clearer the walls, the easier it is to paper them. Mark the positions of the wallplugs with matchsticks, then let these poke through the paper as you hang it to mark the holes.

Electrical fittings don't need to be removed – normally, you can loosen them and paper behind, but be sure to turn off the mains first.

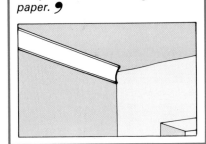

Trade tip
Hide the join
❛ If there is an uneven line between the wall and ceiling, and you're hanging a covering which contrasts strongly with the colour of the ceiling, it's worth putting up cornice, coving or scotia to give yourself a clean line to paper up to. Fill any gaps and paint before starting to paper. ❜

Easy does it – hanging the critical first drop (left).

GETTING STARTED

Before you start cutting or pasting, establish the following points.

Colour consistency Unwrap the rolls and check the colour under both daylight and artificial light. If there is any variation, plan to keep identically coloured rolls together on the same wall – any changes will be less noticeable if they occur at corners.

How the pattern works If the wallpaper has any sort of pattern, make sure you know where to cut and hang it so that it matches between drops. The panel on the right shows the four most common variations; there should also be advice on pattern matching on the manufacturer's label.

Where to start If the paper is plain, or there is no strong motif in the pattern, start somewhere which doesn't call for an exact pattern match (your starting point will also be your finishing point).

Bold patterns look better centred on the most prominent wall in the room (usually the chimney breast or wall opposite the door).

Finally, check that your chosen starting point doesn't leave any awkward, narrow drops.

PLUMBING A LINE

When you've decided roughly where to start, mark exactly where to hang the first drop. Don't rely on anything in the room being true; draw a vertical line with a plumbline or spirit level to ensure the paper will be straight.

If you start at a corner (or against a window or cupboard), mark the line 500mm (20″) away from it. This allows you to hang a full-width drop to one side of the line, then hang and trim the corner drop (which has to be trimmed at the side as well as top and bottom). Work round the room and back to the starting point.

If you start on a prominent wall, find the midpoint, then draw the line exactly half a roll's width from here. Hang the central drop first, against this line, then work around the room from *both* sides towards the least conspicuous corner (often the one nearest the door).

Usually, it's best to start close to a corner, fitted cupboard or full-length window. But if the pattern is bold, centre the first drop on the most prominent wall.

MATCHING THE PATTERN

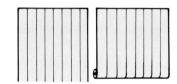

A continuous pattern won't need matching – you can cut the drops wherever you like.

With some random patterns, drops have to be hung in alternate directions so that any repeat in the pattern isn't obvious. This should be specified on the label.

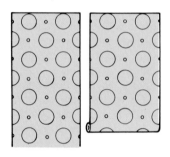 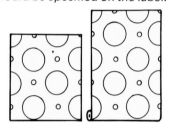

A straight match pattern has the same part of the pattern running down each side of the paper. When cutting, simply ensure there is enough overlap top and bottom to align the motifs exactly.

A drop match pattern has the motifs staggered between drops, which means allowing extra when cutting. The amount of stagger should be specified on the label. If it is large, you may be able to save on paper by cutting alternate drops from different rolls.

1 Draw a vertical line to mark your starting point – ie where to hang the first drop. To use a plumbline, pin it against the top of the wall and rub with chalk . . .

2 . . . then let the line hang vertically, press it against the foot of the wall with one hand, and snap it with the other to leave a chalk impression.

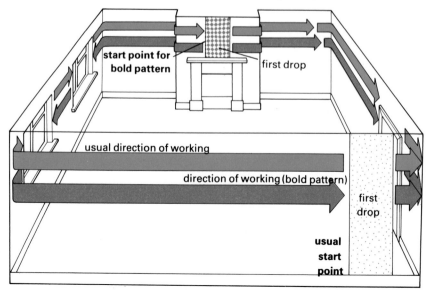

start point for bold pattern

first drop

usual direction of working

direction of working (bold pattern)

first drop

usual start point

CUTTING AND PASTING

For coverings that need pasting, it's up to you whether you cut several drops at a time or cut and paste as you go. If you are working with a partner, it is usually easiest if one person cuts and pastes while the other hangs and trims. And a helper definitely comes in handy when matching and cutting long drops.

Mixing paste

Powder paste usually has to stand for a while before it's ready for use, so mix it before you start measuring and cutting. Follow the instructions carefully (normally you mix the powder to a creamy consistency with a little water, then dilute it) and stir thoroughly.

Ready-pasted paper is soaked a piece at a time to activate the paste. Cut each drop to size, then place the soaking trough directly below where you're going to hang it.

Measuring and cutting

■ On the first drop, measure from the cornice or picture rail to the top of the skirting board, and add 100mm (4″) for trimming top and bottom.
■ On subsequent drops, allow extra for matching the pattern; in other words, check before you cut that the drop has the same number of pattern repeats, plus at least 50mm (2″) trimming allowance top and bottom.

■ Keep any short pieces to fill in gaps above doors, or above and below windows. Normally, a full length roll provides four drops.
■ Use the edge of the pasting table as a guide when cutting, to ensure you cut straight and at the correct point in the pattern.
■ Always cut before you paste – not when the paper is pasted and folded, as is sometimes recommended when cutting a drop lengthways (this method creases the folds and makes it hard to follow the pattern).

After pasting and folding, be sure to let the paste soak in for the recommended time – if you don't, it will bubble.

1 *Always use long wallpapering scissors for cutting. Use the edges of table to square up the paper, crease along the side edge, then slide along and cut.*

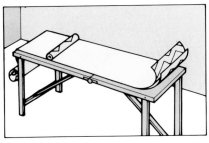

2 *After the first drop, don't forget to allow extra for matching the pattern – plus the usual 100mm (4″) trim allowance – when measuring and cutting.*

Trade tip

Draw a scale

❛ *To make measuring and cutting easier, I mark a scale along the edge of the pasting table in 100mm increments using a biro. This way, you can measure off lengths rather like a shop assistant measures fabric along the counter.* ❜

PASTING TECHNIQUES

1 *Lay the drop wrong side up with the nearest long edge and the top edge overhanging the table slightly. Leave the rest of the drop loosely rolled.*

2 *Paste in a criss-cross pattern, from the centre towards the overhanging edges. Then slide the paper away from you and paste the far edges.*

3 *Fold the pasted part over on itself and slide it off the table. Paste the rest of the drop in the same way, making sure you don't get paste on the table.*

4 *Having pasted the rest of the drop, fold this part in on itself too. Leave the paste to soak into the drop for the time recommended on the label.*

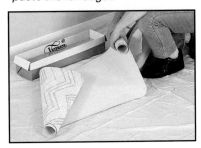

For ready pasted paper, *half fill the soaking trough with water. Roll the cut drop loosely from the bottom, right side out, and immerse it in the trough . . .*

*. . . **leave it to soak** for the time recommended by the manufacturer. Then simply grasp the drop by the top corners and lift it out on to the wall.*

HANGING AND TRIMMING

Once the paper has been pasted and soaked, the next step is to hang it. Be sure you know which is the top of the paper: with ready-pasted papers, it should be the end which comes out of the trough first; with other types, it will be the end you pasted and folded first.

Always try to hang a complete drop (ie full width, no obstacles) first, so that you get the 'feel' of the paper. And keep a clean, damp cloth ready to hand to wipe the tools you use to smooth down the paper (smoothing brush, seam roller and scissors).

1 Unfold the top half of the first drop and press it gently against the wall, leaving an overlap at the top. Check the pattern starts where you want it.

2 Slide the paper gently to and fro until the side edge aligns exactly with the plumbed line on the wall – but don't forget to maintain the top overlap.

3 Smooth the paper with the brush, working from the middle outwards. With the top half flat, unfold and smooth out the lower half in the same way.

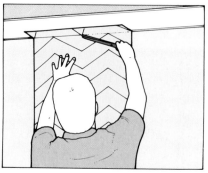

4 To trim top and bottom, gently press the paper into the angle of the ceiling, moulding or skirting with the back of your wallpapering scissors.

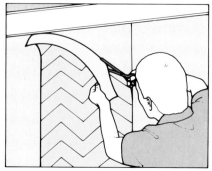

5 Then peel back enough paper to expose the crease that's formed and cut along it with the scissors. Smooth the paper back, then wipe off any excess paste.

Always smooth down the top before unfolding the lower portion of the drop.

6 With the second length pasted, folded and soaked, repeat the process so the next drop butts up to the first length. Check that the pattern matches.

7 After smoothing, marking and trimming the second drop, run the seam roller up and down the length of the seam, to ensure the edges do not lift.

DOORS AND WINDOWS

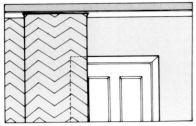
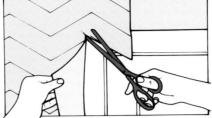

When you come to a door or window align the drop with the previous one and let it flap over the architrave or reveal. If there is a lot of waste, hold the paper against the wall and trim off some of the excess so that it doesn't pull away . . .

. . . then cut diagonally into the paper as far as the architrave or reveal and smooth down the rest of the flap with the brush. Afterwards, mark and trim along the top and side in the usual way, taking care not to tear the corner.

COPING WITH CORNERS

You can never rely on internal and external corners being square, so the rule is:
■ Cut a drop lengthways to fit the gap on one side of the corner, plus a little extra.
■ Paste this in position and turn the overlap around the corner.
■ Plumb a new line on the return wall the same distance from the corner as the width of the offcut.
■ Paste the offcut in position to cover the overlap on the first drop.

Using this method, you can be sure that the corner is filled with paper and that the pattern is maintained. The only points to watch are:

■ That the offcut is a reasonable width. If it isn't, use a fresh drop (which, ideally, you should trim lengthways to hold the pattern).
■ That the corner is reasonably square. If it's badly 'out', you'll need to increase the recommended overlap to take up the variations.
■ That you cut the corner drop accurately. Take your time, and use the edge of the table as a guide.
With vinyl wallcoverings, you may have difficulty getting the overlap to stick – use overlap/repair adhesive to stick the overlap down, or trim away the bulk of it with a sharp knife and metal straight edge.

Trade tip

Measure the repeat

❛ With small patterns and vertical stripes, I always measure the width of the pattern repeat before I come to the corner. Then, rather than allow the usual 25mm overlap, I adjust it to the width of the pattern repeat. This makes it easier to get a closer pattern match. ❜

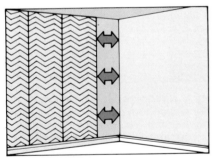

1 At internal corners measure into the corner from the edge of the last drop at several points. Add 25mm (1") to the widest measurement.

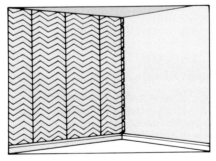

2 Cut a measured length to this width, then paste and hang it so that it just overlaps the adjacent wall. If wrinkles appear, clip or notch the edge.

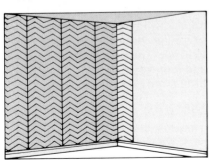

3 Plumb a new vertical the same distance from the corner as the width of the offcut. Hang the offcut so it slightly overlaps the previous strip.

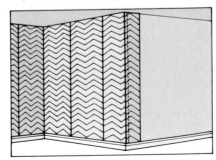

4 Treat external corners in the same way: turn the first part of the drop around the corner, then plumb a new line and hang the offcut to cover the overlap.

When hanging vinyls, you can avoid sticking down the overlap by cutting through both layers of paper, then peeling back and discarding the waste.

PAPERING AWKWARD AREAS

Unfortunately, no room is completely problem-free, and you're likely to have to cope with light switches and radiators as well as larger problems such as arches and window reveals.

SMALL OBSTACLES

Deal with small obstacles such as light switches and radiators as shown below. (Don't use the light switch technique for foil wallcoverings – they conduct electricity, so trim instead.)

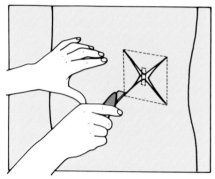

1 *Turn off at the mains* before papering around a light switch. Press paper over the edges of the switch so that it creases, and make diagonal cuts to each corner.

To paper behind a radiator, smooth down the drop as far as you can, then make vertical cuts in line with the bracket positions. Smooth the flaps down behind the radiator with any convenient padded tool.

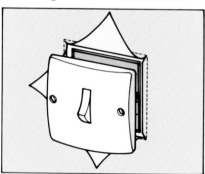

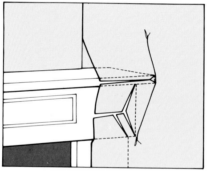

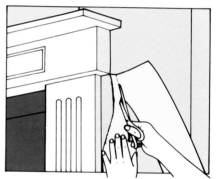

2 *Loosen the faceplate screws and trim off the flaps of waste paper to leave a 9mm (⅜″) margin all round. Smooth down the paper behind the faceplate.*

1 *Fireplace and window sills* may have extra angles to cut around. The rule is: clip into the waste part of the paper up to each change in angle . . .

2 *. . . then smooth and trim each flap in turn against the obstruction. You may find it easier to use ordinary scissors to make the smaller cuts.*

▌PROBLEM SOLVER ▐

Creases and wrinkles

These occur when the paper hasn't been smoothed out properly, or because it has been smoothed out working from the outside inwards.

To cure, peel the paper back to the problem area and smooth out again. If the paper has started to dry, apply a little more paste to the wall.

Always double-check that there are no wrinkles – especially along the fold line – before you start trimming the top and bottom edges.

Bubbles

Bubbles indicate that the paper hasn't been sufficiently pasted or that it hasn't soaked for long enough.

If the paper is still wet, lift it away from the wall and smooth it out again – if necessary applying a little extra paste to the wall.

If the paper has partly dried, make a pin-prick in the bubble to release the air and press down. If this doesn't work, make a cross-shaped cut with a sharp trimming knife and squeeze in some repair adhesive.

Bumps

If the wall has been properly prepared, bumps which suddenly appear will be caused by lumps or foreign matter in the paste. Peel back the paper immediately and remove; if necessary, brush a little more paste on the wall.

Blotches

These are simply the result of the paste showing through the paper. They may look awful just after hanging, but should disappear as the paste dries out – which can sometimes take several days.

WINDOW REVEALS

The diagram on the right shows the sequence for papering a reveal with reasonably straight sides:

■ Hang a full-length drop at one side (1), overlapping the reveal. Cut into the overlap at the soffit and the sill, then try to wrap the paper into the reveal.

■ Continue with short drops above the reveal, turning them back under the soffit (2,3,4).

■ Hang similar short drops below the sill, maintaining the pattern (5,6,7).

■ Hang a second full-length drop in the same way as the first, aligning it carefully against the last two short drops (8).

■ Fill in the spaces in the corners of the soffit with offcuts, tucking under the surrounding paper (9,10).

■ If the full-length drops aren't wide enough to fit to the back of the reveal, hang further narrow width strips (11).

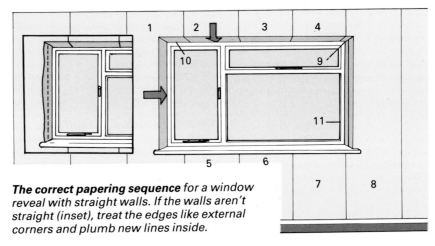

The correct papering sequence for a window reveal with straight walls. If the walls aren't straight (inset), treat the edges like external corners and plumb new lines inside.

With uneven walls, treat the edges of the reveal as any other external corner – leave a 25mm (1") overlap and plumb a line inside the reveal.

Planning the job

To make this sequence work, you need to ensure the full-length drops overlap the reveal by a sufficient amount, and that you're left with an exact number of widths in between. For this reason, it's probably easier to paper the reveal first, before tackling the rest of the room.

1 Hang the first full-length drop to overlap the reveal. Fit at the ceiling, then cut horizontally at the soffit and sill using a sharp blade.

2 Wrap the overlap into the reveal and fit the back edge, then fit at the skirting and sill. Hang short drops above window, wrapping under soffit.

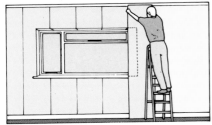

3 Hang the short drops beneath the window, then hang the second full-length drop as in step 1, matching the edge to the short drops as closely as possible.

4 Prepare patches to fill the gaps under the soffit, making them 25mm (1") larger all round with one machined edge matched to adjacent strip. Lift paper around reveal, paste patch in position then smooth down.

ARCHES AND ARCHED ALCOVES

On an open archway which is being papered both sides, paper the inside of the arch with the least dominant of the two patterns.

■ Paper the faces of the two walls first, trimming and turning the drops 25mm (1″) into the arch; make toothed cuts (called 'clipping') to stop the overlap crinkling.

■ Then paper the inside of the arch with a single long strip, pasted and folded concertina-fashion for easy handling. (If you haven't enough paper left, use two strips with a seam at the crown of the arch.)

In an arched recess paper the face of the wall as above, then plumb a line on the back of the recess. Paper the back of the recess using this line as a guide, taking care to match the pattern both horizontally and vertically with the paper on the face. Trim the paper, wrapping 25mm (1″) on to the inside of the arch, and cut notches so it lies flat.

Finally, paper the inside of the arch to cover the overlaps.

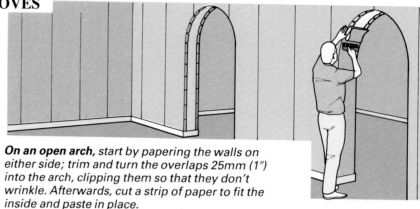

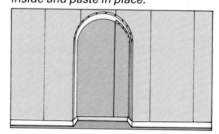

On an open arch, start by papering the walls on either side; trim and turn the overlaps 25mm (1″) into the arch, clipping them so that they don't wrinkle. Afterwards, cut a strip of paper to fit the inside and paste in place.

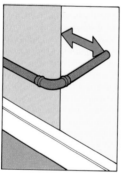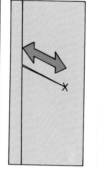

With an arched recess paper the outer wall first. Plumb a line down the back of the recess and paper this, ensuring the pattern aligns, then paper the inside.

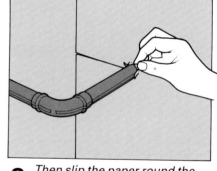

With some patterns it's easier to get a match if you use two strips for the inside of the arch. Arrange for the seam to be at the crown of the arch.

SMALL ROOMS

Lack of working space is one of the main problems in a small room. Set up the pasting table in a nearby room, and use the concertina method (see page 79) for folding the paper so that you can carry it easily. Leave the pasted lengths to soak on a small table outside the room being decorated.

Pipes and shelves may have to be papered around using small patches. Mark any patches directly on to the unpasted roll, leaving a small overlap. Cut and paste them one at a time, to be sure of getting a good pattern match.

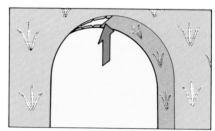

1 Around pipes, measure the distance from the edge of the paper to the pipe. Cut into the paper and cut a cross at the position of the pipe.

2 Then slip the paper round the pipe and smooth down to match the edge of the previous drop. Clip into the paper so it fits around the pipe, then trim.

PROBLEM SOLVER

Disguising joins and overlaps

Making perfect butt joins on a clear, straight wall presents few problems. But when wallpapering awkward areas, you often have to join drops or patches at points other than the manufactured edge of the covering. There are several ways to make such joins less noticeable, depending on the covering:

■ On all types, choose an easily identifiable part of the pattern motif to cut through, so that the match between offcuts is consistent.

■ With heavily textured coverings (such as blown vinyls), overlap the layers with the pattern matching, then cut through both together to make a perfect butt join.

■ With thin wallcoverings and those which don't tear easily, cut the underlapping layer in a wavy line as this makes the joins less obvious.

■ With good quality papers, coated wallpapers and paper-backed vinyls, tear the underlapping layer to make a 'feathered' join.

Cut through heavy vinyls.

Tear for a feathered edge.

WALLPAPERING CEILINGS AND STAIRS

Papering a ceiling is not as difficult as you might think, though unless you've got plenty of wallpapering experience it's definitely a job for two people. Compared with walls, there are usually fewer obstructions, and no awkward corners to turn. The only real problem is organizing the equipment to get you up there.

Prepare a ceiling for papering by stripping off old wallcoverings, washing off distemper or chipping off polystyrene tiles and glue. If the ceiling was previously decorated with texture paint, either remove it or plaster over it (easier). If it was flat but gloss painted, rub down to provide a good key. Seal or size absorbent surfaces.

Choosing a ceiling paper

If you want a pattern on the ceiling, choose it carefully. Small or random match patterns are easier to align on long strips than large patterns. And in most cases a soft, pale pattern is more appropriate than a bolder one, which could draw the eye to the ceiling and create a slightly oppressive effect.

If the ceiling has a poor finish, choose a textured effect: either a white relief decoration, or a pastel blown vinyl, for example.

Another consideration is the weight of the wallcovering. Remember, the heavier it is, the more your arms are likely to ache at the end of the day.

Special techniques, such as using a broom support, help to make ceiling papering straightforward.

HOW MANY ROLLS?

For standard width rolls – 530mm (21″) – and a regularly shaped ceiling area, simply measure the distance around the room and then read off the number of rolls required from the chart on the right. If the room is L-shaped, divide it into smaller rectangles. Measure the distance around each of them, read off the rolls required on the chart, then add the figures together to find the total number of rolls.

To double check, you should come to the same result by working out the area of the ceiling in square metres and dividing by five (or working out the area of the ceiling in square feet and dividing by 50).

For non-standard rolls, use a calculator to divide the length of a roll by the length of the ceiling area to find how many full strips you can get from each roll. Then divide the width of the area by the width of the roll to find how many strips are needed to cover the area. Finally, divide the total number of strips needed by the number of strips you can get out of one roll, to give the number of rolls. Round up to the nearest whole number.

Distance round room		No of
m	ft	rolls
10	33	2
11	36	2
12	39	2
13	42	3
14	46	3
15	49	4
16	52	4
17	55	4
18	58	5
19	62	5
20	65	5
21	68	6
22	72	7
23	75	7

ACCESS AND SAFETY

The main problem when decorating ceilings is getting yourself to the right level so that you don't have to stretch too far.

The simplest arrangement is to rest a pair of sturdy planks between two stepladders as shown. Scaffold boards, which measure around 38×225mm (1½×9") are ideal for this – they are available for hire, or you may be able to borrow them from your local builder's merchant.

If you only have one stepladder, support the other ends of the planks on a sturdy pair of kitchen steps, a portable workbench or even a stout table, depending on the height of the ceiling.

In rooms with fairly low ceilings, a pair of sturdy milk or beer crates may be just as good. But if you have a whole house to decorate, it may be worth investing in one of the new lightweight aluminium ladders that double as hop-ups and trestles.

Safety points

■ If the boards bow, reduce the span between them or sandwich two together. There's little point in trying to span the entire length of the room: use a soft broom wrapped in a clean cloth to support the paper while you shift the platform from one part to another.
■ Never stretch or try to reach too far to either side of the platform – always get down and move it.

Arrange ladders and scaffold boards so that you can reach the ceiling with the palm of your hand, and your head is just below the level of the ceiling.

Trade tip

Getting up there

❛ As a tall person, I never go on any decorating job without my hop-up – made from glued and nailed offcuts of 12mm (½") plywood and blockboard.

If the ceiling is low I can usually paper it with the hop-up alone, simply by shuffling it along the floor as I go. A shorter person would find the hop-up just as useful for reaching the tops of walls or above fitted cupboards. ❜

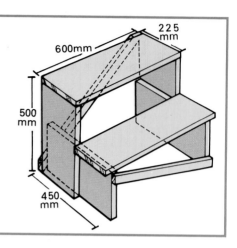

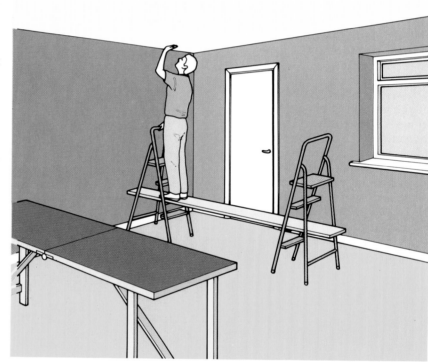

WHERE TO START

When ceilings were papered with overlapping joints, it was usual to start along the main window wall so that the joints didn't catch the light. But if you butt-joint the strips, this no longer applies. Instead, paper across the width of the room – the shorter the strips, the easier they are to hang and the less you have to move the platform.

On an unobstructed ceiling start just under a roll's width from the wall with the fewest obstacles. Hang a full-width strip first, so you can fit and trim the strip along the wall once you have got used to the basic hanging technique.

If there's a large plaster rose, it's easier to start just beside this and then work outwards.

On a clear ceiling, measure 500mm (20") out from the wall at each end. Stretch a chalk-covered line between the two points and snap it to give a straight start line.

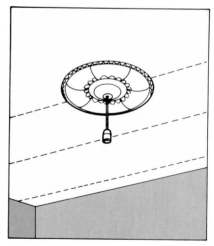

At a ceiling rose, work out the easiest way for the strips to fall (normally one either side), then measure and mark a starting line accordingly.

CUTTING, PASTING AND HANGING

You measure, cut and paste ceiling strips in the same way as drops for walls, allowing a 50mm (2″) margin for trimming both ends. But gravity, combined with the length of the strips, means you need to fold the strips concertina-fashion before carrying them up to the platform. Don't forget to leave the strips to soak for the recommended time.

You'll find it easiest to set up the platform slightly to one side of the start line. If there are two of you, one person should paste, fold (and if necessary support strips) while the other smooths and trims.

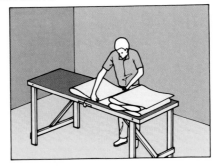

1 After cutting and pasting the first strip, fold concertina-fashion allowing 300–500mm (12–20″) between folds. Fold a further 500mm (20″) at the end.

2 Carry the folded strip up to the ceiling, supported on a spare roll or wood dowel. Align with the start line, allow for the overlap, and smooth down.

3 Work back down the platform, unfolding and smoothing along the start line. If you need to move the platform, support the remaining folds with a broom.

4 Crease and trim the ends of the first strip, then hang the second. Ensure a perfect butt join as you unfold by smoothing out towards the trimming edge.

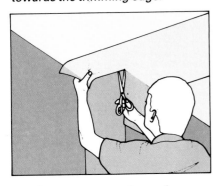

5 At a recess – an alcove, for example – make a straight cut down the strip in line with the edge of the corner, then smooth down the flaps and trim.

6 When fitting a strip into a corner, make release cuts by clipping diagonally into the paper. Afterwards, smooth the paper into the corner, then crease and trim in the usual way.

LIGHT FITTINGS

As with a socket or light switch, the neatest way to deal with a light fitting is to paper behind it. Before you do so, **turn off the power at the consumer unit**. If this leaves you in darkness, remove both lighting circuit fuses (marked '5 amp', or with a white dot), switch the power back on, and then run a side lamp from a nearby power socket.

When cutting and trimming:

■ Paper up to the ceiling rose fitting as you mark its position, and press on the flex outlet to indicate the centre of the cross.

■ Don't cut the cross back too far: slip the pendant and the rose cover gently through it, unscrew the rose cover, then trim back the triangular flaps just enough to clear the rose itself. Finally, refit the cover.

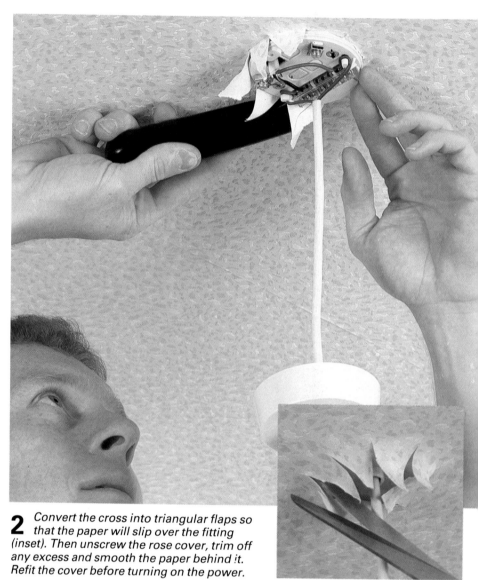

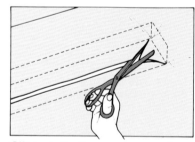

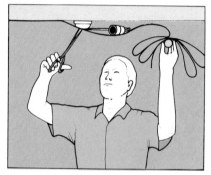

1 *When you come to the light fitting, press the strip against it to leave a mark. Cut a cross at this point and slip the lampholder through.*

2 *Convert the cross into triangular flaps so that the paper will slip over the fitting (inset). Then unscrew the rose cover, trim off any excess and smooth the paper behind it. Refit the cover before turning on the power.*

PROBLEM SOLVER

Dealing with other obstructions

Decorative plaster roses often have intricate shaping round the edge, making it difficult to trim the paper neatly.

Start by cutting into the side of the strip and trimming it roughly to shape so that it begins to lie flat. Then make further radial cuts every 25mm (1") or so into the waste, following the line of the rose. Smooth the paper down as you do so, and trim off any remaining excess. (On some roses, there is a lip around the edge which disguises the trimmed ends completely.)

Strip lights, spots and tracks are treated differently according to how they are fixed.

Spot clusters can be papered behind like a pendant light fitting, but with tracks it's usually easier to turn off the power and remove the track altogether prior to papering.

With a fluorescent strip light, or a track that's difficult to remove, make a slit in the paper roughly corresponding to the centre of the fitting, then clip out towards the corners. Press the paper down over the light and trim in the normal way to butt up to the fitting.

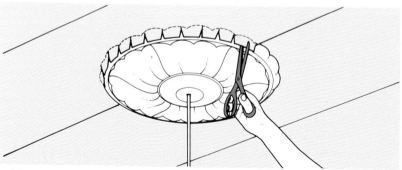

Slit and clip the paper around a fluorescent fitting or track.

Make radial cuts around the edge of a plaster rose, then smooth down and trim the excess.

ACCESS FOR STAIRWELLS

There are numerous ways of arranging working platforms on stairwells, depending on the shape of the stairs and what's available.

If you are lucky, the stairs will be straight with a solid head wall above, a few steps from the bottom. But many houses have at least one quarter turn, necessitating a more complex arrangement.

The examples shown here are based around simple ladder/scaffold board set-ups and can be adapted to fit most staircase layouts. However, for a large or double-flight staircase it may be less trouble to hire a scaffold tower (see overleaf).

Whatever the arrangement, check before you start that you can reach everywhere you need to without stretching.

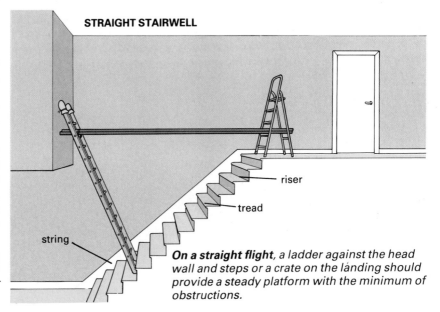

STRAIGHT STAIRWELL

riser

tread

string

On a straight flight, a ladder against the head wall and steps or a crate on the landing should provide a steady platform with the minimum of obstructions.

QUARTER-TURN STAIRCASE

Try to plan the job so that you don't have to lean a ladder support against a newly decorated wall. Where this isn't feasible, wrap the top of the ladder in old cloths to protect the surface.

Avoid resting ladders or scaffold boards on banisters – they are seldom strong enough.

Test other supports for strength before using: a portable workbench and milk or beer crates are all suitable; small tables and tea chests are suspect. Never use anything mounted on wheels.

Use proper scaffold boards measuring at least 225×38mm (9×1½"). On spans of more than 1.5m (4½'), sandwich two boards together.

Hold scaffold boards in place by lashing them around nails driven in the ends, or by clamping them with G-clamps.

Stepladders used as supports should be tied securely together. Anchor the foot between wood battens.

Get your assistant to steady the foot of any ladder you are climbing.

Position the foot of a ladder in the angle between a tread and the adjacent riser. Nail a batten to the tread to steady it.

Remove stair carpets if possible. Otherwise, pin cloth dust sheets along the strings and treads, or tape pieces of brown paper to each tread. Don't use plastic sheets.

Trade tip

Steadying influence

❛ If you are using your own scaffold boards, try this tip where they have to cross each other at right angles.

Set the boards up and steady the supports. Then, where boards cross, drill a hole through both and slip in a coachbolt, large nail or screw. This braces the boards laterally – the only way they can fall – and helps to strengthen the entire structure. Don't drill hired boards though – use G-clamps instead. ❜

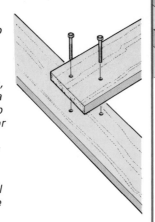

With a deep quarter turn, adapt the basic arrangement to form a cross-over platform. If the quarter landing is wide enough, open out the steps and lash to nails driven into the floorboards. Otherwise, tie the steps together and sandwich the feet between a pair of battens. Pad the top to guard against slipping.

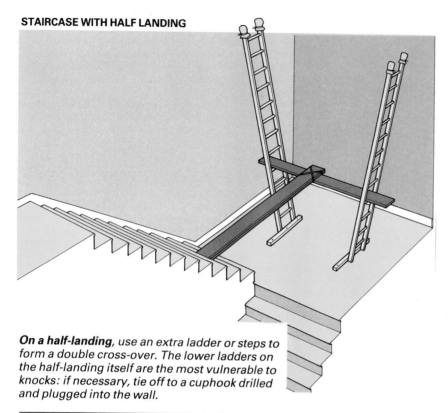

On a half-landing, *use an extra ladder or steps to form a double cross-over. The lower ladders on the half-landing itself are the most vulnerable to knocks: if necessary, tie off to a cuphook drilled and plugged into the wall.*

A hired scaffold tower *may be the only way to reach all parts of a large staircase. Miss out one or more tube sections to fit the treads and level with wood planks.*

GETTING STARTED

Prepare the walls in the normal way, stripping off existing wall-coverings and washing down paint-work. Size bare plaster before hanging a new wallcovering.

If possible, remove stair carpets; if you can't, cover the treads individually with tough brown paper or pieces of dust sheet, taped or pinned in place. Do not use plastic sheeting, which would be dangerously slippery on most stair carpets. And pay particular attention to any protective covering while you are working: rucks and wrinkles are a common cause of accidents.

As a general rule, you should start near the corner of the stairwell which has the longest drop. This will help to keep awkward trimming to a minimum in what is probably the area which is most difficult of all to reach.

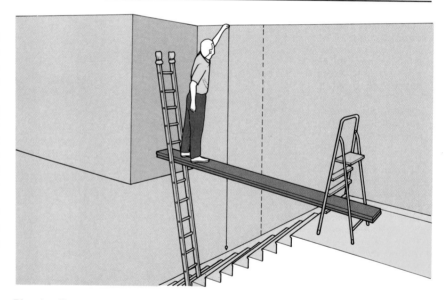

Plumb a line *to mark your starting point 500mm (20") from where the floor/ceiling or head wall meets the side wall of the well. Hang the first drop away from the obstruction, to get the feel of the paper.*

1 Measure the first drop, allowing for extra for the angle of the strings (skirtings). Cut, then paste generously so the paper doesn't dry out as you work.

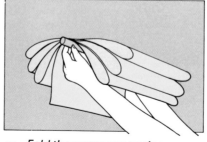

2 Fold the paper concertina-fashion and support it on a spare roll or wooden dowel. Get your assistant to hold it while you get up the ladder.

Trade tip

A short soak

❛ When using a wallcovering with a long soaking time on a stairwell, I always reduce the manufacturer's recommended time by five to ten minutes. Soaked paper is more likely to stretch, so by reducing the time, you should avoid some of the problems of matching unevenly stretched drops. ❜

RENOVATING CERAMIC AND QUARRY TILES

Ceramic and quarry tiles are among the most hardwearing of all wall and floor surfaces – but like anything else they may begin to show their age after years of exposure to steam, dirt and accidental knocks. Their most valuable qualities – solidity and permanence – can also be a problem if you don't like the colour, or you're in the process of making major alterations to the rest of the room.

Hacking off tiles and starting from scratch is a major job which more often than not involves replastering or rescreeding. Fortunately, there are simpler solutions – whether you just want to give the existing surface a facelift, or blend it subtly into a new decorative scheme.

CLEANING AND RESEALING

Although giving tiles a quick wipe-over is usually enough on a day-to-day basis, they need more vigorous cleaning occasionally to remove grease and stains on the grout.

■ Use a household cleaner recommended for tiles and apply with a nylon (not metal) scouring pad. Rinse afterwards to remove smears, especially on unglazed quarries.

■ Where there is mould on grout, scrub it off with a solution of 1 part bleach to 6 of water. If the grout starts to chip away, however, then renew it (see overleaf).

■ Scrub discoloured epoxy grout (as found on worktops) with a nylon scourer moistened with neat bleach.

Resealing

Wherever the tiles meet other surfaces, renewing seals which have become damaged or discoloured can work wonders for the appearance of a tiled wall, as well as guarding against damp problems.

For the new seal choose from:
Silicone or acrylic sealant, both of which come in a variety of colours. If the seal is to be white, choose acrylic – it doesn't discolour so much. Don't use on gaps over 6mm (¼″) as the sealant is likely to sag and look uneven.

Quadrant tiles which are sold in kits containing end and corner pieces. If you can't get an exact match, consider a contrasting colour. Bed in ready-mixed tile adhesive/grout unless the surface is likely to move, in which case use flexible sealant as the adhesive instead.

Sealing strips, which come in both flexible and rigid types in a variety of colours. Many are self-adhesive; if not, use contact adhesive.

Trade tip

Cleaning quarry tiles

❝ For really stubborn stains on old quarries which won't respond to bleaching or scouring, use hydrochloric acid – available from chemists as Spirits of Salts. Use neat or mix up a strong solution in warm water, and wipe over the surface. Leave for a few minutes, then rinse off with lots of clean warm water. When dry, apply 3 to 4 coats of linseed oil. ❞

SAFETY NOTE
Hydrochloric acid is dangerously corrosive.
■ Wear goggles and PVC gloves.
■ Add acid to water, not water to acid.
■ Store out of children's reach.
■ Work in a ventilated room.
■ Rinse splashes immediately with plenty of water.

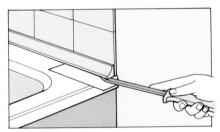

Prise off badly fitting quadrant tiles or sealing strip with an old kitchen knife, being careful not to damage the surrounding surfaces. Clean off old adhesive.

Old sealant must be patiently gouged out and scraped off with an old chisel. Afterwards, clean and degrease the surface with a cloth soaked in white spirit.

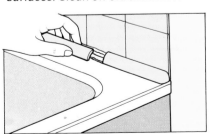

Bed new quadrant tiles in tile adhesive or flexible sealant, depending on whether or not there is likely to be movement. Grout between tiles in the normal way.

Apply new sealant from the tube or in a gun, working away from you. Do each gap in one pass, steadying your arm against the wall so your hand doesn't shake.

Flexible sealing strips are often self-adhesive – unpeel the backing as you stick the strip in place. Mitre the corners and fill any gaps with matching sealant.

RENEWING GROUT

Grout which is simply badly stained or faded can easily be given a complete facelift with paint-on grout colouring.

However, if the grout itself is badly damaged – chipped or flaking away – it's not worth trying to patch it. Instead, rake it out and replace it with new grout. You can buy a special tool for raking out; alternatively use an old wood chisel or a stripping knife.

Afterwards, regrout in the normal way (see page 90). If you're tired of plain white, you can buy powdered grout colouring pigment for adding to the basic mix.

Stained grout which is otherwise sound can simply be painted over with tile grout colouring. Apply with a brush, then wipe away the excess from the tiles with a damp cloth.

Badly chipped or flaking grout must be raked out joint by joint and replaced. You can buy a special tool (above), or use a wood chisel or stripping knife. For a fresh new look, you could consider using powdered grout colouring in the new mix.

REPLACING BROKEN TILES

Cracked and chipped ceramic tiles should be replaced, particularly if they are on a kitchen work surface or splashback. They not only look unsightly, but also harbour germs.

How difficult the job is depends on the thickness of the tiles. Wall tiles normally splinter fairly readily when smashed, allowing the bits to be dug out without disturbing neighbouring tiles. On floors and worktops, ensure the force of your hammer blows is concentrated on the centre of the tile, not the edges. If you don't, there's a possibility that you may crack the surrounding tiles and make matters worse.

Epoxy grout presents a special problem, since it is very hard. The easiest way to release it is by drilling a series of small holes around the edge of the broken tile. Trim off the remains with an old wood chisel once the tile has been removed.

With the old tile out of the way, chip off all traces of the old adhesive. Coat the back of the replacement tile with fresh adhesive and bed in place, applying firm but even pressure and letting any excess squeeze out of the joints. Afterwards, regrout in the normal way.

On walls, use a hammer and piece of cloth to smash the broken tile into fragments. Lever out the pieces with an old chisel, starting from the centre.

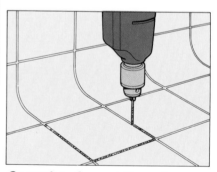

On work surfaces, drill a series of small holes in the epoxy grout to release it from the broken tile. Afterwards, proceed as for walls.

On floors, hack up the broken tile with a hammer and cold chisel, wearing gloves and goggles for protection. Again, work from the centre outwards.

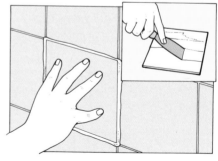

After chipping away the remains of the old adhesive, spread the back of the replacement tile with a generous layer of adhesive and press firmly in place.

FIXING WALL TILES 1: PREPARATION

As any professional will tell you, the secret of successful wall tiling is to plan the job properly. Before you actually buy any tiles, you should be thinking about what sort of surface you'll be tiling on, and how to avoid fiddly cuts. And if you want to incorporate a design or pattern, it pays to work this out on paper first; mistakes made on the wall can be expensive!

WHAT YOU CAN TILE ON

There are no short cuts to preparing surfaces for tiling: they must be structurally sound, flat, dry, and free of dust and grease – otherwise the tiles won't stay up.

Wallpaper Definitely unsuitable. Strip it and treat the wall as below, depending on what you find.

Paint Start by making sure the wall is flat: remove any bumps on solid walls by bashing them with a hammer, and fill depressions over 3mm (1/8″) deep with general purpose filler. Pull out old wallplugs.

For gloss, rub down any flaky patches back to a sound surface, then rub over the entire area to provide extra grip for the adhesive. Finally, wash down with Sugar Soap to remove dust and grease.

For emulsion, it's essential that the paint itself is firmly stuck to the wall (see Tip). Rub down flaky or powdery paint and then seal with tile adhesive primer (available in cans from tile suppliers). Wash down sound paint with Sugar Soap.

Plaster Leave new plaster for at least a month before tiling. Seal all types of bare plaster with tile adhesive primer.

Plasterboard Fine, providing it is on a proper framework that doesn't allow it to flex. Treat as for paint or plaster, whichever is appropriate.

Old tiles Perfectly suitable so long as they're firmly fixed; remove any that aren't and level with filler. Rub over the surface with coarse silicon carbide paper to 'key' (scratch) the glaze, then wash down with Sugar Soap. Bear in mind that on old tiles the adhesive will take much longer to dry; you need to leave it at least 72 hours before grouting.

Wood Existing panelling is best removed as you can't guarantee it will remain stable. Hardboard panelling is totally unsuitable. New panelling should be at least 12mm (1/2″) thick and preferably in either blockboard or WBP (water and boil-proof) plywood. Using chipboard is risky, particularly in a bathroom; it swells when wet.

Panels must be supported every 300mm (12″) so that there is not the slightest chance of them flexing. Screw, rather than nail, them to the supporting framework. Paint **all** bare wood with an oil-based primer, preferably a couple of days before tiling, otherwise the adhesive may fail as it dries.

Trade tip

Know the score

6 Tiles stick perfectly well to emulsion paint, but in my experience the paint itself often stops sticking to the wall – the tile adhesive softens it.

As a precaution against this happening, I always advise people to score the emulsion criss-cross fashion with the corner of a paint scraper, making the scores about 100mm (4″) apart. This way, the adhesive can penetrate and grip the plaster behind. 9

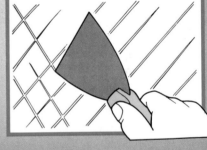

TILE ACCESSORIES

PLASTIC EDGING & SEALING STRIPS

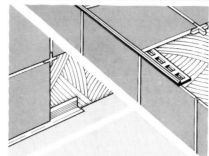

Plastic edging gives a neat finish to corners and edges where the tile edges are unglazed.

Sealing strip forms a watertight seal along the joints with worktops, baths and basins.

Both types are simply bedded in the tile adhesive before fixing the last row of tiles. They are sold in various lengths in a range of colours.

'TRUTILE' TILING GRID

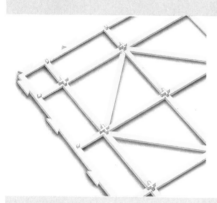

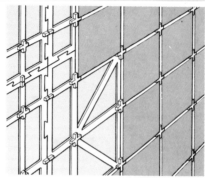

Ingenious system of plastic interlocking grids which are stuck to the wall with tiling adhesive or household glue. Small cross pieces within the grids then allow tiles to be spaced and levelled automatically. Obstructions are easily cut around with scissors or a knife.

Does away with the need for traditional setting out with battens, but can work out expensive on large areas, and only available for certain tile sizes.

FLEXIBLE SEALANT

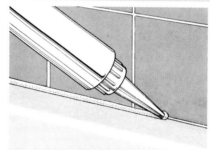

Silicone or acrylic-based sealants used to fill gaps up to 6mm (¼") wide between tiles and worktops or plumbing fixtures (sealants slump in wider gaps – use quadrant tiles or sealing strip instead). Also used in place of grout on tiled panels that need to be removed.

Best bought in cartridge form. Several colours are available; white quickly discolours.

WALL TILE ADHESIVE

Most wall tile adhesives are sold ready mixed in a range of different sized litre tubs. The standard type is PVA-based and only semi-water resistant; for walls prone to dampness or condensation (such as showers, bath splashbacks) use a water resistant acrylic-based adhesive. Acrylic-based adhesives also have better non-slip characteristics and some types can be used to grout the tiles as well; however, they are generally more expensive.

Cement based tile adhesive (more usual for floor tiling), can be used where the unevenness of the surface makes it necessary to apply a bed thickness of more than 3mm (⅛"). It comes in powder form in bags, and is mixed with water in a bucket.

Many tile adhesive ranges include a special surface primer, sold in cans, which reduces the risk of failure.

Cover guide: Ready mixed – 1sq m per litre; powder form – 1sq m per 3.5kg.

WALL TILE GROUT

Standard wall tile grouts come either ready mixed or in powder form. Ready mixed grouts are acrylic based and sold in tubs. Powder grouts are cement based, and come in bags for mixing with water; they are slightly easier to apply.

Both types are reasonably water resistant and can cope quite happily with showers or splashbacks. They cannot, however, take prolonged soaking (in a swimming pool, for example), and they are unsuitable for

worktops since they can harbour germs. In situations like these, use a two-part epoxy resin grout – sold in a pack consisting of resin and hardener. This is impervious and non-toxic, but more expensive than standard grouts and much harder to apply.

Grouts are now available in a range of colours. Or, you can colour powdered grout with pigment additive.

Coverage guide: Ready mixed: 6–8sq m per kg. Cement-based: 1sq m per kg.

FIXING WALL TILES 2: SPLASHBACKS

Thanks to modern tools and materials, fixing wall tiles has become one of the most satisfying and rewarding of all decorating jobs. But if you've never done any tiling before – or you have, but it hasn't worked out too well – it's best to start with a small area like a kitchen splashback or bath surround.

After preparing the surface (see page 85), remove obstructions wherever possible. Shaver and power points look better if the tiling fits behind them – isolate the supply and loosen their fixing screws. If necessary, get this done by an electrician before you start.

Tools for the job

The next stage is to get together a set of tiling tools.

Tile cutter For tiles up to around 150×200mm (6×8″), buy an inexpensive cutting set consisting of a measuring jig/cutting guide, and a combined cutting wheel/tile snapper; you'll find this easier to use than the old method of scoring and snapping tiles over a matchstick.

For larger (and therefore thicker)

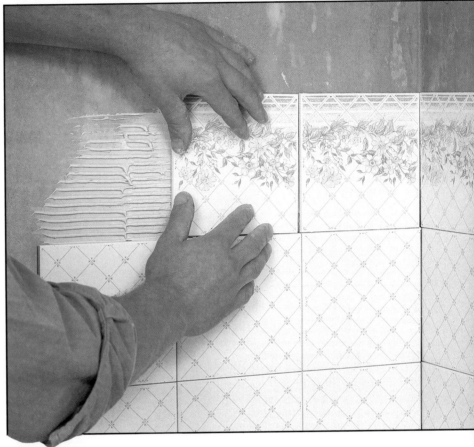

.... Shopping List ....

Plain tiles Divide surfaces to be tiled into rectangles, measure areas and combine; add 5% for breakages and waste.

Motif/border tiles Plan individual designs on squared paper; use this to estimate quantities and as a positioning guide.

Edging strip Measure exposed edges around tiled area; choose strip colour to complement or contrast with tiling.

Quadrant tiles Measure total length required; kits include corner and end pieces.

Sealing strip Normally sold in 1.8m (6′) lengths.

Spacers For spacing non-universal tiles; to estimate quantity, multiply number of tiles required by 1.5. .

Adhesive For wall tiles, average coverage is 1 litre per sq m.

Grout – for 2mm spacing, average coverage is 0.15kg per sq m.

Tools checklist Tile cutter, tile edge sander, adhesive and grout spreaders, spirit level, tape measure, bucket, sponge.

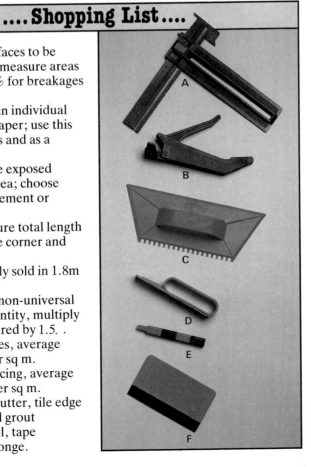

tiles, or if you plan to do any floor tiling, invest in a proper cutting jig; these make light work of even the toughest tiles. (Some tile suppliers have jigs available for hire.)

Tile edge sander An inexpensive tool which smooths the edges of cut tiles and makes all the difference to the finish; the abrasive pads are replaceable.

Adhesive and grout spreaders A notched adhesive spreader is a must: the furrows it creates aid suction, helping the tiles to stick. Sometimes spreaders are supplied with the adhesive, otherwise buy one. Just as important is a rubber bladed grout spreader for spreading and removing excess grout.

Grout joint finisher A cheap plastic tool for rubbing grout joints to a smooth finish. Alternatively, use a piece of 6mm (¼″) wooden dowel (*don't* use your fingers).

A typical set of tiling tools for small-scale jobs: tile jig and cutting guide (A), combined cutter/snapper (B), notched adhesive spreader (C), edge sander (D), four-stage grouting tool (E) and grout spreader (F).

SETTING OUT

For a splashback or bath surround only a few rows high, there's normally no need to bother with traditional supporting battens. However, you *must* have a firm, level surface – such as a worktop or bath edge – to use as a base.

Your aim should be to place the tiles where they look easiest on the eye, and to avoid unsightly cuts. Usually, this means finding the middle of the wall, and then tiling outwards from here so that any gaps at the ends are the same width.

However, narrow gaps look ugly, so you need to decide now whether to start tiling *on* the midpoint, or *to one side* of it. The illustrations on the right show how to do this for three common situations – either by laying out the tiles in a 'dry run', or measuring along the wall in tile widths. (In both cases, don't forget to allow for 2mm (1/16") for the grout if the tiles are square edged.)

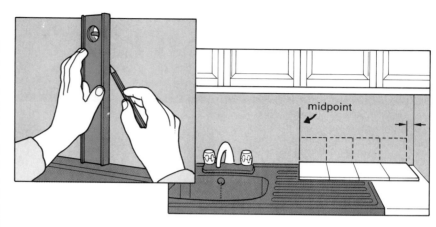

Find the midpoint by measuring the wall, then draw a vertical line using your spirit level (above). The line isn't strictly necessary, but it makes it easier to align the tiles when you come to fix them.

Lay out a row of whole tiles in a dry run, starting from one side of the midpoint (above right). If the gap at the end of the wall is too narrow, fix the tiles with the first tile centred over the midpoint instead (right).

FIXING TILES

Spread out the adhesive and fix tiles in 'blocks' of roughly one square metre, working *along* the wall.

If you're using sealing strip at the bottom, or finishing strip at the top, remember to bed this into the adhesive before fixing the adjoining row of tiles (if it won't stay put, tack it in place temporarily with a couple of nails). With sealing strip, you might find you have to apply the adhesive quite thickly to take up the lip at the back.

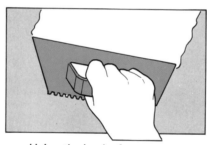

1 Using the back of your spreader, scoop the adhesive out of the tub and press it against the wall to one side of (or on) the midpoint.

marking the end line

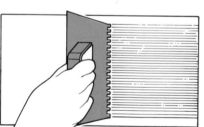

2 Gripping the spreader as shown, spread the adhesive in an even layer 2-3mm (1/16") thick. Apply enough to cover roughly 1 sq m (1 sq yd) of wall.

3 If you're using sealing strip, bed this into the adhesive. Then grip the first tile between your fingers and press it gently on to the wall.

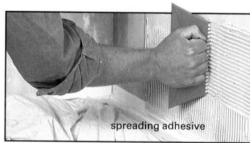

spreading adhesive

4 Having checked the tile sits square to the base or strip, bed spacers into the adhesive top and bottom and position the next tile in the same way.

5 Continue spacing and fixing, making sure the tiles engage the spacers. Stop every so often and check with your level that the tiles are sitting flush.

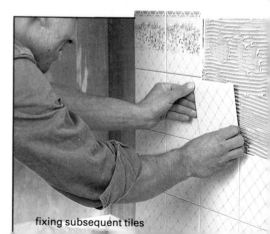

fixing subsequent tiles

For a basin splashback, mark the midpoint as shown on the previous page and then see which layout looks best by marking off in whole tile widths. Don't let the tiles overhang the edge of the basin too far: they won't have sufficient support.

midpoint

Around a bath, plan things so that any cut tiles on the end wall(s) are in the corner, allowing you to finish on whole tiles. (If necessary, let the tiles overhang the bath slightly so the cut tiles aren't too narrow.) Having worked out the layout, draw a vertical line where the whole tiles end to use as a guide when fixing.

Trade tip

Start level

6 If you're unlucky, the worktop or bath you're tiling above has an upstand or moulded edge which makes it impossible to 'sit' the first row of tiles.

In this case, you have to fix up a support batten. Nail it to the wall a tile's height above the base, making sure it is level; leave the nail heads protruding, for easy removal.

Tile above the batten in the usual way then, when the tiles have set, remove the batten and fill in the bottom row. 9

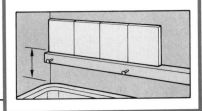
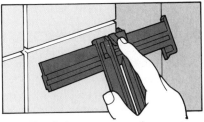

CUTTING TILES

On a splashback or bath surround there should be no need for anything other than straight cuts. Marking and cutting awkward shapes is covered on pages 91-94. Tile cutting jigs like the one shown have a built-in marking gauge which you set to the width of the gap prior to cutting. However, this assumes the wall is square – which it often isn't – so double check by measuring the gap top and bottom, allowing for the grout.

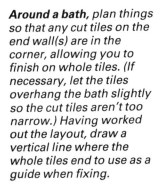

sizing up sealing strips

placing the first tile

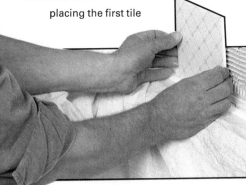

using a cutting jig

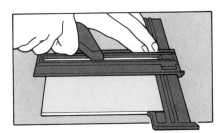

1 Check that the space for a cut tile is square by measuring it top and bottom. If it is, set the jig as shown; if not, transfer the measurements to the tile.

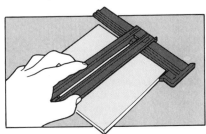

2 For a square cut, simply lay the tile in the jig. For an angled cut, rule a line on the glazed side in felt pen and align it with the slotted cutting guide.

4 To break the tile, hold it as shown and position the snapping jaws of the cutting tool directly over the cutting line; squeeze gently to snap.

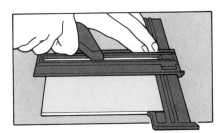

3 Holding the tile and jig steady with one hand, place the cutting tool in the guide and draw it firmly towards you along the slot. Keep the pressure even.

5 Without disturbing the adhesive bed, check that the cut piece fits. If it does, support it, then smooth the edge with your tile file.

GROUTING AND FINISHING

Leave the tiles to set for the time recommended by the adhesive manufacturers (normally at least 12 hours) before grouting.

If the grout is in powder form, add it to the specified amount of water in a bucket and mix to a smooth, but fairly stiff, consistency. If it's ready-mixed, stir in the tub and then apply direct to the wall.

Bear in mind that grouting is a messy job, so cover everything else before you start. Time is of the essence, since the grout hardens rapidly and becomes impossible to work into the joints, so make sure you have enough to do the job in one go. And – just as important – don't allow any grout to dry on the surface of the tiles; it's *very* difficult to remove once hard.

When you apply the grout, leave the joint along the adjoining surface clear (or scrape out the grout before it dries). Later, when the grout has set, fill the joint with silicone or acrylic sealant. This provides a flexible seal that won't disturb the tiles if there's any movement.

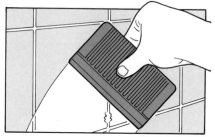

1 Use your adhesive spreader to daub grout over tiles, then quickly work it over the surface and into the joints with the grout spreader.

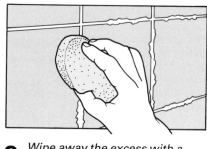

2 Wipe away the excess with a sponge, washing it out frequently. Take care not to leave any ungrouted 'pin holes' between the joints.

3 When the grout has begun to harden, rub down the joints to smooth them off to an even width. Check for any stray grout still on the tiles.

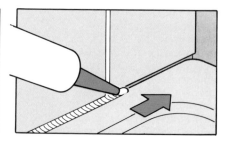

4 Finally, seal any gaps along the adjoining bath edge or work surface with sealant. Remember to push the tube away from you.

PROBLEM SOLVER

Tiles not flush

Check constantly while you are fixing to make sure all the tiles sit flush with one another. If one stands proud of, or below, the surface (and assuming you've prepared the surface properly), the problem is almost certainly that the adhesive bed is uneven at this point.

Remove the tile immediately by prising it from behind with an old kitchen knife, taking care not to disturb the others. Then scrape off **all** the adhesive from both surfaces, spread a fresh bed, and continue as before.

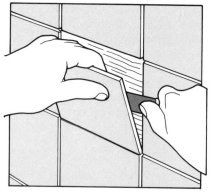

Ease the tile away gently with a kitchen knife to break the suction of the adhesive bed.

Use the kitchen knife to scrape the tile. It's easier to clean down the wall with your spreader.

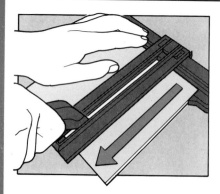

Draw the cutter towards you in a single firm stroke when cutting tiles in a jig.

Cutting problems

If your tiles aren't snapping cleanly when you cut them, it's probably because you are being too hesitant with the cutter. As with glass, you need to score in one firm, even pass so that the cutter's wheel penetrates the glaze to a consistent depth. If you hesitate, press too lightly, or go back over the same line more than once, you'll find yourself left with a jagged edge that no amount of filing or grouting can disguise.

Tiles slumping

If the tiles begin to slump downwards as you build up the rows, it means you've gone too far without arranging proper support. The method shown here relies on starting from a solid, level base and only fixing 4-5 rows in a single session. If you want to fix more, leave the first batch for at least 12 hours before continuing.

Unfortunately, the only cure for slumping is to start again before the adhesive dries.

FIXING WALL TILES 3: LARGE AREAS

Wall-tiling a whole room involves much the same fixing and cutting techniques as those described in the previous section. But this time you are working on a larger scale, which means taking a lot more care over the way you set out the job. Also, unless you're lucky, you'll find yourself having to cut and shape tiles to clear obstructions and awkward corners.

Tools and materials

In addition to the basic tiling tools listed on page 87, you need to make yourself a marking stick (see below). Also, because of the amount of cutting, it's worth hiring a professional-style cutting jig.

The best tool for cutting fiddly shapes in tiles is a tile saw (if you have a carpenter's coping saw, buy an Abrafile blade and use this instead). Sawing is far more efficient than the old 'score and nibble' method, though you must take care to support the tiles properly or they may crack.

If you plan to drill tiles, buy a special spear-shaped bit.

Apart from the usual tiling materials, get in a supply of wood for the support battens – 50×25mm (2×1″) is the ideal size, since it's light and easy to fix.

How the job runs

Setting out is the most crucial stage of tiling a whole room, and the one that many people get wrong.

Normally you'll be tiling to the floor or skirting, both of which are likely to be too uneven to use as a base. So your first job (shown below) is to draw a horizontal base line which allows every row of tiles to be level.

The next stage is to adjust your base line, depending on what's in the room, to avoid having to make unsightly cuts anywhere between floor and ceiling level.

From here you can judge where to place the setting out battens that support the rows of tiles above and keep them level. Having fixed all the tiles inside the battens, you then remove the battens and fill in the remaining gaps.

....Shopping List....

Tile materials checklist:
Plain tiles, motif and/or border tiles, edging strip (for borders and external corners), quadrant tiles (for finishing wide gaps), sealing strip (alternative to quadrant tiles), spacers (square-edged tiles only), adhesive (average coverage 1 litre/sq m), grout (covers 0.15kg/sq m).
Other materials:
Battens Buy enough wood to cover the length and height of the walls.
Nails For fixing battens (on a solid wall use masonry nails).
Tool checklist:
Tile cutting equipment, marking stick, tile sander, tile saw, adhesive and grout spreaders, spirit level, tape measure, bucket, hammer.

Right: Using a batten to check that the tiles lie flat.

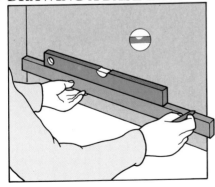

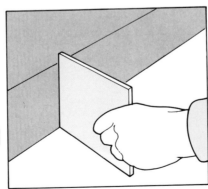

DRAWING A BASE LINE

1 *Using a batten and spirit level, draw a level line right around the room just under a tile's width above where the tiles are to finish.*

2 *Nowhere should the line be more than a tile's width above the finishing point. Check that this is so: if it isn't, draw a new base line lower down.*

─Trade tip─

Make your mark

❛ *No tiler would be without his marking stick, a tool allowing him to gauge at a glance how many tiles fit between two points. To make one, take a piece of 50 ×25mm (2×1″) batten about 1.5m (4″) long and mark it off in whole tile widths; allow for the grout gaps if necessary.* ❜

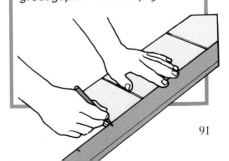

SETTING OUT THE ROOM

Setting out allows you to place cut tiles where they'll be least noticeable, and shows where to fix the support battens.

Start by using marking stick to measure the tile widths between the base line and any fixtures on the wall. Follow the sequence shown on the right, and mark where the cuts fall. Then adjust the height of the base line to get rid of cuts where you don't want them – for example along a window sill, or the top edge of the bath panel. Try to keep the cuts you *do* have to make even.

When you've done this, redraw the base line right around the room. This shows where to fit the horizontal support battens.

Use the same technique to check from side to side. Mark out each wall so that you avoid cut tiles at external corners and at the sides of windows. Where cuts are required at both ends of a wall, find its midpoint and measure out from here so that both lots are equal.

Finally, mark where the last column of whole tiles finishes on the left hand side of each wall. Plumb lines here, showing where to fix the vertical battens.

Follow the sequence shown for checking where to place cut tiles. The red lines show floor to ceiling checks; the blue lines show checks to be made from side to side on each wall.

9 last column of whole tiles – plumb vertical line here

8 measure out from midpoint to keep end cuts equal

cut tiles here

cut tiles here

7 start with whole tiles at either side of external corner

cut tiles here

1 base line to top edge of bath

TILING WITH BATTENS

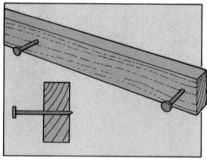

1 After marking your base line (previous page), part-drive nails into the first batten at 300mm (1') intervals; the points should just show through.

2 Offer up the batten level with the base line and drive in the nails until they hold; leave the heads protruding so you can remove the batten later.

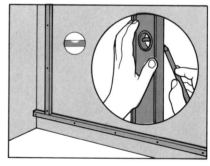

3 Having evened up the cuts from side to side, draw a vertical line to mark the last column of whole tiles. Fix the side batten against this line.

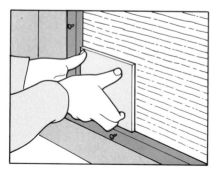

4 Spread about 1 sq m (1 sq yd) of adhesive in the usual way and fix the first tile in the corner of the two battens. Continue, working along the wall.

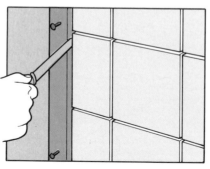

5 After completing the area inside the battens, leave it to set for an hour. Then slide a knife blade along the battens' edges to clear the joints.

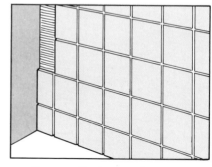

6 Remove the battens by pulling out the fixing nails with pliers. Measure and cut tiles to fit the gaps, and fix them in place in the usual way.

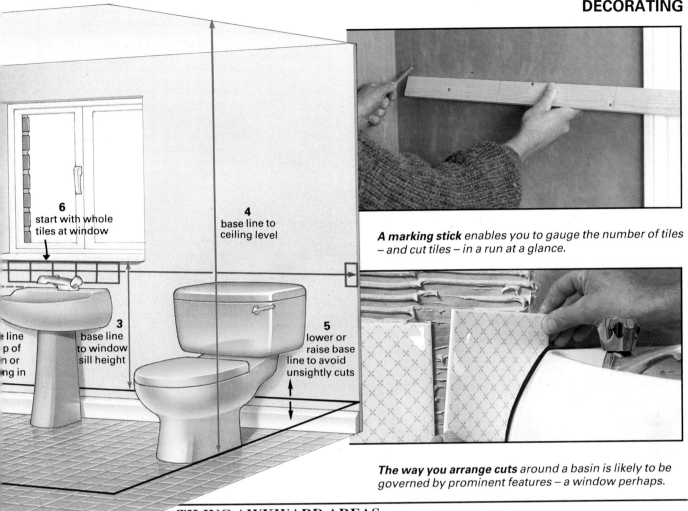

6
start with whole
tiles at window

4
base line to
ceiling level

e line
p of
n or
g in

3
base line
to window
sill height

5
lower or
raise base
line to avoid
unsightly cuts

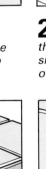

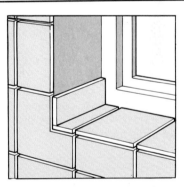

*A **marking stick*** enables you to gauge the number of tiles – and cut tiles – in a run at a glance.

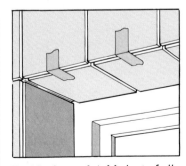

*The **way you arrange cuts*** around a basin is likely to be governed by prominent features – a window perhaps.

TILING AWKWARD AREAS

1 *At internal corners, you overlap one set of cut edges with another. Work out in advance which way to arrange the overlap so it's least noticeable.*

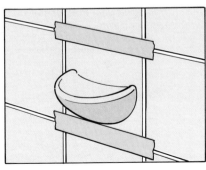

2 *External corners can be finished with trim strip. Bed the strip in the adhesive, then simultaneously fix both 'columns' of tiles so you can align them.*

*Tile a **window recess*** after the main wall. Arrange for equal size cuts on either side.

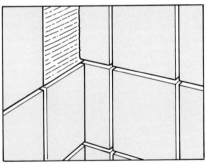

3 *Alternatively, overlap tiles in the direction that's least noticeable. (Around a bath, tiles on a horizontal surface must overlap those on a vertical one.)*

4 *Give a heavy insert tile extra support by taping it to the neighbouring tiles. Use decorator's masking tape – you'll find it easier to remove later.*

*Tackle the **underside*** last of all (the tiles on the wall above should overhang slightly to hide the edges). Tape the tiles for extra support.

Tiling curved areas

Objects like a pedestal basin or soil pipe have large-radius curves that can be difficult to tile around. The answer is to make templates for each tile (see Tip), then mark and cut the tiles individually to fit. In most cases, the object will be symmetrical so you can use the templates twice – once for each side. Do the actual cutting with a tile saw.

When you come to fix the pieces of cut tile, you may find that the adhesive bed has thinned out around the obstruction. Allow for this by adding an extra dab of adhesive, press the tile home, and let the excess squeeze out around the edges. Scrape off immediately.

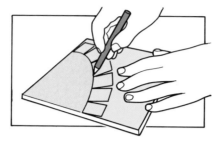

Use a paper template to mark the curve on each tile.

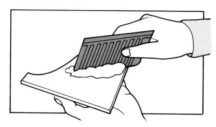

Add extra adhesive when you fit the cut piece.

Trade tip

Making a template

6 I find the best way of making templates is the 'cut and tape' method. Cut some paper into tile size pieces, then cut strips about 12mm (½") wide in the sides. Press the paper 'tiles' against the object so that the strips fan out, describing the line of the curve. Afterwards, stick tape across them to hold the line; tear off the waste. 9

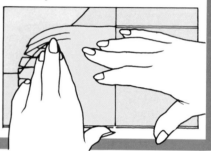

CUTTING AND SHAPING

A tile saw makes light work of cutting awkward shapes out of tiles, though you need to clamp them securely – use pieces of cloth to protect the surface glaze.

This leaves you with just one problem – marking the tiles to fit. Where possible, use something the same (or nearly the same) size as the object you're tiling around as a template (see step 5).

For pipes, don't attempt to cut all the waste out of one tile – it will break. Instead, cut the tile level with the centre of the pipe, then make equal sized cut-outs in each piece using a template.

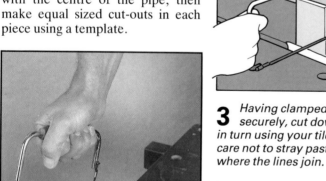

A tile saw cuts awkward shapes quickly and accurately – a lot more efficient than 'nibbling' the tiles with pincers. You may prefer to support a tile as shown.

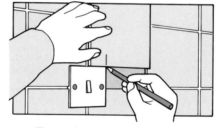

1 To mark a tile for an L shaped cut, start by holding the tile up to one side of the obstruction as shown and mark off against the edge with a felt tip pen.

3 Having clamped the tile securely, cut down each line in turn using your tile saw. Take care not to stray past the corner where the lines join.

5 After cutting the tile, lay the two pieces together and mark the pipe cut-outs – preferably using an offcut of pipe of the same diameter.

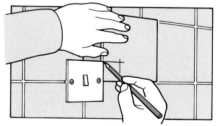

2 Now hold the tile against the other side of the obstruction and mark off again. Use your jig to convert the marks into squared cutting lines.

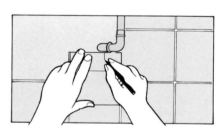

4 Use the same technique around a small pipe. Mark the pipe's position on a tile, then mark the tile for cutting level with the pipe's centre line.

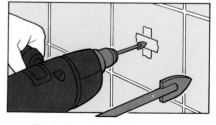

6 To drill holes in tiles, use a spade shaped tile bit and switch your drill to a low speed setting. Stick tape over your marks to stop the bit slipping.

LIFTING AND REPAIRING FLOORBOARDS

Floorboards which creak or wobble are both a nuisance and a potential danger. And splinters, bumps or protruding nail heads will shorten the life of any floorcovering laid over the top.

Faults like these can often be put right quite easily using only basic tools, once the offending boards have been exposed. But sometimes during the course of repairs it's necessary to lift and replace boards – a job calling for much more specialized tools and techniques. The same applies if you need to get to the cavity under the floor – for example, to lay pipes or cables.

Loose boards creak at best, and at worst may trip someone up. Punch all existing nails below the surface, then drive in extra nails (preferably proper *flooring brads*) or secure with countersunk screws.

If the creaking persists, try driving a short, thick countersunk screw **between** the boards to jam them together.

Knots are harder and less prone to shrinkage than the wood around them, which often leads to bumps. Level them with a plane or Surform – if you try to sand them, you're likely to remove more of the surrounding wood.

Watch out for concealed cables or pipes which may be notched into the tops of the joists. They should have been laid in the centre of the boards, so always nail about 20mm (¾") from each side.

POSSIBLE FAULTS AND SIMPLE REPAIRS

Nail heads may protrude due to wear or shrinkage of the boards. Hammer level and punch just below the surface. If the boards are to be left exposed, fill the indents with a slightly darker wood filler – it's less noticeable than a light one.

Broken or split boards are dangerous – remove and replace.

Sagging points to problems in the supporting joists. See Problem Solver.

Warped boards can be trimmed to remove high spots using a Surform or power sander. If the warping is bad, it's easier to replace.

Splintering may have developed in an old board. If minor, glue the loose pieces with woodworking adhesive and clamp in position with a weight on a plastic bag to stop it sticking. Otherwise, replace the board.

Gaps cause draughts. They also look unsightly if left exposed, and can set up ridges in carpet laid over them. Fill with wood or papier mâché (see below) or cover with hardboard before laying carpet.

Trade tip

Stopping squeaks

❝ Squeaking in floorboards is often the result of two boards rubbing together. Where this is the case, lubricate the gap between the boards by puffing in talcum powder or French chalk and working it down with an old table knife blade – the squeak should soon stop. ❞

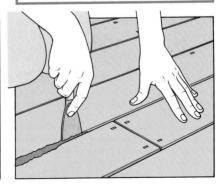

Fill large gaps between boards with strips of wood shaped to a slight taper. Coat with glue and hammer into the gap, then plane level after the glue dries.

Fill narrow gaps with papier-mâché. Mix up some torn-up newspaper, wallpaper paste and boiling water (you can also add wood stain to match the boards) . . .

. . . then force the pulp between the boards with a filling knife. Leave the filler slightly proud of the surface, then sand it smooth when hard.

LIFTING INDIVIDUAL BOARDS

Lifting floorboards which have been lifted before isn't generally too difficult: neither end will be trapped, so once you've checked for extra screw fixings you can simply insert a bolster or crowbar into the gaps and lever gently.

Removing a full-length board is a different matter. One or both ends will be trapped under skirtings or partition walls, so before you can lift it you have to saw through it somewhere along its length.

First, check whether the board is square edged or tongued and grooved (T&G): poke a blade between the gaps and see if it slips through easily; if it stops halfway, the board is T&G and you need to saw through the tongues on both sides to release it.

There are two ways of sawing through the board itself:
■ Over a joist, using a special curved-bladed floorboard saw or a tenon saw.
■ Next to a joist, using a jigsaw. This is much quicker, but risks harming underfloor cables or pipes. Adjusting the sole plate on the saw to cut at an angle of 30° gives a much neater join. For extra safety, cut over a block of wood as shown below to restrict the blade depth.

For T&G boards, saw a short way down both sides to sever the tongues using a tenon saw or floorboard saw. The rest should split away when you start lifting.

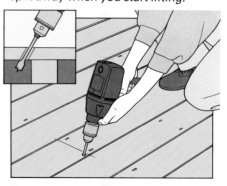

To saw beside a joist, find the edge of the joist with a blade and mark a cutting line across the board. Drill a hole big enough to admit the sawblade . . .

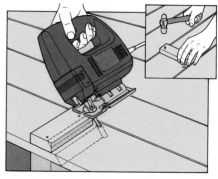

. . . then nail a block of wood parallel with the line. Adjust the jigsaw sole plate to 30°, insert the blade, and saw through the block and board together.

To saw over a joist, look for the rows of nails indicating its position and mark a cutting line just inside one of the rows. Cut along the line using short, flat strokes, then if necessary sever the unreachable ends using a woodworking chisel.

1 To lift the severed board, prise up the cut end from one side using a bolster. Apply enough force to get the jaws of a claw hammer under the end.

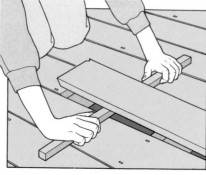

2 Continue levering until you can slide a length of batten under the raised board. Using both hands, force the batten towards the next joist.

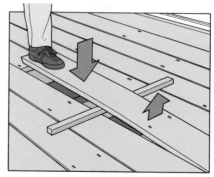

3 When the batten will go no further, put your weight on the cut end to 'spring' the board from the next joist. Repeat this until you reach the end.

PATCHING IN A NEW BOARD

Floorboards exist in a range of widths and thicknesses, but if you're only patching the odd section there is little point searching timber merchants for an exact match. Instead, buy the nearest size you can find and then adapt it to fit:
■ If the board is too wide, plane down the edges to a slight taper.
■ If the board is too thick, mark the joist positions and then cut shallow notches with a chisel.
■ If the board is too thin, fit cardboard or plywood packing over the joists before fixing.

Where you've sawn beside a joist, screw on a batten to support the replacement board before fixing. Screw, rather than nail, the board for future access.

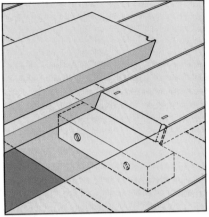
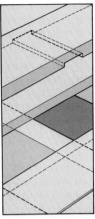
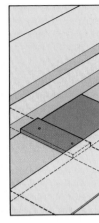

If you've sawn next to a joist, screw a batten to the side of the joist to support the new board. Bevel the end of the board if you cut the old section at an angle.

Notch a board which is too thick where it passes over the joists. *Pack underneath* a board which is too thin using slips of cardboard or plywood.

▉ PROBLEM SOLVER ▉

Problems with joists

Numerous warped, split or damaged boards – or serious sagging in the floor as a whole – point to faults in the floor joists below. Joist problems are more common on ground floors, where the danger of damp is ever-present. But in any event, it's worth checking on the condition of the joists whenever you have to lift more than one or two boards.

Rot or woodworm should be immediately obvious, and need prompt treatment. Any signs of dampness, dark staining or general deterioration suggest that the joists are beginning to rot, in which case they can be rescued if caught in time. By far the best course of action is to have a damp/rot survey carried out by a preservation specialist.

Sagging in an otherwise sound joist could be due to one of several things:
■ Overloading, either now or at some time in the past.
■ Over-weakening, where the joist has been notched to take pipe and cable runs.
■ Weakness in the timber itself.

These faults can usually be cured by strengthening the joist with a new section of timber, or by bracing it against its neighbours with timber struts. Bear in mind, however, that you may have to remove a considerable number of boards to gain sufficient access for putting in the struts.

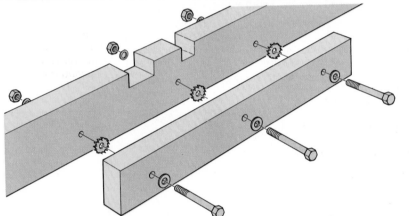

Strengthen a weakened joist by coach-bolting a matching piece of timber alongside it. The new section should be at least 900mm (3') long to be effective. Bolt at 300mm (12") intervals, using star washers (timber connectors) between the sections to lock them together.

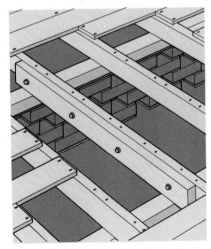
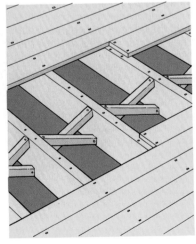

On a ground floor only, you may be able to strengthen a sagging joist by coach-bolting a new section of timber to it and supporting the ends on the two nearest sleeper walls . . .

. . . alternatively, for all joists make up herringbone struts from lengths of 50×50mm (2×2") timber. Nail the struts between the affected joist and its neighbours at 600mm (2') intervals.

RELAYING FLOORBOARDS

Relaying larger areas of floorboards is generally more difficult and disruptive than replacing individual sections. Although it's easy to prise up the boards once the first one is out of the way, you have to make sure the ends are free before you can lift them.

Where the boards are trapped by a skirting, remove this first: prise it away from its wall fixings with a bolster or crowbar, using a block of wood for leverage. Where boards disappear under a partition wall, you have no choice but to saw them off at the nearest convenient joist.

Replacing boards

With the boards up, pull out the old nails and then repair any boards that are salvageable. Boards with only surface damage can often be re-used the other way up.

Take a sample of board with you when buying replacements. New boards are stocked by timber and builders' merchants, but for older properties you may be better off going to an architectural salvage yard for secondhand boards.

Relaying

The main problem when relaying a number of floorboards – especially the square-edged type – is forcing them tightly together so that the gaps are as small as possible. There are two ways of doing this: with a pair of folding wedges (which you can make), or using a *floorboard cramp* (which you can hire).

In both cases it's worth buying a supply of purpose-made *flooring brads*, which are generally sold by the pound or ½kg (equivalent to around 80 2″ nails). Use brads at least twice as long as the boards are thick, allowing two per joist. Screw down any boards which you might need to lift for access in the future (and if they are T&G, saw off the tongues).

Joints and edges

Aim to relay the boards with as few joints as possible, and vary the lengths so that no two joints are next to each other. Wedge or cramp after every four or five boards.

If you're relaying the whole floor, decide whether or not you need to remove the side skirtings; often, they can be left in place and the edge boards slipped underneath.

When you reach the far side of the room, you may have to cut the last board along its length to fit the gap. There's no need to do this neatly, as the cut edge will be concealed by the skirting.

With T&G boards, start with the groove side towards the wall. At the far side, lock the last three boards together and 'spring' them under the skirting before fixing.

Trade tip

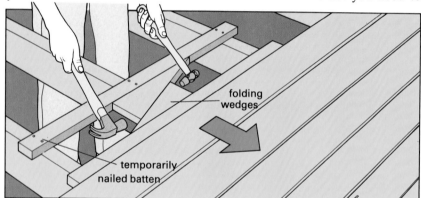

If you use folding wedges to pack the boards, nail a batten temporarily across the joists and place an offcut against the edge of the nearest board. Drive in the wedges from both sides to force the boards tightly together. Repeat every four or five boards.

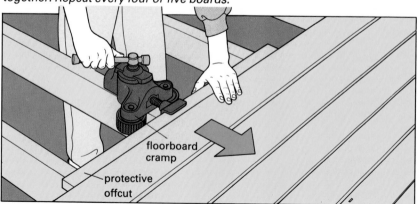

If you use a floorboard cramp, start by positioning the tool on a convenient joist and tightening the clamp. Place an offcut against the floorboards being packed, then turn the handle on the clamp to force them tightly together. Take care not to over-clamp.

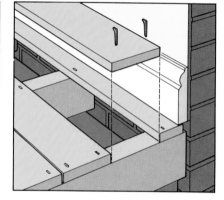

A square-edged end board may have to be sawn along its length and slid underneath the skirting to hide the cut edge. Do this before nailing the previous board.

T&G boards should be interlocked and 'sprung' under the skirting as shown. Again, you may have to cut down the last board to fit the remaining gap.

STRIPPING AND SEALING FLOORBOARDS

In older homes, the original pine floorboards (or, if you are very lucky, oak ones) can be sanded and sealed to give a warm, natural finish that provides the perfect complement to rugs or loose-laid carpet. Sanding and sealing is also among the most economical ways of finishing a floor, although equipment hire and the cost of the sealant can push up the price further than you might expect. Much depends, too, on the condition of the boards: if they are badly damaged or deeply stained already, lining them with hardboard and laying a budget floorcovering such as sheet vinyl or foam-backed carpet is likely to be more sensible.

If you decide to go ahead, make sure you are well prepared. Clear the room completely of furnishings and ensure that any repairs to the boards have been carried out before committing yourself to hire charges.
■ Punch nails below the surface and fill large gaps.
■ Replace or turn over damaged and stained boards.

The same principles apply to sanding and refinishing other types of wood floor, such as solid wood strip and traditional parquet.

Old floorboards in almost any condition can be renovated and sealed to give a durable floor surface.

.... Shopping List ....

Floor sanding equipment can be hired from virtually any hire shop. You need a *floor sanding machine* to deal with the main area, plus an *edging sander* for finishing the edges and any awkward corners. (If you have an orbital sander this may do instead, but it will take heavy punishment).

The hire shop should supply *abrasive sheets* to fit both machines on a sale-or-return basis. Ask for a mixture of coarse, medium and fine grades in both cases.

Protective gear is essential for floor sanding, which is a very noisy and messy job. Make sure you have a dust mask, ear defenders, overalls, and goggles.

Sealant may also be sold by the hire shop, though a DIY store will offer a wider selection.

Polyurethane varnish is the usual choice. It is economical, but slow to dry and picks up dust easily; you need at least 3 (and preferably 4) coats. *Two-part plastic coating* is tougher and dries within the hour, but is more unpleasant to apply and can work out costlier, even though you only need 2 coats. An *oleo-resinous sealant* is the best choice if you plan to give the floor a wax polished finish, though this will be hard work to maintain. You could also consider staining or coloured varnish (see overleaf).

When buying sealant, be sure to check the recommended coverage per coat. For polyurethane, you need white spirit for thinning.

floor sander

oleo-resinous sealant

edge sander

sealant

two-part plastic coating

polyurethane varnish

protective gear

SANDING THE FLOOR

The dust and noise raised by sanding a floor can be considerable, so warn family and neighbours. Immediately before you start:

■ Double-check that the boards are firmly fixed and that there are no sharp nail heads or screws protruding above the surface.

■ Seal up the cracks around doors with parcel tape, and block the gaps underneath with newspaper.

■ Keep any windows open while actually sanding. Close them again after each stage, and vacuum to keep the dust level down.

Follow the sanding sequence shown on the right, checking the abrasive sheets every so often to make sure they're not clogged. With badly marked floors, work diagonally in both directions before working along the grain. Don't change to fine abrasives until all the marks have gone.

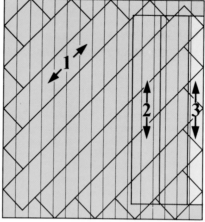

The correct sanding sequence.
Start with the floor sander and work diagonally across the boards using coarse, then medium, abrasives (1). Next, run along the grain of the boards using medium, then fine, abrasives (2). Switch to the edge sander (3): use coarse and medium abrasive to clear the marks; fine to finish.

Trade tip

Using a drum sander

❝ Floor sanders are powerful machines, to be used with care.

■ Always unplug before changing abrasive sheets.

■ Make sure the sheet is taut and firmly locked in place.

■ Never start the machine while the drum is in contact with the ground. Rock the machine back to lift it, then lower gradually when it reaches full speed. Be prepared for it to pull forward.

■ Similarly, rock back to lift the drum before switching off.

■ Empty the dust bag regularly; they have been known to catch fire spontaneously if allowed to become over-full.

■ If the sheet catches on a nail it may shatter with a resounding bang, so be prepared. ❞

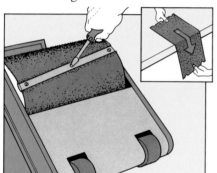

The floor sander sheets are wrapped over the drum, and held by a screw-down bar. Scrape the backing over the edge of a bench to give the sheet a curl before fitting, then pull it taut.

The sander will naturally pull away from you. Use it like a lawn mower and keep the lead over your shoulder so it is out of the way. Avoid 'resting' during a pass, as you risk gouging the boards.

Use the edge sander running in the direction of the grain wherever possible, and keep it flat to avoid score marks. Take care not to scrape the disc against the skirtings.

FINISHING AND SEALING

However you plan to seal the surface, leave the bare boards for as long as possible – and at least a day – to give the dust a chance to settle. (A few squirts into the air with an indoor plant spray will help to speed up the process). Afterwards vacuum the floor thoroughly, along with the skirtings, door and window frames, and any other places where dust might have collected.

Immediately before sealing, wipe over the floor with a cloth soaked in white spirit (don't use water, as this raises the wood grain).

Polyurethane varnish should be thinned with white spirit on the first coat, following the maker's instructions. This allows it to soak into the grain of the wood.

Close all doors and windows. Apply the varnish running with the grain, using a 100mm (4") brush.

After each coat, sand the surface lightly using fine glasspaper on a block, or a wad of medium grade steel wool. Vacuum again and wipe over with the white-spirit-soaked cloth before applying the next coat.

Two-part coatings give off strong fumes, so keep the room well ventilated; put sheets over windows to stop dust entering.

Mix the coating in the container in which it is supplied following the maker's instructions. Apply with a brush that you won't want to use again – it will be ruined – or use a sponge mop. Sand, if necessary, and vacuum between coats.

Oleo-resinous sealants do not need mixing or thinning. Decant the sealant into a paint kettle and apply with a large brush.

Trade tip

Adding colour

❝ The natural tones of the wood can be altered by staining, or by using coloured polyurethane varnish.

■ Apply the stain before sealing: use a spirit-based stain, and apply it with a cloth pad, not a brush. This gives a more even coverage.

■ If using coloured varnish, choose the gloss type. Apply a thinned coat of clear varnish first. This seals the surface so that it will absorb the colour evenly, then follow with two or more coloured coats. Finish with another clear coat – gloss, matt or silk, according to your preference. ❞

LEVELLING A WOODEN FLOOR

Wooden boarded floors, although strong and hardwearing, make a less than ideal surface on which to lay modern floorcoverings such as sheet vinyl, vinyl tiles and foam backed carpet.

Most boarded floors are now at an age where years of lifting and patching have taken their toll, leaving a loose or uneven surface that quickly shows through a thin floorcovering and sets up localized patches of wear. Wooden floors also tend to flex under load and shrink in dry weather, either of which can play havoc with tiles laid on top.

The solution is to prepare the floor – and level it at the same time – by nailing down sheets of hardboard or plywood. Although time consuming, this is a relatively simple job that requires only basic carpentry skills. The time taken will be well repaid in terms of extra comfort, and prolonged life for the floorcovering going on top. And on a ground floor, levelling has the added advantage of reducing heat loss through gaps between boards.

Hardboard is ideal for levelling wood floors: it's easy to cut and leaves a flat, smooth surface.

.... Shopping List ....

The usual material for lining floors is 3mm (⅛″) hardboard, which comes in several sheet sizes. The most useful are 2440×1220mm (8×4′) and 1220×610mm (4×2′). It also comes in two grades. *Standard* grade is perfectly adequate providing you 'condition' it first with water (which some experts

argue creates a more level surface). *Oil-tempered* board is more durable and needs no conditioning, but costs about one and a half times as much.

If you plan to lay ceramic tiles, use 9mm (⅜″) or 12mm (½″) plywood instead, depending on the condition of the floor. This is very much more expensive but the cheapest grade will do. It comes in various sheet sizes, most commonly 2440×1220mm (8×4′).

When calculating how many sheets to buy, bear in mind that some material will inevitably go to waste filling the margins around the edge of the floor. This is where smaller sheets are useful. Ideally, draw a quick scale plan of the room (in this case it's easiest to work in feet) and fill in the plan sheet by sheet.

Nails Use *ring shank nails* – 19mm

(¾″) for hardboard, 25mm (1″) for plywood. These have ridged shanks and round heads that grip the sheets securely. A 0.5kg (1lb) bag should be enough for most rooms.

Tools checklist: Panel saw, string or garden twine, small piece of chalk, plant spray, hammer, plane or planer, nail punch, trimming knife, steel rule or spirit level.

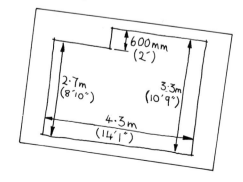

A typical sketched floor plan.

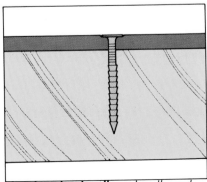

Use ring shank nails on hardboard.

PREPARING THE SHEETS

When you get the sheets home, begin by cutting them in half with a panel saw. This makes them easier to manoeuvre and lay, especially around the edges of the room. If you are using standard hardboard, condition it before laying. Place the cut sheets on edge and lightly spray the mesh sides with clean water from a garden spray. Use about 0.5 litre (¾ pint) of water per board.

Stack the sheets flat in pairs, mesh sides together, and leave them for at least 48 hours in the room being boarded. This allows them to acclimatise as they dry, and prevents buckling when you lay them. The drying process continues after laying, causing the sheets to shrink and form a tight, flat skin.

Spray sheets of standard hardboard with water on the mesh side. Stack them flat, mesh sides together, in the room they are going in and leave for 48 hours.

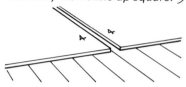

Trade tip

Match the sheets

❝ When you cut the sheets in half, keep track of which halves go together by numbering each pair on the cut edges. Otherwise, there will be gaps in the joints and they won't line up square. ❞

Setting out against chalk lines avoids leaving awkward spaces around the edge of the room. If you need access to underfloor pipes or cables, arrange for narrower strips to be fitted at these points so that you can lift them easily in an emergency.

Trade tip

Underfloor access

❝ Mark any boards which might need lifting in the future to get at pipes or cables. Then, when you come to set out the sheets, arrange things so that small panels are laid over these areas.

   This allows you to gain access to the floorboards without disrupting the entire surface. ❞

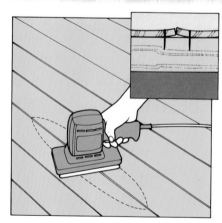

separate panel for underfloor access

adjust positions of sheets to avoid narrow strip on return wall

chalk line 2

chalk line

PREPARING THE FLOOR

Check the floor for boards that are loose or curled at the edges, and for protruding nail heads. These faults must be put right before you go ahead. Do not line the floor if there is any suspicion of damp, rot or woodworm in the boards or in the joists below.

Loose boards can be secured with screws, but lift them first to check that there are no pipes or cables notched into the joists below.

Badly damaged boards must be lifted and replaced. If you have difficulty finding timber as thick as the old boards, fit slips of hardboard or thick card underneath to make up the difference when you nail down the new boards.

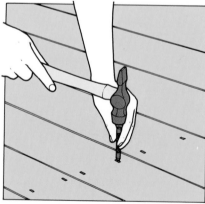

Curling edges are a problem on boards which have shrunk with age. Plane down, or flatten with a belt or orbital sander (wear goggles for protection).

Punch nail heads below the surface, working systematically across the room so that you don't miss any. Secure loose boards with extra nails or screws.

SETTING OUT

Lay the sheets in a staggered pattern, working out from the middle of the room. This breaks up the joints and makes it more economical to fill in the spaces around the edge of the floor.

Mark two lines at right angles across the room as a laying guide. Use a chalked string line for this (it's easier than drawing the lines).

Next, lay out your half sheets in pairs as a dry run to see what spaces are left around the edges. Adjust the sheets to avoid leaving small, fiddly gaps.

1 Pin a length of string at one end of the room, halfway along the wall. Stretch it taut, rub it thoroughly with chalk, and pin it at the opposite end.

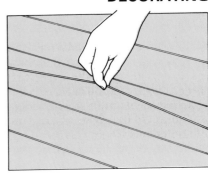

2 Grasp the string between finger and thumb and snap it against the floor to leave an impression in chalk. Snap another line at right angles to it.

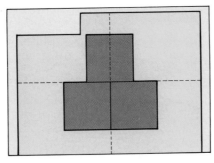

3 Butt the first two sheets against each other where the lines meet. Then lay two more sheets against them, staggered by half their width.

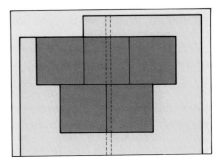

4 Lay out the remaining whole sheets, then adjust their positions to even up the spaces around the edges and avoid awkward cuts.

Trade tip

Which way up?

6 Opinions differ as to which way up to lay hardboard I follow the rule that if the floorcovering is going to be stuck down lay it mesh side up, otherwise lay it smooth side up. Often, though, flooring and adhesive manufacturers specify which surface best suits their products on the packaging. 9

position first sheet between chalk lines

NAILING THE SHEETS

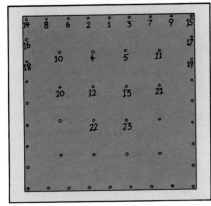

Fix the sheets working clockwise from the middle of the room. Nail hardboard in a pyramid pattern, starting from the middle of one edge, to stop it buckling.

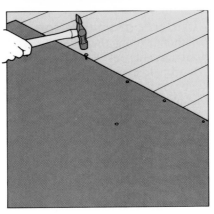

1 Nail sheets 12mm (½") in from the edges, spacing the nails 150mm (6") apart. Space the nails at 225mm (9") intervals over the rest of the sheet.

2 Use pieces of wood cut to length as spacers, but adjust the spacing if you nail through a gap between boards. Make sure no nail heads are left protruding.

DEALING WITH EDGES

The sheets don't have to be an exact fit around the edges of the room, but you'll waste time and material if you try to cut them by eye alone – it's better to scribe the edges first using a block of wood and a pencil.

Scribe sheets to fit straight edges as shown on the right, making use of any offcuts where you can. Deal with corners as shown below: butt the straightest edge against the skirting, scribe the adjacent edge, then mark off where to trim against neighbouring joints.

Trimming sheets

Hardboard Don't bother to saw hardboard to size where you are trimming straight pieces. Score the sheet on the marked side using a trimming knife and steel rule or spirit level. Then kneel on the main board, grasp the waste on both sides, and snap along the score.

Plywood Normally it's easiest to trim sheets with a panel saw, though you may find a jig saw more useful for making fiddly cuts around awkward edges. Bear in mind that since the floor will be tiled, there's no need to get an exact fit – 12mm (½") gaps are perfectly acceptable.

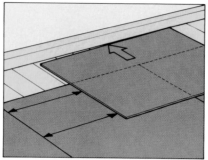

1 To scribe a sheet, centre it over the neighbouring whole sheets. Keeping the sheet square to the others, slide it forward until it touches the skirting.

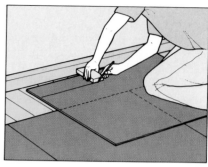

2 Run a block and pencil along the wall edge as shown, marking the profile of the skirting. Trim the sheet along this line.

3 Lay the sheet back in position and butt the scribed edge against the skirting. Mark off the waste against the two neighbouring sheets and trim.

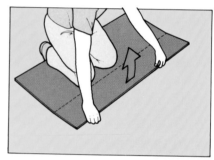

To cut straight edges of hardboard, score with a trimming knife and metal straightedge, then kneel on the main piece of board and snap off the waste.

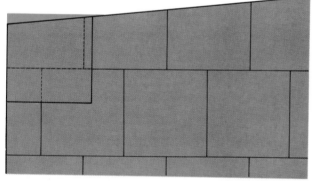

At corners, scribe and trim one wall edge (red area) then mark where to trim the remaining waste (blue lines).

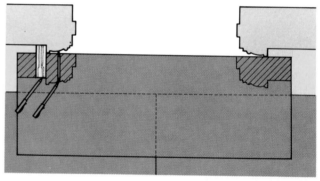

At a doorway, swap the scribing block for a pencil so that you can trace the profiles of the architraves.

PROBLEM SOLVER

Dealing with doorways
Lining the floor will raise the level (substantially in the case of plywood) so lift any inward opening doors off their hinges before you start. The final level will probably be higher still, depending on what type of floorcovering you plan to lay, so leave trimming the bottoms of the doors until later.

Concrete hearths
Sheets can't be nailed over a concrete fire hearth built into the floor. Instead, glue them down with impact adhesive.

Underfloor ventilation
Although lining the floor cuts out draughts between the floorboards, on a ground floor it can also restrict the circulation of air in the space beneath the joists. This is a major cause of wet and dry rot, particularly in older houses where there may be damp. Check that all airbricks at ground floor level are intact and unblocked. If any have been partially covered – for example, by a raised patio – the area immediately in front of the airbrick must be dug out to restore the flow of air.

Check airbricks around the foot of the house walls to make sure they are unblocked and in good condition.

LAYING SHEET VINYL FLOORING

Sheet vinyl flooring is ideal wherever you need a hardwearing, waterproof surface that's easy to keep clean and comfortable to walk on. This makes it a good choice not only for kitchens, bathrooms and halls, but for playrooms, dining areas and utility rooms as well.

There's a wide choice of patterns, ranging from plain geometric to simulated quarry tile and woodgrain. Most have some surface texture, and in the case of simulated types this is pronounced enough to give a realistic effect.

Sheet vinyl comes in widths of 2m (about 6'6"), 3m (9'9") and 4m (13'). This means that most rooms can be covered with one sheet – although sometimes it may be easier to join two narrower sheets.

Overleaf is a guide to estimating how much (and what width) to buy, depending on the shape of the room. But you may not find wider sheets in all patterns, so check availability before making a final choice.

There are two main types of vinyl, both of which come in a wide range of styles and patterns:
Unbacked vinyl consists of a single layer of solid vinyl; only the thicker types are textured. Most unbacked vinyls won't lay flat naturally and must be glued to the floor.
Cushioned vinyl consists of multiple layers, the most important of which is a foam backing that makes it softer and warmer to walk on in bare feet. The surface is usually textured.

Some cushioned vinyl is designed to lay flat naturally and doesn't need gluing. (One exception is under a heavy kitchen appliance, such as a cooker, where gluing stops the vinyl dragging if the appliance has to be moved.) Non-'lay flat' types only need to be glued near

the edges and along any joins.
Other materials: If the vinyl needs sticking down, check the maker's instructions for details of suitable adhesives. Most types come with a spreader.

Seam adhesive gives a professional finish to joins between sheets (see page 110).

Adhesive tape is essential for several stages, and you may need metal cover strips for doorways. Use brown wrapping paper or heavy lining paper to make templates (see page 109).
Tools checklist: Trimming knife, soft broom, metal rule or straight edge, blocks of wood. (Extra tools are needed if the floor has to be prepared first – see overleaf.)

Cross-sections of unbacked vinyl and a typical cushioned vinyl.

unbacked vinyl
'wear' layer
solid vinyl layer

clear 'wear' layer
embossed pattern
solid vinyl layer
foam backing

cushioned vinyl

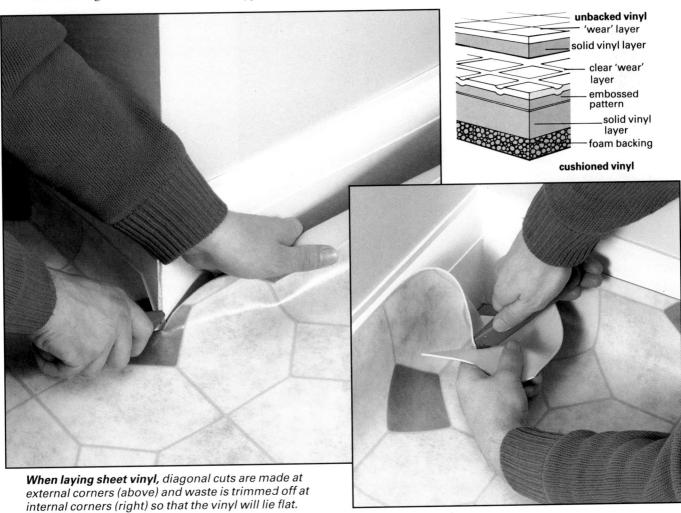

When laying sheet vinyl, diagonal cuts are made at external corners (above) and waste is trimmed off at internal corners (right) so that the vinyl will lie flat.

PREPARATION AND PLANNING

The plans given here show what's involved in laying sheet vinyl in three different situations. Start by seeing what needs to be done to the existing floor surface, then work out the best way to lay the sheet.

Preparing the floor

Vinyl must only be laid on a surface which is even, clean and dry. Any bumps or hollows will eventually show through, and damp can damage a cushioned backing as well as being a problem in its own right.

Floorboards Level old pine boarded floors with sheets of hardboard. With new boards or chipboard, ensure all nail heads are punched below the surface, fill any gaps with general purpose filler, and vacuum.

Concrete Make sure the floor is not damp. If the surface is smooth but dusty, vacuum and apply a coat of concrete sealer; if it is uneven, level with self-smoothing compound.

Quarry/ceramic tiles Check that the tiles are securely fixed and level the joints with filler.

Old glued floor coverings Lift old lino or felt backed vinyl; to remove any remaining backing felt, soak with one part household ammonia to three of water and scrape off.

Old vinyl tiles can stay if firmly fixed; otherwise warm with a hot air stripper to soften the adhesive and lift, scraping off all traces of old adhesive. Old thermoplastic tiles discolour vinyl sheet, so either lift them or screed over the top with latex-based self-smoothing compound.

In all cases it's a good idea to remove inward opening doors and trim the undersides.

Planning how much to buy

Measure the maximum width and length of the room – going right into any recesses or door openings – then draw a sketch plan and put in the dimensions. Take the longest and widest measurements and add 200mm (8″) for a trimming allowance on each side. This represents the minimum sheet size needed to fill the room.

Aim to choose a width that allows you to cover the whole area with a single piece. (If the room is seriously out of square, allow extra for trimming or you may get caught out.) Most stockists sell in lengths to the nearest metre or half metre so you may end up with a bit extra.

Where the size or shape of the room makes it impossible to use a single piece, use your plan to work out the best way of fitting in two or more pieces bearing in mind the following points:

■ Joins between sheets tend to lift and curl in time, so place them where they won't receive heavy wear.

■ A join which runs at right angles to the main light source is less noticeable than one running parallel.

■ It's not normally a good idea to use sheets of different widths on the same floor – they will have been made on a different run and are seldom an exact colour match. However, you can save a lot of wastage this way, especially if the second piece is small and not in a prominent place.

■ Allow extra overlap between pieces for matching the pattern. Makers normally specify the size of the pattern repeat.

EXAMPLE 1: A REGULARLY SHAPED ROOM

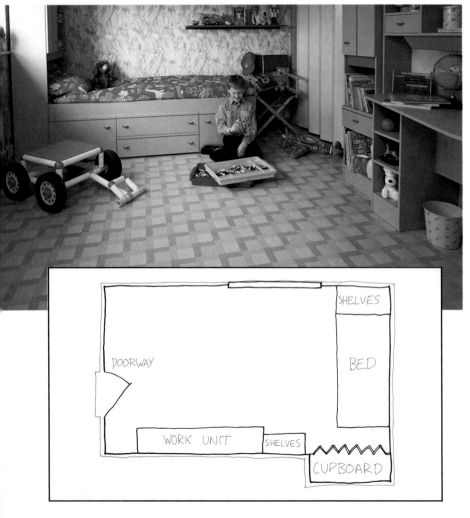

Most rooms are fairly regular in shape with no awkward areas, except perhaps a chimney breast. Providing the maximum width is less than 4m (13′) you should be able to use a single piece.

If you choose a vinyl with an irregular pattern, it won't matter if the walls are slightly out of true. Otherwise, take into account that the pattern must line up with the longest wall or dominant feature (eg a run of kitchen units), or the floor won't look 'right'.

And if the vinyl has a large pattern, like tile squares, it's a good idea to allow extra for trimming so that you can balance the breaks in the pattern between all sides of the room – small slivers of pattern always look like patched mistakes.

A rectangular room with few obstructions (above) can usually be covered in one piece. Check this by drawing a sketch plan (left), not forgetting to allow extra where the sheet has to fit into alcoves and doorways. Lay the vinyl by unrolling it in the room and trimming the sides to fit each wall in turn.

EXAMPLE 2: A THROUGH ROOM

If you want to lay vinyl in two connected areas, such as a kitchen and breakfast room, you have two choices:

■ Lay a single piece trimmed to fit both rooms and the partition between them. This can be tricky – especially if there is a narrow opening or a thick partition – and is only feasible if the maximum width of the area (plus trimming allowance) is less than 4m (13′).

■ Lay two pieces with a join between the rooms or in a convenient area of one of them. This is less neat, and it can be hard to match the pattern, but it's much easier to do.

In an L-shaped through room, like the one shown, it's tempting to place the join across the partition. But a better solution in this case is to lay a single piece over the part receiving the heaviest wear – usually the area between two doorways – then fit a second piece in the corner which gets used the least. A sensible furniture arrangement may help here.

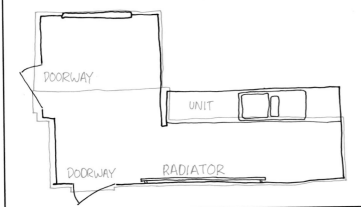

An L-shaped through room (above) poses the problem of what width to buy and where to place the joins. Try out different layouts on a sketch plan (left).

Here, the most economical way is to cover the area between the doorways with one piece, then fit a second in the relatively unused area by the dining table. If the kitchen were wider, it might be possible to cover both rooms with a single piece.

EXAMPLE 3: AN OBSTACLE-FILLED ROOM

Some rooms are an awkward shape or full of obstacles, such as a small bathroom with a toilet, pedestal basin and towel rail. In these situations, it's very difficult to lay vinyl directly and cut round the various shapes.

A better method is to make a paper template of the whole area, showing the obstacles, and use this as a pattern to cut the sheet before you fit it (see page 109). However, don't use this method for a room larger than a couple of metres square, as the template is unlikely to be accurate enough. Instead, unfurl the vinyl in the room as best you can, then make separate templates of the obstacles.

In small rooms full of obstacles, it's easier to cut the vinyl following a paper pattern. Cut on the generous side, then do a final trim with the sheet in position.

LAYING THE VINYL

Unless the supplier has done it for you, start by cutting the sheet roughly to size, allowing about 100mm (4″) trim on all four sides. If you have to work outside, make sure it is dry. Use a trimming knife or kitchen scissors, and check every measurement; pull the waste down and away from the sheet to ensure a clean edge.

Re-roll the sheet across the shorter dimension to take it into the room (large sheets are difficult to handle, so get a helper).

If possible, leave the vinyl rolled loosely in the room for 1–2 days – with the heating on if the weather is cold. This acclimatises it and makes it easier to handle. Immediately before you start work, reverse-roll the sheet so that the pattern will be face up when it is unrolled.

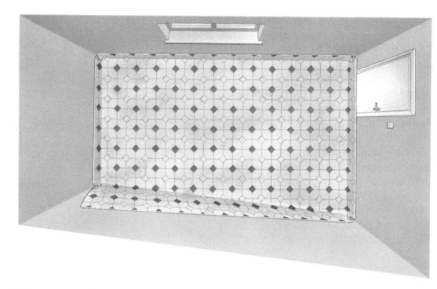

Always try to line up the pattern with the longest wall or most prominent feature. If either of these are out of true, align the pattern so that it runs at right angles to the wall with the most used doorway.

1 Lay the roll at a slight angle to the longest wall or dominant feature. Unroll about 1m (3′) and ease the sheet round so it rides up by about 100mm (4″).

2 Align the pattern, then unroll fully – allowing the edges to overlap the walls and ride over obstructions. Flatten out the air pockets with a soft broom.

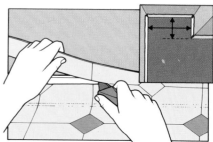

3 Trim off any excess to leave roughly 100mm (4″) overlap all round. At recesses, measure the depth, add a further 100mm (4″), and leave this much overlapping.

SCRIBING AN EDGE

Once you're satisfied that the sheet is lying square to the walls with the pattern in the right alignment, start cutting and trimming to fit. Experts trim all sides freehand like carpet (see *Direct Trimming*) but this is very difficult to get right first time – it's much easier to fit the longest side by scribing the edge.

When cutting, always trim off less than you think you need, then re-trim if necessary – it's difficult to patch an overtrimmed sheet.

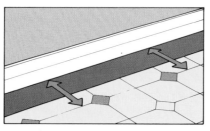

1 Take the edge along the longest wall or dominant feature. Pull the sheet slightly away from the wall, maintaining the alignment of the pattern.

2 Hold a marker pen against a block of wood about 100mm (4″) square. Draw the block along the wall or skirting so the pen marks the wall's profile on the vinyl.

3 Cut along this line with a trimming knife or scissors. Slide the sheet back to the wall so that the cut edge butts up to it and re-trim where necessary.

Trade tip

Get it taped

6 Once you've scribed and trimmed the longest edge to fit, it's a good idea to tape it securely to the wall or skirting so that the sheet doesn't 'creep' out of position while you are trimming the rest. **9**

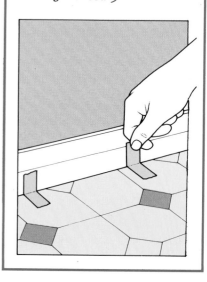

DIRECT TRIMMING

Start by making release cuts at the corners as shown (right) so that the sheet begins to lie flat.

When you come to the edges, don't forget to compensate for the way the vinyl curves into the angle between the floor and the skirting or wall – it's easy to cut it too short. Practise with an offcut before you start trimming the main sheet.

Until you get used to the 'feel' of the vinyl, you may find the knife blade wanders off-line when trimming long edges. In this case it's safer to use the *Step at a time* technique shown below. Begin at a corner next to the scribed edge, and deal with obstacles as shown below.

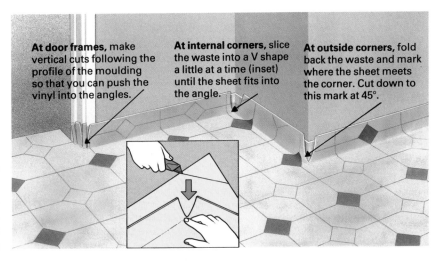

At door frames, make vertical cuts following the profile of the moulding so that you can push the vinyl into the angles.

At internal corners, slice the waste into a V shape a little at a time (inset) until the sheet fits into the angle.

At outside corners, fold back the waste and mark where the sheet meets the corner. Cut down to this mark at 45°.

Make release cuts, starting at external corners, so the sheet lies flat.

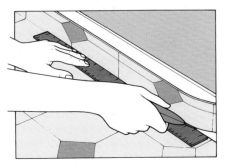

To direct-trim, *push the sheet hard into the angle with a metal ruler, adjust the ruler to allow for the curve, then cut along it. Holding the knife with your thumb 'trapped' against the waste helps to control the blade.*

Trade tip

A step at a time

❝ Try this technique when you first start trimming to be sure of getting a straight cut:
- Cut a rectangular pocket in the waste about 50mm (2") wide and continue the cuts down to where the wall and floor meet.
- Cut further pockets along the wall at 300mm (12") intervals.
- Fold back the flaps which this creates and check the fit.
- Run a straight edge along the folds and cut off the flaps. ❞

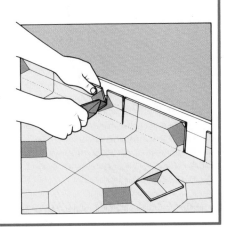

DEALING WITH OBSTACLES

Use paper templates to deal with obstacles like a basin or WC. (In a very small room, tape several sheets of paper together and make a template of the entire floor area as shown on page 107.) Use brown wrapping or heavy lining paper; newspaper is too flimsy. Scribing the outline of the obstacle avoids having to cut the template to an exact fit – but be sure to scribe back again on to the vinyl or you'll end up trimming it in the wrong place.

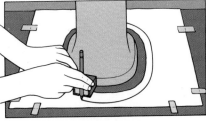

1 *Rough-cut the paper to fit around the obstacle leaving a 25mm (1") gap all round. Then scribe around the obstacle with a wood block and pencil.*

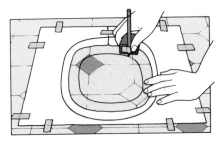

2 *Lay the finished template in position on the vinyl and tape it down. Now scribe back on to the vinyl from the outline marked on the template.*

3 *Make the cut-outs in the vinyl following the marked lines, then make a straight cut to the edge of the sheet in a place where the join won't be noticeable.*

For a room-sized template, *rough-cut and tape together enough sheets to fill the floor. After scribing the obstacles, scribe around the walls too.*

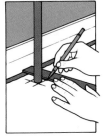

Mark a pipe's position *on the template by drawing a square around it. Transfer the square to the vinyl, then draw a circle just touching the lines.*

JOINS, EDGES AND FINISHING

Where you need to join sheets, start by scribing and direct-trimming the first sheet to fit. Leave plenty of overlap along the joining edge so that you can match the pattern.

After matching and trimming the join with the second sheet as shown, stick down the edges with a 150mm (6″) band of adhesive (see below) before you trim the rest of the second sheet to fit. This stops it slipping out of position.

At doorways, take care to cut the overlap to the full width of the doorway – not just the width of the door stop in the middle. Finish the join between the two coverings with an aluminium cover strip.

Gluing and finishing

Unbacked vinyl must be glued all over. Spread the adhesive over half the floor following the maker's instructions, lay the trimmed sheet lightly in position, then smooth out towards the edges with a soft broom to remove air bubbles. Repeat for the other part of the floor.

Cushioned vinyl normally only needs sticking down with a 150mm (6″) band of adhesive at joins, but glue it all over where it is laid under heavy appliances. Both jobs can be done with the sheet in position.

Afterwards, smooth down the glued areas with a piece of wood wrapped in a soft cloth.

At doorways, fit a metal cover strip with a ramp to match the thickness of the floorcovering in the adjoining room. Nail or screw the strip in place over the vinyl.

1 *To join two pieces,* fit the first sheet and lay the second on top. Align their patterns, leaving at least 100mm (4″) overlap on the opposite wall.

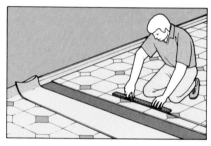

2 Fold back the second sheet and choose where to make the join (a 'line' in the pattern is ideal). Mark this line and cut along it against a straight edge.

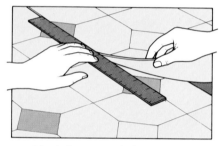

3 Tuck the second sheet under the first sheet. Butt a straight edge against the trimmed edge, fold back this edge, then cut the second sheet.

PROBLEM SOLVER

Tight fits

Trimmed edges sometimes become a tight fit along walls as the sheet begins to settle and flatten. If this happens, mark where the sheet fits perfectly on either side of the problem area, then fold back the sheet and join the marks with a straight line. Re-trim along this line using a straightedge.

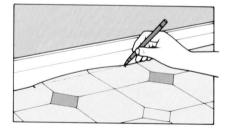

Marking a tightly fitting edge.

Accidental cuts

If the knife slips or you cut in the wrong place, repair the cut with non-stain double sided tape and seaming adhesive – both available from vinyl suppliers.

Cut a length of tape and run the sticky side down the cut on the underside of the sheet. Remove the backing from the tape and press down the sheet.

Now run a thin bead of seaming adhesive along the full length of the cut so that it just fills it. The adhesive will bond the edges together so that they are barely noticeable.

Patch cuts with double sided tape and seaming adhesive.

Sheet overtrimmed

When you've fitted the first edge and come to trim the second, you still have room for manoeuvre if you trim too much: slide the sheet along a bit, scribe the first edge again, then re-trim.

If the problem occurs after you have fitted two or more edges and you're left with an unsightly gap, one answer is to pin softwood quadrant moulding around the skirting or wall to disguise it (see below).

Alternatively, patch in a strip using tape and seaming adhesive. Disguise the join in the patch by running it along a line in the pattern.

Hide gaps with quadrant moulding.

LAYING CORK FLOOR TILES

Cork tiling is a warm, resilient and very economical floorcovering. The tiles are light and relatively easy to handle, and the pre-sealed types require little finishing work.

Choosing tiles

Most cork tiles are 12″ (305mm) square, and are sold in packs of nine to cover 1 sq yd (just under 1 sq m). Although they are available in different grades to suit different levels of wear, the main choice is between *sealed* and *unsealed* – some have a protective coat of acrylic varnish, lacquer or PVC applied in the factory, while others are sanded but left 'raw'. You can also get cork tiles with a self-adhesive backing, in which case they can be treated like self-adhesive vinyl tiles.

Sealed tiles are ready to walk on as soon as they are laid, but the square-edged type must be closely butted together or there is a risk of water seeping down between the joints. Some better quality tiles have lipped edges which interlock to seal the joints.

Unsealed tiles must be sealed before taking any foot traffic. The normal method is to give them at least three coats of polyurethane varnish, allowing each coat to dry thoroughly before applying the next, so it could take several days before the floor is ready for use.

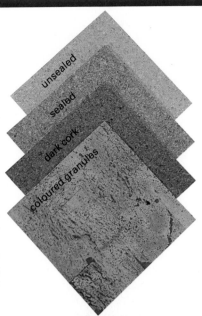

unsealed

sealed

dark cork

coloured granules

....Shopping List....

Most manufacturers provide charts on their packaging indicating how many tiles you need for a given area allowing for wastage. But to make use of this information, you must first measure the floor.

In a regularly shaped room, simply multiply the length by the width. In a room full of awkward shapes it's safer to draw a sketch plan and divide the area into a number of rectangles; find the area of each one, then add them together to get the total area.

Adhesive choice is critical, and will make all the difference to the durability of the floor. In theory, most water-based PVA flooring adhesives are suitable, but recent research suggests that some brands cause certain types of cork to expand and contract as they dry out, leading to shrinkage and gaps.

The problem is less acute on unsealed tiles, where the adhesive can evaporate more easily, and on vinyl-backed tiles, where it doesn't come into contact with the cork. But in all cases, follow the maker's recommendations where given.

Coverage depends on the porosity of the subfloor and on the tiles. As a rough guide, 1 litre will cover around 3–4 sq m (4 sq yd) on a concrete screed – more if the floor is lined with hardboard or the tiles have a smooth backing.

Sealant is usually gloss polyurethane varnish, but again you should follow the manufacturer's own recommendations. You need at least three coats, but on a floor taking heavy wear it's worth applying an extra one for good measure.

One litre of polyurethane covers about 16 sq m (19 sq yd) per coat, but allow for the fact that the first coat should be thinned half and half with white spirit to help it soak into the cork.

Tools checklist: Adhesive spreader (often supplied), string and chalk, tape measure, try square, trimming knife and spare blades, steel wool, wall brush (for applying sealant).

Trade tip

Matt finish

6 If you want a satin or matt finish on cork tiles which you plan to seal yourself, apply a couple of gloss coats first – it is much tougher. You can then use your chosen varnish for the top couple of coats to give a more subdued effect. 9

FLOOR PREPARATION

The first step is to prepare the underlying floor surface.

Boarded floors need lining with sheets of hardboard. Arrange the sheets so they don't coincide with the joints between boards and nail at 225mm (9") centres (150mm (6") around the edges).

Solid floors must be level, smooth and dry. If the surface is simply dusty, coat with concrete stabilizer. Localized damage can be repaired with concrete floor repair compound.

If the floor is slightly uneven, heavily patched or covered with small lumps and bumps, resurface it with self-levelling compound. But if the level is badly 'out' – over 12mm (½") say – or there are signs of dampness, have it rescreeded.

Existing floorcoverings may provide a suitable surface – for example, old cork tiles, vinyl tiles or glued-down sheet vinyl can all be overlaid with cork tiles, as long as they are level and

firmly fixed. Ceramic tiles may be more of a problem if the joints are deeply indented (though you could consider filling them). Old quarry tiled floors need treating with caution, as they may have been laid without a damp-proof membrane underneath. It's safer to lift them and rescreed.

Always check the adhesive manufacturer's instructions – they may recommend priming or sealing a particular surface to ensure a good bond.

DECIDING WHERE TO START

Few rooms have walls which are exactly square to one another, and even fewer are the right size to take a whole number of tiles. So the standard procedure for laying floor tiles is to start from a point near the centre of the floor, and work out towards the edges.

The exact starting point depends on how the gaps fall around the edges. By laying out the tiles in a 'dry run' as shown below, you can adjust it so that the gaps are more or less even right around the room, with no unsightly narrow strips.

Taking a line

If there is a major feature in the room which catches the eye – for example, a run of units – it may be better for the line of the tile joints to run parallel with this, rather than the walls. (Otherwise, the tiles could appear to be askew when in position.)

Arrange for this by making sure that one of the setting-out lines runs parallel to the feature concerned. Then reset the other line at right angles to it.

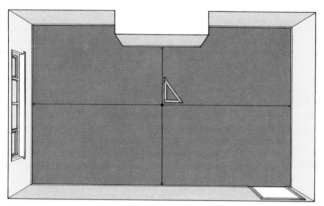

Find the centre of the room by measuring and marking the midpoints of the four walls, then stretching string between them. Check with a try square where the lines cross, and adjust one line until you get a right angle.

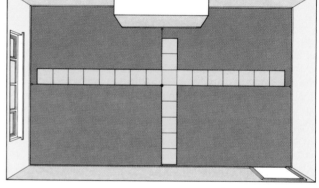
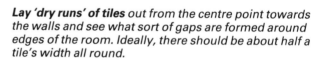

Lay 'dry runs' of tiles out from the centre point towards the walls and see what sort of gaps are formed around edges of the room. Ideally, there should be about half a tile's width all round.

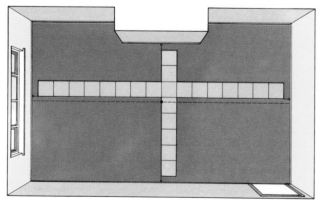

Reposition the centre tile(s) if necessary so that the gaps are evened up – for example, position the first tile over the cross instead of in the angle. If none of the positions is satisfactory, try moving one or both of the string lines.

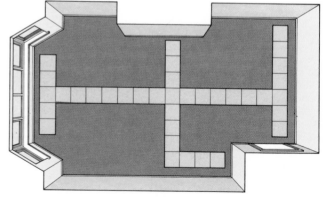

If the room is an awkward shape, lay further dry runs towards each obstacle and check the gaps here. Some awkward cuts will be unavoidable, but try to keep them to unobtrusive areas.

Trade tip

Check the tiles

❝ Before you start laying the tiles, check them carefully for grain pattern and colour. This is easiest while you have them laid out in a dry run.

Some tiles have very definite markings, with chips of cork aligned in rows. If a grain like this is laid running the same way right across the floor, it makes the tiles less obvious; conversely, alternating the grain direction actually strengthens the tiled effect. Decide which you prefer and lay the tiles accordingly.

At the same time, check for colour variation between packs. Unlike wallpaper, cork tiles aren't produced in batch numbers since some colour variation occurs naturally. Even so, you can avoid blocks of lighter or darker tiles by mixing the packs and then laying different tones at random. ❞

When laying cork tiles use a recommended adhesive. Spread the adhesive on the subfloor then position the tiles.

LAYING WHOLE TILES

Once you have decided on your starting point, adjust the strings to align with the central tile(s), then cover them with chalk and snap them against the floor to mark two straight guidelines.

Lay the tiles in a pyramid shape, working from the centre of the room to the wall furthest from the door. Fill in the corners with whole tiles, then work back towards the door in the same way.

When all the whole tiles are in position, leave the adhesive to set for 24 hours before filling in gaps. This way, there's no danger of them becoming dislodged.

1 Starting from the marked point, use a notched spreader to apply enough adhesive to lay about nine tiles. Work towards the wall furthest from the door.

2 Lay two or three tiles along one line, then start outwards along the intersecting line. Fill in the angle, butting to two edges where possible.

3 Use a clean cloth to wipe off any adhesive which squeezes out of the joints on to the tile surface. Moisten the rag with white spirit if necessary.

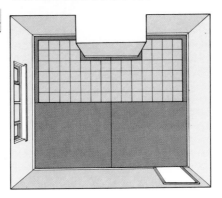

4 Work out from the centre line until half the room is covered. Then repeat for the second half, until all the whole tiles are laid.

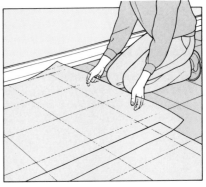

5 If you are using unsealed tiles, protect them by laying sheets of polythene over the surface of the tiles. Leave until the next day before sealing.

FILLING IN THE EDGES

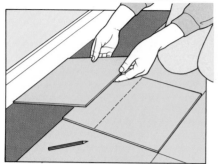

1 Lay the tile to be cut over the last complete tile, aligning the edges exactly. Position an uncut tile on top, so one edge butts against the wall.

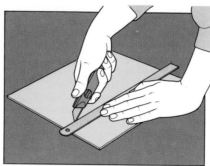

2 Using the top tile as a guide, mark a cutting line on the tile to be cut. Then lay the tile on a hard surface and trim along the marked line with a trimming knife.

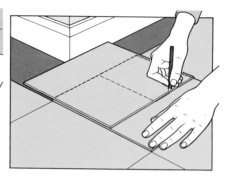

3 At external angles, use the same technique twice to mark both cutting lines. If you are using unsealed tiles, be careful not to mark beyond the angle.

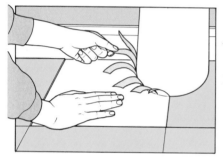

4 For rounded shapes like a basin pedestal, use a paper template. Tear back the paper so it fits round the obstacle, then use it to mark the tile.

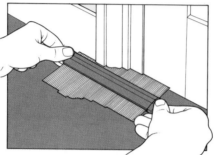

5 For fiddly obstacles, such as the ornate architrave around a doorway, use a profile gauge to trace the exact shape then cut it out a notch at a time.

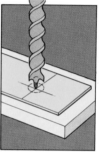

6 Around pipes, trim the tile to fit the gap, then measure the position of the pipe and cut or drill a suitable hole. Finally, slit the tile and slide in place.

SEALING THE TILES

Unsealed tiles have to be coated to protect the surface from everyday wear and tear. Cork in its natural state is highly absorbent, leaving it vulnerable to grease marks and water penetration (which could cause the tiles to lift).

If there is any unevenness in the surface (there shouldn't be if the floor has been properly prepared), sand down with medium glasspaper. Before you start, vacuum the floor thoroughly, and wipe over to remove all traces of dust (see Tip).

Trade tip

Dealing with dust

6 To ensure a dust- and grease-free surface before and during sealing, wipe down the tiles with a clean, white lint-free cloth moistened with white spirit. Keep the rag just moist enough to pick up the dust without wetting the tiles. The same trick can be used for other wooden surfaces before painting or varnishing – white spirit doesn't raise the grain the way water would. 9

Apply at least three coats of polyurethane varnish to unsealed tiles. Rub down with a pad of fine steel wool and wipe off the dust after each coat.

LAYING VINYL AND RUBBER TILES

Vinyl floor tiles give a hard wearing, easy-to-clean surface that's ideally suited to splash-prone rooms such as kitchens and bathrooms. And in a room containing lots of awkward corners, they are likely to be considerably easier to lay than a fitted carpet or sheet vinyl; if you do mis-cut, only a single tile gets wasted.

An expensive, but very durable, alternative to conventional vinyl tiles is synthetic rubber stud flooring – originally developed for airports and other public places. This also comes in tile form, and is laid in virtually the same way.

Decorative possibilities

One of the most appealing things about vinyl tiles is that different colours and styles can be mixed to create a range of decorative effects – for example, you could combine a pale, plain-coloured tile for the main floor area with a 'border' of darker patterned tiles.

Preparation and planning

To prepare the floor and to decide where to begin, follow the instructions given on page 112 for laying cork tiles.

follow the instructions given on page 112

.... Shopping List ....

Vinyl tiles vary widely in price, from relatively economical to very expensive. Some are solid vinyl, others have a cushioned layer, and patterns vary from gently flecked, soft geometric and floral to imitations of brick, cork and other surfaces.

Practically speaking the main choice is between *self adhesive* and *plain* tiles. Self-adhesive tiles are less messy to lay, but stick instantly and don't allow much margin for error. For plain tiles, always use the adhesive recommended by the makers – and where appropriate, buy a supply of suitable *solvent* for cleaning.

Most vinyl tiles are around 300mm (12″) square, and are sold in packs of varying sizes. Coverage per pack is always given on the packaging, so simply divide this figure into the floor area (measured in square metres) and round up to the nearest whole pack to find the total number of packs required. Don't forget that if the room is an awkward shape, it's easier to divide it into smaller rectangles, work out their areas, then add the figures together.

Rubber stud tiles are generally 500mm (20″) square and come in packs of 4. They must be laid with a heavy-duty neoprene rubber-based adhesive, which means taking extra care over preparing the subfloor.

Tools and other materials: Tape measure, pencil, string, chalk, trimming knife, metal rule or straightedge, notched adhesive spreader (if not supplied with the adhesive), white spirit, a supply of clean rags.

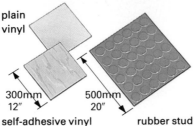

plain
vinyl

300mm
12″

500mm
20″

self-adhesive vinyl   rubber stud

Vinyl tiles are available in many styles, appropriate for many different situations. In the kitchen (top) they are a practical choice: this fresh, basketweave pattern is a classic style which will not date easily. Softer patterns (above), with floral motifs, are an appropriate choice in a sun room.
Rubber stud flooring gives a stylish look to this bathroom with a sunken bath.

LAYING THE TILES

Check vinyl tiles carefully before you start. Some designs have patterns with a 'right' and a 'wrong' way, so make sure you know which is which; if necessary, lay out all the whole tiles in a dry run and then stack them in the correct laying sequence.

Self-adhesive tiles are less messy to lay, but the backs of the tiles are *very* sticky and can't be slid around if you position them wrongly. When you start, use the tips of your fingers to hold the tiles just above the floor surface, align the edges with the guide lines, then lower gently into place. Smooth down the tiles with a soft cloth, and keep some white spirit handy to wipe any

adhesive marks off the face of the tiles.

Lay all the whole tiles before cutting the edge tiles. You can do the cutting straight away, since the adhesive acts instantly. When cutting tiles to fit, make all the necessary cuts before you peel off the backing paper.

Do the cutting on a piece of board, using a sharp trimming knife and a steel rule or metal straightedge. Depending on the thickness of the tile, you may not be able to cut it in one go: make repeated passes instead, and keep the straightedge steady.

Plain tiles can be laid in much the same way, but this time spread an

area of adhesive large enough to lay four tiles at a time. At the beginning, take care that the adhesive doesn't obscure the guide lines. Wipe off any excess on the face of the tiles immediately.

Lay all the whole tiles, then leave the adhesive to dry for at least 12 hours before fitting the edge tiles. For cut tiles, glue the tiles themselves, not the floor.

Rubber stud tiles are larger than plain vinyl, and the neoprene adhesive is much stickier. So it's advisable only to spread enough adhesive for one tile at a time.

The tiles are designed to create a 'continuous' floor surface, so lay them staggered to hide the joints.

Start tiling where the setting out lines cross. Position the first tile in the angle, then work outwards over the quadrant furthest from the door.

With self-adhesive tiles, peel off the backing and hold the tile just above the floor. Adjust until its position is correct, then press down and smooth.

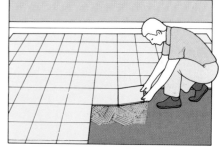

For plain tiles, spread enough adhesive to lay four tiles at a time. Butt the tiles closely, then wipe off any adhesive which squeezes up through the joints.

A profile gauge is handy for tricky obstacles: press in place, transfer the shape to the tile, and cut. Then trim the square edge of the tile to fit the gap.

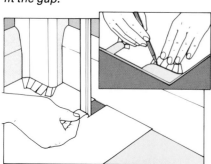

Use sheets of paper the same size as the tiles – or the paper backing on self-adhesive tiles – to make up templates for large obstacles and pipes.

To fit edge tiles, place the tile to be cut on the adjacent, whole tile (inset). Butt a spare tile to the skirting and use the opposite edge to mark the cutting line.

LAYING WOOD MOSAIC FLOORING

The most economical form of hardwood flooring comes as square mosaic panels in a basketweave pattern. These panels are often referred to as 'parquet' or 'woodblock', but they are much thinner and easier to lay than the brick-sized tongued and grooved blocks used on a traditional parquet floor.

The fingers of hardwood making up the panels are generally stuck together with a felt, net or paper backing, though some are strung together with wires which makes cutting slightly trickier. Both methods allow room for expansion and contraction of the wood itself – always the major consideration with a solid wood floor.

Even so, you should ensure the sub-floor is perfectly dry, as well as firm and level. Lift any existing floorcovering and remove all traces of the old adhesive. A concrete floor will probably then need re-finishing with self-levelling compound; level a wooden floor with hardboard.

As with other types of wood flooring, you have to leave a small expansion gap around the edges of the room. One way to hide this is to remove the skirtings and notch the door architraves before you start, or you can cover the gap with cork strip or moulding (see below).

Warm and welcoming, hardwood mosaic panels (above) provide a long-lasting and naturally resilient floorcovering for relatively little cost.

....Shopping List....

Wood mosaic panels These are usually sold in packs to cover about 2 square metres, although this varies from supplier to supplier. Allow a few extra panels in case you cut them badly. Always check the panels are square, by comparing them carefully, turning through 90° to check they are square in both directions.

There are two finishes, sealed and unsealed. When making a choice, bear in mind that the *sealed* panels probably have a better surface than you could apply, and you will save a lot of time because you will not have to apply coats and wait for them to dry before using the room.

With *unsealed* panels, you have to finish them yourself: the varnish will bring out darker and richer tones in the wood.

Adhesive Check the maker's recommendations given with the flooring. You may be able to use a PVA-based general *flooring adhesive*, but many types require a heavier black *bituminous adhesive* to protect the wood from moisture.

Sealant Unsealed panels must have a protective finish, while sealed ones will benefit from an extra coat after laying to stop moisture penetrating the joints.

Polyurethane varnish is the usual choice. Alternatives include quick-drying *two-part lacquer*, which is very hardwearing but considerably more expensive, and *oleo-resinous sealant* which provides a good base for wax polish.

Trim materials The expansion gap around the edge of the room can be filled with *compressible cork strip* (usually stocked by the flooring supplier) or covered with softwood *quadrant* or *scotia moulding*. Avoid using cork strip in small rooms, however, as it detracts from the floor's appearance.

Use moulding or *aluminium threshold strip* to finish the floor at doorways.

Tools checklist: Pencil, tape measure, string and chalk, trimming knife, tenon saw, work bench and hacksaw or pliers (for wired panels), sanding equipment, paintbrush. Extra woodworking tools may be needed for finishing the edges and fitting trim strips.

LAYING THE PANELS

Before you start, double-check that the floor surface is completely smooth. Sand down bumps, punch nail heads below the surface, and vacuum thoroughly.

As with conventional floor tiles, lay the panels in dry runs outwards from the centre of the room so that you can start at a point which avoids fiddly cuts. (Professionals often start in a corner which is easier for them but trickier for DIY). Note these points when setting out:

- In a room where the walls are square to each other, the joints between panels should run parallel to them.

- If the walls are not square, align the joints with the most dominant feature – the longest wall, or a row of units, for example.

- Allow for a 10mm (⅜″) expansion gap (or thereabouts) around the edges of the room.

- Where cuts are unavoidable, try to confine them to the least obvious parts of the room. Aim to make cuts along the joints between the individual fingers, rather than across the fingers themselves (which is more difficult).

- If you need underfloor access – to a stopcock, for example – ensure the mosaic panel joints coincide with those of the panel in the floor, even if this means more cutting.

Trade tip

Avoiding problems

❝ Half the problems with wood mosaic floors are caused by laying the panels straight from a cold warehouse: in a centrally heated home, they are likely to expand or contract quite dramatically to start with.

Anticipate this by buying the panels at least two days before you plan to lay them. Unwrap them and stack them in the room they are going in so that the wood has a chance to acclimatize. ❞

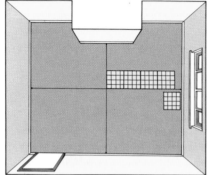

1 Fix string lines at right angles across the centre of the floor and lay dry runs of panels to check the fit at the edges. Aim for cuts to coincide with the joints between 'fingers'.

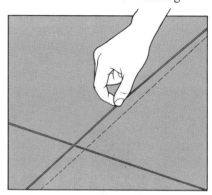

2 When the fit is as good as you can possibly get it, cover the string lines with chalk and snap them to leave guidelines across the floor. Start laying in the quadrant furthest from the door.

3 Starting where the lines cross, spread adhesive over an area slightly larger than a single panel. Position the first panel against the lines.

4 Spread another panel-sized patch of adhesive, then position the second panel so that it butts tightly against the first. Continue spreading and laying, a panel at a time. Avoid letting adhesive squeeze out of the joints on to the surface of the wood.

5 Complete the first quadrant, laying all the whole panels, then work on the other quadrants, finishing at the door. Leave to dry before walking on the panels.

CUTTING PANELS

Cut along the joints between fingers wherever possible. On backed panels, you can simply slice through the backing to separate them. Panels which are wired together along grooves on the underside of the fingers can be severed with tin snips, pincers or a junior hacksaw.

Cutting across the fingers themselves is a little more tricky due to the flexibility of the panels.

■ Begin by marking the cutting line, preferably in pencil.
■ Place the panel on a workbench over an offcut of hardboard. The cutting line should just overhang the edge of the bench.
■ Place a batten on top, as near to the cutting line as you can, and clamp in place.

The panel will now be rigid enough to cut accurately (saw through the hardboard at the same time). Use an electric jigsaw, tenon saw or coping saw as appropriate.

In awkward areas, it may be easier to separate the panels into single fingers and then trim these individually to fit (but avoid it if you can, since it's difficult to align them). Trim back the backing material to avoid fouling the joints.

Cut through the backing with a trimming knife to separate individual fingers.

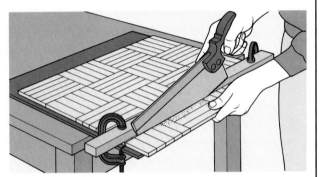

Clamp panels between an offcut of hardboard and a batten to cut across fingers.

FINISHING AROUND THE EDGES

1 To check how much to trim around edge panels, lay the panel to be cut on the last complete panel, then use a spare panel to mark the cutting line.

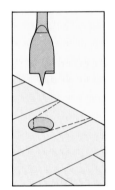
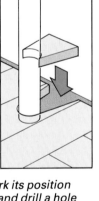

2 At a pipe, mark its position on the panel and drill a hole of a slightly larger diameter. Follow by cutting out a wedge to fit behind the pipe.

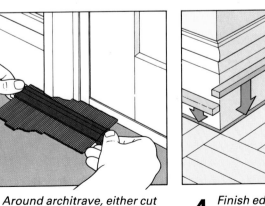

3 Around architrave, either cut a paper template, or use a profile gauge to copy the shape. Transfer to the panel, then cut (preferably with a jigsaw).

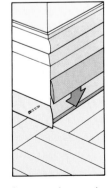

4 Finish edges by pressing cork strip into the expansion gap. Alternatively, cover the gap with softwood moulding tacked to the bottom of the skirting board.

5 At doorways, you can fit a tapered moulding or hardwood fillet to stop feet catching on the edge of the floor. Or, use an aluminium threshold strip.

SEALING THE FLOOR

After laying and finishing the edges, the final stage is to seal the panels with varnish or lacquer.

Using polyurethane, unsealed panels need at least three coats. Thin the first coat with white spirit to help it soak in.

Sand and vacuum thoroughly between coats. You can use fine glasspaper on a sanding block, or even a power sander, but many professionals prefer to use a large wad of medium grade steel wool.

Sealed panels require just a single coat, applied unthinned.

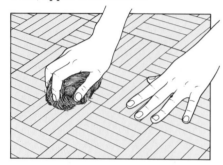

1 *Thin the first coat with 1 part white spirit to 10 parts polyurethane. Sand between coats using a wad of medium grade steel wool, then vacuum well.*

2 *As the finish builds up, the rich tones of the wood will start to emerge. Before the final coat, take extra precautions against dust: close any windows, then vacuum the floor and wipe over the surface with a damp cloth.*

■ PROBLEM SOLVER ■

Repairing damaged panels

It's worth keeping a few spare mosaic panels in case of accidental damage – dents from sharp, heavy objects are the most likely cause. In severe cases, you may have to replace an entire panel; it's more likely that the damage is confined to one or two fingers.

■ On backed panels, the fingers can be loosened by scoring around the edges with a trimming knife. With wired panels, you have to sever the wires by tapping sharply along the joints with a bolster or an old wood chisel.

■ Afterwards, prise out the fingers with a claw hammer or old chisel, using an offcut to protect the surrounding surface. Scrape away all traces of the backing and adhesive below.

■ Cut new fingers from a spare panel and check the fit.

With unsealed panels bed the new fingers in place on a fresh layer of adhesive. (If you haven't the correct type, woodworking adhesive should do).

Leave the repair for a couple of days to let the patch acclimatize. If it stands proud, sand level with the surrounding surface, taking care not to remove wood from the other fingers. Finally, sand the entire panel and revarnish.

With sealed panels, check if the replacement fingers stand proud of the surrounding surface. If they do, peel off any backing and sand them on the back to allow them to lie flush when bedded in adhesive. When stuck, sand the top lightly and give one coat of varnish to blend with the surrounding panel.

Sever wired fingers by tapping sharply along the joints with a thin bladed bolster, old wood chisel, or stripping knife. Use a trimming knife on backed panels.

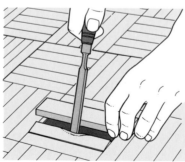

Lever out the damaged fingers with a claw hammer or an old chisel. Afterwards, scrape away all traces of the old adhesive and backing.

Sand the patched area if necessary, then sand the entire panel so that any colour change in the finish occurs between the panel joints.

LAYING FITTED CARPETS

Laying and fitting carpets yourself isn't always a good idea, particularly on large floors or awkwardly shaped areas such as the stairs. Indeed, many suppliers offer free fitting on carpets over a certain value, and professional laying should ensure you get the best wear out of top quality carpets – which have to be stretched tightly so that the pile stands upright.

Even so, there are times when it simply isn't worth calling in the professionals – for example, when laying a cheap foam backed carpet or remnant. You might also want to take carpets with you if you move.

Laying methods

There are three ways to fix carpets. **Foam backed** carpets are normally held around the edges of the room with *double-sided carpet tape*.
Canvas backed carpets can be stretched on gripper strips tacked to the floor around the edges of the room. Alternatively, if the subfloor is wooden, the edges can simply be turned over and tacked in place.

Underlay and lining

Foam or felt underlay should always be laid under canvas backed carpets to prolong wear and add a luxurious feel. It is unnecessary under foam backed carpets.
An extra lining (of paper or nylon) is essential for canvas backed carpet laid over floorboards, to prevent dirt from being drawn up from the void beneath the floor. And under foam backed carpets, a lining can help to prevent the backing from sticking to the subfloor.

Preparation

The subfloor must be clean and free from grease, particularly if you are using adhesive or carpet tape. Remove any doors for clearance if necessary (see Problem Solver).
Wooden floors should be level, with no movement in the boards and all nails punched home. If the boards are at all uneven, line the floor with hardboard, as for sheet vinyl.
Solid floors must be level and free from damp. If they are slightly uneven, level with self-levelling compound; if they are crumbling or 'out' by more than 12mm (½″), get them rescreeded.

PLANNING AND MEASURING

Before buying, measure the room.
■ Measure the overall area, taking measurements along and across the room at several points to allow for moderate irregularities. Measure into bays and alcoves where appropriate.
■ Check how square the walls are to one another by measuring the diagonals as well; if they are equal, you should have little trouble deciding how much carpet to order. If one diagonal is considerably longer than the other, allow extra width and length to ensure a good fit.
■ Allow at least 100mm (4″) extra all around so you can trim the carpet for an accurate fit.
■ Underlay and lining paper should be laid leaving a 50mm (2″) gap all around for double-sided tape, gripper strips or turning and tacking.

Which way round?

Choose a carpet which is wide enough to fit right across the room if possible. If you do have to join widths, plan the job so that seams fall in the areas of least traffic, and make sure that the pile on each piece runs in the same direction.
■ Check the width of the carpet and decide which way to lay it according to the room's proportions. For example, on a floor measuring 2.5×3.8m (8′2″×12′6″), a single piece of 4m (13′) carpet could run the length of the room.
■ A woven carpet should ideally be laid so that the direction of the pile runs away from the door (and towards the window if possible). This helps to prevent indentations from footmarks showing as you enter the room.

A patterned, tufted carpet in 80/20 wool/nylon is an ideal choice for a living room. Measure across the room at several points (inset) and check the diagonals as well before ordering.

For fixing buy *double-sided tape, tacks,* or *carpet gripper strip* according to your chosen method, plus a tack hammer for driving in the nails. Note that grippers come part-nailed, so be sure to state whether you're fixing to floorboards or concrete. *A staple gun* is handy for fixing lining or underlay to wood floors.

For joining seams use *double-sided tape* on foam backed carpet, or *woven tape* and *latex adhesive* on canvas backed carpet. *Single-sided carpet tape* is used to join widths of underlay.

For cutting use *scissors* and/or a *trimming knife,* plus a *metal straight edge* and *tape measure.*

Professional tools aren't essential, but make it easier to get a good finish. Aim to hire or improvise the following items, as they are expensive to buy.

A knee-kicker is used to stretch carpet across the room. The head spikes are adjustable to suit the carpet pile.

Position the kicker head near the edge of the carpet, at a slight angle to the run of the gripper strip. Knock the knee pad to force the carpet closer to the wall, then tuck the edge over the gripper.

A carpet layer's hammer has a long slim head for knocking in nails close to skirtings. It can also be held sideways and used for pressing carpet on to grippers.

A carpet layer's bolster is for tucking carpet between gripper strips and the wall. You can use a clean, blunt bricklayer's bolster or wallpaper scraper instead.

Un-nailed grippers are used in the trade where there's a risk of nailing through pipes. These need a special adhesive – ask your supplier.

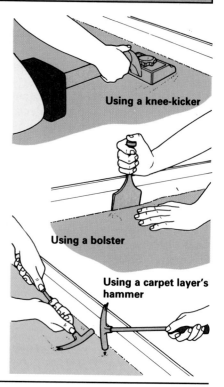

Using a knee-kicker

Using a bolster

Using a carpet layer's hammer

LAYING FOAM-BACKED CARPET

Foam backed carpets are relatively easy to lay – no underlay is used and they don't need stretching.

■ Start by laying the lining if needed. It doesn't have to be fixed, but taping or stapling it in place will stop it shifting around.

■ Check which way the pile runs, and unroll the carpet so it lies the right way round. When it is as flat and smooth as possible, trim to size leaving at least 50mm (2") lapping up the walls all the way round.

■ Make 'freeing cuts' diagonally into the corners so that the carpet lies as flat as possible.

■ Turn back the edge of the carpet and stick down the tape, leaving the backing paper in place.

■ Start to fit the carpet along one long straight wall. You may be able to butt the edge straight to the wall, but usually it's safer to trim it to fit. Stick the carpet down, unpeeling the tape backing and pulling the carpet tight as you go.

■ With one side held firmly, tread the carpet in place, shuffling across the room to remove wrinkles. Repeat to get the carpet as taut as possible.

■ Trim and fit the opposite edge to the one you fixed, making diagonal cuts to fit it into internal or external corners. Stick it in place.

■ Finally, work up and down the room in the same way and stick the remaining edges.

1 Lay the lining if necessary, stapling or sticking it with double-sided tape. Align the end of the carpet with the wall and unroll. Trim waste to 50mm (2").

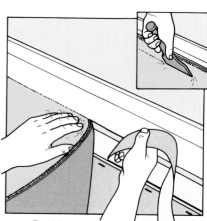

2 Position tape on the floor around the edge of the lining paper. Use a bolster to mark the trim line: ensure the carpet is taut before cutting and sticking.

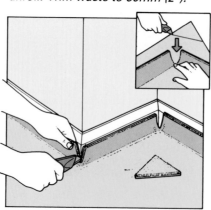

3 Cut across the carpet where it is to fit into internal corners before trimming. At external corners, cut diagonally to the obstruction.

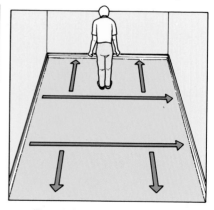

4 Tread the carpet in place across the room, then stick the opposite edge. Finally, work up and down the room and stick the remaining edges in place.

LAYING CANVAS BACKED CARPETS

Canvas backed carpets should be stretched tightly across the room, whether they are turned and tacked or fitted to gripper strips. You can stretch the carpet by shuffling it into place with your feet, but for a professional finish hire a knee-kicker. Proper tensioning ensures that the pile stands as upright as possible, improving its life. Some types of carpet also tend to stretch as they wear in; tensioning should prevent this too.

Lay the lining and underlay first, with a 50mm (2") border. If using grippers, fix them and any threshold strips (see overleaf) next. Watch out for buried pipes and cables.

Before stretching and fitting the carpet, trim it to fit the room allowing about 100mm (4") extra all around. Then, starting from one corner, trim the waste to 20mm (¾") along adjacent edges. Fix these edges for 300mm (1') out from the corner, then stretch the carpet and fit it to the gripper strips along the longer wall. Next stretch it along the shorter wall, out from the same corner. Stretch the carpet across the room towards the corner opposite the starting point, then fit along the remaining walls.

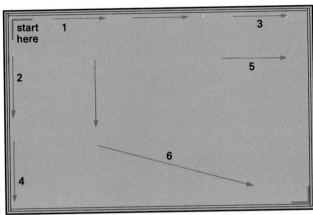

The basic stretching plan is to start from one corner. Fix firmly on both sides of the corner, then stretch and fit along each adjacent wall. Stretch down the longer wall to the opposite corner before fitting the carpet along the remaining walls.

1 Lay the lining and then the underlay, fixing them with staples or tape. Join seams with carpet tape. Nail gripper strips around the room about 5mm (¼") from the wall. At curves, cut short lengths of strip leaving at least two nails for fixing.

2 Unroll the carpet and trim to fit roughly. At the starting corner, trim diagonally across it. Trim the waste to 19mm (¾") and press over the gripper strip.

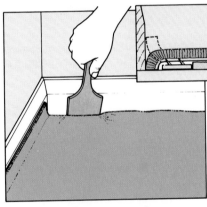

3 Tuck the edge waste between the gripper and skirting. Stretch the carpet along the first edge, pressing it on to the gripper and tucking in as you go.

4 Work around the room in the order shown above, treading the carpet as flat as possible before stretching it taut and fitting over the grippers.

Trade tip

Working with tufteds

If tufted carpets are stored in an unheated place, the backing stiffens up. Leave the carpet in a warm room so that it becomes pliable again – particularly if you plan to lay the carpet in an awkward area. Never fold a tufted carpet, as you will have great difficulty removing the creases.

If turning and tacking fit the first corner by turning under about 50mm (2") and tacking it in place every 100mm (4"). Trim away excess fabric across the corner.

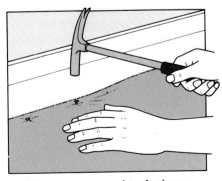

Continue to turn and tack along one edge, stretching it as you go. Repeat for the other edge. Then stretch the carpet across the room, trim, turn and tack.

JOINING WIDTHS

Traditionally, seams between widths of carpet were sewn. Nowadays adhesives and carpet tape are more commonly used. Where possible, join machined edges; otherwise, overlap the two edges to be joined and use one edge as a cutting guide to trim the layer underneath.

With foam backed carpets use the same double-sided tape used to fix the carpet but strengthen the joint with latex adhesive.

With woven backings use woven tape and latex adhesive to make the join. You should join widths before stretching the carpet to fit.

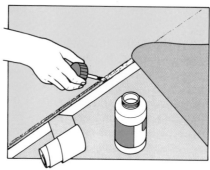

With foam backed carpets position the tape on the floor along the seam line. Apply latex adhesive along the cut edge, peel off the backing and press firmly.

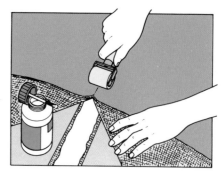

For canvas backed carpet lay woven tape along the seam line, coat it with adhesive, then press the edges in place. Roll the seam afterwards for a good bond.

THRESHOLD STRIPS

Choose a threshold strip *without* spikes for foam backed carpet, *with* spikes for gripper fixing. The type of strip is also governed by what's on the other side of the doorway: where carpets butt up to each other, use a double-sided strip designed to hold carpets on both sides; use a single-sided strip if the carpet finishes here

The threshold strip should be fitted directly under the position of the door when closed. But if there is a hard floorcovering on the other side of the door, the threshold strip must cover its edge.

Position the carpet over the strip, mark the cutting line and trim any waste. Then simply tuck the edge under the cover strip.

To hold foam backed carpets in place, hammer the strip over the edge of the carpet using a piece of wood to protect the metal surface.

Problems with doors

Laying a thick new carpet could involve removing and trimming any inward-opening doors.

◼ To remove a door, open it wide and slip magazines underneath to take the weight while you release the hinges.

◼ After fitting the carpet, measure down the frame from the lower hinge to the surface of the new carpet, and compare this with the equivalent measurement on the door. Mark the bottom edge for trimming.

◼ To trim a small amount – less than 6mm (¼″) or so – simply plane down to the marked line.

◼ To trim more, use a panel saw and plane smooth, or use a power plane.

◼ Check the fit of the door by holding both open and closed. If all is well, place it back on the magazines to align the hinge plates, then refit the screws.

Support the door with magazines while unscrewing the hinges.

Measure and mark the amount to be trimmed.

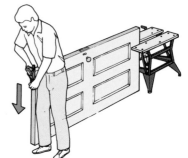

Plane to the marked line.

BUILDING

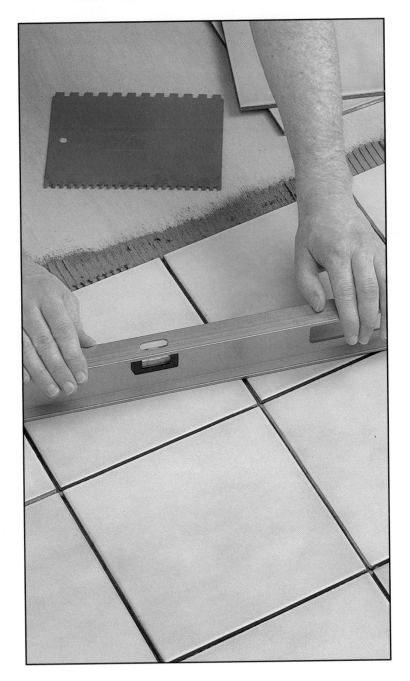

FIXING TO SOLID WALLS

Fixing to a solid wall of plastered brick, block or concrete calls for special fixing devices that will grip the surrounding masonry securely. Here are some basic rules for making sure that they do:

■ Where possible, choose fixings to suit the wall in question, and make sure that they're capable of carrying the load (see pages 129-130).

■ Check that the screws you're using are large enough. Most general purpose fixings take screw gauge Nos. 6, 8 and 10, or else are colour coded for a particular gauge. Some types specify a certain size. The length of the screw will depend on what you are fixing.

■ Make sure the holes for the fixings are the right diameter and depth. Most fixings have the correct size of drill to use marked clearly on the packaging; if not, don't buy. Depth depends on the type of fixing – plastic plugs sit flush with the wall, while the fibre type needs a deeper hole so that the end of the plug doesn't expand and crack the surrounding plaster.

■ Ensure the wall is in good condition. If the plaster or brickwork is crumbly enough for the fixing to pull out easily when inserted, use plugging compound instead (see Problem Solver).

Safety First

Drilling through water pipes buried in the wall is very inconvenient; drilling through cables can be fatal. If the wall you're drilling contains electrical fittings of any sort, avoid the danger zones shown in the diagram – cables are usually run horizontally or vertically between outlets, though you can never be sure.

A better solution is to hire or buy a metal detector (nowadays they are quite cheap) which will show the presence of both cables and pipes. Use this to pinpoint possible danger zones before you start work, and keep a 'map' of any such zones in your 'Home File' for future reference.

BASIC DRILLING TECHNIQUE

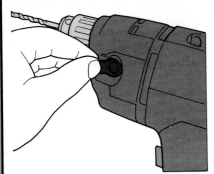

1 For plaster, set the drill speed to 'low' and the hammer facility (if fitted) to 'off'. If you hit brick or concrete, switch the hammer to 'on'.

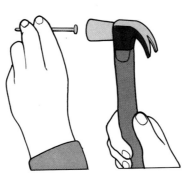

2 Measure the position of each hole twice to avoid mistakes. Then 'spot' the holes by punching them with an old nail to stop the drill bit from slipping.

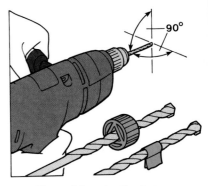

3 Fit a rubber depth stop or a piece of tape to the drill bit so you know how deep to drill. Check the drill is square to the wall before pulling the trigger.

AVOIDING MESS

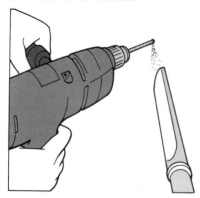

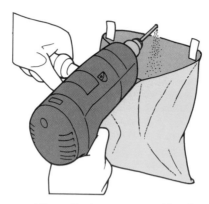

1 One way to reduce the dust thrown up by drilling into a solid wall is to have a helper standing by with a vacuum cleaner – use the dust nozzle.

2 Alternatively, tape one side of plastic bag to the wall just below the holes. Let the bag fall open or grasp it in your fingers to catch the debris.

3 When drilling upwards, use an empty yoghurt pot to catch the debris: bore a hole in the base, then fit the pot over the drill bit so it rests on the chuck.

PROBLEM SOLVER

if the drill bit slips . . .   . . . tilt to correct

Missing the point
If the bit slips away from the mark when you start a hole, tilt the drill in the **same direction** as the slip and you should find that it rights itself.

When holes don't align
If you're fitting brackets and one of the holes doesn't line up, try enlarging the bracket hole with a small file rather than re-drilling the wall.

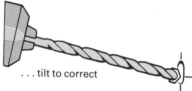

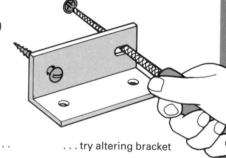

if plugs don't align . . .   . . . try altering bracket

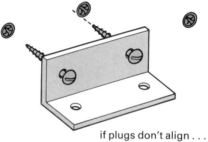

fit plugs to screws where vision is obscured

Plugging blind
Where you can't see to line up screws with their plugs, fit the plugs to the ends of the screws instead and juggle the entire assembly into position.

Using plugging compound

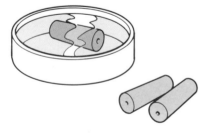

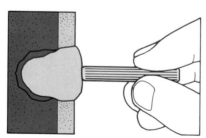

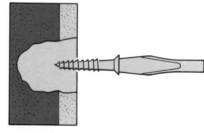

1 Use plugging compound to repair holes in crumbling plaster. Start by soaking a plug in water for one minute to soften it.

2 Force the softened plug into the hole with the dowel supplied and smooth off level with the surface of the wall.

3 Then drive in the fixing screw a third of the way and leave to set for 30 minutes before fitting and fixing as normal.

TYPES OF FIXING

Plastic wallplugs are the most commonly used type of solid wall fixing, and since most sizes of plug each accommodate a range of screw sizes, you should find that with careful selection just two plug sizes cover you for most jobs around the house.

The exception will be where the screws you're using are very long – say, over 32mm (1¼″) 'in the wall'. In this case, ask yourself if such a deep fixing is really necessary, and if it is, use plastic extruded strip cut to length: otherwise, use shorter screws.

Most of the other fixings shown below have more specialized uses, and many are only available from hardware stores. Expandable wall bolts are quite common, but only as fixings for structural members – joist hangers, wall plates and the like. They are expensive, so buy them when you need them and hire a drill bit of the appropriate size.

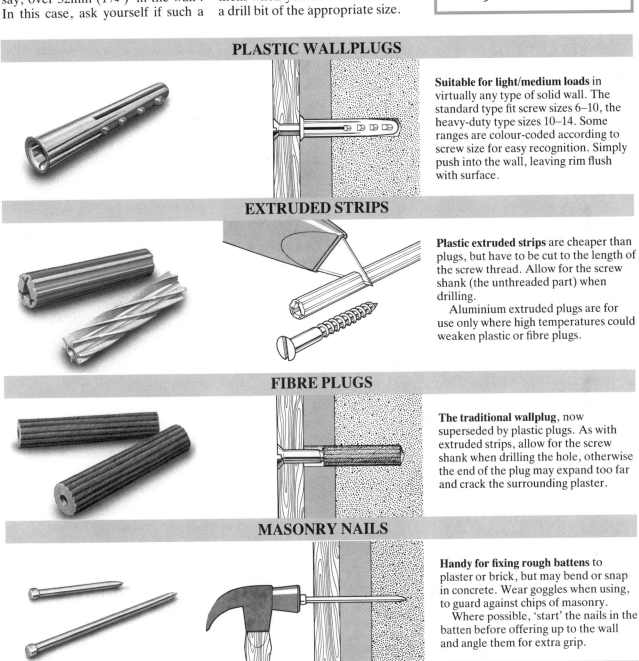

PLASTIC WALLPLUGS

Suitable for light/medium loads in virtually any type of solid wall. The standard type fit screw sizes 6–10, the heavy-duty type sizes 10–14. Some ranges are colour-coded according to screw size for easy recognition. Simply push into the wall, leaving rim flush with surface.

EXTRUDED STRIPS

Plastic extruded strips are cheaper than plugs, but have to be cut to the length of the screw thread. Allow for the screw shank (the unthreaded part) when drilling.

Aluminium extruded plugs are for use only where high temperatures could weaken plastic or fibre plugs.

FIBRE PLUGS

The traditional wallplug, now superseded by plastic plugs. As with extruded strips, allow for the screw shank when drilling the hole, otherwise the end of the plug may expand too far and crack the surrounding plaster.

MASONRY NAILS

Handy for fixing rough battens to plaster or brick, but may bend or snap in concrete. Wear goggles when using, to guard against chips of masonry.

Where possible, 'start' the nails in the batten before offering up to the wall and angle them for extra grip.

BLOCK FIXINGS

Special plugs that provide extra grip in lightweight cellular blocks.

One type is screwed into hole and fixed in position by tapping in a locking pin down the side. Another has fins which expand as the plug is driven into the wall.

NAILABLE PLUGS

Nails with 'built-in' plugs; particularly useful where a large number of not-too-strong fixings have to be made, such as on batten frameworks and skirtings. Wall and batten are drilled in one go, then plug is driven in with a hammer (expanding as it does so). Removable *hammer screw* has a slotted head.

FRAME FIXINGS

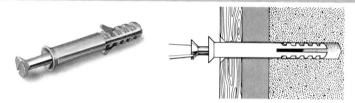

Screw version of nailable plug, invaluable on jobs where alignment of the screw and plug holes may be difficult – for example, when screwing a window frame to the surrounding masonry.

SPECIAL PURPOSE FIXINGS

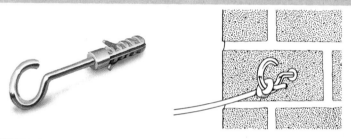

A variety of purpose-made steel fixings are sold complete with heavy-duty high-grip plugs, so if you want to fix anything out of the ordinary it's worth asking your hardware supplier. Shown left is a hook fixing for securing a washing line or cable support wire to an outside wall.

EXPANDING WALL ANCHORS

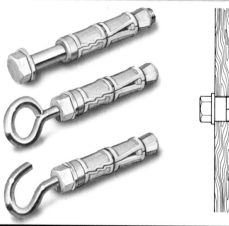 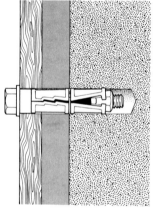

Heavy-duty fixings for securing wooden beams, joist hangers and the like.

On some types the outer metal shell expands as the built-in bolt is driven in. On others, driving the bolt causes the shell to compress and thicken, gripping the wall as it does so. Several types of bolt heads are available, including stud, hook and eye.

Holes for wall anchors must always be drilled in the centre of bricks or blocks – *not* in the intervening mortar joints, or the fixings may fail.

MASONRY DRILLS AND BITS

■ It's absolutely essential to use a tungsten carbide tipped masonry bit (below) for drilling solid walls; you can tell one by the spade-shaped insert in the tip.

■ By far the best type of drill for concrete or rendered walls is a hammer drill, which punches as well as bores its way through the small stones in the material. If you don't own one it's worth hiring – but make sure your drill bits are *'suitable for impact use'*.

■ If your drill has a speed setting, keep it on low unless you feel particular resistance. If it is a variable speed model, start off slowly and increase to medium speed as you go or when you feel extra resistance.

■ Older single speed electric drills will just about cope with blocks and common brick, but operate the drill in bursts to stop the bit blunting.

MASONRY DRILL SIZE CHART

Screw size*	Drill No.	Imp. size	Equiv. metric size
	6	$5/32''$	4mm
	8	$3/16''$	4.5mm
	10	$7/32''$	5.5mm
	12	$1/4''$	6.5mm
	14	$9/32''$	7mm
	16	$5/16''$	8mm
	18	$11/32''$	9mm
	20	$3/8''$	10mm

*Screw heads are shown lifesize, and as a guide only. For drilling plug holes, always use the bit size recommended by the plug maker.

FIXING TO HOLLOW WALLS AND CEILINGS

Fixings for *solid* walls are designed to expand in their holes and get a grip on the surrounding masonry. But in most homes, some of the walls and all the ceilings are hollow, with only a thin plaster or plasterboard skin. This means that there's nothing much for an ordinary wall plug to get a grip on, and you must use cavity fixings instead.

The right fixing

Although there are many types of cavity fixing, they all work by fitting through a small hole in the surface skin and then expanding behind it so the screw won't pull out. Because each one is suitable for different jobs, and because the surface of a cavity construction is relatively weak, it's even more important to choose the right fixing method.

The first step is to take a look at what you're fixing to. In older houses, *some* of the interior walls are probably cavity constructions. But in modern homes, even exterior walls can have a hollow timber frame. So if you suspect a wall's hollow, test it to make sure.

Right: Hollow wall fixings like this Rawlplug collapsible metal type bear on the inside surface of the cavity skin – in this case plasterboard.

IDENTIFYING A CAVITY CONSTRUCTION

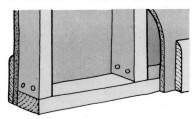

Plasterboard constructions are easily identified because they sound hollow when tapped, except where there are frame timbers behind the skin.

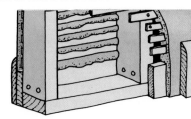

Lath and plaster is much thicker, but may sound hollow if the plaster covering the laths is on the thin side. Drill a small hole to confirm your findings.

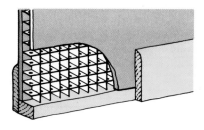

Dry ('Paramount') partition is thinner than other walls (50-63mm). Made of double sheets of 9.5mm (⅜") plasterboard with a cellular core, on wooden frame.

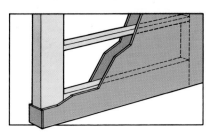

Hollow door Modern interior doors are made from sheets of hardboard or plywood on a wood frame. The cellular core may not sound hollow, so drill to check.

Most cavity walls are based on a framework of substantial vertical timbers called *studs*, usually 350-610mm (14-24") apart, which are braced by crosspieces called *noggins*. Ceilings are fixed to the underside of the supporting timbers (*joists*). These are generally spaced 400-610mm (16-24") apart.

In houses built after 1945, the framing timbers are usually finished with sheets of 12mm (½") thick plasterboard.

In older houses, lath and plaster was used. With this type of construction, thin strips of wood (the laths) are nailed up at roughly 12mm (½") intervals, then covered with a skin of (often thick) plaster.

Other constructions

There are two other types of cavity construction which you might have to fix to: dry partitioning (used only for walls and not common in ordinary houses), and hollow internal doors.

HOW STRONG?

When you have checked what you are fixing to, think about the weight of what you want to put up. The table on the right shows how to group various items as Heavy, Medium and Light. When deciding how to group something, don't forget to allow for the weight of what's going inside or on top.

Light or Medium fixtures can be put up with the right type of cavity fixing, shown on the following pages. For anything Heavy, do not try to use a cavity fixing. The only really secure way to fix it is to screw directly to the timber frame as shown below.

WORKING OUT THE LOAD		
HEAVY 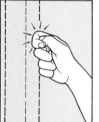	**Walls:** kitchen cupboards, bookshelves, track shelving, radiator, row of coathooks, curtain tracks and poles, large framed mirrors and pictures,	**Ceiling:** hanging plant holders, heavy light fittings, pull-cord switches, curtain tracks and poles
MEDIUM 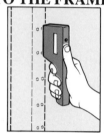	**Walls:** small bathroom cabinet, ornamental shelves, framed pictures, medium sized mirrors, kitchen base units	**Ceilings:** lightweight light fittings, track lighting tracks, spotlights
LIGHT	**Walls:** small pictures/prints, message board, clock, small mirror	

FASTENING TO THE FRAME

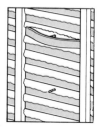

1 Find the timbers by tapping at regular intervals to detect a change in the sound, or use a metal detector to trace rows of fixing nails.

2 The only way to locate the timber precisely is by straddling its position with test holes using a bradawl or thin drill bit.

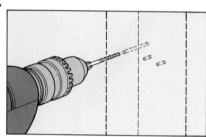

3 Once you have found two timbers, you can find others by measuring the gap and then measuring the same distance along. Drill and test to check.

4 Fixing screws should project at least 32mm (1¼") into the wall. If you can't fix to the studs, screw a batten to them, then screw to the batten.

Trade tip

Drilling hollow walls

❛ Most cavity fixings need quite large holes, usually about 9mm (⅜"). Drill at low speed with little pressure and no hammer – be prepared to break through very suddenly. Plaster and plasterboard are quite soft, so if you haven't a masonry bit this size, use an old wood bit instead. This can even give a cleaner hole, though the drill will be spoilt for other jobs. ❜

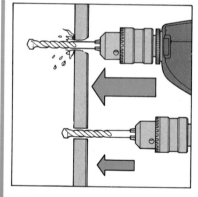

PROBLEM SOLVER

Springing a lath

If the point of the drill pushes a lath away from the plaster instead of going through it, change to a smaller wood bit and try again. If this doesn't get through, try drilling another hole slightly higher or lower.

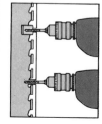

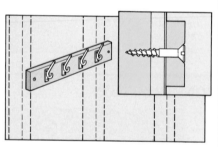

Filling misdrilled holes

The large holes used by cavity wall fixings can be hard to fill if you break through in the wrong place. Mix the filler to a stiff consistency with newspaper or cotton wool to pack out the hole, then smooth over with a final layer of filler when dry.

Fixing to hollow doors

Hardboard hollow doors are sometimes too weak to support a fixing and glued-on fittings may be more secure. If an existing fixing comes out, it will probably split the surface. Try gluing it back in using epoxy adhesive.

TYPES OF CAVITY FIXING

Cavity fixings must be suitable for your wall and the load you are putting up. The table below classes the types of fixings which are suitable for Light or Medium loads and tells you what surfaces they can be used on. If you are in doubt about the weight, choose a fixing from the Medium category.

There are some other points to think about which may affect your decision:

■ If you have to use particular screws with whatever you are putting up, make sure these are suitable for the fixing. Some can only be used with their own built-in screws.

■ If you are buying separate screws, check how far these need to project through into the wall fixing.

■ Note that several types of fixing cannot be used more than once, because if you remove the screw,

they fall into the cavity. If you might have to take down the fixture temporarily – for painting, say – use one listed in the table as reusable.

■ A few fixtures are put up by leaving the screw head projecting and then slotting the fixture over it. Very few cavity fixings expand properly unless the screw is tightly home, so be sure to find a suitable one if you have to fix something which uses this method.

PLASTIC WING PLUG – LIGHT

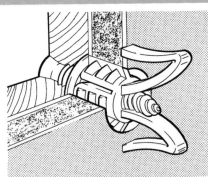

Designed specifically for plasterboard. Requires a 6.5mm hole and accepts standard No. 8 woodscrews. Reusable and inexpensive.

Drill the hole in plasterboard, then tap the plug home and attach the fixture. As you tighten the fixing screw, the legs are forced apart so that they grip the back of the plasterboard.

PLASTIC WEDGE PLUG – LIGHT

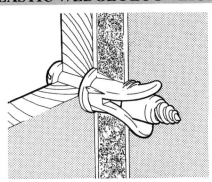

Two versions available – one for plasterboard walls, and a smaller one for hollow doors. They need 9mm/6.5mm holes and take standard No. 8/No. 6 woodscrews respectively. Reusable and inexpensive.

Fit in the same way as a wing plug. Tightening the fixing screw causes the sides of the plug to expand and grip the back of the cavity skin.

PLASTIC PETAL ANCHOR – LIGHT

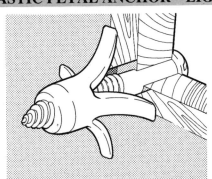

Suits any cavity thickness but is particularly useful for narrow cavities where space for a fixing is limited. Different sizes are available accepting Nos 6, 8 and 10 woodscrews (hole sizes are 6mm, 8mm and 10mm). Very cheap but not reusable.

To fit, drill hole, then attach anchor to fixing screw. When inserted, petals spring back against cavity skin and are drawn into it as screw is tightened.

EXPANDING RUBBER NUT – LIGHT

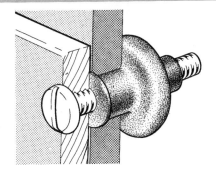

Suitable for various thicknesses of cavity skin, therefore ideal for wood panelling, perforated blocks etc. Also useful if you're not sure what you are drilling into. Different sizes are available (smallest hole size 8mm). Comes with own fixing bolt (hexagonal or slotted head). Reusable but not cheap.

To use, remove bolt and refit through fixture. Then drill hole, insert fixing and tighten bolt.

HOLLOW DOOR FIXINGS – LIGHT

lightweight plug

plug with integral hook

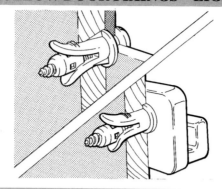

Lightweight wedge plugs for hollow doors need 6.5mm holes and take No.6 screws.

Hollow door hooks with integral plugs are also available, in both single hook and double hook versions - the double hook comes with a drilling guide. They require 6mm holes.

COLLAPSIBLE FIXING – LIGHT/MEDIUM

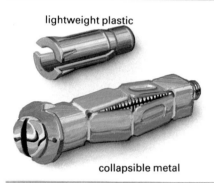

lightweight plastic

collapsible metal

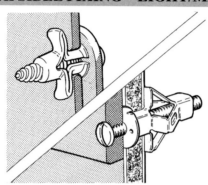

Suitable for different thicknesses of cavity skin, depending on size. Two broad groups – metal and plastic. Plastic types are cheaper, but the cheapest only accept light loads; they accept standard woodscrews (typically Nos 6, 8 and 10). Metal types come with their own machine screws. Hole sizes vary, but are normally 6mm, 8mm or 10mm. Reusable. Fit as for wing plug.

SELF-HOLDING STRAP TOGGLE – MEDIUM

Suitable for different cavity thicknesses up to 50mm (2″). Screw doesn't need full tightening for fixing to hold, so ideal for 'keyhole slot' fixtures. Needs a 10mm hole and No. 8 woodscrews. Reusable, but not cheap. Cavity must be wide enough to allow fixing to open.

To fit, ease toggle through hole, position collar, then pull strap to engage. Trim strap after inserting fixing screw.

GRAVITY TOGGLE – MEDIUM

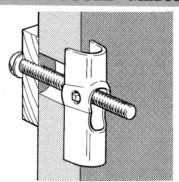

Suitable for different thicknesses of cavity skin, but needs space behind to open. Special type available for ceilings. Robust metal construction, and supplied with own machine screw or hook fixing. Requires large (16mm hole). Expensive and not reusable.

To fit, push right through hole into cavity, allowing backplate to drop. Then pull pack to engage backplate and tighten fixing screw against it.

SPRING TOGGLE – MEDIUM

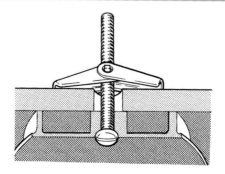

Suitable for different thicknesses of cavity, depending on size chosen, but like gravity toggle needs space behind to open. Particularly suitable for lath and plaster. Robust metal construction, and supplied with own machine screw or hook bolt. Hole size between 11mm and 18mm, depending on size. Expensive and not reusable.

PATCHING HOLES IN PLASTER

The one thing you need when patching holes in plaster is patience. Modern materials have made the job much easier than it used to be, but if you rush, the chances are you'll take twice as long to get a finish that's fit for redecorating.

On small holes and cracks use general purpose filler, building it up in thin layers and allowing each one to dry before applying the next. For the final layer, use fine surface filler

– it is much smoother and takes paint well.

For larger repairs up to around 1 sq m (1 sq yd) you have a choice of using ready-mixed DIY repair and skimming plaster, or mixing your own conventional plaster in a bucket. Each have their advantages and disadvantages (see page 138), but the repairs which are shown here all make use of the ready-mixed type of plaster.

Applying ready mixed skimming plaster.

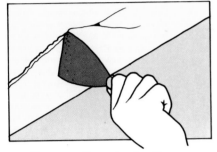

1 For a small crack, give the filler something to grip by enlarging the crack slightly with the corner of your filling knife. Dampen with water afterwards.

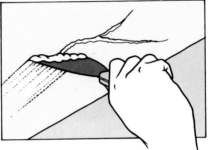

2 Press the filler into the crack, smoothing as you go. Then hold the knife edge-on to the surface of the wall and scrape away the excess.

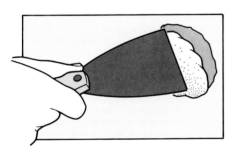

3 For a hole, brush away any loose material and dampen with water. Apply a first layer of filler to a depth of no more than 5mm (¼″) and leave to dry.

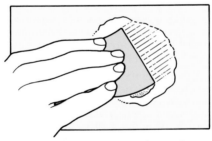

4 Build up subsequent layers in the same way until the filler is just below the surface of the wall. Finish by smearing on a layer of fine surface filler.

─Trade tip─
The spray way

❝ People often fill a hole in plaster roughly, then spend ages sanding it down only to find they have to fill it again. It's far better to get it smooth first time – by using clean tools, and spraying the surface with water as you smooth it using a garden hand spray. It takes a light touch, but with a little bit of practice you soon learn. ❞

MENDING CHIPPED CORNERS

1 Knock some nails into a batten so the tips just show through. Then nail the batten level with the edge of the corner leaving one side of the chip exposed.

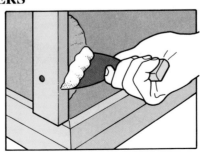

2 Prepare the chipped area as for an ordinary hole, then press in some filler or repair plaster and smooth off against the edge of the batten.

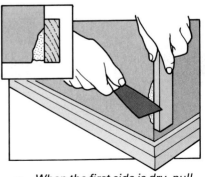

3 When the first side is dry, pull out the batten nails with pliers and fill the second side. Use the batten as shown to get a clean edge to the repair.

RESURFACING AN UNEVEN WALL

Ready mixed skimming plaster is the perfect material for finishing off a patched repair like the one on the previous page.

However, if there are lots of patches in the same wall, it's worth giving the entire wall another coat after you've finished so that the repairs are completely hidden. The technique is exactly the same in both cases.

Use a large, wide paintbrush to apply the skimming plaster; the better the condition of the bristles, the easier the job is.

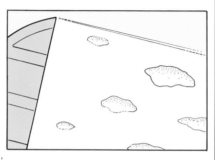

1 Apply the plaster with broad upward sweeps of the brush. When you've covered about a square metre, run the brush gently over it to smooth.

Holding the brush like this when smoothing gives you more control.

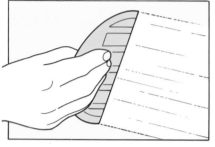

2 Wait until the plaster starts to 'go off' (dry), then use the applicator supplied to smooth out the brushmarks, dipping it frequently in a bowl of water.

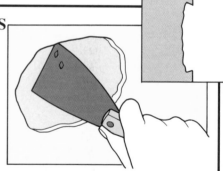

3 Pits like these show that you are 'stretching' the plaster too far; refill them immediately. Don't worry about the ridges – they can be sanded afterwards.

Press the float into the wall as you sweep it across the repair.

PATCHING LARGER HOLES

Holes up to around 1 sq m (1 sq yd) can be patched fairly successfully, but you must make sure the backing is sound. Chip off any loose material (even if this enlarges the hole) using a scraper, an old wood chisel or a bolster chisel. If the plaster is crumbly, paint it with stabilizing fluid or PVA adhesive (see overleaf).

The best tool for applying the repair plaster is a metal float. Don't spend a fortune on this – a cheap one is perfectly adequate.

1 Prepare the hole by brushing away any loose material, and if necessary paint on some stabilizer (see overleaf). Then chip back the edges.

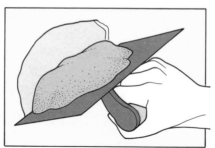

2 Scoop a lump of ready mixed repair plaster on to the back of your float and press it into the hole. Sweep the float upwards to stop it falling out.

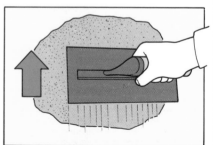

3 When the hole is roughly filled, dip the float in water. Smooth the plaster with gentle sweeps, pressing the blade against the edge of the hole.

MENDING PLASTERBOARD

Use plasterer's scrim tape (from builder's merchants) to reinforce a small plasterboard repair.

For larger holes, ask your local builder's merchant or superstore for an offcut of plasterboard to use as a patch – you don't want to be landed with a whole sheet. Finish the repair with ready mixed skimming plaster as shown opposite. Finding studs in hollow walls is described on page 132.

1 For a small repair, stick small pieces of scrim tape criss-cross over the hole with PVA adhesive. Fill over the top, feathering away the edges.

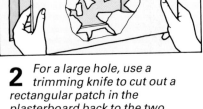

2 For a large hole, use a trimming knife to cut out a rectangular patch in the plasterboard back to the two nearest studs.

3 Cut a new patch to fit from an offcut of plasterboard and nail it to the studs. Plaster over the top using ready mixed skimming plaster or repair plaster.

4 Alternatively, fix string to a piece of plasterboard narrow enough to pass through the hole. Fix it from the back with dabs of filler; then, when this is dry, spread more filler over the top.

Trade tip

Close to the edge

❝ Here's a trick I use for hiding the edges of a plasterboard repair. Before you cover the patch with plaster, dent the edges with a small hammer or screwdriver blade so that you form a shallow groove right the way around it. This ensures an invisible join when you plaster over the top. ❞

Use a trimming knife to cut out the damaged plasterboard.

PATCHING LATH AND PLASTER

Patching a hole in a lath and plaster partition wall is no problem if the laths are intact: simply fill with repair plaster, then finish off with skimming plaster or fine surface filler. But if the laths are broken, you need to make a more substantial repair as shown right.

Zinc gauze provides the perfect reinforcement; if you can't find it at your local hardware store, try a car accessory shop.

Prepare the hole in the usual way by brushing or chipping away all loose material. If the plaster is crumbly brush on a coat of stabilizer or PVA adhesive.

1 Cut the gauze a little smaller all round than the size of the patch using an old pair of scissors. Wear gloves for protection.

2 Push back the broken laths and press the gauze into the hole so that its edges are just below the surface of the plaster.

3 If possible, secure the patch to any unbroken laths using small nails or staples. Alternatively, glue it in place.

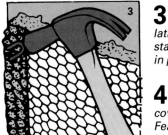

4 Form a depression in the middle of the gauze and cover with repair plaster. Feather away the edges to blend them into the wall.

TYPES OF FILLER

CELLULOSE FILLERS

general purpose fillers

fine surface filler

General purpose cellulose fillers are fine for small holes but don't spread well. In a deep hole, they must be built up in thin layers or they slump.

Ready mixed fillers are more convenient but don't keep well and are too stiff and bulky for some jobs. You can mix powder-type filler to the consistency you want – a definite advantage where you are 'feathering' the edges of a repair to hide them.

Fine surface filler comes ready mixed. It is super-smooth and easy to spread, but must be applied *very* thinly or it won't dry properly. Use it to finish off repairs made with ordinary filler.

READY MIXED DIY PLASTERS

Ready mixed plasters are sold in medium and large size plastic tubs. They are expensive, but their excellent adhesion and long 'open' time (the time they stay workable) makes them perfect for DIY repairs. Also, they are easy to sand down once dry.

Skimming plaster is applied thinly with a large brush, then smoothed using the plastic applicator provided.

Repair plaster is best applied with a metal float, but will fill holes up to 50mm (2″) deep in one coat. Finish afterwards with skimming plaster.

CONVENTIONAL REPAIR PLASTER

Conventional plaster is sold in various sized bags by hardware and DIY stores. *Bonding* plaster is for filling out the hole; *finishing* (skimming) plaster is for creating the final smooth surface. You can also buy *one coat* plaster which can be used (in layers) for both jobs.

All types are much cheaper than ready mixed plaster, but need conventional plastering skills to apply properly.

FOAM FILLER

Aerosol foam fillers are ideal for filling cracks around skirtings or door architraves, but too costly to use for larger holes.

As the foam is injected via the plastic tube nozzle, it expands and hardens to fill every crevice. It dries hard, but is easily sanded down.

PATCHING ACCESSORIES

stabilizer

scrim tape

gauze

PVA adhesive

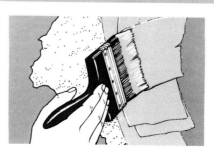

Plaster stabilizing fluid is a brush-on liquid that binds the surface of crumbly old plaster so the filler stays in place.

PVA adhesive (such as 'Unibond') does the same job when painted on neat and left to go tacky. It also aids adhesion if you're using conventional plaster.

Scrim tape and zinc gauze add strength to repairs made in plasterboard and lath and plaster respectively.

REPAIRING A CONCRETE FLOOR

Solid concrete floors can suffer from several faults, all of which need to be cured before laying a new covering.

General unevenness could be due to the floor not being laid properly in the first place, or to localized wear and tear. It may not be noticeable while the floor is bare, but will show after covering.

If the level is 'out' by less than 12mm (½″) – see *Checking the floor* overleaf – the cure is to resurface the floor using self-smoothing compound. See Problem Solver for how to cope with serious unevenness.

Dampness can be a problem in houses built before 1945, where the floor has been laid over bare ground without a damp-proof membrane (DPM). As the concrete becomes more porous with age, moisture rises to the surface and either ruins the floorcovering or works its way up the surrounding walls.

Newer floors can also suffer from damp if the DPM has been accidentally punctured during the course of earlier building work.

Providing the floor isn't soaking wet (in which case it needs rebuild-

Repairs are essential *before laying a new covering.*

ing), the cure is to give it a waterproof coating and resurface.

Local damage may be caused by dampness as well as physical damage. Or perhaps the original surface layer has broken down through age, leaving flaking areas and deep pits.

Faults like these always show through soft coverings, and make

hard coverings more difficult to lay. The cure is to patch with repair mortar and resurface.

Dusting is another symptom of old concrete, in which the top surface becomes powdery and starts to break down. If the floor is otherwise smooth, paint with concrete sealer; if uneven, resurface as well.

....Shopping List....

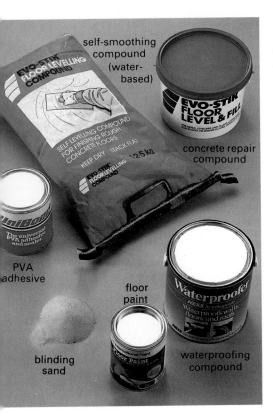

self-smoothing compound (water-based)

concrete repair compound

PVA adhesive

floor paint

blinding sand

waterproofing compound

Self-smoothing compound is the standard material for resurfacing a concrete floor. It's sold in 10, 15 and 25kg (11, 33 and 55lb) bags.

Water based compound comes in powder form for mixing with water. It is the easiest to use, but is not strong enough if the floor is being left bare.

Latex based compound is more resilient and resists structural movement. It comes in powder form and is mixed with *latex liquid* which you buy separately.

Acrylic based compound is the strongest, and also the most expensive. It is sold in two-part powder form for mixing with water.

As a rough guide, a 25kg bag of water based compound covers around 6–7 sq m (7–8 sq yd) when laid to the recommended depth of 4–5mm (³⁄₁₆″).

Repair mortar Either use dry-mixed repair mortar, or special *concrete floor repair compound* which comes ready-mixed in 2.5 and 5 litre tubs.

PVA adhesive (eg 'Unibond') acts as a primer when making patched repairs. Added to repair mortar, it helps it bind to the floor.

Waterproofing compounds for concrete floors are now widely available. The most effective are epoxy resin based (often with bitumen additive), and come in two-part form. Two coats are required; coverage is around 1 sq m (1.2 sq yd) per litre, depending on the smoothness of the surface.

If the floor is being resurfaced (which it must be if laying an adhesive-laid covering), the coating must be *blinded* – sprinkled with sand while tacky so that the compound will stick to it. Special blinding sand is available for this, or use clean sharp sand.

See page 142 for details of finishes for bare concrete.

Tools checklist: Plasterer's steel float, pointing trowel, 2 buckets, wood batten, spirit level, old paintbrush, squeegee.

CHECKING THE FLOOR

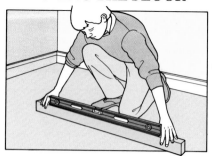

Test for unevenness using a spirit level and wood batten. Try the floor in both directions, and measure the difference between the high and low points.

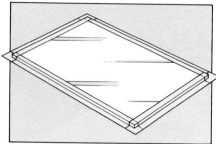

Test for dampness by taping a piece of glass or polythene to the floor. Leave for two days, then inspect: if the underside is cloudy, moisture is present.

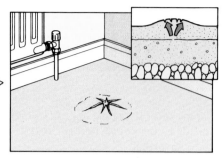

'Swelling' patches suggest localized dampness – possibly the result of a punctured DPM. Look for nearby alterations which might confirm your suspicions.

PATCHING HOLES

1 **For a hole**, brush or vacuum away any dust or loose chips. If filling with mortar, paint on a solution of 1 part PVA adhesive to 3 parts water and leave to dry.

2 Press in some repair compound or mortar and smooth off with a pointing trowel. (For a mortar repair, add a little PVA adhesive to the mixing water.)

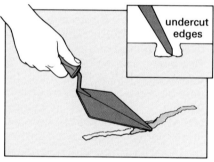

3 **Open out a crack** with the corner of a bolster and brush away the dust. Then patch with repair compound or brush with PVA solution and fill with mortar.

DEALING WITH DAMP

Before waterproofing a damp floor, it's advisable (though not essential) to remove the skirtings and strip any plaster behind to a height of 100mm (4″). This allows you to extend the coating 75–100mm (3–4″) up the walls to the damp-proof course (DPC).

■ Prise the skirtings away from the wall using a claw hammer, bolster or crowbar. Use a block of wood to lever against, and to protect the wall surface above.

■ Chop back the plaster using a club hammer and bolster. Wear goggles to protect your eyes.

For a localized patch, carefully chop out the concrete using a hammer and bolster until you reach the old damp-proof membrane – either a black pitch-like substance or a layer of plastic sheet. Vacuum away the dust and check for holes in the membrane. To repair, coat the area with waterproofing compound, then patch with repair mortar.

If you are resurfacing, lightly sprinkle the surface with sand while the coating is still tacky. This gives the smoothing compound something to grip.

1 Pour the waterproofing compound hardener into the resin following the maker's instructions. Stir until thoroughly mixed.

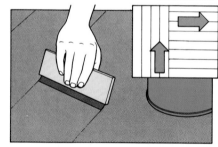

2 Apply the first coat in wide parallel bands using a squeegee. When dry, apply a second coat of waterproofer at right angles to the first.

Self-smoothing compound is thin and flexible enough to need only a light sweep with a steel float. Any nibs and ridges disappear as it dries, leaving a smooth, level surface. Most types are hard within two hours and can be walked on after eight, but leave for a day to dry.

Although the compound is reasonably easy to use, you need to work fast – particularly if you're mixing batches. A bucketful only stays workable for about half an hour, so don't mix more in one go.

Preparation Self-smoothing compound won't stick to concrete that's dirty or greasy, so wash down the surface with sugar soap. Any old floor adhesive must also be removed; soften with a hot-air gun and scrape off.

Seal off the edges of the area being resurfaced using strips of batten. This includes doorways and junctions with other floor surfaces.

Thickness Aim to spread the compound to an average thickness of 5mm (³⁄₁₆″). If this isn't enough to level the floor, apply a second layer once the first is completely dry.

Trade tip

Mixing trick

❝ Mixing is often the trickiest part of using self-smoothing compound: if there are lumps in the mixture when you pour it, you'll never get it to settle.

You need an efficient mixing tool. A lot of people use wood, but this isn't good at breaking up the powder. I prefer an old fish slice, but any similar kitchen implement will do.

Also, be sure to mix in the right sequence. Start with a little of the mixing liquid, add some of the powder and mix to a paste. Then add more liquid, followed by more of the powder, stirring all the time. ❞

Mix the smoothing compound powder in a bucket with the water (or latex fluid, for the latex type). Stir thoroughly to remove the lumps and adjust the mixture until it is the consistency of thick cream.

1 Scrub the floor thoroughly using a mixture of water and sugar soap, then rinse with cold water. Try not to wet the concrete any more than necessary.

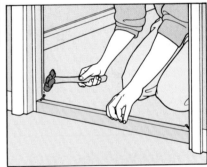

2 Nail battens across doorways and anywhere else you don't want the compound to spread. Screen pipes etc with pieces of cardboard.

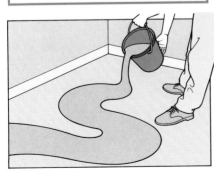

3 Starting furthest from the door, pour the mixture in a 'trail' over the area stirring as you go. Smooth out immediately with a steel float.

4 Check the depth at several points, then smooth again. Use the float in a light, sweeping motion, angling the blade so that just the back edge makes contact.

5 As the compound settles, any ridges and nibs disappear. If you need to pour another batch, do so immediately before the first begins to dry.

FINISHES FOR BARE CONCRETE

If the floor being levelled is in a garage or utility room, you may not want to go to the trouble of laying a new covering – self-smoothing compound is smooth enough to be finished direct, although it won't stand up to heavy abuse.

Paint with clear sealer/hardener if you want to leave the concrete bare. This soaks into the floor and gives greater long-term protection than ordinary concrete sealer.

Paint with floor/lino paint for a coloured finish. This is only available in a limited range of colours (normally red, green, stone and grey), but is easy to apply by roller and dries to a hardwearing finish. Coverage is in the region of 10 sq m (12 sq yd) per litre.

Before applying either finish, make sure the floor is free of dust and wash down with sugar soap.

A painted finish (right) is ideal for brightening up a garage or playroom/utility room.

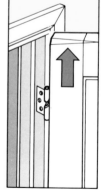

■ PROBLEM SOLVER ■

Serious unevenness

If the floor level is 'out' by more than 12mm (½″), don't try to make up the difference using self-smoothing compound alone; above this thickness, it isn't strong enough to take any weight. Instead, build up the low point with screed mortar, then resurface over the top.

■ Start by coating the area to be built up with a solution of 1 part PVA adhesive to 3 parts water. Leave to dry.

■ Make up a fairly dry mortar mix of 1 part cement to 6 of sharp sand, adding a splash of PVA adhesive to the mixing water. Trowel over the area using a steel float.

■ Use a spirit level on a wood batten to check the level, and add more mortar to pack any low spots. Level high spots by slicing off the mortar with the wood batten.

■ Leave for a day to dry, then resurface in the usual way.

Use a batten and spirit level to level repaired patches.

Dealing with doorways

Resurfacing inevitably raises the floor level a few millimetres, which could cause problems at a doorway. However, adding a new floorcovering will raise it further still, so don't forget to take this into account when finding a cure.

If the floor in the next room is lower, fit a metal or hardwood threshold strip to make up the difference.

If the door jams against the new floor, either trim the base or rehang it on rising butt hinges. These have the effect of lifting the door as it opens, allowing it to clear the floor, while maintaining a snug fit in the frame when the door is closed.

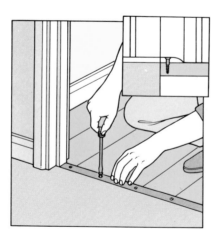

Fit a threshold strip to make up the slight difference in level at a doorway. Screw down the strip if the adjoining floor is wooden, otherwise use impact adhesive.

Rehang the door with rising butt hinges if it looks like jamming against the new floor when opened. You may also have to trim a fraction off the top.

LAYING CERAMIC AND QUARRY FLOOR TILES

Of all the readily available coverings for floors, ceramic and quarry tiles are the longest-lived and hardest wearing. Laid properly, a hard-tiled floor should add substantially to the value of your home, and the huge range of styles available leaves plenty of scope for expressing your own personal taste.

Before going ahead, however, it's as well to consider the limitations:

■ Most hard tiles raise the level of the floor substantially, which could involve removing skirtings, trimming doors, and fitting wooden ramps with adjoining floor surfaces.
■ Hard tiles are as good as permanent, so you should think twice before laying them around built-ins – for example, kitchen units; the chances are the units will be the first to go, leaving holes that you may

not be able to match.
■ Solid floors are better suited to hard tiling than suspended wooden ones. It is *possible* to tile a wooden floor, but only if it is absolutely free of structural movement, and properly lined with plywood. Remember, too, that you won't have access to services running under the floor once the tiles are firmly fixed in place.

Ceramic tiles (left) and quarry tiles (below) are hardwearing and practical in halls and kitchens.

PRELIMINARY WORK

Aim to get as much preliminary work as possible done before buying the tiles (see overleaf).
■ Skirtings should ideally be removed so that they can be refitted to hide the cut tiles around the edge of the floor. However, this may be more trouble than it's worth if the skirtings are the deep ornate type.
■ Remove as much built-in furniture as you can. Again, ideally, the tiles should run from wall to wall.
■ Line a wooden boarded floor with exterior grade plywood.
■ On a solid floor, check the level: a *thick-bed adhesive* (see overleaf) will accommodate variations of up to about 12mm (½") but for anything greater, fill hollows then resurface with self-smoothing compound.
■ Remove inward-opening doors ready for trimming later.
■ Nail battens temporarily across doorways to give yourself something to tile against.

Prise off skirtings with a bolster or crowbar, using a block of wood to protect the plaster.

Line a boarded floor with sheets of 12mm (½") plywood, staggering the joints.

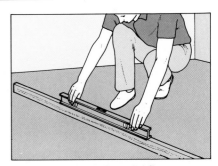

Check the level of a solid floor at various points. If it varies by over 12mm (½"), resurface.

Temporarily nail battens across doors to provide an edge for tiling against.

CHOOSING AND BUYING THE TILES

DIY shops, builders' merchants and superstores stock limited runs of the more popular ranges of ceramic floor tile, but their choice of quarries is generally limited. For the widest selection of all types, visit a tile supplier: most have panels showing the finished effect, which may not be as you imagined.

Floor tiles are normally sold by the square metre or square yard, so make sure you're armed with the room dimensions and add 8–10% extra for wastage depending on how much cutting you anticipate.

Wherever you buy the tiles, the same outlet will also be able to supply the adhesive, grout, and any special tools (see opposite).

Ceramic tiles

Ceramic floor tiles are thicker than wall tiles – most are at least 6mm ($\frac{1}{4}$") – but have the same glazed finish. The majority are machine-made; hand-made floor tiles are harder to lay and often expensive.

Many floor tile patterns look identical to wall tiles, so be sure to specify 'floor tiles' when ordering. Others imitate materials such as stone flags, marble or granite. And as well as a choice of colour and pattern style, you are likely to come across a variety of surface finishes – for example, matt or gloss, smooth or textured.

Popular square and rectangular sizes are 150×100mm, 150×150mm, 200×150mm and 200×200mm (about 6×4, 6×6, 8×6 and 8×8"). There are also hexagonal and interlocking shapes.

Decorative insets for ceramic floor tiles are often sold as part of a range. But whereas wall insets are usually tile-sized (or multiple tile-sized) motifs, floor insets tend to take the form of much smaller decorative tiles which you interlock with the main tiles or 'build in' at the corner joints.

Quarry tiles

Unglazed quarry tiled floors have enjoyed a revival over the past few years, and their warm, natural tones are well suited to more rustic decorative schemes. Even so, the subtle colour ranges, plus the chance to use contrasting ceramic insets, can create exciting effects.

Quarries are sold in the same way as ceramics, and come in similar sizes and shapes, but they are much thicker – from around 10mm ($\frac{3}{8}$") to as much as 25mm (1"). They are also never uniform in size, which is part of their appeal.

When choosing quarries, always ask to see a finished panel so that you can gauge the effect.

Adhesives and grout

Ceramic tiles are generally laid using a *thin-bed adhesive*, spread to a thickness of around 3mm ($\frac{1}{8}$"). This comes ready mixed in tubs of various sizes, or slightly more cheaply in powder form for mixing

with water; one type has a latex additive and is designed specially for wooden floors. Coverage is about 2.5litres ($\frac{1}{2}$ gal) per sq m (1.2sq yd) for ready mixed; 2.75kg (6lb) per sq m for powder.

For thicker ceramic tiles and all quarry tiles, use a *thick-bed adhesive*. This is spread up to 12mm ($\frac{1}{2}$") thick, and so is capable of taking up the natural variations in the thickness of the tiles. (Professionals usually lay quarries in a sand and cement screed, but this is a lot harder than it looks and is not recommended for DIY.)

Thick-bed adhesive comes in powder form and looks like cement (on which it is based). Coverage is around 11kg (24lb) per sq m (1.2sq yd), but always order on the generous side.

Grout for floor tiles is generally sold in powder form. There is a range of colours for ceramics, plus more natural looking cement-based types for quarries. Coverage depends on the thickness of the tiles and on how wide you decide to make the joints – ask your supplier's advice.

For quarry tiles, you also need a means of sealing the unglazed surface. Most professionals favour 2–3 coats of *boiled linseed oil* thinned with 50% white spirit. One litre of the mixture covers about 20sq m.

Practical ideas include diagonal tiling in narrow rooms (below) and non-slip finishes (left).

DESIGN CHECKLIST – CERAMICS

- Is the floor in a bathroom, utility room or entrance hall likely to get wet? If so, the tiles should have a non-slip surface.
- Do you prefer a gloss or matt glaze? Floor tiles can have either.
- Have you a basic preference for flat or broken colour? Flat colours produce a clean, streamlined effect but you may find it too clinical if used over a large area.
- Is the room long and narrow? In this case, tiling diagonally – ie at 45° to the walls – will give an impression of greater width.

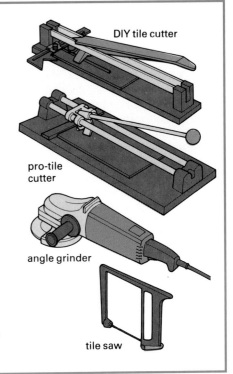

When choosing quarry tiles for a kitchen, a glazed or sealed finish is more practical (left). Larger tiles may help to give a feeling of space (above).

.... Shopping List ....

As well as the tiles and adhesive, you'll need a complete set of tiling tools.

A notched spreader for applying the adhesive; the plasterer's trowel pattern is best for floors.

A tile cutter – see Tip.

A tile file for finishing the edges of cut tiles.

A spirit level and wood or metal straightedge for keeping a check on the floor level.

A try square, chalk lines and tape for squaring things up.

Softwood battens for setting out – 50×25mm (2×1″) is a useful size. You also need a hammer and nails to fix them.

A bucket and stirring implement (an old slotted spoon is ideal) for mixing the adhesive and grout.

A rubber squeegee and sponge for applying the grout, plus a wooden dowel for finishing the joints.

Trade tip

Cutting floor tiles

❝ Even the thinner floor tiles are much harder to cut than wall tiles, and an ordinary wall tile cutter won't do. Alternatives are:
■ A lightweight floor tile cutter – reasonably cheap to buy, and suitable for most ceramic tiles up to around 6mm (¼″) thick.
■ A professional tile cutter – available for hire from most hire shops, or where you buy the tiles. This copes easily with ceramic tiles and with thinner quarries.
■ An angle grinder – easily hired – is the best tool for cutting thick quarries, and is useful for 'nibbling' awkward shapes. You also need full protective gear – goggles, gloves and a mask.

If you're not using an angle grinder, a tile saw is the best tool for cutting out small pieces. ❞

DIY tile cutter

pro-tile cutter

angle grinder

tile saw

SETTING OUT

As with all floor tiles, the first stage is to set out the tiling so that you avoid awkward cuts and narrow gaps around the edges of the room. The procedure is basically the same for both ceramics and quarries, but differs slightly from that used for other types of floor tile.

Start by snapping chalked string lines to cross at right angles to one another in the centre of the room. The first chalk line represents the 'line' of the tile joints as seen from the main doorway: it must run parallel to the dominant visual line in the room – the longest wall, the bath, or a run of kitchen units – otherwise the tiles will appear 'crooked' as you walk into the room.

If you have difficulty deciding on a dominant feature, draw the line from the centre – and at right angles to – the main doorway.

After snapping the second line, measure off in whole tiles along the arms of the cross to see what sort of gaps are left at the edges. You can do this by laying out the tiles themselves (not forgetting to allow the correct joint gap – see below), but it's easier to make up a tiling gauge (see Tip).

Ideally, no edge gap should be less than a third of a tile's width. If your measuring reveals otherwise, shift the position of one or both lines so that the gaps are evened up and then try again.

Fixing setting out battens

When you are happy with the positions of the lines, decide in which quadrant to begin tiling, bearing in mind that you'll be starting in one corner and working back towards the door. Use your tiling gauge to mark the positions of the last whole tiles in the quadrant, then join the marks into guidelines using a straightedge.

Next, cut two battens roughly to the length of the guidelines. Nail them along the lines as shown, so that they sit on the 'gap' side, not the 'whole tile' side. Use a carpenter's try square to check that the battens are at 90°. You are then ready to start laying the tiles.

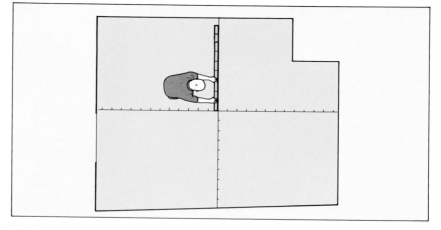

Setting out stage 1: chalk lines across the room to align with the dominant visual feature, then use your tile gauge to find out how the gaps fall at the edges.

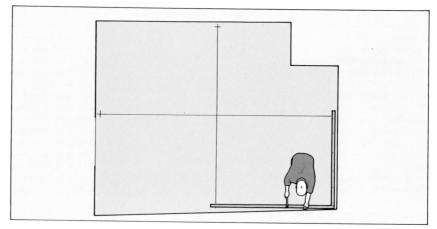

Setting out stage 2: having adjusted the chalk lines as necessary, draw guidelines around the edge of the first quadrant to be tiled and nail battens against them.

WHAT JOINT SPACING?

Unlike many wall tiles, floor tiles are always square edged and must be laid with an allowance for the joint spacing. Nor are there any hard and fast rules as to how wide the spacing should be; much depends on the tile, and on the sort of look you want – the wider the joints, the more obviously 'tiled' the finished effect becomes.

As a general rule, for ceramics the spacing should be narrow – between 2 and 4mm ($\frac{1}{16}$–$\frac{1}{8}$). For quarries, which don't have straight edges, it must necessarily be wider – approximately 4–10mm ($\frac{1}{8}$–$\frac{3}{8}$").

Unless you've seen finished samples of the tiling, it's worth experimenting before you start setting out. When you've decided on the spacing, find something to use as a gauge – a piece of thick card, a thin wall tile or a slip of plywood are all popular choices.

— Trade tip —

Make a gauge

❝ A tiling gauge makes it easy to measure off whole tile widths with an allowance for the joints.

For ceramics, simply mark off tile widths and joint spacings along a straight batten.

For quarries, where neither the tiles nor the gaps are a consistent width, pick 8–10 tiles at random and lay them out in a row. Adjust the joints until they look more or less even, then mark off. ❞

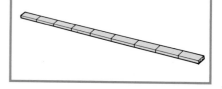

LAYING CERAMICS

The basic laying procedure for ceramics is to start tiling against the setting out battens, then continue laying whole tiles back towards the door. With all the whole tiles laid, leave the adhesive to set for at least 12 hours. Then remove the setting out battens and cut and lay the edge tiles.

Spread the adhesive in batches roughly a metre square. Use the spacing tool to make sure that each tile sits square to its neighbours.

Check regularly that the tiles sit level. In particular, make sure that the tiles on one patch of adhesive are level with those on the next, as this is where problems usually occur. If you find that the level is 'out', lift the tiles immediately and re-trowel the adhesive bed to bring it to the correct thickness.

When it comes to fitting the edge tiles, mark them individually using a whole tile to gauge the profile of the wall. For straight cuts use the tile cutter; see Problem Solver for how to deal with awkward shapes.

When laying the edge tiles, spread the adhesive on the backs of the tiles, and spread it slightly more thickly than you did on the floor.

1 Using a notched spreader, spread a 1m (1.1yd) square layer of adhesive in the corner formed by the battens. Thickness of the bed should be around 3mm (⅛").

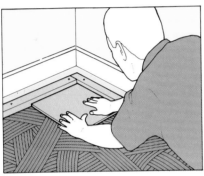

2 Slide the first tile into the corner and press down gently. (Note that if adhesive squeezes up over the edges you are pressing too hard.)

3 Position the next tile, using your spacing gauge to ensure it sits square to the first. Continue in this way until the adhesive area is filled.

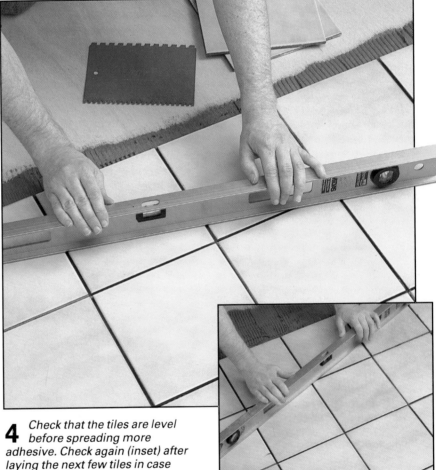

4 Check that the tiles are level before spreading more adhesive. Check again (inset) after laying the next few tiles in case the two areas don't match.

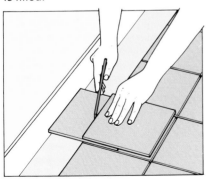

5 Having laid all the whole tiles and allowed the adhesive to dry, mark the edge tiles individually to fit using a whole tile to gauge the wall profile.

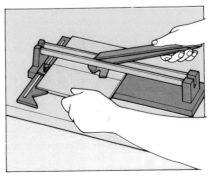

6 To make straight cuts, lay the tile face up in the cutting jig. Score down the marked line, then depress the lever – the tile should snap cleanly.

7 Apply adhesive to the backs of the cut tiles with the notched spreader and position them with the cut edge against the wall. Press gently into place.

LAYING QUARRIES

Quarry tiles stuck with thick-bed adhesive (as opposed to mortar) are laid in virtually the same way as ceramic tiles. The main difference is that the thickness of the adhesive (and the unevenness of some quarries) makes it slightly more difficult to keep everything level.

■ Mix and spread the adhesive in 1m (1.1yd) square batches to a depth of around 10mm (⅜″).

■ Set the tiles in place using only very light pressure – don't worry about levelling them.

■ When the patch of adhesive is covered, use a sturdy wood block to press the tiles down level with one another; avoid putting pressure on any one tile in particular.

Repeat this sequence for all the whole tiles, then leave to dry before fitting the edge tiles.

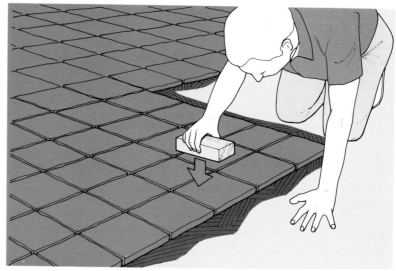

Set quarry tiles in place with very light pressure, spacing the joints as evenly as you can. After covering each spread batch of adhesive, use a stout block of wood to tap the tiles down level with one another.

GROUTING AND FINISHING

Both ceramics and quarries are grouted in the same way as wall tiles – preferably at least 12 hours after fitting the edge tiles.

Mix up the grout in a bucket according to the maker's instructions and stir thoroughly to remove lumps. Use immediately and work fast – it doesn't take long for it to become unworkable. Make sure, too, that you remove the excess grout from the face of the tiles before it dries; quarries in particular are susceptible to staining, since they are unglazed.

Sealing quarry tiles is best done before you grout, to protect the surface from staining, but take your supplier's advice. Apply two coats of thinned linseed oil with a clean cloth and leave to dry overnight.

  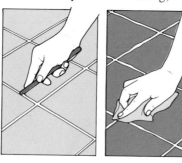

1 Mix up the grout according to the instructions and spread it over the tiles. Work it into the joints using a rubber squeegee, then sponge up the excess.

2 Check that there are no air pockets, then leave the joints until just hard. Finish with a piece of dowel (ceramics) or rub with a coarse cloth (quarries).

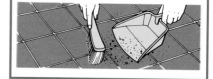
PROBLEM SOLVER

Cutting awkward shapes

Don't be too ambitious when cutting edge tiles to fit tricky shapes such as architraves or pipes – stick to simple, straight cuts (if you try to notch tiles, they'll break), then rely on the grout to fill any gaps.

Ceramics are best cut clamped in a workbench using a tile saw. For quarries, use an angle grinder; work outside, wear full protective gear and take great care – especially to avoid cutting the lead.

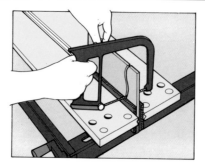

Awkward shapes are best marked by measuring direct. Most ceramic floor tiles can be cut with a tile saw; clamp them in a bench with protective padding.

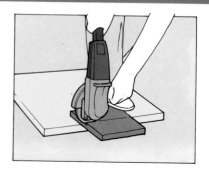

Thick tiles such as quarries are best cut with an angle grinder – wear stout boots and support the tile as shown. Don't put down the grinder until the wheel stops.

REGLAZING WINDOWS AND DOORS

The usual reason for reglazing a window is because of accidental breakage, but there are several other good reasons for renewing existing glass:

■ Low level glazing (below about 750mm – 2'6") is an accident hazard, especially if there are young children about. It is advisable to reglaze with a shatterproof safety glass.

■ Ordinary glass can be replaced with a practical improvement, such as warmer double-glazed panels, or tougher security glass.

■ Plain or ugly patterned glass can be swapped for a variety of decorative types, ranging from patterned or coloured glass to a leaded, stained glass panel.

Before you repair . . .

When glass is broken accidentally, DIY may not be the best option. Check first whether your house contents insurance policy covers fixed glass (ie glazing): if it does, you should be able to claim for a professional repair.

Replacing a small pane is a simple and cheap job.

Trade tip

Temporary security

❛ If you can't reglaze a broken window at once, or if the repair isn't completed the same day, you may need to make temporary arrangements.

Where the window is a security risk, use a sheet of plywood cut to fit the frame. Either screw it to the woodwork or drill a hole through the middle and insert a long bolt which can be tightened through a locking bar fitted on the inside.

Simply to keep the weather out, seal a cracked pane with waterproof tape. If the glass is missing or smashed use a sheet of polythene taped to the frame on the inside. ❜

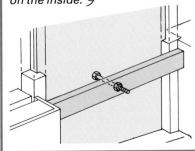

.... Shopping List ....

Glass is made in many different types (see page 151) so check your options carefully. Measure the pane(s) you are glazing and buy glass to fit; the supplier should cut it either free or very cheaply, so there is rarely any need to do it yourself.

Putty comes in several forms. *Linseed oil putty* is for wooden frames, *metal casement putty* is for galvanized steel frames, and *general purpose putty* suits either type. *Non-setting putty* is for sealed unit glazing panels. *Brown putty* is for natural hardwood frames.

All types are sold by weight; 1kg (2.2lb) is enough for about 8m (24') of frame rebate.

Other materials Check your frame (see page 152) to see what other fixings hold the glass. The main alternatives are *glazing sprigs* (special nails) for wooden frames or patent *clips* for metal frames. On doors and some windows you may need wooden beading instead. If the frame is damaged in any way, make sure you have whatever is

needed to repair it. You also need a little general purpose primer.

Protective clothing You need heavy leather gloves, preferably with wrist protection, and safety glasses. Wear long sleeves made from a tough fabric to protect your arms from flying splinters and stout shoes in case pieces drop on your foot.

Tools checklist: General tools include a hammer, pincers, paintbrush, dustpan and brush.

Specialized glazing tools are fairly cheap, although it is possible to improvise.

A hacking knife is designed for rough chopping work with a hammer and makes it easy to remove the old putty and chips of glass. An old chisel or stripping knife will do.

A putty knife is specially shaped for applying a neat bead of putty, but you can manage with a filling knife instead.

A glass cutter is needed if you don't buy glass cut to fit. It also helps when removing old glass.

BUYING GLASS

If you are buying plain glass, all you have to worry about is what size and thickness you need; it should be available from stock. Some special glazing materials may need a little more planning to buy, especially as they might have to be made to order.

Local glass merchants stock a surprisingly wide range of glass and will normally order special or unusual types. It's easiest to ask for exactly the sizes you need and get them cut for you. This costs either nothing or very little (usually depending whether you need a special shape or not), so there is little need to cut glass yourself. Glass merchants can also cut shapes and holes (eg for a ventilator fan).

However, having glass cut to size does make it important to measure accurately as you cannot check the glass itself against the frame. Cutting a small sliver off a sheet that is fractionally too large is tricky (see Problem Solver), and if you order the glass too small it will be wasted.

For large panes it is always worth asking the glass merchant to deliver (local journeys may even be free). Otherwise, if you have a suitable vehicle, have the glass wrapped and then strap it down on a board to keep it safe in transit. Make sure that it can't slide around.

MEASURING UP

For accuracy, you must measure right into the *rebate* – the slot into which the glass is fitted. In some cases it may be easier to remove the old glass first (see page 152), but much depends on how easy it is to secure the window temporarily and whether the glass is in stock.

Measure in millimetres. Check the frame for squareness by measuring the diagonals – they should be more or less identical. Then measure the height and width at three or more points each. Minor variations here (up to about 5mm) don't matter; just take the smallest dimension. Large differences mean the frame is warped.

Where the frame is true, order the glass by quoting its dimensions after deducting 3mm from both the height and width figures to allow a fitting clearance. The exception is if you are buying sealed unit double glazing panels. These need a clearance of about 6mm (¼").

If the frame is very uneven, cut a template from paper, stiff card, or even hardboard, depending on which is easiest. Take this with you when you have the glass cut.

Use the same technique if the glass is a complicated shape, but make the template from stiff card to ensure an exact fit. If you want a patterned glass, mark the template 'Outside' to ensure that the glass will be cut smooth side out.

Trade tip

Measuring tips

❝ Avoid using a tape measure for checking the frame – it can all too easily flex and cause inaccuracy. If available, a steel rule is ideal. Otherwise, mark the dimensions on a straight wooden batten and lay this down to measure it with your tape.

■ When buying glass with a directional pattern, the convention is to quote the height before the width – this ensures that the glass merchant gets the pattern running in the right direction. To replace patterned glass with an identical type, always take a sample with you to check.

■ Old glass was sold by weight, not thickness, and also tends to be less even than modern glass. If you are replacing a pane that must match, measure its thickness in millimetres and order the nearest available (if there is no close match buy the glass slightly thicker rather than thinner for safety reasons). ❞

Measure the diagonals to check that the frame is square. They should match to within a millimetre or two. If they differ, the frame isn't true.

Check the dimensions at three or more points across the frame's width and height. Take the measurement right into the rebate in both cases.

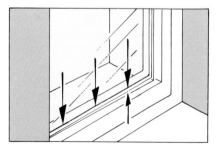

The glass size should be 3mm smaller than the height and width measurements. If these vary slightly, buy to fit the smallest dimension of the frame.

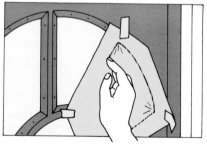

For irregular shapes make a template from paper or card. If you have cut this to fit the frame exactly, tell the suppliers so they can leave a clearance.

TYPES OF GLASS

Float glass is the normal form of flat sheet glass and is sold by thickness in millimetres.

■ 3mm glass is only suitable for very small panes.

■ 4mm glass is for panes up to about 1 sq m (11 sq ft).

■ 6mm glass is used for panes over 1 sq m (11 sq ft).

■ 10mm glass is occasionally used in picture windows. For very large panes or low-level glazing, safety glass is preferable.

Toughened (tempered) glass is a fairly low-cost form of safety glass which breaks into harmless chips like a car windscreen. It cannot be cut, so must be ordered and made to size – although standard sizes are often held in stock.

Laminated glass is a more expensive safety glass with a plastic centre layer that holds the fragments together in the event of a breakage (making it more secure as well as safer). It comes in thicknesses from 4mm to 8mm and can be cut to size by many glass merchants.

Wired glass is 6mm glass with a fine steel wire mesh cast into it. One common type has a 13mm (½″) square mesh and an obscure face, and is called *Georgian wired glass*. Wired glass is no stronger than float glass but the mesh stops it shattering. Its main use is in fire doors and windows to stop fire spreading – it is not really a security glazing material.

Patterned glass is embossed on one surface – the other is usually smooth. It provides both decoration and some privacy, depending on the pattern. Clear patterned glass is 4mm or 6mm thick and costs little more than flat glass. It also comes in several colours, and toughened for use in doors and screens.

Coloured glass is available in a wide range of shades, but glass merchants are only likely to hold a limited number of popular ones. For the more subtle colours used to replace a leaded light panel, try a specialist in stained glass work.

Solar control glass is tinted or coated to reflect heat without stopping much light. It is costly, but useful on problem windows where direct sun makes the room very hot. It also comes laminated, toughened

obscure glass

clear float glass

Georgian wired glass

laminated glass

toughened glass

coloured glass

and double glazed.

Double glazing panels (sealed units) are the type used in modern double glazed windows. They can also be fitted to conventional frames although they tend to be a little less efficient unless the frames seal very well. There are two types; both are expensive and normally to order.

Square edge sealed units consist of two panes spaced between 6 and 12mm (¼–½″) apart and sealed around the edge – total thickness is about 15mm (⅝″) upwards. Special types of glass can be used and it is best to discuss your exact needs with the supplier.

Stepped sealed units are similar, but used where the rebate in the window frame is too shallow to take a square edge panel. Only the outer pane fits into the rebate, the inner one fits through the frame.

REPLACING GLASS

If the window or door is already glazed, the first thing to do is to remove the existing pane and make any necessary repairs. The new pane can then be fitted in its place.

On upper floors, it's far easier if you can take out the whole window or sash and then reglaze it in safety on a workbench. If this is impossible and you are forced to work at a height, make sure you have a sturdy working platform. Bear in mind that you may also need help to lift the new pane into place. Don't attempt to reglaze anything more than a small pane working from a ladder – hire an access tower and anchor it securely before use.

The job itself depends on the type of window frame and how the glass is fixed. Special types of glass such as sealed units may also need special techniques (see page 154).

How glazing is fixed
Glass is held into the frame in one of four ways:

On wooden frames it is normally bedded in a thin layer of putty and held by flat nails called sprigs. A fillet of putty is applied to seal the glass into the frame.

On sliding sashes, the inner sash may have a groove in the underside of the top rail. The glass fits into this, bedded in putty, but is conventionally puttied on the other three sides.

On galvanized steel frames the glass is bedded in a thin layer of putty and held by spring clips. A fillet of putty is then applied to seal it to the frame.

On aluminium and plastic (uPVC) windows the glazing is normally held in special rubber seals. With this type of window, it is worth

contacting the manufacturer or a glazier to find out what is involved in repairing that particular make.

On doors and some wooden windows the glass is bedded in a thin layer of putty but retained by thin strips of wooden beading. These are nailed or screwed to the frame and may be glued up with old paint.

Remove old glass
If broken, this is mainly a matter of carefully breaking away large pieces, then removing whatever fixed it and chopping away remaining slivers. Unbroken panes can sometimes be removed in one piece, which is preferable.

Handling broken glass is the most dangerous part of the job, so wear full protective clothing, keep children and pets away, and use plenty of care.

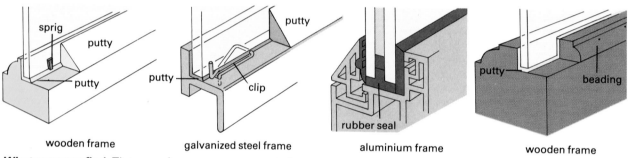

wooden frame   galvanized steel frame   aluminium frame   wooden frame

What you may find. *There are four common ways to fix glass into the frame, usually depending on the frame material but possibly also on the type of glazing.*

1 If the glass is intact, tape across in case of breakage and chop out the putty to release it. Pull out any sprigs or clips, then gently tap the glass free.

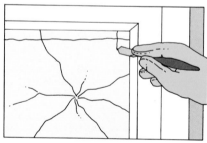

2 Alternatively, score across near the edge with a glass cutter and carefully break large pieces away, working from the top downwards.

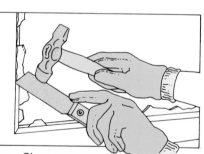

3 Chop out any remaining putty using a hacking knife. Be careful, as it may contain small glass splinters. Prise out any sprigs or clips you find.

4 On sash windows where the glass is held in a groove, clean this out with an old 6mm (¼") chisel, working it in under any glass left in place.

5 Clean and tidy the rebates with an old chisel. Apply quick-drying primer to protect the bare frame and to stop the oil in the putty being absorbed.

Trade tip

Dangerous rubbish

❛ Dispose of broken glass safely. Small pieces can be dropped in a nearby bottle bank. Otherwise wrap in thick newspaper and take it to a local authority tip or leave it in a bag or box beside your dustbin, labelled 'Broken Glass'.

Some glass merchants also take it in to be recycled. ❜

FIXING THE NEW GLASS

Before applying putty to the rebate, try the glass in place to make sure it fits. The job of fixing the new pane is tackled in a similar way whether the glass is held in putty and sprigs, or whether it is retained by beading.

To putty-in the glass, start by lining the rebate with a thin layer of putty – the *bedding putty*. The putty should be soft and easily workable without being sticky.

In cold weather, or if it has been allowed to dry out, the putty may be hard and crumbly. If this is the case, knead it in your fingers to warm and soften it; linseed oil putty can be further softened by adding a little oil and working this in the same way. If the putty is too sticky, roll it on wadded newspaper to absorb some of the oil.

Press the glass on to the bedding putty until it is evenly supported, then fit sprigs or clips to retain it. On a sash window with a groove in the top rail, slot the top edge of the pane into this first, then lower into the rebates.

Finish off by applying more putty to the outside to form a weather-proof seal, sloping it off neatly. For ease of working, this putty should be slightly stiffer.

To retain with beading, apply bedding putty in the same way. Prime the new beading and coat the backs of the strips with non-setting putty, then press them into place. Fix by carefully tapping in panel pins or pre-drilling the beading and then inserting small brass countersunk woodscrews.

Trade tip

No slip-ups

❝ As soon as the glass is bedded in, tap sprigs into any two edges to hold it in place and prevent it from falling forward. Also, make sure you leave the tools and some sprigs within easy reach – you must not risk letting go of the glass until it is held firmly. ❞

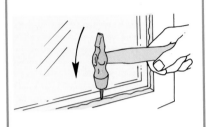

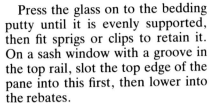

1 Press in a layer of bedding putty by holding a ball in your palm and feeding it through your finger and thumb to fill the rebate to a depth of 3mm (⅛").

2 Set the glass in place, bottom edge first, and rock it back into the frame. (On sashes with a top groove, set the glass in this first, then lower.)

3 Press the glass home gently, using your hands around the edges only – never the middle – until the putty squeezes out to about 3mm (⅛") thick all round.

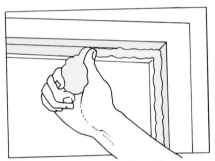

4 Tap in sprigs every 200mm (8") using the back of the hacking knife or a chisel. Slide the tool across the glass as shown to avoid cracking it.

5 On metal frames, fit spring clips at intervals instead of sprigs. The clips hook round the glass and press into holes at convenient points on the frame.

6 Leave the clips or sprigs protruding about 5mm (³/₁₆"). Apply more putty to the face of the glass until it completely fills the rebate.

7 A putty knife is shaped to rest on the woodwork and glass so that you can smooth the putty to a neat 'mitred' finish; dip the blade in water if it sticks.

8 Cut away surplus putty and clean off smears with white spirit. Leave for about three weeks to harden before painting to protect the putty.

Fit glazing beads after coating the back with a thin layer of putty. Press into place and fix with panel pins or screws, being careful not to crack the glass.

FITTING SEALED UNITS

Sealed unit double glazing panels are fitted much like conventional glass. The main differences are that non-setting putty is used, and that the panels are held with wooden beading on the outside. Because the putty does not set hard, it's also important to use special spacers to keep the glass free of the frame.

Prepare the rebate as normal and check that the panel fits, remembering that a stepped edge panel must fit through the frame as well as into the rebate. Then line the rebate with putty and press in spacers at two points along the bottom. Stand the glass in place and drive in pins to hold it temporarily. Coat the back of the beading with putty and screw it to the frame to retain the glass.

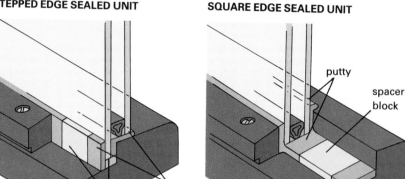

STEPPED EDGE SEALED UNIT

SQUARE EDGE SEALED UNIT

putty

spacer block

non-setting putty

spacer blocks

Both types of double glazing panels are bedded in non-setting putty and retained with beading. The spacer blocks are essential to keep the panel standing just free of the frame.

■ PROBLEM SOLVER

Cutting glass

If you don't get the glass cut by the glass merchant or if the piece which you bought turns out slightly oversized, you may need to cut it yourself. You need a glass cutter, and a flat, padded surface to work on – lay old carpet or layers of newspaper on the worktop.

■ Lay a straightedge along the cut. For a shaped cut, put a paper pattern under the glass. For patterned glass, cut from the flat side. Allow for the distance of the wheel from the face of the cutter.

■ Wet the glass cutter using paraffin or light oil. Holding it like a pencil at about 60°, draw it towards you in a single smooth movement maintaining firm pressure on the glass.

■ Without waiting, lubricate the cut with white spirit then snap it. Either place a thin strip of wood under the glass and press down both sides with even pressure, or tap along the underside of the score with the back of the glass cutter and flex the glass downwards with both hands.

If only a thin strip needs to be removed, you can't snap it in this way. Instead, nibble it away with pliers or the breaker slots on the back of the glass cutter. If the edge is uneven, it can be smoothed with an oilstone or wet and dry paper wrapped over a block – but beware of small, sharp splinters.

Score the cut line using a glass cutter in one smooth movement. Practise on a piece of scrap to see how much pressure is needed for an even mark on the surface.

Lubricate the cut with white spirit, then break over a thin strip of wood using even pressure from both hands on each side of the cut.

Another way to break the glass is to tap along the underside of the cut using the back of the cutter. Then flex the glass downwards using both hands.

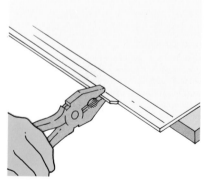

To remove a thin strip, score the cut, then nibble off pieces using a pair of pliers or the breaker slots in the back of many patterns of glass cutter.

SIMPLE DOUBLE GLAZING

Double glazing is an effective cure for the heat loss, condensation and draughts which plague conventional windows in cold weather. Problems like these arise because a single sheet of glass is such a poor insulator. The idea of double glazing is to trap a thin layer of air – a very good insulator – up against the panes.

For the do-it-yourselfer, the least expensive way to provide this insulating layer is by fitting *secondary double glazing* – a second set of panes up against the originals. There are several systems for doing so, all widely available in kit form.

The other options are to reglaze the window with double glazed *sealed units*, which involves considerably more work, or to have double glazed *replacement windows* fitted. Both are costly, and won't pay for themselves in terms of heat saved for many years, but they may be worth considering if your windows are in poor condition and need to be replaced soon.

Fixed panel secondary glazing kits provide an inexpensive and simple means of double glazing.

Trade tip

Soundproofing

❛ People often forget that for double glazing to provide effective sound insulation, the air gap between the panes must be at least 150mm (6") – as opposed to the 10–20mm (⅜–¾") needed to keep the heat in. Fitting a secondary system is the only way to provide this. ❜

TYPES OF SECONDARY GLAZING

Secondary double glazing kits are effectively fixing systems for the new panes, which you buy separately. There are three main types available:

Fixed panel systems aren't really fixed – the glazing panels are designed to be removed for cleaning or ventilation, though not on a regular basis.

Hinged systems work on a similar principle to fixed ones, but have hinges built into the fixing frames which allow the glazing panels to be swung open.

Sliding systems have a track frame which fits to the face of the main window frame or to the sides of the reveal, allowing the glazing panels to be slid open at will.

GLAZING OPTIONS

For the new glazing panels, you have a choice between glass and plastic. Thickness depends on the kit and on what sort of panels you choose, but will be specified on the kit packaging. Some kits can be adapted to take a range of thicknesses – commonly 2–4mm plastic or 4mm glass.

Glass is robust and medium priced, but is unwieldy to handle and too heavy for the lighter types of fixed frame.

Acrylic plastic is light and easy to handle, as well as cheap, but it scratches easily, and needs careful cleaning.

Polycarbonate plastic is the costliest option, but combines the lightness of acrylic with the toughness of glass.

Glass must be cut to size by the supplier. Plastic glazing is sold in various sized sheets by glaziers and DIY stores, and you can cut it yourself.

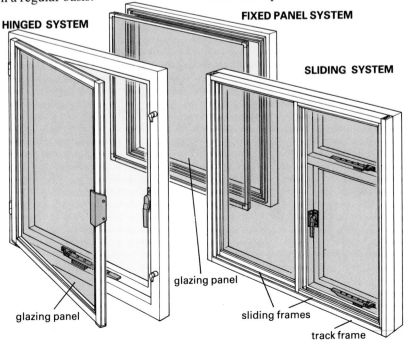

HINGED SYSTEM

FIXED PANEL SYSTEM

SLIDING SYSTEM

glazing panel

glazing panel

glazing panel

sliding frames

track frame

ASSESSING THE OPTIONS

Which type of system you choose to install will depend partly on how much you want to spend, and partly on your windows.

Fixed panels are inexpensive and easy to fit, but inconvenient for windows that get opened frequently – choose an equivalent hinged system instead. Fixed panels are also a potential hazard in the event of a fire, since they could block your escape route, so make sure that at least one opening window in every room has a hinged panel.

On larger windows with both fixed and opening lights, a combination of the two systems is likely to be the best choice.

Sliding systems are costlier and involve more work, but they are much more substantial and often look less obtrusive. It may be worth fitting sliding panels in the most important rooms of the house, and cheaper fixed or hinged panels elsewhere.

Kit compatibility

Not all systems (or kits) fit all windows, and where they do, some look better than others. So once you have a system in mind, note down the following points on the window concerned.

■ Is the frame wood or metal? If it is metal, you could have problems making the panel fixings (see Problem Solver).

■ How wide is the frame? Fixed and hinged panels have to overlap the frame by a certain amount to provide a decent seal.

■ How deep is the frame? If the cockspur handle and other fittings protrude too far, you could have difficulty fitting certain types of fixed or hinged panel.

Armed with this information, see what kits are available at local suppliers and check the instruction leaflets. How you measure up and buy the glazing depends on the system, so check the notes in the appropriate section.

FITTING FIXED AND HINGED PANELS

With fixed and hinged panels, you measure up and buy the glazing before fitting the kit. The diagrams show the options – either fix panels to individual lights, or use a single panel to enclose the entire window.

Refer to the kit instructions to check the thickness of glazing panels required. If you're using plastic, measure on the generous side and then cut the sheets to fit (see page 160) when you get them home. For glass, the exact dimensions are those of the inside of the frame, plus whatever sealing overlap is specified in the kit.

Kits themselves are sold in standard 'height' and 'width' packs, or as complete sets to suit common sizes of window. In all cases, you simply buy the next size up from the actual dimensions of the window, then cut the various parts down.

Fixed panels

There are two common types of fixed panel kit:

Magnetic kits consist of a coated metal strip that goes around the window frame, and a magnetized

plastic strip which you cut to fit the edges of the panel. The metal strip is self-adhesive; the magnetic strip is either self-adhesive or clips to the edges of the glazing, depending on the kit.

Clip frame kits use push-on sections of moulded plastic channel to frame the panels. The sections normally fit over a rubber sealing gasket and butt-joint at corners, so there is no tricky mitring.

In one kit, the framed panels are then fixed to the window frame with plastic turnbuckle clips. In another, they are a snap-fit into a matching self-adhesive channel which you stick all around the window frame. (In practice aligning the two frames is easy: you simply cut and assemble all the channel sections while they are still clipped together – see steps).

Hinged panels

Some hinged panel kits work on the same principle as the clip-frame fixed type, except that in this case one of the side sections of channel is hinged along its length to allow the

panel to swing open. Such kits are ideal for use on large windows, where some lights are fixed and others open.

The hinged section is self-adhesive, enabling you to offer up the panel and position it correctly on the frame. However, because of the extra weight, the fixing then has to be reinforced using the screws supplied with the kit.

Fully hinged panels employ a more complex system of channelling and sealing gaskets to frame the panels. The channel sections are cut to size and joined with special corner pieces in a similar way to sliding panels (see page 158). Hinge pins then slot into the side section and hang from receivers screwed to the window frame.

The panels are sealed against the frame with brush-type draught-proofing strip. Again, you simply cut this to size and slide it into slots in the channel.

Tools checklist: Junior hacksaw, trimming knife, tape measure, drill and bits, screwdrivers (possibly).

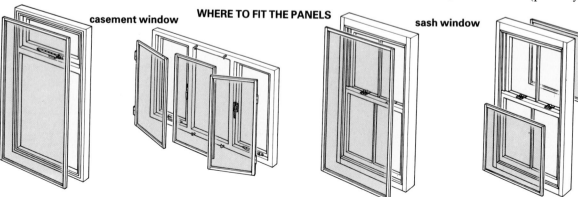

WHERE TO FIT THE PANELS

casement window   sash window

single panel fitted to main window frame

fixed and hinged panels fitted to individual lights

single panel fitted to main window frame

fixed panels on inside of inner sash and outside of outer sash to allow for opening

PREPARING THE WINDOW

It isn't worth double glazing a window that's in a poor state of repair, so check for rotten patches, re-putty any loose panes, and repaint if necessary.

Poor draughtproofing can lead to condensation on the insides of the new glazing panels and make the insulation less efficient. Plug gaps between the frame and the wall with flexible sealant or expanding foam filler. Other sealing measures depend on the window (see right) and on what draughtproofing products are readily available.

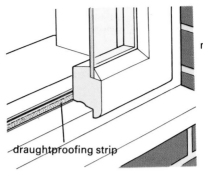

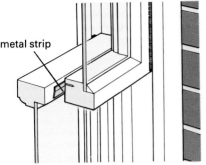

draughtproofing strip

metal strip

On casement windows, seal the frame with good quality self-adhesive draughtproofing strip. Make sure the surface is clean and dry or it won't stick.

On sash windows, seal between the sashes with plastic or metal sprung strip nailed to the outer sash. Seal the sides with stick-on brush pile strips.

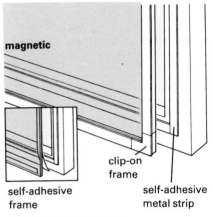

magnetic

self-adhesive frame

clip-on frame

self-adhesive metal strip

FIXED PANEL SYSTEMS

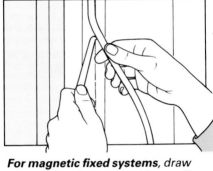

For magnetic fixed systems, draw around the glazing panel in pencil, then use this line as a guide for positioning the self-adhesive metal strip.

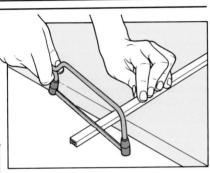

Cut the framing strip for the panel to size, allowing for butt joints at corners. Clip the strip sections around the edges (or stick to the inside) and offer up.

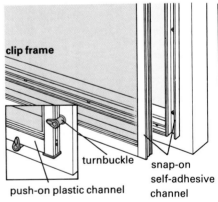

clip frame

turnbuckle

push-on plastic channel

snap-on self-adhesive channel

For clip frame fixed panels with channel fixings, measure off against the panel and cut the combined channel sections to size. Slip on around the panel.

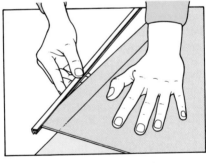

Peel off the backing on the inner channel, then offer up the panel and press firmly against the frame. You can then unclip it, leaving the inner channel stuck.

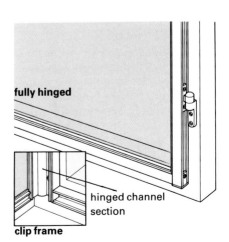

fully hinged

hinged channel section

clip frame

HINGED PANEL SYSTEMS

For clip frames with hinges, press the framed panel against the window frame to locate the channels. Open it, support the weight, and screw down the hinge.

With a fully hinged panel, fit the channels, draughtproofing strips and hinges, then offer up the complete panel and mark the receiver positions on the frame.

FITTING SLIDING PANELS

Like fixed and hinge systems, sliding panel kits are sold in 'height' and 'width' packs or as standard 'window' sets, both of which you cut down to size. The typical kit consists of track sections – in white uPVC, or in white coated or brushed aluminium – plus plastic channel sections to make the sliding frames around each panel. The channels push on over sealing gaskets clipped over the edges of the panels, and are held by screw-on corner pieces.

Depending on the kit, the track sections can be screwed to the face of the window frame or to the sides of the reveal. The first is usually easier, but there may not be enough clearance; the second looks neater.

Fitting the tracks

In contrast to fixed and hinged systems, with sliding panels it's safer to fit the track sections to the window **before** you measure up for the glazing. This way, you can be sure the panels fit.

Measure the lengths of the track sections direct from the frame or reveal. The sections normally butt together at corners, in which case it's easier to cut and fix the top and bottom tracks, then cut the side tracks to fit. Opposite sides should of course be the same length, or the track frame will be out of square. Also, make sure you don't muddle the different sections up – they aren't normally interchangeable.

Having cut the track sections to length – and on some kits, drilled the screw holes – mark the fixing positions. Then screw to the frame, or into drilled and plugged holes in the reveal.

Use a try square or spirit level to check that the track frame is absolutely square. If it isn't, loosen the screw fixings and pack behind the tracks with pieces of card where necessary.

Fitting the panels

Measure the height and width from the **inside** edges of the track frame to find the total glazing area. Individual panels can be up to 2 sq m (20 sq ft), so two should be enough for most windows. If you need more, it looks better if they are arranged so that the seals between them line up with the frame members between the lights. Typically, to work out the size of each panel:

■ Measure the height and width, then deduct the recommended allowance for fitting the sliding frames.

■ Divide the width measurement by the number of panels.

■ To each width figure, add the recommended allowance to cover the overlap between panels. This gives you the final panel width.

With the panels cut to size, assemble each one as follows:

■ Measure off and cut the channel sections for the sliding frames, allowing for the amount taken up by the corner pieces.

■ Cut and fit the sealing gasket around the edges of the panel. (On some kits this is used to convert between 2mm and 4mm glazing.)

■ Lay the panel on a flat surface and tap on the channel sections. Then fit the corner pieces and tighten their securing screws.

With the panels framed, cut the draughtproofing strip that seals the gap between them and slide it into the appropriate channel sections. Then fit any other bits and pieces, for example PTFE slide assisters, and clip-on handles. The panels can now be slotted into the tracks.

Tools checklist: Hacksaw, trimming knife, tape measure, electric drill and bits, screwdrivers, metal file.

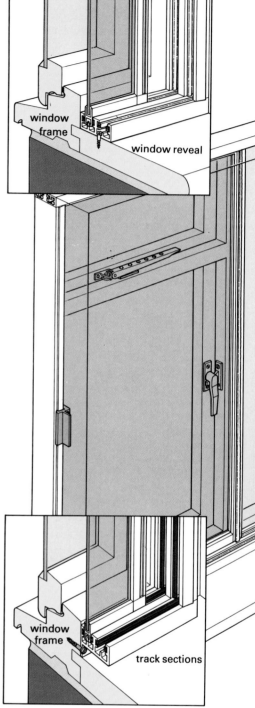

REVEAL-MOUNTED SLIDING PANELS

window frame

window reveal

window frame

track sections

FACE-FIXING SLIDING PANELS

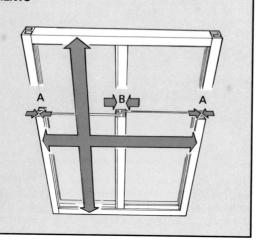

CRITICAL GLAZING MEASUREMENTS

Measure the inside dimensions of the track frame from inside the channels. Then deduct the recommended allowances for the sliding frames (A) and (maybe) add the overlap between panels (B).

A   B   A

SASH WINDOWS

Vertical sliding panel kits are available for sash windows, which tend to be taller than they are wide (use one on a narrow hinged window as well). The system relies on special sprung tracks, which grip the panel frames and stop them sliding under gravity. The frame sections where the panels meet are designed to interlock, forming a weatherproof seal.

The kits are intended for use with plastic glazing panels. They are suitable for windows measuring up to 2.4×1.2m (8×4').

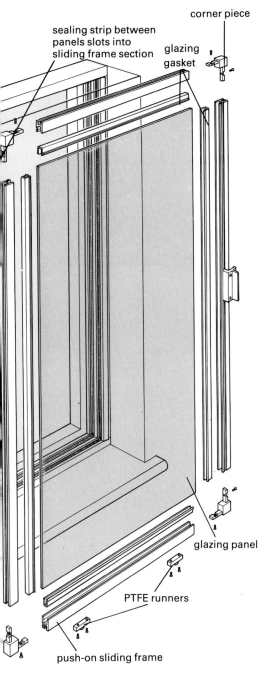

sealing strip between panels slots into sliding frame section

corner piece

glazing gasket

glazing panel

PTFE runners

push-on sliding frame

glazing panel frame

glazing panel with seals

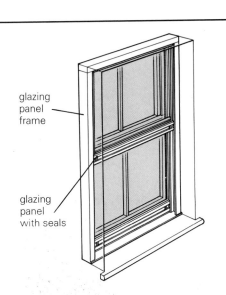

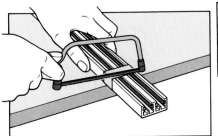

1 Cut the track sections to size with a hacksaw, wrapping tape around the cutting lines to ensure cuts are square. File off any burrs, then remove the tape.

2 Hold a spirit level against the track sections when marking the fixing holes on the frame or reveal. Drill and plug holes where necessary.

3 Check that the track frame is square. If necessary, correct any misalignment by loosening the screws and packing behind the track with pieces of card.

4 Cut the glazing gasket with a trimming knife and clip over the panel edges. It mustn't overlap at the corners or you won't get the channel on.

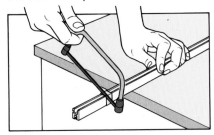
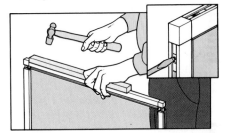

5 Cut the sliding frame sections to size, deducting the recommended amount from the panel dimensions to allow for the corner pieces.

6 Tap the channel sections over the gasket, using a wood block to protect them. Fit the corner pieces (inset) and tighten their screws to lock the frame.

After fitting draughtproofing strip to seal between the panels, lift each panel up into the top track, engage the runners, then lower on to the bottom track.

CUTTING PLASTIC GLAZING PANELS

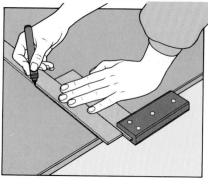 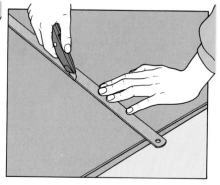 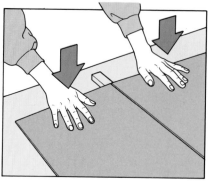

1 Leaving the protective cover sheet on, lay the panel on a flat, stable surface. Measure off the cutting lines, and mark using a try square and felt-tip pen.

2 Using a metal straight edge and trimming knife with laminate cutting blade, score repeatedly through each line until you're half way through.

3 Place a batten under the scored line and apply gentle pressure until the sheet snaps. Afterwards, sand any rough edges using coarse paper on a block.

PROBLEM SOLVER

Metal framed windows

Metal framed windows – or wooden ones with very thin frames – may present problems with certain types of kit. It could be that the frame is too narrow to take the panel fixings, or that the cockspur handle protrudes too far for you to fit panels against the frame at all.

One way out may be to use a sliding panel system mounted in the window reveal. The alternative is to make up a simple butt-jointed softwood sub-frame and screw this in front of the frame as shown.

In many cases you should be able to fix the sub-frame to the reveal. If you have to fix to a metal window, use self-tapping screws.

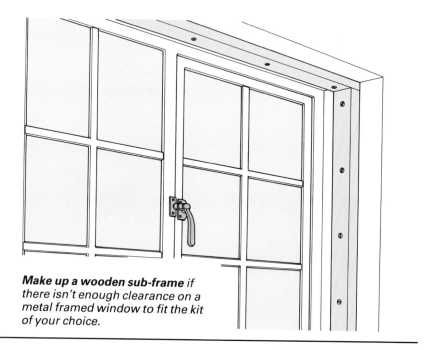

Make up a wooden sub-frame if there isn't enough clearance on a metal framed window to fit the kit of your choice.

Curing condensation

If you find that condensation builds up on the inside of the new panels, try curing it with moisture-absorbing crystals – available from most glazing kit suppliers. Simply place the box of crystals in the cavity between the two panels.

After a couple of months the crystals will stop working, but they can be rejuvenated by drying them out in an airing cupboard or a warm oven.

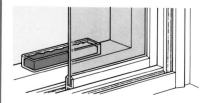

Drilling lintels

Concrete and metal lintels above window reveals can be devilishly difficult to drill and plug – if the kit demands it, it's almost worth drilling a test hole to check.

For concrete, you must have a hammer-action drill and a sharp, fairly new masonry bit. Even so, be prepared for the job to take some time – and pause frequently to let the bit cool down.

If you strike metal, you'll find you make no progress at all; poke the hole with a nail to check, then swap for an ordinary high speed steel twist bit.

When drilling a tiled reveal, don't forget to start the holes with a spearpoint bit and use tape to stop it from slipping.

Drilling a concrete lintel takes time under the best of circumstances, and won't be possible at all unless your drill has a hammer action.

INSULATING PIPES AND TANKS

Insulating cold water supply pipes and storage tanks is a vital precaution against winter freeze-ups. But on hot pipes and the hot water cylinder, insulation can play another, equally important role – by keeping valuable heat sealed in and cutting down on fuel bills.

What to insulate

■ Top priority must go to pipes and tanks in the roof space, particularly if loft insulation has already been laid between the joists. This has the effect of lowering the temperature in the roof space, increasing its vulnerability to frost.

As well as the cold water storage tank and supply pipes, don't overlook the central heating feed and expansion tank, and the overflow pipes running from both tanks to the eaves. (Ice plugs here can easily cause ballvalve failures to pass unnoticed until it's too late.)

Next on the list are pipes passing through a cellar, garage, outhouse, utility room or non-centrally heated extension. These may survive cold snaps quite happily while the rest of the house is fully heated (ironically,

Trade tip

Is your house safe?

6 Even if your pipes and tanks are already insulated, it pays not to be too complacent. Older insulation materials aren't particularly robust, and in time they have a habit of disintegrating or slipping off (especially in areas where repairs have been carried out).

It's also possible that whoever installed the insulation skimped on the job. Sadly, I've had plenty of customers over the years who thought they were safe from freeze-ups – but weren't. 9

the escaping heat protects them). Yet it only takes one severe frost while the family is away to create complete havoc.

■ Check boxed-in pipes. If these run along cold walls, the boxing will insulate them from warmth in the house but not from cold outside.

■ Finally, check the hot water system. Hot pipes which pass through rooms can be left, as the heat they give out won't be wasted. But the hot water cylinder and any pipes inside cupboards are prime candidates for insulation – you can save around 75% of heat this way.

The instructions overleaf give suitable insulating materials for each location, so check before you buy. In some places you may be able to use up any materials left over from insulating the loft.

Insulate vulnerable pipework (below) using flexible foam sleeve insulation.

INSULATING PIPES

Protect pipes with *sleeve*, or *pipe-wrap* insulation. Each has its pros and cons, and it's often best to use a combination of both.

Using sleeve insulation

Insulating sleeve comes in two materials – plastic foam and felt.

Foam sleeve takes the form of rigid or semi-rigid tubes which come in various lengths, and in sizes to suit 15mm, 22mm and 28mm pipes. The tubes are slit lengthways – allowing them to be slipped over pipes – and either clip shut or are fixed with tape or wire depending on the make.

Foam sleeve is the most costly form of pipe insulation, but also the easiest to fit. To estimate, measure each pipe end to end (this covers wastage at joints) and total the figures. Round upwards to the nearest multiple of the sleeve length.

Make a note of any stopcocks, valves or other fittings. Some makes include special two-piece sleeve sections for these; otherwise, insulate them with pipe-wrap.

Felt sleeve is cheaper than foam and comes in rolls around 20m (22yd) long to suit 15mm and 22mm pipes. Although designed to be slipped over pipes before they are installed, it can be fitted to existing pipes by slicing open the stitched seams, then tying or taping in place.

Other materials: Suitable adhesive tape (see Tip), garden tie wire.

Tools checklist: Sharp knife, mitre box, tape measure, pliers.

rigid foam sleeve

traditional felt sleeve

home-made blanket roll bandage

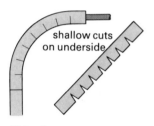

shallow cuts on underside

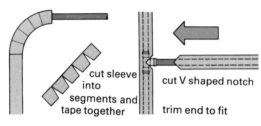

cut sleeve into segments and tape together

cut V shaped notch

trim end to fit

Trim foam sleeve *as shown to deal with elbows, bends and T-junctions.*

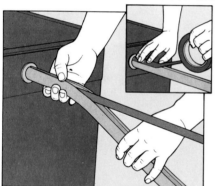

1 To fit foam sleeve insulation, prise the lengths apart and slip them over the pipe. On the non-moulded type, cover the split lengthways with tape.

2 Tape lengths together where they butt-join. At corners, it's neater to mitre the ends in a mitre box – use a sharp kitchen knife to cut the sleeve.

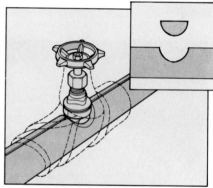

3 Cut notches in the sleeve to clear stopcocks and other fittings (see also Problem Solver). Where necessary, add an extra layer of pipe-wrap.

BOXED-IN PIPES

Insulate boxed-in pipes with **loose fill** loft insulation, which comes in bags of various sizes. Mineral wool loose fill is easier to handle than the granule type, but wear gloves – the fibres irritate the skin.

Open up the boxing at places which give good access to the entire pipe run, then push in the loose fill. Use an opened out wire coathanger for this part of the job, and channel the material through a home-made cardboard tube. Distribute it evenly over the pipes until they are completely covered.

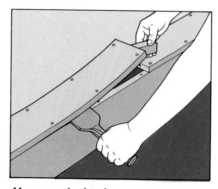

Unscrew the boxing *at convenient points, or prise it open using a sharp bolster or old wood chisel. If necessary, prop the loosened end with a block of wood.*

Force the loose fill *into the boxing through a home-made tube of cardboard. Use a stick to push it through, then spread it evenly with an opened-out coathanger.*

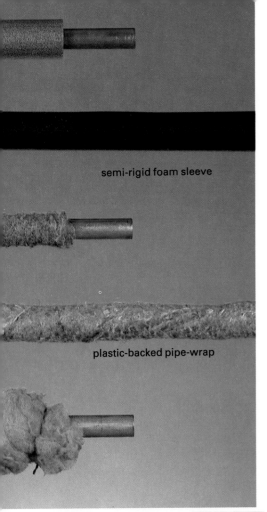

semi-rigid foam sleeve

plastic-backed pipe-wrap

Using pipe-wrap

Pipe-wrap (also called *bandage*) comes in rolls in a variety of materials, including felt, mineral wool and glass fibre. Some makes have a plastic or metal foil backing; others are self-adhesive, which makes fitting easier. Rolls are typically 50mm or 75mm (2–3″) wide and 5m (16′5″) or 10m (33′) long. Make sure you compare like with like when checking prices.

Pipe-wrap is simply rolled around the pipes, overlapping on each turn. It is particularly useful on runs full of bends or joints, and for insulating stopcocks and valves.

Coverage is around half a metre of pipe per metre of roll, but treat this as a rough guide and err on the generous side – your supplier should be prepared to take back unused rolls if they're unopened.

Clean the pipes with a damp cloth before fitting self-adhesive pipe-wrap. For other types, cut lengths of wire to secure the ends.

Pipe insulation (left) comes in several different types.

Blanket roll left over from the loft can be used instead of pipe-wrap providing it is at least 50mm (2″) thick. Cut the roll into 75mm (3″) 'slices' using a panel saw. Then fix the home-made bandage in place with twists of wire or plastic tape.

Tools checklist: Trimming knife, panel saw (for blanket roll).

Other materials: Stiff wire or suitable adhesive tape (see Tip).

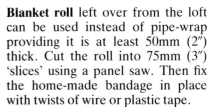

Trade tip

Tape tip

6 At a pinch, you can use virtually any type of self-adhesive tape to secure foam sleeve, pipe-wrap and polystyrene slabs – but some types are better than others.

Some insulation manufacturers include purpose-made glass fibre reinforced or PVC tape as part of their ranges. A good alternative is 50mm (2″) plastic parcel tape, sold by stationers. Don't use insulating tape, as it tends to lose its adhesion. 9

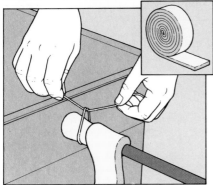

1 To fit pipe-wrap, start with a double turn and secure with a twist of garden tie-wire. Wind it around the pipe in a spiral, overlapping ⅓ of its width.

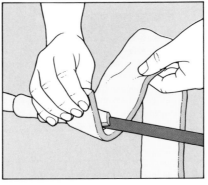

2 Allow a double overlap where lengths join. Secure the non-adhesive type with wire or tape – but not too tightly, or you'll reduce its effectiveness.

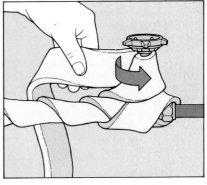

3 Wrap stopcocks and valves in an 'X' pattern so that the body of the fitting is completely covered, leaving only the handle exposed.

INSULATING THE HOT CYLINDER

Insulating jackets, consisting of quilted plastic sections filled with mineral or glass fibre wool, are available to fit all common sizes of cylinder. The sections are linked via a wire collar fitted around the topmost pipe, and held in place with elastic or adjustable straps. You'll find it easier to assemble the jacket if you fit the straps first.

If there is an immersion heater fitted, arrange for it to coincide with a joint between sections and leave the cap exposed. The same applies to a cylinder thermostat.

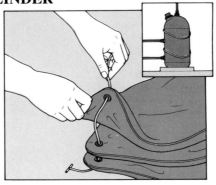

1 Fit the jacket's straps loosely around the cylinder, a quarter of the way from the top and bottom. Then thread the jacket sections through the wire collar.

2 Fit the collar around the top pipe and drape the sections over the cylinder. Tuck the sections under the straps, one by one closing any gaps as you go.

INSULATING TANKS

If you have the choice, insulate tanks **after** the pipework so that the vulnerable connections are doubly protected. Leave the area below a tank free of insulation to take advantage of rising heat.

Tank insulation kits consist of specially tailored slabs of polystyrene foam, plus tape or straps to secure them. They are made to fit all common sizes of plastic tank, but are unsuitable for round tanks and may not match older, galvanized steel types. Kits are not the cheapest solution, but they are easy to fit.

Slip-over insulating jackets similar to hot water cylinder jackets are available for round tanks.

For either of the above options, be sure to measure the tank dimensions before you buy.

Polystyrene slabs used for loft insulation are easily cut to fit square-sided tanks. The slabs should be at least 25mm (1″) thick. Fix with cocktail sticks and tape.

Left-over blanket roll or batts (minimum 75mm [3″] thick) can also be used, but they are less robust than slabs and trickier to fit. Secure the pieces with string, and tape over

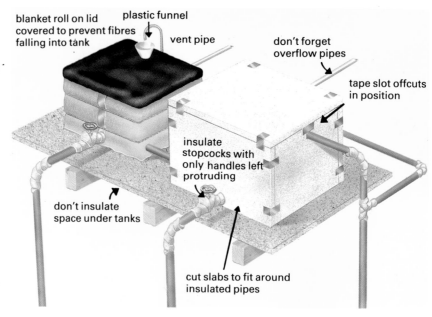

blanket roll on lid covered to prevent fibres falling into tank — plastic funnel — vent pipe — don't forget overflow pipes — tape slot offcuts in position — insulate stopcocks with only handles left protruding — don't insulate space under tanks — cut slabs to fit around insulated pipes

any vertical joints. Cut another piece to fit on top of the lid and wrap them both in a bin liner.

Where the tank is without a lid, make one from an offcut of 12mm (½″) chipboard or 9mm (⅜″) plywood. Cut slots to clear pipes, then drill out the waste wood.

Other materials: Suitable adhesive

A properly insulated cold storage tank/central heating expansion tank set-up showing polystyrene slab and blanket roll insulation.

tape (see previous page), string or twine, cocktail sticks, funnel.

Tools checklist: Sharp kitchen knife, tape measure, felt-tip pen.

1 **Cut foam slabs** to fit around the sides of the tank using a sharp kitchen knife. Cut slots to clear any pipes, but save the offcuts for taping back on.

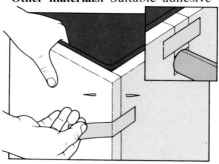

2 Fix the slabs together at the corners with cocktail sticks and reinforce with PVC tape. Then tape back the offcuts where slots were cut for pipes.

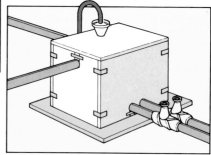

3 Cut a fifth slab for the lid and secure to the sides with tape. Where there is an overhead vent pipe, drive a cheap plastic funnel through the slab.

PROBLEM SOLVER

Awkward areas

There are likely to be places where space is too restricted to fit conventional insulation. In particular, watch out for outside taps and the holes where their supply pipes pass through walls. There may be a similar problem at the eaves, where overflows pass to the outside.

Pack these gaps with expanding foam filler, available in aerosol form. Although not cheap, it provides better weather protection than loose fill and is easier to handle.

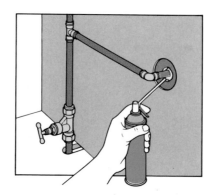

Squirt foam filler into the gaps where supply or overflow pipes pass through outside walls.

Cover outside tap pipes in a 'sleeve' of foam. This can be sanded smooth when dry.

LAYING INSULATION IN YOUR LOFT

Keeping your house warm can be expensive at the best of times, but inadequate insulation sends heating costs literally through the roof.

An uninsulated loft lets through 25% of the heat below. And even a layer 50mm (2″) thick loses more than 10%, which makes it well worth 'topping up'. Apart from the extra comfort, the saving on fuel bills can cover the cost of the insulation within a few years and you may also qualify for a grant (see page 167).

If your loft isn't used as a living space, the easiest place to insulate is between the ceiling joists, using one of the materials shown below. Any part of the loft used as a living area must be insulated at rafter level to retain heat rising from the rooms below. This is covered elsewhere.

Flat roofs are more difficult to insulate – see Problem Solver for possible solutions.

Insulation slabs are easy to handle and can be cut to fit any joist spacing.

TYPES OF INSULATION MATERIAL

Fibre mat insulation is made from mineral or glass wool. It comes in continuous rolls and as slabs (also called *batts*). *Rolls* (in various lengths) are commonly available in thicknesses ranging from 50mm (2″) to 150mm (6″) and in standard widths to fit the usual 400mm (16″) joist spacing. Wider 1200mm (48″) rolls can be cut into three pieces with a panel saw to fit 400mm (16″) joists or two to fit the less common 600mm (24″) spacing. A few makes have an integral polythene or foil vapour barrier to keep out moisture; the 150mm thick rolls sometimes have a separate top layer that can be offset to cover the tops of the joists. *Slabs* are 50mm thick and have to be cut in three for 400mm joists or two for 600mm. Separate 'kits' are available for the loft hatch.

Loose fill consists of mineral wool fibres or vermiculite granules and is sold in bags. A bag of mineral wool fibre covers roughly 1 sq m (11 sq ft)

to a depth of 50mm (2″). A bag of vermiculite covers 2.25 sq m (24 sq ft) to the same depth, but must be laid thicker to provide the same degree of insulation.

Polystyrene comes in sheets up to 2400×1200mm (8×4′) in size, to a thickness of 100mm (4″).

An alternative to DIY is to hire a contractor to 'blow' cellulose or mineral fibre into the loft. This is very efficient but expensive.

With loose fill or blanket insulation special **eaves vents** and **soffit vents** are available to prevent condensation in the loft.

Mineral wool roll

Glassfibre roll

Eaves vents

Polystyrene sheeting

Mineral wool slab

Fibre loose fill

Granule loose fill

Soffit vents

Hatch kit

CHOOSING THE RIGHT MATERIAL

Measure the depth of the joists and the spaces between them, checking to see if they are evenly spaced. They may not be suitable for standard width rolls, or could be too shallow for some types of loose fill.

If you want to use loose fill and your loft is very draughty, it's better to use the mineral fibre type as vermiculite granules can drift.

The chart below shows the options for different joist spacings and any existing insulation thickness. The depths for each type of material are the minimum recommended and give a rough indication of their relative efficiency. You can put in a thicker layer, but it is unlikely to be as cost-effective.

To calculate how many rolls or slabs you need, multiply the joist length by the number of spaces to be filled. Divide this figure by the length of each roll or slab section.

For loose fill, multiply together the overall dimensions of the loft in metres for the total area in square metres. The coverage for loose fills given on page 165 includes the area taken up by the joists.

INSULATION OPTIONS

Joist layout	Suitable insulation	Minimum extra insulation needed if existing insulation thickness is:		
		None	Under 30mm (1¼")	Around 50mm (2")
Regular gaps: approx 400mm (16")	Roll: standard width or 1200mm cut in three	100mm (4")	100mm (4")	50mm (2")
	Slab cut in three	100mm (4")	100mm (4")	50mm (2")
	Fibre loose fill	90mm (3½")	70mm (2¾")	50mm (2")
	Granule loose fill	155mm (6")	not suitable	100mm (4")
	'Blown' fibre	85–110mm (3½–4½")	not suitable	not suitable
Regular gaps: approx 600mm (24")	Roll: 1200mm cut in two	100mm (4")	100mm (4")	50mm (2")
	Slab cut in two	100mm (4")	100mm (4")	50mm (2")
	Fibre loose fill	90mm (3½")	70mm (2¾")	50mm (2")
	Granule loose fill	155mm (6")	not suitable	100mm (4")
	'Blown' fibre	85–110mm (3½–4½")	not suitable	not suitable
Irregular gaps and awkward corners	Slab cut to fit	100mm (4")	100mm (4")	50mm (2")
	Fibre loose fill	90mm (3½")	70mm (2¾")	50mm (2")
	Granule loose fill	155mm (6")	not suitable	100mm (4")
	'Blown' fibre	85–110mm (3½–4½")	not suitable	not suitable

PREPARING TO LAY INSULATION

Make sure there is enough light to work in and if necessary lay on a temporary light source. Clear the loft and take up any flooring inspecting the joists beneath for rot or woodworm. Step only on the joists and use a board to kneel on.

Fix any wires that run over the ceiling to the joists above the insulation level – this stops them overheating. Wiring that passes through joists must be removed and refixed over the top. If you find any old rubber sheathed wiring, this is due for replacement.

Pipes running between the joists can be left covered with insulation. Other pipes and any cold water tanks must be individually insulated as shown in the following section.

It's important to ensure that there is constant air circulation through the loft above the insulation. This prevents condensation forming and causing damage to the insulation and roof timbers. Vents can be fitted between the rafters at joist level to ensure the ventilation gaps in the eaves remain unblocked. A vapour barrier of polythene sheeting or foil backed-paper fixed between the joists stops water vapour entering the loft.

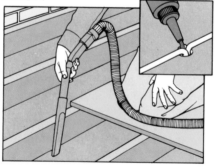
Clean thoroughly between the joists with a soft brush or vacuum cleaner. Seal any gaps where pipes and wires enter with mastic or filler.

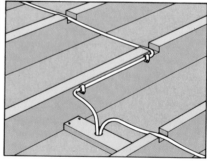
Staple wires to the joists above the level of the insulation. If you are boarding over joists, chisel shallow notches in tops to accept the wires.

Check that there are gaps or holes along the eaves. If there isn't enough air getting in, drill holes or install ventilation grilles in the soffit.

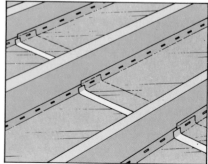
Lay a vapour barrier between the joists, leaving 25mm (1") flaps at each side. Overlap the sections, tape joins and staple or tape to the joists.

GETTING A GRANT

Local authority grants may be available if *all* these conditions apply:

■ You or your partner receives family credit, income support or housing benefit.
■ Your house was built before 1976.
■ The loft has no insulation or less than 30mm (1¼").
■ The loft forms your ceiling.
■ No insulation grant has previously been awarded.

If you qualify, you are eligible for a grant of 90% of the material and labour costs or £137, whichever is less.

You must use local authority approved materials to recommended depths. And work cannot begin before the grant has been approved.

The whole loft must be insulated (except under the cold water tanks and in inaccessible areas) plus all cold water tanks, pipes and the hot water cylinder.

Flat roofs do not qualify.

Protection
Some mineral or glass wool fibres can irritate the skin and lungs so wear a face mask and gloves when handling insulation made from either of these materials.

LAYING ROLLS AND SLABS

Take the materials up into the loft in their packages – rolls expand to up to four times their original size when unwrapped and if you're cutting to size, it's easier to do so before you remove the wrapping.

Rolls are designed to fit snugly between standard spaced joists so only trim them to fit the odd non-standard spacing.

If you're not using a kit to insulate the loft hatch cover, cut a piece of the material to size and tie loosely on to the cover. Tape or staple a sheet of polythene or a bin liner over the material to prevent stray fibres escaping into the house.

Trade tip

Getting into the eaves

❝ If you can't get right into the eaves because of the slope of the roof, unroll a convenient length of blanket and push the end gently into the eaves with a broom. Be careful not to push it is so far that it blocks off the air holes. ❞

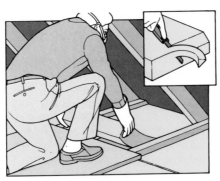

1 Start laying insulation at the eaves, leaving a 50mm (2") air gap or fitting vents. With slabs, trim the ends at an angle to help the airflow.

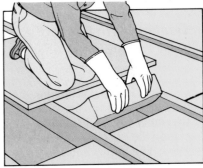

2 Unroll or fit the material gently without compressing it. Fit tightly up against the joists and butt the pieces up to each other where they meet.

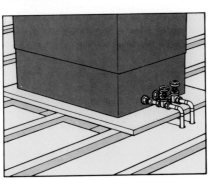

3 Cut the roll or slabs to fit snugly around any obstacles or pipes using heavy scissors or a kitchen knife. Leave the space under the cold tank free.

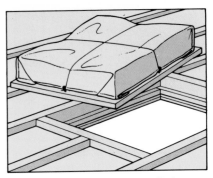

4 Hammer some clout nails into the sides of the hatch cover, leaving them 25mm (1") proud. Cover the insulation with polythene and tie on with string.

PUTTING IN LOOSE FILL

Cover over any cold pipes that run close to the ceiling with pieces of cardboard or thick paper to stop the loose fill from flowing underneath them. This lets heat from the room below keep the pipes warm.

Do not lay loose fill under the cold tanks for the same reason. Fit boards between the joists to block off this area.

The simplest way to insulate the hatch cover is to use a slab kit or 100mm (4") thick polystyrene sheeting.

1 Fix eaves vents or pieces of board near the ends of the joists to avoid blocking the ventilation gap. Block off the areas under the cold tanks.

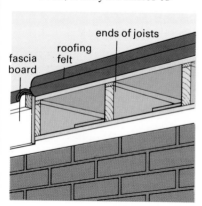

2 Cut a piece of polystyrene sheet to size and glue it on to the inside of the hatch cover. Use adhesive designed for polystyrene ceiling tiles.

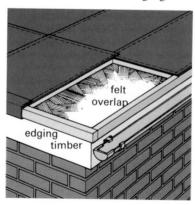

3 Spread or pour the loose fill evenly between the joists, except under the cold tanks. Gently separate and fluff up mineral wool fibre.

4 Level off the loose fill at the top of the joists. Use a garden rake for wool fibres and a piece of shaped board for vermiculite granules.

PROBLEM SOLVER

Dealing with flat roofs

There are three ways to insulate a flat roof:

Option 1: Internal insulation is only possible if you are prepared to remove the fascia boards and expose the gaps between the joists. This allows you to slide sheets of polystyrene or mineral wool slabs into the roof space. However, it may be easier to have fibre material blown in by a contractor. This is more expensive but could save you time and trouble.

Option 2: A new roof can be laid using special weatherproof insulation slabs bonded to the existing roof with mastic. These are pre-felted, but must be finished with a timber edging.

Option 3: Ceiling insulation is a last resort if access to the fascia or roof is very difficult. For a minimum of insulation, you can stick polystyrene tiles to the ceiling with tile adhesive. But if the ceiling is high enough, it's possible to line it with polystyrene sheeting (plus a polythene vapour barrier) and cover it with a false ceiling.

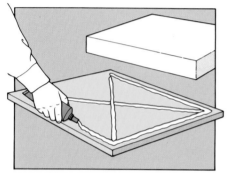

Removing the fascia boards gives access to the spaces between the joists, so they can be filled from the outside with polystyrene sheets or mineral wool slabs.

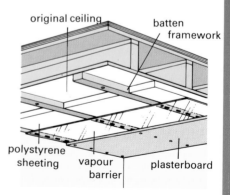

Prefelted roof slabs have flaps which overlap to make a weatherproof roof surface, but require a timber framework to finish the edges.

A false ceiling on a timber framework can be built to conceal a layer of polystyrene insulation so long as it still leaves 2.3m (7'6") headroom.

IDENTIFYING AND CURING CONDENSATION

Condensation is the scourge of modern homes, and like weeds in the garden it can be frustratingly difficult to get rid of. In a well-designed and sensibly run home there is no reason why it should occur at all, but that's little consolation if you are a condensation sufferer. A more realistic approach is to understand why condensation happens, then set about eliminating the causes one by one.

What is condensation?

Air always contains a certain amount of moisture in the form of water vapour. Like a bath sponge, there's a limit to the amount it can carry, and when it can hold no more it is said to have reached *saturation point*. Unlike a sponge, however, the saturation point of air varies according to its temperature – warm air can hold more moisture than cool air.

When air at saturation point is suddenly cooled – for example, by coming into contact with a cold window pane on a chilly day – its ability to hold moisture as water vapour is immediately reduced. At this point, the excess vapour *condenses* into minute water droplets and the process of condensation begins.

The droplets appear first as a fine film that mists up the glass and causes other cold, smooth surfaces to feel damp. But as more moisture is deposited, the droplets combine into the trickles of water that leave tell-tale pools on window sills and the like.

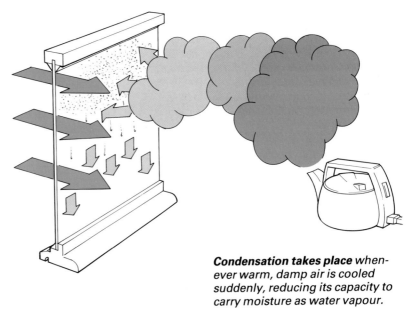

Condensation takes place whenever warm, damp air is cooled suddenly, reducing its capacity to carry moisture as water vapour.

THE CONSEQUENCES OF CONDENSATION

Surfaces which are continually damp can be a nuisance – even unpleasant – to live with. And owners of condensation-prone homes need no reminding of the damage which continued trickles of water can do to wallcoverings and soft furnishings. But condensation can have more serious consequences too:

Mould growth is the most common, particularly around window frames. Air-borne fungal spores searching for water to help them germinate find an ideal breeding ground on the damp surfaces of a condensation-prone room.

Materials which retain moisture, such as wallpaper or the edges of window frames, are particularly at risk. So are other areas where poor ventilation – itself a prime cause of condensation – keeps the air moisture content high.

Structural decay is less common, but much more serious. Surface condensation can penetrate the cracks in painted woodwork, creating perfect conditions for rot to develop. In walls, the same process causes plaster to break down and crumble.

There is also *interstitial condensation* – condensation which takes place naturally within the structure. In a properly designed and ventilated home, this should quickly be dispersed. But if the condensation is excessive, or is allowed to become trapped, any porous materials – especially timber – soon begin to decay.

INDENTIFYING THE CAUSES

Somewhat surprisingly, we are ourselves a major source of moisture in the air. Our breath is moist and our sweat evaporates; one person 'produces' a quarter of a litre of water during eight hours of sleep, and as much as a litre and a half during an active day.

Our domestic activities create even more moisture. Cooking, washing up, bathing, washing and drying clothes and so on produces up to between 10 and 12 litres of water a day, and every litre of fuel burnt in a flueless oil or paraffin heater give off roughly another litre of water vapour.

We expect the air in the house to 'soak up' this liquid for us. Condensation becomes a problem when it can't, for one or more of the reasons given here.

THE CONSEQUENCES OF CONDENSATION

POOR VENTILATION

The normal way in which moist air is removed from the house is by ventilation. Sometimes this is intentional – for example, when we open windows or switch on an extractor fan. But in the average home there's a fair degree of unintentional ventilation too, as moisture-laden air escapes through old chimney flues and other gaps.

Unfortunately, the quest for warmer homes and reduced heating bills has led to houses becoming much more air-tight than they used to be. Flues are blocked off, windows are double glazed, doors are draught-proofed and floors, walls and ceilings are insulated. Such measures increase comfort but reduce ventilation, increasing the condensation risk.

Poor ventilation is not only a problem within the house; it can affect the structure too, and in particular the roof space. When a loft floor or flat roof is insulated, the air in the space above remains cold. This causes any warm, moist air which finds its way into the space to 'lose' its moisture as condensation. The condensation in turn soaks the insulation, rendering it less effective and encouraging rot.

It is now realized that efficient ventilation of roof spaces by means of special eaves vents and ridge ventilators is essential, and you will see these features on all new houses. However, many older homes don't even benefit from 'ac-cidental' ventilation – especially if the eaves have been packed with loft insulation – and may be beginning to suffer serious problems as a result.

Possible solutions

Top priority must go towards providing a controllable means of getting rid of excess moist air.

■ In kitchens and bathrooms, an extractor fan is usually the answer. This expels the unwanted air quickly, minimizing heat losses, and has the added benefit of dispersing unwanted smells too. In severe cases, you could consider wiring the fan to a *humidity detector* so that operation is automatic.

■ Elsewhere, the simplest solutions are to fit window- and door-mounted slot ventilators, or extra wall-mounted airbricks. But first make sure that any existing airbricks are unblocked, and that rooms with secondary double glazing have at least one openable light for emergency ventilation.

■ Unused chimney flues must be vented top and bottom, which serves as a useful back-up to other ventilation measures. If a flue is left blocked, condensation inside can result in damp patches on chimney breast walls.

■ In the roof space, check that there is a vapour barrier of polythene or building paper below the loft insulation. Make sure the insulation isn't carried right to the eaves, and fit eaves vents if necessary away from pipes and cisterns.

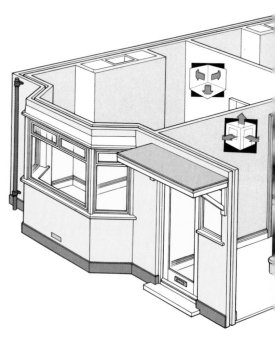

Check the house room by room for condensation problems. The symbols above show the most common trouble spots and indicate the probable cause – see main text for details.

DEHUMIDIFICATION

Where ventilation problems can't be solved by other means, it may be worth investing in an *electric dehumidifier*. These remove moisture from the air and produce heat as a by-product (although they are most effective where heat and humidity are the main problem, rather than low temperatures).

Portable dehumidifiers can be intrusively noisy to run. *Whole-house* versions are mounted in the roof space and operate through a system of ducts. They are comparitively expensive, but quieter and more efficient.

POOR INSULATION

Wall, floor and ceiling surfaces – not to mention window glass – all become cold as external temperatures fall, even if the interior is adequately warm. This results in condensation as soon as warm, moisture-laden air within the room comes into contact with them.

A poorly insulated home is left wide open to condensation – particularly in areas where natural air circulation is restricted – for example, the corners of rooms, or behind furniture (especially where this is built-in against a cold outside wall). But even where the structure is basically well insulated, condensation may still occur at 'cold bridges' with the outside – for example, window and door reveals and lintels.

Possible solutions

Over and above normal insulating measures – including double glazing – you may need to take additional steps to keep walls warm. One possibility is to redecorate with heat-retaining materials (see overleaf). Very severe cases may call for *cavity wall insulation,* which must be professionally installed by a qualified contractor using approved materials.

INADEQUATE HEATING

Improving insulation must go hand in hand with providing adequate heating; even a well insulated room will eventually become cold enough for condensation to occur, even though the rate of heat loss has been reduced. This applies particularly to rooms which are traditionally heated only for part of the day, such as bedrooms.

Possible solutions

In centrally heated homes, which now make up over 70 per cent of the UK's housing stock, the solution is to avoid intermittent heating so that room temperatures are maintained at a sufficient level to stop condensation occuring. This needn't mean an increase in fuel bills – often it is more wasteful to keep warming up a building from cold every time the heating is switched on.

In homes without central heating, the solution is to provide a local heat source in every room. Appliances such as balanced flue gas heaters or electric night storage heaters are ideal for main rooms, and small electric heaters with thermostatic control can be used in small rooms such as bathrooms and WCs. Avoid paraffin heaters: they produce water vapour.

ABSORBENT SURFACES

Condensation is naturally retained for longer by absorbent surfaces and materials than by smooth ones. Not only does this make them harder to clean; it also encourages mould.

Remember this when choosing decorations and furnishings. Vinyl wallcoverings and sheet vinyl, vinyl tiled or sealed cork flooring are good choices for these rooms. For painted surfaces, consider redecorating with *anti-condensation paint* (see overleaf). This absorbs excess water vapour until it can evaporate harmlessly, so preventing run-off.

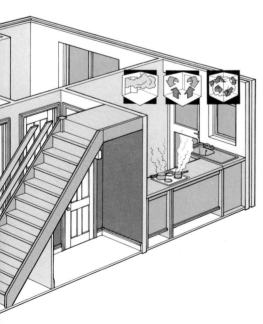

BAD HABITS

You can make a personal contribution towards reducing condensation by a simple change of habits.

■ Keep doors to steamy rooms closed so that moist air can be expelled through proper ventilation instead of finding its way into other (colder) parts of the house.

■ Dry clothes in the open air wherever possible, or invest in a tumble drier. Where you have to dry them indoors, make special ventilation arrangements.
■ Make sure bathrooms and shower rooms are warm before you use them.
■ Keep bedrooms ventilated at night. If it's too cold to have a window open, leave the door ajar.

SIMPLE CURES

Apply anti-condensation paint *using ordinary brush or roller techniques. It can be left as a finish in its own right or overpainted when dry.*

DECORATIVE IDEAS

When redecorating rooms such as kitchens or bathrooms which have a condensation problem due to cold walls, choose materials which help to prevent condensation.

Anti-condensation paint dries to a white, finely textured finish which resists the formation of condensation and also inhibits mould growth. Once dry it can be overpainted with any emulsion paint to blend in with your colour scheme; the anti-condensation properties are unaffected.

Insulating wallcoverings also help to prevent condensation on cold walls. Two options are to apply an expanded polystyrene or polyethylene lining, or to use a blown vinyl wallcovering. Both contain minute air bubbles which help to retain heat.

WINDOW VENTS

A window vent fitted in a fixed pane is a simple way to allow fresh air to ventilate a room. Wind-driven designs are dependent on there being some airflow outside. There are also static types with an outer wind shield which should permit a constant exchange of air with the minimum of draughts. For areas of heavy condensation you could even install a powered extractor fan.

All such vents are fitted by bolting them together through a hole in the glass. Don't try to cut this yourself – get a glass merchant to supply a pane of glass with a hole cut in it, and reglaze the window.

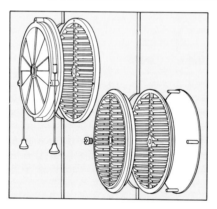

Vents come in two parts which bolt together through the hole. There are various designs, but the main choice is between a revolving or static type.

Trade tip

Soak it up

❝ For minor condensation on windows, self-adhesive foam strip will absorb the water run-off. Don't use it where the window is constantly wet as it must get a chance to dry out. ❞

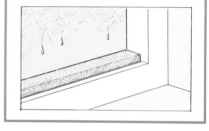

EAVES VENTS

Eaves vents are cheap plastic barriers which hold the loft insulation a short distance away from the roof covering to provide vital air circulation. Fitting is simple – just tuck the bottom flap under the edge of the insulation material to retain it in place.

If the construction of the roof leads you to suspect that air flow through the eaves is insufficient, you can fit *soffit vents* – plastic grilles to trim holes cut in the soffit board. This must be done from the outside, using a ladder or access tower, so try to combine it with other outdoor repairs requiring similar access arrangements.

Fit eaves vents *where none are present, or when insulating from scratch. These keep the cold roof space well ventilated, minimizing the risk of condensation.*

IDENTIFYING DAMP PROBLEMS

Damp is one of the most common and potentially serious problems facing housing in temperate climates. Left to its own devices, continual dampness can ruin decorations and cause the structure to deteriorate rapidly. But worse still, it can create the ideal conditions for wet and dry rot – associated problems which cost homeowners millions of pounds each year to put right.

What is damp?

For a building, suffering from damp is not the same thing as simply getting wet.

All houses are constantly in contact with moisture in the ground and air, and they frequently get pelted with rain. But if they are properly designed and structurally sound, ground water will be stopped from penetrating, rainwater will run off, and any moisture which does get in should evaporate quickly. At the same time, areas which could suffer if they got wet – the plaster and concealed woodwork for instance – should be well protected.

Damp occurs when structural defects cause one or more of these built-in safeguards to break down. Moisture gets in and, instead of disappearing, becomes trapped in the house structure. Once inside, it remains where it is or finds its way into more vulnerable areas – by which time the damage has been done.

For this reason alone, preventing damp is a lot more sensible than trying to cure it once it has taken hold. You can do a lot by giving your home an immediate 'damp survey' to check out the most vulnerable areas.

TYPES OF DAMP

Builders and damproofing specialists classify damp by the way in which it is caused. In many cases the symptoms – mould, spoilt decorations, rotten woodwork – are the same, but where damp is concerned you can't possibly hope to put things right unless you identify the cause first.

Rising damp occurs when the house structure sucks moisture out of the ground. Old houses without a damp-proof course (DPC) and damp-proof floor membrane (DPM) are especially vulnerable, and brick walls also tend to become more porous with age. But rising damp can affect newer houses, too, if there are defects in the built-in damp-proofing measures.

Penetrating damp, the most common kind, occurs when water penetrates and becomes trapped in the house structure. All houses are vulnerable, but older ones particularly so since they are likely to have more structural defects which allow water to get in unhindered.

Damp caused by leaks from water pipes and the seals around plumbing fittings can pass by unnoticed, but it is very common. All houses are vulnerable.

Hygroscopic damp occurs when the house absorbs moisture from the atmosphere. It is rarer than the other types, but may be present at the same time as them. Older houses are particularly vulnerable.

Condensation is where water vapour in the air turns to water as it contacts a cooler surface. Although not the same as structural dampness, it can produce the same symptoms, and may be confused with it. Dealing with condensation is covered in separate sections.

The poor condition of the brickwork shown below was caused by a combination of hygroscopic salts, frost attack, rising damp and leaking rainwater pipes.

FINDING THE CAUSE: OUTSIDE

Under the right conditions, virtually any structural defect can lead to dampness. But some areas of a house are more vulnerable than others and a few are notorious trouble spots.

When matching symptoms inside the house to faults outside, bear in mind that dampness often shows up some way away from the defect which caused it. In walls and ceilings, the moisture tends to 'creep' along structural joints or gaps, then emerge at a weak point – such as a patch of repaired plaster.

Pitched roofs are surprisingly resistant to penetrating damp, but that doesn't mean you can ignore them.
■ Slipped slates or tiles may let in rain, and this water penetration often shows up as cracking in first floor ceilings. If there is a layer of felt under the roof covering, this may channel the water away from the hole – possibly as far as the walls.

Flat roofs are a common trouble spot. When water penetrates a flat roof, it gathers above the ceiling below, or runs with the fall to the edges. As well as leaks in the roof covering itself, check for:
■ Damaged flashings where the roof meets the walls. These can cause damp patches lower down inside the house.
■ Cracked or missing stone cappings on parapet walls, which lead to similar problems. Brick-capped parapets should have a DPC.

Trade tip

DPC or not?

❛ If your house was built after 1900, you can be pretty sure it has a damp-proof course – either engineering bricks, slate, or bitumen felt. Before this date, there's a chance it may not.

Over the last 20 years, many DPC-less houses have had a damp-proof course added, usually by chemical injection, but sometimes by fitting ceramic respirators or electro-osmotic equipment. Unfortunately, none of these methods has a 100 per cent success rate – much depends on how efficiently the DPC was installed – so even if your house has been 'damp-proofed', you can't rule out the possibility of some rising damp. ❜

Chimneys are another recognized trouble spot.
■ Cracked mortar flaunching around the pots allows water to soak into the stack, causing rapid deterioration.
■ Damaged flashings where the chimney meets the roof covering lead to penetrating damp in the chimney breast. In time, this may spread to first-floor level.
■ Uncapped chimneys, if left unused, can raise the level of moisture throughout the entire chimney breast. Often this results in small patches of hygroscopic damp on walls.

Leaking rainwater systems are responsible for most penetrating damp problems. The best time to check is immediately after a period of heavy rain.
■ Blockages and leaks in joints should be obvious. On PVC guttering, check, too, that the run isn't bowing and causing overspill at the edges.
■ Check cast-iron downpipes for rusting, especially around the backs.

Walls which have been allowed to deteriorate may cause penetrating damp.
■ Check that the pointing is intact.
■ Watch for missing, cracked or *spalled* (deeply pitted) bricks.
■ Check that rendering hasn't cracked or 'blown' by tapping to see if it sounds hollow.
■ On cavity walls, make sure that earlier alterations haven't allowed the cavity to become blocked or 'bridged'. Debris left from replacing a window, and badly sealed waste pipes are two common problems.

Leaking overflows may not be obvious, since they usually drip intermittently to start with. Look for tell-tale green moss patches on the area of wall immediately below.

Windows are a common cause of penetrating damp.
■ Check that the putty around the panes is intact.
■ Check stone or concrete sills for signs of cracking.
■ Look under each sill and check that the drip groove is clear and intact (some sills have a protruding drip bead). The groove stops rainwater hugging the underside of the sill and running into the wall below; if it is clogged with old paint, there may be penetrating damp inside the house, below the window.
■ Check the seals around the frames; these are particularly vulnerable if made with fillets of mortar rather than flexible sealant.

DPC faults lead to rising damp. If you can see the DPC, check for cracks caused by subsidence and any other obvious signs of damage. If you can't see the DPC, take it as being at the same height as the lowest doorstep and check right around the house up to this level.
■ Earth or other debris piled up against the walls can 'bridge' the DPC. So, too, can an incorrectly laid path or patio.
■ Paths and patios laid less than 150mm (6″) below DPC level may cause rainwater 'splashback' on the walls. The effects of this inside the house are likely to be most noticeable in winter.
■ Rendering may bridge the DPC if it is continued as far as ground level. (In older houses there may be a rendered plinth hiding a DPC consisting of several courses of engineering bricks. This is acceptable.)
■ Adjoining walls will bridge the DPC unless they have one too. Garden walls without a DPC need a vertical DPC where they join a house wall.

Airbricks protect the ground floor structure from rising damp by helping moisture under the house to evaporate. Check that they aren't blocked. There may be airbricks higher up the house as well, to ventilate the wall cavity.

Poor surface drainage mainly affects older houses where the DPC is either missing or defective. Its effects inside the house are likely to be seasonal.

Trade tip

Make a sketch

❢ When checking the outside of the house, do what the professionals do and make a sketch plan of each elevation – front, back and sides. As well as noting any obvious faults, don't forget areas that look suspect but which you can't inspect closely – they may need further investigation. ❡

FINDING THE CAUSE: INSIDE

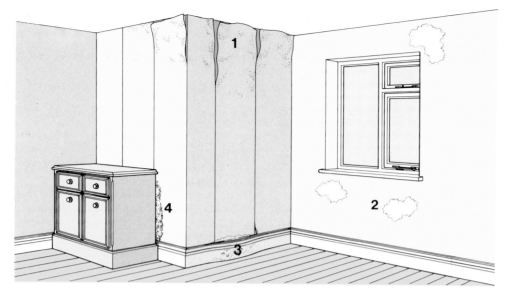

The classic symptoms of damp include:
(1) stained or peeling wallpaper,
(2) salt deposits (efflorescence) on painted or bare plastered walls,
(3) swollen or blistered painted woodwork,
(4) black mould in badly ventilated areas or behind furniture.

As with the outside of the house, when checking the inside it helps if you make a rough sketch plan of each room and note potential trouble spots.

In some places the symptoms of damp may be obvious (see above) – as may the cause once you know where to look. But it's areas where the damp lies unseen that frequently cause the most problems. In particular, be sure to check:
■ Behind large cupboards or wardrobes – move them away from the wall if possible.
■ Behind areas of boxing-in – remove panels wherever convenient and shine in a torch to inspect.
■ Beneath wooden floors – lift a few boards and shine in a torch; often a musty damp smell is immediately obvious.
■ Around plumbing fittings and (in the loft) storage tanks – remove the bath panel to check the all-important seal around the bath rim.

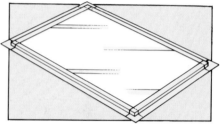

Check for a damp solid floor by taping down a piece of glass and leaving it for a few days. If the glass mists up after this time, there's damp present.

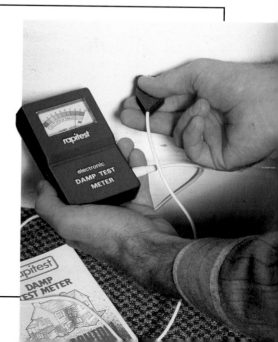

Lift floorboards to check a wooden ground floor. The 'sleeper' walls supporting the joists should have DPCs above them – but these are often missing in older houses.

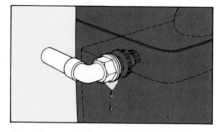

Faulty seals around bathroom fittings are a common source of dampness – often only revealed when enough water has collected to bring down the ceiling below!

Overflow pipe connections may have lain untested for years – only to leak undetected as soon as a ballvalve fault occurs. Check tanks for leaks too.

USING A DAMP METER

If your house is old or prone to damp problems, a damp meter could prove a worthwhile investment. The latest battery powered models cost no more than a cheap electric drill, and come with a comprehensive instruction booklet.

The meter has a pair of sharp prongs which you insert into different surfaces – walls, woodwork and so on – during the course of making your damp checks. The dial on the meter then registers whether the moisture level in the surface is safe, in need of some attention, or a problem that needs urgent action.

When using a damp meter:
■ Make sure the prongs penetrate any decorative coverings, or you won't get a true reading.
■ Hygroscopic salts in a wall may produce an 'Urgent action' reading, even though the wall may appear dry. But since these salts may cause damp themselves in the future, they need attention before too long.

When using a damp meter on a wall (see right), make sure the prongs are pushed well in.

REPAIRING DAMP PATCHES IN WALLS

Damp patches on walls are unsightly and unhealthy, so it makes sense to repair them as soon as possible. But first, and most important, you need to pinpoint and cure what is actually causing the damp.

Penetrating damp

If the patches are *penetrating damp*, resulting from a leak or an outside structural fault, they should begin to recede as soon as the fault is repaired. You can speed the drying out process by clearing away all nearby furniture and other fixtures, and then stripping the decorations back to dry plaster.

After a week or so, check the condition of the plaster.

If the plaster is sound, you should be able to do a 'cosmetic' patching job once it has dried fully – see *Curing mild dampness* overleaf. Salt deposits (efflorescence) may appear in the meantime, but this is normal; if possible, leave them until they stop spreading.

If the plaster is ruined – either because the dampness has turned it soft and crumbly, or because it has 'blown' (parted) from the wall, it will need to be chopped back to sound material and replaced (see *Patching damp-soaked plaster* overleaf). The same applies to a patch of **hygroscopic damp**, where the plaster has become laden with water-attracting salts (usually the result of a previous damp fault).

Rising damp

Where the damp patches are caused by rising damp, it's often less easy to cure the dampness at source. Some faults will be obvious, such as bridging of the damp-proof course. Others may be less so, but should still be traceable – for example, a localized damp patch in a cavity wall suggests that the DPC has been punctured at or around this point.

The real problems tend to occur in older houses where the brickwork has become porous with age and the DPC (if there is one) has ceased to be fully effective. This often results in damp patches all over a wall, usually coinciding with weak points in the brickwork. A badly installed chemical DPC will produce similar symptoms.

Faced by rising damp patches, you have two choices.

Have a new DPC installed. In this case all the affected walls must be stripped and replastered – preferably from floor to ceiling. Depending on the severity of the problem, a damp-proof 'skin' may have to be added between the brickwork and the new plaster.

All this is expensive and highly disruptive, but it should cure the problem once and for all.

Patch up the dampness as and when it occurs, as you would for penetrating damp. This is not a long-term answer – no matter how well you do the job, the damp will return in time. But if the dampness isn't too extensive, it's a much less disruptive solution than full-scale replastering.

Most of the special compounds used for interior damp-proofing are chlorinated rubber- or solvent-based, and give off strong fumes. Unlike dust, wearing a face mask is no protection – so **never** apply any waterproofing compound in a confined or unventilated space. Open all windows, and stop at the first sign of dizziness. Don't smoke or allow naked flames near the working area.

Make sure, too, that you have a supply of the appropriate cleaner or solvent close to hand. If the waterproofer gets on your skin, wipe off with a rag soaked in the cleaner and wash immediately.

CURING MILD DAMPNESS

Begin by stripping off all traces of old decorations. If the wall is painted, and the paint has bubbled or flaked, scrape it back to a sound surface with a paint scraper and then sand to 'feather' the edges.

If possible, remove any joinery mouldings – skirtings, architraves – around the affected area. You won't be able to seal the wall completely if they are left in place, and they may have been affected by the damp in any case.

The area of wall behind the mouldings may have to be made good, in which case see *Patching damp-soaked plaster*.

Trade tip
Stir it up

❦ *Interior waterproofer separates far more readily than ordinary paint, and won't be effective unless thoroughly stirred. If you use a stick, work it right down to the bottom of the can and keep stirring until the waterproofer is completely uniform in colour.*

Alternatively, do what I do and use a paint stirring attachment for an electric drill. ❧

Surface preparation

Brush off any traces of dust and efflorescence. If there are signs of black mould, wash down the wall with a solution of one part bleach to four of water (or use a proprietary fungicide) and leave to dry.

Apply the waterproofer, following the manufacturer's recommendations on coating and drying times. Two coats are normally sufficient, but leave up to 24 hours between them otherwise the second coat may cause the first to blister. Coverage is in the region of 5–6 sq m (6–7 sq yd) per litre per coat.

After treatment, touch in any 'missed' areas where the old surface still shows through. The wall can be repainted or papered as desired.

Tools and materials: Interior waterproofer, decorating preparation tools, old wall-size paintbrush, brush cleaner (for removing spills).

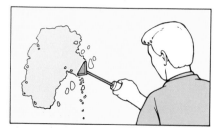

1 Scrape old flaking paint back to a sound edge using a paint scraper. Sand the edges of the stripped patch so that they don't show through.

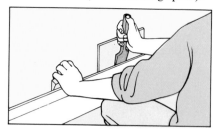

2 Prise off nearby mouldings with a bolster, using a block of wood as a lever. Check the back of the mouldings for rot and replace if necessary.

3 Having prepared the surface, apply waterproofer with broad sweeps, working on a square metre (or yard) at a time. Make sure you don't miss any patches.

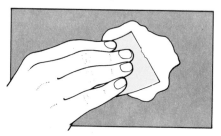

4 After recoating, fill any hollows and smooth over old paint edges with fine surface filler. Sand down, but avoid puncturing the coating.

USING DAMP-PROOF FOIL

This is applied in much the same way as a foil wallcovering – ie by pasting the wall, not the covering itself – and is ideal for use in confined spaces.

Prepare as for interior waterproofer, brushing off all signs of efflorescence and killing any mould patches. Some kits also recommend that the wall is sized first, using a brushed-on coat of the special adhesive.

Cut the strips with scissors to avoid tearing, allowing the usual overlap for trimming. Plumb a line on the wall, then 'paste' with the adhesive.

Hang the first strip against the line and trim in the normal way. On subsequent strips, overlap the joints by around 12mm (½") and brush in more of the adhesive to seal them. Finally, smooth down with a damp cloth.

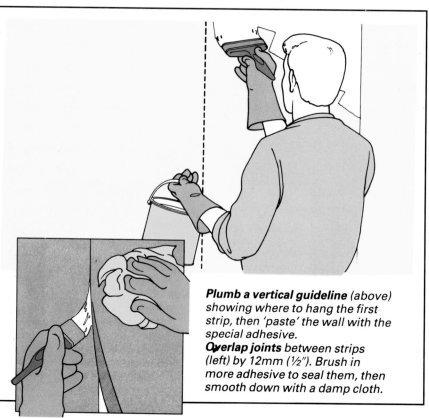

Plumb a vertical guideline *(above) showing where to hang the first strip, then 'paste' the wall with the special adhesive.*

Overlap joints *between strips (left) by 12mm (½"). Brush in more adhesive to seal them, then smooth down with a damp cloth.*

PATCHING DAMP-SOAKED PLASTER

If the plaster is soft and crumbly or has 'blown' from the wall and sounds hollow when you tap it, you have no choice but to hack it out and repair the patch.

Obviously, the smaller the patch the easier this will be. But there is no point in creating several small patches close together, or leaving some unsound plaster on the wall because the patch looks like getting too large. Generally, the larger and more complete the repair, the greater the chances of success.

Getting prepared

Even a small repair of this type is very messy, so prepare the room as if you were decorating and make sure everything is set up in advance. Bear in mind that the repair may take up to a weekend to complete.

When removing the old plaster, lay dust sheets to catch the debris and close all doors – there may be a lot of dust. Protect yourself, as always when using a bolster, with safety spectacles or goggles and a mask.

What to use

Having removed the old plaster, you patch the brickwork with repair mortar and apply a waterproof coating prior to making good. This can either be a thick, black brush-on liquid membrane (cheaper and easier to apply) or a clear moisture-curing resin (costly, but more effective if applied in sufficient coats).

When it comes to filling the hole, use a heavyweight bonding plaster such as Sirapite – ordinary repair or ready mixed plasters will quickly absorb any dampness left in the surrounding wall. You can, however, use ready mixed skimming plaster to finish off the repair.

Materials: Dry mixed repair mortar, heavyweight bonding plaster (eg Sirapite), liquid membrane (eg Aquaprufe) or moisture-curing resin (eg Bondaglass G4), ready mixed skimming plaster, sharp sand, solvent for waterproofer.

Tools checklist: Club hammer, bolster, steel float, bucket, mixing stick, old piece of board, old paintbrush, wire brush, safety spectacles/goggles, face mask.

1 Chop out the area of damaged plaster using a bolster and club hammer. Try to 'undercut' the edges of the patch so that the new plaster can get a grip.

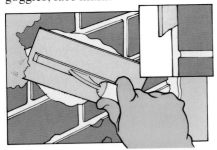

2 Brush away dust from the brickwork, dampen down, then patch with repair mortar to fill any deep holes and leave a reasonably flat surface.

3 When the mortar has dried, apply the first coat of liquid membrane. Work it well in, but take care not to splash the surrounding plaster.

4 Recoat as directed. As the final coat dries, sprinkle with clean, sharp sand so that the surface is 'keyed' for the bonding plaster.

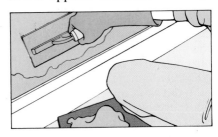

5 Turn out the mixed bonding plaster on to an old board and apply with a steel float. Level off with the surrounding wall using a wooden straightedge.

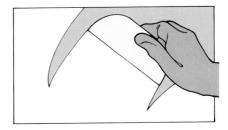

6 The bonding plaster should be just below the surrounding surface. This allows you to finish with a skim of ready mixed plaster and sand smooth.

MOISTURE-CURING RESINS

In serious cases, use a moisture-curing resin compound in preference to brush-on liquid membrane. This comes in one- or two-part form; mix in an old container following the manufacturer's instructions. Like interior waterproofer, the compound gives off strong fumes; make sure the area is well ventilated and avoid breathing the fumes in.

Three to four coats are normally required. Work the first well into the mortar-patched brickwork, then apply subsequent coats as the ones before become just touch-dry. Sprinkle the final coat with sharp sand while still tacky.

You can speed the drying process by warming the patch gently with a fan heater or hair dryer; **don't** use a naked flame.

Moisture-curing resin can be applied directly to the brickwork – as here – but where there are large holes, patch them with mortar first.

EXTERIOR DAMP-PROOFING

If you suspect that the dampness inside the house is caused by porous brickwork on the outside, it makes sense to coat the brickwork with clear silicone-based water repellent at the same time as carrying out any other repairs. On old walls, this is a wise precaution anyway, since even occasional rain splashing can 'reactivate' dampness left inside the masonry and cause efflorescence. Silicone water repellent also helps to prevent badly weathered bricks from deteriorating any further.

Before you start, check the condition of the mortar joints and brickwork following the diagram on the right. Any faults must be put right before the wall is treated.

Applying the repellent

Do this during a dry spell, and at least two days after any rain. To be effective you need to coat the entire wall – which may mean using access equipment. Coverage is around 3–4 sq m (4–5 sq yd) per litre per coat, and one coat is sufficient on all but the most absorbent surfaces.

Tools and materials: Silicone water repellent, soft brush, paint kettle, ladders (maybe). For repairs: dry mixed repair mortar, spare bricks (preferably to match wall), club hammer, bolster, pointing trowel.

Scratch the mortar joints with an old penknife. Areas which crumble must be raked out and repointed using 1:3 dry mixed repair mortar.

Wash off green algae using a fungicide for exterior masonry. Let the wall dry completely before treating.

Fill small holes with 1:3 dry mixed repair mortar.

Chop out damaged bricks with a bolster and replace.

Check the wall for faults before starting.
Apply the repellent from a paint kettle using a wall brush or soft hand broom. Work it well into the brickwork and leave to dry.

PROBLEM SOLVER

Damp around sockets

Channelling electrical cables through walls can weaken the plasterwork's resistance to damp, causing damp patches to appear on or around power sockets – a potentially very dangerous situation.

In this case, turn off the power at the mains before you do anything else.

Unscrew the socket faceplate and disconnect the circuit cables. Then unscrew and prise away the backing box from the wall, and check the cut-out for signs of moisture.

If the damp follows the line of one of the cables, gently ease this away from the wall too, chipping off the plaster or filler covering it as you go.

Curing the problem If the plaster appears sound and the damage is limited, simply coat the socket cut-out and cable channel with waterproofer.

But if the damp extends into the surrounding plaster, repair the entire area as if it were a single patch. Afterwards, re-run the cable along the surface of the wall using plastic mini-trunking and convert the socket to a surface mounted type with plastic backing box.

Dampness from floors

Damp caused by a punctured or missing damp-proof membrane (DPM) in a solid floor often continues up the wall. Parts of the floor which have been channelled for pipes or cables are particularly suspect.

In this case, repair the wall and floor together. Hack away a margin of screed along the affected wall and continue your damp-proofing treatment down as far as DPM level.

If there is no DPM, apply a waterproofing treatment to the surface of the floor and carry the wall treatment on to this.

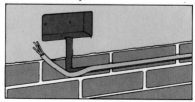

Dampness around sockets can often be cured simply by coating the cut-out and cable channel with waterproofer . . .

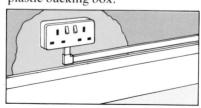

. . . but in severe cases, repair the entire area as if it were a large damp patch and refit the cable and socket on the surface.

Where damp from a solid floor has passed into the walls, extend the damp-proofing treatment down below the level of the screed.

REPAIRING ROTTEN WOODWORK

Rot is the most common problem affecting woodwork in damp climates – and left to its own devices, the structural decay it causes can have expensive consequences. Softwood is more susceptible than hardwood, but either can be affected.

What is rot?
Wood rot is caused by fungal spores circulating in the air which settle on the timber and use any dampness present to germinate. The fungus then decomposes the wood fibres to obtain food, and eventually destroys the timber completely.

There are two main types of rot fungus – *wet rot* and *dry rot* – and it's vital to know the difference before carrying out any repairs.
Wet rot is the more common of the two, and only affects wood which is actually damp.

Once wet rot has taken hold, it can be repaired by patching in new wood or using a rot cure system. At the same time the surrounding area must be treated with preservative, and steps taken to make sure the timber doesn't become damp again.
Dry rot is far more serious: although the fungus requires damp,

warm conditions to germinate, once established it can spread like wildfire through dry, perfectly sound timber – and even through masonry. Also, unlike wet rot, it doesn't die when the affected wood is removed; the entire area must be treated.

If you have even the slightest suspicion of dry rot (see below), it's worth arranging a damp survey through a preservation specialist. Treating dry rot is nearly always a professional job, and it doesn't pay to take chances – especially where structural timbers are at risk.

WET AND DRY ROT – THE TELL-TALE SIGNS

The symptoms of rot are easily spotted and you can test the extent of the damage by using a bradawl or the point of a knife. Sound wood will resist the point; on decayed wood it will go in easily.

Deciding whether the problem is caused by wet rot or dry rot may be more difficult: use the following checklist as a guide.

Wet *or* dry rot
- Affected areas easily penetrated.
- Affected areas produce a different sound when tapped.
- Outward warping on panelling, skirtings etc (on its own, this also can be due to natural shrinkage).
- Deep cracks across the grain (most common with dry rot but can appear with wet rot).

Wet rot only
- Timber feels wet and spongy.
- Paint is lifting from discoloured patches of wood, possibly with white or grey fungal strands below.

Dry rot only
- White, yellowish or rust red fungal growth evident on surface of wood and nearby masonry.
- Timber dry and brittle, often discoloured light brown.
- Characteristic deep cracks, with the wood split into 'cubes'.

Other fungal problems
You may find black spots (due to damp mould) or blue-grey marks (due to a fungus called *sapstain*) on the surface of otherwise sound timber. Neither presents any

Wet rot (above) is more common but less serious than *dry rot* (right), which under the right conditions can spread rapidly through walls and sound timber.

danger to the wood, though mould could warn of impending damp.

Where appearance is important, treat with a decorating fungicide (though this may not remove deep sapstain marks completely).

KEEPING ROT AT BAY

Prevention is always better than cure, so save yourself expensive and complicated repair work by doing an annual check on timber which is exposed to damp. Late summer is a good time for this: dry weather often causes joints to shrink and paint to crack; and if there is a problem, the weather should be good enough to allow you to fix it before the rainy spell starts.

Windows and doors should be checked to see that the paint, putty and joints are in good condition. Make good any damage and refinish to stop water penetrating the wood.

Fascia boards and other exposed roof timbers need regular repainting. Leaky gutters may cause local rot. **Fences, etc** should be brushed down to remove mould, moss and lichen. Apply preservative every 2–5 years. If the wood has been creosoted. renew this every 2–5 years.

WINDOWS: THE TROUBLE SPOTS

Gaps around frames allow moisture to reach unprotected timber. Seal with frame sealant.

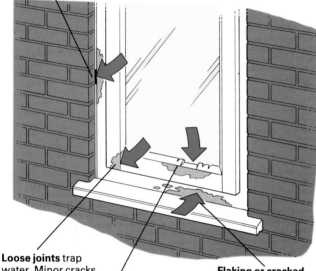

Loose joints trap water. Minor cracks can be filled with flexible filler before repainting or varnishing.

Cracked putty lets water penetrate. Rake out and renew.

Flaking or cracked paint provides no defence against moisture. Rub down and repaint.

DOORS: THE TROUBLE SPOTS

Splash back off the doorstep causes paint to flake on the front of the frame.

Gaps around frames allow moisture to reach unprotected timber. Seal with frame sealant.

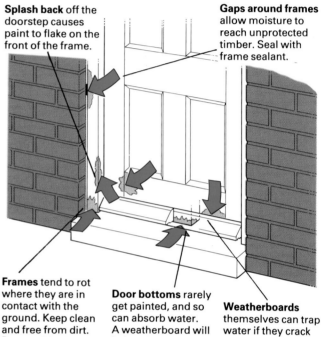

Frames tend to rot where they are in contact with the ground. Keep clean and free from dirt. Renew old paint after treating bare wood with preservative or rot killer.

Door bottoms rarely get painted, and so can absorb water. A weatherboard will help to keep this area dry; prime or varnish the back before fitting.

Weatherboards themselves can trap water if they crack loose; fill behind with flexible filler.

PRESERVATIVE TREATMENTS

Preservative treatments are a sensible precaution for any wood which is particularly at risk from rot, whether on a repair or a new project.

Pre-treated timber

Treated timber is rather more expensive than ordinary timber (around 15–20%), but worth using for outdoor work and wherever wood is in contact with the ground. There are various processes for applying the preservative under pressure to ensure deep penetration; trade names include 'Tanalized' and 'Celcure'. Cut ends and holes must be given a further coat of preservative fluid.

Preservative fluid

To prevent rot from starting in new or existing sound timber, apply timber preservative. This is made in a range of colours, including clear for use under paintwork. Some makers provide different formulations for use on hardwood items like doors and window frames, and for cedar sheds and garden furniture.

On existing timber, remove any dirt or mould and treat with fungicide or a solution of one part bleach to six of water. Allow to dry thoroughly.

Sand new planed timber with fine grade glasspaper to help the preservative soak in.

Either brush on liberally, applying two or three coats, or soak the timber for better penetration. Fence posts need soaking for at least an hour to the depth they will be sunk.

Rot killer fluid

Where wet rot has caused decay, an application of rot killer helps to ensure that it does not recur. After cutting away the damaged wood, brush or spray three coats of the rot killer fluid on to the surface of both the existing timber and any patches. If it is possible to dip the parts in the fluid for ten minutes, this provides even better protection.

The fluid can also be used on new timber as a preservative, in which case two coats are sufficient. If timber is in contact with the ground, it should be soaked in the fluid for between an hour and one day.

Treated timber can be given any type of surface finish once it has dried.

Preservative pellets

These are part of a rot cure system, but can also be used on sound wood to prevent rot. Insert them at 50mm (2″) intervals in high-risk areas, and cover with resin-based filler (see opposite).

USING A ROT CURE SYSTEM

Rot cure systems consist of chemicals designed to stop the rot and preserve the existing timber, plus resin-based filler to make good the damage. The result should be at least as strong as the existing wood.

A big advantage of rot cure systems is that they can cope with complicated frames where replacing the timber would be difficult, if not impossible. But while they are excellent for patching, you cannot expect them to replace structural timber – for example, if the whole corner of a window has rotted.

Making the repair
Start by removing all the decayed timber, although it is not necessary to go right back to sound wood.

1 Pull or cut away decayed wood fibres (see left) to leave a reasonably firm surface. Strip back any paint or varnish and allow damp patches to dry out.

Then brush on a wood hardening solution which binds the remaining loose fibres. One type incorporates a preservative treatment to prevent further decay; with other systems this is done separately (see below).

The damaged area is then built up with quick-setting filler. Once this is hardened, it can be shaped and painted just like wood.

Preserving the wood
Systems which don't include preservative treatment at an earlier stage then incorporate a further process, which consists of drilling small holes around the affected area and inserting pellets of solid preservative. Then cap with wood filler and finish off.

2 Brush on the clear hardening fluid, applying several coats to make sure it penetrates the area fully. Cover to protect from the rain and leave to dry.

3 Mix the resin filler and apply with a filling knife. To reinforce deep holes, drive screws into the wood below leaving the heads projecting.

4 When set, use a shaper plane or file to carve the filler to shape. Sand smooth, then prime and repaint to match the surrounding timber.

With another system, you finish off the treatment by drilling holes for preservative pellets at 50mm (2″) intervals into the sound wood around the repair.

Insert the pellets and push them well below the surface. (Be sure to wear rubber gloves when handling them as they contain strong fungicide.)

Cap the holes with small amounts of the resin filler and sand smooth when dry. The pellets are only activated if the wood becomes moist again.

PATCHING WOODWORK

Patching the damaged area with new wood is rather harder than using a rot cure system, but it is the only solution where:

■ The wood is varnished or stained.
■ You are repairing a frame which has been weakened by decay.

The repairs shown below are typical. In all cases, use wood which matches the original timber in both its appearance and dimensions. If you are dealing with a shaped part of a window or door frame, see if you can buy a matching moulded section to cut down the amount of reshaping required.

Treat the existing timber and any new patches with preservative to prevent further decay. Refinish the area as soon as possible.

1 **To repair the foot of a door frame,** saw through it about 75mm (3") above the decayed area. Make the cut square across the wood and sloped downwards at 45°.

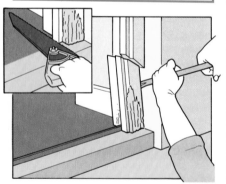

2 Prise the cut section away from the wall – it may be held by nails or screws. If you find it is set into the sill, saw off square across the bottom.

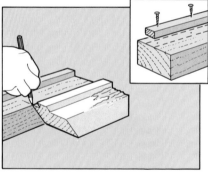

3 Cut a patch from matching timber using the old piece as a pattern. If you can't match the section exactly, join two pieces to make up the right shape.

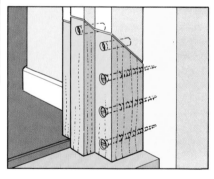

4 Treat with preservative and screw to drilled and plugged holes in the wall. Reinforce the sloping joint with screws or dowels, then fill any gaps.

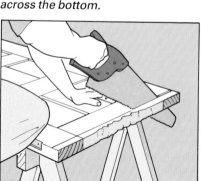

1 **To repair the base** of a door or opening window frame, remove it from its hinges. Saw along a line parallel to the bottom and above the rotted area.

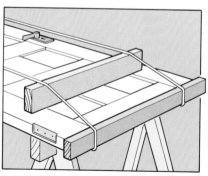

2 Cut the new section slightly oversize and treat both parts with preservative. When dry, apply waterproof woodworking adhesive and clamp together.

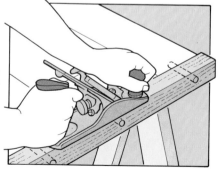

3 Reinforce by inserting glued dowels through both parts (or screws, providing they are well recessed into the timber). Plane to the exact size and rehang.

BUILDING A STUD PARTITION WALL

Constructing a timber-framed *stud partition* wall is generally the easiest way to divide one room into two semi-permanently. Unlike a solid block wall, it is light enough not to need extensive loadbearing support; it is also fairly easy to remove should your space requirements change again at a later date.

From a DIY point of view, the great advantages of stud partitions are that they require no great skill to build, and use cheap, readily available materials. The simplest method (shown here) is to use taper-edge plasterboard and simply fill the joints before decoration; an alternative is to use square-edged sheets and give the whole wall a thin surface skim of plaster.

ANATOMY OF A STUD PARTITION

Head plate – a single length of timber screwed to ceiling joists and used to locate tops of studs.

Studs – vertical lengths of timber nailed between the head and sole plates at both ends and at 400mm (16") intervals.

Cladding – plasterboard or similar sheet material nailed to each side of the framework. Using standard sheet sizes, the edges of panels should fall neatly over the centres of studs spaced at 400mm (16").

Joints. The V-shaped notches formed by taper-edged plasterboard can be covered with paper tape and special joint filler.

Noggins – horizontal lengths of timber nailed between the studs to brace the frame and provide support for the edges of the cladding panels.

Sole plate – a single length of timber nailed or screwed to floor to locate bottoms of studs.

400mm (16")

1220mm (4')

....Shopping List....

Plan the layout and constructional details of the partition (see overleaf), then measure up and draw a sketch of the wall showing all the frame members and their relevant dimensions. List the materials on the drawing, then work out the quantities.

Timber for the framework is cheap *sawn softwood* rather than planed. Minimum size is 75×50mm (3×2"), but for a substantial partition that may have to take wall-hung shelves, cupboards or a washbasin, increase this to 100×50mm (4×2").

Cladding You can clad the frame with virtually any sheet material, but *plasterboard* is generally the easiest to fix and finish. It is also one of the cheapest.

For simple filled joints, use 12.5mm thick *taper-edged* board. This is commonly available in ceiling-height 2440×1220mm (8×4') sheets, though half sheets and smaller sizes may be available for dealing with small gaps.

Joinery mouldings You'll need softwood skirting moulding to finish the bottom of the wall on both sides, plus lining boards and architrave moulding to finish any openings you have to make (see overleaf). Try to match existing mouldings where possible.

Finish the joints at the ceiling with stick-on plastic or plaster *coving*, which will be sold with the appropriate adhesive.

Other materials

■ Galvanized plasterboard nails for fixing the cladding, and 100mm (4") round wire nails for the frame.

■ 100mm (4") frame fixings or 100mm (4") No.10 countersunk woodscrews (plus suitable wallplugs) for securing the head and sole plates and the end studs.

■ Plasterboard *paper tape* and *joint filler* for covering the joints between boards. (At the same time it's worth buying the special *applicator* and *jointing sponge* sold with them.)

Tools checklist: hammer, drill and bits, screwdrivers, bradawl, spirit level, plumbline, filling knife, trimming knife, tape measure, panel saw, chisel and tenon saw (possibly).

taper-edged plasterboard

joint filler

sawn softwood

paper tape

plasterboard nails

jointing sponge

PLANNING THE PARTITION

You don't need Building Regulations approval to build a stud partition wall, but there are certain restrictions on how the job is done. For this reason, make sure you consider all of the following points before starting.

■ Will the new rooms formed by the partition both be big enough? Don't forget to allow for the thickness of the wall itself when working out their areas, and make sure the partitioned space is usable. You may have to include a right angle turn in the new wall to ensure this.

■ Both new rooms must have some natural light, unless one or the other is a bathroom or WC. If possible, position the wall to allow for this. Otherwise, you'll have to provide a glazed door or window (see below) so that light can pass from one room to another.

■ Proper ventilation is essential. In a bathroom or WC without windows, you can satisfy the Building Regulations by fitting an automatic extractor fan. In any other 'habitable' room, the Regulations require that the area of openable window in each room must be equal to at least 5% of the room's total floor area. Also, at least part of the opening section must be more than 1.75m

(5'8") from the floor. This could mean changing an existing fixed window to one that can be opened or has a vent.

■ How will you get into the new rooms? Whatever the walls are made of, it's much easier to build a doorway into the new partition (see below) than to cut an opening in an existing wall.

■ Where the floor is wooden, can you gain access to the joists? And are the upstairs ceiling joists accessible too? If the answer is no in either case, you may be restricted on where you can position the new wall (see below).

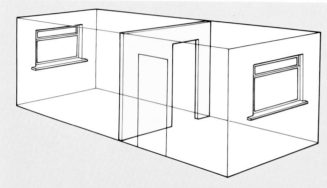

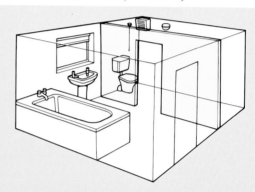

Ideally, the partition should leave more or less equal amounts of natural light and openable window in both the new rooms.

The rules are relaxed, however, in a bathroom/WC: if there is no natural light or ventilation in the new room, fit an automatic extractor fan.

Adding a room 1: a semi-partition with open arch (left) makes it possible to create a self-contained washing/dressing room within a fairly small bedroom without either appearing cramped.

Adding a room 2: partitioning a double windowed room (above) solves the problem of where to put a new arrival in the family. The old room is easily restored if needs change at a later date.

CONSTRUCTIONAL DETAILS

Ideally, a stud partition wall built over a suspended wooden floor should run at right angles to the joists to spread the load.

If it must run parallel to the joists, you have a choice: either sit it directly over a joist (which may be easier – see Tip), or lift the surrounding floorboards and fix extra trimmers across the existing joists as shown right. The trimmers should be the same size – and spaced at the same intervals – as the joists themselves. Fix them using metal *joist-to-joist hangers*.

Use the same method where the head plate of the new wall falls between two joists, but space the trimmers at 600mm (2') centres.

Making openings

Door and window openings should be made to suit standard 'off the shelf' joinery, so choose your door or window first.

There are two methods for framing the opening. One is to fit studs on each side and nail the lintel (and sill for a window) between them after cutting housings with a tenon saw and chisel. The other method – costlier but easier – is to support the cross-pieces on short *cripple studs* nailed to the full-height studs. In both cases, wide windows need short *trimming studs* above the lintel and below the sill.

Line the openings with 25mm (1") thick softwood, wide enough to conceal the edges of the cladding.

When measuring up for a door, space the studs at the door width plus an allowance for the thickness of the lining and an extra clearance of 6mm (¼") to allow for hinging.

When measuring up for a window, space the studs to fit the frame plus an allowance for the thickness of the lining. The window is nailed directly to the lined opening.

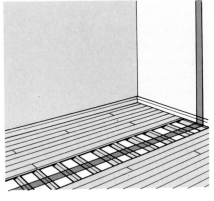

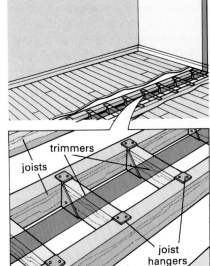

No reinforcement is normally needed if the wall runs at right angles to the floor joists. Where the wall runs parallel, fit trimmers between the joists using metal hangers (inset). Use a similar arrangement where the line of the wall falls between two ceiling joists.

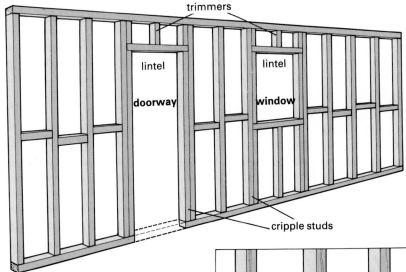

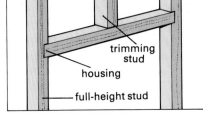

Openings for doors and windows can either be created using cripple studs (above) or by cutting housings for the lintels in the existing studs (inset). With a doorway, the sole plate is cut away after the framework has been nailed together.

Trade tip

Reinforce or not?

❝ One of the trickiest questions facing a builder is whether or not to reinforce a floor joist if a stud wall has to go directly on top of it.

By and large, if the wall is normal height, uses a light frame, and won't have anything heavy fixed to it **and** the joist itself measures at least 100×50mm (4×2"), there should be no need to reinforce. But if the wall is likely to be heavier, or the joist is lighter, you'd be advised to err on the safe side.

Providing reinforcement means coach-bolting a new joist of the same size to the existing one. It should be supported at each end in the same way. ❞

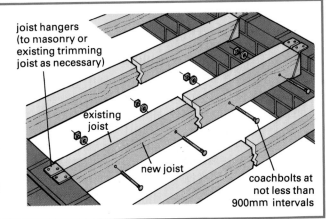

BUILDING THE FRAMEWORK

Start by doing any strengthening work necessary on the floor and ceiling joists. You shouldn't have to lift every floorboard to fit trimmers, but there is bound to be some disruption and you should clear the room as far as possible.

Afterwards, mark the trimmer positions on the floor and ceiling, and replace the boards. Make sure the floorboards are firmly fixed and reasonably level along the full length of the new wall.

If you don't need to fit trimmers to a wooden floor, just lift a few boards to find the joist positions, then establish where the ceiling joists are by knocking with your fist until you hear a dull sound, then poking with a bradawl.

Setting out

Measure and mark the positions of the head and sole plates and end studs on the floor, wall and ceiling. Use a spirit level or plumbline to mark the verticals, so you can be sure the head plate will sit directly above the sole plate.

This is also the time to decide what to do about any skirtings or other mouldings fixed to the adjoining walls (see Problem Solver).

Frame assembly

Assembly of the frame starts with the sole plate, which can be nailed to a wooden floor or screwed to a concrete one. Follow by screwing on the head plate and end studs, then nail on the studs and noggins.

In general, studs should be spaced equally at 400–450mm (16–18″) intervals (and to suit the positions of any openings) with noggins fixed in a line 1200mm (4′) from the floor. However, you should work out the actual positions so that the edges of each plasterboard sheet fall over the centre of a frame member. Most likely, this will mean fixing an extra stud or two to support part of a sheet. In a high ceilinged room, you may also have to fit an extra row of noggins.

Mark the stud positions on the sole plate. Then measure each stud individually and cut them slightly oversize, so they can be wedged in place while you nail them.

1 Having cleared the room and removed any floorcoverings, inspect the floor. If it is wood, lift a few boards to check the joist positions and spacing.

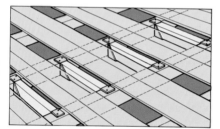

2 If the wall has to run between joists, lift boards at intervals across the room so that you can fix trimmers across the joists using metal hangers.

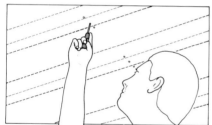

3 Probe the ceiling with a bradawl to locate the joists above and mark their positions. If necessary, fit trimmers as for the floor joists.

4 Taking into account the positions of the floor and ceiling joists, mark out the position of the partition on the floor, walls and ceiling.

5 Having removed any mouldings, cut the sole plate to size and nail or screw it to the floor, except in doorways. (Over a joist fix at 400mm (16″) centres.

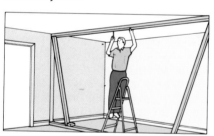

6 Cut the head plate to size and prop in place as shown. Check it is aligned with the marks on the wall and ceiling, then drill and screw to the ceiling joists.

7 Cut the end studs to fit exactly between the two plates, drill clearance holes, then drill and plug the wall. Screw the end studs in position.

8 Cut intermediate studs about 3mm (⅛″) oversize so they're a tight fit between the plates. Wedge in place, check they sit plumb, then skew-nail both ends.

9 Cut and fit the noggins. Nail through the next stud into one end, then skew-nail the other end to the previous stud to fix the noggins in line.

OPENINGS AND CORNERS

Assemble the frames for openings as you build the wall, either by housing the lintels in the studs or by fitting cripple studs.

If you have to turn a corner, simply butt the separate sole and head plates against each other, then fit three studs at each turn.

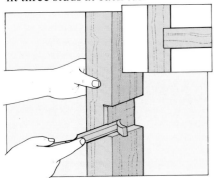

Cut housings for a lintel using a tenon saw, then pare out the waste with a broad woodworking chisel. Don't notch the studs by more than half their thickness.

At a doorway, check that the opening framework is secure and make additional fixings where necessary. Then carefully saw off the unwanted section of sole plate.

At a corner, use three studs as shown to provide adequate support for the cladding panels on each side of the angles and to strengthen the structure.

PROBLEM SOLVER

Dealing with mouldings

There are three ways to deal with skirtings and other such obstructions on adjoining walls.

The simplest method is to cut the stud into sections to fit above (and below) the moulding and to fit a short section of stud over the moulding itself where this is possible. The disadvantage is that you may find it difficult to achieve a neat joint between the existing and new sections of moulding.

Another method is to notch the studs around the mouldings, if they have a reasonably simple profile and don't protrude far. The same disadvantage applies.

The third method is to remove sections of moulding so that the studs, and ideally the cladding, fit against the wall. You may be able to do this in situ, as shown, or you may have to prise off the whole length, then refit it after you have constructed the wall. This way you can mitre the cut ends for a neat finish.

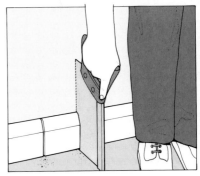

Scribe and notch the end studs to fit around a narrow skirting. On a heavier skirting, cut out a section using a tenon saw.

Running services

If you need to fit sockets or plumbing fittings on the new wall, run the pipes and cables while you're building the frame so that they can be hidden in the cavity.

Cables and supply pipes can simply be fed through suitably sized holes bored in the centres of the studs. For a basin waste pipe, cut 60mm (2¼″) deep notches in the studs, and cut housings for lengths of 50×25mm (2×1″) batten to cover the notches once the pipe is in place. (Don't do this unless you are using 100×50mm – 4×2″ – studs).

Make up mountings for socket backing boxes, basin brackets

and so on from offcuts of frame timber and plywood. There's no hard and fast rule on how to fix them, though if the mountings are to take any weight they should be screwed to the studs.

Run any pipes and cables within the framework, and fit backing panels for socket outlets (below). Do not run a basin waste through the studs unless they are the 100×50mm (4×2″) size.

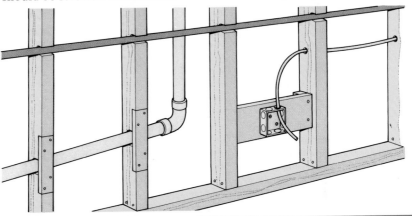

CLADDING THE FRAME

In most houses, full-size sheets of plasterboard nailed on end using a footlifter (see right, and Tip) can go straight on the frame without cutting. There will be a small gap at the bottom, to be concealed with skirting later.

If the ceiling is lower than the height of a full sheet, simply cut the sheets to size leaving a 25mm (1") gap for lifting. Where the ceiling is high, however, you may find it easier to nail the sheets lengthways. In this case, nail the upper row first, ensuring the edges are supported on a row of noggins.

In all cases, it's also worth checking that you won't be left with awkward gaps to fill around openings and at the end of the wall. Sheets are easily cut down, but they must be supported by frame members on all sides; you may have to nail on extra noggins to ensure this.

Cutting and fixing

The easiest way to make straight cuts in plasterboard is to score a line with a trimming knife, snap the board over a timber straightedge, then cut through the paper on the other side. If you need to make shaped cuts, mark out both sides and score with a trimming knife, then cut the board using an old panel saw.

Nail the sheets using plasterboard nails – spaced at 100mm (4") around the edges, 150mm (6") elsewhere. The heads must go below the surface.

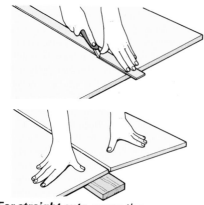

For straight cuts, score the plasterboard with a trimming knife and snap over a wooden straightedge. Then turn over and cut through the other side.

FINISHING THE WALL

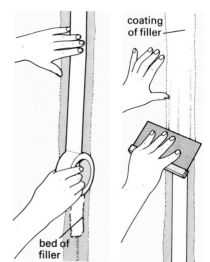

Cover taper joints with strips of paper tape bedded in filler. Press well down and spread more filler over the top. Then feather the edges with a plastic applicator or squeegee and buff with a jointing sponge.

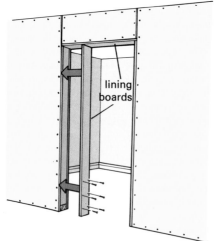

Line openings with boards cut to finish flush with the edges of the plasterboard. Nail them to the lintel and the studs. If you are not fitting architraves to conceal the joint, fill gaps flush with the boards.

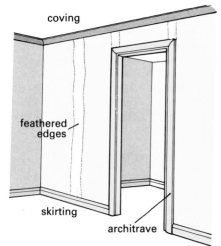

Finish the top of the wall with stick-on plastic or plaster coving, mitred at the corners. **Cover the gap at the bottom** – and finish any openings – with softwood skirting and architrave mouldings, nailed to the frame.

CARPENTRY

THE RIGHT WOOD FOR THE JOB

Whatever sort of carpentry work you're doing – whether it's putting up shelves, boxing in pipework, or repairing a window – the job starts with choosing suitable lengths of timber. Wood, in one form or another, is among the most basic of all DIY materials.

This section is about softwood, the least expensive, most common and easily worked form of solid timber. Hardwood is much costlier and has far more specialist uses. Man-made boards such as plywood, chipboard and hardboard, are covered on pages 197-200.

What is softwood?

The term softwood does not refer to the wood's hardness but to the way it grows – softwood covers any timber from trees with needles and cones. These are generally quick-growing, with pronounced rings at seasonal intervals – they grow much faster in summer.

When the tree has been felled and stripped of its bark it is converted into usable timber. The usual method is *slash-sawing*, where slices are cut right across the trunk. This exposes the growth rings to produce a sharply angled grain (which increases the chance of warping), while the ends of any branches appear as knots. A costlier method called *quarter sawing* results in a more even grain.

Before use, the wood is dried in the open air or in a kiln. This removes much of the moisture, although a fair amount (around 20%) is left, and in fact the moisture content varies according to the humidity of the surrounding air.

Below Slash sawing (left) is more economical, but quarter sawing (right) produces better timber.

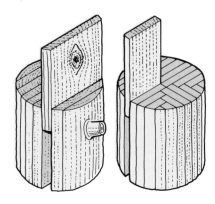

KNOW YOUR TIMBER

Pine A common name for several types of timber. Usually European redwood (also called deal or Scots pine), you may also find spruce (sometimes called white deal). Grain is coarse, and the wood is often very knotty. Spruce is lighter than redwood, but both darken with age.

Fir Also called British Columbian pine, Oregon pine, Douglas fir. Stronger than pine (but prone to split) and, as the trees are larger, is straight grained and knot-free. Useful for structural work, window frames and interior joinery.

Parana pine Widely used for interior joinery, such as stairs. Parana pine is available in large boards with an even texture and is often free of blemishes such as knots – but can be prone to warping or splitting as it dries out. Pale colour with darker spots along grain.

Cedar (Western Red Cedar). Contains natural preservative oils so is widely used for fences, sheds etc. The oils attack steel fittings so use brass or plated instead. Knot-free with a close, straight grain, it resists warping well and withstands heat (allowing it to be used near radiators). Has a warm, reddish brown colour, but does not take varnish well – use a cedar preservative.

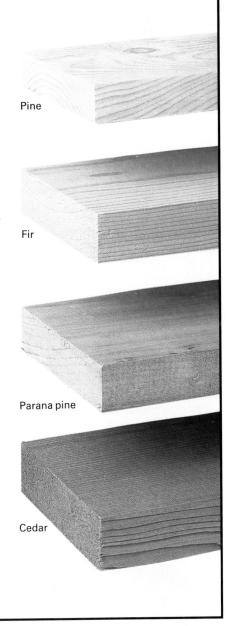

Pine

Fir

Parana pine

Cedar

TIMBER SIZES

Softwood logs are cut into a range of standard dimensions between 6mm and 300mm, although most shops only carry the more popular sizes.

Timber is supplied in two forms. *Sawn* timber is cheaper, and is used

Sawn timber *is closer to its quoted (nominal) size than planed, because some wood is lost during machining*

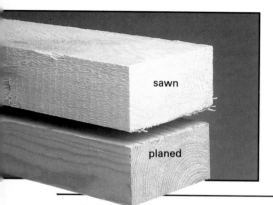

for rough or concealed work where appearance isn't important. *Planed* ('prepared') timber is for finished work that is to be painted, stained or varnished. Most planed timber is smoothed on all four sides (called PAR, for 'Planed All Round') although you may occasionally find only two or three finished surfaces.

Timber sizes can be confusing. Few suppliers give the exact measurements but use a *nominal* size based on the original dimensions. Some wood is wasted when sawing, and even more during planing. So, for example, nominal 50mm is usually about 47mm sawn and 44mm planed.

Also, although metric dimensions are supposed to be used in the UK, these are virtually equivalents of Imperial measurements and many people still say '10 feet of 2 by 1' rather than '3 metres of 50 by 25'.

BUYING TIMBER

The best buys depend on what you are after, and how much you want. A specialist timber merchant should have a far wider selection if you are after unusual sizes or a specific type of wood. This is also your best bet if you need timber machined to size, although a few superstores do offer a cutting service. For small pieces, a timber merchant is more likely to sell you what you need since most carry a stock of short offcuts.

On the other hand, if all you want is a few lengths of battening then the nearest DIY store, superstore or builder's merchant will probably all have what you need at more or less the same price. Also, superstores often sell bundles of common sizes (for example, twenty 1.8m lengths of 25×25mm) which may work out cheaper if you want a large quantity. There are no rules as to how many may be in a bundle – it varies from supplier to supplier.

Prices are generally calculated on the *total volume* of timber, so a given length of 100×50mm costs roughly twice as much as the same length of 50×50mm and four times as much as 50×25mm. Small sections can cost proportionately more in view of the wastage and extra work involved, and non-standard sizes carry a price premium.

Value for money is harder to assess. If the appearance or strength of the wood is important, it may be worth paying extra to be able to pick sound lengths.

Trade tip

Bargain buys

❛ Where appearance isn't important I often use secondhand softwood – old floorboards, joists, rafters and so on – which is readily obtainable from demolition sites or salvage merchants. Not only is it cheaper than new – it's also thoroughly seasoned, and may even be better quality.

However, almost all secondhand wood has holes in it, and many pieces contain old screws and nails (or even just dirt) which will damage cutting tools. Also, make absolutely sure that there is no evidence of woodworm or rot attack. ❜

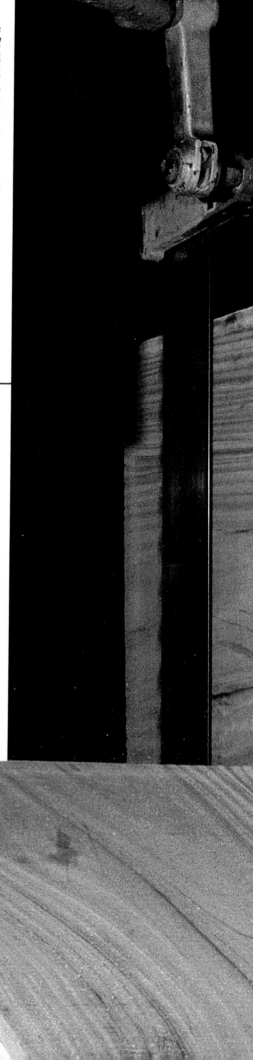

Natural timber *logs are converted into usable timber at the sawmill. After sawing into planks which are left to season, the rough-sawn timber may be planed smooth.*

STANDARD SOFTWOOD SIZES

BOARDS

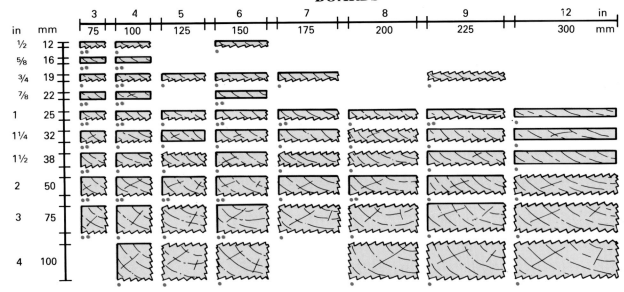

BATTENS

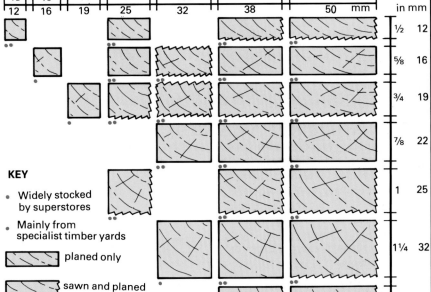

Based on surveys of suppliers, these tables show commonly available sizes of sawn and planed solid softwood. They also show which are likely to be stocked by DIY superstores, and which are generally only available at timber merchants.

All sizes are *nominal* and Imperial measures are approximate. Smaller sections are sometimes sold, but these are covered separately under *Wooden mouldings*. Wide planks of softwood strips, glued together come under *Choosing man-made boards* (pages 197-200).

Common uses

50×25mm Shelf bearer, wardrobe frame, slatted shelf, wall batten
25×25mm Lightweight shelf bearer, batten support for boxing-in
100×50mm sawn Stud partition wall
50×50–100×100mm Table legs
75×19–100×32mm Table frame
19×19–38×38mm Coffee table legs
32×19–75×19mm Coffee table frame
75×19–150×19mm Plinth
100×19–300×25mm Shelf

KEY

- Widely stocked by superstores
· Mainly from specialist timber yards

planed only

sawn and planed

sawn only

Below *The standard lengths for softwood start at 1.8m and go up in steps of 300mm (to a rare maximum of 6.3m). Many stores only stock a selection of the shorter lengths, up to a maximum of 3.0m.*

Timber faults

Timber is a natural material, and varies in quality, but its condition also depends on how well it is stored. As wastage can be costly, it is worth finding a supplier who will let you check for any of the faults described below.

Knots There are two types of knots, both harder than the wood around them.

Live knots are the result of cutting through the ends of growing branches. They can be a decorative feature and shouldn't affect the strength of the wood too much. However, they need to be sealed with *knotting* before painting because they can ooze sap which stains the paint.

Dead knots are old branches which have a dark ring of bark around them. They are weak points, prone to fall out.

Splitting Also called *checks* or *shakes,* splits can occur in the drying process. Normally you have to saw the wood short of the split before it can be used.

Compression shakes are cracks across the grain caused by damage when the tree is felled. Affected timber is weakened.

Fungal staining Pine is sometimes stained blue-grey by fungus. This does not affect its strength but is unsightly when varnished and resists paint.

Waney edge The remains of the bark are sometimes left on the edge of the board. This may be intentional, as for rustic fencing, but where it is accidental it has to be planed off before the wood is used, adding to the wastage.

Warping This depends how the timber was cut, dried and stored and may not be apparent when you buy. See below for details on how to avoid later problems.

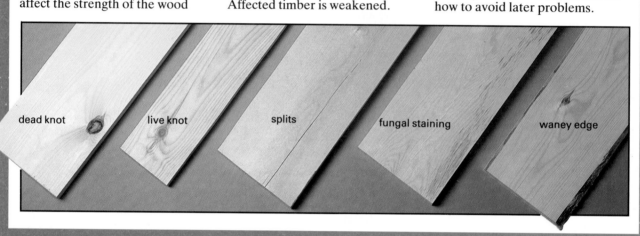

dead knot   live knot   splits   fungal staining   waney edge

CARE AND PREPARATION

Timber which has been stored in the open or an unheated shed contains 15-20% moisture. If the wood is then brought into a centrally heated home it loses around half of this, and as a result shrinks slightly. Such shrinkage is most noticeable through the thickness of the growth rings.

Timber which has the growth rings at a pronounced angle tends to bow more severely as it dries. Timber which has growth rings running squarely throughout its thickness shrinks the same amount, but is less likely to warp, so it's worth looking out for – especially if you are buying wide planks.

Below Look for timber with straight growth rings (bottom) – it's much less likely to warp.

Store wide planks as shown to help air circulate and avoid warping.

Avoid timber which bows sideways (above), from end to end (below)…

…or has a pronounced twist (below); these cannot be cured.

Avoid buying timber which already has a curve across its width, or a pronounced end to end bow or twist (sight along it to check). Such defects are almost impossible to cure, and they are unlikely to improve as the wood dries out.

Storing timber

Wood that is too damp for the room in which it is going to be used will always tend to shrink or warp, no matter how securely it is fixed or how accurately it is cut.

Ideally, keep it in the house for two or three weeks before use to allow it to acclimatize. Stack the timber flat with scrap pieces between to allow air to circulate.

Don't on any account store timber in damp conditions, even for a short time, as this encourages it to absorb moisture and accentuates shrinkage problems when the wood starts to dry out again.

CHOOSING MAN-MADE BOARDS

Solid wood, versatile as it is, has several disadvantages:
- It's expensive.
- It contains faults such as knots.
- Its width is limited by the thickness of the tree.
- It's prone to warping and splits.
- Softwood rots when it is exposed to damp – unless specially treated.

These are some of the reasons why man-made boards were developed. They are all made from wood, so they have many of its properties. But the disadvantages can be controlled by the manufacturing process.
- They can be made in large sheets with an even thickness and no flaws.
- They can be made damp resistant.
- They can be cheaper than the equivalent-sized timber.
- They can have a variety of surfaces, some needing no finishing.

The chart below summarises the main characteristics and uses of different boards. Overleaf are more detailed descriptions of each type.

Modern man-made boards come in all shapes and sizes. This tongued and grooved chipboard flooring is specially designed for loft work.

WHICH BOARD TO USE AT-A-GLANCE

BOARD	USES	STRENGTH	DURABILITY	CUTTING/JOINING	FINISHING
PLYWOOD **Price range** Medium price to expensive depending on grade.	Most constructional jobs from furniture to building material depending on size and type of board.	Good both along and across board, but can warp. Strength depends on number of plies.	Excellent moisture resistance if the right grade (ie Marine or WBP).	Cuts cleanly. Holds screws and nails well, even close to the edge. Easy to glue.	Varnish or prime and paint. May have decorative surface or special veneer.
BLOCKBOARD **Price range** Expensive.	Cupboards, doors, worktops, table tops, wide shelves, general furniture.	Good along board, fair across it. Resists warping but may split in dry, heated rooms.	Unsuitable for exterior applications or in very damp conditions.	Ensure core runs *along* the piece. Takes screws, nails and glue well except in end grain.	May have decorative surface. Varnish or prime and paint. Exposed core needs lipping.
CHIPBOARD (particle board) **Price range** mostly cheap, but special types more costly.	Cheap material for flooring, cladding, rough framework, furniture making.	Stiffness poor, but good resistance to warping. Strength depends on density of core chips.	Fair moisture resistance if exterior grade, otherwise poor.	Hard on tools; tends to crumble. Use chipboard screws and fixings. Glues well; edge joints weak.	Fill and prime before painting. Edges may need lipping to conceal core.
FACED & COATED CHIPBOARDS **Price range** Medium, but range of sizes means little waste.	Shelving, built-in furniture, cupboard doors, general DIY constructions.	Not quite so strong as plain chipboard – and not available in stronger grades.	Unsuitable for damp conditions. Core will disintegrate if it gets damp.	Surface may split when cut. Use special fixings or dowels and glue to conceal joints.	Finish cut edges with matching veneer/plastic edging. Varnish veneered boards.
HARDBOARD **Price range** Cheap unless special purpose type.	Lightweight cladding and panelling, including curves. Levelling wooden floors.	Poor stiffness and can warp. Standard hardboard may expand and buckle when exposed to damp.	Poor resistance to moisture – use oil tempered board in damp conditions.	Support while cutting. Holds fixings poorly – glue, pin or screw to frame.	May be white painted or have decorative coating. Prime and paint unless pre-finished.
MEDIUM DENSITY FIBREBOARD (MDF) **Price range** Medium, but ease of working keeps costs down.	Furniture making, built-in cupboards, most things that can be made in wood.	Uniform strength – fair in both directions. Resists warping well.	Unsuitable for exterior use. Absorbs moisture fairly readily.	Use any woodworking technique. Holds screws and nails well; easy to glue.	Varnish or prime and paint. Very little preparation needed – no sanding or surface filling.
LAMINATED SOFTWOOD **Price range** Expensive.	Wide shelving, cupboards, tabletops where natural wood look is required.	Good in both directions, but can warp. Slightly more stable than solid wood.	As solid timber. Unsuitable for exterior use.	As solid timber. Holds screws and nails well; easy to glue.	Varnish or stain (primer and paint hide decorative grain of the material).

PLYWOOD

Plywood is made from several layers *(plies)* of thin sheets of wood. Each ply is laid with its grain in the opposite direction to the ones on either side. This reinforces the board.

The number of plies vary for a given thickness – in general the more plies there are, the stronger and better quality the plywood. The type of wood used also varies, and more expensive plywoods have decorative facings such as birch or oak.

Plywood resists splitting and can be nailed or glued close to the edges. It is much stronger than solid timber.

The durability of the plywood depends partly on the wood used and partly on the glue used in its manufacture. If ordinary plywood comes into contact with water for any length of time, the individual plies separate and the wood starts to rot.

Weather and Boil Proof (WBP) plywood and **Marine Ply** are both names for plywood which can be used in exposed situations. Other abbreviations you may come across include **Int** (Interior), **MR** (Moisture Resistant – should not be exposed for long periods), and **BR** (Boil Resistant – unsuitable for prolonged exposure).

Shuttering plywood is designed for supporting concrete castings, but can be used for other outdoor constructions as it is WBP quality. Normally only one side is finished smoothly.

Laminated plywood is faced with patterned plastic and is used as a decorative panelling. Some versions are also suitable for worktops – they are stronger than chipboard, and need not be so thick and heavy.

Birch faced plywood

Sapele plywood

Shuttering plywood

Redwood plywood

> **Widely available sheet sizes:**
> 610×610mm to 2440×1220mm
> **Most common sheet sizes:**
> 2440×1220mm
> **Widely available thicknesses:**
> 3mm to 25mm
> **Most common thicknesses:**
> 6mm to 18mm

BLOCKBOARD (LAMINBOARD AND BATTENBOARD)

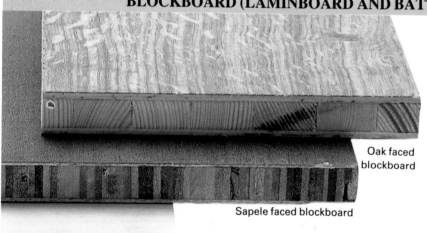

Oak faced blockboard

Sapele faced blockboard

Birch faced blockboard

Malayan blockboard

Blockboard is made from strips of wood laid parallel to one another and glued between continuous sheets of thick veneer. The strips are normally about 25mm (1″) wide, and are arranged so that their grains run in opposite directions to minimize warping.
Laminboard has narrower strips.
Battenboard has wider, batten-sized strips.

There is at least one veneer on each side, and sometimes two – the grain of the first veneer running across the strips. The outer veneer forms the facing of the board and can be a decorative timber like oak, teak or mahogany.

Boards normally need edging as the core is visible and there may be gaps and flaws on show.

> **Widely available sheet sizes:**
> 2440×1220 and 3050×1525mm
> **Most common sheet sizes:**
> 2440×1220mm
> **Widely available thicknesses:**
> 12 to 25mm
> **Most common thicknesses:**
> 12 to 25mm

CHIPBOARD (PARTICLE BOARD)

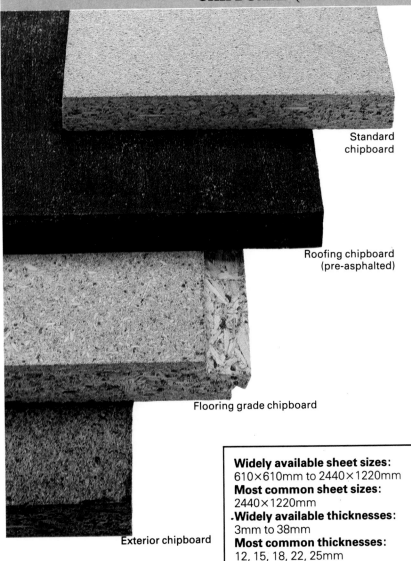

Standard chipboard

Roofing chipboard (pre-asphalted)

Flooring grade chipboard

Exterior chipboard

Chipboard is made from small fragments of softwood, such as the scraps left over when logs are cut into usable sizes. The fragments are chopped and bonded with resin to form solid sheets.

Its strength depends on the way the chips are arranged, and on the type of bonding resin. The cheapest form has a single layer of chips, all the same size. But most boards have *graded density* chips so that there are fine, closely packed particles on the outside and coarser ones at the core.

Standard grade chipboard has sanded faces which need filling and sealing before painting.

Flooring-grade chipboard is stronger, with more densely packed particles, and can be used in place of floorboards. It is also made in easy-to-lay small sheets, and as tongued-and-grooved boards with jointed edges.

Most chipboard quickly deteriorates when exposed to moisture and should not be used outdoors.

Exterior and **moisture resistant** grades are available for outside use, and for inside jobs where dampness or condensation may be a problem.

Roofing board, for flat roofs, has an extra felt or bitumen coating. It is still necessary to cover the roof.

Chipboard contains a lot of glue, which quickly blunts ordinary tools. If you do much cutting with a power saw or router, it's worth fitting more costly *tungsten carbide tipped* tools.

All types are prone to crumbling, so use *chipboard* screws or fixings. Exposed edges need finishing with lipping or edging veneer.

> **Widely available sheet sizes:**
> 610×610mm to 2440×1220mm
> **Most common sheet sizes:**
> 2440×1220mm
> **Widely available thicknesses:**
> 3mm to 38mm
> **Most common thicknesses:**
> 12, 15, 18, 22, 25mm

COATED CHIPBOARDS & WORKTOPS

Post-formed worktop

'Mahogany' veneered chipboard

Melamine-coated chipboard

Chipboard is often given a decorative facing for furniture making. The commonest finishes are mid-brown 'mahogany' type wood veneer, and white melamine (a coating made from layers of plastic-impregnated paper).

Faced and coated boards are made in a wider range of sheet sizes than standard chipboard, including 'planks' of various lengths in widths upwards from 150mm (6″). These have facings on four sides, and sometimes the ends too.

Shelving lengths of melamine coated chipboard are made in finished sizes, edged all round and may be given a decorative profile. Cut edges normally need covering with a strip of the facing material where the chipboard core is exposed.

Kitchen worktop is mostly made from thick chipboard with a scratch-resistant plastic coating. The front edge is usually rounded (postformed), giving a seamless surface which is easier to keep clean than square-edged worktops covered with separate laminate.

> **Widely available sheet sizes:**
> 2440×1220mm, and in widths of 150, 225, 300, 375, 450, 525, 600, 675, 750mm, lengths of 1800 and 2440mm. Worktops are 600mm wide, 1000, 1500, 2000, 3050mm long.
> **Most common sheet sizes:**
> 2440×1220mm
> **Widely available thicknesses:**
> 15 and 18mm. Worktops are normally 30mm thick
> **Most common thicknesses:**
> 15mm

HARDBOARD

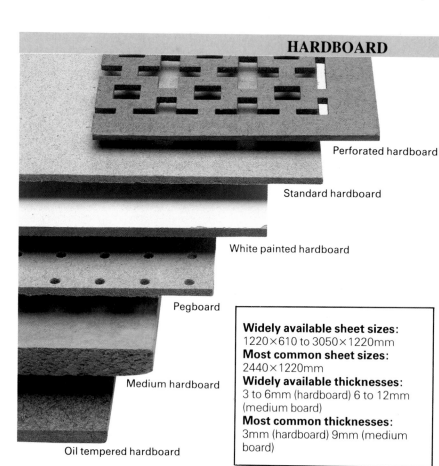

Perforated hardboard

Standard hardboard

White painted hardboard

Pegboard

Medium hardboard

Oil tempered hardboard

Hardboard is compressed wood fibre.
Standard hardboard has a smooth, hard finish on one side and a 'woven' texture on the other.
Double-faced hardboard (relatively rare) has a smooth finish both sides.
White painted hardboard is finished on the smooth side with melamine.

Standard hardboard absorbs water and may warp or buckle in use. Avoid this by *tempering* – wetting the back and drying in the room it's to be used in. Sheets can be bent over a former, or by soaking and bending for tighter curves.
Oil tempered hardboard contains oil to make it water resistant. It is commonly used for levelling wooden floors.
Perforated hardboard is stamped with holes in a regular pattern and may be smooth both sides. There are patterned boards for partitioning and boxing in.

Pegboard has small holes at 20 or 25mm intervals, and is used for noticeboards and racks.
Faced hardboards have a plastic coating with a pattern like wood grain or tiles. Commonly used as wallboards.
Medium hardboard (Sundeala, softboard, fibreboard) is thicker and softer; used for pinboards/insulation.

> **Widely available sheet sizes:**
> 1220×610 to 3050×1220mm
> **Most common sheet sizes:**
> 2440×1220mm
> **Widely available thicknesses:**
> 3 to 6mm (hardboard) 6 to 12mm (medium board)
> **Most common thicknesses:**
> 3mm (hardboard) 9mm (medium board)

MEDIUM DENSITY FIBREBOARD (MDF)

6mm Medium density fibreboard

12mm MDF

18mm MDF

This smooth, stable material is formed by bonding fine wood fibres together. As the fibres run in all directions, there is no grain and the material is equally strong in every direction.

MDF can be cut and shaped using any woodworking technique and will accept any of the standard finishes for wood such as paint or laminate. No edging is necessary as there is virtually no grain. It doesn't warp or split and can be jointed like solid wood as well as by using screws or nails.

However, the fibres are fairly absorbent, so the material must be protected from water, and it cannot be used in exposed situations.

> **Widely available sheet sizes:**
> 2440×1220mm
> **Most common sheet sizes:**
> 2440×1220mm
> **Widely available thicknesses:**
> 6 to 25mm
> **Most common thicknesses:**
> 12mm

LAMINATED SOFTWOOD & HARDWOOD

Laminated pine shelving

Laminated hardwood worktop (beech)

Laminated softwood boards consist of battens glued side by side with the grain running in opposite directions to minimize warping. They look and behave like solid timber, but come in widths suitable for deep shelves, cupboards and tables.

Apart from looks, they have no particular advantages. They are less prone to warp than solid timber, but not as stable as other boards.
Laminated hardwoods are a luxury, specialist material for use as worktops. Woods used include beech and maple. Boards are sometimes available in standard sizes, but are usually only made to measure by specialist suppliers.

> **Widely available sizes:**
> Widths of 150, 225, 300, 375, 450, 525, 600, 675, 750mm. Lengths of 1800 and 2440mm
> **Widely available thicknesses:**
> 18mm and 28mm
> **Most common thicknesses:**
> 18mm

WOODEN MOULDINGS

Mouldings are made by running strips of wood through shaped cutters. Their main uses are:

■ As general purpose trims and decoration in woodwork.

■ As decorative features for interior design.

■ As the stock materials for a wide range joinery and furniture.

The cheapest mouldings are made from pine, but if this is stained or varnished rather than painted, it may show unattractive knots and blemishes. Better quality mouldings are made from redwood (which has a more regular grain) or hardwoods such as ramin, luaun and sapele.

Most modern mouldings are fairly plain, but copies of older, ornate designs can be found. DIY stores stock the common mouldings and some keep decorative patterns.

For the more unusual feature and constructional mouldings, you will probably need to visit a timber merchant – some specialize in period designs, which is useful if you need to match an existing door frame, say. There are also specialists who will machine a hard-to-match shape (an expensive option).

Many mouldings are cut from European redwood which is even grained and free from blemishes.

Trade tip

Size it up

❝ Moulding sizes often confuse people. Like ordinary softwood, they are quoted as a nominal or 'ex-stock' size based on the wood from which the moulding was cut; because of the wastage in machining, the actual size of the moulding is normally quite a lot smaller. The exception to this rule is dowelling, which is usually very close to the stated diameter. ❞

GENERAL PURPOSE MOULDINGS

Quadrant mouldings are shaped like a quarter of a circle and are commonly used to trim the joint between two panels which meet at a right angle.

Half round mouldings are for trimming joints or the edge of a board. The smallest are a full half circle, but larger sizes have a flatter curve.

Cover mouldings are used for similar purposes, but are more decorative. They are also available prefinished and with *embossed* decoration.

Dowels (also called *rounds*) are full circles, used for things like legs, pegs and rails.

External angles are 'L' shaped and normally fit over the edge and face of a board. They come in various sizes and with different length 'arms' on each side. There are square, rounded and moulded patterns. One of the most useful is called *hockey stick* because of the shape of its cross section.

Internal angles are also 'L' shaped, with the finished face on the inside of the L. They are used to trim the joint between two panels at a right angle.

Scotia mouldings are used for the same purpose. They have one square corner and one scooped out in a curve.

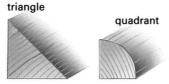

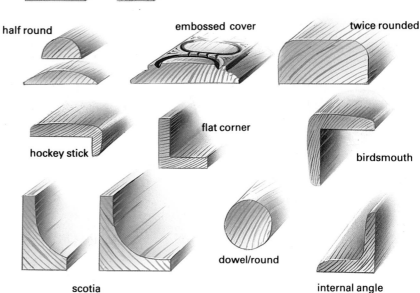

triangle

quadrant

half round

embossed cover

twice rounded

hockey stick

flat corner

birdsmouth

scotia

dowel/round

internal angle

FEATURE MOULDINGS

Feature mouldings are used throughout houses as decorative features. All types come in a wide range of patterns (many with traditional names). Some of the most common of each type are illustrated.

Skirtings trim the joint between the wall and the floor, and also protect the plaster. It's common for the skirting to match the architraves.

Architraves are the mouldings which 'frame' a door or window.

Cornices cover the joint between the wall and the ceiling, though wood cornices are less common than plaster or plastic. They are also used to trim the tops of dressers and wardrobes.

Picture rails have a grooved top into which *moulding hooks* fit for hanging pictures.

Dado rails (chair rails) are fixed part-way up the wall – usually at about waist height – for protection and to provide a visual break.

Panel mouldings are used to frame areas on a flat wall. They can also be used to decorate the front of a plain, flush door by simulating panels (ready cut kits are available for this). *Rebated* panel mouldings have a grooved edge so they can be used to frame a thin panel.

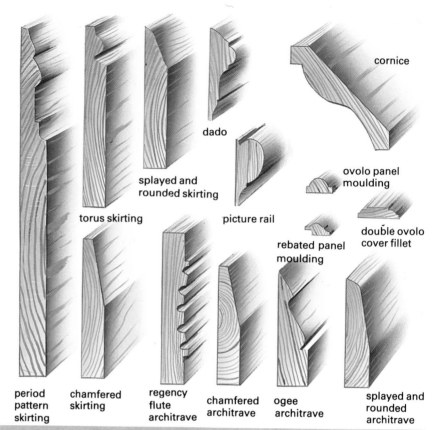

cornice

dado

splayed and rounded skirting

torus skirting

picture rail

ovolo panel moulding

rebated panel moulding

double ovolo cover fillet

period pattern skirting

chamfered skirting

regency flute architrave

chamfered architrave

ogee architrave

splayed and rounded architrave

CONSTRUCTIONAL MOULDINGS

Softwood mouldings are used for the specially shaped timbers which make up things like window frames, staircases and doors. These are useful for repairs as well as new constructions, but check that the design and dimensions are identical to the original.

Window mouldings are available to make all parts of the frame, including: *Rails* (in different sections for top and bottom). Sliding sashes have special mouldings for the two *meeting rails* in the centre.

Stiles, the sides of the window. *Glazing bars* where the window is split into smaller panes. *Greenhouse bar* is heavier, and is used for greenhouses and conservatories.

Beading for retaining the glass or the sliding sashes.

Window board and *window sill* to trim the bottom of the frame.

Door mouldings are made for all parts but those in common use are: *Weatherboard* (weatherbar) to keep the rain away from the base of the door. *Transom* (drip moulding) to keep the rain off the upper part of the frame and top of the door.

Sill (sometimes spelt 'cill' in catalogues) to form a threshold.

Stair mouldings include: *Handrails* in different patterns for wall mounting or use on a balustrade. *Nosings* to form the rounded front edge of a tread.

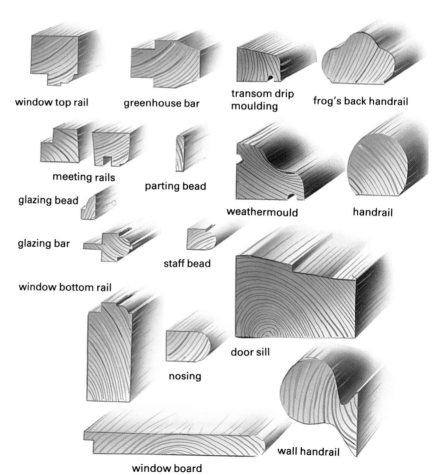

window top rail

greenhouse bar

transom drip moulding

frog's back handrail

meeting rails

glazing bead

parting bead

weathermould

handrail

glazing bar

staff bead

window bottom rail

nosing

door sill

wall handrail

window board

202

CUTTING TIMBER AND BOARDS

A secure work surface and a means of clamping the job to it are essential for all kinds of carpentry, as well as a host of other DIY jobs. But since few people have the luxury of a purpose-built workshop, most workbench arrangements have to be more or less temporary.

A portable folding workbench is by far the most popular option, as it is relatively cheap, takes up little space, and has the added benefit of built-in clamps. Even if you have a more permanent workbench set up in a shed or garage, a portable bench is still invaluable for jobs that need to be done on the spot.

Trestles and a top are another way to provide a versatile, low-cost bench, with the useful advantage that the work surface can be as big as you want to make it. Clamping can be a problem, however.

A permanent workbench (folding or free-standing) in a shed, garage or workroom gives you the advantage of a large, sturdy worktop with lots of handy accessories. If you have the space, there is no substitute for really serious carpentry.

A workbench provides a sturdy working platform and a way to clamp things which need to be sawn or planed.

PORTABLE FOLDING WORKBENCHES

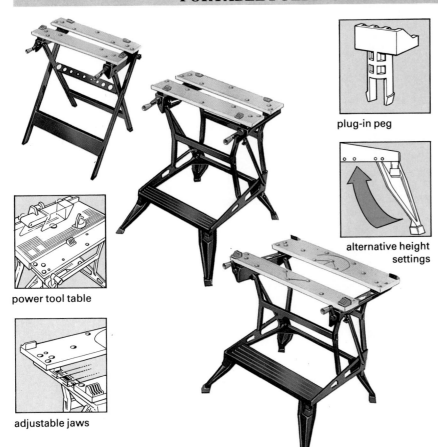

power tool table

adjustable jaws

plug-in peg

alternative height settings

Folding workbenches have become virtually indispensible to do-it-yourselfers and professionals alike. There are several different models, all of which pack flat and have a two-part top that can be screwed in and out like vice jaws. The inner edges of the top are so shaped that rounded and tapering objects can be clamped as easily as square ones.

More sophisticated models have *alternative height settings*. Use the lower setting for sawing and related jobs, and the higher setting for fine work such as planing and chiselling. Larger workbenches also have a wider jaw opening facility, allowing a greater variety of objects to be clamped in the top.

Various accessories include:

Plug-in pegs – standard accessories which allow the worktop to be used as a clamp for objects which are too big to fit the vice jaws.

Extension arms – optional extras fitted into the worktop so that it will clamp objects too large to fit on top.

A power tool table – an optional extra which clips on to the top and accepts a variety of tools such as saws and routers, turning them into more stable fixed machinery.

CUTTING TIMBER BY HAND

Even if you have a power saw, hand sawing is likely to be quicker for small jobs and possibly more accurate, too.

Use a tenon saw for fine, accurate cutting of battens and small pieces of wood up to a maximum of 100×50mm ($4 \times 2''$).

A tenon saw also comes in handy for small widths of plastic-coated board, where its fine teeth help to minimize surface splintering (see *Cutting Boards*, pages 206-207.

Use a panel saw where speed is more important than accuracy, and for cutting larger pieces of timber.

Whichever saw you use, it's essential to support the wood firmly. For small pieces you'll find it easier to work at table or worktop height, preferably with the wood supported in a bench hook or a vice (in which case protect the surface of the wood with offcuts).

For larger timber and when using a panel saw, use a folding workbench, trestle or old chair to support the wood just above knee height and steady it with your own weight.

Posture is all-important when using a panel saw. Choose a position that lets you saw comfortably at an angle of roughly 45° – if you're off-balance or pinched up, the cut won't be straight.

STARTING THE CUT

Start the cut off in the right place and there's a good chance it will stay there. You'll find it a big help to hold the saw with your index finger pointing along the side of the handle in line with the blade to steady it.

If you push the saw down to start, the forward angle of the teeth makes them skip on the edge of the wood before cutting into it, and it's hard to get a proper start. The trick is to form a small nick in the edge first by drawing the saw backwards towards you so that the shallow angle of the teeth rides smoothly over the wood.

Remember to start the cut on the waste side of the cutting line, to allow for the thickness of the saw kerf. In practice the kerf should just brush the line – something which you can easily check as you draw the saw back to make the initial nick in the edge.

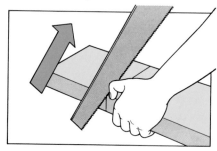

1 Line up the near end of the saw blade against the top joint of your thumb so that it's fractionally to the waste side of the cutting line.

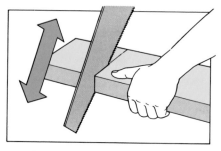

2 Draw the blade towards you, letting its weight carve a nick in the edge of the timber. Then push forward gently so that the teeth can bite.

USING A PANEL SAW
■ Never force a panel saw – the blade will flex and bind in the cut. Hold it at about 45° to the wood and use a slightly curving stroke, as this helps to prevent the blade from sticking.

■ Cut with light pressure on the forward stroke only. Saw from the shoulder, working up to long strokes of the saw, rather than short bites. It's difficult to bring a panel saw back on line, so make sure it doesn't wander from the initial nick. Watch the cutting line on the top of the wood, checking that the kerf stays just clear of the mark, and at the same time keep an eye on the edge to make sure the cut stays square.

■ When sawing down the length of a piece of wood, you may find the cut starts to close up, pinching the blade in the process. If this happens, keep it open by driving in a small wedge.

1 As the teeth begin to bite, exert gentle pressure on the forward stroke only. Move your arm from the shoulder and look straight down the blade.

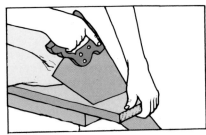

2 Near the end, lower the cutting angle and shorten your strokes. Support the offcut with your free hand so it doesn't tear as the saw breaks through.

Trade tip
Stop it sticking
❛ If the saw binds in the cut for no obvious reason, it may be because of moisture in the wood. You'll find the blade cuts much more easily if you lubricate it by rubbing with a piece of candle. ❜

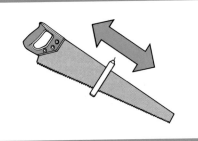

USING A TENON SAW
The tenon saw's stiff back makes it easier to keep on line, but you still need to keep a constant check for squareness along the edge or the cut won't be straight.

The sawing position is flatter, but otherwise the same – cut with light pressure on the forward stroke only, working from the shoulder, and gradually increase the length of your strokes.

If there is a long offcut, don't forget to support it to prevent splintering at the end of the cut.

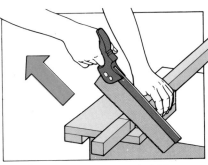

1 Start a tenon saw cut at an angle of around 45°, then gradually lower the blade until it cuts horizontally. Keep checking that the cut is square.

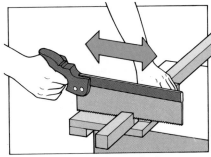

2 As you reach the end, shorten your strokes to reduce the chance of splintering. If you use a bench hook, saw into its base to finish the cut cleanly.

Trade tip
Trimming a short end
❛ You can't easily saw less than 5mm off the end of a piece of wood – and you shouldn't need to if you've marked up accurately!

But if the worst does happen, you'll find it easier to clamp on overlapping pieces of scrap wood, then saw through them all together. The scrap wood holds the saw on line and stops the short end splitting away. ❜

Trade tip
Get a grip on it
❛ Holding the timber firmly is half the battle, and a home-made bench hook is one of the most useful holding tools you can own – particularly for dealing with small pieces. I use one even if I'm working on a portable workbench – it's quicker than the bench's built-in vice, and it's a positive advantage to be able to cut into it.

Make your own bench hook from a piece of stout ply or chipboard about 300mm (12") square and two lengths of 50 × 25mm (2 × 1") batten glued and screwed together as shown. To use it, lock one side against the edge of the bench and press the timber firmly against the back stop to hold it in place. ❜

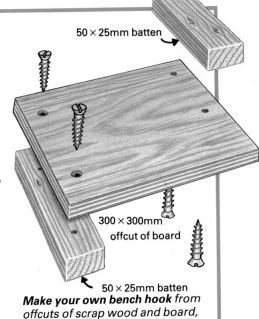

50 × 25mm batten

300 × 300mm offcut of board

50 × 25mm batten

Make your own bench hook from offcuts of scrap wood and board, nailed and glued together.

CUTTING BOARDS

Although there are several types of power driven saw for cutting boards, this section features only the jigsaw – the safest and easiest to use. It will cut both straight lines and curves in a wide variety of different types of board. If you don't own a jigsaw and don't want to buy one, use a panel saw instead.

Whatever the saw, the key to cutting a large board is to support it securely. It's no good propping it both ends and sawing across the middle – this causes the saw blade to pinch as the board begins to sag, and risks the two halves snapping as you near the end. The trick is to imagine the board is already in two pieces and prop it so that each half is individually supported from the beginning.

A portable folding workbench makes a useful trestle for one side; for the other, try two kitchen chairs with lengths of wood stretched between them. Aim to support the board at just above knee height so you can steady it with your weight.

USING A JIGSAW

A power jigsaw cuts on the up-stroke, so if your board is only finished on one side (like a work-top), cut from underneath. Otherwise, cut where any splintering will show least. To minimize splintering, run masking tape along the cutting line and saw through this.

To keep straight cuts on line, use a guide fence. Some jigsaws have a metal fence for following a nearby edge, but for a more accurate guide clamp or nail a straight piece of batten to the board.

Jigsaw safety
- Don't wear loose clothes that could get tangled in the blade.
- Loop the flex over your shoulder to keep it safely away from the cut.
- Don't use a blunt blade.
- Unplug before changing blades.
- Begin a cut slowly and gently, so the blade doesn't buck back.
- Give the saw blade time to stop moving before you put it down.

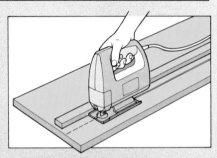

Position a guide batten so that the blade follows the cutting line as you slide the edge of the sole plate along it. Check its position before you start to cut.

Start the saw and advance the moving blade to the line, resting the sole plate on the edge of the board. Don't force or twist the blade – it will break.

Trade tip
Means of support

❝ Supporting large boards is easy in a fully equipped workshop, but a lot more difficult at home. Here are some ways to improvise your own supports, assuming you can use a portable workbench for one side of the board. ❞

USING A PANEL SAW

Hold the board firmly with your weight on your knee and one hand. Keep your eye over the cutting line, and start the cut as for solid timber (see page 205).

A panel saw will splinter the underside of the board. So with faced boards, such as melamine, mark the line on the face that shows, then score along it with a trimming knife to stop the surface chipping. Saw with the blade as flat as possible to reduce the amount it tears the surface.

Score the cutting line with a trimming knife and straight edge to help prevent the surface veneer or plastic coating from chipping off.

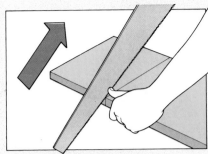

Start the cut as you would for solid timber – draw the blade back gently, steadying it with your thumb, to form a small nick in the edge.

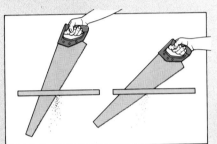

For rough work, you can saw faster at 45°. But keep the saw as flat as possible if you want to avoid splintering the underside of the board.

If you run off line, twist the blade slightly as you saw to bring it back on course. Correct the fault gradually, though, or it will leave an unsightly notch.

Trade tip

Stop it flapping

❝ Very thin boards such as plywood or hardboard sheets often tend to whip up and down with each saw stroke, making it difficult to saw them cleanly.

I stop a board like this from flexing by laying two lengths of batten across my supports, one just to each side of the cutting line. ❞

PROBLEM SOLVER

Cutting corners

The way you deal with a corner depends on whether you're using a panel saw or a jigsaw, and also on the shape of the corner.

External corners Where possible, saw past the corner in both directions so that you get a clean cut. Attempting to stop exactly on the spot usually means ending short and splintering the last little bit.

Internal corners You can't cut past the corner, so take care and stop short if necessary. Any splintering is likely to be on the waste part, so you can trim it off later.

With a jigsaw, slow down and watch carefully as you approach the corner. With a panel saw, change the angle so you cut vertically into it.

Cutting holes

For these, you need a jigsaw or a hand saw with a thin blade (such as a padsaw or keyhole saw).

There are two ways to start the cut. The easiest (and only way with a hand saw) is to drill one or more large holes somewhere in the waste area. Insert the blade through the board before you switch on, then cut in the ordinary way.

The alternative if you don't have a large drill bit is to make a *pocket cut*. Stand the jigsaw on the end of its soleplate inside the area with the blade not touching the surface. Switch on, and gently angle the blade down to contact the board. It should gradually cut its own way through – but be prepared for it to buck if it touches suddenly.

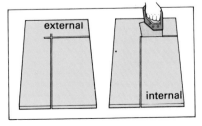

Internal and external corners need to be finished carefully.

Start a pocket cut by standing the jigsaw soleplate on its end.

THREE ESSENTIAL SAWS

TENON SAW

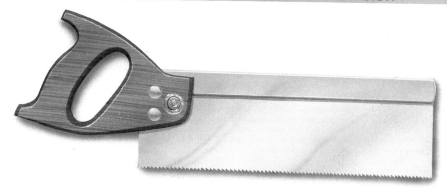

A tenon saw is designed for making accurate cuts in small pieces of wood. The blade is short – there are various lengths from about 200mm (8″) to 350mm (14″) – with fine teeth running right along the cutting edge.

The top of the blade is fitted with a stiffening rib made of brass or steel. This keeps the blade in line, and provides sufficient weight for you to cut through the wood without having to apply much pressure.
Typical ppi range: 12-14

PANEL SAW

A panel saw has a long, flexible blade ranging from around 500mm (20″) to 660mm (26″) in length, with fairly coarse teeth along the cutting edge. The length of the blade should match your sawing stroke, but the longer the blade, the less easy it is to control. Unlike a tenon saw there is no stiffening back, allowing the blade to cut right through a wide board.

Strictly speaking, there are two teeth patterns – *cross-cut*, designed to saw across the grain, and *rip*, for sawing along it. In practice, only specialists bother about this and most people have a general purpose panel saw which is a compromise cross-cut type for tackling a range of jobs.
Typical ppi range: 8-12

POWER JIGSAWS

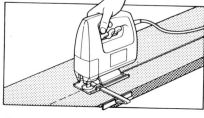

Some models have a guide fence.

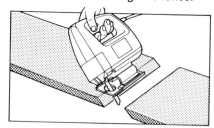

The sole plate can be angled at 45°.

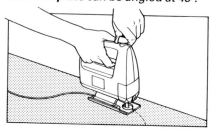

Scrolling jigsaw blade control.

A power jigsaw has a narrow blade which works up and down and cuts on the up stroke. They are excellent tools for sawing sheet materials and can also be used to cut smaller pieces of timber.

The simplest type has a single speed and cuts wood up to around 50mm (2″) thick. (With a suitable blade, it also cuts sheet metal up to around 3mm (⅛″) thick.) It can be used freehand for curved or straight cuts, but many models have a guide fence and circle guide for straight lines and regular curves.

The *sole plate* which contacts the surface of the wood normally pivots to an angle of 45° for mitre cutting and retracts to allow you to cut right up to an obstacle.

More sophisticated models may incorporate *variable speed* – for different materials and tight curves – and *orbital action*, in which the blade swings back and forth as well as going up and down. Both result in an easier, cleaner cut.

Scrolling jigsaws have a separate hand knob which controls the blade plunger. This allows you to rotate the blade to cut in any direction regardless of the position of the body. As a result you can cut awkward shapes more accurately.
Typical ppi range (for wood): 8-12

MEASURING WOOD TO FIT

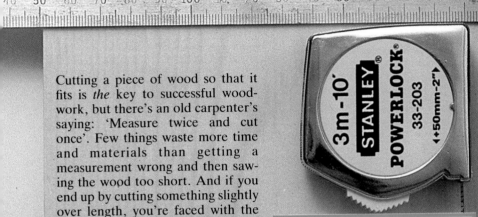

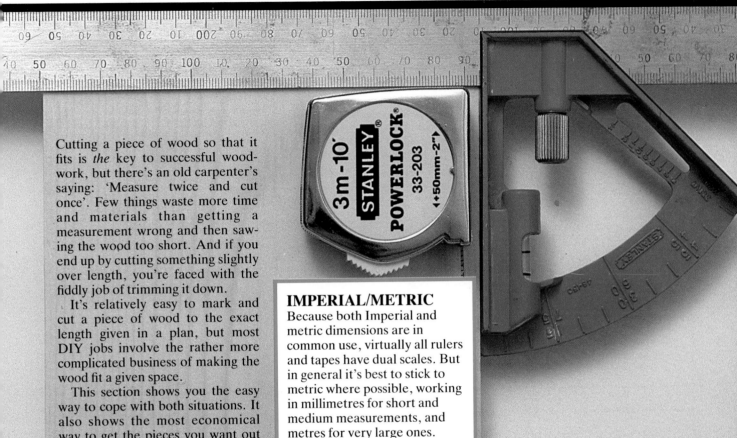

Cutting a piece of wood so that it fits is *the* key to successful woodwork, but there's an old carpenter's saying: 'Measure twice and cut once'. Few things waste more time and materials than getting a measurement wrong and then sawing the wood too short. And if you end up by cutting something slightly over length, you're faced with the fiddly job of trimming it down.

It's relatively easy to mark and cut a piece of wood to the exact length given in a plan, but most DIY jobs involve the rather more complicated business of making the wood fit a given space.

This section shows you the easy way to cope with both situations. It also shows the most economical way to get the pieces you want out of standard timber sizes.

IMPERIAL/METRIC
Because both Imperial and metric dimensions are in common use, virtually all rulers and tapes have dual scales. But in general it's best to stick to metric where possible, working in millimetres for short and medium measurements, and metres for very large ones.

MEASURING UP
Short distances are easy to measure accurately. A tape measure is simple to use up to a comfortable arm span – a metre or so – because you can pull it taut with both hands.

Rulers are even easier to handle and are more accurate for short measurements. You can also use the edge of a ruler to draw a straight line on the material. Use a metal ruler for marking with a knife.

If you have to measure something which extends beyond your arm span, or beyond the length of the tape, always double check – it's all too easy to introduce errors.

If you have a helper, they can ensure that the tape is taut. Otherwise you will have to fix the end while you take the measurement. If you are working single handed, the locking button on the tape is useful to stop it springing back if you let it go accidentally. Masking tape is also handy for securing the tape measure temporarily in awkward situations.

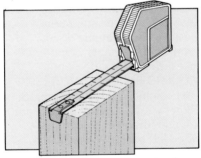

1 A tape measure can only give an accurate reading if it is pulled tight. Don't let it sag, bow or twist, or your measurement will be too long.

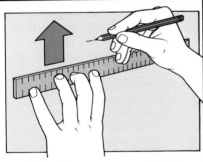

2 Rule a line more accurately by positioning a pencil on the starting point first. Hold the pencil firm, then bring the edge of the ruler up to contact it.

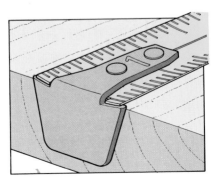

3 If you can't hold the end of the tape, secure it with the hook provided. This automatically aligns the end of the tape with what you are measuring.

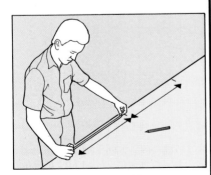

4 To measure something longer than the tape itself, it's best to lock it at a manageable length, then work along in steps, marking at each stage.

MEASURING INTERNAL DISTANCES

There are many situations where you need to know the exact distance between two fixed sides, for example when putting up shelves in an alcove.

You can do this with a tape measure up to a comfortable arm span, but beyond this it gets difficult to keep the tape taut. So a good alternative is to use a pair of extending rods – just lengths of stiff batten, each cut to between two-thirds and three-quarters the opening's width.

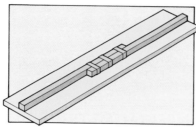

To use a tape measure accurately beyond your reach, get a helper to pull it taut. Add the width of the case to the measurement on the tape.

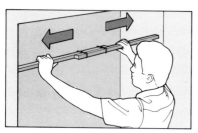

1 Use extending rods by sliding them out until both ends touch the sides. This makes it easy to see whether the width of the opening varies.

2 Tape the rods together securely to retain the dimensions of the opening, then use them to transfer the measurement to your wood.

Trade tip

Direct measuring

❝ Where you just want a piece of wood to fit a given space, in many cases I find that taking the measurement and transferring it to the wood makes the job more complicated and less accurate. Unless you are dealing with very large pieces it's often better to use the wood as its own ruler.

For example, if I want a piece of batten the same length as the depth of a worktop, I lay the batten itself across the surface and strike off the exact measurement. ❞

CHOOSING THE RIGHT SIZE

If you refer to the timber size chart on page 195, and the sheet sizes for man-made boards on pages 198-200, you will see that a limited number of standard lengths and widths are available.

You may be able to get your supplier to cut the material for you, but if this isn't possible or too expensive you'll need to choose standard sizes from which to cut your own.

Length If you're buying standard lengths of timber, pick the ones which allow you to cut the pieces you need with the minimum wastage. For example, if you want a large number of battens measuring 1.15m, don't buy bundles 1.8m long; 2.4m, the next commonly available length, allows you to cut two pieces from a single strip with hardly any wood left over.

Width mainly applies to man-made boards, where you can cut several pieces out of a sheet. For example, if you want strips 175mm wide, it's more economical to cut two from a 375mm wide board than one from a 225mm wide board.

If you want a large number of odd-sized pieces, see if you can get them all out of a bigger sheet of the same material.

timber

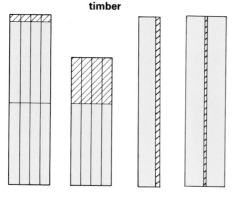

Think carefully about the length and number of pieces of wood you need for a job. Often, what seems the most obvious standard size leaves a lot of wastage, and you need to switch to a larger one.

boards

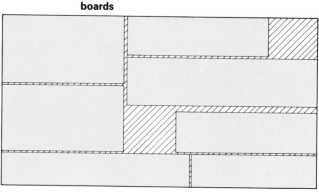

The safest way to see how many pieces you can get out of a standard sheet of board is to draw them all to scale, cut them out, and shuffle them around on a plan. On coated boards you can slot pieces in crosswise; but if there is a grain they should all run the same way.

GETTING A SQUARE END

Before you can transfer the measurement you want on to your material, you need a starting point to measure it from. Normally, this will be one end of the length of timber or board. But unless the end is cut straight and square you will never get a true measurement.

The first rule of accuracy is never to trust something until you have checked it. In particular, solid timber is unlikely to be supplied with ends which are square *and* in good condition. And even though man-made boards are usually machined true, the ends may have been knocked or damaged, so you should still check them first.

Inspect the end for damage, including splits or unsightly discoloration in the case of solid wood. Then use a try square to check that the end is cut squarely across its length *and* through its thickness.

Unless this is the case, it is best to use the try square to mark a new, dead square end a little way along the wood.

Use the try square to mark a line across the surface of the timber. Turn the wood over and starting from the same point, square another line down the edge.

MEASURING TO LENGTH

Measure the right distance along from your square end and make a clear but thin mark on the material. Square across to mark the cutting line.

If you have to cut a number of short pieces from a single length of wood, *don't* try measuring them all in one go before cutting them: the result won't be accurate because a small amount of wood is wasted in the width of the saw cut.

It's better to measure, cut, then measure and cut again, even if this takes longer. There are shortcuts you can use if you want several pieces the same size.

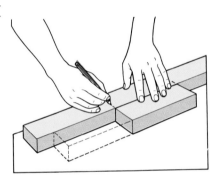

If you want to cut a number of pieces of the same length from one longer piece, cut the first and use it as a template to mark the rest. For maximum accuracy use the same template to mark all the pieces.

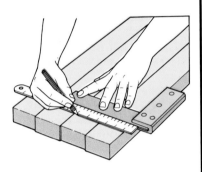

To cut a number of pieces down to the same length, it's best to measure them all at once. Align the ends with a square, tape or clamp them together, then measure the correct length and square a line right across.

DEALING WITH ANGLES

The most common angle you're likely to encounter in woodwork apart from the right angle is the 45 degree mitre, used for things like picture frames and architrave mouldings. Mitre boxes can be used to cut thin sections of wood directly, but to mark out a mitre on a larger piece of wood, you need a combination or mitre square.

You may also find odd angles like the slope of a stair rail or ceiling in the loft, say.

If you have to cut something to match, it's sometimes possible to mark it directly but otherwise you need a pattern. There is a special tool for this called a sliding bevel – basically a try square with a movable, lockable blade.

Trade tip

Angle templates

❝ A sliding bevel is such a specialized tool that it really isn't worth buying one for a single job. Make your own angle template from two thin strips of wood fixed together at the correct angle, or by cutting a piece of stiff card to the right shape. ❞

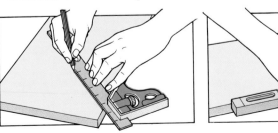

Combination and mitre squares are tools that let you rule a 45 degree cutting line across a wider surface than you can fit inside a mitre box.

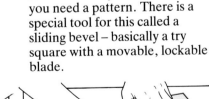

You can swivel the blade of a sliding bevel to reproduce any angle, and lock it in position. You can then use it to transfer the angle to your piece of wood.

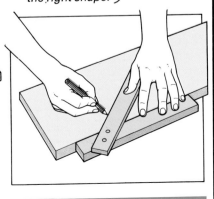

DEALING WITH
AWKWARD SHAPES

Although most DIY woodwork involves simply cutting pieces to length from standard sized material, there are times when things aren't quite so straightforward because the wood or board you're using has to be trimmed to a complicated shape.

A case in point is where you want a board to fit snugly against a surface which is irregular or uneven, or where there's an awkward projection. The technique for doing this is called *scribing to fit*.

Use a similar technique where you need to mark along the edge of the material, rather than across it – either to trim a board down by an even amount, or because you want to fit something parallel to the edge.

There may also be times when you have to mark a piece of wood with a curve, or some other irregular shape. Jobs like this require special tools, though luckily you can make some of them yourself.

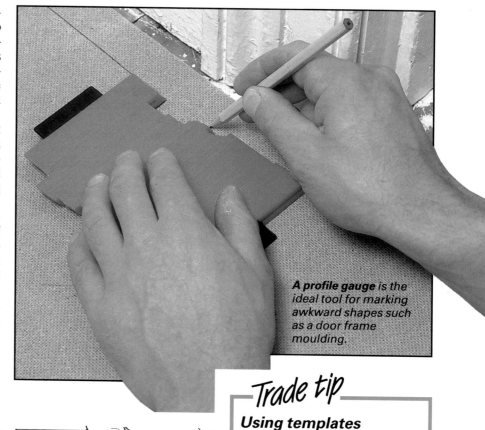

A profile gauge is the ideal tool for marking awkward shapes such as a door frame moulding.

SCRIBING THE EDGE

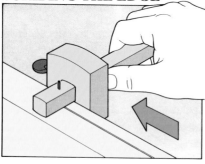

1 A marking gauge is used to mark a line running at a true parallel to the edge or end of a board. Set it to the width you want and run it gently along.

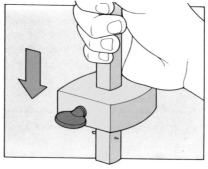

2 To make fine adjustments to a marking gauge, don't use the adjusting screw but knock the end gently on a solid surface to jar it along a fraction.

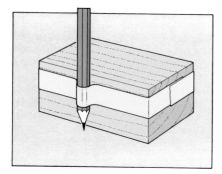

1 A scribing block traces an irregular line along the edge of a board. Improvise your own by taping a pencil to a small block of wood as shown.

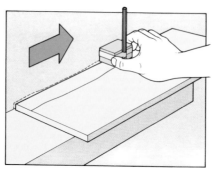

2 To scribe the edge of a board, butt it up against the irregular surface, then run the scribing block along the board so that it transfers the outline.

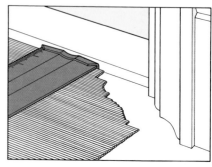

Use a profile gauge to take the pattern of more complex shapes. Press against the object so that the needles mimic the shape, then transfer to your material.

DRILLING HOLES IN WOOD

As materials go, wood is soft and fairly easy to drill. But making clean, accurate holes in exactly the right spot isn't always so simple – it needs care, and the right tools.

The normal choice for drilling is a power drill, which in most cases is quick, accurate and takes very little effort. But drilling by hand has certain advantages too:

■ You don't need a power source (though cordless drills get round this problem too).

■ You can work slowly – and therefore often more accurately.

■ Hand drills are smaller and lighter, making them easier to use in awkward corners; they are also less likely to snap thin drill bits.

Whichever method you choose, you also need bits of various shapes and sizes. Some wood bits are designed specifically for power or hand drills and aren't interchangeable, while larger bits (particularly those for hand drilling) are also fairly expensive. Most people find it best to collect a set of general purpose bits in small and medium sizes and then add to them as the need arises. The full range of drilling tools and bits is described on pages 215-216.

BASIC DRILLING TECHNIQUES

Whatever the hole, make sure you use the right bit and the correct technique:

Small holes (up to 6mm – ¼″) are mainly for screws – either straight-through shank clearance holes, or pilot holes for the thread. Accurate positioning is important, but depth is rarely critical since in softwood and most man-made boards the screw cuts its own way in.

Holes like these are normally drilled with twist bits or wood bits, but for small pilot holes it's often easier to use a bradawl, a gimlet or a push drill.

Medium sized holes (6 to 19mm – ¼ to ¾″) are mainly for dowels, bolts, pipes and metal fittings. They must be positioned accurately, and often have to be drilled to an accurate diameter and depth (see overleaf for details of drilling dowel holes). Use a wood bit, flat bit or auger bit, depending on the size and accuracy required.

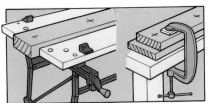

1 Unless the wood's own weight holds it steady, always clamp the work securely. Make sure there is no risk of drilling through into something important.

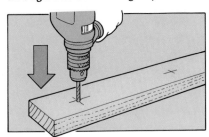

3 Position the bit over the marked point and apply steady pressure, keeping it square to the work. Don't force the bit as this, too, can make it wander.

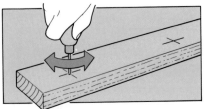

2 Mark the centre of the hole with a punch, bradawl or even a nail. This ensures the drill bit goes where you want it, and stops it from wandering off line.

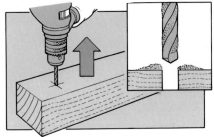

When drilling deep holes, back off periodically to make sure the bit isn't clogged with wood dust. A clogged bit will quickly overheat and go blunt.

Trade tip

Avoid splinters

❛ To stop the underside of a piece of wood from splintering as you drill through it:

■ Clamp a piece of scrap wood firmly to the back and drill through into this.

■ With a flat bit or auger bit, use a double-drilling technique: stop as soon as the centre point breaks through the wood, then turn the work over and drill back through the other side. ❜

For greater accuracy, use a try square to align the drill. For perfect accuracy and steadiness – particularly when drilling a series of holes – use a drill stand.

DRILLING LARGE HOLES

Large holes – 19mm (¾″) to 75mm (3″) – are used for a variety of purposes, including housings for cylinder locks, recesses for concealed hinges, and cut-outs for pull handles. Almost always, they must be drilled to an exact size and position and should be finished very cleanly.

Most of the time you'll need a large flat bit or a hole saw, though hinge recesses are cut with a special hinge boring bit (*end mill*) made to suit a normal 35mm diameter hinge boss.

Such bits are tricky to use in a hand-held drill, though a drill stand makes things simpler. Some types of end mill have a raised rim to limit the depth of cut; if yours doesn't, take extra care not to drill too far, or use a drill depth stop.

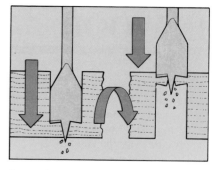

Large flat bits can only be used on fairly thick wood. They are almost certain to tear it if you drill right through, so use the double-drilling technique.

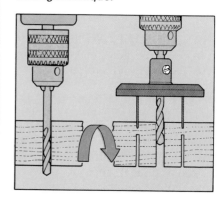

A hole saw cuts thin material very cleanly, but will overheat if forced. On thicker materials, bore through with the centre bit, then use the saw from both sides.

To use a hinge boring bit with a hand-held drill (see left), start by rocking the bit gently from side to side. Continue until you reach the right depth.

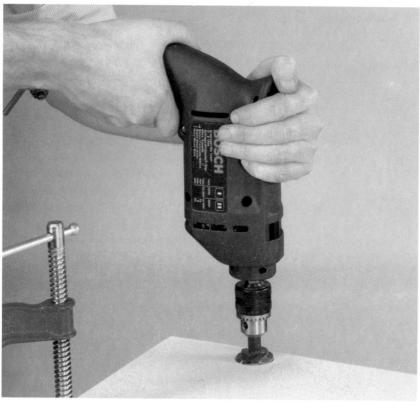

ALIGNING HOLES FOR DOWEL JOINTS

Dowel holes must be drilled cleanly to the right depth and diameter. It's also important that the holes in each part line up perfectly.

Jointing dowels are often sold with matching dowel bits – your best guarantee that the holes are the right size. If your drill hasn't a built-in depth stop, fit one to the bit (or use tape) to gauge the depth.

You can align the holes by carefully measuring and marking both parts, but a safer way is to use a cheap set of *dowel centre points* – again, sold to suit various dowel sizes. If you have a lot of joints to make, an inexpensive *dowelling jig* could be a worthwhile investment. A vertical drill stand also helps to ensure straight holes.

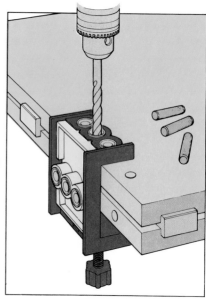

A dowelling jig ensures that both sets of holes get drilled straight and that they align with each other. The jig simply clamps in position on the work.

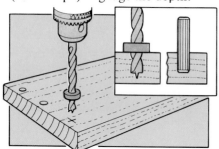

1 Use a dowel bit to make the holes in the first part, taking care to keep the drill square to the wood. Fit a depth stop to check on the depth.

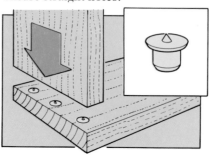

2 Insert dowel centre points in the holes you have drilled and press the two parts together to mark the hole centres on the second part ready for drilling.

DRILLING BY HAND

Hand drilling is slower than using a power tool, but gives you far more control. For small holes up to about 10mm (⅜″), use a *hand drill* with a twist bit or wood bit; larger holes must be drilled with a *brace*.

If you have a hand drill as well as a power drill, you'll find that on jobs requiring a number of holes of two different sizes it's easier to use both tools together than to keep swapping bits.

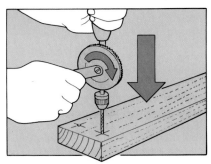

Guide a hand drill and apply pressure with the end handle while you turn the crank. The slow speed makes it simple to keep the bit in alignment.

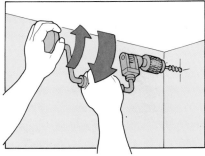

A ratchet brace can be used in a confined space by setting the rachet mechanism and cranking the handle repeatedly through part of a full swing.

Trade tip

Keep your edge

❝ Blunt bits cut poorly and overheat; they also make inaccurate holes. Small bits are cheap to replace, but larger ones are worth sharpening.

Twist bits can be sharpened in a cheap drill-powered sharpener costing about the same as a set of bits. Sharpen wood bits, dowel bits and auger bits by hand using a fine triangular file on the spur and cutters. ❞

DRILLING TOOLS

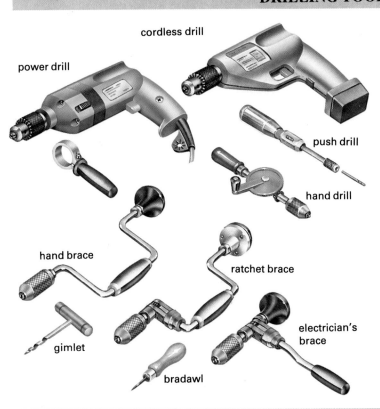

cordless drill

power drill

push drill

hand drill

hand brace

ratchet brace

gimlet

bradawl

electrician's brace

Power drills used for woodworking don't need a hammer action, but it's worth having a two speed model with variable speed control for large or accurate holes. *Cordless drills* come into their own for carpentry, and on many jobs can be used instead of a hand drill.

Hand drills are convenient, lightweight tools for working away from a power source or in confined spaces. On better models the crank wheel generally drives twin gears for more even power. There are various handle designs.

Braces are traditional woodworking tools measured by the size of their sweep (the diameter of a full turn of the handle). The larger the sweep, the greater the power, but the harder the tool is to use in a restricted space. The *electrician's brace* is a specialized tool for drilling holes between joists and similarly restricted areas.

Most braces have a ratchet action, enabling them to be used in confined spaces by cranking the handle. Plain braces are about two thirds the price of ratchet models.

Bradawls are for boring small screw pilot holes in softwood.

Gimlets (*hand augers*) come in a range of sizes from 3 to 6mm (⅛ to ¼″) for boring small holes.

Push drills to fit *spiral ratchet screwdrivers* can be used instead of a bradawl or gimlet.

DRILLING AIDS

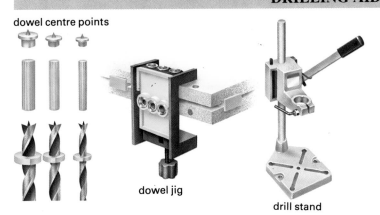

dowel centre points

dowel jig

drill stand

Dowel centre points are made in various sizes to suit corresponding dowel and dowel bit sizes.

Dowelling jigs consist of a series of guides for positioning dowel holes accurately and drilling them straight. There are various patterns, all designed to clamp to the edge of the work.

Depth stops, on the bit or fitted to the drill itself, enable you to drill to pre-set depths.

Drill stands for power drills help to ensure alignment and depth – especially when drilling large, accurate holes or a series of identically sized holes in different parts. Some stands are made to suit particular drills, but there are universal models, too.

BITS FOR POWER OR HAND DRILLS

twist
bit

wood
bit

countersinks

Twist bits have a blunt point and long spiral flutes. They are available in *high speed steel* (HSS) for drilling wood and metal, or carbon steel for drilling wood only.

Twist bits are commonly sold in sets. A typical metric set contains bits from 1 to 6.5mm in 0.5mm steps, the Imperial equivalent being ¹⁄₁₆ to ¼″ in 64ths of an inch. Bits over 6mm (¼″) are usually expensive. When power drilling, use a fast drill speed.

Wood bits resemble twist bits but have a central spur and angled cutting edges for more accurate, cleaner holes. *Dowel bits* are similar, but are accurately matched to various sizes of jointing dowel. When power drilling, use a fast drill speed.

Countersinks are used to make the angled recesses for countersunk screw heads. Not all types are interchangeable. Use at a moderate speed.

SPECIAL BITS FOR POWER TOOLS

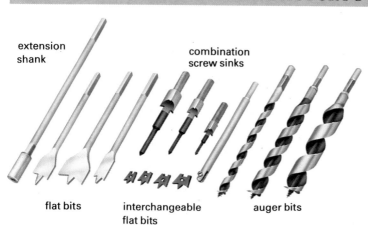

extension
shank

combination
screw sinks

flat bits

interchangeable
flat bits

auger bits

plug cutters

hinge
boring bit

hole saw

Flat bits are for rapid drilling of medium-sized holes in wood and must be used at a fast drill speed (at least 1,000 rpm). Sizes normally range from 6 to 38mm (¼ to 1½″) in 3mm (⅛″) steps, but as well as separate bits you may also find sets of interchangeable cutters to fit a universal shank. *Extension shanks* are available to fit some types of flat bit for drilling very deep holes.

Combination screwsinks, for drilling screw holes, have stepped cutters that form a pilot, clearance and countersink all in one go. They are exactly matched to particular screw sizes and are unlikely to be worth buying unless you have to fit a large number of identical screws.

Combination auger bits are dual-purpose bits for power drills and hand braces (but not hand drills), the wide spiral and single cutter making them very accurate for large, deep holes. Sizes range from 8 to 32mm (⁵⁄₁₆ to 1¼″). Use a slow drill speed.

Hole saws have a central pilot bit surrounded by a ring of saw teeth. They are designed for large holes in thin materials and won't work at all at thicknesses over around 38mm (1½″).

Sizes range from 15 to 75mm (⅝ to 3″), and you can also buy combination sets with a series of interchangeable blades. Use a fast drill speed, but take care not to force the blade.

Plug cutters remove a plug (core) of scrap wood which can then be glued into a hole in the work itself to conceal a deeply recessed screw head.

Hinge boring bits (*end mills*) are specialized tools for boring the large (35mm) recesses needed to fit modern-style concealed cabinet hinges.

SPECIAL BITS FOR BRACES

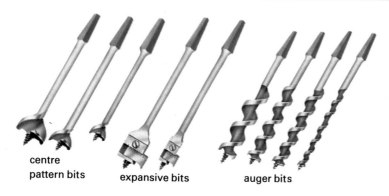

centre
pattern bits

expansive bits

auger bits

Centre pattern bits drill shallow holes cleanly and quickly. Sizes range from 9 to 38mm (⅜ to 1½″).

Expansive bits are similar to centre pattern bits, but have movable cutters with an adjusting screw which allows the cutting diameter to be changed. They are more expensive, but a small bit adjusts from 12–25mm (½–1″), a large one from 22–75mm (⅞–3″).

Auger bits are more accurate for deep holes. The central lead screw is surrounded by cutters which give a clean finish, and the shank has long spiral flutes that help to centre the bit and channel waste out of the hole. There are various patterns, each with different designs of spiral and cutters. Sizes range from 6 to 38mm (¼ to 1½″).

CHISELS AND CHISELLING

Chisels are among the most versatile of all woodworking tools, and on some jobs – such as fitting a hinge or mortise lock – you can't do without one. Yet simple as they are, they need handling with skill and care for best results.

In general carpentry, chisels are mainly used for *paring* (trimming) excess wood from a piece of timber, and for cutting *housings* (recesses) or *mortises* (enclosed holes) for joints and fittings. But chisels are also the main tools for carving wood, and in this area there are many special blade shapes for making particular kinds of cut.

Safety first

A sharp chisel can cause serious injury, so always follow these simple safety precautions before using one:
■ Make sure the work is clamped or held securely to keep it under control.
■ Keep your hands and fingers behind the cutting edge at all times.
■ Keep the chisel as sharp as possible – blunt chisels encourage you to apply too much force and increase the likelihood of something slipping.
■ Keep a blade guard on the chisel when it is not in use.

CUTTING A HOUSING

The term housing covers the slots, notches and recesses found in all areas of woodworking.

Housing joints are used in frames for furniture and built-in units, usually with *through housings* in which the wood is notched across its entire width. Although part of the notch can be made by cutting across the wood with a saw, you still need a chisel to remove the waste.

A chisel is even more important for cutting *stopped housings*, which range from the shallow recesses enclosing a hinge plate to the deeper slots used to support shelf boards or stair treads.

Cut the sides of a housing first (left). On shallow housings such as hinge recesses, you can do this with a trimming knife. Or press in the chisel (flat side outwards) to the correct depth right around the outline.

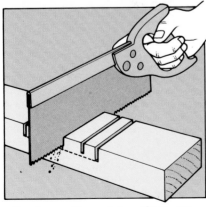

On deeper through housings, cut the sides with a tenon saw. On wide housings, make a further series of saw cuts across the centre of the waste.

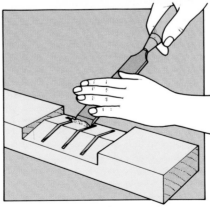

Use the chisel to chop out the waste. Don't attempt to trim to the bottom of the housing first time; take it in easy stages and leave some waste . . .

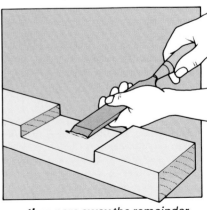

. . . then pare away the remainder using your fingers and palm to guide the blade. Again, cut in thin slices to stop the chisel digging into the grain.

CUTTING A MORTISE

Before cutting a mortise, mark it out accurately. It's much easier to finish the sides of the mortise squarely if you make it the same width as the chisel. But where this isn't possible, use a narrower chisel and trim the sides afterwards.

Proper *mortise chisels* have extra-strong blades and handles so that they can be struck with a mallet. But if, as is likely, you have to use an ordinary *chisel* with a mallet, don't give it anything other than light taps or you risk snapping the blade. Drill out the waste instead, and then use the chisel to square up the sides.

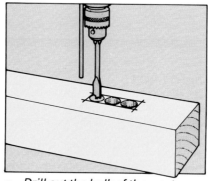

1 Drill out the bulk of the waste by making a series of holes using a bit the width of the mortise. Gauge the depth with a stop, or tape the bit.

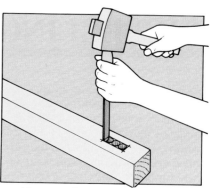

2 Use a mallet to drive in the chisel at one end of the mortise with the bevel inwards; don't drive it too far, though, or the blade may jam.

3 Lever the chisel forward and work along the slot to remove the waste, starting with shallow cuts and then going progressively deeper . . .

. . . until you reach the correct depth. At this point, reverse the blade and pare away the back of the mortise, ensuring your final cuts are square to the edge.

Trade tip
Gauging the depth

❝ Keep a check on how deep you're going by wrapping a piece of masking tape around the chisel blade. ❞

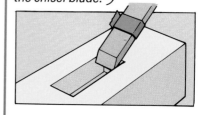

4 If the mortise edges need trimming, use the widest bladed chisel possible to pare away thin slices. Take care to keep the sides parallel.

TRIMMING WITH A CHISEL

Chisels can be used to trim and shape the ends of a piece of wood by paring across the grain. But before you start, make sure the wood is held firmly and put a piece of scrap timber underneath (thick plywood is ideal).

You shouldn't need to use a mallet. If the wood is difficult to cut, either you are trying to remove too thick a slice in one go, or the chisel needs sharpening.

For rounded cuts – concave or convex – use a gouge (a chisel with a curved blade) in a similar way.

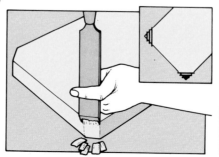

To cut a chamfer, pare vertically in a series of thin slices. Use your weight to push the chisel through the wood, guiding the blade with your fingertips.

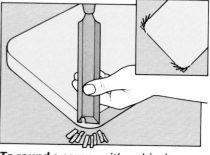

To round a corner with a chisel, chamfer as much as you can. Then work round the rest in a series of small slices, starting on the edge and working towards the end.

SHARPENING A CHISEL

Sharp chisels cut more accurately and take less effort, so it's worth keeping them in good condition.

A chisel blade is sharpened to a double angle. The first angle, called the *grinding bevel*, is produced on a grindstone or coarse oilstone. The second, *honing* angle is the actual cutting edge and is produced on a fine oilstone.

Chisels need honing fairly often to keep the cutting edge in trim, but grinding is normally only necessary where the edge has been accidentally chipped, or has thickened up due to frequent sharpening.

A new chisel may be sharpened to a grinding angle only, leaving you to hone the final edge before use. Old, blunt chisels may need to be reground first to restore them to use.

Honing the edge

Use a fine oilstone and clamp it firmly (preferably in its box) so that you can use both hands to guide the chisel. Wet the stone with a little oil (olive oil is ideal) to reduce friction. Then, keeping the chisel at the correct angle, rub it back and forth with light pressure.

Grinding the edge

Grinding can be done on a grindstone (electric or hand-powered), or by hand on the coarse side of an oilstone – which is much slower.

Grinding wheels can be dangerous, if you don't take proper precautions. Powered wheels should have an eyeshield to guard against the shower of sparks and abrasive particles which are thrown off. Drill and hand-powered wheels may not have these, in which case you must wear goggles or a face mask. Don't wear loose clothing in case this gets caught in the wheel.

Trade tip

Checking the edge

❝ To test whether a chisel is sharp, try the edge against your fingernail. A properly honed blade won't slip. ❞

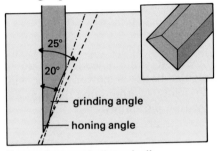

For paring work, the grinding angle should be 20° and the honing angle 25° . . .

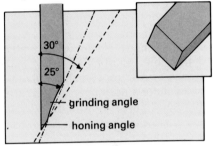

. . . but for mortising this may be too weak – increase the angles to 25° and 30° or 35°.

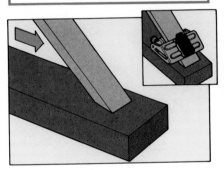

1 *If you hone the blade by hand, take care not to rock it or the sharpening angle will be curved. A honing guide helps to keep the angle consistent.*

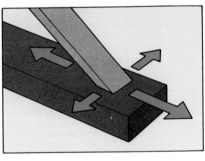

2 *Move the chisel across the stone occasionally to stop it from wearing a hollow. When sharpening a narrow blade, use an area near the edge of the stone.*

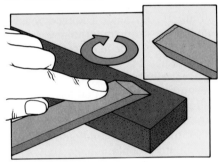

3 *Honing produces a slight burr. Flatten the back of the chisel by rubbing it lightly over the stone, then remove the remaining burr on a piece of scrap wood.*

Grind a chisel with the wheel revolving towards you and the blade on the rest at the correct angle. Work the blade from side to side to keep the wear even.

A grinding attachment (right) for an electric drill has special clamps to ensure that the blade is held at the right angle.

USING PLANES AND RASPS

Planes are the traditional tools for trimming, smoothing and shaping wood. Use one whenever you need to reduce a piece of wood by an amount which is too thin to cut with a saw, or you want to smooth a rough surface rapidly. Although powered sanders make light work of many finishing tasks, they are no substitute for a plane when it comes to jobs like hanging doors and scribing wood to fit uneven walls.

Modern technology has made the hand plane much easier to use. A plane is only efficient when really sharp, but sharpening aids and planes with replaceable blades mean there's no longer any excuse for blunt tools. And with the advent of power planes, most of the hard work has disappeared, too.

Other tools

It's also worth considering one of the many types of Surform or wood rasp. These don't need sharpening, and cope with a much wider range of materials – although the surface they leave often lacks the smoothness of a planed one.

There are other planes designed for cutting rebates, grooves and mouldings, but these are expensive, specialized tools and only worth buying if you do woodwork on a regular basis. A power router will do many of the same jobs more cheaply and simply.

WHAT TO USE WHERE

Use a smoothing plane for surfacing pieces of timber and a block plane for fine trimming or work on end grain. If you have a longer bench plane, use it for smoothing work on large pieces as it helps to keep the surface flat. Fix the wood securely.

Before starting, take a few seconds to check the plane and make sure it is set properly (see page 222). Then inspect the wood.

Don't plane secondhand wood, which may contain nails that will wreck the blade. On old painted wood, strip the surface first or use a Surform planer instead.

Check which way the grain runs, as this will avoid problems when you start to plane. Wherever possible, plane with the grain – not against it, which may cause the blade to dig in. Where the grain runs in different directions ('curly grain'), hold the plane at a slight angle to stop it digging in.

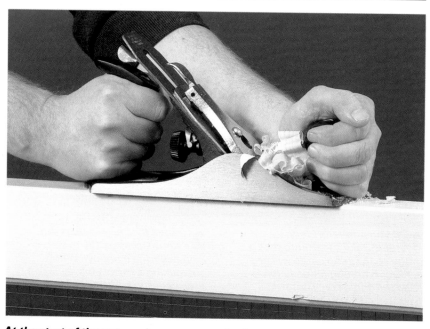

At the start of the cut, apply pressure to the front of the plane. Aim to run right along the wood with even pressure, easing the weight onto the back of the plane as you reach the end so that it runs off smoothly.

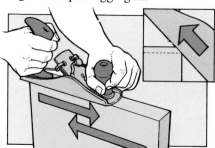

On end grain, avoid splintering the corners by planing from one side and then the other towards the middle. Alternatively, plane off the vulnerable corner first.

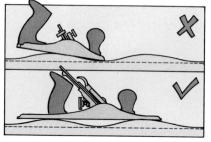

On large boards, use the longest plane available. A short one tends to ride up and down the hollows instead of knocking down any high spots first.

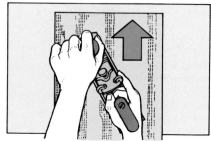

On wide boards, end grain or 'curly grain', it may be easier to hold the plane at a slight angle so the blade slices across the wood instead of digging in.

USING A POWER PLANE

Power planes demand very little effort and can be used for almost anything you would tackle with a hand tool, including rebating. The drawbacks are that they are larger than hand planes – making them difficult to use where space is restricted – and they produce a lot of small shavings.

Some models can be mounted upside down in a workbench so that you pass the wood over the plane. This makes things much easier when trimming the surface of strips of wood, but check that your power plane is designed to be operated in this way and be sure to take proper safety precautions.

 Mind the cutters

It's essential to take some simple precautions: the spinning cutters will rapidly slice through anything they touch and they go on revolving for some time after you switch off.

Always unplug the plane before adjusting it, and when the tool is not in use. Some models have an automatic guard over the cutters; on those which do not, take care not to touch the cutters or allow them to contact anything until they have stopped revolving.

When working with the plane mounted upside down, always feed the wood through with a push stick.

Start the plane and let it reach full speed before allowing the cutters to touch the wood. Push the wood forward with light pressure to avoid gouging.

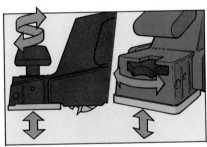

Set the depth of cut required. Some models have a separate adjuster – on others you slacken the front knob and move the front of the sole plate up or down.

For chamfering the edge of a board, some models have a guide groove. Do not hold the body with your fingers underneath so that you risk contacting the cutters.

USING A SURFORM OR RASP

Surform planes/files come in a range of sizes and shapes, allowing them to cope with most of the jobs you might otherwise tackle with a plane. They can also be used on a variety of materials – not just wood – which makes them ideal for use on old painted wood containing nails or filler (both of which could damage a plane).

The blades on these tools are designed to be replaced as soon as they become blunt. Some models accept different blades, according to the material being planed.

In general, you use a Surform exactly as you would a plane, except that the direction of the grain is not as critical. A Surform can even be used to plane across the grain, but the cutting action depends on how you angle the tool relative to the direction of the cut. Similarly, you can use a rasp in any direction.

Use a long Surform plane for jobs like levelling floorboards and planing old timber.

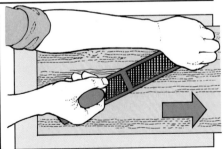

The cutting action depends on how you angle the tool relative to the direction of cut.

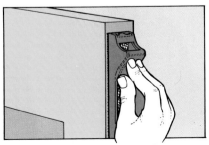

A Surform block plane can be used one-handed for jobs like easing a sticking door or window.

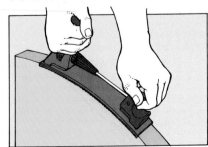

Flexible rasps can be adjusted so that they produce an evenly curved surface.

SHARPENING AND SETTING

Easy, efficient cutting depends on the plane having a sharp blade which is set correctly. On replaceable blade planes, you simply unscrew or unclip the blade and slot in a new one; traditional plane blades need sharpening on an oilstone.

Sharpening blades

Sharpening a plane blade is very similar to sharpening a chisel (see instructions on page 219). If the blade has a separate *cap iron* screwed to it, you should remove this before you sharpen the chisel.

Rub the blade on a fine oilstone moistened with a light machine oil, keeping the angle to a more or less constant 30°; a *honing guide* makes this part of the job much easier. Then, if you're planing a lot of wide boards, use the old carpenter's trick of rounding off the corners very slightly to stop them digging in (you can also get replacement blades made this way). Complete the sharpening process by rubbing the back of the blade on the stone to keep it flat and remove any burr.

Have the blade reground to an angle of 35° whenever the bevel produced by sharpening becomes larger than about 1.5mm (¹⁄₁₆″), or if the edge of the blade becomes nicked too deeply to remove on the oilstone. Re-sharpen as above.

Setting the cap iron

A cap iron is designed to curl away the shavings as they are cut, so if fitted it must be set in the right position relative to the blade. The actual distance varies from plane to plane, and also depends on what you are doing, but is normally in the range of 0.5–1.5mm (¹⁄₆₄–¹⁄₁₆″).

Setting the blade

Sight down the sole to check the position of the blade – it should be just visible as a very thin line. Use the adjusting screw to advance or retract the blade as necessary.

If one side is higher than the other use the sideways adjusting lever to level it.

If a cap iron is fitted it is held by a retaining screw which fits into a slot. This is used to alter the position of the cap iron depending on the work you are doing.

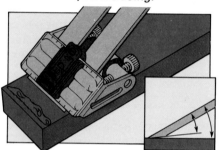

The blade should be ground to an angle of 35° and then honed on an oilstone to 30°. Use a honing guide to ensure the sharpening angle is correct.

GENERAL PURPOSE PLANES

Modern planes are almost always metal with some plastic parts, although old planes had wooden or composite bodies.

Block planes are for one or two-handed use on end grain and general trimming. They have a plain blade with no cap iron, set at a low angle of about 20° to the base. A special version made for trimming plastics has the blade set at 12°.

Bench planes are for smoothing large boards, mainly along the grain; the blades are fitted with separate cap irons. There are several types divided in order of size: *smoothing* planes range from 200–250mm (8–10″), *jack* planes range from 350–375mm (14–15″), and *fore*, *try* or *jointer* planes from 450–550mm (18–22″). Special versions are also made with a *corrugated base* for use on resinous timbers.

Rebate planes are made in various sizes and have cutters which extend the full width of the body so they can be used for planing a rebate into the edge of a piece of wood. Some models incorporate an optional guide fence to keep them parallel to the workpiece.

Replaceable blade planes are made in both bench plane and block plane versions. Short, disposable blades are held in the body by a special retaining clamp; when they become blunt, simply undo the clamp and replace the whole blade. The block plane version has an additional advantage in that the blade can be fitted at the front, enabling you to plane right into corners. The bench plane version can be fitted with a guide fence for cutting rebates.

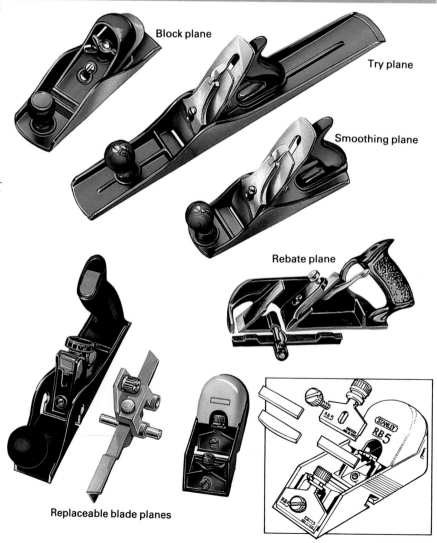

Block plane

Try plane

Smoothing plane

Rebate plane

Replaceable blade planes

JOINT SYSTEMS FOR BOARDS AND FRAMES

There are many ways to join two boards or two pieces of wood without having to cut joints into them. All the fittings shown here are capable of making a strong joint and need no more than a few holes drilled. Many are available for DIY use while some are widely employed in manufactured self-assembly furniture.

Before choosing any joint system, think about:
■ Appearance. Most systems are visible from one side or the other; often this doesn't matter, but sometimes it is critical.
■ Neatness. Some systems project inside the furniture. This is important where it obstructs the fitting of drawers or restricts the amount of storage space.
■ Ease of use. A few joints require the use of special drills or other assembly tools.
■ Price. However cheap an individual fitting may be, a furnishing system might use dozens of them.
■ Security. Is the joint ever likely to need dismantling? If so, choose a knock-down fitting. Where a joint is intended to be permanent, a continuous glue line (possibly reinforced by screws) is stronger than knock-down fittings.

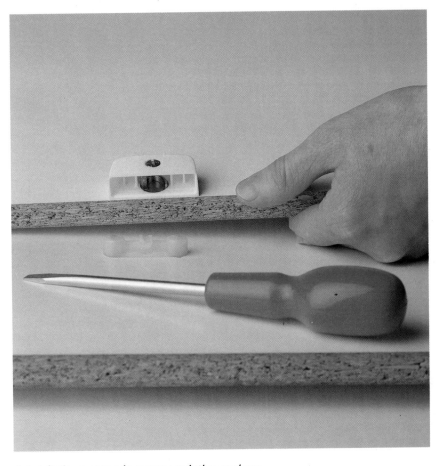

Joint fittings *come in many varieties and are designed to give speedy, reliable joints – especially with man-made boards.*

PLASTIC BLOCK JOINTS

Plastic block joints are medium-priced fittings which are common for both DIY use and on bought furniture. They are visible on the inside of the carcase and because they project up to 20mm (¾") are unsuitable for some applications, such as when drawers are to be fitted. They come in white, brown and beige; choose the colour to suit the material.

One piece blocks have two sets of holes drilled at right angles. They are fixed with screws and are designed for joints which do not need to be undone.

Two piece blocks come in pairs. One part is screwed to each side of the joint and a locking bolt is used to draw them together; use them where the assembly may need to be dismantled. The fitting is quite large but a miniature version is available.

Miniature blocks are plastic plugs which screw into a hole drilled in one part. A chipboard screw is then inserted to join the other part.

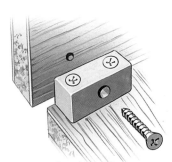

one piece joint block

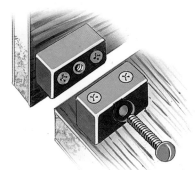

two piece joint block

miniature joint block

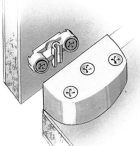

two piece joint block

CAM FITTINGS

Cam fittings are a form of knockdown joint which come in two parts that can be locked together or unlocked by twisting one part of the fitting. As this makes assembly a matter of seconds, they are popular on 'flat pack' self-assembly furniture, where a large variety of different fittings in plastic or metal are used.

A few types are also available for DIY use. They have no advantage for furniture which does not need to be dismantled, and disadvantages include a fairly high cost, plus the need for specialised tools to make holes to fit them into the cabinet parts.

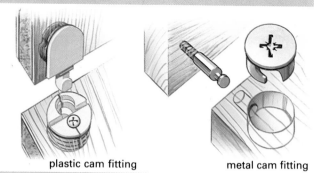

plastic cam fitting   metal cam fitting

SCREW FITTINGS

Use screws for a cheap, permanent fixing. For maximum strength, the joint can be glued as well. Screws do not project on the inside of the cabinet, and by using plastic covers, the heads can be concealed fairly well.

Chipboard screws are designed with special threads for better grip in man-made boards. Most have crosshead slots and can be power driven. Plastic covers can be fitted into the cross of a screw; two piece covers fit on slotted screws.

Connector screws for man-made boards are much larger in diameter and have a coarse thread which bites into the sides of a pre-drilled hole. The head sinks flush and is unobtrusive, but can be fitted with a plastic cap. The hole must be accurately drilled with the aid of a simple jig and depth stop

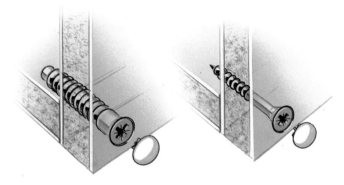

chipboard connector   chipboard screw

METAL BRACKETS

Metal brackets are cheap fittings for use with screws. Their appearance means that they are best used where they will not be on show. As well as making corner joints they are good for joining worktops to frames or carcases.

Corner brackets join and strengthen the corners of a cabinet and have a central hole which can be used for hanging it. There are several types, commonly made from plated steel. *Angle plates* are flat and are fixed to the back edge. *Corner plates* have turned-over flanges for fixing to the inner faces of the cabinet. Plastic versions are available with clip-on covers to conceal the fixing.

Right angle brackets made of mild steel or plated steel come in various lengths. *Shrinkage plates* are similar but have slotted screwholes designed to allow for a small amount of shrinkage and expansion in the wood.

Interlocking plates are mainly for frame constructions. They come in two halves which are screwed to both parts and then pressed together to make a firm joint.

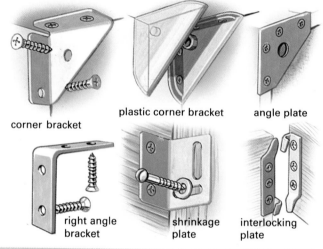

plastic corner bracket   angle plate

corner bracket

right angle bracket   shrinkage plate   interlocking plate

BOLT FITTINGS

Bolts are mainly used for frame construction. Unlike screws, they are designed for joints which have to be dismantled.

Hanger bolts have one end with a machine screw thread, and one end with a woodscrew which can be screwed into the wood after locking two nuts together on the thread. The joint is then made with a *wing nut* or an ordinary nut.

Tee nuts are hammered or pressed into the surface over a predrilled hole so a bolt can be screwed into it.

Screws and cross dowels are mainly for frames. The cross dowel is inserted into a hole in one part, and a screw fitted through the other part screws into it. The screws have socket (Allen) heads and decorative collars are fitted to trim the holes.

Socket head nuts can be used with the above system in conjunction with plain threaded rods (*studding*).

Cabinet connecting screws are used to link two boards back to back – for joining cupboards through their sides.

Worktop connectors (panel connectors) are used to join two panels end to end, particularly worktops.

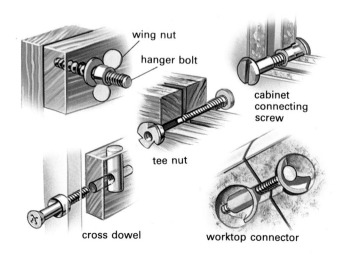

wing nut

hanger bolt

cabinet connecting screw

tee nut

cross dowel   worktop connector

FIXING WOOD WITH NAILS

It's wrong to think of nails as being a 'second-best' way to fix things together. Properly used, they make a quick, strong and permanent joint – in fact, the loadbearing timberwork of the average house is put together using nothing else. Nails also find many applications in quality furniture, and for lots of DIY jobs there is no sensible substitute.

For any job you need to know:
■ Which type of nail to use (you may also have to think about its finish, or what it's made of).
■ What size of nail to use.
■ What quantity to buy.

Types of nails
The chart on page 227 shows all the main types of nail and lists their uses. Each different shape is designed to drive easily and grips well in the materials it is intended for.

Most nails are made from steel wire or stamped out of sheet steel. As a result, they bend quite easily and rust in damp conditions. Some types have a rust-resistant galvanized (zinc) coating, and a few have special or decorative finishes.

Sizes
Nails are made in a range of sizes to cope with different thicknesses of materials. When buying, you only need to specify the length in millimetres or inches; unlike screws, a nail's thickness is fixed by its length.

***Drive nails** squarely (right) using the full length of the hammer.*

BUYING NAILS

Nails are sold in several ways, depending on their type, where you shop, and on whether you want a large or small quantity:

Pre-packs are nails sold in small boxes, tubes or bubble packs. They are a convenient way to buy small nails, and many of the more specialised types are only sold in this form. However, buying larger nails in pre-packs can be expensive unless you only need a few. The packs may be made up by weight (30, 40 or 50gm – 1⅛, 1½ or 1¾oz), or sometimes by number.

Loose Larger nails are commonly sold loose by ironmongers and builders merchants. Some superstores also stock loose nails. You buy them by weight – usually in steps of 100gm (3½oz), ½kg (1lb) or ½lb (0.25kg). The chart on Sheet 14 shows roughly how many nails of common lengths you can expect to get to the 100gm. Small nails and pins may be sold in 50gm (1¾oz) quantities.

Bulk packs are some superstores' equivalent of buying nails loose. Standard quantities (often 200gm, 400gm or 2kg) are sold in sealed polythene bags which are good value for large nails unless you only need a few.

***Large nails** are usually sold loose, but small or specialised nails come in pre-packs.*

NAILING WOOD

Successful nailing is a matter of applying the right basic techniques. shown here, and using the correct nails (see chart opposite).

Where there are special nails for the materials you are fixing, use them. If there is a choice, as in general woodwork, there are some basic rules to follow:

■ Don't use nails unless the joint is designed to be permanent.

■ Where the appearance doesn't matter, large heads give a better grip. If you don't want the nails to show, use ones with heads which can be driven flush.

■ Where the nail may be pulled out or the material is weak, ring shank nails grip better than ordinary ones.

Trade tip

Get the right length

❝ When the two things you are joining are nearly the same thickness, choose a nail that will go right through the thinner one, and half to three-quarters through the other.

When joining something thin to something thicker, always nail through the thinner material. The length of the nail should be 2½ to 3 times the thickness of the thinner material.

When driving nails into the end grain of solid wood or boards, use the longer measurements in both cases. ❞

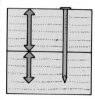

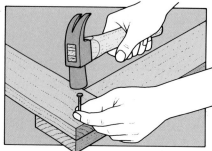

1 To start a nail, grip it firmly and give it a few light, short taps with the hammer until it grips the wood by itself. Make sure it goes in straight.

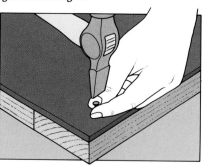

2 A cross pein hammer's wedge shaped head makes it easier to start small nails which are so short that there's a risk of hitting your fingers.

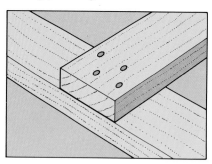

4 Where you are securing a joint with several nails, stagger them along the grain. This reduces splitting and makes a stronger joint.

Trade tip

Holding small nails

❝ A good way to start small nails is to push them through a piece of corrugated cardboard. Rip the card away before you drive them fully home. ❞

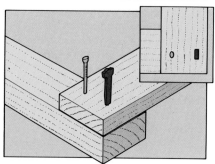

3 Drive in oval and rectangular nails so the longest dimension runs along the grain of the wood. This helps to avoid splits and makes a stronger joint.

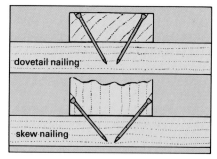

dovetail nailing

skew nailing

5 For extra strength, drive the nails at an angle as shown. Dovetail nailing and skew nailing both prevent nails from coming loose or being pulled out easily.

PROBLEM SOLVER

Avoiding splits and dents

Accidental splits can be minimized by using these methods:

■ Blunt the nail by tapping the point with a hammer. It then punches its way through the wood instead of wedging it apart.

■ Start the hole with a bradawl and then use a hammer.

■ When nailing close to the end, leave the wood overlength and saw it off after nailing.

To avoid dents in the surface, stop a fraction short and use a punch to drive the nail the rest of the way home.

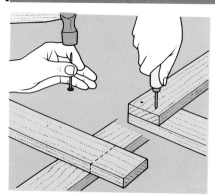

To prevent splits, blunt the nail or start the hole with a bradawl. You may be able to avoid nailing near the end of the wood by leaving surplus to cut off later.

Drive the nail fully home using a nail punch to avoid dents. To conceal the head, punch it right below the surface and cover the hole with filler.

NAILS FOR GENERAL WOODWORKING

TYPE		USES	SIZES	No per 100gm (size)
Round wire nail		• rough carpentry, eg making frames; shuttering concrete	19-150mm (¾-6")	17 (75mm), 42 (50mm)
Oval wire nail		• finished carpentry and joinery, eg door frames	25-150mm (1-6")	14 (75mm), 38 (50mm)
Lost-head nail		• carpentry; secret nailing of tongue and groove boards	25-150mm (1-6")	35 (50mm), 68 (38mm)
Panel pin		• furniture making; glued joints; fixing mouldings	12-75mm (½-3")	302 (25mm)
Moulding pin (veneer pin)		• similar to panel pin, but used for finer work	12-25mm (½-1")	568 (25mm), 1666 (15mm)
Hardboard pin		• fixing hardboard or plywood panels to frames	12-25mm (½-1")	347 (20mm)
Ring shank nail (annular nail)		• fixing man-made boards, and for extra holding power	19-75mm (¾-3")	201 (19mm)
Cut clasp nail	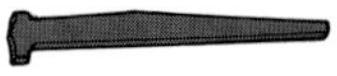	▮ rough carpentry; also for fixing to blockwork walls	38-100mm (1½-4")	27 (50mm)
Cut floor brad		▮ fixing floorboards to joists (unlikely to split wood)	50-65mm (2-2½")	15 (65mm)

NAILS FOR SPECIAL PURPOSES

TYPE		USES	SIZES	No per 100gm (size)
Clout nail		• fixing roofing felt, building paper, slates	12-75mm (½-3")	96 (19mm), 34 (38mm)
Plasterboard nail		• fixing plasterboard and insulation board to frames	38mm (1½")	64 (38mm)
Masonry nail		• fixing timber to brickwork and concrete	12-100mm (½-4")	sold by number
Corrugated fastener (wiggle nail)	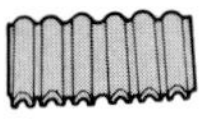	making corner joints in batten frameworks	12-25mm (½-1") deep, widths vary	sold in pre-packs
Galvanised roof nail (drive screw)		• fixing corrugated sheet roofing to rafters	65-100mm (2½-4")	14 (65mm)
Wire slate nail		• fixing slates to roof battens	32-65mm (1¼-2½")	35 (38mm)
Glazing sprig		▮ fixing glass to window frames, lies flush	12 or 16mm (½ or ⅝")	260 (15mm)
Netting staple		• fixing fence wires or netting to posts	12-50mm (½-2")	237 (15mm)
Insulated staple		fixing electric cables to woodwork	12-25mm (½-1")	sold by number
Escutcheon pin		• fixing metal fittings to furniture and joinery	16-19mm (⅝-¾")	300 (16mm)
Tack		▪ fixing webbing or fabric to frames; laying carpet	6-25mm (¼-1")	200 (19mm)
Gimp pin		· like fine tacks, for fixing gimp and braid	9-25mm (⅜-1")	770 (12mm)
Upholstery nail (chair nail)		• used as decorative trimming in upholstery	12-19mm (½-¾")	sold by number
Wire staple		use with a gun for fixing sheet materials and fabric	6-15mm (¼-⁹⁄₁₆")	sold by number
Nail plate (timber connector)	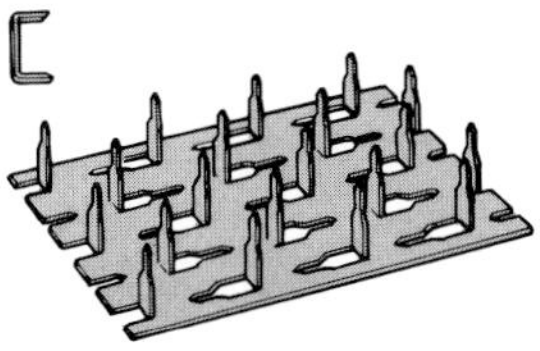	fastening roof trusses and other heavy frames	various rectangular sizes	sold by number

TOOLS FOR NAILING

HAMMERS

Woodworking hammers are divided into two main types, and both come in various weights.

Claw hammers have a head with one round face for driving nails and a claw for pulling them out. They are for general use in carpentry, especially heavy work. The weight ranges from 450gm (16oz) to 675gm (24oz); a 450gm (16oz) hammer is a good general purpose tool. Handles are commonly wood, but may be metal or fibreglass for extra durability.

Tack hammers for carpet laying and upholstery are like miniature claw hammers, weighing about 175gm (6oz); the heads are often magnetised which makes it much easier to drive in very small nails.

Cross pein hammers (also called *Warrington* hammers) have a head with one round face for driving nails and a tapered wedge face which makes it easier to start them. They are lighter than claw hammers, ranging from 110gm (4oz) to 450gm (16oz) and are mainly used for furniture making and light hammering. Smaller cross pein hammers weighing 110gm (4oz) or less are often called *Pin hammers* and are used for very light work.

It's well worth buying a good quality hammer. Cheap ones may be prone to various faults including loose heads, poorly hardened striking faces, badly formed claws and weak handles. All of these can affect the hammer's safety as well as its comfort in use.

OTHER NAILING TOOLS

Staple guns are an alternative to using a hammer and pins or tacks, if you have to fix a lot of sheet material. They can be loaded with staples of varying lengths to suit the job.

Pincers are the best tool for removing nails on which a claw hammer cannot get a grip, but are not suitable for very large nails. Some types have a tack lifter blade built into the handle.

Tack lifters are for removing small nails with large heads – particularly tacks. They are not suitable for heavy work and cannot grip nails with small heads.

Nail punches are used with nails which are made for driving in flush or below the surface, such as lost-head nails. There are various sizes given in terms of tip widths. The hollow pointed type is best for small pins; it prevents the tip slipping off the head.

PROBLEM SOLVER

Removing nails
Always remove bent or wrongly angled nails rather than trying to correct them. Use a claw hammer or pincers, and protect the wood from damage with a scrap of plywood or thick pad of card. For tacks and similar nails, use a tack lifter.

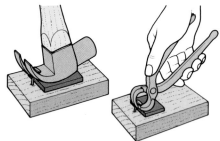
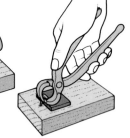
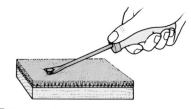

Extract nails with a claw hammer, pincers or a tack lifter. Protect the wood with scrap wood or card.

Loose hammer heads
Loose heads on hammers with wooden handles should be fixed as soon as possible. You can make a temporary repair with a metal wedge, but it's safer to buy a replacement handle of the same size – plus some metal wedges to secure it – from a specialist tool shop.

Remove the old handle by drilling out enough of the wood inside the head to loosen it.

To fit the new handle, make two or three saw cuts in the end and push on the head. Saw off any protruding waste, then drive the wedges into the cuts.

Drive in metal wedges (right) to secure a new hammer handle.

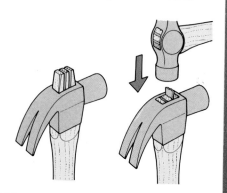

MAKING JOINTS WITH SCREWS

A properly made screwed joint looks neat and is unlikely to fail. Faults usually arise because the screws are the wrong size or type (see overleaf) or have not been fitted correctly.

Screw sizes

Screws come in various lengths, given in millimetres or inches, and in a range of thicknesses – given gauge numbers in the UK. The higher the number, the thicker the screw. No.4 to No.12 are the most common. Other countries use metric measurements and this is likely to become the case in the UK, too.

Materials

Mild steel screws are for general purposes. They are cheap and fairly strong, but rust rapidly outdoors or in damp air, and react with some hardwoods, like oak, causing stains.

Brass screws are decorative and rust resistant, but relatively weak.

Stainless steel screws are less commonly available. They are strong and almost completely rust-proof.

Aluminium screws are less common. They are rust resistant, but weak.

Bright zinc plating (BZP) is a pale silver colour, and is widely used for chipboard screws. The plating resists rust unless damaged.

Black iron screws are painted (japanned) or chemically blacked to make them rust resistant. If damaged they rust easily. Their main use is outdoors and for black iron fittings.

Chrome screws have a shiny plating and resist tarnishing, although the plating may eventually fail. Often used in bathrooms.

SCREW HEAD AND SLOT SHAPES

There are three main shapes:

Countersunk heads sink flush into a recess in the wood or fitting. A deeply recessed head can be concealed with filler.

Roundhead screws project from the surface – mainly for things too thin to countersink.

Raised head screws have a shallow dome with a countersink below, mainly used for fixing metal fittings.

All head shapes can have different shapes of slot:

Slotted heads vary widely in size with screw gauge so need a wide range of screwdrivers.

Cross head screws only need four screwdrivers to fit all sizes, and tolerate slight misalignment when driving, but are hard to clean if they get clogged with paint. There are three different patterns. *Pozidriv* and *Supadriv* have four small points between the arms of the cross and use the same screwdriver. *Phillips* screws (mainly used on machines) don't have the extra points and need a different screwdriver.

countersunk	roundhead	raised head

slotted head	Pozidriv	Phillips	Supadriv

Buying screws

DIY stores sell packs of various sizes. You can also buy screws loose in tens from ironmongers and hardware stores, or in boxes of 500 or 200 (popular sizes), 100 or 50 (less popular sizes). Large packs are often the most economical way to buy common sizes – if there are some left over, they can be used for another job. Small pre-packs are usually the most expensive.

Trade tip

Get what you want

❛ To make sure you're given exactly what you want when buying, remember to check all these points:

Quantity
Length
Gauge
Head pattern
Material
Type

For example:
Twenty 38mm No.8 slotted head countersunk brass woodscrews. ❜

TYPES OF SCREWS

WOODSCREWS

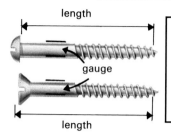

length

gauge

length

COMMON SIZES

No.4 (2.7mm)	No.6 (3.5mm)	No.8 (4.2mm)	No.10 (4.9mm)	No.12 (5.6mm)
12mm (½″)	12mm (½″)	19mm (¾″)	25mm (1″)	50mm (2″)
16mm (⅝″)	16mm (⅝″)	25mm (1″)	32mm (1¼″)	63mm (2½″)
19mm (¾″)	19mm (¾″)	32mm (1¼″)	38mm (1½″)	75mm (3″)
	25mm (1″)	38mm (1½″)	50mm (2″)	
	32mm (1¼″)	50mm (2″)	63mm (2½″)	
	38mm (1½″)	63mm (2½″)	75mm (3″)	

Woodscrews have a long, tapering tip and are threaded for about two-thirds of their length. The remaining portion under the head is a plain, unthreaded *shank*. The thread is a single spiral which gets a good grip in the grain of most timbers and some boards, but not in chipboard. Woodscrews come in the widest range of materials and sizes.

CHIPBOARD SCREWS

COMMON SIZES

No.4 (2.7mm)	No.6 (3.5mm)	No.8 (4.2mm)	No.10 (4.9mm)	No.12 (5.6mm)
9mm (⅜″)	12mm (½″)	19mm (¾″)	25mm (1″)	50mm (2″)
12mm (½″)	16mm (⅝″)	25mm (1″)	32mm (1¼″)	63mm (2½″)
16mm (⅝″)	19mm (¾″)	32mm (1¼″)	38mm (1½″)	50mm (2″)
19mm (¾″)	25mm (1″)	38mm (1½″)	50mm (2″)	
	32mm (1¼″)	50mm (2″)	63mm (2½″)	
	38mm (1½″)	63mm (2½″)	75mm (3″)	

Chipboard screws are mainly for joining things to chipboard, but can also be used in solid wood, where they help to get a better grip if you have to fix into the end grain. They do not taper as much as woodscrews, the thread is cut deeper and runs the full length of the screw. It often has a double spiral to give it extra grip. Chipboard screws come in a wide range of sizes and are usually made of BZP or mild steel.

SPECIAL PURPOSE SCREWS

Mirror screws with head covers

Coach screw

Security screw

Dowel screw

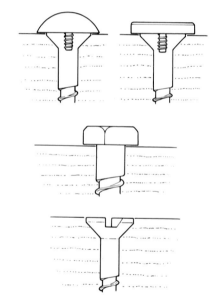

Mirror screws are countersunk woodscrews with a threaded hole in the centre of the head. They have screw-on decorative covers, which hide the head after the screws have been inserted.
Coach screws are like very large woodscrews with a square head designed to be driven with a spanner. They are for heavy constructions – like timber frames and garden furniture – and are sold by diameter, rather than gauge number. Common sizes range from 6mm (¼″) to 12mm (½″) and lengths up to 150mm (6″). Made of mild steel, which may be galvanized.
Security screws have a 'one-way' slot in the head so they can be done up but not removed. Ordinary screws can be made into security screws by filing the slots or burring them after insertion.
Dowel screws are for joining two pieces of wood invisibly – eg fixing wooden knobs. They have a thread at each end so they screw into both parts together.

SCREW ACCESSORIES

Inset screw cup

Screw cup washer

Screw covers

Screw cap

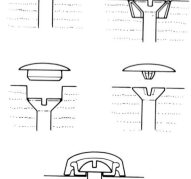

Screw cups give a decorative finish and help the screw grip better without damaging the wood. They are only used with countersunk and raised head screws. There are two sorts: *cup washers* (surface screw cups), normally in brass or chrome, and *insert screw cups,* normally in brass, which plug into a recess in the wood.
Screw caps, made of white or brown plastic, plug into the slot of a crosshead screw or a recess drilled into the wood over the head.
Screw covers, made of white or brown plastic, are in two parts. One goes under the head of a screw and the other clips over it to hide the head.

MAKING SCREW HOLES

Only one size of hole in a given material allows any particular size of screw to turn easily and get the best grip from its threads. This hole is called a *pilot hole*, and should be slightly shorter than the screw.

Woodscrews have an unthreaded shank which must be free to turn easily, so this part must have a wider *clearance hole*. If it doesn't, the screw will be hard to drive and you risk damaging it. Chipboard screws don't have a plain shank, but still need a clearance hole in the part you are fixing so it will be pulled up tight. The chart on the right shows what hole sizes to drill.

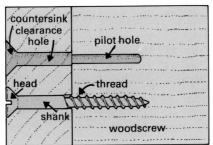

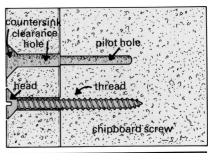

SCREW AND DRILL SIZES

Screw gauge	Clearance	Pilot (softwood)		Pilot (board/hardwood)	
		Woodscrew	Chipboard	Woodscrew	Chipboard
No 4 (2.7mm)	3mm (1/8″)	bradawl	1mm (3/64″)	1.5mm (1/16″)	2mm (1/16″)
No 6 (3.5mm)	4mm (5/32″)	1.5mm (1/16″)	1.5mm (1/16″)	2mm (1/16″)	2.5mm (3/32″)
No 8 (4.2mm)	4.5mm (3/16″)	2mm (1/16″)	2mm (1/16″)	2.5mm (3/32″)	3mm (1/8″)
No 10 (4.9mm)	5mm (7/32″)	2mm (1/16″)	2.5mm (3/32″)	2.5mm (1/8″)	3mm (1/8″)
No 12 (5.6mm)	6mm (1/4″)	2.5mm (3/32″)	2.5mm (3/32″)	3mm (1/8″)	3.5mm (1/8″)

DRILLING AND FIXING

The holes drilled in each part must align and must be the right depth.
■ If you are fixing a pre-drilled fitting, mark the position of the screw holes using a bradawl. Then drill a pilot hole in the thing you are fixing it to, and open out to a clearance size if necessary.
■ If the part you are fixing is not pre-drilled, start by drilling clearance holes in it so you can mark through them, or clamp the parts together and drill the pilot holes through both. Enlarge the holes in the first part to clearance size.

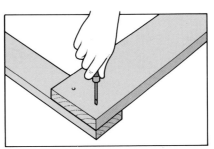

1 *Mark the holes with a bradawl – this stops the drill bit wandering off line. With small screws in softwood, a bradawl hole is all you need.*

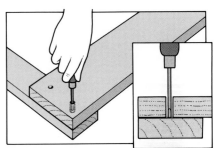

2 *If you are fitting something which is not predrilled, either drill clearance holes first and mark through them on to the other part so you can drill it...*

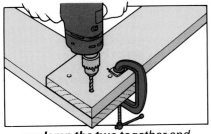

...or clamp the two together and drill pilot holes followed by clearance holes. This ensures that the screws align perfectly through both parts.

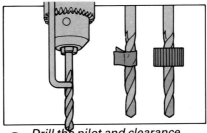

3 *Drill the pilot and clearance holes with the right sized bit. Use a depth stop or put tape on the bit so you stop just short of the length of the screw.*

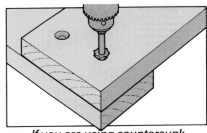

4 *If you are using countersunk screws, finish off with a countersunk bit to the size of the head. Don't let the bit 'chatter' causing a ragged hole.*

Trade tip

Trouble-free fixing

❝ ■ If you are fixing two pieces of wood together, use a screw twice as long as the thickness of the first piece of wood.
■ If you are fixing something very thick, avoid using over-long screws by 'counterboring' part of the clearance hole. Use a drill bit just larger than the head of the screw.
■ Don't put screws near the edge of a piece of wood – it may split. If you have to screw into end grain,

use chipboard screws.
■ If you are fitting lots of screws in a line, 'stagger' them to avoid splitting the wood.
■ Make screws easier to drive and remove by rubbing them on a candle to lubricate the threads.
■ To avoid breaking a brass screw, drive a steel screw in first to open out the hole.
■ Don't change bits unnecessarily – it's less work and less likely to cause mistakes. Do all the pilot holes, then the clearance holes, then the countersinking. ❞

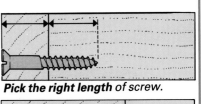

Pick the right length of screw.

drill to size of head

Counterbore thick pieces of wood.

TOOLS FOR MAKING SCREW JOINTS

BRADAWL

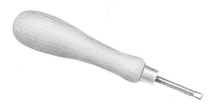

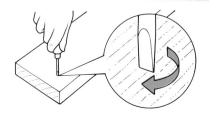

A bradawl has a slim, short blade like a screwdriver, sharpened to a knife edge. It is used for starting small screws in softwood or marking the hole before drilling. Hold it so the blade crosses the grain of the wood, then press and twist it into the surface.

DRILL BITS

Push drill bit

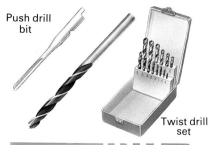

Twist drill set

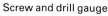

Screw and drill gauge

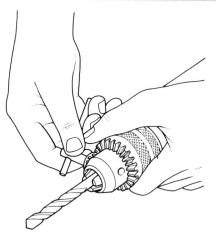

Twist drills fit an electric or hand drill. A typical 10-piece set contains drills from 1.5-6.5mm or $\frac{1}{16}$-$\frac{1}{4}$" and should cope with all normal screws. They are made in High Speed Steel (HSS) for use in wood or metal, or carbon steel which is for wood only and blunts easily. Blunt drills cut badly and overheat, causing even more blunting. Drill sharpeners are available, but few people bother for small, cheap bits.

Screw and drill gauges help you pick the drill size to match the screw.

Push drill bits fit a spiral ratchet screwdriver for small holes and rough work in softwood. The pointed cutter twists its way gradually into the wood.

COUNTERSINKS

Hand countersink

Countersink bits

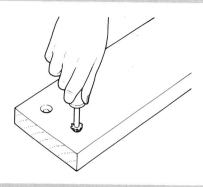

Countersink bits for drills are made in High Speed Steel for metal as well as wood, or in carbon steel, for wood only. It's worth having an HSS one for recutting recesses in metal fittings.

Countersinking with a drill is the least work, but using another tool saves swapping bits. Countersink bits are also made for push drills, while **hand countersinks** have a bit with a stubby handle which you twist back and forth. Both are only suitable for wood.

SCREWDRIVERS

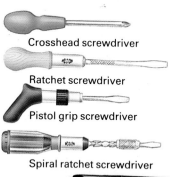

Crosshead screwdriver

Ratchet screwdriver

Pistol grip screwdriver

Spiral ratchet screwdriver

Electric screwdriver

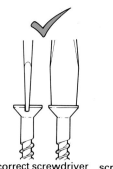

correct screwdriver   screwdriver too small

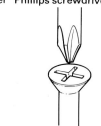

Pozidriv screwdriver   Phillips screwdriver

Flat blade screwdrivers for slotted head screws come in many sizes and must fit the screw head accurately.

Crosshead screwdriver sizes vary less. A No.2 Pozidriv driver fits most woodworking screws but not Phillips screws (Phillips drivers work with Pozidriv but don't fit so well).

Both kinds may have rigid plastic or wooden handles. You can also get a range of 'easy action' screwdrivers.

Ratchet screwdrivers have a 'one-way' action which drives or undoes without changing grip or locks rigidly. Some have interchangeable bits. 'Pistol grip' handles apply more pressure.

Spiral ratchet screwdrivers have a push action handle to exert more force than by twisting. They have interchangeable bits and can be locked rigid.

Electric screwdrivers have rechargeable power packs and interchangeable bits, while **electric drills** can be fitted with screwdriver bits if they have a low speed and have a reverse action.

MAKING GLUED JOINTS

Modern woodworking adhesives give a bond which is often much stronger than the materials they are fixing. And as a result, many of the traditional ways of joining wood have been superseded by methods which rely on the strength of the glue alone.

One of the main advantages of using adhesive is that you can often make joints which are virtually invisible. But glued joints are also permanent, quick to make, and can be used where there is no room for screws or nails.

Possible drawbacks

Adhesives have disadvantages, too, so when deciding how to fix something, bear in mind the following:
■ Most adhesives don't give you an 'instant' joint; they may need to be held in position, then left anywhere from an hour to a day to gain full strength.
■ Don't expect butt joints to be very strong, especially when gluing end grain. Although the adhesive is unlikely to fail, the wood fibres themselves may well pull away.
■ Be careful which adhesive you choose when gluing anything subject to changes in temperature and humidity.
■ Don't glue any joint you might need to dismantle.

Many adhesives set slowly to give you time to work – so the joint must be held until it bonds.

THE RIGHT ADHESIVE FOR THE JOB	
IF YOU'RE GLUING	**CHOOSE**
Indoor woodwork (dry conditions)	PVA adhesive or waterproof resin adhesive
Indoor woodwork (damp conditions)	Waterproof PVA adhesive or waterproof resin adhesive
Outdoor woodwork	Waterproof PVA adhesive or waterproof resin adhesive
Plastic laminates on to wood	Contact adhesive
Loose joints	PVA adhesive, or waterproof resin adhesive if large gaps need filling
Wallboards to walls	Special wallboard adhesive
Laying wooden flooring	Special flooring adhesive
See full adhesives guide overleaf for product details.	

Trade tip

Stick with it

6 Many general purpose repair adhesives will stick wood quite well, including epoxy resins, 'super' glues, and multi-purpose clear adhesives. All these can be useful in an emergency – and epoxy resin is excellent for gluing metal and plastic fittings to wood.

In general, though, repair adhesives tend to work out a lot more expensive than adhesives designed for the job. And even though some of them might in theory give a stronger bond, this is probably stronger than you actually need. 9

ADHESIVES FOR WOODWORK

PVA ADHESIVES

Apply PVA adhesive from the bottle or tube. On large areas, you can spread it more evenly using a brush or spreader. Clean the tools with water.

PVA adhesive is often sold under the name 'Woodworking adhesive', and is a good choice for all kinds of indoor woodwork. However, the standard type is not recommended for anything which might get damp, as moisture can cause the bond to fail. There is a special formulation called *Waterproof* PVA adhesive for situations like this.

Both types are sold in squeeze bottles, tubs and tins of various sizes. PVA adhesive tends to 'go off' if stored for a long time, so buying more than you're likely to use in the near future may not be worthwhile.

WATERPROOF RESIN ADHESIVES

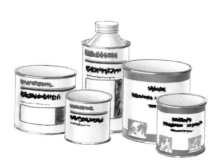

Mix resin adhesive in a plastic or glass container, not a metal one. Spread it with an old brush or notched spreader and clean the tools as quickly as possible.

Waterproof resin adhesives normally come in small tins similar to paint tins. They all need to be mixed before use. Some types come in dry powder form for mixing with water. Others are in two parts, one of which may be a liquid hardener.

Resin adhesives give a very strong waterproof bond, so are excellent for work which will be used outdoors or in damp conditions. They fill gaps better than PVA adhesive, and can be used where maximum strength is important.

CONTACT ADHESIVES

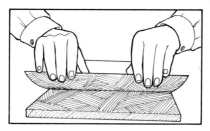

Spread contact adhesive on both surfaces using a spreader. Allow to dry, then bring the two parts together. Most bond instantly, so take care when positioning.

Contact ('impact') adhesive is used for bonding sheet materials to boards. The adhesive is spread on both surfaces and allowed to dry before bonding; most then bond instantly, but *thixotropic* (gel) types allow some repositioning.

Many formulations are inflammable and give off a toxic vapour until dried; they also need special solvent/cleaner. Non-toxic versions are available.

Contact adhesives are sold in various sized tins, and also in tubes for very small quantities. Most come with a spreader, although some non-toxic types are spread with a foam pad instead.

GLUE GUNS

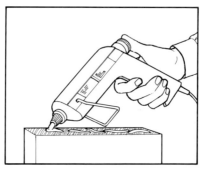

Glue from a gun can be used as soon as the gun is hot enough for the glue to flow evenly. Bring the parts together as soon as you can and hold for a few moments.

Glue guns use special sticks of solid adhesive which melt when heated. The molten adhesive is then forced out of the nozzle either by pressing the other end of the stick (on cheaper models) or by pulling a trigger. There are different adhesive sticks to suit wood and other materials, and because they harden on cooling, all types give a strong bond very rapidly. This often eliminates the need for clamps, because the joint can simply pressed together and held until it bonds.

The main drawback is price – guns are fairly expensive and the adhesive sticks themselves may cost more than liquid and powder types. You also need a power source within reach of the job.

HOW TO MAKE GLUED JOINTS

There are three basic ways to stick wood using adhesives.

Glue only. This is a perfectly adequate way to join pieces of wood, providing you can hold the parts firmly enough to stop them from moving before the glue dries.

Normally, the best way to do this is with clamps; but cutting conventional woodworking joints in the parts also helps to secure them and increases the gluing area to.

Glue and pin. After spreading the adhesive, the parts are secured using panel pins or nails. These contribute a certain amount to the strength of the joint, but their main function is to hold the assembly firmly until the glue has set.

Glue and dowel. This is a simple method for increasing the joint area and adding strength. It is frequently used to join veneered chipboard, where it enables you to glue to the core of the wood, rather than the surface veneer (which is weakly bonded to the chipboard and may be too shiny to take glue well).

Avoiding marks

For a good finish, it's important to clean off surplus glue. But be careful how you do it: if woodworking adhesive is smeared over the surface, even thinly, it often leaves marks which show up through varnish.

One method is to use a rag moistened in the right solvent (water or chemical cleaner as appropriate) to remove all traces. In practice, though, it's often safer to wait until the glue has dried and pare or scrape off the excess.

Glued joints need to be clamped or otherwise held in place until the adhesive has hardened.

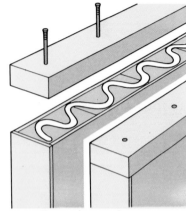

Pins or nails can be used to reinforce a joint and hold it while the adhesive sets.

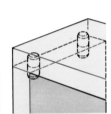

Dowels set into drilled holes help to strengthen glued joints, especially in man-made boards.

1 Lightly sand the area to be glued and dust it off. This cleans the surface and provides a 'key' for the glue to bond on to. Remove any old glue or paint.

2 Apply the adhesive to one surface only, except in the case of contact adhesives. For maximum strength, it should form a thin, even glue line.

3 If you are gluing end grain, seal it first with a thin coat of glue and allow this to dry. Then spread another layer and make the joint.

PROBLEM SOLVER

Gluing difficult surfaces

Oily woods, eg teak are best glued as soon as possible after sawing or sanding. If the oil content of the wood is left to rise to the surface, it may affect the bond.

Preservative-treated timbers need to have their joining surfaces sanded down immediately before gluing. If you are applying preservative, allow it to dry first for several days before using glue.

Loose joints are best filled using resin adhesive, which has better gap-filling properties than PVA types.

Otherwise, avoid filling gaps with adhesive if at all possible.

Damp conditions can swell wood and ruin a glued joint. If there is a chance your work will be exposed to damp, let the timber acclimatise to the conditions for about a week before gluing and be sure to use a waterproof glue.

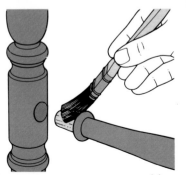

Worn joints are common on old furniture. Resin adhesives can help fill gaps here.

HOLDING THE JOINT TOGETHER

GENERAL PURPOSE CLAMPS

G-cramps

plug-in peg

folding workbench

quick-acting cramp

G-cramps can be used for clamping many different kinds of joints. They come in a range of sizes, measured by their maximum jaw opening, and you can get specially deep versions for holding work which is a long way from the edge. Some G-cramps have soft pads on their jaws.

Folding workbenches have a pair of clamping jaws which can be used to hold a joint (although the bench will be out of action until the glue has hardened). The design of the jaws allows them to grip material up to around 100mm (4″) thick and to cope with tapering shapes.

Larger objects, such as frames, can be gripped using plug-in pegs and extension arms which fit into holes in the worktop.

CLAMPS FOR SPECIAL PURPOSES

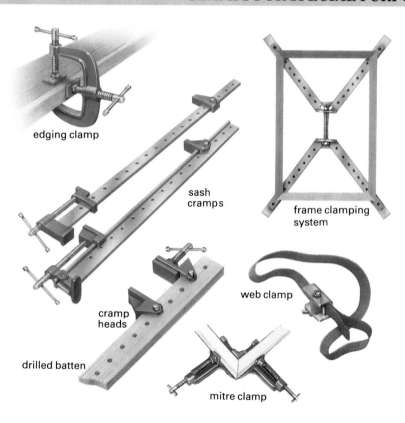

edging clamp

sash cramps

frame clamping system

cramp heads

web clamp

drilled batten

mitre clamp

Edging clamps are for holding edging strips in place and may be worth buying if you use a lot of material which needs finishing in this way. (For a one-off job you can usually improvise with adhesive tape or string bindings, protecting the edges with card.)

Mitre clamps are worth using if you make pictures frames or anything with similar corner joints. There are cheaper plastic or metal *frame clamping systems*, or you can improvise with string and adhesive tape.

Web clamps are for holding large jobs, such as frames, and can be used even on irregular shapes. The webbing is tightened using a spanner or screwdriver and has a ratchet release.

Sash cramps are the best way to hold large objects, such as doors or table tops. They are expensive to buy (particularly as you often need to use them in pairs), but can be hired.

Cramp heads, consisting of end stops plus screw clamps for applying pressure, are a cheaper alternative to sash cramps. The heads are designed to fit into holes drilled in a batten, allowing you to make up a sash cramp to any length required.

IMPROVISED CLAMPS

spanish windlass

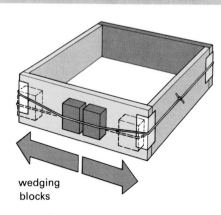

wedging blocks

String can be used to improvise all sorts of clamps – particularly for frames and edgings. Use strong string of a type which doesn't stretch too much, and always protect the surface using card or scraps of wood.

The two most effective ways to pull the string tight are by twisting it with a piece of stick (a 'Spanish windlass'), or by using pairs of blocks to give a wedging action. In both cases, you may need to use tape to hold the tightening devices in position.

SIMPLE JOINTS FOR SOLID TIMBER

Making things from solid timber means that you need to join a number of small pieces together. Traditional woodworking used many different forms of joint which were often complicated by the need for them to have a strength which did not depend on the rather weak glues then available. Some joints were also intended to give a decorative appearance to the finished job.

Although modern glues and joint systems have made it easy to join two pieces of wood together strongly, there are still many occasions when it's essential to cut a joint. In some cases this is for added strength; sometimes it makes a neater finished job.

The illustrations below show the most useful joints for things like built-in furniture and household joinery – together with examples of where to use them.

ANGLED JOINTS

Butt joints are simple to make but depend entirely on the strength of their fixings. They can be glued or reinforced with nails or screws. When panelling is applied to a butt jointed frame it helps to lock and strengthen the joint.
Common uses: Frames for panelling.

Mitre joints are a form of decorative butt joint in which no end grain is visible. The mitre is normally cut at 45°, but different angles can be used for non-square frames.
Common uses: Picture frames, decorative mouldings.

Halving (half lap) joints are used when two pieces meet at right angles on the wide face. They give a flush surface, while interlocking for strength, and can be used for corners, T or cross shapes.
Common uses: Frames for panelling or in view.

Housing joints are used when two pieces meet at right angles on their narrow face. Stopped housings are used when one piece of wood is narrower than the other.
Common uses: Shelving, steps.

Bridle joints are used for corners when more strength is needed, and for a decorative appearance.
Common uses: Furniture frames.

Mortise and tenon joints are the traditional corner joint for sturdy frames. Fairly complicated to make, they are neat and strong.
Common uses: Door, window, table and bed frames.

BOX JOINTS

Dovetail joints interlock strongly and resist being pulled apart. The version shown is machine cut.
Common uses: Drawer sides.

Comb joints are simpler to cut but less strong.
Common uses: Boxes.

LENGTHENING JOINTS

Scarf joints are designed to give maximum strength. Each half can be made with three saw cuts, but these require accurate marking.
Common uses: Repairs to door frames, lengthening rails.

WIDENING JOINTS

Edge glued joints are very strong, but rely on the timber being planed true. The joint can be reinforced with dowels or corrugated fasteners.
Common uses: Worktops, tables.

Tongued and grooved joints can be made using special pre-cut timber.

TECHNIQUES FOR MAKING JOINTS

The techniques shown here are for making the most common and useful forms of joint. The other joints, which are shown on the previous page, are all based on those covered in detail here and can be made by adapting the techniques described below.

Tools needed

As with most woodwork, accurate marking and measuring is the key. As a minimum you need a straight-edge, ruler and try square. A marking gauge is also useful, although it is possible to manage without one.

Most joints are cut with a tenon saw and cleaned up with a chisel, which must be kept sharp. The simpler joints can be cut with a saw alone. For halving joints, finishing them with a chisel is likely to be more accurate, while a chisel is essential for making mortise and tenon joints.

MAKING BUTT JOINTS

Butt joints are the simplest of all to make, but because the two parts don't interlock in any way, they rely on the fixings (glue, nails or screws) for strength. It's also important to cut the wood accurately so that the contact patch is made as large as possible.

Mitre joints and scarf joints are made in much the same way, except that the ends are cut at an angle. And similar techniques apply when making edge to edge joints to widen a piece of timber. These are effectively just a long butt joint, but it is essential to plane the wood true and clamp the joint while the adhesive is drying.

1 Cut the parts to length after marking the cutting lines with a try square to ensure that the ends are true. Take care to saw on the right side of the line.

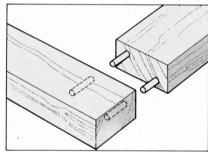

2 Nails make quick and easy fixings. Screws can be used instead, but tend not to grip well since they are driven into end grain.

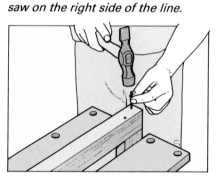

3 A plain glued butt joint is satisfactory for unstressed areas, where the joint can be held firm until it sets. Pin through for extra strength.

4 For a concealed joint use dowels and glue. The holes in each side must be drilled accurately using a dowel jig or dowel centre pins.

Trade tip

Headless pinning

‘For a quick and easy concealed joint, drive nails into one part then cut their heads off with wire cutting pliers. Hammer the second part on to the points this produces. ’

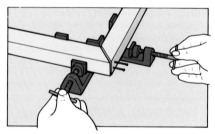

Make a mitre joint by cutting the ends at 45° using a mitre box. For strength it helps to clamp the joint in a mitre clamp, glue and pin or dowel.

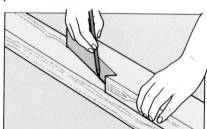

Make a scarf joint by marking one part carefully and sawing to shape. Use this to mark and cut the second, then glue and screw them together.

Joint cutting clamps are one of a number of useful aids. They help to guide the saw at the correct angle, and can be adapted to suit a range of joints. They can also be used to hold the pieces together during assembly.

MAKING A HALVING JOINT

Halving joints are the most basic form of cut joint, used wherever two frame members meet or cross without gaining thickness.

There are two types of halving joint; the T halving and the cross halving joint. The technique varies slightly depending on which one you are making since it is possible to cut a halving joint on the end of a piece of timber by using two saw cuts. A halving joint in the middle of a piece must be cut with a chisel; housing joints are cut in very much the same way.

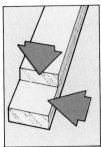 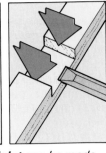

An end halving joint can be made with two saw cuts. A cross halving joint must be chiselled out after sawing down each side to the right depth.

1 Mark each piece to indicate where the other crosses it. Draw the lines with a square, exactly the same width apart as the width of the wood.

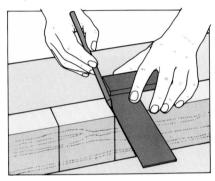

2 Align the square accurately against each side of the wood and continue the lines which you marked across the top all the way down both sides.

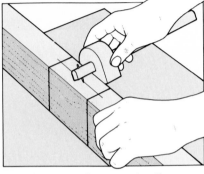

3 On each piece, mark a line halfway through its thickness. The easy way is to use a marking gauge (see Tip) but you can measure and then rule it.

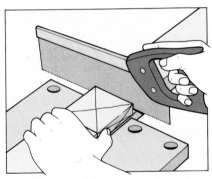

4 Check which part is to be cut away, then saw squarely along the cross lines on each side of the joint down as far as the halfway mark.

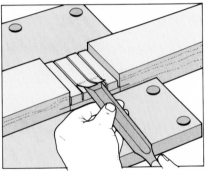

5 Pare out the waste with a chisel working down in shallow steps. On wide joints, a few extra saw cuts in the middle make this easier.

Trade tip

Halving with a marking gauge

❝Set a marking gauge to half the thickness of the wood this way:
■ Set it to what you think looks right and mark in from both sides to check.
■ If the two marks don't meet or if they overlap, the gauge needs adjusting.
■ To make small adjustments, tap the end of the gauge on the worktop to jar it along.
■ Recheck until the two marks align perfectly. ❞

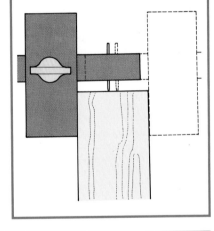

MORTISE AND TENON JOINTS

Mortise and tenon joints rely on accurate marking out. A few basic rules can be applied when doing so.
■ Put the mortise in the vertical part and put the tenon in the horizontal.
■ Make the tenon about one-third the thickness of the wood.
■ Adjust the size of the mortise and tenon to suit the sizes of drill bit and chisel you have available.
■ Where the tenon runs right through the mortised part, the joint will be neater if you make the tenon overlength and trim it off after the joint has been made.

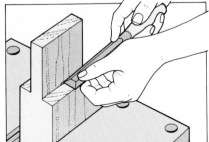

1 Make a tenon by sawing across the two shoulders, then sawing down from the ends. Clean up with a chisel for a neat, accurate joint.

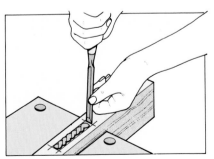

2 Cut the mortise by drilling out most of the waste with a drill bit of the same width, then cut out the rest by chopping down with a chisel.

Joint doesn't fit

Although care in marking and cutting should produce a perfect fitting joint, a mistake can easily leave the joint loose and badly fitting.

The best solution is to make a new piece, but when you can't, you need to ensure that the joint fits together as well as possible, concealing any gaps later if need be.

Where the gaps are small, one solution is to use a resin-based woodworking glue. Whereas a general purpose type such as PVA tends to run out of the joint, resin glues are far better at filling gaps.

If you are driving in nails or screws, make sure these don't pull the parts out of alignment by trying to close up the gap. If necessary, pack any cracks out with slips of wood to prevent this.

Fill remaining gaps with a general purpose filler if painting, or a wood-coloured stopping if the joints are going to be on view.

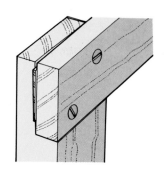

When joints are badly cut *ensure that nailing or screwing them together does not pull them out of line. Pack out if necessary to avoid this.*

TOOLS FOR MAKING JOINTS

Mitre boxes are used with a tenon saw and are an aid to cutting timber squarely or at a 45° angle. They may be made of wood or plastic, and some have metal inserts. Most boxes are not capable of taking wood over about 50mm (2″) wide; if you buy a wider box you will need a very long tenon saw to use it properly.

It is essential to treat a mitre box with care – once the slots become worn and inaccurate it is useless.

Mitre blocks are like an open version of the mitre box. While they have only one set of slots, making them less accurate, they can take wood of a greater width.

Joint cutting guides are like multi-angle mitre boxes. They come with a range of attachments and instructions showing how to set them up for a range of different joints.

Mitre clamps are designed to hold a corner joint steady while glueing or nailing it together.

Frame clamping systems hold four or more corners together at once. Particularly useful for picture frames, some types are sturdy enough to make them also suitable for heavier constructions.

Dowelling jigs come in various forms. All are designed to do the same job, ensuring that two pieces of wood can be drilled so that the holes in them align perfectly. Most clamp on to the edge of the wood, and may have different guides to fit various sizes of dowel bit.

Dovetailing jigs are drill attachments used for making dovetail or comb joints in thin boards – especially for making drawers and boxes. The wood is clamped in the jig which has a series of parallel guides. A special cutter is then pushed into each guide slot in turn to make one half of the joint – a straight cutter makes a comb joint, and an angled one makes a dovetail. This is then repeated for the other piece of wood.

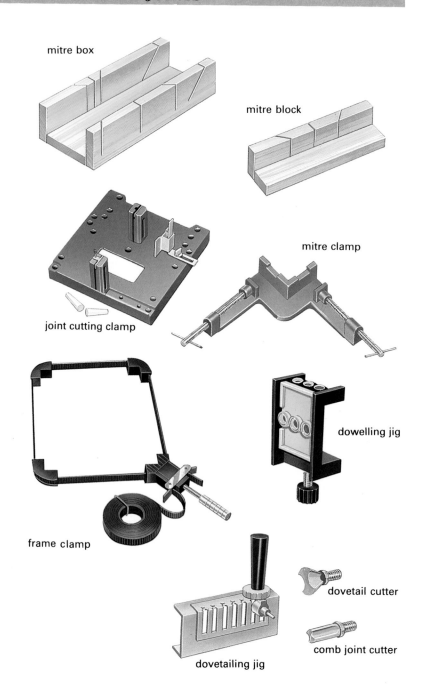

mitre box

mitre block

mitre clamp

joint cutting clamp

dowelling jig

frame clamp

dovetail cutter

comb joint cutter

dovetailing jig

CLEAR FINISHES FOR INTERIOR WOODWORK

As the final stage in renovating or making wooden furniture and fittings, wood finishing is among the most satisfying of all DIY jobs. The products available for bringing out or enhancing the natural beauty of wood can be numbered in their hundreds, but most fall into one or other of the following groups.

Colourings for modifying the wood's natural colour.

Fillers for disguising blemishes.

Traditional finishes, such as oils and shellac-based polishes.

Varnishes, based on natural oil or synthetic polyurethane resins.

Modern lacquers, which give a much tougher finish than varnishes.

There are also various factory finishes for modern furniture, including cellulose lacquer and polyester or melamine coatings. These need special equipment to apply and are not discussed here.

When choosing a clear wood finish, you need to take into account not only the finished effect, but also the type of wood and the amount of wear and tear it can be expected to receive. The materials described in this section are suitable both for new wood, and for old wood that has been stripped for refinishing. But remember that no clear finish will hide surface imperfections entirely – either repair these first, or choose paint instead.

Clear finishes can bring out or enhance the natural beauty of wood, as well as protecting the surface.

WOOD COLOURINGS

Bleaches have to be used if you want to lighten wood, or dye it to a shade which is paler than its natural colour.

Two-part bleaches come in a pack with two bottles of solution. The first, which is alkaline, may darken the wood slightly when applied; the second is then added to start the chemical reaction which bleaches the wood.

Oxalic acid (available from chemists and specialist suppliers) can also be used to lighten wood, but is less effective than two-part bleaches and highly poisonous. The acid must be neutralized by washing off with methylated spirits before further finishing can take place.

If you plan to polish wood which has been bleached, use *white French polish* (see overleaf).

Dyes and stains are used to colour wood before finishing. Until a few years ago, the terms 'wood dye' and 'wood stain' were interchangeable, but

confusingly some manufacturers now produce *exterior wood stains* – coloured surface coatings which simply obscure the grain. A true wood dye or stain penetrates deep into the wood, and when dry must be sealed with some other form of clear finish.

Solvent-based dyes are penetrating, quick drying and do not raise the grain. Some contain translucent pigments which stop them fading, and different colours from the same range can be mixed to produce the shade you want. The disadvantage of solvent dyes is that they dry very quickly, making it difficult to maintain a 'wet edge' and sometimes leading to a rather blotchy effect.

Water and alcohol-based dyes are easier to apply, but tend to raise the grain of the wood and are not as colourfast as solvent-based dyes. They are only available from specialist wood finish suppliers.

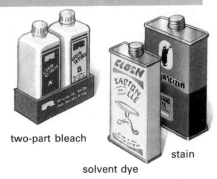

two-part bleach

solvent dye

stain

Apply wood dye with a cloth

CRACK AND GRAIN FILLERS

Wood filler or 'stopping' is used to fill cracks in the wood, or cover marks such as screw and nail heads. Some types come in tins or tubes as a ready to use *stiff paste*; others are in *two parts*, with a hardener which is mixed with the stopping immediately before application. Various shades are available, but the filler always stays visible under a clear finish since it breaks up the natural grain lines.

Plastic wood actually contains real wood flour, but tends to shrink more than other stoppers. Apply a little at a time, to allow for drying and shrinkage.

Grain fillers are specifically for filling the grain of wood to make it easier to apply a high gloss finish.

Woods such as oak and teak have an open grained texture that quickly soaks up any finish. And while this is fine for oils or waxes, without grain filler a thinner varnish or lacquer needs multiple coats – with a lot of rubbing down in between – before the surface

is smooth enough to produce a satisfactory gloss.

Traditionally plaster of Paris was used, then wiped over with linseed oil to make the plaster transparent. This is incompatible with modern finishes, so use *ready-mixed paste grain filler* instead.

In some cases, you may be able to use wood dye to colour the grain filler so that staining and filling can be carried out in one operation.

paste stopping

ready-mixed grain filler

Trade tip

Colour matching
❛Manufacturers claim that fillers take up wood dyes, but they are likely to do so in a different way to surrounding wood. The solution is to stain the wood first, then stain the filler to match this colour as closely as possible. ❜

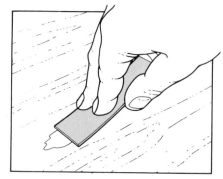

Apply filler with a putty knife or filling knife.

TRADITIONAL CLEAR FINISHES

Oiling is the easiest of all clear finishing processes – you simply rub the oil into the wood. The traditional oil used in Europe is *linseed oil*, derived from the flax plant. This takes about three days to dry in its raw form, so many people prefer to use *boiled linseed oil* which dries in about 18 hours.

Teak oil is specially formulated for teak, normally with extra resins for a tougher finish. *Danish oil* contains oil from the Chinese tung tree, and gives a lustrous finish with less sheen than teak oil or linseed oil.

Waxing is probably the oldest method of treating wood: *beeswax* – the original ingredient – has been known and used for thousands of years. You can make your own wax polish by dissolving blocks of beeswax in an equal quantity of pure turpentine: heat it very gently in a bowl over a saucepan of water to speed up the process.

Many proprietary wax polishes are also available, often including *carnauba wax* (from a Brazilian palm) to make the beeswax less sticky.

French polish was invented by a French cabinet maker nearly 200 years ago. It gives a deep, lustrous gloss, but is nothing like as durable as modern varnishes and is particularly susceptible to heat and alcohol. It also takes real skill to apply.

French polish is based on *shellac* – a substance derived from the lac insect which lives on trees in India and the Far East. There are various grades.

White French polish should be used on bleached and pale wood. *Button polish* is golden brown, and is often used in antique restoration. It takes its

French polishes

wax polish

raw beeswax

wood oils

name from the shellac used to make it, which is in thin discs, like buttons. *Garnet polish* is a darker form of French polish, for use on mahogany and other dark coloured woods.

When applying French polish with a cloth in the traditional way, you also need linseed oil to lubricate it, and methylated spirits for 'rubbing off' to a high gloss – the tricky part.

Shellac varnish contains similar ingredients to French polish, and can be applied by brush, rather than by rubbing. *Sanding sealer* is also based on shellac, and can be used to seal the surface before applying most types of finish. (*Knotting*, too, is based on shellac, but is not generally necessary under clear finishes.)

Oiled finish

Waxed finish

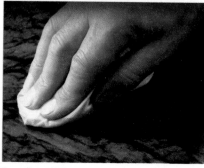

French polish

MODERN VARNISHES

Varnish is a tough brush-on finish which is easier to apply than many traditional types, hence its popularity for tables and natural wood joinery.

Traditional varnishes were based on natural oil resins and tended to be very brittle. Most modern types contain more durable synthetic resins, and offer a choice of high gloss, satin or matt finishes. *Solvent-based polyurethane* varnish (which has to be cleaned off the brush with white spirit) is usually glossier than *water-based* varnish (which contains alkyds). Some types are also available in aerosols, for intricate shapes like wicker chairs and louvre doors.

The quality of polyurethane varnishes varies; the better ones contain a high proportion of solids – the part which is left when the solvents evaporate. Unfortunately, it is difficult to assess this by eye, since some makes have thickeners added, or are formulated as gel rather than liquid.

Varnish stains are varnishes which have been coloured with dyes or translucent pigments (or a mixture of both) so that colour and finish can be applied in one go. This is the best way of colouring wood where the existing varnish has not been stripped off. It is also recommended for colouring pine, which doesn't take wood dyes very well because of the difference in absorption rate between the heart and sap wood.

Unlike wood dyes, varnish stain deepens in colour the more coats you apply. If you reach the colour you want before the coat is thick enough, switch to clear varnish instead.

Coloured transparent finishes are similar to varnish stains, but instead of being wood coloured they come in a range of bright primary and other attractive colours. They colour wood in the same way as paint, but because the pigments are translucent, the grain of the wood can still be seen. They look particularly good on woods with a strong grain, such as pine and ash.

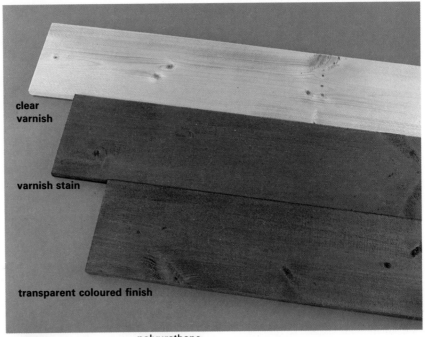

clear varnish

varnish stain

transparent coloured finish

polyurethane

traditional oil-based varnish

water-based resin varnish

transparent coloured finish

Trade tip

Thinning it out

❝When using polyurethane varnish on bare wood, it is usually advisable to thin the first coat so that it soaks in quickly and seals the grain.

Solvent-based polyurethanes are thinned with white spirit. The amount depends on the quality of the varnish, and could be anything from 10% to 30% – check the manufacturer's instructions. Thinner varnishes obviously need less thinning.

Afterwards, the sealed wood can be finished with further coats of full strength varnish, or wax polished for a more natural finish. ❞

WOOD LACQUERS

Two-part lacquers (properly called *catalysed cold cure lacquers*) represent the greatest advance in wood finishes. They contain resins and plastics which are activated by mixing in a hardener just before application. Special formulations are available for floors.

Very quick-drying, lacquers are paler in colour than white French polish but can be polished to a similar – though much tougher – finish. The naturally glossy surface can also be rubbed down with steel wool and wax polished for a more natural matt or satin effect.

Special thinners are needed for cleaning brushes and spills, so make sure you get some when you buy.

Mix lacquer in a china or glass bowl.

Once the surface of the wood has been prepared, you need only a minimum of tools to apply clear finishes.

Filling knives or **putty knives** are used to apply wood fillers, stoppers and plastic wood. You may need finer tools for working them into small cracks.

Lint-free rags are used to apply many traditional finishes, including dyes, grain filler, oil, wax, and French polish; it's also possible to apply varnish this way.

Old cotton or linen handkerchiefs and sheets are ideal, as are old cotton shirts. You also need some unmedicated cotton wool to absorb the polish and to form the rag into a polishing pad.

Steel wool (medium and fine grade) is most convenient for rubbing down and for applying wax polish over hard finishes such as polyurethane varnish

Brushes for applying varnish should be top quality natural bristle, and free from loose hairs and dust. Keep them separate from those used for painting, as it's almost impossible to remove paint sediment entirely. You will need a selection of different widths.

For applying shellac, use broad, (preferably bear hair) artists brushes, which are finer and give a better finish.

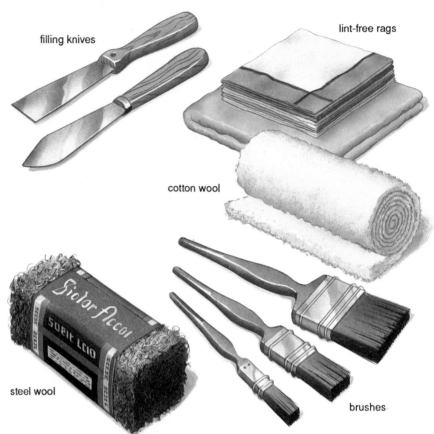

filling knives

lint-free rags

cotton wool

steel wool

brushes

CHOOSING A FINISH				
FINISH	**EFFECT**	**BEST USED FOR**	**APPLICATION**	**MAINTENANCE**
Oiling	Dark, rich, very slightly lustrous finish	Draining boards, kitchen worktops, tables subject to wear and tear	Easily done with a cloth	Re-oil every couple of months
Waxing	Soft satin sheen	Popular for stripped pine furniture but susceptible to heat, water and alcohol	Fairly easy: the more elbow grease, the higher the sheen	Dust and buff regularly; re-wax every couple of months
French polish and shellac	Produces a very high gloss if traditionally applied; may be finished with wax for a softer look	Traditionally used for fine furniture. Particularly susceptible to heat and alcohol	Traditional French polishing requires practice; easier option is to brush on and wax polish	Dust and polish regularly; if the surface becomes dull or damaged, apply a home-made 'reviver'
Polyurethane varnish	Gloss, satin or matt finish; tends to add a tinge of orange to the wood	Primarily for areas taking heavy wear (including floors) and those which might otherwise be painted – doors, skirtings, window frames, stairs	Easy to apply, but care must be taken for a good finish	Dust regularly and wipe down with a damp cloth when necessary; wax polish if preferred
Two-part lacquer	Very clear finish; polish for a high gloss or apply wax for a satin finish	Table tops, work surfaces, floors; home-made furniture	Work in a well ventilated room. Easy to apply	Wipe down with a damp cloth, or apply wax polish every few weeks

APPLYING SYNTHETIC WOOD FINISHES

As well as being easy to apply, modern synthetic finishes give bare wood a tough protective coating that brings out the grain and enhances its natural colour. 'Traditional' finishes still have their place, but tend to be less hardwearing and may need a fair degree of skill and practice to apply successfully.

Choosing a finish

Polyurethane varnishes come in matt, satin and high gloss finishes. Even with a gloss varnish, it takes careful preparation to get a mirror-like surface. Use a *grain filler* to fill the natural pores in the wood, and wood *filler* or *stopper* to repair larger cracks and damage.

Two-part lacquers (plastic coatings) dry very rapidly and can be applied thicker than polyurethane, but you still have to get the surface as smooth as possible for best results. They naturally give a high gloss but can be buffed to a matt sheen.

Coloured finishes can be achieved by dyeing the wood under a clear varnish, or by using a coloured varnish. Polyurethane varnish comes in several 'natural' wood colours and strong tints. Wood dyes come in an even wider range of shades and can be used under polyurethane or two-part lacquers. Where you are going lighter than the original colour bleach the wood first.

Preparing the surface

The ideal surface is sanded new wood, but even this may need sealing and filling. On old wood, the

Varnish and stain to bring out the grain of the wood.

amount of preparation needed depends on any existing finish, as well as on the type of finish you plan to apply.

■ Previously varnished surfaces which are in good condition just need a light rub down with abrasive paper. Any peeling or cracked varnish should be totally stripped.

■ Waxed and oiled finishes – and all traces of wax polish which have been applied to wood or over varnish – must also be removed (see below).

■ If the original finish was French polish, think twice before removing it. It may be easier to refinish.

Tools and equipment

Lint-free rags are used for applying stain, and rubbing in grain filler.

Brushes for varnishing should never be used for anything else – it's almost impossible to remove all traces of old paint. Choose good quality bristle brushes, and work them through your fingers or brush them over bare brickwork, to tease out loose hairs, before starting.

REMOVE OIL AND WAX

Modern varnishes and lacquers must only be applied to surfaces which are free from dirt, grease, oil and wax.

Wax can be removed with wire wool and white spirit, whether applied directly to the wood or used as a polish over varnish.

Oil can also be removed in this way, but the job is more difficult because the oil soaks deep into the wood.

French polish and other shellac finishes can be dissolved and cleaned off with methylated spirits or chemical strippers.

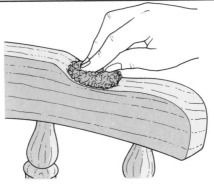

1 To remove all traces of wax or oil, use grade 00 steel wool dipped in white spirit. Rub along the grain, so that you do not scratch the surface.

2 Before the white spirit evaporates, wipe the surface with a clean, dry rag. Avoid handling the wood after wiping as even clean hands are greasy.

FILLING AND COLOURING

There are several ways to improve the appearance of wood before applying varnish or lacquer. It is important to carry out each process in the right order, so work out which you want to use according to the item you are working on, the type of wood, and the finish required.

You can often omit some stages. For example, dyeing and staining won't be necessary if you use a coloured varnish – but you may want to bleach the wood, and you still need to fill it.

Bleaching must always be done first, since the process usually raises the grain of the wood and leaves it in need of further sanding. Use bleach to lighten the colour of dark wood, or before using a pale wood dye to alter the shade *and* lighten the colour.

Grain filling – which helps to produce the smooth surface required for a glossy finish – is the next stage. (You may be able to dye and fill the grain at the same time.)

Dyeing or staining to change the colour of the wood is the next job to do.

Wood filling or stopping should always be done after dyeing – it makes it easier to match the filler to the wood colour.

Trade tip

Keep it clean

❝Once you have finished preparing the wood, keep the room as clean as possible. Any dust particles which settle on the varnish while it is drying will ruin the finish, leaving spots which must be sanded off.

When working on items which have been stripped, don't rest them on old newspapers; marks from the printing ink can easily get transferred to the surface. Use lining paper or old wallpaper instead. ❞

USING WOOD BLEACH

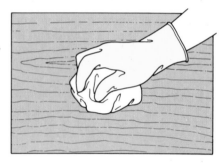

1 Tip the first solution into a clean, empty jam jar. Apply liberally with an old paint brush, and leave for 10 minutes. This tends to darken the wood.

2 Apply the second solution and leave it for several hours or overnight. If a scum appears, remove it with a scrubbing brush and clean water.

3 Finally, rinse with a solution of 50% white vinegar and 50% water. This will raise the grain, so sand smooth before dyeing or finishing the wood.

FILLING THE GRAIN

Even the most carefully planed and sanded wood is full of minute cracks and pores which follow the grain. Some woods show this more than others – mahogany being a prime example – but in all cases the grain should be filled if you want a really fine, glossy finish.

- Sand the surface with very fine abrasive paper (flour paper).
- Thin the grain filler to a thin paste with white spirit.
- Apply with a coarse rag, rubbing it in across the grain.
- Wipe off excess filler across the grain, using a clean rag.
- Leave overnight to harden.

Improve the surface (above) by smoothing with grain filler before applying a gloss finish. Apply with a coarse cloth across the grain.

Trade tip

Coloured filler

❝If you plan to dye or stain the wood as well as filling the grain, save work by using spirit-based dye to colour the grain filler. Simply mix the filler to a paste using the dye instead of white spirit. ❞

Minute cracks and pores in the grain of unfilled wood (right) deflect the light in different directions, dulling the surface. Using grain filler makes the surface more reflective and therefore glossier.

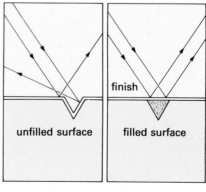

unfilled surface

finish

filled surface

DYEING WOOD

There are several ways to change the colour of the wood to imitate more expensive wood, to disguise mismatched panels and repairs or simply to add colour.

If you want a darker colour you can apply a wood dye or a coloured varnish direct. Coloured varnish is often harder to apply evenly, but can be used over old varnish. It is also easier to remove in the future.

If you want a lighter colour you have to bleach the wood, then use a dye or coloured varnish. Remember that even clear varnish will yellow the wood when applied, and continue to darken with age.

Whatever type of dye or stain you choose, start by testing the effect on a piece of wood as similar as possible to the work in hand, or in an inconspicuous spot such as the back of a door or drawer front.

■ Use a cloth rather than a brush to apply wood dye; a brush tends to give an uneven finish, particularly where it first contacts the surface.

■ If you are not happy with the colour of the first test, try a second coat, or mix the dye with other colours from the same range to get the shade you want.

■ New pine often has very uneven absorbency, so more dye will soak into the wood in some places, giving a darker colour. To prevent this, seal with thinned clear varnish.

■ On end grain, the dye will soak in more, giving a darker colour. To preven this, seal the end grain first with thinned varnish.

■ Glue which has squeezed out of the joints will not take the colour. Scrape or sand back to bare wood.

Use a cloth to apply dye more evenly. Tip the dye into a saucer, so that you can judge how much the cloth soaks up each time you charge it. If you apply the dye with a brush more dye will soak into the wood when you first touch it with the bristles.

Seal end grain and uneven surfaces by using a thinned coat of the finish. This stops the dye being absorbed more by some areas than by others.

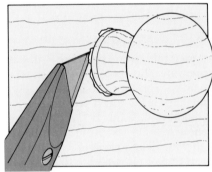

Glue will not take dye, so smears on the surface or where it has oozed out of the joints must be removed. Scrape with a blade or sand with fine abrasive paper.

FILLING BLEMISHES

Cracks and gaps which are not due to the natural grain of the wood need extra attention. The choice is between using a paste stopping, plastic wood, or a two-part wood filler. The main problem is getting the filler the same colour as the wood you are filling – most manufacturers make a limited range of colours, which are unlikely to give a perfect match.

■ Dye or stain the wood first, to the colour required.

■ Choose a filler or stopper which is paler than the colour you require if you can't get an exact match.

■ Some fillers can be blended with wood dye for a better colour, but test this first in case the dye stops the filler hardening properly

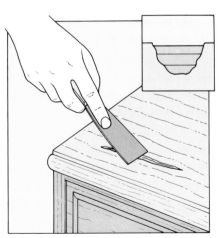

1 When filling deep cracks, apply filler or stopper a little at a time, leaving it to harden (and shrink) according to the manufacturer's instructions.

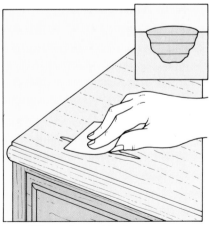

2 Fill cracks and holes very slightly above the surface of the wood, then use a fine grade abrasive paper to sand the surface smooth.

APPLYING VARNISH

Most manufacturers recommend thinning the first coat with one part white spirit to 10 of varnish. Then apply at least two full-strength coats of varnish – more if it will be subjected to heavy wear.

■ Gloss polyurethane is usually tougher than matt or satin. For maximum protection without a gloss finish, build up gloss undercoats and apply a matt or satin topcoat.

■ The first coat may be easier to apply with a cloth.

■ Don't overload the brush. Dip it in the varnish and touch the ends of the bristles against the side of the tin – don't scrape them across the lip as this tends to form bubbles.

■ Minute bubbles may appear in the first coat due to air trapped in the pores of the wood. Thinning the first coat and using a cloth should prevent this; otherwise rub down well before applying the next coat.

■ Allow the varnish to dry hard before sanding and recoating – this could take anything from 2 hours to 12 hours, depending on the type of varnish, and the conditions.

Coloured varnish

Apply this with extra care – if it is uneven, the colour will appear patchy. The more coats you apply, the darker the effect. If you get the colour you want before applying enough coats for protection, finish off with clear varnish.

If the colour you want to use is not available in the right finish (matt, satin or gloss), use the appropriate clear varnish for the topcoat.

1 Work on an area about 500mm (20") square at a time. Apply the varnish along the grain first, drawing the brush backwards and forwards. If using two-part lacquer, remember that it dries rapidly – work quickly and do not over-brush.

2 Using lighter pressure, brush at right angles across the grain. Then finish off along the grain as lightly as possible using the tip of the brush.

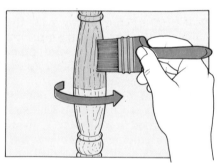

3 When varnishing mouldings, work only along the grain or you may find you get a lot of drips. On turnings such as stair spindles work round the pattern.

USING TWO-PART LACQUER

Two-part lacquers (plastic coatings) are applied much like varnishes but harden by chemical reaction instead of drying. This happens very rapidly and gives off strong fumes, so there are several points to watch:

■ Make sure you have a supply of the special cleaner to suit (ordinary brush cleaner will not work). If you buy a kit, this should include a small amount of brush cleaner but it may not be enough to clean the brush more than once.

■ Always provide good ventilation as the fumes are much stronger than those of ordinary varnish.

■ Mix the lacquer and hardener in an old glass or china container (not metal or plastic). Never mix more than you need for each application.

■ Apply the finish liberally using a paintbrush – do not over-brush.

■ A second coat can be applied as soon as the first is dry (after 1–1½ hours).

■ There is no need to rub down between coats unless there are obvious imperfections.

■ Build up three coats, then rub down with fine wet and dry paper until you get a matt surface; shiny patches indicate hollows, and a further coat will be necessary for a smooth finish.

■ Finish the surface with wire wool and wax or burnishing cream (see Tip).

Trade tip

Finishing touches

To give a sheen to a high gloss finish, use fine wire wool and solid wax polish or liquid brass polish. Dip the wire wool in the polish and work it gently along the grain. The wax acts as a lubricant, to help the wire wool run smoothly over the surface.

For a high gloss finish (on two-part lacquered surfaces in particular) use a burnishing cream. This is often included in a two-part lacquer kit, otherwise use car body refinishing cream (eg T-Cut). Rub down the surface with fine abrasive paper, then polish using a soft rag (such as cotton stockinette).

REPAIRING WOODEN MOULDINGS

Wooden mouldings are used all round the house – for skirtings, architraves around doors and windows, and sometimes for picture or dado (chair) rails. As well as providing a decorative feature, they have the important practical function of protecting the plasterwork from damage. This makes them prone to knocks and chips, while other problems include loose fixings, splits, warps and even rot.

Where a moulding is basically sound and the damage is minor, patching is the simplest option; most repairs involve little more than using the right filler, plus a few basic carpentry tools.

However, where a moulding is badly damaged or so scruffy that repair would involve extensive work, replacement may be simpler. Several factors affect your decision:
■ Is a similar moulding easily available? If not, replacement could be difficult and expensive.

Common mouldings are sold by many DIY stores, while a larger range is stocked by timber merchants or specialist moulding suppliers (try under 'joinery' in Yellow Pages). But older houses often have elaborately carved mouldings which may no longer be made, although they can sometimes be replaced by making up from several sections of

replacement mouldings or by modifying a similar moulding to match (see Problem Solver).

In the last resort, you can have a moulding made up specially, but this may be expensive.
■ How much redecoration do you intend to do? If the plaster is in poor condition, removing a moulding could loosen it so much that extensive patching is required.
■ If the damage is caused by rot, this may indicate a serious problem, either now or in the past. Replacement of the affected timber is usually essential, but where you suspect dry rot or active damp, have this checked out first.

SIMPLE REPAIRS

Odd dents and chips, splits, or loose fixings are normally easy to repair. Where filling is needed, there are basically three choices:
■ Use general purpose interior filler for repairs where the moulding is firmly fixed and is unlikely to receive heavy knocks.
■ Use a resin wood filler if the patch is in a position where it may receive further knocks.
■ Use a flexible filler if the patch is at all subject to movement – often the case where skirtings and architraves are fixed to partition walls.

If a large piece is missing, use a wooden block to replace it and then finish off with filler to match the contours. This is stronger and cheaper than using filler for the whole repair.

Finally, prime the patch and either paint to conceal it, or refinish the whole section.

Loose fixings often cause cracks or splits. Refix with nails, screws or frame fixings, depending on what there is to fix to behind the moulding.

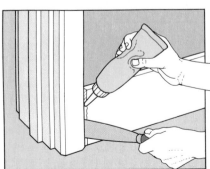

Repair cracks at joints with flexible filler if there is any sign of movement. Ordinary filler is fine for splits along the grain of the wood.

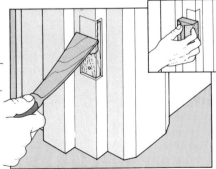

Fill large gaps by pinning a wooden offcut into the hole slightly below the surface. Finish off with filler and sand when dry to match the moulding.

Trade tip

Getting to grips

❛ Dents are best repaired with resin filler.

Scrape off the paint first. Then, if the hole is large, hammer some panel pins into the dent so that the filler has something to grip. Sand level with the surface when dry. ❜

REPLACING MOULDINGS

Where a moulding is seriously damaged or badly battered and a matching section is available, replacement is a sensible option.

Before you begin, however, check what's involved. In particular, see if it is necessary to remove a full length of moulding, or if the damage is limited to a section of the run. Replacing a section is cheaper, but it must be cut neatly (using a tenon saw and mitre block) if the repair is not to show. It is also vital that the replacement is an exact match in every detail.

It is sometimes difficult to know whether a replacement is available without removing the original to use as a pattern (see Problem Solver). If you need to do this, try not to damage the old piece too much; if replacement proves impossible, you then have the option of replacing it and patching it up.

REMOVING SKIRTINGS

Skirtings are fitted in several different ways (see below). In some cases, it won't be obvious what you are dealing with until you begin to remove a section from the wall. Be careful not to damage the plaster; put a small piece of offcut wood between the wall and any tool used.

■ To remove a whole run of skirting, lever it from the wall with a bolster then prise it away with the claw of a hammer.

■ To remove a shorter section of skirting, prise it away from the wall with a bolster until it can be wedged out enough to be sawn at both ends with a tenon saw; use a mitre block for an accurate mitre cut.

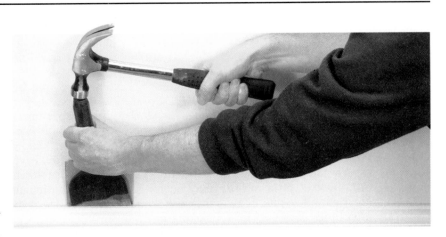

To remove a run of skirting, start at one end and place a bolster at the top edge where it meets the wall. Hammer the bolster in gently, then prise the board away with a claw hammer. Continue along the run until free.

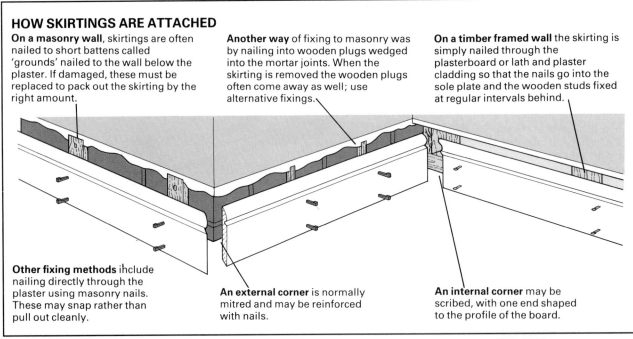

HOW SKIRTINGS ARE ATTACHED

On a masonry wall, skirtings are often nailed to short battens called 'grounds' nailed to the wall below the plaster. If damaged, these must be replaced to pack out the skirting by the right amount.

Another way of fixing to masonry was by nailing into wooden plugs wedged into the mortar joints. When the skirting is removed the wooden plugs often come away as well; use alternative fixings.

On a timber framed wall the skirting is simply nailed through the plasterboard or lath and plaster cladding so that the nails go into the sole plate and the wooden studs fixed at regular intervals behind.

Other fixing methods include nailing directly through the plaster using masonry nails. These may snap rather than pull out cleanly.

An external corner is normally mitred and may be reinforced with nails.

An internal corner may be scribed, with one end shaped to the profile of the board.

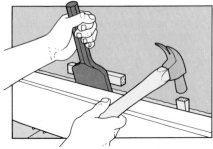

1 **To remove a section** of skirting prise it away from the wall with a bolster. Gently hammer in wedges to hold the damaged section away from the wall.

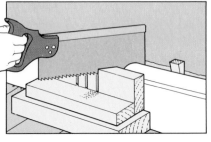

2 Rule a line to show the cutting point, then place a mitre block against the board to guide the start of the cut. Raise it on packing if necessary.

3 Continue the cut to the bottom of the board, following the vertical pencil line to help keep the cut straight. Repeat for the other end of the section.

REMOVING ARCHITRAVES

Architraves around door and window frames are normally either nailed to the wooden lining of the opening or to the frame itself. In both cases they can simply be prised away by levering under the edge, using an offcut to gain purchase.

However, before removing a run of architrave, it's usually advisable to score down the edges with a trimming knife to release any overlapping decorations – otherwise you may find they tear away with it.

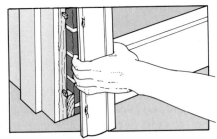

1 To remove an architrave, gently hammer a bolster or old wood chisel under its edge. Start at one end and work from the wall side, not the frame.

2 Work along until the whole architrave can be levered free. Avoid denting the wood of the door frame, and pull out any nails which remain.

REMOVING PICTURE RAILS AND DADOS

Most picture rails and dados are simply nailed to the wall and mitred at the corners. If you don't need to remove a whole run, cut the ends to a mitre as you saw out the damaged piece. (It is usually possible to do this without having to prise the moulding away from the wall as you would for a skirting board.)

The nailed fixings make rails easy to remove, but prising them free often causes minor damage to the plasterwork. Repair any holes with filler before replacing the rail, which doesn't have to be fixed the same way – or in the same place.

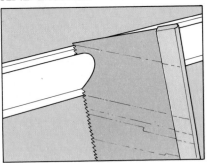

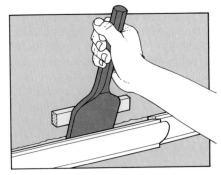

1 Saw across the rail with a tenon saw where you are only removing a short section – a mitre block helps to start the cut. Avoid sawing into the wall as you finish.

2 Lever off the moulding with a bolster using a block of wood to protect the plaster. The old nails may snap rather than pull out – remove them later.

PROBLEM SOLVER

Matching mouldings

Modern mouldings have simple profiles which are easy to match, and in many cases you just need a note of the dimensions. But when buying a replacement for more complicated shapes, take a pattern or a piece of the original moulding along to ensure an exact match. The simplest way to make a pattern is to use a profile gauge to copy the shape.

The mouldings in older houses are often much more elaborate and may be difficult to match. This applies particularly to skirtings, which may be very deep with a complicated shape at the top. If no exact match is available, the options are:

■ Mouldings can be specially machined – at a price. Some timber merchants offer this service, otherwise try a specialist joinery workshop.

■ Deep skirting can sometimes be matched by building up several sections of standard mouldings.

■ You may be able to plane or sand a similar piece to the required profile.

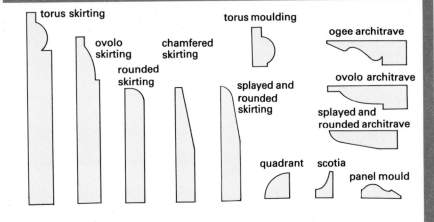

torus skirting
ovolo skirting
rounded skirting
chamfered skirting
torus moulding
splayed and rounded skirting
ogee architrave
ovolo architrave
splayed and rounded architrave
quadrant
scotia
panel mould

Standard mouldings cover an extensive range. Common, widely available shapes are shown here; for more elaborate ones you may need to go to a specialist.

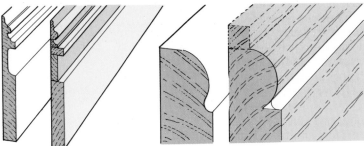

Deep skirting profiles can be built up by putting together a number of standard mouldings, although this will not produce an exact match.

Sandpaper or a plane can be used to smooth rounded profiles. You may also be able to improve the contours by using filler, then sanding to shape.

FITTING NEW SKIRTING

To replace either a whole run or short section of skirting, the new piece must be cut to the right length and its ends must be shaped to fit the existing board.

■ Mitred ends are used on external corners and also where you have cut out a short section. Take care to mark the overall length of the board from the outside of the mitre and ensure that the mitre slopes the right way.

■ Scribed ends, shaped to fit over the existing board, are needed at most internal corners.

Accuracy in measurement is very important to obtain a tight fit. If the piece you removed is in reasonable condition, you may be able to use it as a pattern to mark the replacement; simply allow a fraction extra on the length for the thickness of the saw cut. Otherwise, either measure the gap or lay the new skirting against it and strike off the measurements directly.

It is better to cut the board slightly too large as it is easier to trim it down than to fill a gap.

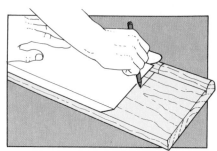

1 Transfer the dimensions of the gap to be filled on to the new board – by striking off directly, measuring, or using the removed piece as a guide.

2 Mitre an end by marking a cutting line across the board and using a mitre block and tenon saw to start the cut. Remove the block to saw right across.

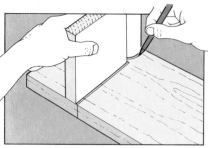

3 To scribe an end, cut a piece of old skirting and hold it tightly down the cutting line. Draw the outline on the back and cut to shape with a coping saw.

4 Check the fit of the new board in the gap – if tight, plane or sand it down. Refix with nails, or use wallplugs and screws for a more secure fixing.

REPLACING ARCHITRAVES

Use a tenon saw to cut the replacement moulding to the right length. Although the corners of architraves must be mitred like a picture frame, they may not be exactly square so you cannot always do this in a mitre box.

Check the exact length, either by using the old moulding as a pattern or by copying the dimensions of the gap. If the corners are a true 45°, use a mitre box to guide the cut. Otherwise, mark an accurate cutting line and saw along them freehand.

Nail the new length to the lining using panel pins or oval wire nails and patch with filler.

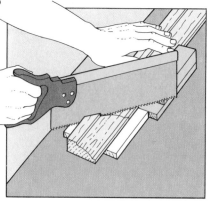

1 Measure and mark carefully. Cut mitred ends in a box if they are true – otherwise, mark the cutting line and use the tenon saw freehand.

2 Nail through the replacement close to the edge so that the nails go into the thickness of the timber lining the opening – not into the wall plaster.

REPLACING PICTURE RAILS AND DADOS

Rails can be refixed with masonry nails if the plaster is sound. Where the plaster is weak, or where a picture rail is to carry heavy pictures, screws and wallplugs or frame fixings are more secure.

Measure the length accurately, and cut any mitres using a mitre box and tenon saw. Cut too long rather than too short and trim to an exact fit – gaps are difficult to conceal.

If you are replacing a short section, glue the ends at the joint and insert one or two pins to strengthen it. Finish off with filler then sand to conceal.

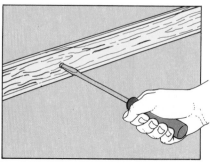

1 Cut a matching section and check that it fits. Fix with masonry nails or screws and plugs at 750–900mm (2′6″–3′) intervals. Plug holes with filler.

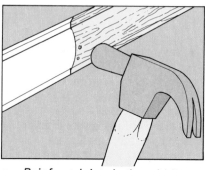

2 Reinforce joints in the middle of a run by gluing and pinning the ends together. Then use filler to patch any gaps, and sand smooth to hide the repair.

REPAIRING SASH WINDOWS

Sliding sash windows were standard fittings in the majority of Victorian houses, but went out of favour early in the 20th century. This is partly because their construction is more complicated than hinged casements, with a large number of parts. As a result of their age, many original sash windows now need regular repairs to keep them in good working order.

Common faults (apart from rot damage) centre around sticking sashes and broken sash cords. Cures for rot and minor sticking are covered on pages 181-184 and 257-258; other repairs are described here.

Modern improvements and changing tastes have seen a return to the old style of window in some recently built homes. However, these have a completely different form of mechanism requiring much less maintenance.

SASH WINDOW CONSTRUCTION

Conventional sash windows have two sliding frames (the *sashes*), balanced by heavy *weights* on each side. These weights are concealed in deep side frames (sometimes called a *cased* frame) and are attached to *cords* which pass over *pulleys* at the top. (Occasionally, chains are used instead of cords.)

In most windows a thin strip of wood down the centre of the case keeps the weights separate and stops them jamming, but this is not always present. There is also a removable cover which gives access to the weight pockets.

The two sashes slide in separate grooves. The outer sash is trapped by the outside lining of the frame on one side and is retained on the other by a thin batten called a *parting bead* which is fitted into a grooved channel in the frame. The inner sash slides between the parting bead and an inner moulding called the *staff bead* or *stop bead* nailed to the frame.

Modern sash windows have a completely different construction. In place of the deep cases, the side member is solid. Depending on the design, either the frame or the sash have channels up each side in which there are *spring mechanisms* held inside thin tubes. These take the place of weights to balance the weight of the sashes. In some designs the sashes themselves are retained by beading as in a conventional window; in others, they are retained by catches which clip on to the spring mechanisms and can be released quickly.

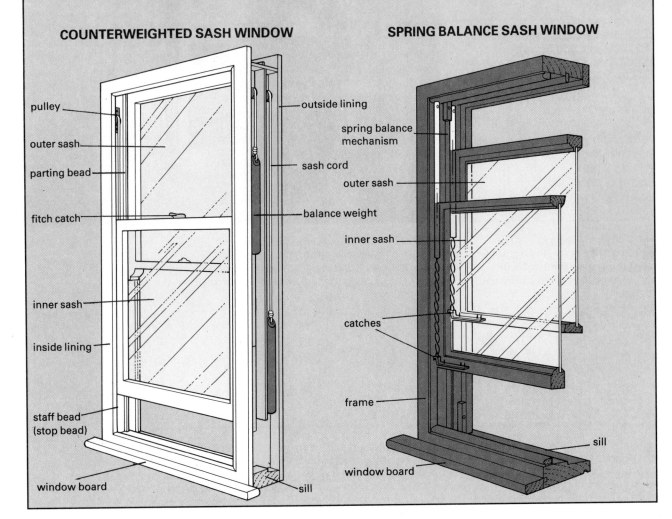

COUNTERWEIGHTED SASH WINDOW

- pulley
- outer sash
- parting bead
- fitch catch
- inner sash
- inside lining
- staff bead (stop bead)
- window board
- outside lining
- sash cord
- balance weight
- sill

SPRING BALANCE SASH WINDOW

- outside lining
- spring balance mechanism
- outer sash
- inner sash
- catches
- frame
- window board
- sill

REMOVING A SASH

To take out a sash, the beading must be prised away. If you are careful, it is possible to do this without seriously damaging the paint finish or denting the wood. But if any of the strips of beading do get damaged, buy a replacement section. Staff bead and parting bead are standard mouldings and should be readily available, although you may find that new ones are rather heavier looking than the originals.

■ Insert a broad chisel or stiff stripping knife between the window frame and one of the staff beads, somewhere near the middle. Tap with a mallet and prise gently until it bows away from the frame. The nails should then be clearly visible.

■ Carry on prising close to each nail, as there is less risk of snapping the wood. With luck, the bead will then bow enough to free it from the mitres at each end.

■ Where the bead is too tightly fitted, allow it to spring back and then pull the nail heads through the moulding – after which it should be easy to slip out.

When both staff beads have been removed, the inner sash should lift away from the frame. At this stage it will still be suspended on the intact cord(s), so if you don't plan to renew the cords, carefully support the sash on a pair of steps or other suitable stand. Otherwise, release each cord by prising out any fixing nails – or by cutting it. Don't allow the cord to fly back due to the weight on the other end; jam it in the pulley (see Tip).

To remove the outer sash, prise out the parting bead on one side, starting at one end; it will be held in its groove by very few nails. You should then be able to lift out the outer sash in the same way.

Trap the cord

6 Where possible, stop the cord running back into the weight pocket; it will save work later. One way to do this is to tie a knot in it or jam a wooden wedge into the pulley to stop it turning. An alternative is to take a couple of turns round a scrap of wood – or even a screwdriver as shown. 9

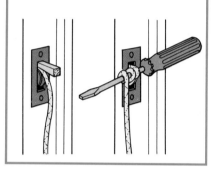

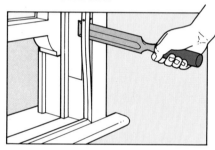

1 Prise the centre of the staff bead so that it bows away from the frame. When the fixing pins are visible through the gap, prise near each one.

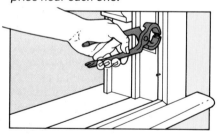

2 If the moulding cannot be freed easily by prising, allow it to spring back then pull out the nails by their exposed heads to free it.

3 Lift out the sash. Any intact cords will still be attached, so if you don't want to replace them, support the sash to one side. Otherwise, remove the cords, making sure the ends do not fall through the pulley.

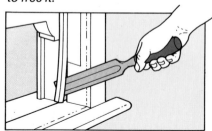

4 To remove the outer sash, prise the parting bead out of its groove at one side. This may not be nailed at all, but at most there will only be two or three.

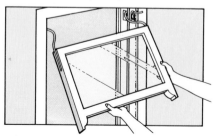

5 It should be possible to lift away the outer sash without disturbing the other bead. Deal with its cords in the same way as for the inner sash.

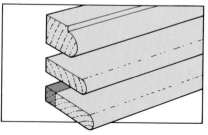

If any of the beads are damaged buy a replacement moulding, standard sections are available. If the parting bead is too wide plane the back edge.

RENEWING A SASH CORD

Replace a broken or worn cord with a new length. It is often better to replace all the cords at once – if one has broken, it's likely that the others are well worn.

Sash cord is specially woven to resist stretching or wearing. The modern type is made from synthetic fibre and can be prevented from fraying by melting the end over a match. You also need some 25mm (1″) *galvanized clout nails* to fix it.

At the bottom of the channel in which the window slides is a small cover which gives access to the weight pocket. This may be held by a screw, which must be removed (it can be tricky to locate if it is covered in old paint). Prise out the cover using an old chisel and lift the weight out of the frame.

If the old cord still runs over the pulley, tie a length of string to its end and use it to pull the string through; it will be used to thread the new cord. Otherwise, you need a slim weight which can be tied to one end of the string and which will fit over the pulley – examples are a large bent nail or a length of old bath chain. Pass this over the pulley and let it pull the string down until you can catch it through the weight pocket.

Take the old sash cord and cut a new piece to the same length or a little longer. Tie the cord to the end of the string and pull it through. Thread the end through the hole in the weight and tie it off, copying the old knot.

Nail the other end of the cord into the groove in the sash using a single clout nail. Make sure that the nail is further down the sash than the distance between the centre of the pulley and the top of the window frame. Tap the nails in

carefully, as it is easy to shatter the glass.

With both cords fitted, try sliding the sash up and down:
■ If it will not go to the bottom of the frame, the cord is too short.
■ If the weight hits the bottom of the pocket when the sash is at the top, the cord is too long.
■ If the sash jams before it reaches the top, the nail is too far up.

Adjust the cord if necessary, then insert two or three more fixing nails below the first one.

Tap the pocket cover back into place and tighten the screw if one was fitted. Fit each sash in turn and refix the retaining beads. In most cases, new 25mm (1″) panel pins can be inserted in the old holes and tapped back in. If a beading was damaged, cut a new piece and nail it in place. Fill over the nails before redecorating.

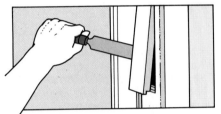

1 Prise off the cover of the weight pocket. Often this is simply wedged in place, but there is sometimes a screw concealed under the old paintwork.

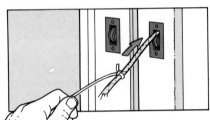

2 If the cord is in place, tie a length of stout string to it and then lift away the weight so that the string is pulled over the pulley.

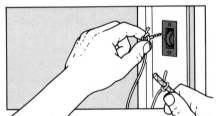

3 If the cord has snapped, pull the string over the pulley using a weight tied to the end. This weight must be slim enough to pass over the pulley.

4 Pull the new cord through and tie it to the weight. (If there are different weights, ensure you don't muddle them up at this stage).

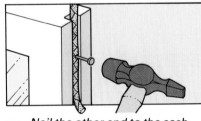

5 Nail the other end to the sash using a single clout nail. It must be fitted at least the distance shown from the top of the sash.

Trade tip

New pulleys

❝ Old pulleys may have rusted or have developed sharp spots on the rims. They are simply held by two screws and are easy to renew. ❞

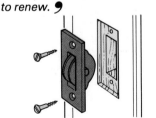

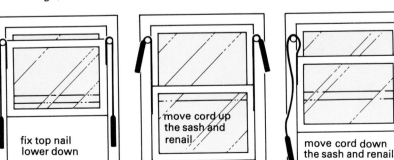

fix top nail lower down

move cord up the sash and renail

move cord down the sash and renail

6 Try the sash back in place temporarily and test the action to ensure that the cord is the right length. Pull out the single fixing nail and adjust its position to correct any of the faults shown.

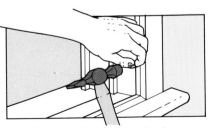

7 Finish nailing the cords, then refit the pocket cover. To retain the sash, refit the beads and nail them; use the old nail holes where possible.

SPRING SASH REPAIRS

Modern sash windows with spring balance mechanisms are much easier to repair than the traditional type. The most common fault is that the spring loses its tension, but this is easy to adjust using the special tool provided by the window maker (or failing that, a stiff piece of bent wire). If the sash sticks at one point, the most likely cause is that the spiral needs oiling.

To tension a spring, lift the sash as far as it will go and support it with a length of batten. Hook the adjusting tool into the exposed end of the spiral mechanism and pull it down to free it from the catch.

Pull the mechanism down about 150mm (6″) without allowing it to untwist and lose the spring's tension. Turn the tool two or three times anti-clockwise to add tension, then hook it back in place.

Remove the prop and test the action – if the sash continues to drop, add a turn until it just stays in position.

To oil the spiral mechanism, unhook the mechanism as above, but this time allow it to untwist. Wipe down with an oily rag, then push it back up and wind to add tension.

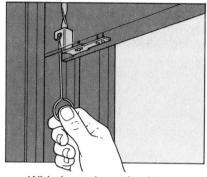

1 With the sashes raised to their full extent and propped in place, unhook the spiral mechanism using the maker's adjusting tool.

2 Pull the mechanism down about 150mm (6″) without allowing it to untwist. Add tension by turning anti-clockwise two or three turns.

3 Refit and test. The sash should just stay in place against spring tension – if not, repeat the process adding a turn at a time.

Oil the spring mechanism by allowing the spiral to untwist fully, then wiping down with an oiled rag. Twist it back up, then tension using the adjuster.

PROBLEM SOLVER

Curing rattling sashes

Sash windows rattle because the sliding sashes are loose in their grooves – a problem which affects the inner sash more than the outer. The most common causes are that the staff bead is fixed too far out, or that the parting bead is too thin.

To cure a loose inner sash, remove and refix the staff beads. If the parting bead is worn, replace this first.

If an outer sash is loose and the parting bead is not worn, the only solution is to pack out the sides of the sash frame. A simple way to do this is to line it with strips of *iron-on plastic edging strip*. This is thin enough to take up the wear gradually and provides an ideal wearing surface.

Further cures are to fit cam-type or screw-type *fitch catches* (whether or not window locks are also fitted). These tend to draw the two sashes tightly together at the meeting edge. If there is a gap here, fit a brush or spring strip draught excluder.

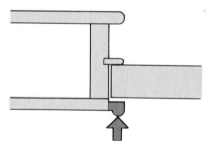

Refix the staff bead closer to the frame to stop the inner sash from rattling. Check the state of the parting bead first, though, and renew it if worn.

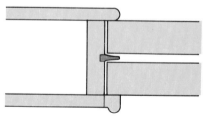

Replace the parting bead if the outer sash is loose. If this does not cure the problem, iron-on plastic strips will take up the wear on the frame.

Cam-type and screw-type fitch catches are both designed to draw the two sashes firmly together. Don't rely on them for security – fit bolts or locks as well.

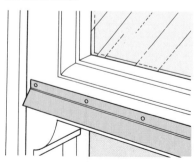

Fit brush strip or spring strip draught excluder to the bottom rail of the outer sash. This will improve the draughtproofing and cut down any rattling.

CURING STICKING WINDOWS

There are three main reasons why wooden windows stick:

Swollen timber caused by damp is normally a seasonal problem which only appears in wet weather. Treat by allowing the wood to dry out and preventing further damp penetration. The frame may also need to be trimmed down and repainted.

Paint build-up – often the result of poor preparation when the frames were last painted – is a problem which affects sash windows in particular. Treat by removing excess paint and refinishing. In bad cases where the window is stuck shut, extra care is needed to free it.

Dropped frames due to loose joints are the most serious problem. The frames must be repaired and strengthened, then trimmed if necessary and refinished. If a window frame is seriously weakened by rot damage, it may need extensive repairs – or even replacement.

Sticking on sash windows may also be caused by a broken sash cord, covered on pages 253-256.

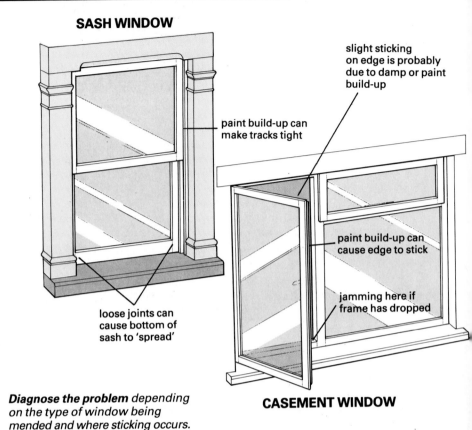

SASH WINDOW

slight sticking on edge is probably due to damp or paint build-up

paint build-up can make tracks tight

paint build-up can cause edge to stick

jamming here if frame has dropped

loose joints can cause bottom of sash to 'spread'

CASEMENT WINDOW

Diagnose the problem depending on the type of window being mended and where sticking occurs.

CURING SEASONAL SWELLING

When casement windows stick at the onset of damp weather, it's a sign that the wood is swelling as it absorbs moisture. Sash windows are less likely to be affected as they work with larger clearances.

A small amount of swelling is virtually inevitable because all timber expands and contracts as the weather gets warmer or cooler. So on a new window, it could simply be that the moving parts are too close a fit – a problem aggravated by redecorating during the summer months (see overleaf).

In many cases, however, swelling shows that moisture is getting into the wood – either because the paint isn't doing its job properly, or because water is seeping in through loose joints and cracked putty. If damp penetration like this is left untreated, there is a risk of wet rot developing.

The cure is to wait for a period of dry weather or arrange a temporary screen over the window so it can dry out. You may have to plane it to ease the sticking, then fill any gaps and repaint to prevent the problem from recurring.

1 *When the wood has dried out, you may need to plane the frame a little to let it shut properly. Use a Surform, which won't be damaged by old paint.*

3 *Sand down any areas of thin or flaking paint. Repaint bare wood using primer, undercoat and topcoat, but avoid applying any of these too thickly.*

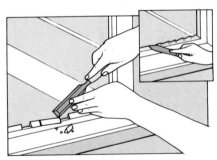

2 *Fill any gaps or cracks between the frame members with a flexible wood filler. If the glazing putty is cracking, chip it out and replace.*

─Trade tip─

Easing the way

❝ On sash windows, slight sticking is often caused by friction between the sides of the sashes and the beading which holds them in the frame. In many cases this can be cured simply by rubbing a wax candle down all the surfaces in contact with one another. ❞

CURING PAINT BUILD-UP

Test the window to find out where the sticking is occuring (see Tip). If there is only a minor problem you may be able to cure it without refinishing the paintwork.

On hinged casements, thick paint normally causes localized sticking, often visible as scuff marks at a few points down the edge. This is easy to treat.

Similarly, sash windows which jam at odd points when raised are easily freed. But sashes which are stuck fast because they have been incorrectly painted pose greater problems. There is even a chance you may damage the sash beads while freeing them, though these can be replaced with purpose-made mouldings from a timber yard.

Trade tip

Where does it stick?

❝ To test for tight spots, slip a piece of stiff paper into the joint and close the window. Slide the paper down and mark any points where it sticks. ❞

On casement windows, sand or plane down the area which is sticking. If you go back to bare wood, prime, then apply thin coats of undercoat and topcoat.

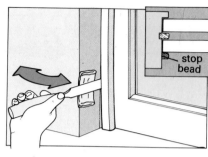

1 **On sash windows,** free a stuck inner sash by levering off the stop beads. Use a chisel or a bolster and try to prise each bead free in one piece.

2 Free a stuck outer sash by prising out the parting bead set into a groove in the frame. Use a screwdriver or chisel and work it in under one end.

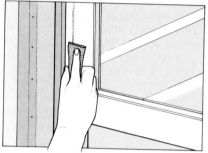

3 Sand or scrape off excess paint. Refit the sashes and replace the beads in the order they came off. Pin in place, punch in the heads, and fill.

REPAIRING A LOOSE FRAME

Loose joints often allow a frame to drop out of square, causing it to bind or jam. Where possible, it is better to remake the original joint; but if this is too badly damaged, use angle plates instead.

Hinged windows are simple to unscrew and can be repaired more easily once out of the frame. Sash windows can be removed (see above) to remake the joints, but when fitting angle plates it may be easier to leave the sashes in place.

In all cases, be very careful how you go about the job as it is easy to crack the glass.

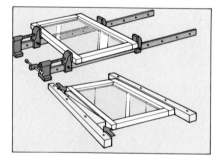

After removal, a frame can be pulled square with sash cramps. Alternatively lay it on a board or wood floor between two nailed-down battens and wedge.

With a sash window, it is sometimes preferable to leave the sashes in the frame and knock in wedges to force the corners of the sash frames back together.

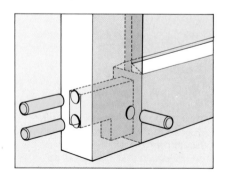

Reinforce a mortise and tenon joint by drilling into it as shown then inserting glued dowels. Sand smooth and refinish any exposed wood.

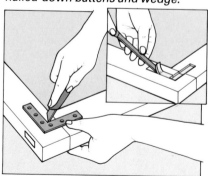

To fit angle plates, lay them on the surface and cut round the outline using a trimming knife. Chisel out a shallow recess, slightly deeper than the plate . . .

. . . then screw the plates in place and fill flush with the surface using a resin wood filler. Fill any cracks with the same material, then repaint.

HANGING A NEW DOOR

There's more to hanging a door than just fitting hinges. Hanging a new door in a new frame shouldn't be too difficult, particularly if you are installing the frame yourself: choose the door first and then build the frame around it. By contrast, hanging a new door in an old frame generally means tailoring the door to fit – and possibly repairing the frame, too.

Both situations involve a wide range of carpentry techniques. The first step is to trim the door so it fits the opening exactly, using a saw and a plane. Chiselling the hinge recesses and fitting the hinges comes next. Finally, you need to fit a lock or latch and any other door furniture.

The secret of success is to work gradually, rather than attempt to get a perfect fit first time. Even the experts often take several goes to make a door fit snugly, as well as opening and shutting smoothly.

*A **power plane** or sharp smoothing plane is essential if a door needs to be trimmed to fit the existing frame.*

....Shopping List....

New doors come in a wide range of styles:
Panel doors have a heavy frame made from solid wood set with four or more thin panels of wood or plywood. Interior quality doors are thinner and cheaper than exterior ones.
Flush doors have smooth sides made from veneered plywood or hardboard. Interior doors have a hollow core filled with a lightweight honeycomb, and solid wood around the edges as reinforcement for the hinges and locks. Exterior doors often have a solid core.
Pressed hardboard interior doors are a form of flush door with an embossed surface resembling a panel door, although they are much lighter and cheaper.

All doors come in a range of standard sizes. The most common for exterior doors are:
- 2134×914mm (7′×3′)
- 2032×838mm (6′8″×2′9″)
- 2032×813mm (6′8″×2′8″)
- 1981×838mm (6′6″×2′9″)
- 1981×762mm (6′6″×2′6″)

Interior doors are generally 1981mm (6′6″) high and 838, 813,

762, 686 or 610mm (2′9″, 2′8″, 2′6″, 2′3″ or 2′) wide.

Hinges can be either 75mm (3″) or 100mm (4″) butt hinges, depending on the size and weight of the door. Use pressed steel hinges for an interior door or flush exterior door, cast iron for a panel door which is to be painted, and brass for varnished doors. Buy screws to suit.

If you are replacing an old door, it helps to use the same size hinges (although new ones may not be a perfect match). If the new door is heavier, it may need larger hinges.

Door furniture includes a lock or latch, plus any other security fittings. In the case of a front door, you may also need a knocker or letter plate.

Finish is either varnish or primer, undercoat and paint, depending on the quality of the wood which the door is made from, and the style you choose.

Tools checklist: Panel saw, plane, chisels, screwdriver, trimming knife, drill and bits, finishing tools.

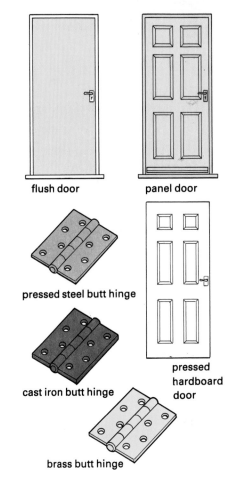

flush door

panel door

pressed steel butt hinge

cast iron butt hinge

pressed hardboard door

brass butt hinge

TRIMMING A DOOR TO FIT

Buy the door to fit the opening as closely as possible – either the exact size, or a little larger to allow for trimming down. If no standard sizes come close, you have a choice:

■ Buy the next size up (if there is a larger one) and cut it down to suit. The disadvantage is that this may involve removing so much timber that the door is seriously weakened. You can safely remove about 20mm (¾") from a panel door and about 10mm (⅜") from a flush door.

■ Buy a size too small and glue strips of wood on the sides and top to bring it up to size. This is only possible if you are painting the door and can conceal the joins.

■ Have a new door made to measure by a door specialist or joinery workshop. This is the best solution; although expensive, it may not be unduly costly.

After trimming, the door should fit into the opening leaving a small gap all round – if it is too tight it will catch on the frame as it opens and shuts. Exterior doors also tend to expand and contract as the seasons change, so need a little more clearance to allow for this.

The normal clearance is around 3mm (⅛") down the sides and 6mm (¼") at the bottom, but it is best to work slowly and keep trying the door in the frame itself until the fit

feels right. You can always trim more off if the door is too tight, but you can't easily restore it if too much has been trimmed off so always err on the cautious side.

If the door is more than a few millimetres too big, aim to take off an equal amount from both sides. On a panel door this keeps the panels in proportion; on a flush door it avoids weakening one side more than the other.

Where an old door was a good fit, use this as a guide to the dimensions. If you are fitting a door for the first time or the old one was a poor fit, measure the door against the frame.

1 If a panel door has 'horns' (extensions of the frame), mark across these square with the top and bottom rails and then cut them off flush using a panel saw.

2 Measure the inside of the frame and transfer its dimensions to the door. You may be able to mark the door directly by standing it in the opening.

3 If the door has to be trimmed by a large amount, use a panel saw or power saw to cut most of the waste wood away. Make sure you keep well clear of the cutting line to allow for final trimming with a plane.

4 Using a plane, trim the door gradually to size. The height is least critical, so trim the ends first. Stand the door against the frame to check.

5 Trim the sides of the door a little at a time. Test it in the frame until it stands in place, leaving about a 3mm (⅛") gap all down one side.

Trade tip

Easier opening

❝ For a snug-fitting door that doesn't bind on the frame, it helps to plane the lock side to a slight bevel as shown. This counteracts the natural tendency of the inner corner to jam as it swings outwards. ❞

FITTING THE HINGES

Interior doors are hung using two hinges; heavy exterior doors are best hung on three. If there are no hinge recesses already cut in the frame, the top hinge goes about 150mm (6″) down, the bottom hinge goes about 225mm (9″) up, and a third goes midway between them. Where hinge recesses already exist, put the hinges in the same positions, but inspect the old recesses first in case you need to patch them (see Problem Solver).

On a flush door, check whether there are reinforcing blocks for the hinges and locks. Their positions will be marked on the outside.

Fit the hinges to the door first, then attach them to the frame making sure you leave a small clearance at the bottom of the door. The easiest way to do this is by standing the door on a thin piece of scrap plywood or other material.

You may find it easier to fit the lock or latch to the door before hanging it. But if you do so, bear in mind that it will be harder to give the door a final trim if it does not fit perfectly. In any case, don't fit the handles or the lock body (in the case of a rim lock), as these are easily damaged; attach those parts after the door is in the frame, then fit the striking plate to align exactly with the lock.

1 Mark the hinge positions by standing the door in the frame and copying the old recesses. If you are fitting to a new frame without existing recesses to copy, fix the hinge positions by measuring the door itself.

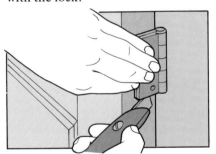

2 Hold each hinge against the edge of the door with the knuckle just projecting as shown. Cut round the hinge with a sharp knife to the depth of one leaf.

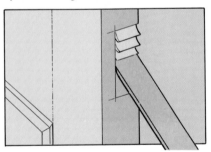

3 Chisel out the wood within the cut, taking care not to splinter it. Test the hinge in place until it just sits flush with the timber of the door.

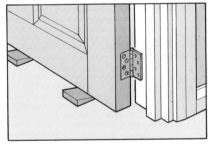

4 Fix each hinge using only one screw until you have tested the fit. Stand the door in the frame, propped up so that it just clears the floor.

5 Check the hinge positions on the frame. If you are making new recesses, mark the positions then cut round a spare hinge before chiselling the frame.

6 When the hinges align, insert one screw in each and test the swing of the door. Adjust as necessary (see Problem Solver), then add the remaining screws.

─Trade tip─

Out of sight

❝ The bottom of an outside door is hard to reach and normally doesn't get painted, making it vulnerable to damp. To give long-term protection, one alternative is to give it two coats of primer and then at least one of topcoat before hanging, or brush on timber preservative – allowing plenty of time for it to dry before hanging the door. ❞

Adjusting the hinges

It's not easy to cut the hinge recesses dead right first time around.

If the recesses are too shallow, the door will be too far from the frame, causing binding on the lock side. Chisel a fraction more wood out of one or both sets of recesses to move the door over.

If the recesses are too deep, the door will resist closing fully and tend to spring open; it is said to be 'hinge-bound'. Cure this by packing behind the hinge with slips of thin card – pieces cut from a breakfast cereal packet are ideal. (Contrary to opinion, this isn't bodging – even professionals need to do it sometimes.)

Check also that the problem isn't simply due to a screw not being driven fully home.

If the hinges are misaligned, the door will be hard to move and the hinges may squeak. Cure this by setting each hinge parallel to the edge of the door and cutting sections out of the recesses, as necessary, to fit the hinges in new positions.

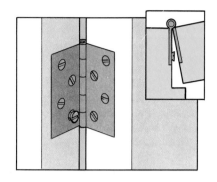

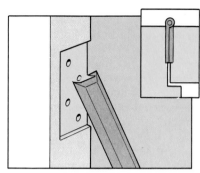

With any hinge problem check first that the hinge itself is not faulty and that the screw heads are not protruding, stopping the door closing properly.

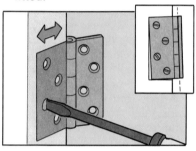

Recut shallow recesses to cure a door which binds on the lock side. Don't try trimming the edge of the door until the hinges are correctly fitted.

Cure hinge-bound doors by packing out the hinges with card slips. Add extra slips one by one until the leaf of the hinge is flush with the woodwork.

Misaligned hinges can cause all sorts of problems. Recut the recess parallel with the edge, refit the hinge, and test using a different screw hole.

Drill out damaged screw holes and pack with glued slips of wood or short lengths of dowel. Allow to dry before drilling new screw holes.

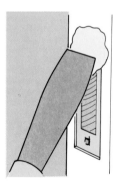

Fill large holes with glued blocks of wood. Small gaps can be plugged with resin filler to help strengthen the repair, then sanded smooth.

Patching the frame

Where possible, you should try to fit the new hinges and locks in the same position as the old ones. But this may mean that damaged existing recesses need to be patched before hanging the new door.

Hinge recesses often need to be repaired because the old screw holes are damaged or slightly offset from the new ones, making it hard to redrill the holes. You may also find that the hinges are a slightly different size, leaving unwanted gaps at the ends or down the sides.

Lock recesses may be a slightly different size, leaving part of the hole to patch. And if the new door has to have a lock in a different place, you need to finish the old hole flush.

General-purpose filler can be used, but is prone to cracks if there is any movement at all in the frame. It's better to use blocks of scrap wood wherever possible, then fill any remaining cracks with resin filler for extra strength.

CHOOSING HINGES

Hinges have countless uses in woodwork, from hanging house doors, cupboard doors and gates, to building folding tables and fitting flaps in furniture. Such a variety of applications has led to an equally varied number of hinge types – an additional complication being that many hinges come in a range of sizes and materials.

In practice, choosing hinges is seldom too difficult, since most DIY stores only stock a small range of popular types – for example, butt hinges for doors, strap hinges for gates and concealed cabinet hinges for kitchen furniture. But if you're keen on woodwork, you'll find that architectural ironmongers stock a wide selection of specialist and decorative hinges.

Parts of a hinge: *most forms of hinge are broadly similar in construction.*

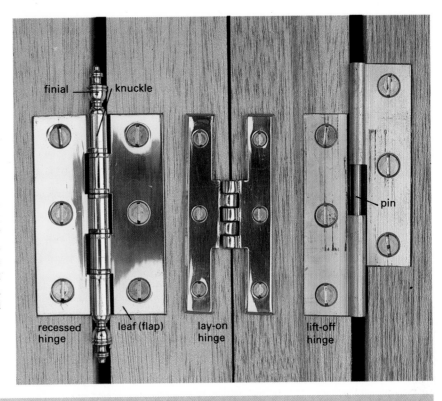

finial — knuckle

recessed hinge — leaf (flap) — lay-on hinge — lift-off hinge — pin

DOOR HINGES

Butt hinges are the normal type of door hinge, and come in different sizes, referred to by the length of the knuckle; 75mm and 100mm (3″ and 4″) hinges are commonly used for house doors – smaller ones are used on furniture and larger ones on very heavy doors. They are usually sold in pairs or sets of three ('1½ pairs').

Butt hinges are made in different materials. *Pressed steel* hinges are for fairly lightweight interior doors and must be painted to resist rusting. *Cast iron* hinges have thicker leaves to suit heavier interior or exterior doors; they, too, must be painted. *Brass* hinges don't need painting and are used to decorate varnished doors.

Rising butt hinges lift a door as it opens – for example, to clear a thick floorcovering – and also tend to make it swing closed by itself. They are made in pressed steel and come in left or right handed sets depending on which way the door opens.

Rising butts are a form of *lift-off hinge*: the door can be lifted free of the hinge pins when fully opened.

T hinges are a traditional type of hinge used on cottage doors and also on gates. A similar looking hinge in black iron is fitted to some 'Tudor' style front doors, but on modern versions the strap is often purely decorative and is fitted over an ordinary butt hinge.

Double spring hinges are for swinging louvre doors often used in kitchens.

pressed steel butt hinge

cast-iron butt hinge

brass butt hinge

rising butt hinge

T hinge

black iron decorative strap hinge

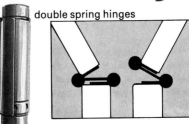

double spring hinges

GARAGE AND GATE HINGES

Strap hinges are for light or medium gates which lie flush with the fence. Painted or galvanized and sold by length. Heavy duty *reversible strap hinges* have separate pivot bosses and are made for garage doors or heavy gates. Also for garage doors are *hook and pin sets* which allow the door to be lifted off. Both of the latter types are normally plain steel and must be painted before fitting.

T hinges are for hanging light and medium gates flush with a post. Painted black or galvanized, and sold by length.

Hinge pins and straps are made for hanging gates. Different pins are available for mortaring into brickwork or bolting or nailing to a post. Double straps are used for heavy gates.

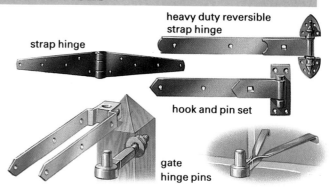

strap hinge

heavy duty reversible strap hinge

hook and pin set

gate hinge pins

CABINET LEAF HINGES

Suite hinges are smaller versions of the butt hinges used on house doors, and are designed for use on cabinet doors and chest lids. They are mostly made of brass or plated steel. Size is given in terms of the length of the knuckle, but hinges are also made with wide and narrow leaves for heavy and fine work, so the width of the leaf may also be quoted.

Decorative leaf hinges are made from brass and are for flush fixing on the face of furniture. They come in different styles – 'H' and snake patterns are two common examples.

Backflap hinges are similar to a very wide butt hinge but have offset screw holes for a stronger fixing. They are used for drop-leaf flaps and tables, where strength is important.

Flush hinges have very thin leaves which fit within each other and therefore don't need recessing – they simply screw to the edge of the door.

Piano hinge (always described in the singular) resembles a continuous lightweight butt hinge. It is cut to length with a hacksaw for use on doors and flaps without recessing.

Table and counter hinges are heavy brass hinges for use on drop-leaf tables and counters. There are several styles.

Mortise hinges are let into holes cut into the edge of doors and furniture panels for a neat, concealed fixing.

Cranked hinges ('angle hinges') are a form of *lay-on* (ie non-recessed) hinge designed to give a strong fixing and extra support. The crank also makes it possible to fix a door so it opens within its own width.

Pivot hinges have short pivot pins and thin fixing plates or studs in place of flat leaves. They are mainly for doors that cannot be fastened along the edge.

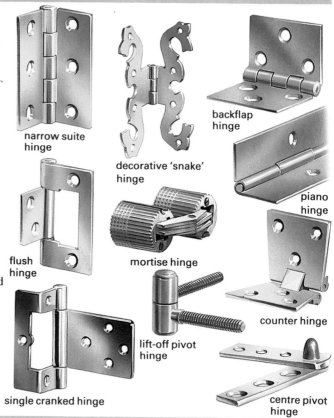

narrow suite hinge

decorative 'snake' hinge

backflap hinge

piano hinge

flush hinge

mortise hinge

single cranked hinge

lift-off pivot hinge

counter hinge

centre pivot hinge

CONCEALED CABINET HINGES

Modern built-in and modular furniture depends on this type of hinge, which is invisible when the door is closed.

The hinge itself fits into a large hole drilled in the door, the hinge arm then locks on to an adjustable fixing plate screwed to the side of the cabinet. All types are designed for use with furniture made from either 15mm (⅝″) or 19mm (¾″) board.

The hinges are available either sprung or unsprung. Unsprung hinges are for doors with a catch to hold them closed; sprung hinges stay closed without a separate catch.

100° hinges are the standard type, allowing the door to open straight outwards.

110 and 125° hinges are for units with internal drawers or wire baskets which need the door to open wider.

170° hinges open flat back against the adjacent cupboard to provide full access; because the door doesn't project, they also fulfil an important safety role.

Glass door hinges have a special boss designed to fit a hole drilled through a glass door panel.

Most hinges need a 35mm hinge boring bit (end mill) but some miniature versions take a 26mm bit. *Height adjustable base plates* are standard on some hinges and can be fitted to allow for extra adjustment.

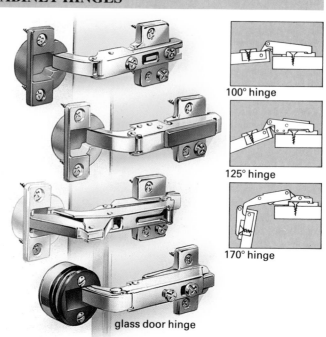

100° hinge

125° hinge

170° hinge

glass door hinge

CURING STICKING DOORS

A door may stick if you've laid a new floor covering, or for several other reasons (see right). Fix it as soon as you can – continual sticking can weaken the joints and hinges.

Check where the door sticks using a thin slip of card: close the door and run the card round the gap, marking where it jams. Afterwards, trace the fault using the checklist below.

Before going any further, make sure that the door itself is sound.

Serious warping is shown by a door which won't sit flush in its frame.
Dropping due to loose joints is common on older, heavier panel doors. It's often shown by cracks in the finish over the joints.
Wet rot reveals itself on outside doors, usually at the base, as cracked wood or flaking paint which gives way if prodded with a knife.

Repairing these faults is beyond the scope of this book. It's often easier to replace the door.

Check all round to find out where the door sticks. Then use the checklist (left) to identify possible causes and their cures.

DOOR FAULT CHECKLIST

PROBLEM	POSSIBLE CAUSES	CURE
A: Sticks at bottom Symptom: Scrapes floor or flattens carpet	Poor trimming when fitted Swelling due to damp Thicker floor covering Dropping due to loose joints	Sand or plane Sand and seal Trim off surplus Repair/replace
B: Sticks at lock side Symptom: Scuffs frame	Paint build up Poor trimming when fitted Swelling due to damp	Sand or plane Sand or plane Sand/plane and seal
C: Sticks at top Symptom: Scuffs frame	Paint build up Poor trimming when fitted Swelling due to damp	Sand off Sand or plane Sand/plane and seal
D: Jams at hinge side Symptom: Tends to spring open	Paint build up on edge Paint/rust build up on hinge Projecting hinge screws Hinges recessed too deeply	Sand off surplus Clean and oil Refit screws Pack out hinges

SANDING EDGES

If the door only sticks slightly, you can often cure it by sanding down the high spots. Often there is no need to remove it.

Wait until a warm, dry spell, particularly if you suspect the problem is caused by damp weather. If you are trimming the side or top, use a wedge to keep the door open while you work. And be sure to sand the door down enough to allow for the thickness of the paint coats you will apply.

Unless you want to refinish the whole door, sand and repaint the entire edge, not just patches. This way the area of new paint won't be obvious if the colours don't match exactly.

Prime and paint (or revarnish) the bare wood as soon as possible. Remember that you need to leave the door open until it dries, so start in the morning if it's an outside door.

Sticking at the side can be cured by sanding the high spots – use a block of wood to keep the paper square to the door. Refinish the whole edge afterwards.

Slight sticking at the bottom can often be cured by taping coarse sandpaper to the floor and working the door over it. Replace the paper as it wears out.

Trade tip

Take the easy way out

✍ Don't be in too much of a hurry to remove wood from the door if the sticking is slight. Doors and frames expand and contract if the weather is very damp or very dry, and you may find that a minor problem which appears in the autumn goes again in the spring.

If the sticking is occasional and not too serious, I start by rubbing a candle along the edge of the door and frame to ease the tight spots. Often, this cures the problem. 🍗

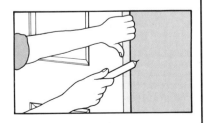

REMOVING A DOOR

The first step to curing more serious sticking is to take the door off its hinges. How difficult this is depends on the weight of the door, and also on whether you are working on your own. Tackling any door is easier if you work this way:

■ Open the door so that it clears the frame and you can get at the hinge screws easily.

■ Slip something underneath to support the weight. A pair of wedges, or even a couple of old magazines, will do.

■ It's helpful to put something behind the door – a small chair, say – so that it doesn't fall backwards when you unscrew the hinges. Don't bother, though, if the door is a lightweight type or if you have an assistant to help you.

■ Undo the screws on the frame, not on the door.

■ Clean the screw slots and slacken each screw half a turn so that they turn easily when you want them to.

■ Remove all but one screw in the bottom hinge, then repeat for the top hinge.

■ Remove the last screw in the bottom hinge. Then take the weight of the door and remove the final screw in the top hinge.

To replace the door, prop it back in position. Steady it with one screw at the top, then add the others.

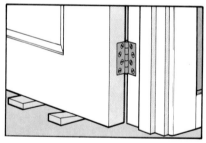

1 Open the door far enough to expose the hinges. Slip some magazines or a pair of wooden wedges underneath so that the weight of the door is supported.

Remove all but one screw from each hinge. Undo the last screw at the bottom, support the door, then remove the top screw and lift away from frame.

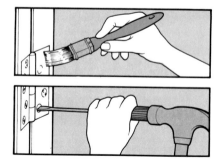

2 Clean old paint out of the screw slots. Either dab on paint stripper, or tap the slots using an old screwdriver to chip away the built-up layers.

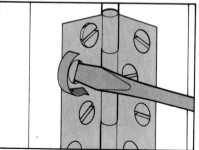

3 Slacken each screw half a turn so you can be sure they unscrew easily when you need them to. Make sure your screwdriver fits the slots exactly.

CURING SERIOUS STICKING

If sanding won't cure sticking at the bottom, use a plane to remove up to 6mm (¼″) of waste wood. Mark a trimming line parallel to the floor, allowing a 2–3mm (⅛″) gap.

■ You could need to trim more than this from the bottom to clear a thick floor covering. It's much easier to saw this off (but see Problem Solver for another solution).

It's worth waiting for a warm, dry spell before starting. Refinish the door as soon as possible, so the bare wood doesn't have a chance to swell. If the bottom has been sticking due to damp, prime and paint (or varnish) it before rehanging.

Trade tip

Avoid splintering

❛ Stop the corners splitting by planing them off at an angle first, then gradually flattening the cut towards the middle. ❜

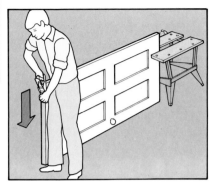

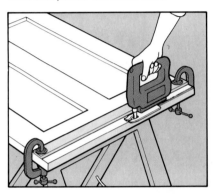

1 *When a door sticks badly at the bottom, use a scrap of hardboard or ply to rule a line along it parallel to the floor and about 3mm (⅛″) up.*

2 *Remove the door and support it on a side edge. Plane the bottom, working from one corner towards the middle, then turn it over and plane the other side.*

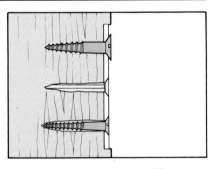

Mark the clearance *for a new floor covering with the door placed against the frame. Mark off the clearance at the top, then transfer to the bottom.*

To saw off a larger strip, *support the door on trestles or a portable bench. Use a panel saw, or jig saw and guide batten. Finish with a plane or sandpaper.*

CURING HINGE FAULTS

If the door won't shut properly and tends to open itself, the cause may be that the hinge side of the door is jamming against the frame. This problem is often made worse on old doors by the build up of several coats of paint, but the most common causes are:

■ The hinge recesses are too deep. You need to pack out the hinges so they can shut correctly.

■ The heads of some of the screws are protruding, preventing the hinges from closing. You need to improve the fit of the screws.

In both cases you may not even need to remove the door, but wedge it open and pack it underneath to support the weight. If packing out the hinges causes the opposite side of the door to stick, sand off the surplus or remove the door and plane the edge.

It's also worth checking the condition of the hinges. Old paint or rust could be jamming them, so scrape this off and oil them if necessary. Replace hopelessly worn or rusty hinges.

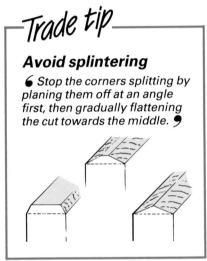

Remove misaligned screws *and plug the holes with matchsticks dipped in glue. Redrill the holes straight when the glue has dried, then replace the screws.*

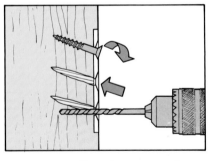

Replace oversize screws *with thinner ones that fit the recesses better. If they don't grip, again pack the holes with matchsticks dipped in glue.*

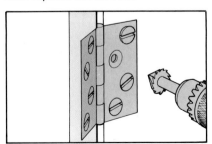

An alternative *is to remove the screws one by one. Drill out each screw recess with a countersink bit suitable for metal, then refit the screw.*

Trade tip

Pack with card

❛ The ideal way to pack out the hinge recesses is with pieces of thin, stiff cardboard, added layer by layer until the hinges close properly. Plug the holes if the screws become loose. ❜

Uneven floors

It's quite common for the door to open over a floor which slopes, has a bump, or is fitted with a thick carpet. In any of these cases, removing sufficient wood from the bottom of the door to clear the obstruction is likely to leave a wide, draughty gap when the door is closed.

An alternative is to fit **rising butt hinges**. These replace the ordinary hinges and are designed to lift the door about 10mm ($7/8''$) as it opens, providing extra clearance. They also have the effect of making the door close automatically – which may or may not suit you.

Rising butts are *lift-off* hinges; they come apart so that the door can be removed by lifting it upwards off the hinge pins. They are sold in right or left handed sets, and it's important to choose the correct ones so that the door goes up – not down – as it opens.

Rising butts aren't always an exact size-for-size replacement for the existing hinges, so you could have to enlarge or fill the hinge recesses. You may also need to trim the top of the door so that it doesn't jam on the frame when it lifts during opening.

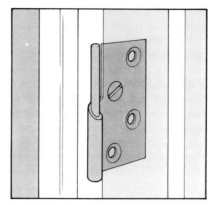

1 Remove the door by unscrewing the existing hinges from the frame. Fit the hinge pin halves of the rising butts to the frame, using one screw each.

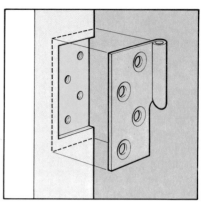

2 If the rising butts are larger than the original hinges, enlarge the recesses with a chisel. If they are smaller, the gaps can be filled later.

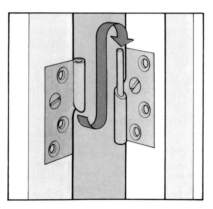

3 Screw the other halves of the rising butts to the door using one screw each. Lift the door onto the pins of the fixed halves and check that they align.

4 Swing the door to check its action. If all is well, fix the other screws. If not, remove the door and realign the hinges before trying again.

Choose right handed hinges if the door opens this way.

right hand

Choose left handed hinges if the door opens this way.

left hand

--- *Trade tip* ---

When to trim

6 Unless the door is a very loose fit, you'll probably need to plane away the top at a slight angle to clear the frame as it closes. Take care when you first fit the door, as it is easy to damage the frame by accident. Close it gently, watching the top as you go, and mark where it touches. 9

SECURING DOORS – 1

Front and back doors fitted with nothing more secure than a simple nightlatch provide an open invitation to burglars. And even doors which are already fitted with a mortise lock may not be as secure as they should be – particularly if the lock itself has a simple *two or three lever* mechanism (see below).

The illustrations on the right show what's needed to provide a reasonable level of security for front and back doors. This section describes how to choose and fit mortise locks and bolts; the other fittings shown – deadlatches, chains and viewers – are covered on pages 273-276, which also deal with french windows and patio doors.

Check your doors

Good locks can make things hard for a thief, but there is no point in fitting them to a flimsy door with glass panes and thin wood panels that can be smashed to gain access. If the door itself is weak, replacing it may be the only answer.

Likewise, you can't fit a mortise lock unless the woodwork is sound and thick enough to take it. The outer frame member (stile) of the door must be at least 45mm (1¾″) thick and 75mm (3″) wide to fit a standard lock, although *narrow stile* locks fit 64mm (2½″) stiles.

.... Shopping List ....

Mortise locks are mostly lever action, with a conventional key which slides a *deadbolt* into a striking plate on the door frame. ('Deadbolt' means it can't be pushed back in without the key.) For extra strength, the striking plate is often reinforced with a *box staple* around the bolt.

Two-bolt mortise *sashlocks* are similar but incorporate a handle-operated latch which keeps the door closed without turning the key. Some sashlocks are left or right 'handed', others are reversible.

Cylinder mortise locks use a flat key which operates a tumbler-type mechanism. This fits right through the door and is retained by a screw through the end of the lock case.

High security locks are commonly awarded British

Fit a deadlatch one third of the way down from the top of the door.

Door viewers and chains provide added security against unwanted callers.

Hinge bolts can be used to reinforce a weak door, especially where it opens outwards.

Fit a five lever mortise lock near the centre of the edge of the door. Use a sashlock if the door is opened frequently.

Fit a five lever mortise deadlock one third of the way up from the bottom of the door.

Bolts fitted near the top and bottom of the door protect it against forcing and can be fastened before you go out.

The front door is normally the one you leave the house by, so it must be lockable from the outside. Fit two locks as shown and fasten both when you go out. Use the latch for convenience when you are indoors.

Back or side doors only need a single mortise deadlock, as they can be bolted before you go out. If the door is used a lot, fit a two-bolt mortise sashlock to ensure it stays shut without using the key.

narrow stile mortise lock

five lever mortise lock

box staple

two bolt mortise lock (sashlock)

striking plate

lever lock-type key

horizontal mortise sashlock

cylinder lock key

cylinder mortise lock

Standard 3621 which checks both strength and security. Among other requirements, no lever lock is considered thief resistant unless it has at least five levers.

Door bolts come in a range of styles, some for flush mounting, others for fitting within the woodwork.

Tools checklist: Electric drill and bits (see lock instructions for sizes), trimming knife, screwdriver, chisels, try-square.

Trade tip

Key cutting

If you're fitting deadlocks to two or more exterior doors, use locks of the same make and get a locksmith to change the levers or tumblers so they work with the same key. Some cylinder locks are supplied with spare cylinders for this purpose.

FITTING A MORTISE LOCK

The amount of work involved in fitting a mortise lock depends on whether you are replacing an old one with a more secure model or installing a lock where none exists. Sashlocks and cylinder mortise locks are fitted in much the same way as a simple mortise lock, except that you need to drill extra holes after cutting the mortise.

Replacing an existing lock

Although there are standards for the size of mortise locks, there is no guarantee that a replacement lock will slot straight into the hole left by an old one. To check how to proceed, it's worth removing the existing lock and measuring its exact dimensions before buying a replacement.

Take the opportunity to inspect the mortise, too. Even if the hole is in good order, you may have to trim or enlarge it; and if you fit a lock with a box staple striking plate, this will probably need an enlarged recess as well.

If the mortise is mis-shapen, oversized or the surrounding wood has cracked, you have two alternatives:
■ Fit metal reinforcing plates to the area of the lock on both faces of the door.
■ Fill the old mortise and striking plate recess (see Problem Solver), then cut a fresh mortise elsewhere on the stile. This is also the best solution if the old lock was fitted in the wrong place – either too far up or down the door.

CUTTING A LOCK MORTISE

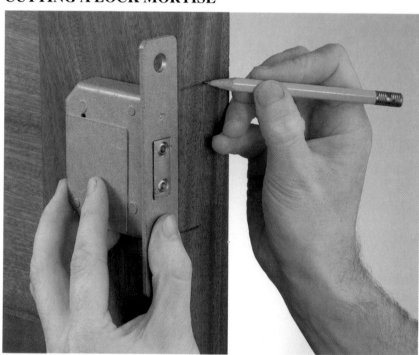

1 Offer up the lock to the door and strike off marks in line with the top and bottom of the body. Remove the lock and use a try square to extend lines right across the edge. Then rule a line down the centre of the edge between them.

A new lock mortise must be cut as accurately as possible to avoid weakening the door unnecessarily. If the door already has a mortise which is unusable, site the new one at least 150mm (6″) away from it.

Some mortise locks have a double end plate which comes with a polished outer trim section. You need to remove this to fit the lock, but remember to allow for its extra thickness when recessing the end plate or working out the position of the keyhole.

2 Drill a series of holes down this centre line, square to the wood. Use a bit the same width as the lock case, and mark it to show the lock's depth.

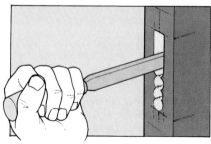

3 Chisel remaining wood away to square up the mortise, then test-fit the lock. Extend the bolt first so you have something to grip if it sticks in the hole.

4 Cut round the end plate of the lock with a trimming knife, then chisel a recess. To check the fit, reverse the lock and try the end plate in place.

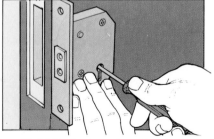

5 Hold the lock against the side of the door to mark the holes for the key, cylinder or spindle. Drill holes across and cut a keyhole slot with a saw or file.

FITTING THE STRIKING PLATE

Fit the striking plate to the frame after fitting the lock so that you can be sure the bolt slides cleanly. The alignment is especially critical on a sashlock, where even a slight mismatch may stop the latch engaging.

If the door is a tight fit, you have no choice but to chisel out a recess and set the striking plate into the frame. But where there is plenty of clearance, simply cut a recess for the bolt hole and screw the plate itself to the surface of the door frame.

See Problem Solver for how to deal with alignment difficulties once the lock has been fully fitted.

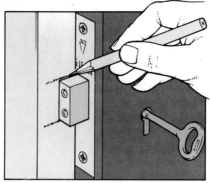

1 Fit the lock into the mortise and add the mounting screws. Test the operation with the key, then close the door to mark where the bolt contacts the frame.

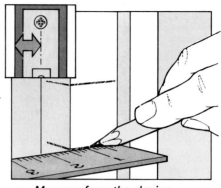

2 Measure from the closing edge of the door to the centre line of the bolt. Mark this distance out from the door stop to show the centre of the striking plate.

3 Cut a recess to fit the hole in the striking plate using the marks to guide you. A box staple needs a hole much larger than the bolt itself.

4 Test fit the striking plate. If it needs to be sunk flush with the frame, cut around the outside edge using a trimming knife and chisel out a recess.

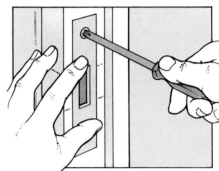

5 Fit the striking plate in place and test the lock before inserting the fixing screws. This allows you to move the plate or enlarge the recess if necessary.

FINISHING OFF

On a simple mortise lock, trim the keyholes by fitting escutcheon plates. A sashlock also needs operating handles or knobs – often supplied as a combined set on a plate incorporating a keyhole, although separate handles and escutcheons may be used.

Cylinder mortise locks normally have a trim plate to conceal the fitting hole around the cylinder. On versions which incorporate a latch handle, this may be fitted on a mounting plate with a shaped cutout to fit the cylinder.

Fit escutcheon plates over the keyholes. Cylinder mortise locks have shaped side plates to conceal the hole where the cylinder passes through the door.

On a sashlock, pass the spindle through the lock and slip on the handles; bear in mind that you may need to cut the spindle shorter with a junior hacksaw. Use the key to align the keyhole, then screw on the plate.

FITTING DOOR BOLTS

Bolts provide extra security for doors which can be fastened from inside. There are several types, but all should be fitted in pairs near the top and bottom of the door.

Surface mounted bolts only offer security if they are solidly built with stout screw fixings. *Tower and barrel bolts* are utility types, with a round bolt bar which slides in a guide on the door and fits into a staple on the frame. *Locking bolts* normally have an enclosed bolt held in the closed position by a small key-operated lock. *Flush bolts* are recessed into the wood of the door for a neat appearance; on double doors, they can be fitted to the ends of the door to shoot upwards and downwards.

Mortise rack bolts fit into the edge of the door for added strength. They are operated with a special key, making them suitable for use on glass panelled doors where most surface mounted bolts can be slipped by breaking the glass and reaching through.

Hinge bolts provide protection against the door being forced open by attacking the hinges. This is most likely on doors which open outwards where the hinges are exposed. Fit two, 75mm (3″) above and below the top and bottom hinges. They engage automatically whenever the door is closed.

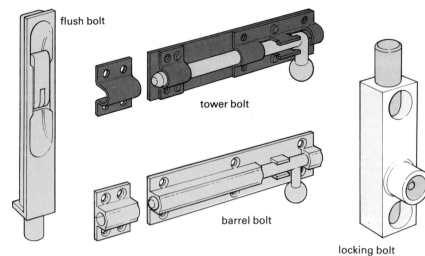

flush bolt *tower bolt* *barrel bolt* *locking bolt*

Surface mounted bolts *screw to the door, although you may need to chisel a recess on the frame to fit the striking plate. They come in several styles.*

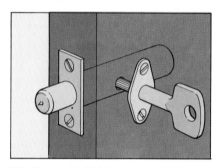

Mortise bolts *fit into a mounting hole in the stile with a crossways hole for the key. They shoot into a striking plate fitted over a hole in the frame.*

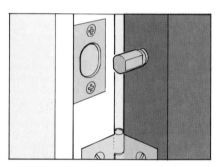

Hinge bolts *screw into mounting holes drilled in the centre of the door edge. As the door is closed they engage with striking plates recessed into the frame.*

PROBLEM SOLVER

Patching an old mortise

Don't rely on general-purpose filler to patch an unwanted mortise hole – it's important to restore as much of the door's strength as possible. The best method is to cut blocks of wood to fit the old hole as accurately as possible and glue them in place with woodworking adhesive.

Cut the blocks so that they are a tight fit in the hole, but don't try to force them in or you may damage the surrounding woodwork. Leave the ends protruding from the hole slightly so that you can plane or sand them off smooth after the adhesive has fully hardened (between 7–16 hours).

To patch any remaining small gaps and holes, use a resin-based wood filler which won't shrink or crack. Resin filler also sets as hard as the surrounding wood itself, helping to add to the strength of the repair.

Fill an old mortise hole *with blocks of wood cut to roughly the right size and glued in place. Then patch with resin filler.*

Where sticking *is due to a misaligned striking plate, enlarge the recess and move it over. Pack behind with glued strips of wood.*

Sticking locks

A stiff or jammed action on a recently fitted lock is most likely to be due to misalignment of the bolt and the striking plate. Open the door and see if the lock works freely. If it does, inspect the striking plate for wear marks to find out where the bolt has been rubbing.

Start by making sure the problem isn't simply the result of the door warping or dropping on its hinges. This is the most likely cause – especially in winter – and is usually easily remedied without having to touch the lock.

Otherwise, remove the striking plate and recut the recess to correct its position. Pack the hole with glued wood strips to maintain a tight fit.

To free a stiff lock, lubricate with powdered graphite (from locksmiths) rather than oil, which tends to attract dust and soon makes matters worse.

SECURING DOORS – 2

Mortise locks and bolts provide a high level of security, but aren't very convenient for keeping doors shut while you are in. You may also find that a door simply isn't substantial enough to take a mortise lock. The alternative is to fit a *deadlatch*.

Using deadlatches

Don't confuse a deadlatch with the similar-looking nightlatch, still standard equipment on most outside doors. Nightlatches are much less secure (see overleaf), and in high-risk situations are best replaced.

A deadlatch engages automatically when the door is closed, ensuring it isn't left unsecured by accident. Although potentially less secure than a mortise lock, it is proof against most forms of attack. And because the lock screws to the surface of the door, it weakens it less than cutting a mortise.

As shown in the previous section, a front door should have a deadlatch as well as a mortise lock. Any door which cannot take a mortise can have a deadlatch instead, so long as it is backed up by bolts.

Completing your security

A front door will also benefit from a *viewer*, enabling unwanted callers to be avoided, and a *chain* for keeping strangers out until you've checked their credentials.

French windows or patio doors need securing with purpose-made locks and bolts. And if your house has an integral garage, you should take steps to ensure the doors can't easily be forced.

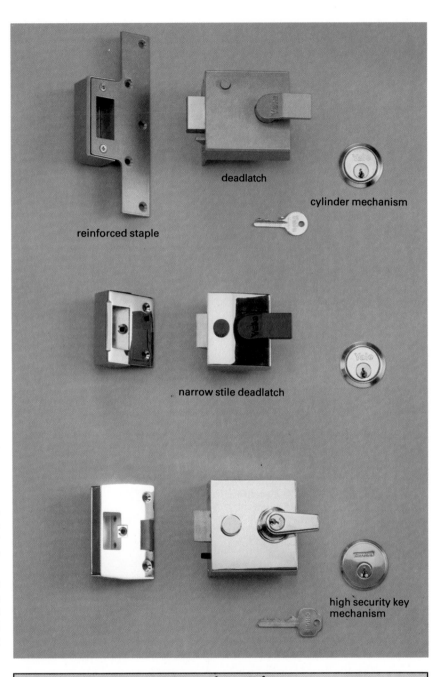

reinforced staple

deadlatch

cylinder mechanism

narrow stile deadlatch

high security key mechanism

Trade tip

Key changes

6 If you lose your keys, or if you have just moved home, you cannot be sure of the security of your locks. If an existing latch is a secure type that is worth keeping, you can avoid much of the expense of a new lock by buying a replacement cylinder mechanism (barrel) and fitting this in place of the old one. You can also buy matched sets for securing the front and back door with the same key. 9

....Shopping List....

Deadlatches come in a wide range of styles and can be fitted to most doors over 38mm (1½″) thick. Standard designs need a door stile around 90mm (3½″) wide – if yours is narrower, alternative models are available for stiles as narrow as 40mm (1½″). All types have a cylinder lock mechanism using a flat key, although there are several variations depending on the make.

High security deadlatches have stronger cylinder mechanisms and reinforced staples (which need to be recessed into the frame). But any

lock approved to British Standard 3621 will have been tested to withstand forcing as well as attack by drilling and sawing.

Chains and viewers are made in several different designs and a range of finishes. See page 275 for details.

Patio door locks and bolts vary according to the doors concerned. See page 276 for details.

Tools checklist: Screwdriver, junior hacksaw (possibly), chisel, electric drill and bits.

HOW DEADLATCHES WORK

Deadlatches are a form of 'rim lock', a term for any lock screwed to the inside surface of the door. They have *cylinder* mechanisms fitted into a hole drilled through the door and operated by a flat key.

A deadlatch is secure because the latch bolt is deadlocked in position when the door is shut, and cannot be pushed back without the key. With some designs this happens automatically when the door is closed; for added security you can lock the internal operating knob/handle. Other types are deadlocked by using the key to throw the bolt further across or to operate a separate bolt.

Nightlatches are another form of cylinder rim lock. They have a springbolt operated by a key from outside and a knob inside. Nightlatches are less secure because they do not deadlock – the bolt can be fixed in position using the snib, but not from outside. This means that the springbolt can often be forced back with a strip of metal or card, while on glazed doors smashing the glass gives ready access to the locking snib. Replace existing nightlatches where security is important.

One other form of rim lock you may come across is the *lever rimlock*, which uses a conventional key. These are normally lightly constructed with simple mechanisms which do not offer any real security. Replace with a deadlatch or mortise lock.

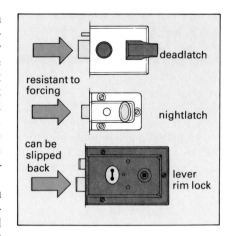

Deadlatches *are the only form of rim lock which offer really high security. This is because the bolt is deadlocked and cannot be forced back.*

FITTING A DEADLATCH

If you are fitting a deadlatch together with a mortise lock, put it about two-thirds of the way up the door. Where the latch is the only lock, fit it about halfway up.

Cylinder locks require a large hole drilled straight through the door, for which you will need a suitable drill or hole saw – check the maker's instructions for sizes.

Although the lock body itself simply screws to the surface of the door, a few designs have an end plate which has to be recessed into the edge of the door. Do this first, otherwise the screw holes will not align properly.

Replacing a nightlatch

When fitting a deadlatch in place of an old nightlatch, it's preferable to avoid using the existing screw holes – they are unlikely to give such a strong fixing as new holes.

If the holes in the new lock line up with the old ones, one option is to fit longer or thicker screws. A better solution is to fill the holes with glued wooden plugs; allow these to dry then redrill the holes.

1 *Some locks come with a template for marking the position of the cylinder hole, otherwise use the lock's backplate. Fit a bit or hole saw of the size specified in the maker's instructions and drill the hole.*

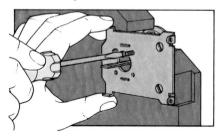

2 *Screw the lock backplate to the door, then fit the cylinder and mounting ring and tighten the retaining screws – trim them to length if necessary.*

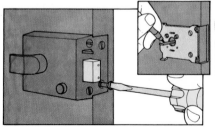

3 *Fit the lock case to the backplate. If it won't go on because the cylinder connecting bar is too long, cut the bar at one of the marked grooves.*

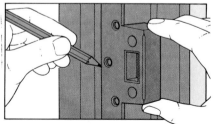

4 *Close the door and mark the striker position on the frame. Align the striker plate, mark round it, then chisel a rebate in the frame and screw it in place.*

FITTING CHAINS AND VIEWERS

Locks and bolts are only effective so long as the door remains shut. Fitting a chain or viewer lets you and your family check on callers before admitting them.

Chains and restraints

Chains and restraints allow the door to open just enough to talk to someone without letting them in.

Chains are generally around 200mm (8″) long. One end is screwed securely to the door frame; the other passes through a slit ring fixed to the door or latches into a grooved slider rail that allows it to be released for full opening.

One design is retained by a lock mechanism which can be released from outside by a keyholder. This is particularly suitable for the elderly or infirm since they can leave it engaged and give keys to their family or other regular visitors.

Restraints work on a similar principle but are generally stronger, with a rigid bar in place of a chain. You can also get door locks which have a built-in restraint strap.

When fitting, position the two parts to ensure that the chain or restrainer can only be engaged or released when the door is closed.

Viewers

Viewers are for fitting to solid wood doors so that you can see callers without them seeing you. For night-time use you really need a porch light as well, and this has the added advantage of deterring intruders.

Fit a viewer through a solid part of the door, not a panel, and at a comfortable level for the shortest user.

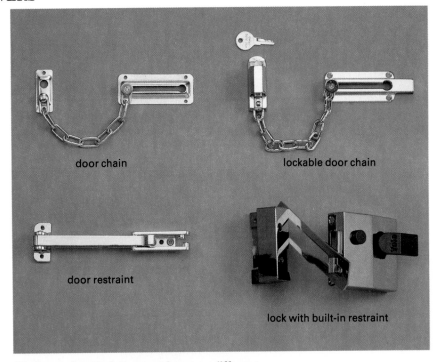

door chain

lockable door chain

door restraint

lock with built-in restraint

Chains and restraints *come in many different designs. When fitting one, make sure it is at a convenient height and can only be released when the door is closed. Remember, too, that it will only be as secure as its fixings.*

To fit a chain, *screw the fixed end firmly to the frame at a convenient height. Link the chain to the keeper and open the door to mark its position.*

Fit a viewer *by drilling a hole through the solid wood of the door and inserting one half from each side. Screw the two parts together.*

PROBLEM SOLVER

Securing integral garages

An integral garage is likely to have an internal door connecting with the house. This poses a special security problem because an intruder concealed in the garage has more time to force it, and there may be tools to hand to aid his efforts.

Fortunately, such doors are normally strongly constructed to meet fire regulations, enabling them to take a high security lever mortise lock. For added protection, fit mortise bolts at the top and bottom of the door, together with hinge bolts.

Keep the garage door locked to restrict access.

Secure up-and-over garage doors by fitting *padbolts* to shoot sideways into the surround and use security padlocks. Position the bolts about 500mm (20″) from the bottom of the door for easy operation, and fix them to the door with coachbolts (don't forget to put the nuts on the inside!).

With hinged double garage doors, fit top and bottom bolts to one door and a mortise lock or deadlatch to the other. Make sure the lock engages securely with the bolted door.

Secure an up-and-over *garage door by fitting padbolts shooting outwards into the frame. With hinged double garage doors, fit bolts to one door and a mortise lock or deadlatch to the other.*

FRENCH WINDOWS AND PATIO DOORS

Wooden french windows may have one or two opening frames. Single frames can be treated like any other external door. Double opening frames often have a mortise sash-lock and a handle operating an *espagnolette* (a double-ended vertical bolt). These are easily opened by smashing a pane, so add extra bolts – two to each frame.

Mortise bolts are ideal. There are different lengths to suit doors and windows, but often the window models are more appropriate because of the narrowness of the frames. Where the frames are too thin to take a mortise bolt, use flush bolts or even surface-mounted locking bolts.

Metal french windows made from galvanized steel usually have their own lock, but this may not be very strong. For added security fit metal window locks to the top and bottom of both opening frames so that they shoot into the outer frame.

Aluminium sliding patio doors come with their own locks, but for extra protection they can be equipped with special bolts designed to fit aluminium frames. The bolts can be mounted on the doors, to shoot up or down into the surround, or on the surround, to shoot sideways into the door frames.

Wooden sliding doors cannot be fitted with a conventional mortise lock or rim lock. Instead, use a mortise lock with a *hook-bolt* or *claw-bolt* (clutch-bolt), both of which grip the striker plate and resist the sideways pull.

In the case of a hook-bolt, there is a locating pin below it which engages the striker plate and prevents the door being lifted to free the bolt.

Fitting is generally similar to normal mortise locks. With a hook-bolt, use the locating pin to line up the striker plate.

WOODEN FRENCH WINDOWS

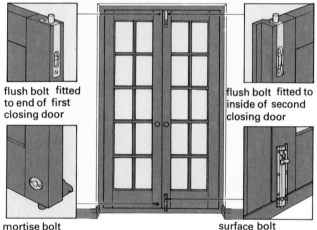

flush bolt fitted to end of first closing door

flush bolt fitted to inside of second closing door

mortise bolt

surface bolt

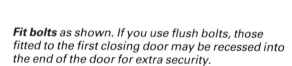

Fit bolts as shown. If you use flush bolts, those fitted to the first closing door may be recessed into the end of the door for extra security.

METAL FRENCH WINDOWS

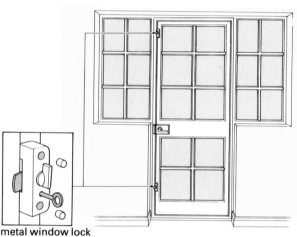

metal window lock

Fit metal window locks to secure the opening frames to the metal surround. Fix the locks with self-tapping screws.

WOODEN SLIDING DOORS

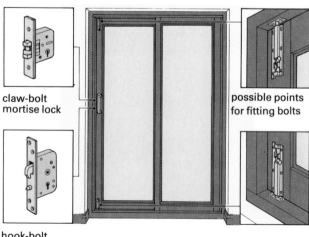

claw-bolt mortise lock

possible points for fitting bolts

hook-bolt mortise lock

Use a mortise lock with a hook bolt or claw bolt to resist the sideways pull. For extra protection, fit bolts to shoot upwards and downwards.

ALUMINIUM SLIDING DOORS

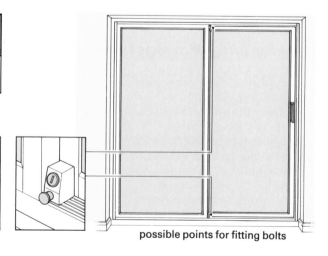

possible points for fitting bolts

Fit patio door bolts to reinforce the existing lock – most types suit single or double sliding frames. Screw in place with self-tapping screws.

DOOR TRIMS AND FURNITURE

DECORATIVE PLATES

Door plates are both functional and attractive. Although primarily intended to protect vulnerable parts of the door from wear, most door plates are prominent decorative features in their own right.

Fingerplates are screwed to the surface of the door to protect the point which receives most wear during opening and closing.

Kickplates are mounted at the base of the door to protect it from knocks. They can also be useful for stopping pets from scratching the door finish.

Nameplates come in many designs, either with the name already printed or left blank for you to fill in.

─Trade tip─

Stick-on nameplates

❛ Screw-on nameplates don't always hold well in the thin panelling of flush doors, so use self-adhesive sticky pads instead. Then, to avoid leaving empty screw holes in the plate, bore holes in the door with a bradawl or snip off the screw shanks with wire cutters. Stick the screws or the heads in place with a smear of epoxy resin adhesive. This technique works on fingerplates too. ❜

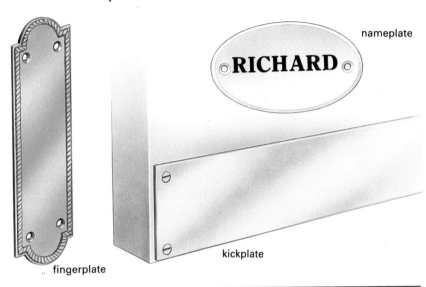

nameplate

RICHARD

fingerplate

kickplate

BOLTS FOR INTERIOR DOORS

Bolts for interior doors aren't strong enough to act as security devices – they are mainly for holding doors shut, or keeping small children out of mischief.

Straight barrel bolts are used where the surface of the door shuts flush with the surrounding frame.

Necked barrel bolts are fitted where the door surface isn't flush or where there is not enough wood directly in line with the bolt to drill a hole for the bolt to shoot into. The offset end of the barrel shoots into a keeper hole drilled in the frame.

Indicator bolts are for bathroom and WC doors; shooting the bolt operates an indicator panel on the outside of the door to show that the door is locked. Most can be opened from the outside in an emergency.

straight barrel

necked barrel

indicator bolt

HOOKS AND HANGERS

Coat hooks come in a wide range of styles. Designs range from ornamental brass to plain white plastic and have one, two or more hooks depending on what you want.

Self-adhesive hooks are suitable only for lightweight items. The bond isn't strong enough to support heavy loads.

Screw-on hooks are easy to attach to solid doors and give a firm fixing. There are special cavity-type fixings for attaching to flush doors. Some hook designs have concealed or integral fixings for a neat finish.

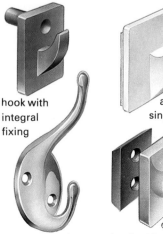

hook with integral fixing

self-adhesive single hook

screw-on hook

hook with concealed fixing

─Trade tip─

More grip

❛ The bond between a self-adhesive fitting and a painted door is only as strong as the bond of the paint to the door. If the paint is at all suspect, I mark the outline of the hook base on to the door and then sand off all the paint layers within this mark. This gives the hook a stronger fixing. ❜

FITTING FRONT DOOR FURNITURE

Door furniture normally fits in one of two ways – with short screws or with through-bolts.

Screwing to doors The main thing to ensure here is that you position the fitting and mark the holes accurately. Misdrilled holes are hard to conceal if you get them in the wrong place, which is easily done if you are putting together separate numerals to make up the house number, say.

Small brass screws such as those used for door furniture are fairly weak. And if they are inserted into a hole drilled in a tough hardwood door there is a risk of them snapping, or of the slots distorting as you tighten them.

Avoid this by driving in steel screws of the same size first, to open out the holes. After that it's simply a matter of replacing them with the brass ones, which go in easier still if you rub them on a bar of soap.

Drilling and bolting Knockers and handles are normally fitted with a bolt right through the door and have projecting lugs which locate the fitting in place. Use these to mark the position for drilling.

Offer up the fitting, taking care to position it centrally, and press against the door so that the lugs leave indents in the timber.

When you are drilling right through a door it pays to be careful: many hardwoods are brittle and when the drill breaks through, it's easy to split the wood. Avoid this happening by using the double-drilling technique shown below.

Mark the position of a knob using the lugs on the back.

1 To use the double-drilling technique, mark the position of the hole on the outside of the door, then drill through with a fine bit to act as a guide.

2 Drill back through from the inside using the correct size bit. When it breaks through, any splintering will be covered by the fitting itself.

Trade tip

In the right place

❝ It's often difficult to position numbers so that they align properly on the door and have the right spacing. And once you have drilled the fixing holes you are usually stuck with them even if they look wrong.

You can fix lightweight numbers temporarily using sticking putty, but for heavier fittings I always cut the shapes out of paper and stick these to the door to check their position. Close up, you can't usually tell whether a set of door numbers are in the right position or crooked, so double check by seeing how they look from the front gate. ❞

FITTING LETTERPLATES

Unless it comes with a paper template, you need to measure the letterplate carefully.

For inward-opening types, the hole through the door needs to be a fraction larger than the flap itself, which you should measure from the back. Take care not to make the cut-out too large, as normally you have to drill holes for fixing bolts close to either side of it.

The hole size is less critical on a lift-up flap; make it the same as the cut-out in the plate.

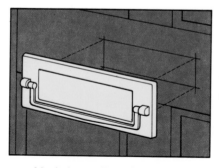

1 Mark the outline of the cut-out for the flap on the face of the door. It may help to make a paper pattern and tape this in place so you can position the hole accurately.

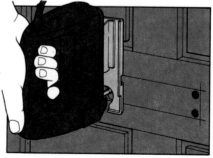

2 Drill four holes inside the corners of the marked area with a large (say, 12mm) bit and saw out the waste with a jigsaw. Try the letterplate for fit, then mark and drill the bolt fixings.

FITTING WINDOW LOCKS

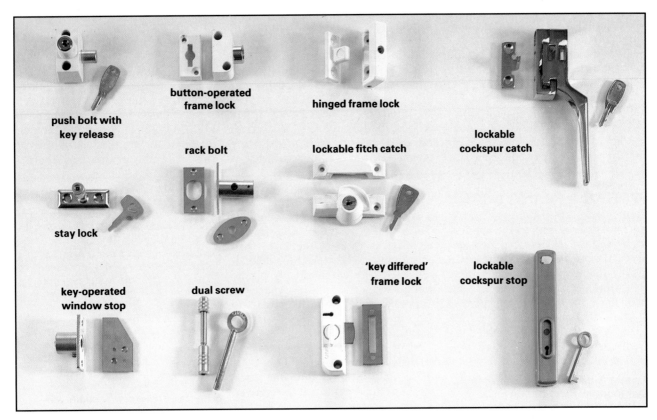

push bolt with key release

button-operated frame lock

hinged frame lock

lockable cockspur catch

rack bolt

lockable fitch catch

stay lock

key-operated window stop

dual screw

'key differed' frame lock

lockable cockspur stop

Around half of the domestic burglaries which occur each year take place through windows. And in the majority of cases the burglar gains entry either by forcing the insecure catches which most windows have fitted as standard, or by breaking the glass to slip those catches.

Window locks stop this happening. For only a modest investment, they leave the would-be intruder with the choice of smashing a pane and climbing through (possibly attracting attention in the process), or moving on to easier pickings. Most burglars choose the latter.

Narrowing the choice

Although individual makes of window locks vary widely, they fall into distinct groups according to the type of window being secured. And within any group, different makes all fit in a broadly similar way.

The following pages show which categories of lock are appropriate, depending whether the windows are:
■ Hinged with wooden frames
■ Sashes with wooden frames
■ Metal framed
(Patio windows form another category, and are covered on page 276.)

Run through this section and list which types are possible options for the windows you want to secure. Then consider the following when choosing between models:

Convenience is important if the window is in constant use. Automatic locking is an advantage if you're forgetful, and combination or push-button locks are helpful if you're apt to mislay keys. Individually keyed ('key differed') locks are more secure, but could leave you with a lot of keys to sort out.

Some types of lock allow windows to be locked partially open for ventilation, though this reduces their security value.

Cost can be difficult to assess. Many cheaper locks must be fitted in pairs to be effective, which adds to the cost but also increases the number of locking points. Complex locks are more expensive, but not necessarily more secure (see below).

Security The more locking points, the better. Surface mounted locks are generally the easiest to fit, but are only as strong as their screw fixings. Locks housed in the frame timber tend to be stronger.

Finish Window locks come in various finishes including white, silver metal and brass. Obtrusive locks are a positive advantage from a security point of view.

Special windows

Double glazed sealed units with frames of wood or metal can be fitted with window locks, but you need to take extra care not to puncture the seals when drilling fixing holes. Modern types usually have adequate locks.

Plastic (uPVC) windows are a fairly recent innovation, and as such should already be fitted with adequate locks. Conventional window locks are unsuitable; contact the window manufacturer if you need extra security.

Trade tip

Security points

❝ On all types of window:
Don't bother with window locks if the frame timber is rotten – it will be obvious to a burglar.
Don't fit locks which weaken the frame to the point where it's no longer secure. Again, burglars will be quick to spot it.
Do use longer fixing screws if you feel that the ones supplied aren't strong enough.
Don't leave keys in locks. ❞

LOCKING HINGED WINDOWS (WOODEN FRAME)

There are basically two ways to secure a hinged window:

■ Fit extra devices to lock the casement to the window frame. This is usually the most effective way.

■ Replace (or fit lockable attachments to) the existing catches.

Surface-mounted frame locks fall into the first group and come in a wide variety of patterns and finishes. Features available include automatic locking (so you don't forget them) and combination locks (no keys to lose). The more expensive types are key differed for greater security.

Frame locks generally screw on, and like all such locks are only as strong as their fixings. A single lock, placed centrally, is perfectly adequate for a fanlight or small window, but for larger casements fit a pair – one at the top, one at the bottom – on the catch side.

Rack bolts for windows (longer ones are used on doors) offer greater security than surface-mounted frame locks because they rely on the frame itself for strength rather than on their own fixing screws. However, they are trickier

to fit, and are only suitable for casement frames measuring over 38×38mm (1½×1½"). Fit a pair – one on either side of the casement, about half way up.

Lockable catches and stays replace or lock the existing catches. They are simple to fit, but only as secure as their screw fixings allow them to be. Also, they secure the window at one point only – which may not be enough to deter some burglars.

Stay locks are most useful on fanlights, allowing them to be locked open for ventilation. However, this makes the window less secure.

FITTING A FRAME LOCK

Frame locks consist of two parts: the *lock body* screws to the window frame and the *lock plate* to the casement (the opening part). With some makes the two parts go the other way round, and some types of lock body have a separate locking plate.

Mark the positions of the two parts with the lock assembled so that you can be sure they will engage cleanly.

Types of surface-mounted frame lock (below). Push-button locks with key release make closure easier. Automatic catch locks need well fitting frames.

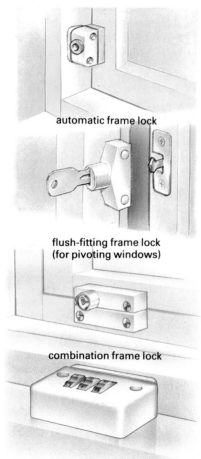

button-operated frame lock

automatic frame lock

flush-fitting frame lock (for pivoting windows)

combination frame lock

If the window frame is moulded, mark the position of the frame-mounted portion of the lock, then chisel out enough wood for it to sit square to the casement. A plastic wedge-shaped backing piece is usually provided with the lock to do the same job on a tapered window frame.

Some makes of lock have plastic security screw covers. Don't fit these until you're sure the lock works as they're difficult to remove.

Tools: Electric drill and bits or bradawl, pencil, screwdriver, 12mm (½") wood chisel (maybe).

1 *Fit the two parts of the lock together and offer up to the closed window. Mark their positions in pencil on the frame and casement.*

On a moulded frame, chisel out a recess for the lock body so that it will sit square to the casement when the window is closed (see also Problem Solver).

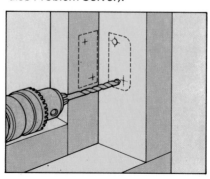

2 *Separate the lock. Hold each part in place and mark the screw holes, then drill or bradawl pilot holes to the same depth as the screw threads.*

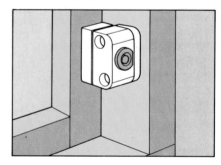

On tapered frames, you need to pack behind the lock in order for it to sit square. Most makes supply a wedge-shaped backing piece for this.

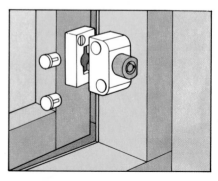

3 *Screw both parts in position and check that they engage cleanly. If all is well, push the plastic screw covers down into the fixing holes.*

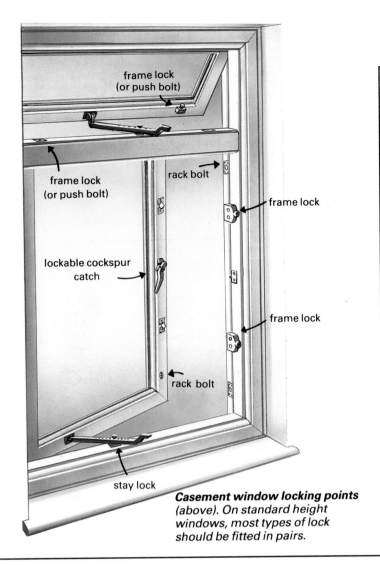

frame lock
(or push bolt)

frame lock
(or push bolt)

rack bolt

frame lock

lockable cockspur
catch

frame lock

rack bolt

stay lock

Casement window locking points
(above). On standard height
windows, most types of lock
should be fitted in pairs.

FITTING CATCH LOCKS
A lockable cockspur catch is a good choice if the original catch is weak or the window is a loose fit. Most types are a straight replacement, and simply screw on.

Stay locks are available for both holed and plain stays, but only holed stays can be locked open. Replacement stays with adjustable ratchets that can be locked in any position are also available.

Tools: Bradawl, screwdriver, electric drill and bits.

stay lock
(hole-type)

cockspur catch

stay lock
(plain type)

FITTING RACK BOLTS
Check the maker's instructions to see what drill bits are required. Normally you need a 10mm (3/8") twist bit for the key hole and a 16mm (5/8") flat bit for the lock hole.

Make sure you drill all the holes absolutely square to the frame, so that the bolt and key engage cleanly. Get a helper to hold the window steady while you drill the casement.

Tools: Electric drill and bits, bradawl, screwdriver, try square, 12mm (1/2") wood chisel.

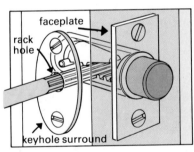

faceplate

rack hole

keyhole surround

The rack bolt sits in a hole in the casement, held by a screw-on faceplate (usually recessed). Turning the key drives the bolt into the frame.

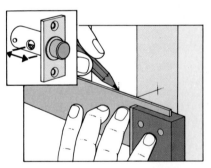

1 Mark the bolt position on the casement edge. Measure the distance from faceplate to rack hole and transfer to the side of the frame with a try square.

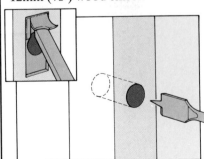

2 Drill a hole for the lock body centrally through the edge of the casement, then test-fit the lock and mark the faceplate position. Chisel out a recess.

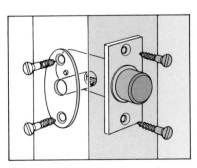

3 Drill a hole for the key at your marked point. Test-fit the lock and check it works, then screw down the faceplate and screw on the keyhole surround.

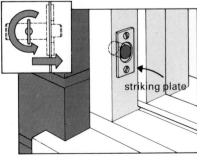

striking plate

4 Close the window and operate the lock so that the bolt marks the frame. Drill a hole for the bolt recess at this point, then screw on the striking plate.

LOCKING SASH WINDOWS

The easiest way to secure a sliding-sash window is to replace the original catch (probably either a screw-barrel or fitch type) with a new lockable catch. But as with hinged windows this only provides a single security point – not enough to deter many burglars.

There are three other options, all of which work by locking the movable sashes together.

Push bolts come in several patterns and may be either button or key operated. They should be fitted in pairs, one each side of the window.

The push lock body screws to the top rail of the lower sash, and shoots a bolt into a hole drilled in the upper sash. Drilling a series of such holes allows the lower sash to be locked open for ventilation.

Window ('acorn') stops are screw-in or key-lockable brass pegs which, when fitted to the upper sash, stop the lower sash sliding up. Like push locks, they are best fitted in pairs.

Dual screws are 'bolts within bolts' which lock the two sashes together. The outer threaded barrel fits into a hole drilled in the upper rail of the lower sash. Inside this goes a screw bolt which is driven into a corresponding hole in the lower rail of the upper sash using a simple key.

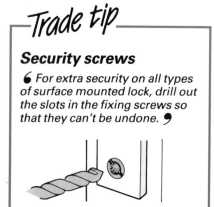

Trade tip

Security screws

❛ *For extra security on all types of surface mounted lock, drill out the slots in the fixing screws so that they can't be undone.* ❜

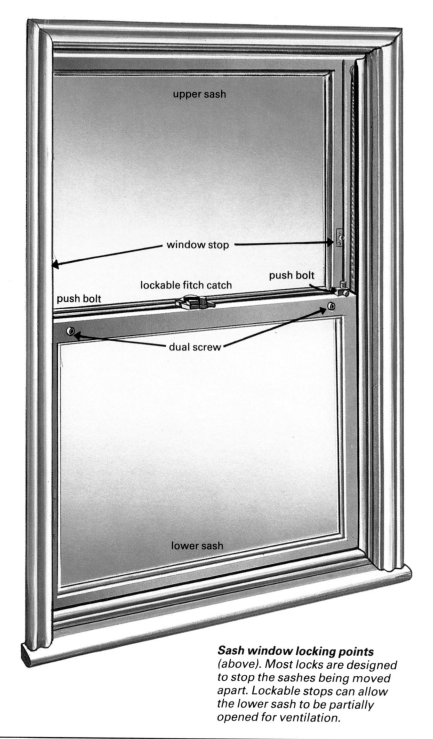

upper sash

window stop

lockable fitch catch

push bolt

push bolt

dual screw

lower sash

Sash window locking points (above). *Most locks are designed to stop the sashes being moved apart. Lockable stops can allow the lower sash to be partially opened for ventilation.*

FITTING A PUSH BOLT

Check the instructions before you start to find out what drill size is needed for the bolt hole – they vary widely. Use the lock bolt itself to mark the position of the hole (if necessary, rub a felt-tip pen over the end).

Repeat the sequence shown to drill a second bolt hole so that the window can be locked open for ventilation. This hole should be no further than 100mm (4″) above the first.

Tools: Electric drill and bits, screwdriver.

1 *Screw the lock body to the upper rail of the lower sash, then operate the lock so that the bolt leaves a mark showing where to drill the upper sash frame.*

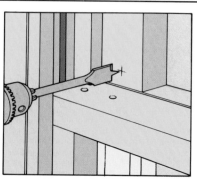

2 *Remove the lock body, then drill the bolt hole and fit the striking cover plate (if supplied). Replace the lock and check that the bolt engages.*

FITTING WINDOW STOPS

Fit stops at the corners where the sashes meet. It's possible to fit two pairs – one to hold the window fully closed, and another 100mm (4″) further up the upper sash to allow the lower sash to be opened for ventilation.

The fixing plates are either screwed to the surface of the sash frame or recessed into the sash for greater strength.

Tools: Electric drill and bits, bradawl, screwdriver, 12mm (½″) wood chisel (maybe), tape measure.

Peg-type stops are designed to be fitted and removed by hand.

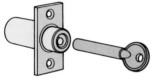

Key-operated versions are more secure, but also more costly.

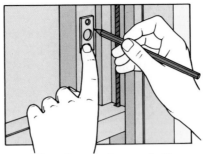

1 *Close the window and offer up the fixing plate to the upper sash. Draw around it in pencil, and mark where to drill the stop peg hole.*

3 *Fit the stop peg chain to the window frame within easy reach. Complete the job by screwing the stop striker plate to the lower sash top rail.*

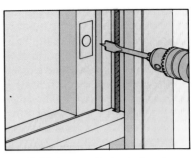

2 *Drill the peg hole to the size and depth recommended. If need be, chisel out a recess for the fixing plate. Then bradawl the screw holes and screw in place.*

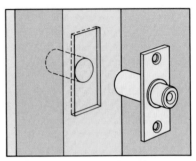

On key operated stops, the stop and fixing plate are combined in a single unit housed in the sash frame. Drill out the housing, then screw in place.

FITTING DUAL SCREWS

Fit dual screws 75-100mm (3-4″) in from the sides of the sashes. You only need to drill one hole per screw (normally 10mm – ⅜″ – diameter), but make sure you don't drill too far.

The most common type of dual screw (shown) has a threaded barrel and receiver which simply tap in. Others have a screw-on facing plate, for which you'll need to chisel recesses.

Tools: Electric drill and bits, hammer, 12mm (½″) chisel (maybe).

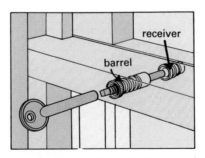

The dual screw inner bolt is driven in with a key. It runs through a threaded barrel in the lower sash into a receiver housed in the upper sash.

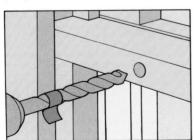

1 *With the window closed, drill a hole through the lower sash top rail. Mark the drill bit with tape, then continue the hole 15mm (⅝″) into the upper sash.*

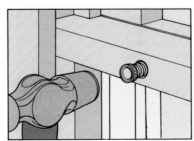

2 *Tap in the threaded barrel as far as it will go, then slide down the upper sash and tap in the receiver. To lock, screw in the bolt flush with the rail.*

LOCKABLE CATCHES

Lockable catches for sash windows are normally a straight replacement for the existing fitch or screw-and-barrel catch. However, it's advisable not to re-use any of the original screw holes – plug them with filler, then drill or bradawl new ones in the two sash frames.

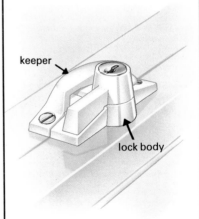

Lockable replacement catches for sash windows come in two parts. The body screws to one rail, the keeper to the other.

LOCKING METAL FRAMED WINDOWS

Metal framed windows can either be secured by locking the existing catch or locking the casement to the frame, but in both cases the number of devices available is more limited.

Catch locks for cockspur catches come in two types. One type clamps on to the catch and is released with a key. The other (which is more secure) consists of a lockable stop bolt that screws to the frame.

Frame locks are similar (and in some cases interchangeable) with those for wooden frames, but are fixed with self-tapping screws instead of woodscrews. Check these are supplied when you buy.

There is also an **integral frame lock** for fitting within the frame. This is secure and unobtrusive, but only suitable for 'H' section frames at least 23mm (⅞") thick.

Fixing to metal

Follow these rules when fixing locks to metal frames.

■ Punch indents for the screw holes before drilling using a hammer and *centre punch*. This stops the drill bit slipping.

■ Be sure to use HSS (high speed steel) drill bits, not carbon steel.

■ Prime any bared metal before fitting the new lock.

frame lock

lockable cockspur stop

frame lock

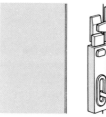

Cockspur locks simply screw on below the existing cockspur catch. The key-operated bolt on the lock slides up to trap the catch in the closed position.

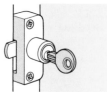

Frame locks for metal windows are fitted to the casement and have a catch which engages with the edge of the frame. Fix with self-tapping screws.

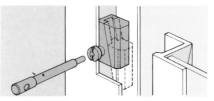

Integral frame locks are specially designed for 'H' section steel frames. The lock body fits within the frame and engages a catch in the casement.

PROBLEM SOLVER

Covering mistakes

■ If you drill a hole in the wrong place, fill it with an offcut of wood. Trim the wood to fit the hole with a sharp knife, and coat the end in woodworking glue. Tap it in place, then saw off the excess flush with the frame. Leave for a few hours before continuing.

■ If a faceplate or striking plate recess is too deep, and the lock bolt won't engage, pack behind it with a slip of card.

Poorly fitting windows

With casement windows that don't fit properly or are prone to seasonal swelling, there's a chance that rack bolts and frame locks with automatic catches won't engage properly because the frame and casement don't align.

In such cases it's a good idea to fit a pair of screw-type surface-mounted frame locks which draw the casement into the frame as you tighten them.

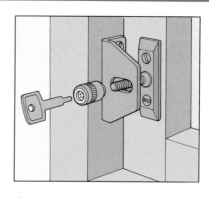

Screw-type locks draw a poorly fitting casement into its frame.

Chiselling recesses

Cutting recesses for faceplates and striking plates could prove tricky if you're unused to handling a chisel. The two golden rules are:

■ Make sure the chisel is sharp.

■ Remove a fraction of wood at a time, so you don't cut too deep.

Hold the chisel as shown, keeping it at a low angle with your fingers behind the blade at all times. You shouldn't need to apply much pressure.

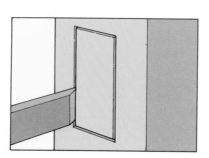

1 Having marked the position of the recess using the plate as a template, pierce around the cutting line as shown with the chisel bevel pointing inwards.

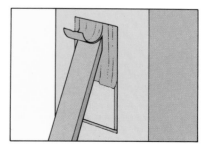

2 Gently pare away slivers of wood, working from the centre of the recess to the edges. Keep the chisel at a low angle, supported by your free hand.

FITTING T&G PANELLING

Panelling a wall or ceiling with T&G (tongue-and-groove) boards is a simple and effective way to give an otherwise ordinary room a smart new look. The new panelling can have other benefits too:

■ It can cover up poor or heavily patched plasterwork, saving on the disruption which renewing this involves.

■ It can hide unsightly pipes or cables, or make it easy to run new ones in the space behind.

■ It gives you the perfect opportunity to fit wall or ceiling insulation and cut fuel bills, as well as offering some degree of insulation in its own right.

The one thing panelling won't do is cure dampness – in fact, it can make the problem far worse. Any dampness already in the walls must be traced, cured and left to dry out before you start the job.

.... Shopping List ....

T&G panelling (matchboard) is widely available from timber yards and DIY superstores. The boards are either sold in separate lengths or in bundles of 10 cut to standard sizes – typically 1.8m (6′) and 2.4m (8′). Most come in nominal widths of 100mm (4″) or 125mm (5″), though the effective span of each board is of course less because of the interlocking tongues and grooves. Common thicknesses are 10mm (⅜″) or 13mm (½″) thick – although you may find thicker boards – and there are various profiles, the most common of which are shown on the right.

Softwood matchboarding ('knotty pine') is the most economical, with a characteristic 'pine' look. More expensive types made from Douglas Fir or Parana Pine contain fewer blemishes and are more durable.

Hardwood T&G boards made from woods such as Hemlock or Philippine Mahogany are more durable still, but appreciably more expensive.

Other options

Cladding boards consist of hardwood-veneered plywood strips – typically 400mm (16″) wide with false 'joints' in between. They represent good value for money, but the width of the strips often means more trimming.

Shiplap cladding boards come in similar styles to T&G, with much the same choice of woods and sizes. They overlap, instead of interlock, and are best fitted horizontally.

Square edged boards are an option if the wall is panelled with fibreboard insulation (see overleaf), in which case they can be fixed with gaps between them.

PVC cladding is fixed in much the same way as wooden boards, and is sold by superstores in similar size bundles. The white finish can be painted after fixing, and there are special profiles for covering gaps and trimming edges.

Battening materials

All types of panelling must be fitted to a batten framework – normally 38×25mm (1½×1″) sawn softwood, though you may need thicker or thinner battens for certain situations (see overleaf). Fix the battens with *masonry nails* or *frame fixings* – screws with built-in wallplugs.

Trimming materials

Most stockists will supply a range of *scotia* and *quadrant* mouldings for finishing corners, and matching *square edged battens* for trimming gaps and edges. You may also need *skirting* and *coving* mouldings, depending on the situation. As mentioned, PVC cladding has its own special trim profiles.

Other materials

Fix boards with *lost head nails* or *T&G clips* (often supplied in packs with the bundles). *Plywood* or *hardboard* scraps will be needed for levelling the batten frame.

Insulation can be provided with sheets of *fibreboard* fixed between the battens and boards. Or you can use *blanket roll* insulation with a *polythene vapour barrier* behind.

Tools checklist: panel saw, tenon saw, electric drill and bits, hammer, screwdrivers, nail punch, spirit level, tape measure.

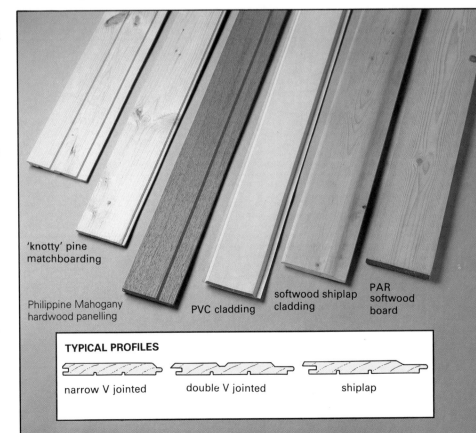

'knotty' pine matchboarding

Philippine Mahogany hardwood panelling

PVC cladding

softwood shiplap cladding

PAR softwood board

TYPICAL PROFILES

narrow V jointed

double V jointed

shiplap

DESIGNING THE PANELLING

Before buying any materials, you have to know:

■ **What direction to fix the boards in.** Most types can go vertically (with horizontal battening) or horizontally (with vertical battening); it's also possible to fix boards at 45°, though this involves more work, since they have to be cut and measured individually.

Many people find vertical boards easiest, since the 2.4m (8′) standard lengths fit most walls with minimal wastage. Horizontal boards have to be butt-jointed, with the joints staggered between rows.

■ **What to do about skirtings and architraves.** It's usually easiest to treat these as battens and fix the boards over them, packing with plywood where necessary. You can then leave a gap, or fix new mouldings to the panelling.

However, heavy skirtings and other mouldings which would stand proud of the battens must be prised off with a bolster or crowbar.

■ **How to deal with windows.** Most window openings can be panelled around then finished with moulding or square edge batten. But it may be better to saw off a protruding window board flush with the wall first.

■ **How to deal with ceiling junctions.** If you plan to panel the ceiling, do this first. Otherwise, boards can be stopped just short of the ceiling (which makes decorating easier), carried up against it, or trimmed with wood coving moulding.

■ **What to do about insulation.** The techniques for arranging this are described on page 288.

■ **What to do about services.** If you want to move lights and sockets or install new plumbing, do this first. Water pipes and cables can usually be hidden behind the panelling, but check first – you may need to increase the thickness of the batten frame to clear them. Drainage pipes will probably be boxed in, in which case remove the existing cladding and incorporate the box frame into the new one, then panel over it.

Study the design points below for ways to deal with these situations.

See Problem Solver for how to deal with switches and sockets.

Versatile T&G boarding is equally at home on the ceiling or on the walls. On the right, 'knotty pine' boards finished with moulding create a totally panelled look, while Douglas Fir boarding (below) brings a homely touch to this large kitchen.

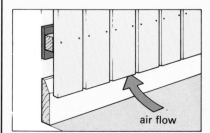

Skirtings 1: Overlap the skirting, leaving a small air gap.

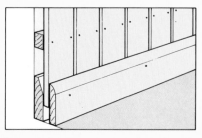

Skirtings 2: Fit new skirting moulding over the panelling.

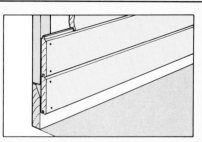

Skirtings 3: Use the skirting as a frame batten and stop boards short.

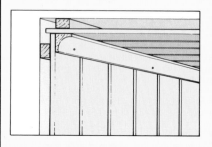

Ceilings 1: Butt boards to old or new ceiling and fit coving.

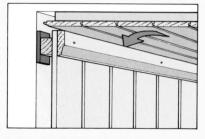

Ceilings 2: Stop boards short to leave an air gap; you can still use coving.

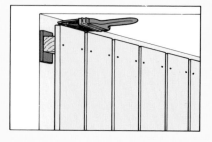

Ceilings 3: (also for inside corners): leaving a small gap eases decorating.

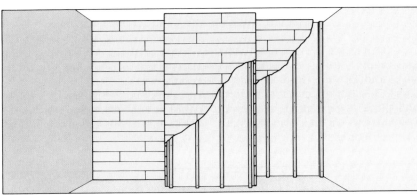

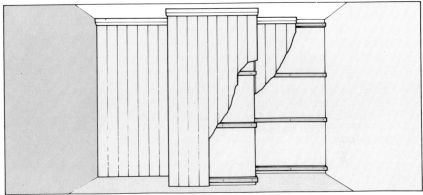

For horizontal panelling, run the battens vertically with extra ones at the end of each run.

For vertical panelling, the battens run horizontally across the wall. Fit extra pieces around obstructions.

Note, too, that you shouldn't panel within 150mm (6″) of a fire, boiler or other heater; stop short, and fit a non-combustible substitute such as plasterboard or tiles over a plywood base. Neither should boards be allowed to touch flues – leave a gap around them and finish with metal edging strip.

When you've worked out what to do, sketch a plan of each wall (or ceiling) giving full dimensions. You should also list on the plan:
■ The total length of battening used – battens are fixed at all edges and at 400–500mm (16–20″) intervals for 10mm (⅜″) boards or 500–600mm (20–24″) for 13mm (½″) boards.

■ The total lengths of each type of moulding and trim batten required.

Take the plan with you to the supplier. From here, it should be a simple matter for the two of you to select board lengths which give minimal wastage, and to work out the coverage for your chosen board width.

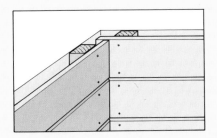

Inside corners 1: butt boards together with one side overlapping.

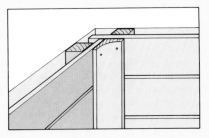

Inside corners 2: finish with square section batten or coving moulding.

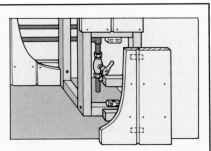

Around boxing, build a separate panelled frame on magnetic catches.

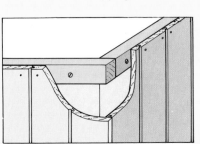

Outside corners 1: butt frame battens and boards (with tongues sawn off).

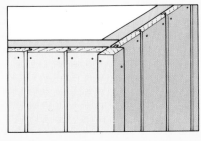

Outside corners 2: saw off tongues of adjoining boards and trim with batten.

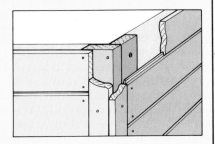

Outside corners 3: saw tongues off boards and trim with separate battens.

FIXING THE BATTEN FRAME

Providing you've planned things properly, fixing the battens should present few difficulties.

If the plaster is reasonably new and sound, using masonry nails saves a lot of time. In older plaster which is likely to crumble, screws and plugs are essential. However, you can still save time by using frame fixings: simply tack the battens in place, then drill through them into the wall (but use two drills, or swap to a masonry bit when you strike the plaster). Fix the battens near the ends, and at 450mm (18″) intervals in between.

Don't drive the fixings fully home until you've checked that the battens all sit plumb with one another. This way, you can slip packing pieces behind the battens, recheck for plumb, then trap the packing against the wall as the fixings are knocked in or tightened.

On a ceiling, find the joists first by poking with a bradawl – they are normally at 400 or 450mm (16″ or 18″) centres. Screw the battens in place, checking for level and packing as necessary.

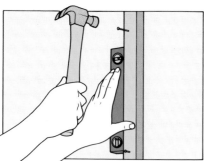

Don't drive masonry nails *fully in until you've checked the battens for plumb and packed behind as necessary. Pre-drilling battens avoids splitting.*

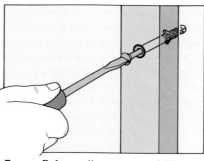

Frame fixings *allow you to drill through the batten into the wall with the batten in place. Again don't drive the screws fully home until you've checked for plumb.*

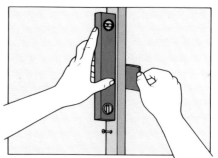

Check for plumb *with a spirit level and timber straightedge to ensure a good 'spread'. Hollows can be packed out with slips of plywood or hardboard.*

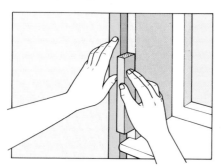

At critical areas *such as around windows, use a piece of board or trimming batten to gauge where to position the frame batten for a neat finish.*

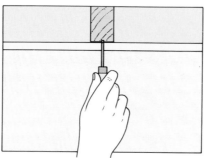

On the ceiling, *the battens can run across the joists or along them. Find and mark the joist positions first, then predrill the battens and screw in place.*

Trade tip

Leave a gap

❝When fixing battens along the edges of walls, don't fix them hard up against the edges – leave a 12mm (½″) gap. This way, you won't have to fix boards close to the ends, where there's a risk of them splitting. ❞

PROVIDING INSULATION

There are two ways to insulate behind the panelling.

Fibreboard sheets are the most expensive option, but also the most substantial. Fit packing pieces behind the batten frame to let air circulate, then nail the sheets to the battens leaving more gaps around the edges. Afterwards, simply nail the boards in place (draw lines to show the batten positions).

Blanket roll insulation can be sandwiched between the batten frame and the panelling, in which case space the battens to suit. Since the insulation restricts air flow behind the boards, it's essential to staple a polythene vapour barrier across the battens first.

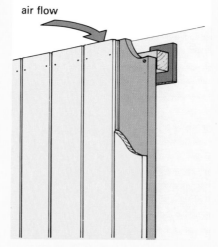

air flow

Option 1 – *nail sheets of 12mm (½″) fibre insulating board to the battens leaving gaps all round to maintain the air flow. Then nail the panelling on top.*

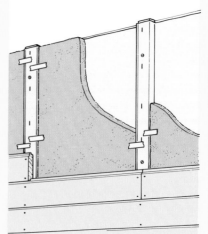

Option 2 – *staple a vapour barrier or polythene sheet across the battens then fit blanket roll insulation between them (it can be taped temporarily in place).*

FIXING THE T&G BOARDS

The illustration on the right shows the three options for fixing the boards to the battens (PVC must always be clipped). The first board in every run – along with any trim battens or mouldings – should be face-fixed with the grooved side towards the edge. Thereafter, you simply slot in the next board, then secret nail or clip fix to each batten in turn. In all cases, don't forget to punch the nail heads below the surface of the wood.

The last board in each run will also have to be face fixed. It is unlikely to fit the gap exactly, so scribe it to fit as shown below then cut it lengthways with a panel saw.

After completing the panelling, face-fix any trim battens and mouldings and fill all nail holes.

Trade tip

Cut them together

❛In most cases you'll be cutting a number of boards to the same length. To save work, measure and cut one, then clamp this to five or six more in a portable workbench and saw through them all together. ❜

BOARD FIXING OPTIONS

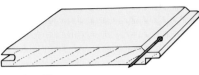

face nailing

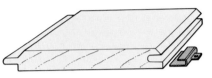

secret nailing

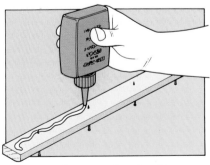

T&G fixing clips

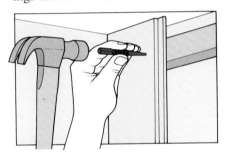

1 *Face-fix the first board to the battens with the grooved side towards the edge. Punch the nail heads below the surface for filling with wood stopper later.*

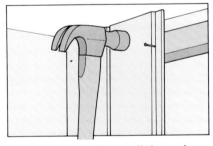

2 *If secret nailing, nail through the tongue of the first board at an angle as shown, then slot in the next board and repeat along the run.*

Using T&G fixing clips *is easier for the unpractised hand – slip the clips into the grooves of the boards, then pin them to the battens. Note that whatever the fixing method, you only fix on one side so that the boards can 'move' as their moisture content changes.*

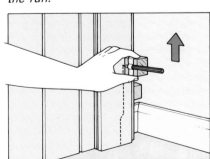

3 *At the end of a run, scribe the last board to fit the gap and cut it lengthways with a panel saw. Face-fix in place, punching down the nail heads.*

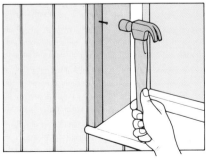

4 *Fix trims and mouldings once the main panelling is completed. Trim battens for the edges can be nailed to the frame battens and/or edges of boards.*

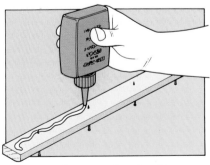

5 *Mouldings can be glued to the boards using PVA glue. Pin for reinforcement, part-driving the nails into the moulding first, to aid positioning.*

FINISHING THE PANELLING

Finish the wooden panelling as soon as possible, to prevent damage and to stop the boards absorbing undue amounts of moisture.

The most popular options are:

Clear polyurethane varnish, which will marginally deepen the wood colour and give it a slight orange tinge.

Varnish stain, which can deepen and darken the wood colour to tone better with existing decorations.

Coloured transparent finish, which on lighter woods can be used to colour the surface without obscuring the panelling's natural grain.

In all cases, apply the first coat thinned to seal the surface. Rub down between this and subsequent coats – you need at least three – with a pad of medium grade steel wool, and be sure to clean off the dust before applying more varnish.

Three ways to finish boards. Clear varnish (above) must be applied in at least three coats, with the first one thinned to seal the surface. Coloured transparent finish (far left) modifies the colour without obscuring the wood grain; while for a more dramatic colour change, you have the option of varnish stain (left) applied with a soft cloth. In all cases, make sure the boards are kept dust-free during application.

PROBLEM SOLVER

Dealing with switches and sockets

Before checking or actually dealing with light switches and sockets, be sure to **turn off the power at the consumer unit**.

In all cases, loosen off the switch or socket faceplate and check there is enough slack in the circuit cables to draw the faceplate as far as the boards.

For a surface mounted fitting, simply unscrew the pattress box. Cut clearance notches in the panel boards for the cables, then refit the box once the panelling is in place. Smooth the notches to prevent the cables chafing.

For a flush mounted fitting, there are two choices:

■ Fix battens around the hole, stop the panelling short, then remove the backing box and pack inside the old hole. You can then refit the box flush with the surface of the panelling.

■ Disconnect the faceplate and change to a surface mounted pattress box.

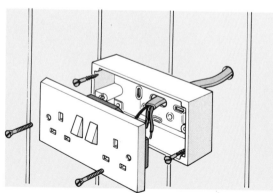

Surface mounted fittings can usually be refitted on the surface of the panelling – simply cut clearance notches for the cables in the boards.

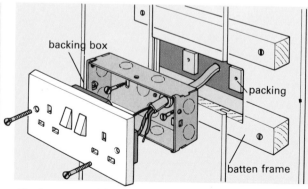

backing box

packing

batten frame

Flush mounted fittings can be battened around. Remove the backing box and pack behind with wood so that it sits level with the panelling, then refit.

STORAGE

PUTTING UP ALCOVE SHELVES

Putting up shelves in alcoves is a time-honoured way of using space that might otherwise go to waste – and this form of storage is perfectly suited to books, records, ornaments and hi-fi equipment.

Over the years, people have devised countless ways of arranging and supporting alcove shelving, but most are variations on one of the five options described overleaf.

.... Shopping List ....

Shelf materials: Work out the size and number of shelves as shown below. Then see overleaf for the options on boards and finishes.
Supports Work out how many shelves to put up, as shown below. Then check the chart overleaf to size up the supports and other fixings.
Wall fixings: Wallplugs, No.8 screws (to gauge length, add 32mm (1¼") to thickness of what you're fixing).
Tools: Panel saw, drill and bits, tenon saw, tape measure, spirit level, screwdriver. You may also need a junior hacksaw, wood chisel, Surform plane or scribing tools.

Alcove shelves *provide an ideal way to store large quantities of books.*

DESIGNING ALCOVE SHELVES

Start by measuring the alcove. If you want to put up more than one shelf, draw a sketch plan showing the alcove dimensions.

Although you can put the shelves at any heights you like, there are some practical guidelines:

■ If you are putting shelves in a pair of alcoves, keep the shelf spacings the same on both sides.
■ Wider-spaced shelves tend to look best at or below worktop/table height – around 750–900mm (30–36"). Set the first level of shelves here, then work out the spacings up and down.
■ Small paperbacks need 200mm (8") height and 125mm (5") depth.
■ Large illustrated books need a spacing of around 330mm (13") and a depth of 225–250mm (9–10").
■ You may want one shelf spaced at around 330mm (13") below the next, to hold hi-fi speakers, records, or a small TV. This shelf needs to be 300mm (12") or more in depth.

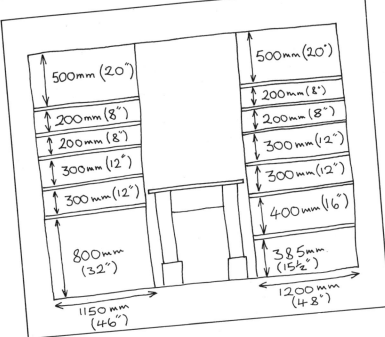

A sketch plan *helps you keep track of what you need to buy, and acts as a reminder of the shelf spacings when you come to mark them out.*

CHOOSING SHELVES AND SUPPORTS

There's a wide range of options for both the shelf boards themselves and the way you support them.

Choosing shelf boards

The panel below shows what materials can be used, depending on the look you want. Your choice will also be affected by:

What you want to store. Books and records are heavy, so need boards which resist warping. If the books are large OR the span is over 900mm (3'), follow the appropriate Bracing Guide and only use boards rated as suitable for 'heavy duty'.

On the other hand, shelves for lightweight ornaments should be as thin as possible so that they don't detract from what's on them.

The size of the shelves. Some materials only come in small sizes, while boards which come in large sheets are wasteful if you are only fitting a few shelves.

Choosing supports

The chart opposite shows the support options available. Again, your choice may depend on:

What you want to store. Small shelves for ornaments need light, unobtrusive supports, but for anything heavier choose one of the stronger systems (options 1, 2 and 3). If you are storing a lot of large books or other heavy items, OR the span is over 900mm (3'), use a back batten/aluminium angle or extra brackets. If you think your storage needs may change, an adjustable system could make sense.

The depth of the alcove. If you are fitting deep shelves in a very shallow alcove, end supports (ie options 1, 2, 4 and 5) may not offer sufficient bracing. Unless at least two thirds of the depth is supported, option 3 is more reliable.

The condition of the walls. Some systems (eg options 3, 5) are well suited to walls which are uneven and out of square with each other.

How the walls are made. Chimney breast walls are always solid, but if the other walls are hollow, options 1 and 2 (which allow you to fix to the studs at any point) are better; don't rely on cavity wall fixings.

The look of the shelves. Aim to choose a system that's in keeping with the style of the room. Track shelves, for example, can look out of place in a traditional setting, while batten supports may not suit a more modern, streamlined look.

CHOOSING SHELF BOARDS

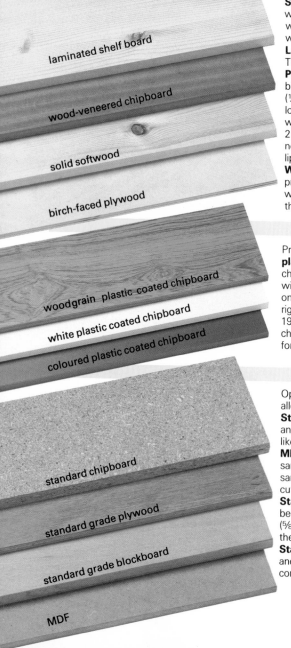

laminated shelf board

wood-veneered chipboard

solid softwood

birch-faced plywood

woodgrain plastic coated chipboard

white plastic coated chipboard

coloured plastic coated chipboard

standard chipboard

standard grade plywood

standard grade blockboard

MDF

NATURAL FINISH

Solid wood is only practical up to a 225mm (9″) width, after which it becomes costly and liable to warp. Boards should be 19 or 25mm (¾ or 1″) thick, which may not suit shelves taking ornaments.
Laminated shelf boards are 19mm (¾″) thick. They are ideal for shelves over 225mm (9″) wide.
Plywood or blockboard should be the high quality birch-faced type, but can be used thinner – 12mm (½″), 16mm (⅝″), or 19mm (¾″), depending on the load. Shelves can be cut to any width, but may work out expensive if you have to buy a full-size 2.4×1.2m (8×4′) sheet and can't use it all. You also need to finish the exposed edges with solid wood lipping or iron-on veneer tape.
Wood veneered chipboard boards come prefinished (see below) in handy lengths and widths, and in 16mm (⅝″) and 19mm (¾″) thicknesses.

BRACING GUIDE
Solid softwood (19mm): add extra bracing over 600mm (24″) for medium duty, or 450mm (18″) for heavy duty.
Solid softwood (25mm): add extra bracing over 750mm (30″) for heavy duty.
Laminated board (19mm): add extra bracing over 750mm (30″) for heavy duty.
Plywood and blockboard (see below for all sizes)
Veneered chipboard (see *Other boards* below)

PREFINISHED

Prefinished shelves can be white or coloured **plastic coated chipboard.** As with wood veneered chipboard, there is a large range of pre-cut 'shelf' widths in standard lengths to choose from, so the only cutting involved should be trimming to the right length. The boards come in 16mm (⅝″) and 19mm (¾″) thicknesses, but as with other chipboard-based materials, choose the thicker size for all but very light loads.

BRACING GUIDE
Coated chipboard (see *Other boards* below)

PAINTED FINISH

Opting for a painted finish involves more work, but allows you to choose cheaper material.
Standard chipboard, which comes in 19mm (¾″) and 16mm (⅝″) thicknesses, is economical but likely to bow over a long span with a heavy load.
MDF (medium density fibreboard) is about the same strength as chipboard and comes in the same thicknesses. It is costlier, but much easier to cut and finish.
Standard grade plywood is stronger and so can be used thinner – choose from 12mm (½″), 16mm (⅝″), and 19mm (¾″) thicknesses, depending on the load.
Standard grade blockboard is similar to plywood and comes in the same thicknesses. It's worth comparing prices at your stockist.

BRACING GUIDE
Plywood (12mm): add extra bracing over 600mm (24″) for medium duty.
Plywood (16mm): add extra bracing over 600mm (24″) for medium duty, or 450mm (18″) for heavy duty.
Plywood (19mm): add extra bracing over 750mm (30″) for heavy duty.
Other boards (16mm): add extra bracing over 600mm (24″) for medium duty.
Other boards (19mm): add extra bracing over 750mm (30″) for medium duty.

	DESCRIPTION	PROS & CONS	WHAT YOU NEED
Option 1: Wooden battens (medium/heavy duty)	Shelves are supported on a pair of wooden battens screwed to the walls. The ends of the battens can be angled or curved to make them less noticeable. For heavy loads or wide spans, add a third batten along the back wall.	Inexpensive and easy to fit if the walls are smooth and more or less square to each other. On hollow walls, the battens allow you to make fixings wherever you want, so there is no need to worry about the stud spacing.	Softwood batten (the thickness of the shelf material by twice the thickness of the shelf material). Wallplugs and screws to fix batten. To fix the shelves to the batten you also need 12mm (½") No.6 screws, plus three or four 3-hole glass plates per shelf.
Option 2: Aluminium angle (medium/heavy duty)	Shelves are supported on lengths of L-section aluminium angle, now widely available from hardware and superstores. As with battens, you can use two or three strips per shelf depending on the load and shelf span.	Less noticeable than battens, but slightly trickier to fit. Like battens, best suited to alcove walls which are even and true.	Aluminium angle the same width as the thickness of the shelving. Wallplugs and screws.
Option 3: Tracks/brackets (medium/heavy duty)	Shelves are supported on a proprietary track system, or on purpose-made metal or wooden shelf brackets attached to batten 'tracks'. Use in pairs for light loads/ narrow alcoves; add a third support on wide spans and heavy loads.	Tracks fully adjustable and easier to fit than brackets, but decorative effect of brackets may be preferable. Cost of parts must be borne in mind. Best suited to uneven walls where shelves can't be an exact fit.	Proprietary track system, or brackets (2–3 per shelf) and 50×19mm (2×¾") softwood batten supports. Wallplugs and screws and 19mm (¾") No.6 screws.
Option 4: Bookcase strip (light duty or narrow spans)	Shelves are supported on side walls only using bookcase strip – a mini track system with adjustable hook supports.	Easy-to-fit supports are unobtrusive and fully adjustable, but unsuitable for uneven walls, wide shelves or heavy loads. Shelves cannot be fixed in place.	Bookcase strip system (2 per side wall)
Option 5: Plug-in shelf supports (light duty or narrow spans)	Alcove is lined with boards scribed to fit. Shelves are supported on side walls only; holes drilled in lining accept plug-in shelf supports designed for fitting in cupboards.	Trickiest option, but worth considering if alcove walls are in very poor condition. Once lining is in place, shelf supports are easy to fit. Drilling extra holes gives full adjustability.	Suitable lining material (eg chipboard, plywood, blockboard, MDF), slips of thin batten, hardboard or cardboard for packing, 50mm (2") No.8 screws for fixing, plug-in shelf supports.

FITTING WOODEN BATTENS

Cut batten supports to length to suit the shelves and the depth of the alcove. Side battens don't have to finish flush with the front edge – stopping them a little way back makes them less obtrusive. You can also shape the ends by sawing off at an angle or smoothing into a curve using a Surform plane.

After cutting, drill fixing holes in the side battens at 75mm (3″) intervals and in the back batten at 300mm (12″) intervals. Fix them in the sequence shown so that you can be sure the shelves will sit level.

Fixing the shelves to the battens is optional, but advisable unless they are heavily weighed down. Glass plates are best where you can see the fixings, but above eye level you can simply screw the shelves to their battens from above.

Trade tip

Keeping shelves flat

❝ If you're fitting a back batten, fix the side battens first, then leave the shelf in place while you mark the fixing holes on the wall. This way, you can be sure the shelf sits level on all three battens. ❞

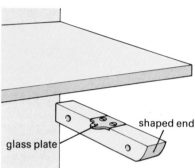

cut end

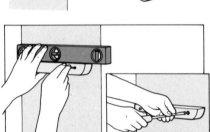

glass plate   shaped end

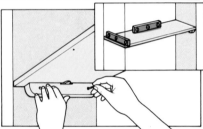

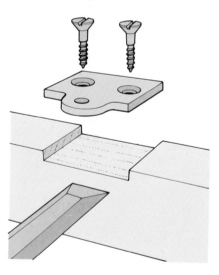

1 Mark the shelf spacings on one side of the alcove, not forgetting to allow for the thickness of the shelves themselves.

2 Offer up one pre-cut batten (allow for a back batten if fitted), level it, and mark the fixing holes. Drill and plug the wall, then screw in place.

3 Resting the shelf on the fixed batten, offer up the other side batten. Check for level both ways, then mark the fixing holes and screw to the wall.

Fix shelves with glass plates where the tops are below eye level and likely to show; use 1 per side batten, 1–2 along a back batten. Chisel shallow recesses for the plates in the battens, screw in place, then refit the shelf to mark the fixing holes.

Wooden battens (left) which are painted the same colour as the shelves are neat and unobtrusive.

USING ALUMINIUM ANGLE

Aluminium angle is easily cut to fit using a junior hacksaw. Smooth the ends with a file or coarse wet and dry abrasive paper.

Drill the screw fixing holes in the side pieces at 75mm (3″) intervals and in the back piece at 300mm (12″) intervals, supporting the angle on an offcut of wood. To stop the drill bit wandering, pop-mark the holes with a centre punch or nail.

Don't forget to allow 4mm (⅛″) for the thickness of the angle when cutting the shelves to fit (see overleaf). Otherwise, follow the same fitting sequence as for wooden battens. Fix the shelves to the angle by screwing through from below with 12mm (½″) No.4 chipboard screws.

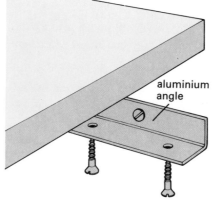

aluminium angle

Aluminium angle is a strong and much less conspicuous alternative to batten supports. Saw it to length and pre-drill the fixing holes.

USING BOOKCASE STRIP

Two strips per side should be sufficient for all but the largest alcoves, but they look best if they run the full height. Space the strips a quarter of the way in from the front and back of the shelf.

Screw the strips to the wall as you would shelf tracks, using a spirit level to check for plumb. The supports can be hooked into the strips at any height.

Cut the shelves 8mm (⅜″) narrower than the alcove to allow clearance for the strips; this is easier than trying to notch the shelves.

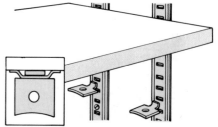

Bookcase strip comes in brass and silver finish and can be screwed directly onto even wall surfaces. Fit clip-in supports to take the ends of the shelf boards.

TRACK AND BRACKET SYSTEMS

When fitting a track or bracket system, choose brackets with a span that suits the depth of the shelves. The only special consideration is how you space the supports.

If there are two sets, aim to position them a quarter of the way in from either side of the alcove. But if this means that the supports exceed their recommended spacing, include a third set running down the middle of the alcove and position the outer two sets one-sixth of the way in from the edges.

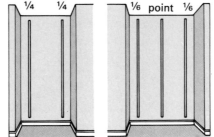

¼ ¼   ⅙ mid point ⅙

Adjust the track spacing (above) to suit the alcove width. Shelf heights can be varied (right) depending upon what you wish to display.

CUTTING SHELVES TO FIT

Don't attempt to cut all the shelves to the same size unless:

1 The walls of the alcove are even and true (or you have lined them).

2 The walls aren't true, but you are using a track system and need adjustable shelves. In this case cut the shelves so they all fit the width of the alcove at its narrowest point,

allowing a small clearance.

In all other situations it's best to measure and cut each shelf individually. You can do this conventionally, using a tape or measuring sticks; but since the sides of the alcove are probably uneven, as well as out of true, it's safer to use the template method shown below.

If the shelves don't need to fit exactly, use a pair of sticks joined with rubber bands to check the minimum width of the alcove, then allow 6mm (¼") clearance.

Trade tip

Perfect fit

❝ To be sure of an exact fit, make up a template for each shelf in turn using an offcut of board and some pieces of card.

Get a helper to hold the offcut against the back of the alcove at shelf height while you place pieces of card on top and slide them against the sides to mimic the alcove's shape. Tape the card to the board, then remove it and use it to mark the shelf board for cutting. ❞

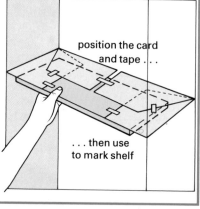

position the card and tape . . .

. . . then use to mark shelf

PROBLEM SOLVER

Alcove not square

If, as is often the case in older houses, the alcove sides are seriously out of true, it's sensible to choose Option 5 – line the sides with boards, then fit plug-in shelf supports (as found inside fitted units).

Select a rigid material for the lining (you may want to match it to the shelving), so that there's no danger of the boards bowing

out of shape as they are being fixed; 16mm (⅝") plywood, and 19mm (¾") blockboard, MDF or chipboard are possible options.

Start by cutting and scribing the boards to fit. Whether they run the full height of the alcove or finish at the skirting is up to you: if the skirting looks easy to remove, a full-height lining will be neater.

Fix the boards at roughly 450mm (18") intervals, using 50mm (2") No.6 screws. Space the screws at 100mm (4") centres, or to coincide with stud positions.

Pack behind the boards to bring them vertical as you screw them to the wall – use thin battens, or strips of board or card, depending on the gap.

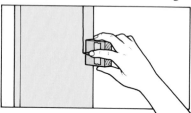

1 *Scribe and cut the lining boards to fit flush with the front of the alcove, using a wood block and pencil to mark the profile of the back wall.*

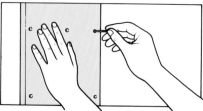

2 *Drill rows of fixing holes in the boards at 450mm (18") intervals, then offer up each board and mark where to drill and plug the wall.*

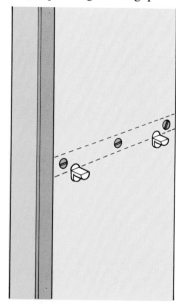

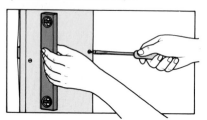

3 *Hold a spirit level against the board as you screw it to the wall. Slip pieces of packing behind – resting them on the screws – to keep the board plumb.*

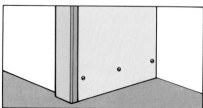

4 *Having lined the other side in the same way, hide any gaps between the boards and the wall with strips of panel moulding, pinned and glued to the edges.*

With the lining boards in place, drill rows of holes for the plug-in supports at regular intervals. You can arrange for the shelf ends to hide the screw heads.

PUTTING UP TRACK SHELVES

Open track shelving systems are the perfect way to store things which don't need to be kept locked away and look good enough to be on show. The shelves are easy to fit, and you can adjust them as and when your storage needs change.

At the heart of any track system are the tracks themselves – long metal strips containing sets of holes at roughly 25mm (1″) intervals into which you lock the brackets.

Because of their length, tracks tend to be more stable than individual brackets. And since the track brackets' positions are already fixed, there's no tricky aligning to do – the only critical stages are fixing the first track vertical, and then getting the others level with it.

Although you can reset the bracket heights in a few minutes, in practice you'll probably find you set them once and then leave them that way. Even so, with the tracks already in place it's easy to add further shelves if you need them.

.... Shopping List ....

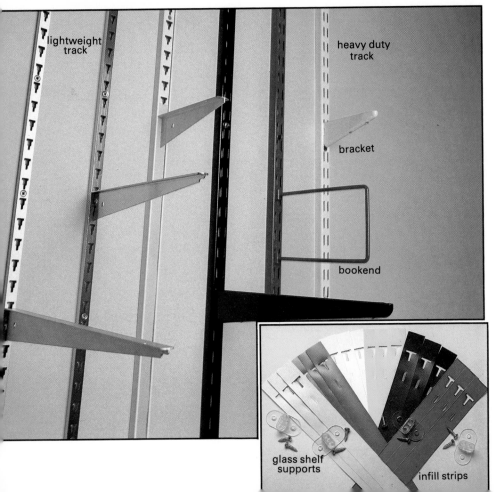

lightweight track

heavy duty track

bracket

bookend

glass shelf supports

infill strips

All systems include uprights and brackets in a range of lengths, but other accessories may also be available depending on the make. These include:

■ Coloured infill strips to cover unused slots and match the uprights to your decor.
■ Bookends.
■ Glass shelf supports.
■ Sloping brackets for display shelves.
■ Panel brackets for fixing wallboards, etc.
■ Cabinet brackets for fixing boxes and vertical panels to uprights.

Some manufacturers also offer a wide range of shelf sizes and finishes to suit their tracks, while others leave you to choose your own. Possible options include veneered chipboard (with a wood or plastic surface finish), blockboard and solid timber. The material you choose may affect the amount of support required (see overleaf).

Tools: Drill with masonry and wood bits, screwdriver, tape measure, spirit level (also a saw and try square if you have to cut shelves).

DESIGNING WITH STANDARD UNITS

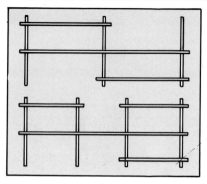

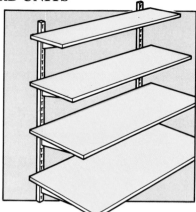

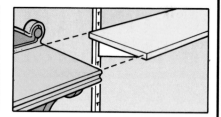

Shelf length Having three or more tracks allows you to fit shelves of different lengths, none of which need necessarily span the entire system.

This is particularly useful if you have to put a few tall items among objects that look best with the shelves closely spaced.

Shelf depth Fitting shelves of different depths makes it possible to store a wide range of items more efficiently within a small space. Always put the shelves in decreasing order of depth, from bottom to top.

Fixed levels If you want the shelving to line up with a feature of the room, such as a mantelpiece, you'll need to take extra care when marking the positions of the tracks.

The only reliable way to work out the final shelf level is to fit a bracket to a track and align it with the feature before you mark the screw holes – not forgetting to allow for the thickness of the shelf itself in your calculations.

WHAT TO FIX TO

On a solid masonry wall, fix the tracks by screwing through each of the fixing holes into drilled and plugged holes in the wall.

On a hollow timber-framed partition wall, you *must* screw the tracks to the solid timber framework itself. It is not sufficient to fix them to the hollow part of the wall using cavity wall fixings – the thin skin covering the wall will not be strong enough.

The tracks are flexible enough to cope with small irregularities in the wall, but if the surface is very uneven it's a good idea to fix battens to it first (see Problem Solver).

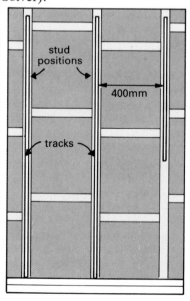

Right Track systems aren't just for shelving; here one of the shelves doubles as a lightweight desk.

HOW MANY SUPPORTS?

If you are fixing to a hollow wall, the track positions are governed by the position of the timber frame. You must screw to *each* stud – approximately 400mm (16″) intervals.

Otherwise, the maximum spacing is fixed by the material you are using for the shelving. The standard 15mm (⅝″) chipboard used as shelving material needs support at 600mm (24″) intervals to stop it bowing. But with very sturdy material, such as 25mm (1″) thick softwood or 19mm (¾″) blockboard, you can extend this to 900mm (3′).

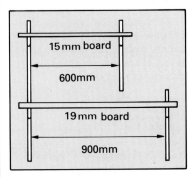

The brackets should either be the same depth as the shelves or a little less.

Remember, the longer the brackets, the *less* the amount of evenly distributed weight they will stand – 150mm (6″) brackets might carry well over 50kg (110lb), whereas 450mm (18″) brackets could be limited to as little as 15kg (35lb).

If you have to put heavy weights on a deep shelf, it's worth fitting tracks and brackets at more frequent intervals.

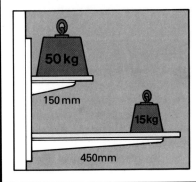

Left Here, short lengths of track are used to create a streamlined run of shelves.

FIXING THE TRACKS

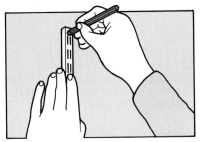

1 Mark the position of the top hole of the first track. If the shelf height is critical you will need to fit a bracket and align it first (see opposite).

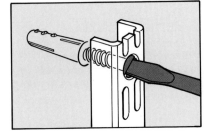

2 Drill the hole for the top screw and fix the track to the wall. Only partially tighten the screw, so that the track is left free to pivot on its fixing.

3 Use a spirit level to set the track vertically, then mark and drill the other holes. Fit the remaining screws, using packing pieces where necessary.

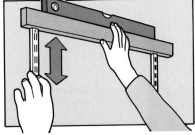

4 Use the level again to set the top of the second track at exactly the same height as the first. If you don't do this the shelves won't sit straight.

301

FIXING THE SHELVES

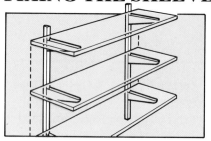

1 Align the shelves so they overlap the brackets by the same amount on each side. Make sure, too, that the ends line up above one another.

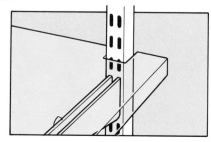

2 If you want the shelves to fit right back against the wall, cut notches in them to accommodate the thickness of the tracks.

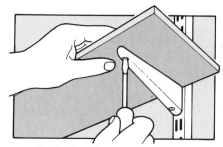

3 Fit the brackets to the tracks, position the shelves and weight them, then mark the screw holes from underneath with a bradawl. Screw the brackets on.

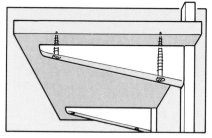

4 With U-shaped brackets, the outer screw is shorter than the inner one. If you are using thin shelves, take care not to screw right through the boards.

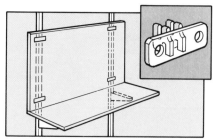

5 Some systems have brackets for vertical panels. If yours doesn't, but you want to fit such panels, you can screw them to the shelves instead.

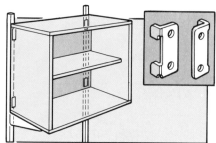

6 If you want to include box units, these can either be home-made or adapted from basic self-assembly cabinets such as kitchen wall units.

Trade tip

Strengthening shelves

❝ I find that a good way to stop thin shelves from bowing is to fix wood lipping along the edge. This also makes them look more substantial. A thin strip of softwood or ramin – about 50 × 12mm (2 × ½") – is usually ideal; fix it either to the front or back of the shelf. ❞

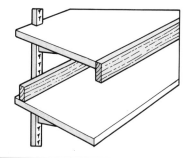

PROBLEM SOLVER

Uneven walls

Very few walls are perfectly flat or square, so when you screw the tracks in place make sure they don't bend because of irregularities in the surface.

Small bumps and hollows can be accommodated by inserting packing pieces of hardboard or cardboard behind the tracks as you drive in the screws.

If the walls are seriously out of square or in poor condition, it's better to screw 50 × 25mm (2 × 1") battens to the wall and then screw the tracks to these. This gives you more scope for packing behind the battens and lets you make the wall fixings where you like, rather than at points fixed by the tracks.

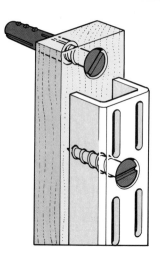

Fit packing pieces (left) to fill small hollows, but fit a batten (above) if the surface is poor.

PUTTING UP BRACKET SHELVES

If you only want a few fixed shelves, separate brackets are an ideal choice. They are often cheaper and easier to fit than track systems – although this advantage is reduced every time you add another shelf. And because there is a much wider range of styles, both brackets and shelves can be chosen to suit your decorations.

Bracket styles range from cheap and functional to stylish or ornate. The basic options are detailed below. Whatever type you choose, use the recommended bracket spacing for the shelf material and the likely load the shelf will have to support (see page 301 for more details).

Alternatives Separate brackets aren't a sensible choice if you want a run of stacked shelving because of the difficulty of lining up all the holes – consider a track system instead. Conventional brackets may also be hard to fit directly above objects such as radiators.

Shelves on brackets provide quick, convenient storage – and can look as stylish as you want.

....Shopping List....

Brackets come in several patterns. The size and number needed depend on the size of the shelves and the weight they will have to support.

Utility pressed steel brackets are a good choice for workrooms or garages and can be painted.

'Streamlined' steel or plastic-covered brackets are strong and inexpensive. The finish is good enough for display shelves.

'Wrought iron' brackets made of steel or aluminium in various finishes are reasonably strong but can be tricky to fit.

Cast-iron and brass brackets can be stylish, but are expensive.

Wooden brackets are sometimes sold separately but are more often part of complete 'shelf packs'.

Shelves Natural wood, man-made boards and glass can all be used. See overleaf for details of what to consider when choosing.

Fixings Normally you need two or three screws and wallplugs per bracket to fix to the wall, and two or three to fix the shelf. Use the heaviest screws that fit the bracket. They should project about 38mm (1½″) into the wall and up to three quarters of the way through the shelf.

Tools: Drill with masonry and wood bits, screwdriver, tape measure, spirit level (and possibly a plumbline), plus a saw and try square if you are going to cut and trim shelves.

lightweight pressed steel bracket

steel bracket with plastic cover

heavyweight pressed steel bracket

heavy duty aluminium bracket

aluminium 'wrought iron' bracket

steel 'wrought iron' brackets

softwood bracket

PUTTING UP THE SHELVES

Lightweight shelves are best fitted with their brackets before fixing to the wall.

■ Mark the bracket positions on the underside of the shelf, drill pilot holes, and screw the brackets in place.

■ Offer up the complete assembly to the wall with a spirit level on top. Check the alignment, then mark the bracket fixing holes. Drill and plug.

Heavy shelves are easier to fit if you fix the brackets to the wall first.

■ Mark the bracket positions underneath the shelf. Check where one end bracket falls on the wall and position it to mark the fixing holes.

■ Drill and plug the wall and fix the bracket in place.

■ Support the shelf (or a straight length of batten) on the fixed bracket with a spirit level on top. Check for level, then mark the position of the other end bracket.

■ Remove the shelf and fix the second bracket to the wall.

■ Rest the shelf on both brackets and mark the positions of the other brackets. Fix them to the wall, then screw the shelf to all the brackets.

A small shelf is easier to fit if you screw the brackets to it first. Position the shelf with the aid of a spirit level, then mark the bracket fixings.

1 *With a heavy shelf*, begin by marking the positions of the fixing brackets on the underside. Then check where one end bracket falls on the wall.

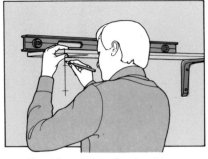

2 Fix this end bracket in place. Offer up the shelf (or a straight batten) with a spirit level on top and mark the other end bracket's position.

3 Add intervening brackets with the shelf resting in place. Check that each bracket supports the shelf correctly, then mark its fixing position on the wall.

PROBLEM SOLVER

Aligning several shelves

If you need to stack shelves one above the other, but don't want a track system, there are two methods of fixing brackets:

Fixing to battens first makes it easier to align the brackets and avoids having to drill a lot of holes in the wall.

Mark the bracket positions with the battens laid together to ensure they line up. Screw the brackets in place, then screw each batten to the wall at 300mm (12″) intervals.

The backs of the shelves must be notched to fit over the battens if you want the shelves to sit flush with the wall.

Fixing independently is neater, and means the shelves don't need to be notched. However, it is more difficult to get the shelves in line, which is essential if the result is to look good.

Mark out the first shelf and use it as a template to mark all the others. Fix the first pair of brackets to the wall and hang a plumbline from each. Then use the lines as a guide to fixing the rows of brackets below.

To align separate shelves (below), fix the top set of brackets and then use plumblines to gauge the positions of the brackets in the rows below.

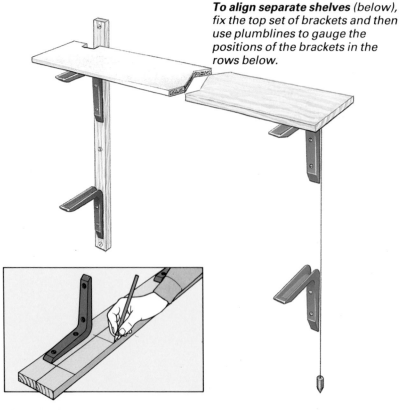

A stack of shelves is easier to align if you fit the brackets to lengths of batten first.

Notch the backs of the shelves to fit over the battens. Fit the brackets to both battens together to guarantee even spacing.

FITTING GLASS SHELVING

Glass can be used with most types of shelf support and is an attractive alternative to more conventional shelving materials. The main reasons for using glass instead of wood are:

■ Glass has a light, delicate appearance which doesn't overpower small objects and ornaments.

■ It is easy to clean and doesn't stain, making it a practical choice for bathrooms and kitchens.

■ It transmits light, so it can be used where solid shelves would cast unwanted shadows, such as in front of a mirror or around a window.

Glass also has disadvantages:

■ It is brittle and broken glass can be dangerous, so glass shelves need good support and shouldn't be fitted within reach of small children.

■ Heavy objects need thick glass shelves to provide adequate strength. As the shelves themselves are heavy, you need more supports than for an equivalent wooden shelf.

The main appeal of glass is its appearance, but it has practical advantages, too. In situations where a shelf could block the light, there is no other choice.

.... Shopping List ....

As with any shelving, you must take into account the thickness of the shelf material and the amount of support it needs to suit the weight it has to carry.

Glass should be at least 6mm thick, depending on the load (see below). The normal choice is flat (float) clear glass, but other suitable types include coloured, patterned and wired glass – all of which can be used to decorative effect.

■ 6mm glass is suitable for light loads if the shelves are supported every 400mm (16″).

■ 10mm glass can be used for normal loads with brackets up to 700mm (28″) apart – reduce this to 500mm (20″) for books.

Get the glass cut to size by a glass merchant. All edges should be ground and polished smooth. Standard shelf widths are available pre-cut and finished.

Brackets depend partly on the situation, but in general glass is heavy so use a medium/heavy duty system. The main options are:

Track systems which can be used either with special plastic retaining clips or self-adhesive glass fixing pads on the brackets.

Metal channels which grip the back of the shelves to give an unobtrusive fixing. These come in a range of colours and are suitable for 6mm glass only (a special insert is used to protect the glass from contact with the metal).

Shelf brackets are often unsuitable because the part of the bracket which is seen through the shelf looks unfinished. A popular option is 'wrought iron' type brackets which look neat used in this way. Some pressed steel brackets can be fitted with special glass shelf clips which grip the shelf neatly.

Glass shelf brackets are commonly made for use in bathrooms. Most are designed to fit over the ends of a shelf which is cut to suit.

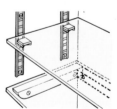

Alcove supports are an option where you are fitting shelves in a recess or a fitted cabinet.

Plug-in end supports include plastic plugs to fit into pre-drilled holes, or metal bookcase strips which screw to the sides ready to take clips at any height you wish.

Battens or metal angle screwed to sides and back of an alcove provide a means of giving continuous support for the shelves.

FITTING GLASS SHELVES

Supports for glass shelves are fitted in much the same way as for any other shelf. However, it is even more important than usual to make sure that they are properly aligned – the shelf needs support across its whole width without undue flexing.

Some systems incorporate clips which prevent the glass from sliding on the brackets. Otherwise, if there is any risk at all of it being knocked, you should use self-adhesive retaining pads to hold it firmly in place on its supports.

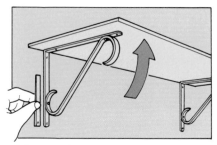

Trade tip

Using a dummy

❝ With many support systems it often helps to line up the brackets by trying a shelf in place. To make it easier to do this and to simplify cutting the glass shelves to size, cut a dummy shelf from an offcut of chipboard or other suitable material and use this for your fitting experiments. **❞**

To retain the glass on plain brackets, use double-sided self-adhesive pads. These also help to cushion it from contact with metal surfaces.

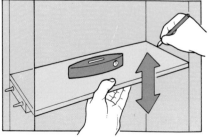

Align track and bracket systems carefully. Pack out behind the fixings if necessary to make sure that the shelf is fully supported and not twisted in any way.

Alcove shelf battens must be carefully aligned. Fix one end first and align the second one by trying a shelf in place and marking along it.

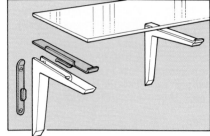

Special clips are needed for some brackets. Take care that these trap the edge of the glass without undue pressure which could cause splintering.

PROBLEM SOLVER

Polishing the edges

In most cases you can buy the glass ready cut and polished by the glass merchant. If you want to use a piece of glass which you have already, you can cut your own shelves with a glass cutter in the conventional way. But before use, you must also grind and polish the edges to prevent accidents.

This isn't very difficult to do, but it does take a little time. The easiest tool to use is an oilstone, but you can get by with a piece of wet or dry abrasive paper pinned to a block of wood. Start with a coarse abrasive and work down to fine.

Wear heavy gloves when handling the unpolished glass. Wet the stone (or paper) lightly and rub the edges of the glass, at an angle of about 45°. Use only downward strokes at this stage in case of splinters being pulled off the rough edge.

Rub down all the edges with the coarse abrasive until the sharp corners are removed, then switch to a medium abrasive. Wet this too and rub it along the edge to round off the ridges left by the first pass. Use this stone to take off the sharp corners.

Finish off with a fine abrasive, again used wet, running it along the edges at several angles until it produces a smooth curve.

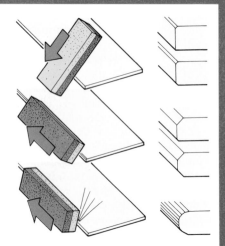

Grind the edges with progressively finer abrasive used wet. Work in the order shown to produce a smoothly rounded edge with a polished surface.

FITTING SLIDING WARDROBE DOORS

Track kits contain double top and bottom tracks, a clip-on fascia panel, and fixings. They come in standard widths which you trim to size.

'DIY door' kits come with tracks, runners and clip-on frames for the doors.

For the doors themselves, use 4mm plywood. This is generally available in 2440×1220mm (8×4') sheets, in two grades.

Sliding door kits for mirror and panel doors are sold in one, two, three and four-door packs. The doors come in one height, but a range of widths.

Tools checklist: Tape measure, drill, junior hacksaw, various screwdrivers. You will need other tools and materials for making your own doors or adapting the opening size, so run through the instructions before you start. Before you decide finally what kits to buy, work out how and where you're going to fit the wardrobe (see overleaf).

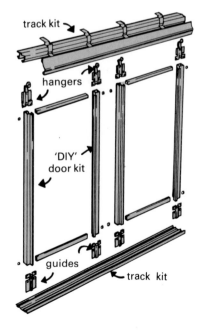

track kit

hangers

'DIY'
door kit

guides

track kit

Installing a set of sliding wardrobe doors is a simple yet effective way to streamline your bedroom storage. The doors enclose as much space as you want and can also be used to conceal untidy features in the room. There's a choice of styles, including mirror and panel fronts.

Two systems are available. One consists of two separate kits – a door pack, which includes standard size doors and runners; and a track pack containing the top and bottom tracks, plus a clip-on fascia.

The other system is based around a 'DIY door' kit containing the tracks, together with clip-on frames for the doors. You provide the actual door panels, which has the advantage that you can cut them to size and paint or paper them to match the room.

Both types are extremely versatile – run the doors right across the room; stop them short with an end panel, or fit them in an alcove.

Once you have enclosed the space, fit out the inside to suit your requirements. Special wardrobe interior kits make this a fairly quick and simple job (see pages 313-318). Alternatively, fit a plain hanging rail.

THE RIGHT COMBINATION

The secret of a trouble-free installation is to balance the look you want against a layout which suits the room and is easy to arrange. So before you order any parts, consider these points:

Which doors? Mirror and panel door kits normally come in a standard height of 2285mm (90"), which rounds off to fit a ceiling height of 2.5m (8'2") by the time they're fitted in their tracks. They can't be cut down, which rules out using them if your ceiling is lower than their standard height. But if the ceiling is higher than this, it's relatively easy to make up the difference with a timber filling piece or even a false 'drop top' panel (see Problem Solver).

With 'DIY' doors, you can cut the plywood panels to any size you like so long as the floor and ceiling are reasonably level. You may prefer this option anyway if you're on a tight budget, or you want to decorate the panels to match the rest of the room.

Which layout? The box below shows the possible variations, depending on how your room is laid out and what other furniture has to go in it. If necessary, draw a sketch plan to make sure the new layout won't be too cramped.

Before making a final decision, read through *Where to fix the top track* opposite. If the ceiling joists are inconveniently placed, it may be easier to alter the depth of the wardrobe than to add bracing.

How many doors? When you've decided on your ideal layout, measure the opening width. Then check the chart at the bottom of the page which shows the width and number of doors needed for a range of given openings.
- If you're fitting 'DIY doors', use the chart to work out what size to make the panels.
- If you choose standard doors, but you're fitting an end panel, arrange for the opening width to match one of the combinations in the chart.
- If you want standard doors to run wall to wall, and the opening width doesn't match any of the standard sizes, you have the choice of shortening the wardrobe with an end panel or fitting side panels to make up the difference.

WHICH LAYOUT?

Run the wardrobe wall to wall *(right) using two, three or four doors as appropriate. If the doors are a fixed size, you may have to fit one or more side panels to take up the extra opening width.*

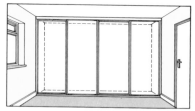

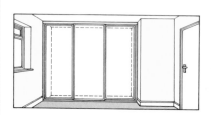

Fit the wardrobe in an alcove *(left) if the alcove is 600mm (24") deep or more. Otherwise, it's more practical to increase the depth with an end panel or continue the doors across the entire wall.*

Where space is limited, *stop the wardrobe short and fit your own end panel. Alternatively, place the wardrobe in the middle of the wall and fit two end panels. Both options allow you to match the opening width to standard doors.*

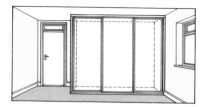

Mirror doors (above) blend easily into any decorative scheme and have the advantage of making a room seem larger. However, they can't be cut, so you may need to fit side panels to make up the opening width.
Panel doors (right) come ready finished and have a pleasingly substantial appearance. Like mirror doors they can't be cut.

WHICH DOOR SIZE?

The chart shows commonly available sizes of mirror and panel doors. If you make your own doors, use one of the combinations shown to work out the width of the plywood panels.

Opening width	Number and size of doors required	Opening width	Number and size of doors required
1190mm (3'11")	2×609mm (2')	2235mm (7'4")	3×750mm (2'6")
1498mm (4'11")	2×760mm (2'6")	2690mm (8'10")	3×900mm (3')
1803mm (5'11")	2×914mm (3')	2950mm (9'8")	4×750mm (2'6")
1778mm (5'10")	3×609mm (2')	3600mm (11'10")	4×900mm (3')

WHERE TO FIT THE TOP TRACK

Your wardrobe should be around 600mm (24")
deep to allow for clothes on hangers, with the top
track positioned to suit (in most kits it goes 25mm
(1") inside the line of the doors).

However, because this track takes the weight of
the doors, it can't be fixed to the thin ceiling
plaster – you need to screw it directly into the
supporting timbers (joists).

Start by finding out which way the joists run. If
the floor upstairs is boarded, the boards will run
in the opposite direction, with rows of nails giving
away the joists' exact positions.

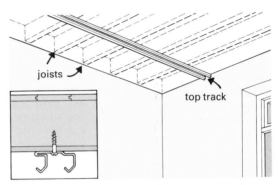

If the joists run at right angles to the track, there
are no problems. Simply drill extra fixing holes in
the track to match the joist spacing, then screw the
track in position.

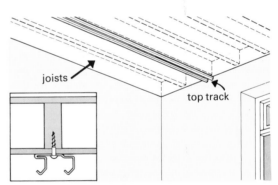

If the joists are parallel to the track, try to arrange
for the track to run along the centre of a joist – if
necessary by increasing or reducing the depth of
the wardrobe slightly.

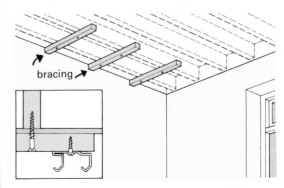

Alternatively, fix the track to 50×50mm (2×2")
bracing pieces fitted between the two nearest
joists. The neat way is to nail these from above; but
if you don't have access, screw them from below
then hide the ends with a piece of timber.

FITTING THE TRACKS

Having taken delivery of the kit parts, check the dimensions of the opening as follows:

Width Measure from wall to wall or to the end panel position. If you need to close up the opening to fit the doors, see Problem Solver overleaf for how to do it.

Height Measure from floor to ceiling at several points. If you need to fit filling pieces or a panel to accommodate the doors, again see Problem Solver overleaf.

If you find the door-plus-track height – 2.5m (8'2") for standard doors – varies by more than 12mm (½"), one or other of the tracks will need packing with slips of stiff card or hardboard to bring them level. Insert the packing before tightening the track fixing screws.

Unless you are fitting a filling piece below it, the bottom track can be fixed directly to the floor through the existing covering. Take extra care that it aligns with the top track.

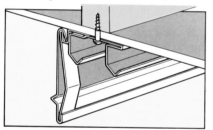

3 Clip the fascia over the top track as shown. When it's in position, tighten the track fixing screws to clamp the fascia against the ceiling.

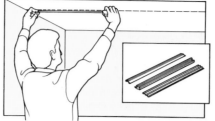

1 Mark the final width of the wardrobe on the tracks and fascia. Square cutting lines across them, then saw them to length using a junior hacksaw.

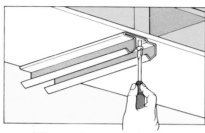

2 Offer up the top track and mark the fixing positions (drill extra holes if necessary). Screw the track in place, leaving the screws slightly loose.

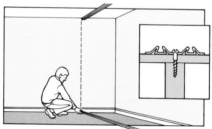

4 Make sure the bottom track aligns exactly with the top one when marking the fixing positions. If necessary, pack underneath to bring it level.

HANGING THE DOORS

If you're fitting standard size doors, the tricky part of the job is out of the way. The hangers and guides are factory fitted, so simply slip the doors into their tracks and adjust the guides following the kit maker's instructions.

If you are making your own doors, now is the time to cut the plywood panels to size.

Measure up with the tracks in place, allowing for the extra taken up by the runners and guides. If you're trimming the width as well as the height, double doors are cut to half the width plus a 25mm (1") overlap allowance, while three-door sets are cut to a third of the opening width, plus the overlap.

Cut the door panels as accurately as you can, but don't worry about finishing the edges: these are hidden by the frames, which you measure direct from the panels and cut separately. Check each panel's fit before cutting the frames.

1 Having transferred the measurements of the opening to the panels, cut them to size using a handsaw or electric jigsaw fitted with a fine blade.

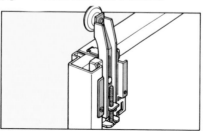

3 The top hangers and bottom guides have tabs which normally clip into slots in the frame. If these were sawn off, fit them with screws instead.

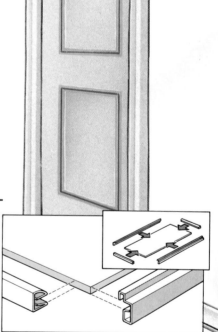

2 Use a junior hacksaw to cut the frame pieces, sizing them directly from the cut panels. Notch the corners where they join, then clip them in place.

4 Hook the hanger wheels on the tracks by offering up the doors at an angle. When in place, align by adjusting the hangers; lastly, fit the runners.

310

top track fixed to ceiling joist(s)

fascia clipped to top track

bottom track fixed to floor

A typical 3-door assembly (above) *using standard size mirror and panel doors. When combining door types, fit the mirror on the front of the two track channels.*
Angle the doors (right) *when slotting in the hangers.*

ADDING AN END PANEL

Where the wardrobe isn't running from wall to wall, fit an end panel of 16mm or 19mm board (such as veneered chipboard). Buy a piece long enough to fit from floor to ceiling and wide enough to fit from the back wall to the front of the fascia.

Almost certainly, you'll need to trim the panel to fit against the wall and ceiling, so cut it on the generous side to begin with, then scribe and fine-trim it afterwards.

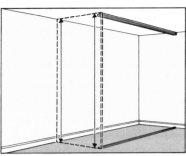

1 Measure the height from floor to ceiling at the front and back of the wardrobe. Mark the dimensions on the panel and cut it to size.

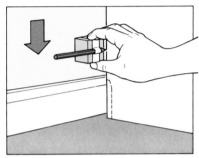

2 Stand the panel up and scribe the back edge to fit the wall and skirting. Then trim it with a hand saw or jigsaw, and finish the edge with a surform plane.

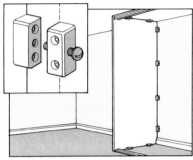

3 Fix the panel with plastic joint blocks. Fit the two top and bottom; along the back edge, space four evenly and screw them into drilled and plugged holes.

Adjusting the opening height

How you approach this depends on the size of the gap.

■ For gaps up to 100mm (4"), fit a timber filling piece under the bottom track using either of the methods shown on the right.

The thickness of the timber doesn't have to match the gap exactly – remember, the runners will accommodate differences up to 12mm (½"). If the floor level is out by more than this, pack under the filling piece with slips of wood or hardboard.

■ For gaps between 100mm and 200mm (4-8"), you can fit a filling piece top *and* bottom – but only if the floor and ceiling are roughly level. Otherwise, see below.

■ For larger gaps, build a 'drop top' frame of 100×50mm (4×2") timber as shown on the right, then screw the top track to this.

Give the frame members as much support as possible, screwing them to the joists where appropriate, and to a bearer fixed along the back wall.

Afterwards, panel the frame with 6mm plywood pinned to the frame and then decorate to match the walls.

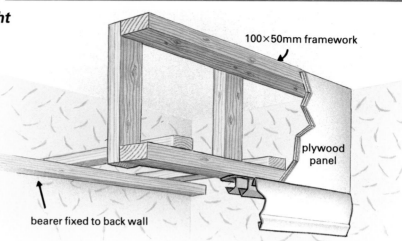

100×50mm framework

plywood panel

bearer fixed to back wall

Make a 'drop top' frame *from 100×50mm (4×2") timber screwed to the ceiling with braces extending to the back wall.*

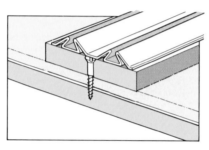

For gaps of up to 100mm (4"), *it's easiest to screw a filler piece under the bottom track. Choose a thickness that comes within 12mm (½") of the gap.*

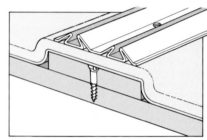

Alternatively, *for a small gap roll back the carpet and fit the filling piece underneath. (This is also better if you need to level the timber with packing pieces.)*

Adjusting the opening width

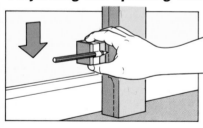

1 *If the filling piece has to clear a skirting, stand it in place temporarily and scribe the skirting's shape as shown using a pencil and block of wood.*

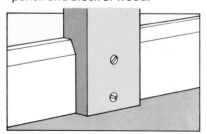

2 *Cut out the notch with a hand saw then screw the filling piece to the wall. Check that it sits vertically – if not, pack behind it.*

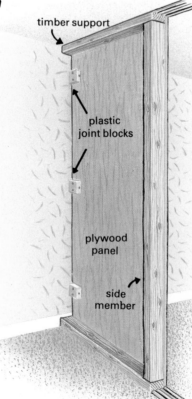

timber support

plastic joint blocks

plywood panel

side member

Like the height, how you deal with the opening width depends on the gap.

■ For gaps up to 100mm (4"), fit a filling piece to the adjoining wall. Screw it just behind the line of the fascia, and pack behind it to ensure that it's vertical. Fill any gaps later.

Use the same technique to clear a projecting skirting board. Shape the end of the filling piece to fit the skirting as shown on the left.

■ For gaps of between 100mm and 200mm (4-8"), fit a filling piece on both sides.

■ For larger gaps, fit a filling panel as shown on the left.

If the panel is running to ceiling height, fix the 100×50mm (4×2") side member to timber supports screwed to the ceiling and floor. If you're building a drop top panel as well, incorporate the side member into the rest of the frame. Fix the panel itself with plastic joint blocks.

FITTING OUT A WARDROBE

Modern fittings make it easy to put together a wardrobe interior that suits your storage needs perfectly – whether you use a ready-made kit or separate units.

If you already have a built-in cupboard or sliding door wardrobe, now could be the perfect time to think about organizing the space more efficiently. And if you are installing wardrobe doors, you can plan and fit out the interior at the same time.

Narrowing the choice

The first step is to think about what's going in the wardrobe, and how you'd like to store it. Broadly, there is a choice between hanging space, open storage, and drawers – with special fittings for things like shoes and ties.

The three basic kit options are shown below, and in larger wardrobes there's no reason why you shouldn't combine them. But before you decide, run through *Planning your storage needs* overleaf.

A typical wardrobe interior kit (right) providing a practical mix of different storage including dividers, hanging rails, drawers and open shelving.

.... Shopping List ....

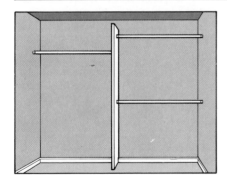

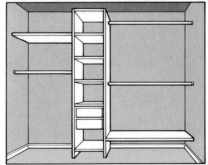

Rail/divider system

The simplest type of interior kit, consisting of one or more vertical panels to divide the wardrobe, plus hanging rails and hooks. Shelves are a make-yourself option.

You need a minimum of 300mm (12″) depth for the unit, but at least 600mm (2′) if you want to hang clothes. A single kit spans up to about 2.4m (8′).

You may need 300×15mm (12×⅝″) melamine-faced boards for shelves.

Shelf/drawer system

This type of self-assembly kit has vertical box frames which include shelves and drawers. Hanging rails fit onto each side and you can make your own top and bottom shelves.

You need at least 400mm (16″) depth for the unit, rising to 600mm (2′) for hanging clothes. A kit typically spans up to about 2.4m (8′); above this, buy two kits.

You may need 450×15mm (18×⅝″) melamine-faced boards for shelves.

Wire basket system

This is based on open frames made of plastic-coated wire which clip together to make rigid supports. There is a wide range of baskets, hooks and rails for varied storage.

You need 300-550mm (12-22″) depth, depending on the system, and at least 600mm (2′) if you want to hang clothes.

You may need 15mm melamine-faced boards for shelving, and hanging rails may be separate.

313

PLANNING YOUR STORAGE NEEDS

Different things need different kinds of storage, but a combination of these four basic types will cope with most needs:

Hanging space: Rails for hanging clothes are a top priority. Long dresses and coats need more height than jackets, trousers, suits, skirts and shirts.

Open shelving and drawers: Shelving is useful for items like bed linen, towels and luggage if this is stored in the bedroom. Drawers are best for small objects, underwear and folded knitwear.

Special storage may be required for things like ties and shoes.

Only you can decide how much of each type you need – people are different sizes, and so are their clothes. To give yourself a clearer idea, draw up a detailed list of what you want to store and divide the items between the four categories listed above. Then allocate space accordingly.

HANGING SPACE

The main hanging rails should be set slightly above eye level, around 1.8m (6′) from the floor – and if there is a top shelf, you need at least 50mm clearance above the rails to unhook a hanger. Clothes are deceptively heavy, so avoid very long, unsupported spans.

Remember that where clothes don't need the full hanging height, you can fit shelves or a second rail below them to make better use of the space.

These are the approximate hanging lengths needed for different types of clothing:

- Long dress: 1.6m (5′4″).
- Dressing gown, robe or long

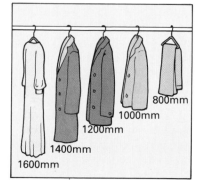

Unless you have lots of full-length clothes you can fit other storage in the unused space below the hanging rail – a second rail, perhaps, or a low shelf unit.

A drawer/shelf system cuts down on clutter by providing easily accessible storage for small or awkward items, as well as folded clothes and towels.

DRAWERS AND OPEN SHELVING

You could easily need anywhere from 10 to 15 drawers for folded clothes, depending on their size and the number you want to store. But some clothes can be kept in open shelves or wire baskets just as well, saving on drawer space.

Spare bedlinen and luggage is likely to need anywhere between about 1m (3′4″) and 3m (10′) total shelf length. But suitcases may be very wasteful of space unless they can be fitted inside one another.

Shoes, handbags, hats and so on will probably require 1-2m (3-7′) total shelving space, with plenty of room above for taller items. But you may be able to store them more efficiently by using purpose-made racks or hooks.

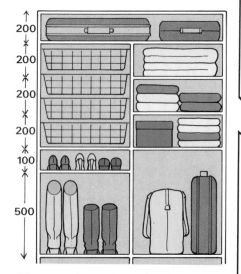

Most people need a mix of shelf and drawer spacing to cope with all that they want to store. Some tall items can be highly wasteful of wardrobe space.

coat: 1.4m (4'6").
■ Medium coat, man's jacket:
1.2m (4').
■ Woman's jacket, skirt: 1m
(3'4").
■ Trousers, shirts: 800mm (32").

A lot obviously depends on
how much you have to store, but
as a rule of thumb most men
need a total hanging space about
650mm (26") wide, while women
need around 1m (3'4").

If you have a lot of clothes
needing hangers, this could go up
to about 1.5m (5') for men and
2.4m (8') for women. And if you
hang shirts and blouses, add
about another 300-500mm (12-
20") to the basic measurements.

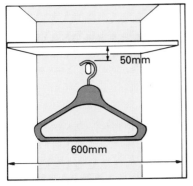

Plenty of clearance *is needed for the
hanging rails. You need room to lift
clothes on and off, and enough
depth for them to hang without
crushing.*

This rail/divider system
*lets you hang short clothes
on two levels to make the
best use of space. You can
add shelves to take other
items which can't be hung
on rails.*

Wire baskets *are a good
alternative storage
solution for the kind of
things which need to go in
drawers or on shelves –
and they ensure that
everything gets properly
aired.*

315

FITTING A RAIL/DIVIDER

The maximum span of a wardrobe rail before it starts to bend or sag is usually about 1200mm (4'). This is narrower than most wardrobes, so the simplest type of rail system consists of upright panels which divide the wardrobe into short sections with hanger rails fitted on either side. All these parts come as a kit, which also includes hooks and other fittings.

For a short two-door wardrobe, you need only one centre panel. This is normally supplied with three rails to span the space from it to the sides of the wardrobe. For wider wardrobes, simply buy an extra kit to make up the kind of layout shown below. Top and bottom shelves aren't included; make these from standard shelf-width boards.

Tools: electric drill and bits, spirit level, tape measure, junior hacksaw, handsaw and screwdrivers.

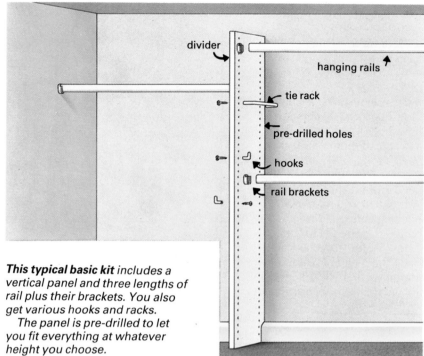

This typical basic kit includes a vertical panel and three lengths of rail plus their brackets. You also get various hooks and racks.

The panel is pre-drilled to let you fit everything at whatever height you choose.

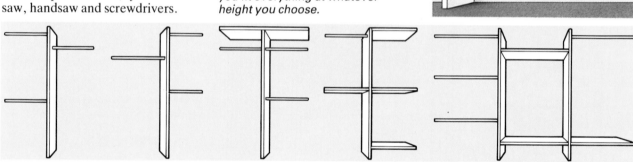

Fit the rails at any height you like on either side of the panel.

Optional shelves can be added by using standard boards.

In a wide wardrobe, combine two kits side-by-side.

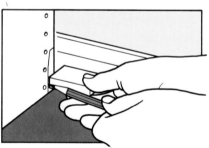

1 Scribe the vertical panel to clear a skirting by standing it the same distance out from the wall as the width of the scribing block. Saw out the notch.

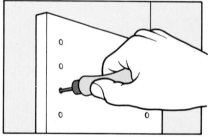

2 Stand the panel against the end of the wardrobe or the side wall and mark off the heights of the rails on both the panel and the side.

3 Screw the hanging rail brackets to the panel and to the end of the wardrobe or side wall. Use wallplugs if you're fixing into masonry.

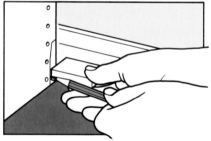

4 Fix the vertical panel in place using plastic joint blocks or brackets screwed into drilled and plugged holes in the wall behind. Screw another block to the floor.

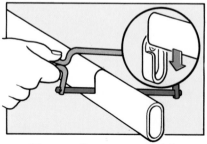

5 Measure the space remaining for each rail between the panel and the end, and cut them to length with a junior hacksaw. Fit the rails to the brackets.

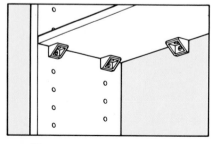

6 If you want to add shelves, cut them from melamine-faced board and attach them to the sides, back and vertical panel using joint blocks.

FITTING A SHELF/DRAWER UNIT

This works in a similar way to the simple rail/divider system on the previous page. It has a number of hanging rails, plus a vertical divider to break up the interior of the wardrobe into short, easily spanned lengths. But in this case the vertical divider is a free-standing box unit containing shelves and drawers. The system comes in flat-packed form, so you can fix the shelves at the height of your choice.

Like the simpler rail/divider system, you can fit a single kit to a narrow wardrobe, or combine two to cope with a wider span (see below). It's also possible to add extra top or bottom shelves to the kit, using lengths of standard shelf-width sized melamine-faced board.

Tools: electric drill and bits, spirit level, tape measure, junior hacksaw, handsaw and screwdrivers.

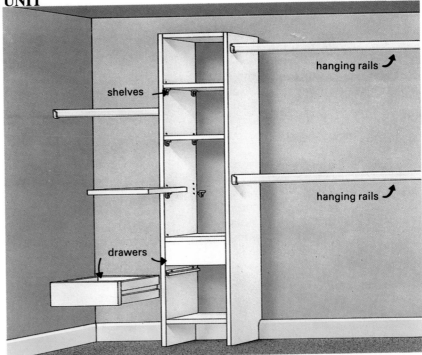

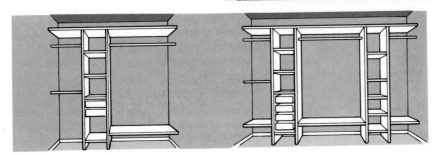

The kit includes(above) a flat-pack storage unit consisting of two sides, connecting shelves and a set of drawers. There are also lengths of rail and brackets to fit on each side of the assembled unit. The rails are often different lengths, allowing you to stand the divider off to one side of the wardrobe.

***Fit the rails** at any height you want and add your own shelves.*

***Two kits** allow for more varied storage in a wider wardrobe.*

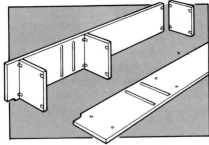

1 Scribe the vertical panels to fit over any skirting. Then fix drawer runners and shelves to assemble the unit – normally using screws and plastic blocks.

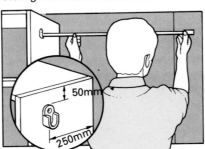

2 Stand the unit up and mark the height of the hanging rail bracket on the vertical panel. Measure to the wall or end of the wardrobe to find the rail length.

3 Screw the bracket to the vertical panel. Cut the rail to length with a junior hacksaw, then find the position of the other bracket and screw in place.

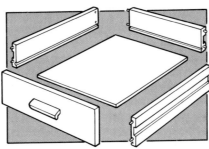

4 Assemble the drawers, which are supplied in flat-pack form with either plastic joints or glued corners. Fit these and the internal shelves in place.

Trade tip

Forward planning

❛ Don't make the mistake I once did and forget the space left when the wardrobe doors are opened. The interior unit must be offset to one side so that it is completely unobstructed by the doors – otherwise you won't be able to pull out the drawers.

Think about this at the planning stage, because it may affect the way you arrange your hanging space. ❜

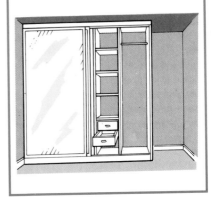

317

WIRE BASKET SYSTEMS

Wire basket storage units can be free-standing, or supported by the side panels of the wardrobe. Kits range from complete wardrobe interiors to individual baskets and small modules which can be fitted into any odd space. Some allow you to use the baskets as ordinary drawers, and you can also get accessories like undershelf baskets and shoe racks.

A typical basic system consists of a set of side panels, crossbars and baskets, made in a range of sizes so that you can assemble sets of units to suit your needs. Most systems are based on a standard unit width (often 450mm – 18″), so you can combine them to span any area.

Wire basket components vary *but this typical system shows many of the fittings available. Open baskets are used as drawers, and shelves or hanging rails clip on.*

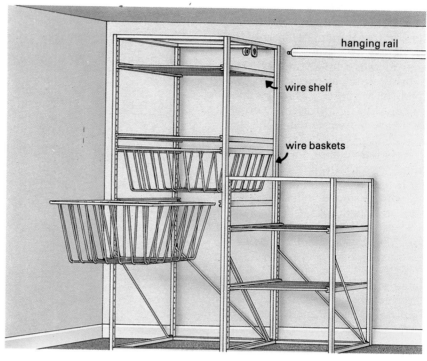

hanging rail

wire shelf

wire baskets

1 *Free-standing frames clip together using crossbars at top and bottom. Press them together by hand or use a mallet if they are stiff.*

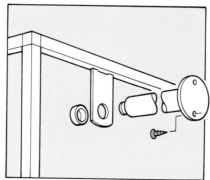

2 *Some systems have attachments for hanging rails. The other end of the rail can be supported by a bracket screwed to the end panel or side wall.*

3 *Many wire baskets can also be used as open drawers in a unit made from solid boards. This is done by fitting separate runners to the insides of the panels.*

PROBLEM SOLVER

Dealing with awkward corners
Shallow wardrobes and ones where the depth is reduced by a projection inside, such as an old chimney breast, pose special problems – because you need about 600mm (2′) to fit in a hanger comfortably.

If you haven't enough depth, one answer may be to hang the clothes facing the front of the wardrobe instead of sideways on. You'll be able to get at them easily by fitting an extending wardrobe rail running from front to back. These are especially good for hanging light clothes like shirts and blouses.

You need a space at least 600mm wide, and a sturdy shelf above it, into which to screw the new extending rail.

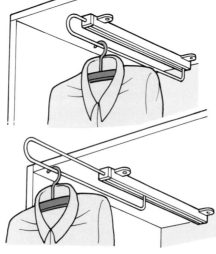

This type of rail *needs less than 400mm fitting depth but can be pulled out for easy access.*

═Trade tip═

Heavy loads
❛ If you've got a lot of jackets and coats to store, they can be surprisingly heavy. Oval hanging rails are much better than round ones at taking the strain and are used in most kits. You can also buy them separately.

Whatever type of rail you are fixing, bear in mind that the heavy weights involved mean that you need good fastenings.

I recommend using chipboard screws in all types of wood, as these are much better at getting a grip. For very long rails or very heavy loads, consider fitting a top shelf and screwing a centre support bracket underneath.❜

BUILT-IN CUPBOARDS

Built-in cupboards are the neatest solution to household storage problems. Unlike free-standing furniture, they can be planned to make the best use of the available space, and you can ensure that they don't obstruct the rest of the room. And although you can't take them with you if you move, most potential purchasers see plenty of built-in cupboards as a real asset.

One way to provide built-in cupboard space is to buy modular furniture such as kitchen or bedroom units. But although this is likely to be the easiest option, it may not always be the best. If you have an awkward space (or it simply doesn't fit the modular unit size very well) you may find that the units fill it little better than free-standing furniture. Modular units can also work out fairly expensive, simply because the makers have to ensure that they are structurally sound regardless of where they are fitted or what is on each side.

Building your own furniture is rather more complicated, but can offer some significant advantages.

First of all, you can ensure that things fit properly. For example, if you have a space which is 1050mm wide, you can build a unit this size rather than having to adapt a stan-

dard unit which is probably 900 or 1000mm wide (or use a combination of 500 and 600mm wide ones).

Secondly, you can save on materials by making more use of the walls themselves (or adjacent cupboards) as supports.

Thirdly, you can produce furniture which simply isn't available any other way. For example, you can make shallow cupboards that fit a shallow alcove perfectly, rather than using deeper standard ones which would project awkwardly.

Types of built-in furniture
There are two basic ways to make built-in furniture:

Traditional styling suits living room alcoves.

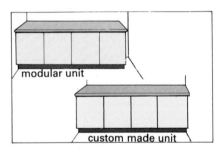

Custom designed built-in furniture can be made to fit an awkward space perfectly – unlike modular furniture which is restricted to set sizes.

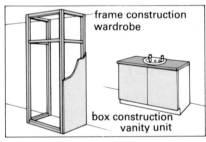

Box furniture is easy to make and most furniture is now built this way. Frame furniture is more complicated but lighter and more economical on materials.

Framed furniture uses battens as the main structural supports, and in many cases – for example, alcove shelving – the battens can be fixed directly to the walls. Any of the framework left exposed can then be clad with non-structural panelling, which also serves to brace it.

Box furniture uses panels of sheet material (eg chipboard) as the main structural supports; most modern self-assembly units are built this way.

In practice, you may find it is best to use a combination of methods. On the following pages are a number of basic designs which can be adapted to many situations.

DESIGNING BUILT-IN FURNITURE

There are no hard-and-fast rules for designing built-in furniture: by its very nature, each piece should be made to suit the situation. This means taking a flexible attitude, and adapting basic design principles as you go.

Start by measuring up the room and drawing a scale plan. This should show all the critical dimensions, and you may find you need to draw two plans (one to show the floor and another showing the walls) to include enough detail. Mark in any fixed points such as electrical sockets and water pipes.

Next draw a rough sketch of the furniture you have in mind. There are two things which you should consider right from the start. First of all, try to stick to the standard dimensions given in the table on the right when it comes to things like worktop height and so on. If you are in doubt about overall sizes, measure some finished furniture as a starting point.

Secondly, bear in mind the available sizes of the materials you plan to use. For example, faced chipboard comes in 300 and 375mm (12 and 15″) widths. Making a unit 325mm (13″) deep means trimming down the wider boards (unless you go up to a larger sheet and can cut several strips from it with less waste). Unless there is an over-riding reason for sticking to a specific non-standard dimension, use standard boards for ease of work and economy. Similarly, work to standard lengths as far as possible.

Finally, it is worth taking advantage of ready made accessories wherever possible – to save time and to ensure a good finish.

■ Standard ready made doors and drawer fronts can save hours of work. See the following construction plans for more details.

■ Drawers are rarely worth con-structing from scratch, since drawer kits are simple, reasonably cheap and very efficient.

When you have roughed out the design to your satisfaction, transfer it accurately to the scale plan. This forms both the basis of your shopping list and a guide to constructing the furniture.

STANDARD DIMENSIONS

Worktop depth	600mm
Worktop/sink height	900mm
Worktop to wall unit gap	450mm
Dressing table height	600–800mm
Wardrobe depth	500–600mm
Seating height	400–450mm
Dining table height	700–750mm
Washbasin height	700mm
Chest of drawers depth	400–450mm
Shelf supports	600–750mm apart

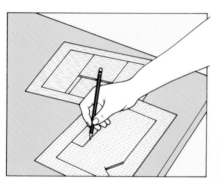

Draw a scale plan and elevation of the room showing all the critical dimensions and the position of any fixed points like sockets and pipes.

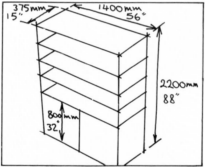

Sketch out your furniture design, roughly indicate overall height and depth. Choose the overall dimensions to suit the materials and fittings you are using.

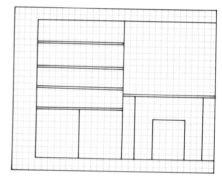

Adapt your drawing to suit the scale plan and then draw it on the plan accurately to scale. This becomes your shopping list and cutting plan.

....Shopping List....

Sheet materials The main material for low-cost box furniture is *faced* or *veneered* 16mm (⅝″) chipboard. This comes in 2240×1220mm (8×4′) sheets and a variety of board widths and lengths.

Alternatives for painting include *MDF* and *blockboard*. Blockboard is very strong and comes in a variety of several thicknesses, is easy to work, stable and easy to finish. *Veneered blockboard* can be used for varnished wood furniture. Both materials come in standard 2240×1220mm (8×4′) sheets.

Where you are panelling over a timber frame, the sheet material is not structural. *Hardboard* may be adequate, although it flexes easily and may 'drum'; it is often used to make furniture backs. Otherwise

use *thin plywood* . You can even use *plasterboard* for furniture which forms the corner of a room, providing the edges are covered and it does not have to take a load.

Other timber *Planed softwood battens* are the stock solution for built-in furniture. 50×25mm (2×1″) is adequate for most jobs.

Softwood mouldings are worth investigating as solutions to design or decor problems. They are particularly useful for concealing exposed edges, or to break up large expanses of flat panelling.

Doors and drawers Blank *door and drawer fronts* come in various styles in a small range of sizes. Common examples are:

■ Widths of 300, 375, 450, 600, 675, and 750mm.

■ Heights of 450, 600, 750, 900, 1200, 1500, 1650, 1800 and 2000mm.

(There may be some variation in the measurement depending on whether they are basically Imperial or metric sizes). Home made doors and drawer fronts can be any size you wish.

Fixings *PVA adhesive, chipboard screws* in various sizes and *panel pins* should cope with most jobs; buy plenty, as it is almost impossible to plan exact needs in advance. It is also worth buying *brackets* or *block joints* in bulk for the same reason.

Fittings *Drawer kits, hinges, knobs* and other fittings can be estimated fairly accurately. DIY superstores often sell such items in bulk.

ADAPTABLE LIVING ROOM UNITS

These units can be used as either a sideboard/dresser or bookcase/entertainments centre by making small modifications to the design and construction. It's also easy to change the appearance to suit different furnishing styles by applying mouldings and choosing different doors.

The construction is straightforward and is intended for use either in an alcove or in a corner – although it could easily be extended right across a room. Essentially, there are two parts; a base unit with worktop and a series of shelves above.

In an alcove, the shelves can be entirely supported on the wall, but where the unit is built into a corner you need to fit an end panel; in this case fit one against the wall too, for the sake of symmetry.

Making the doors

You can either use standard ready made doors which come in a lmited range of sizes, or make your own to fit. Ready made doors guarantee a good finish, but you are likely to have to panel-in gaps in the course of adapting them to fit the space.

Home-made doors can be made simply by using panels of faced or veneered chipboard, or blockboard edged with lipping. If you want a painted finish, MDF is the best choice. All these have a flat, stark appearance which is fine in modern rooms but not so good for period ones. If necessary, give the surface a panelled look by gluing on mouldings.

Finishing touches

There are two main ways to modify the style of the cupboards:

■ Choose materials with either a painted or natural wood finish in mind. If you are painting, use MDF, blockboard or a veneered chipboard; for a natural wood look use solid wood, veneered chipboard or veneered blockboard with matching lipping.

■ Pick mouldings to match other fittings in the room – the key to a real 'built-in' style. Trim the top with a cornice to match the coving in the room, and use architraves and cupboard door mouldings to match those on the other doors. You could also continue the skirting around the plinth, and run any picture rail across the unit at the same height.

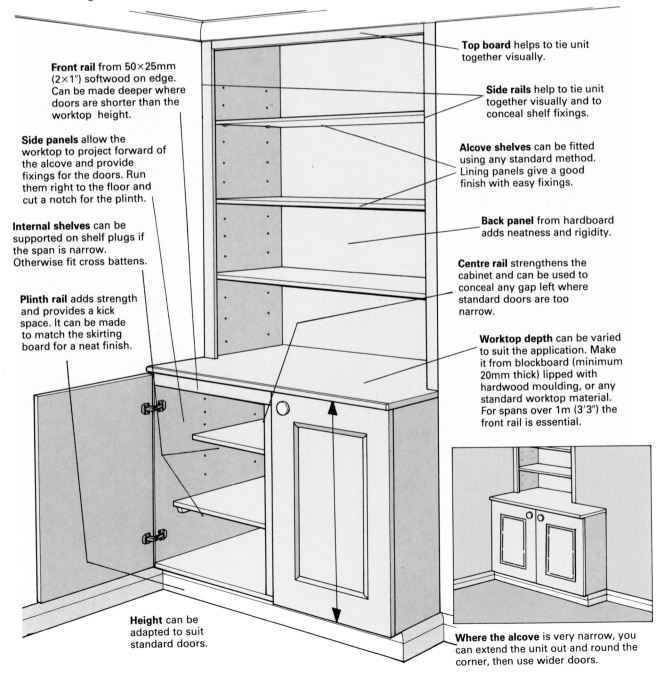

Front rail from 50×25mm (2×1″) softwood on edge. Can be made deeper where doors are shorter than the worktop height.

Side panels allow the worktop to project forward of the alcove and provide fixings for the doors. Run them right to the floor and cut a notch for the plinth.

Internal shelves can be supported on shelf plugs if the span is narrow. Otherwise fit cross battens.

Plinth rail adds strength and provides a kick space. It can be made to match the skirting board for a neat finish.

Height can be adapted to suit standard doors.

Top board helps to tie unit together visually.

Side rails help to tie unit together visually and to conceal shelf fixings.

Alcove shelves can be fitted using any standard method. Lining panels give a good finish with easy fixings.

Back panel from hardboard adds neatness and rigidity.

Centre rail strengthens the cabinet and can be used to conceal any gap left where standard doors are too narrow.

Worktop depth can be varied to suit the application. Make it from blockboard (minimum 20mm thick) lipped with hardwood moulding, or any standard worktop material. For spans over 1m (3′3″) the front rail is essential.

Where the alcove is very narrow, you can extend the unit out and round the corner, then use wider doors.

BASIC KITCHEN UNITS

Kitchen units can be made to suit awkward locations far more efficiently than standard self-assembly units. In general it makes sense to use similar construction methods, and where standard units are being used elsewhere in the kitchen it's a good idea to copy them.

The main reasons for making your own units are where standard ones don't fit a given width very well, or where you want to take top units right up to the ceiling.

All the fittings are easily obtainable from DIY superstores, and are fairly easy to use – although you need to buy a special hinge-boring bit to fit the type of hinges used on kitchen cupboard doors.

Door options

Doors are the major problem with home made kitchen units. If you want plain white flush doors, these are simple to make from sheets of coated chipboard (and you may also find this in a range of colours).

Where you are trying to match existing units, you really have no option but to use identical doors, bought as spares from the unit suppliers. This means that you have to work around standard sizes – which to some extent defeats the object of making your own units in the first place. However, even if you have to panel out the cupboard to suit the doors, you still have the internal space which is not available if you use smaller units.

Standard doors may also be the best option if you want something more interesting than a plain panel. There is no need to stick to kitchen unit doors; ready made cupboard doors are widely available in a range of sizes and can be varnished or painted as you choose.

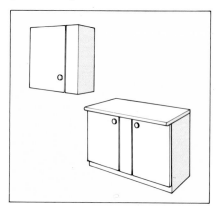

Options for adapting standard doors to fit all involve packing out the sides with extra strips, leaving the internal size unaltered. Don't do this on the hinge side, since the mounting plates need to be screwed to a flat panel.

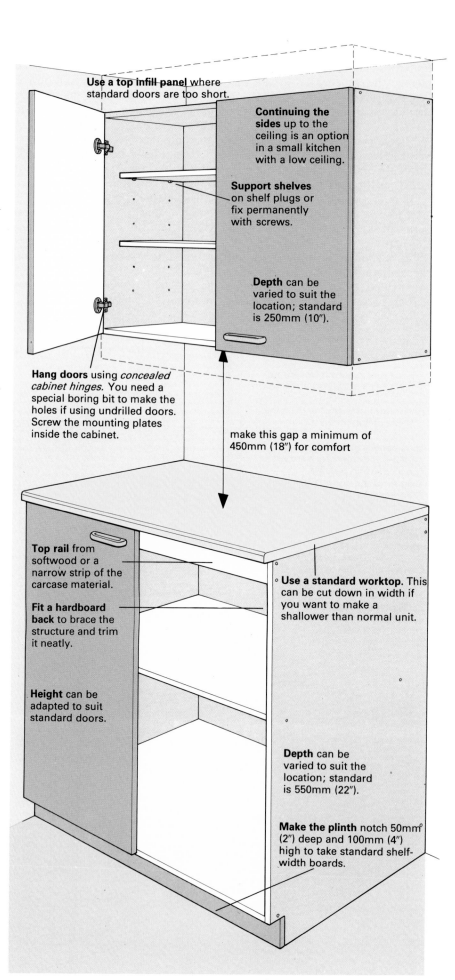

Use a top infill panel where standard doors are too short.

Continuing the sides up to the ceiling is an option in a small kitchen with a low ceiling.

Support shelves on shelf plugs or fix permanently with screws.

Depth can be varied to suit the location; standard is 250mm (10″).

Hang doors using *concealed cabinet hinges*. You need a special boring bit to make the holes if using undrilled doors. Screw the mounting plates inside the cabinet.

make this gap a minimum of 450mm (18″) for comfort

Top rail from softwood or a narrow strip of the carcase material.

Fit a hardboard back to brace the structure and trim it neatly.

Height can be adapted to suit standard doors.

Use a standard worktop. This can be cut down in width if you want to make a shallower than normal unit.

Depth can be varied to suit the location; standard is 550mm (22″).

Make the plinth notch 50mm (2″) deep and 100mm (4″) high to take standard shelf-width boards.

BUILDING-IN WARDROBES

Built-in wardrobes are easily put together using a combination of box and frame construction techniques. Alternatively, you can partition off the end or corner of a room and fit sliding doors.

However, in a small bedroom, it may not be worth going to the trouble of making the basic wardrobe – and a cheaper option may be to adapt a low-cost self-assembly unit. The dimensions of things like hanging space tend to be fairly fixed anyway, and it is rarely necessary to make the basic box fit a particular space with any degree of accuracy.

Whether you make the wardrobe from scratch or adapt an existing unit, the trick is to use the dressing table part to adjust it to fit the room exactly. Gaps can then simply be filled in by using mouldings – a theme which can be continued across the doors and so on.

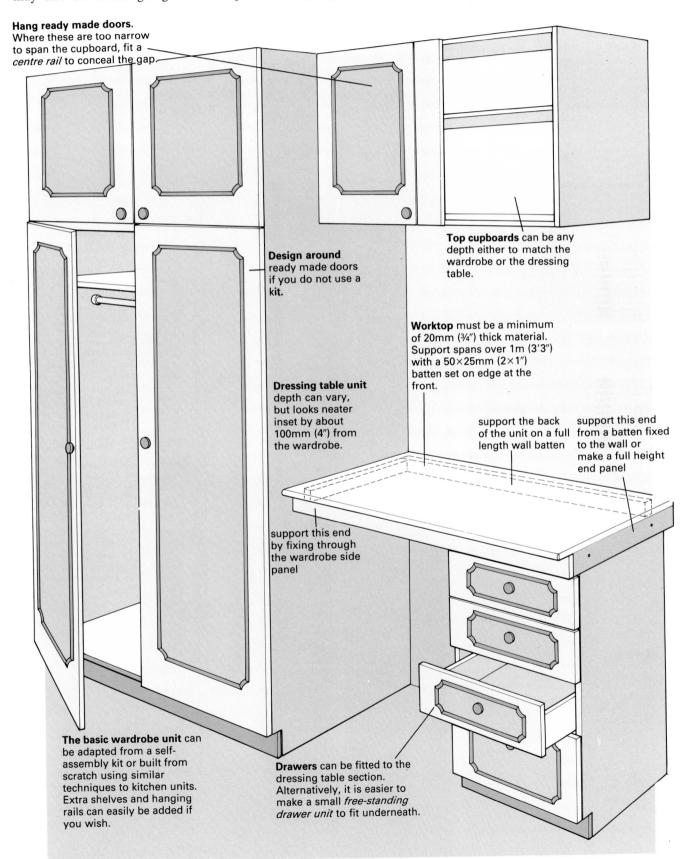

Hang ready made doors.
Where these are too narrow to span the cupboard, fit a *centre rail* to conceal the gap.

Top cupboards can be any depth either to match the wardrobe or the dressing table.

Design around ready made doors if you do not use a **kit.**

Worktop must be a minimum of 20mm (¾") thick material. Support spans over 1m (3'3") with a 50×25mm (2×1") batten set on edge at the front.

Dressing table unit depth can vary, but looks neater inset by about 100mm (4") from the wardrobe.

support the back of the unit on a full length wall batten

support this end from a batten fixed to the wall or make a full height end panel

support this end by fixing through the wardrobe side panel

The basic wardrobe unit can be adapted from a self-assembly kit or built from scratch using similar techniques to kitchen units. Extra shelves and hanging rails can easily be added if you wish.

Drawers can be fitted to the dressing table section. Alternatively, it is easier to make a small *free-standing drawer unit* to fit underneath.

AIRING CUPBOARD

Airing cupboards need to run from floor to ceiling. This makes frame construction the natural choice; it is lighter than solid panels and you aren't restricted by the size of standard boards.

The hot water cylinder will normally be close to a corner, so all you have to do is to frame one side and hang doors across the other. You'll gain useful space by rerouting any intrusive pipes to run down walls.

Louvre doors are normally the best choice since they provide natural ventilation. If you use solid doors, you should fit vent panels to the top and bottom of the unit.

Planning points

■ Choose your doors first and work round their dimensions. Make sure there is room for them to swing.

■ Choose the cladding material – if this comes in sheets smaller than the height of the cupboard you must arrange for the joint to fall over a supporting batten. Suitable materials include plywood, hardboard, or plasterboard (so long as the exposed front edge is protected with a lipping).

■ Make sure you will have easy access to any gatevalves controlling the flow of water to the cylinder, and to the thermostat or switch for an immersion heater.

Construction details

■ Fix the wall battens first, ensuring they are accurately horizontal and vertical.

■ Assemble the side frame.

■ Use a door to measure where the side frame needs to be positioned.

■ Fix the frame to walls, floor and ceiling, making sure the door post is vertical (check from side to side and back to front, too).

■ Fix cross battens and a plinth.

■ Install the shelves.

■ Cover the frame with panelling.

■ Hang the doors.

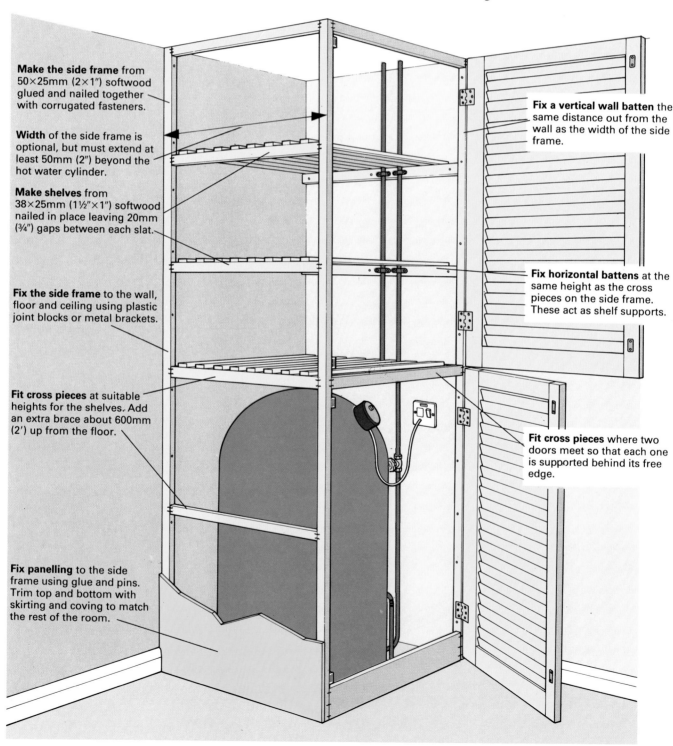

Make the side frame from 50×25mm (2×1″) softwood glued and nailed together with corrugated fasteners.

Width of the side frame is optional, but must extend at least 50mm (2″) beyond the hot water cylinder.

Make shelves from 38×25mm (1½″×1″) softwood nailed in place leaving 20mm (¾″) gaps between each slat.

Fix the side frame to the wall, floor and ceiling using plastic joint blocks or metal brackets.

Fix cross pieces at suitable heights for the shelves. Add an extra brace about 600mm (2′) up from the floor.

Fix panelling to the side frame using glue and pins. Trim top and bottom with skirting and coving to match the rest of the room.

Fix a vertical wall batten the same distance out from the wall as the width of the side frame.

Fix horizontal battens at the same height as the cross pieces on the side frame. These act as shelf supports.

Fit cross pieces where two doors meet so that each one is supported behind its free edge.

6

PLUMBING

WHERE TO TURN THE WATER OFF

Before you can do any plumbing job, whether it's changing a tap washer or mending a leak, you need to know where to turn the water off. This section covers everything you need to know about turning off the hot and cold supplies to carry out DIY jobs, and in case of an emergency (see also pages 333-336).

All household plumbing systems contain stopcocks or gate valves for isolating the water supply. The basic procedure is:

■ Turn off the heating as a safety precaution.

■ Find the nearest stopcock to the pipe or outlet you want to isolate (this will vary from job to job).

■ Turn the stopcock **clockwise** as far as it will go.

■ Open the tap at the end of the pipe run to drain any water left in the pipework (this may take a few seconds).

Unfortunately, there are no 'rules' about where stopcocks might be placed: some houses have more than others, and only rarely is there one for every section of pipe. So before you try to find out which stopcock controls which pipes, have a look at the diagram on the right, which shows how water flows around the house.

Cold supply This enters the house under mains pressure. In many systems the pipe then splits into two, one branch serving the kitchen sink cold tap and the other the cold storage tank in the roof. In some systems, however, there is no storage tank; the pipe simply divides into branches serving the different outlets so all the cold water is at mains pressure. The diagram shows a storage tank system, but all systems work on the same principle.

From the cold storage tank, further pipes serve the remaining cold outlets and the hot water cylinder. The water in these pipes is not under mains pressure: it relies on gravity, which means that the higher the tank, the greater the 'push' the water gets.

Hot supply The pressure of the water in the hot pipes is governed by the pressure of the cold water. This is because as the water gets heated in the cylinder or water heater, it rises above the cold water being fed in below it; the pressure of the cold water then literally forces the hot water out into the pipes. In other words, stop the cold water and the hot water stops too – a useful point to remember when there isn't a stopcock where you'd expect to find one.

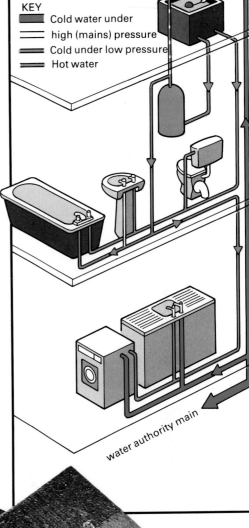

KEY
- Cold water under high (mains) pressure
- Cold under low pressure
- Hot water

water authority main

KITCHEN COLD WATER 4½ TURNS FROM OFF

Trade tip

Now's the time to try

❝ I always tell people to find out where their stopcocks are as soon as they move into a house – far better to do it when you've got the time, than when there's an emergency and you've got a flood to deal with.

As you find each one, turn it off and test which pipes it serves by opening all the likely taps or checking the ballvalves in the cold storage tank and WC cistern.

It's a good idea to label the stopcocks with their function, ie 'bathroom cold water', (you can make a note of their positions in your House File) so that anyone else in the house can find them in a hurry if they need to. ❞

WHERE TO LOOK FOR YOUR STOPCOCKS

BATHROOM APPLIANCES

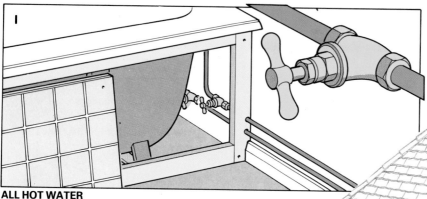

ALL HOT WATER

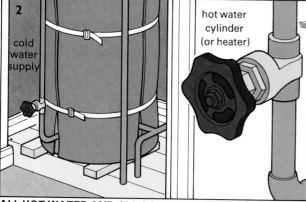

hot water cylinder (or heater)

cold water supply

ALL HOT WATER AND ALL COLD WATER NOT MAINS-FED

vent pipe

cold water supply

cold water feeds

Trade tip

Take it in turns

❛ If the stopcock you're dealing with controls water under mains pressure, note on the label how many turns it takes to shut it off, and turn it on again by the same amount. Stopcocks are often used to reduce the water flow slightly in areas where the mains pressure is high, in which case opening them fully could cause hammering in the pipework.

It's also a good idea to follow the old plumber's rule: 'never assume a stopcock works until you've tried it'; often they don't, and you need to try another one further down the line. ❜

KITCHEN COLD TAP AND APPLIANCES

hot supply

branch from rising main

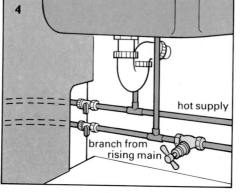

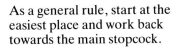

As a general rule, start at the easiest place and work back towards the main stopcock.

Bathroom appliances

1 Bathroom appliances sometimes have stopcocks for each supply pipe, or one set that shuts off all the bathroom water. Be prepared for them to be hidden behind the bath panel or any boxing-in that's been used to conceal the pipes.

All hot water

2 If you can't find any local stopcocks, the ideal place to turn off all the hot water is at the cold feed to the hot water cylinder or heater. Look for a stopcock near the base, and check that the pipe it's on feels cold.

All hot water and all cold water not mains fed

3 Often, stopcocks are fitted to the feed pipes from the storage tank to the hot cylinder and bathroom cold taps.

Failing this, you can isolate all pipes that aren't on the rising main by shutting off the supply to the tank and then draining it down by turning on all the cold taps. This will take some time, and can leave the system prone to airlocks, so only try it as a last resort.

If there is no stopcock on the supply pipe (the one feeding the ballvalve in the tank), tie up the ballvalve itself as shown.

Kitchen cold tap and appliances

4 There may be a stopcock somewhere in the kitchen to shut off the branch of the rising main that feeds the sink cold tap. Other kitchen appliances, such as a washing machine or dish washer, should have shut-off valves on both supply pipes. The same goes for other ground-floor appliances fed direct from the rising main, and also for outdoor taps.

All water

5 The rising main stopcock shuts off all the water, and it's rare for houses not to have one (though not impossible). Look for it where the main enters the house: under the stairs or behind the kitchen sink are the most common locations. In flats and maisonettes it will be on the first branch off the main supply to the rest of the building, probably near the sink or the water heater.

6 Sometimes, however, the main stopcock is found under the floorboards – often near the front door, or, if the kitchen has been extended, where the old sink was.

Search for a small section of floorboard that looks as if it has been cut and lifted in the past. Lever it up with a bolster chisel (at a pinch, use a garden spade).

7 Most houses also have a water authority stopcock which isolates the entire water supply before it enters the building, so if all else fails you can try this. You'll find it under an iron cover on the pavement, or in the garden near the road. The stopcock itself will be about 1m (3ft) below the ground, and may be covered by layers of mud; dig this out by hand with a piece of coat hanger wire.

To turn the stopcock, you need a special key (available from plumber's merchants) or a strong piece of wood with a V shaped notch cut in the end. Alternatively, the engineer's department of your local water authority will do it for you, but give them a day's notice.

ALL WATER

iron cover

7

rising main

ALL WATER

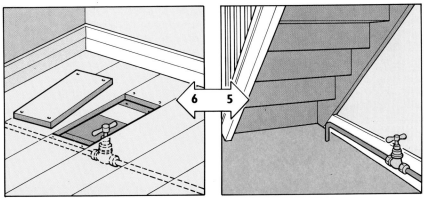

6 **5**

When it won't budge

When stopcocks haven't been used for a while they have a nasty habit of refusing to move (gate valves, which work slightly differently, are more reliable).

In this case, the first thing to do is squirt some penetrating oil around the spindle mechanism and leave it for half an hour before trying again.

If this doesn't work, wrap the stopcock in an old floorcloth and pour on boiling water; the heat may release it.

Your only other options are to apply more heat – from a blow torch or electric paint stripper – or more force. But before you use force a word of warning: if the pipes either side of the stopcock are lead, the chances are they will crack. If possible, find another stopcock further down the line rather than risk a burst.

To get extra leverage, slip a piece of pipe over one side of the handle. Alternatively, use an adjustable wrench with some cloth between the jaws to stop the handle getting chewed up. Relieve the strain on the pipework by supporting it with a piece of wood.

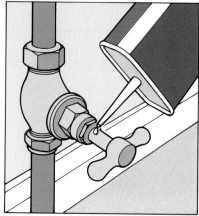

Try freeing a seized stopcock with penetrating oil...

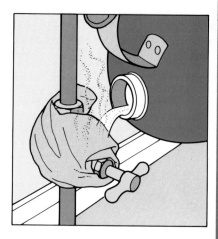

...or wrap it in an old cloth and pour on boiling water.

Minor leaks

After freeing a stopcock you might find that it leaks slightly from around the spindle area. To cure this, loosen the top (gland) nut on the spindle and wind a few turns of plumber's jointing tape (PTFE tape – available from any hardware store) round the threaded spindle body. Then retighten the nut a little over hand-tight – any more, and you won't be able to turn the handle.

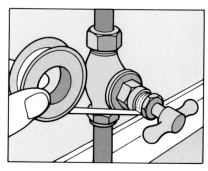

Use PTFE tape to seal a leaking stopcock spindle.

Airlocks

Sometimes, when you turn the water back on, you hear a hissing and gurgling in the pipes and no water comes out of the taps. Usually, the pipes affected are those fed from the storage tank, where the pressure is low.

Depending on where the problem is, you may be able to force the airlock back up the pipe by taking a damp cloth and plunging vigorously against the spout of the affected tap; when the air reaches the tank it will be able to escape.

If this doesn't work, connect a hose between the affected tap and one that's supplied at mains pressure (securing the ends with Jubilee clips).

Turn both taps on and leave them for about 30 seconds, then turn the mains tap off and check to see if the airlock has cleared. Sometimes it takes several goes, so be patient.

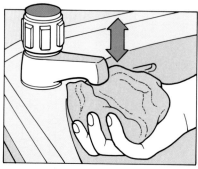

Try pumping an airlocked tap with a damp rag to create suction and force the airlock down the pipe.

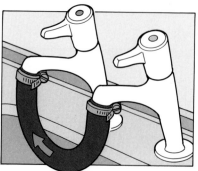

If this doesn't work, see if you can force out the airlock by connecting to a mains-fed tap.

Trade tip

Avoiding airlocks

‘ Airlocks can take ages to clear, so wherever possible I try to avoid them. If I've had to drain the cold storage tank, for example, I'll let the water back in as slowly as possible so that the air in the pipes has a chance to escape as they fill up.

If you then get persistent airlocks, the trouble may be that the storage tank isn't filling up as quickly as it is being drained, so the pipes are sucking in air instead of water. You can check this by watching the tank while someone is filling the bath to see whether the tank empties before the bath is full. If so, the trouble may be that the stopcock hasn't been turned back on fully or that you have a faulty ball-valve controlling the supply to the tank. ’

CHOOSING TOOLS FOR PLUMBING

Considering how specialized plumbing work is, there are surprisingly few special tools. For the vast majority of repair and improvement jobs you can get by with a fairly basic toolkit (see panel right). Only large-scale alterations like installing central heating or putting in a new bathroom demand more specialist items. And since you'll probably only use these once, it's better to hire than to buy.

There is a catch, however. Because most pipes are buried in, or pass through, structural parts of the house, you're quite likely to need many more tools in order to get at the pipework – and, sometimes, to make good the resulting damage.

In practice it pays to think carefully about what tools you need before starting any plumbing job. There is nothing more frustrating than having the right sized spanner, only to find that you can't use it because the joint concerned is inaccessible.

Although it is often possible to 'make do' where plumbing tools are concerned, the correct tools help the job go more smoothly. Shown (right) are a Stillson wrench and an adjustable spanner.

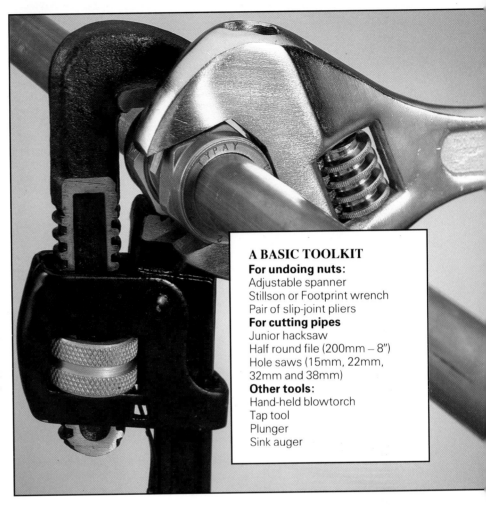

A BASIC TOOLKIT
For undoing nuts:
Adjustable spanner
Stillson or Footprint wrench
Pair of slip-joint pliers
For cutting pipes
Junior hacksaw
Half round file (200mm – 8″)
Hole saws (15mm, 22mm, 32mm and 38mm)
Other tools:
Hand-held blowtorch
Tap tool
Plunger
Sink auger

MISCELLANEOUS TOOLS

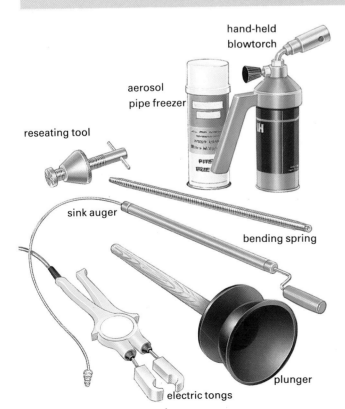

hand-held blowtorch

aerosol pipe freezer

reseating tool

sink auger

bending spring

electric tongs

plunger

Blowtorches are the traditional tools for making soldered joints in copper pipe. For the odd repair or alteration, a hand-held blowtorch with a screw or clamp-on butane canister is perfectly adequate. For major jobs, such as installing central heating, it's worth hiring a propane torch with separate gas cylinder. Blowtorches should always be used with a flame-proof board to guard against scorching.

Plug-in electric tongs are the modern alternative to blowtorches for soldered joints. They are cleaner, safer, and are available for hire from some outlets.

Plungers and sink augers ('snakes') are two tools which are worth buying to deal with minor blockages in sink traps and waste pipes.

Choose a plunger with a 100mm (4″) cup. Augers come in various patterns and lengths; the flexible steel type with a corkscrew tip and cranked handle is ideal for home use. Heavy duty versions for unblocking drains can be hired.

Bending springs stop copper pipe collapsing when bent by hand. Normally the springs fit inside the pipe, though some small sizes go on the outside. They come in three sizes, to fit 15mm, 22mm and 28mm pipe.

Aerosol pipe freezers allow you to work on sections of pipe without turning off the water – particularly useful where a stopcock has failed, or on central heating systems that are difficult to drain down.

Disposable tap reseating tools, for regrinding damaged tap washer seats, can work out much cheaper than replacing the tap. Metal versions are available for hire.

SPANNERS AND WRENCHES

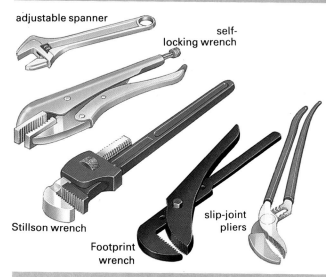

adjustable spanner

self-locking wrench

Stillson wrench

Footprint wrench

slip-joint pliers

Although it's possible to raid your car or bike toolkit for some plumbing jobs, special purpose tools are more versatile and easier to use.

Adjustable spanners are handy general purpose tools and make up in versatility what they lack in convenience. Choose one which opens to around 65mm (2½″).

Adjustable self-locking wrenches (Mole grips) are useful in an emergency but tend to chew up brass plumbing fittings.

Slip-joint ('waterpump') pliers are instantly adjustable, making them convenient to use. But they rely on the grip of the user for strength, as do *Footprint wrenches* (see below).

'Footprint' wrenches can be locked on different jaw openings, each of which is adjustable. They are simple, robust tools and offer good value for money.

'Stillson' wrenches are the most expensive type, but are easy to use and can cope with the most stubborn nuts as well as getting a grip on pipes and fittings. The adjustable head comes in various sizes, but one around 38mm (1¼″) is ideal for home use.

SPECIAL PURPOSE SPANNERS

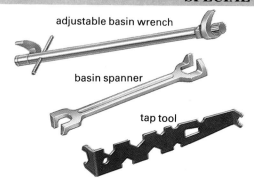

adjustable basin wrench

basin spanner

tap tool

Adjustable basin wrenches are for reaching the backnuts and fixing nuts of inaccessible taps and plumbing fittings. Most types have one or two self-adjusting heads, with a T-bar on the end of the long metal handle.

Basin spanners (sometimes called 'basin wrenches' or 'crowsfoot spanners') are simpler tools designed to do the same job. They have two heads – one to fit 15mm pipe nuts, another to fit 22mm pipe nuts.

Tap tools are inexpensive combination spanners with pressings to fit all the types of nut you're likely to encounter when changing taps. They are not particularly strong, but are good enough to cope with most situations.

CUTTING TOOLS

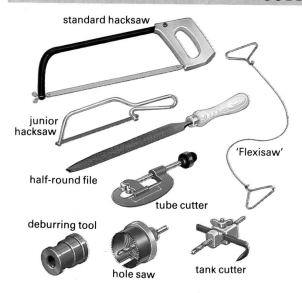

standard hacksaw

junior hacksaw

half-round file

'Flexisaw'

deburring tool

tube cutter

hole saw

tank cutter

Junior hacksaws are fine for cutting copper or plastic supply pipes. **Standard hacksaws** are better for cutting iron pipes and large diameter plastic or cast-iron drain pipes.

Hacksaw blades are measured in teeth per inch (tpi). Standard blades are 18 and 24 tpi, but for copper pipe a finer (say, 32 tpi) blade gives a cleaner cut.

Metal files are for removing the burrs left by saw cuts. The best type for home use is a *half-round second cut* file with a length of around 200mm (8″). **Deburring tools** do the same job, but are less versatile.

Tube cutters have adjustable cutting wheels which bite through the walls of copper pipe as the tool is rotated. They produce a cleaner, more accurate cut than a hacksaw, but must be used with care to avoid distorting the pipe.

Abrafile 'Flexisaw' blades have a wire handle at each end and are ideal for cutting through pipes in confined spaces.

Hole saws are drill attachments for boring large diameter holes in drain pipes, storage tanks or hot water cylinders. They are sold individually to match the common pipe sizes, and in multi-bladed sets. **Tank cutters** do the same job and are adjustable, but they are very expensive.

SPECIAL TOOLS FOR HIRE

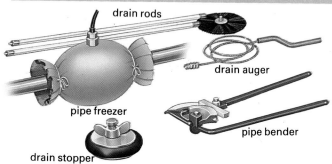

drain rods

drain auger

pipe freezer

pipe bender

drain stopper

Pipe bending machines make fast work of bending pipes – useful for major installations.

Professional pipe freezers clamp around the pipe and are pumped with refrigerant from a small electric compressor or gas canister. They are worth hiring for larger jobs – such as fitting new radiator valves.

Polypropylene drain rods can be hired in sets for unblocking inspection chambers and main drains, as can manual and power operated **drain augers**. Don't use old cane rods.

Drain stoppers are plastic plugs used to block the ends of drains prior to testing for leaks.

WHAT TO DO IN AN EMERGENCY

The floods caused by leaking or burst pipes can result in damage on a grand scale, bringing down ceilings and ruining decorations and furnishings.

In temperate climates, the combination of unexpected frost and inadequate insulation is still the major culprit. But faulty pipework, worn fittings and DIY accidents all account for their fair share of emergencies, so wherever you live it pays to know what to do when disaster strikes – and to be prepared at all times.

■ Make sure you know where your stopcocks are and which pipes they control. Ensure they all work.

■ Keep emergency repair materials (see Shopping List) in the house.

The following repairs are designed to get you by until the damage can be repaired more permanently.

.... Shopping List ....

Shopping is the last thing you want to do when faced with a flood, so be prepared.

Two-part epoxy putty (A) will plug almost any kind of leak and is useful for countless other repair jobs around the home. *Car body filler* is an effective substitute, but less easy to handle.

Two-part adhesive tape (B) is another handy repair material, especially for sealing burst soldered joints in copper pipes.

PTFE tape (C) makes it possible to re-make burst compression joints.

Potatoes (D) have saved many a plumber – if a pipe comes adrift, shove a potato over the end.

Repair kits for pipes (E) are inexpensive, and worth buying.

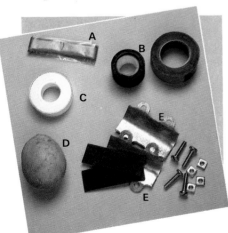

EMERGENCY CHECKLIST

PIPE ALREADY BURST

Don't panic!
If you are alone...
Turn off the water supply
☐ Do this as close to the leaking pipe as possible. If you can't find a stopcock, or it is jammed, turn off at the main stopcock. Failing this, if you have a cold storage tank and central heating expansion tank, tie up their ballvalves to stop water entering.

☐ Switch off the central heating, immersion heater, or any other water heating appliances. (If the flood is near electrical outlets, switch off at the main switch by the consumer unit or fusebox).

☐ Open all the taps to relieve pressure on the leak and get rid of any water left in the system.

If there are others in the house, get someone else to carry out the above steps while you...
☐ Locate the exact source of the leak.

☐ If the pipe has failed at a joint and it will pull apart, shove a potato on the end to stem the flow. (If the water is at mains pressure, bend the pipe or wedge something against the potato to hold it in place.)

☐ Otherwise, tie a cloth around the leak to contain it while you decide what to do next.

YOU BURST PIPE

☐ If you did it with a nail or screw, leave this where it is (it will at least contain the flow) while you turn off the water as described above.

☐ If you did it with a drill, drive a screw part-way into the hole to stem the flow. Then turn off the water and heating.

WATER POURING FROM OVERFLOW

☐ Locate which tank or cistern the pipe is connected to and tie up the affected ballvalve (the cause of the trouble). Turn off the supply to the tank.

WATER BOILING IN PIPES

☐ Turn off water heating.
☐ Leave system to cool down.
☐ Open hot taps to check water supply to hot water cylinder, which if the heating has been off during a frost may be blocked by an ice plug.
☐ If supply is OK, call plumber to replace faulty central heating or cylinder thermostat.

For lead pipes see Problem Solver page 336

AVOIDING DISASTERS

Efficiently heated, properly insulated homes are well protected against bursts caused by freezing. Even so, it's worth checking for vulnerable areas before the start of each cold season.

■ Make sure all pipes and storage tanks are insulated. But don't insulate underneath tanks in a roof space – heat rising from below helps to protect them.

■ Check that the existing insulation hasn't been disturbed or displaced. Watch out for lids left off storage tanks, or insulating jackets which have been allowed to slip down.

Pipe bends and the areas around stopcocks also have a habit of 'losing' their insulation – refix it with lengths of twisted wire.

■ Leave the heating on low if you leave the house during winter. For an extended absence, it's as well to turn off the water and drain down the entire system (but not the central heating).

■ Even in centrally heated homes, pipes against outside walls or in extensions and outhouses are particularly vulnerable to frost. Make sure these areas are kept warm.

■ Check where the rising main enters the house. This area is often overlooked when insulating.

■ Don't forget to turn off the supply to an outside tap before the cold weather starts.

And the rest of the year...

■ Beware of drilling or fixing into walls and floors where pipes may run. Look first, or check with a metal detector.

■ Watch out for pipes around radiators, which are especially prone to accidental knocks.

■ Treat lead pipes and their stopcocks with extra respect. Most lead pipework is at an age where the slightest movement may cause it to disintegrate.

■ Check that your bathroom fittings and tanks all have overflow pipes connected to the drains or to outside. The previous occupants may have 'forgotten' to fit one, probably because it was inconvenient to arrange (though this is against the Building Regulations).

Frozen pipes

If you suspect your pipes have frozen, try all the taps until you've located the approximate location of the freeze-up. If the trouble is on the rising main, storage tank or cold feed pipe to the hot water cylinder, turn off the heating as a precaution.

You can thaw the ice plug using one of the methods shown. But first, be prepared for a leak when the ice melts.

Check your house (below) for areas vulnerable to frost before every cold season. The rest of the year, watch out for blocked or missing overflows, and pipes that are prone to accidental damage.

THAWING FROZEN PIPES

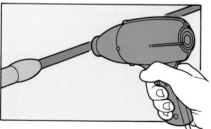

Hot air: If possible, play a hair dryer over the suspect area. Warm the whole pipe, so that the ice plug disperses quickly as soon as it begins to melt.

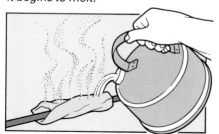

Boiling water: Alternatively, wrap cloth over the pipe and pour on boiling water. Don't apply the water direct, or you risk doing more damage.

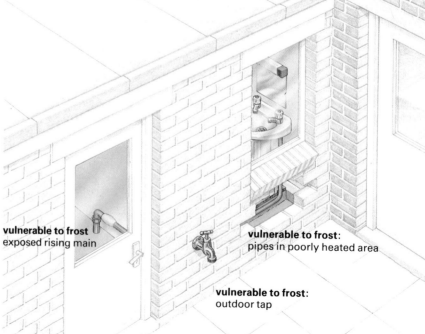

flood danger: overflow blocked or missing

vulnerable to frost exposed rising main

vulnerable to frost: pipes in poorly heated area

vulnerable to frost: outdoor tap

The illustration on the left shows labelled areas of a house:

vulnerable to frost: slipped insulating jacket/lid left off tank

vulnerable to frost: slipped pipe insulation

prone to accidental damage: radiator pipes and joints

prone to accidental damage: pipes under floors and in walls

MENDING A BURST

How you make a temporary repair depends on where the burst is.

- If it's in the middle of a pipe and there's space, use a clamp-type repair kit or improvise your own (see overleaf).
- If it's at a compression joint, undo the cover nut and wrap PTFE tape around the sealing ring, then retighten.
- If it's at a soldered joint, cover the joint with layers of two-part repair tape or a sleeve of epoxy putty (see overleaf).

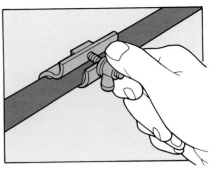

One type of repair kit consists of two clamping plates. Lay the one with the rubber seal over the burst, interlock the other, then tighten the wing nut to hold them.

Another kit uses Jubilee clips. Lay the seal over the burst and position the metal clamping plates. Undo the clips, fit them over the plates, and tighten.

Bind a burst soldered joint with two-part repair tape. Wind on a layer of one tape, cover with a layer of the second, then finish with another of the first.

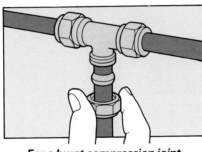

1 **For a burst compression joint,** begin by loosening off the cover nut with an adjustable spanner. Slide back the nut to reveal the sealing ring (olive).

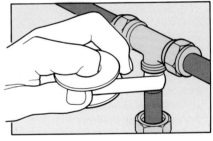

2 Wind a few turns of PTFE tape around the sealing ring, plus a little more around the threaded joint connector. Replace the cover nut and tighten.

STORAGE TANK EMERGENCIES

adjuster screw

If the overflow is running, the ballvalve is at fault. Try bending the float arm down to exert more closing pressure (on a plastic valve screw in the adjuster). Otherwise, tie up the float arm.

To plug a pin-hole leak in an old metal tank, first tie up the ballvalve and drain it. Drill out the hole and fit a nut and bolt with a washer both sides. Replace tank as soon as possible.

ACCIDENTAL DAMAGE

If possible, leave whatever caused the damage in the pipe while you turn off the water and drain down the pipe.

Where the pipe is bedded in a solid wall, you won't have space to use a repair kit – use epoxy putty or car body filler instead. This makes a substantial repair that will last for some time if left undisturbed. However, it's as well to make a proper repair before making good the damage to the surrounding plaster or you could have problems later.

1 Use a builder's bolster or an old wood chisel to hack away the plaster around the area of the burst. Take care not to cause any more damage to the pipe.

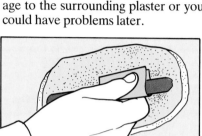

2 Rub the damaged part of the pipe with sandpaper until it becomes shiny. Then clean the whole area with white spirit or methylated spirit (alcohol).

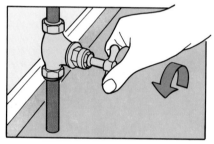

3 For epoxy putty, knead together pieces from both packs. (For car filler, mix up the resin with a little of the hardener on a piece of wood.)

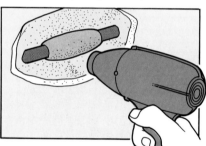

4 Press the repair mixture over and around the hole (but not too hard, or you'll block the pipe). Then play a hair dryer over it to speed hardening.

5 When the repair feels hard, you can restore a low-pressure supply – open the stopcock just a little. After a day, restore the supply to normal.

Trade tip

Your own repair kit

❝ If you're caught unprepared, wrap anything you can around the burst – belt, floorcloth, or some such – and make up your own repair kit as follows:

Take a piece of ordinary garden hose about 100mm (4″) long and slice it down the middle. Lay the two halves opposite each other over the burst – then secure with pieces of thin coathanger wire every 12mm (½″) or so. Twist the wire ends tightly using pliers. ❞

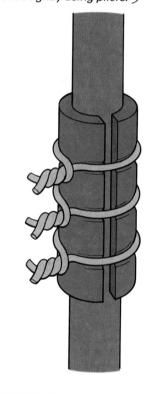

PROBLEM SOLVER

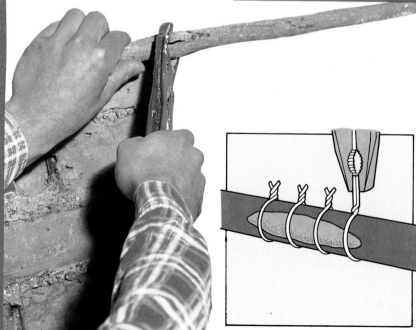

Dealing with lead pipes

When a lead pipe bursts it usually splits, so try the following repair:

■ Pinch the split closed with a self-grip wrench – set the jaws wide open, so they bear on the split area, not the whole pipe.

■ Fill what remains of the split with epoxy putty or car body filler as described above.

■ Wrap stiff wire – 30A fuse wire or thin coathanger wire – tightly around the pipe to support the repair and hold the filler in place.

If a lead pipe disintegrates completely, saw through it with a hacksaw, hammer the end closed, and fill with putty.

Support the epoxy putty repair with twists of stiff wire.

336

MENDING LEAKS IN PIPEWORK

Where a pipe or joint has already burst, calling for emergency repairs, there remains the problem of how to repair the damage permanently. Fortunately, modern plumbing fittings have put the job firmly within the scope of the do-it-yourselfer – even when the damage is on an old iron or lead pipe.

All of the repairs shown here use basic plumbing tools – wrenches for undoing pipes, hacksaws for cutting them, and PTFE tape for remaking the joints. In the case of soldered joints, you'll also need a blowtorch and heat-proof mat, plus supplies of self-cleaning flux and solder. When it comes to buying new pipe and fittings, the important thing is to know what pipe size you're dealing with. If necessary, check the external diameter and quote this to your supplier.

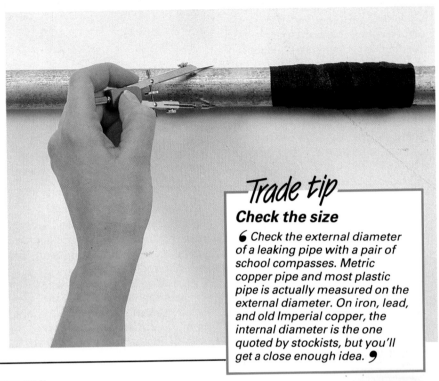

Trade tip

Check the size

❛ Check the external diameter of a leaking pipe with a pair of school compasses. Metric copper pipe and most plastic pipe is actually measured on the external diameter. On iron, lead, and old Imperial copper, the internal diameter is the one quoted by stockists, but you'll get a close enough idea. ❜

LEAKING COMPRESSION JOINTS

Most leaks on compression joints are caused by over or undertightening; the difficulty is knowing which.

If there is some thread left showing, try tightening the nut (clockwise) a half-turn. If this doesn't work – or there is no visible thread to start with – turn off the water, drain down the pipe, and dismantle the leaking side of the fitting.

Check that the pipe end reaches as far as the internal stop, with the sealing ring (olive) hard against the fitting. If the pipe is too short, you'll have to patch in a new section (see overleaf). If the olive is wrongly positioned, you *may* be able to tap it further along the pipe. However, it's safer to saw through the old

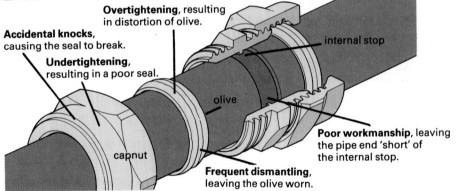

Overtightening, resulting in distortion of olive.

Accidental knocks, causing the seal to break.

Undertightening, resulting in a poor seal.

internal stop

olive

capnut

Poor workmanship, leaving the pipe end 'short' of the internal stop.

Frequent dismantling, leaving the olive worn.

olive with a hacksaw – taking care not to damage the pipe end – then fit a new one.

If everything looks OK, wrap a couple of turns of PTFE tape around the fitting side of the olive, keeping it clear of the cut pipe end, or lightly smear it with jointing compound (eg Boss Blue, Fernox XLS). Then remake the joint.

LEAKING THREADED JOINTS

Old-fashioned threaded joints in iron pipe were sealed with hemp and linseed oil compound. After years in service, the hemp can rot and allow water to seep through – although this usually results in an annoying drip rather than a jet of water.

The problem is easily remedied providing you can unscrew the pipe. But this means starting at a free end or a union, so you may have to dismantle several good joints to get at the faulty one.

1 Undo the necessary joints, using a Stillson-type wrench to grip the threaded pipe. If any are stiff, apply a little heat to soften the old jointing compound.

2 Scrape off all traces of old compound from the thread, and wrap it with at least five clockwise turns of PTFE tape before remaking each joint.

LEAKING SOLDERED JOINTS

Leaks in soldered joints are usually caused by dirt stopping the solder running freely in the first place. So long as the pipe can be drained **completely** it's usually possible to solve the problem by heating the joint with a blowtorch, and then feeding in a generous amount of self-cleaning flux followed immediately by a short length of solder. This works on pre-soldered joints as well as the end feed type.

Otherwise, it's best to fit a new joint. Sever the old one in the middle, then heat up both sides and remove them. Clean and resolder.

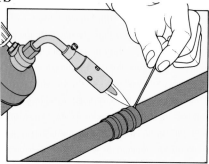

Patch an existing joint by heating until the solder bubbles, then feeding in fresh flux and solder. If the solder is drawn in, you know it has worked.

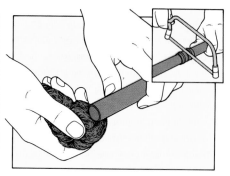

To dismantle a leaking joint, saw through the middle (inset), then heat both sides to remove the cut fitting. Clean off all traces of old solder with steel wool.

REPAIRING COPPER PIPE

Burst or damaged sections of copper pipe are best cut out and replaced with new (but see Tip opposite). A frost damaged pipe is likely to have expanded well beyond the actual burst, making it difficult to fit new joints, so don't be tempted to skimp on materials – cut out at least 300mm (12").

Where the pipe is rigidly fixed between two points it may be difficult to insert a new section with conventional couplings. There are two ways to overcome this problem.
■ Use special *slip couplings*. These have no internal stops, allowing them to be slipped on to the old pipe ends and then slid back again

over the joint once the new section is in position. Slip couplings are available in both compression and pre-soldered form.
■ Fit a *flexible connector*, which can be bent by hand to fit the gap. Flexible connectors are available with compression, soldered or push-fit joints, and come in various lengths. You shouldn't need to fit new pipe as well, but make sure you have the connector with you before cutting out the damaged section, and don't forget to allow some overlap.

On balance, flexible connectors are more convenient than slip couplings but may not look as neat.

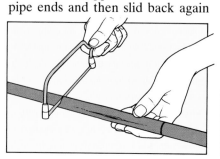

1 Cut out the damaged section of pipe with a junior hacksaw. File off any burrs and clean the pipe ends thoroughly, ready to receive the new couplings.

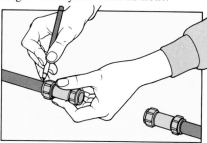

2 If using slip couplings, slide them over the pipe ends and mark their final positions in pencil. This helps when it comes to placing them over the joints.

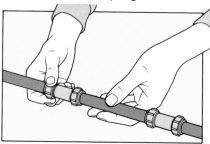

3 Mark and cut the new section to fit the gap exactly. Prepare the ends and offer it up, then slide the couplings over it and make the joints.

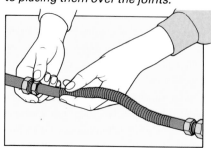

Bend a flexible connector to fit the gap and make the joints. The corrugated type can't withstand repeated bending, so take care to get it right first time.

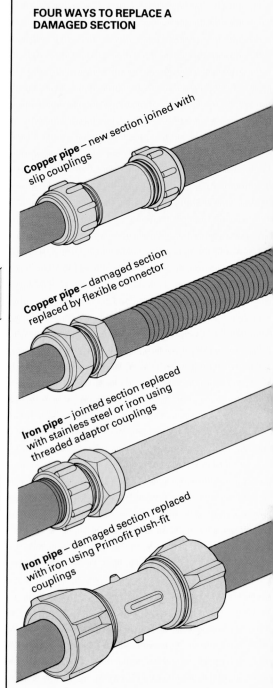

FOUR WAYS TO REPLACE A DAMAGED SECTION

Copper pipe – new section joined with slip couplings

Copper pipe – damaged section replaced by flexible connector

Iron pipe – jointed section replaced with stainless steel or iron using threaded adaptor couplings

Iron pipe – damaged section replaced with iron using Primofit push-fit couplings

Trade tip

Patching holes in copper

❝ Providing you can drain the pipe, patch pin-prick holes in copper with a blob of solder. You can repair larger holes or accidental cuts in a similar way, by soldering on a patch made from a half-section of copper pipe bent to shape.

In both cases, make sure you clean and flux the mating surfaces before applying the solder or it won't 'take'. Leave the joint to cool before testing. ❞

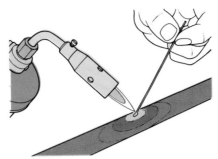

Fill a small hole with a blob of solder. Polish the pipe with steel wool first, smear on some flux, then gently melt the solder over the hole.

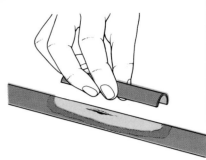

For a larger hole, heat the fluxed pipe and melt on solder to cover the damaged area. Then position the fluxed patch, heat again, and feed in more solder.

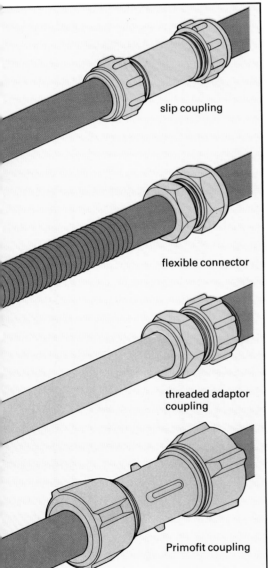

slip coupling

flexible connector

threaded adaptor coupling

Primofit coupling

REPAIRING IRON PIPE

There are three ways to repair iron pipe, depending on the extent of the damaged area, and on what materials you can get hold of.

If the damaged area is small and there is at least 25mm (1″) clearance around the pipe, buy a single *Johnston coupling* and use this to seal the hole.

Where the damage extends over a larger area, you have two choices:
■ Cut out the old section of pipe and fit a new piece of iron pipe between two Johnston couplings or *Primofit* push-fit joints.
■ Unscrew the complete damaged section at the nearest threaded joints, and fit a new section using *adaptor couplings*. This may be easier where space around the pipe is limited, though you could have to remove several sections to get at the damaged one.

In this case, use plastic or stainless steel for the replacement section (but not copper, which sets up an electro-chemical reaction with iron that eventually causes the pipework to corrode). Choose the nearest matching diameter – eg 15mm plastic for ½″ iron – then buy couplings to suit. There are versions for both stainless steel and plastic, with threaded joints on one side and compression joints on the other.

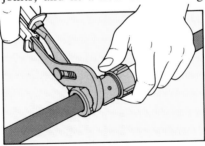

For a small hole, saw through the pipe, ease open the cut and insert a Johnston coupling. Slide it over the cut and tighten the nuts with an adjustable wrench.

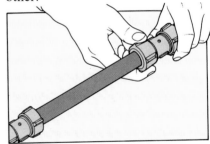

For more extensive damage, cut out a section of pipe and fit a new piece. Use Johnston couplings or Primofit joints to avoid having to make threaded joints.

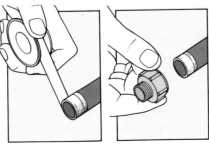

To replace a complete section, dismantle the run back to the nearest threaded joint. Clean the thread, wrap on PTFE tape, and fit a threaded adaptor . . .

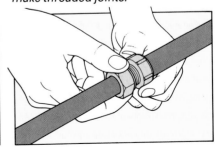

. . . then cut a new section of plastic or stainless steel pipe and compression-joint it to the adaptor. Repeat at the other end, then reassemble the run.

JOINING TO LEAD PIPE

Modern joint fittings like those on the right have made it possible to repair lead pipe without having to worry about traditional 'wiped joints'. After cutting out the damaged section, simply join in a new section of copper pipe of the equivalent internal diameter.

The only difficult part is measuring the old pipe so that you know what size fitting to buy. Lead pipe varies in wall thickness according to its grade, so look for identification marks stamped on it giving the weight and bore size – eg 'BS 602 ¾″ × 11lbs'.

If you can't find any stamp (very old pipe may not have one), either take the old damaged section with you to the merchants, or cut the pipe and then measure both the bore and the wall thickness.

When cutting out the old section, take care to support the pipe so that you don't cause any damage further along the run. Remove any burrs with a file or metal rasp, then cut the new copper section to the exact size of the gap.

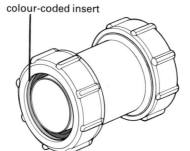

colour-coded insert

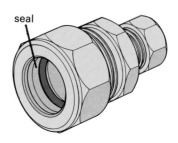

seal

'Philmac' plastic couplings have colour-coded inserts for various pipe materials and sizes.

'Leadlock' fittings come in different sizes and types – eg lead-lead, lead-copper.

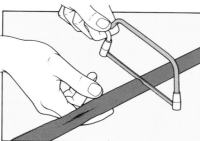

1 Saw the lead pipe with a hacksaw or coarse toothed 'Universal' saw. Cut far enough past the damage to leave you with the true size of the pipe.

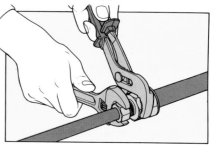

2 Join in the new section of copper pipe using a pair of your chosen fittings. Take care to assemble them in the right order then tighten the nuts.

PROBLEM SOLVER

When you can't turn the water off . . .

If you can't turn the water off – either because of a faulty stopcock, or because there isn't one – use a pipe freezer to stem the flow temporarily.

Professional pipe freezers can be hired, but it's usually easier to buy a freezing kit (eg 'Artic') consisting of an aerosol spray and freezing muff which you tie over the pipe. These kits are perfectly capable of coping with mains pressure pipes – which is usually where they are most needed.

Using a pipe freezer
Plan things thoroughly before you start: have all your tools to hand, plus a suitable size flexible connector, or a new section of pipe and slip couplings. You also need a watch or timer to time the cooling process, which is critical to the successful formation of an ice plug that will completely block the flow of water.

Aim to complete the job as quickly as possible, but don't panic – the ice plug will remain in place for up to half an hour.

Leaks in plastic pipe
The problem with repairing plastic supply pipes is knowing what type of plastic they are. **cPVC** pipe (generally white) has solvent-welded joints. Simply cut back to the nearest joints, then join in a new piece.
Polyethylene-based pipe (blue or black) can be push-fit or compression jointed (using steel reinforcing sleeves). However, its often easier to buy a copper flexible connector and use this to replace the damaged section.

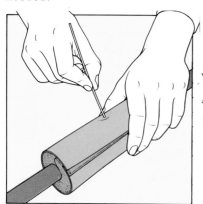

1 **Select an area to freeze**, at least 600mm (2′) **upstream** of the damaged part. Fit the tube to the muff and secure the ends tightly around the pipe.

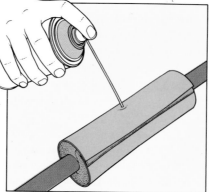

2 Fit the can to the tube and spray in the freezing agent. Wait the recommended amount of time for the ice plug to form, then get to work.

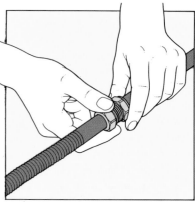

3 Cut out the damaged section and fit a flexible connector or a new piece of pipe and slip couplings. Then simply wait for the ice plug to melt.

REPAIRS TO WC CISTERNS

Niggling WC faults such as hit and miss flushing have a habit of turning into something more serious. Even so, there are surprisingly few problems that can't be fixed with just a few simple tools and the right spare part.

This section explains how flushing faults and leaks occur, and shows what can be done to fix them. Blockages and ballvalve problems are covered on pages 365 and 345-348.

How WCs work

WCs are far from complicated, but knowing how they work makes it much easier to trace and rectify faults.

A modern WC *cistern* is designed to deliver a measured quantity of water to flush the pan. This is done by storing the water in the cistern and then discharging it via a *siphon unit* operated by a lever or button. The siphon only works when the cistern is full, ensuring the right amount of water is delivered.

Flushing causes a *lifting plate* and *diaphragm* inside the siphon to rise, drawing water up and then down again into the flush pipe. From then on, the siphoning action takes over, bending the diaphragm upwards and drawing the rest of the water from the cistern into the flush pipe.

When the cistern empties, the siphoning action ceases, the

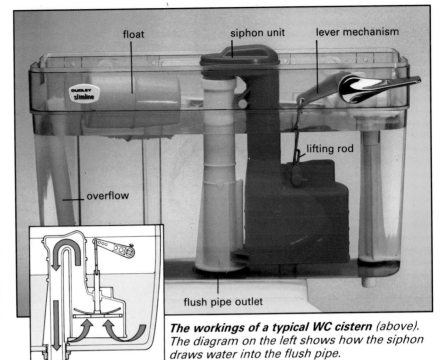

float   siphon unit   lever mechanism

lifting rod

overflow

flush pipe outlet

The workings of a typical WC cistern (above). The diagram on the left shows how the siphon draws water into the flush pipe.

diaphragm falls, and the ballvalve controlling the water inlet admits a fresh supply of water.

Variations on a theme

The description above applies to a *washdown* pan, in which the flushing water simply displaces the water in the pan trap. Modern washdown pans have a dual position siphon, to save water: pressing the lever or button and then releasing it delivers a part-flush; holding the lever down delivers a full flush.

More sophisticated WCs work on the *siphonic principle* and usually incorporate a *double trap* pan. In this case, a *pressure reducing* ('puff') pipe attached to the siphon sucks air out of the chamber between the traps as the diaphragm in the cistern rises. This causes the pan contents to empty before the flushing water enters, giving quieter operation.

TYPES OF WC PAN AND CISTERN

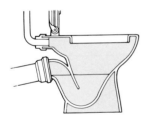

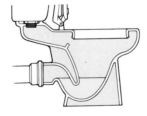

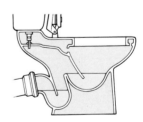

Washdown: the most common type, in which water from the cistern enters through the flush pipe and displaces the contents of the trap.

Single trap siphonic: the narrow trap outlet creates a partial vacuum which sucks out the contents as fresh water enters. Quieter in operation.

Double trap siphonic: flushing creates a vacuum in the chamber between the two traps, sucking out the contents silently as fresh water enters.

High level: the cistern and pan are connected by a long flush pipe – usually of metal, now sold as two-piece plastic.

Low level: the plastic cistern is connected to a separate pan via a length of plastic or metal flush pipe.

Close coupled: the ceramic cistern is joined directly to the pan, both being sold as a matching set.

FAULTFINDER CHART

SYMPTOM	POSSIBLE CAUSES	CURE
Poor or non-existent flushing; no feeling of resistance to flush lever or chain	■ Perished or damaged diaphragm washer ■ Broken lever arm linkage or pull chain arm linkage.	■ Renew diaphragm ■ Inspect mechanism; identify broken part and replace or temporarily repair
Poor flushing (siphonic WC)	■ The water in the pan does not draw away immediately the flush is activated but is only displaced by the new water coming in.	■ Replace the 'puff pipe' sealing washer
Resistance to flush action but only a small quantity of water enters the pan	■ Insufficient water in cistern ■ Damaged diaphragm ■ Blockage in flush pipe	■ Check water level; adjust ballvalve to suit ■ Check diaphragm ■ Check flushpipe
Leaks around cistern base or flush pipe connection	■ Perished seals on flush pipe joints.	■ Replace seals
Cistern continuously filling and emptying	■ Water coming in too fast.	■ Check ballvalve seating; restrict flow by adjusting stopcock.

NB An old-fashioned high level cistern and flushing mechanism may not be worth repairing, or you could have difficulty getting parts. See page 344 for how to replace it with a modern low-level type.

.... Shopping List ....

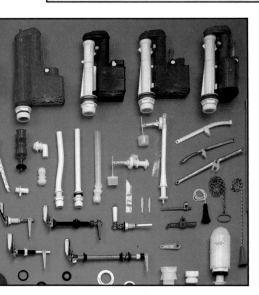

Most plumbers' merchants carry extensive ranges of parts for WCs.

As with other plumbing repairs, it's often difficult to buy replacement parts for WCs without first dismantling the mechanism concerned and then taking the part along to a plumbers' merchant to be matched. Note the make (and if possible the model) of the cistern.

This means thinking ahead: carry out repairs when you know the shops are open, and when the rest of the family won't be too upset by the water being turned off.

In an emergency, you can usually improvise something (ie stiff wire for the lever mechanism, or plastic sheet for a torn diaphragm), but short-term remedies are unlikely to stand much wear and tear.

Tools checklist: Adjustable wrench, slip-joint pliers, PTFE tape.

PERPETUAL FLUSHING

Perpetual flushing is a common condition in which water continues to enter the pan long after the WC has been flushed. It happens because the cistern fills too quickly, stopping the siphon from drawing in the air which halts the flushing sequence. Instead, the siphon and ballvalve work in perfect unison, filling and emptying at the same rate.

The answer is to slow down the filling rate of the ballvalve, either by fitting a High Pressure (HP) seat in the valve itself, or by turning the stopcock on the supply pipe to lower the water pressure.

FLUSHING PROBLEMS 1 – BROKEN LEVER MECHANISM

The weak link in a flush lever mechanism is the 'S' or 'C' hook connecting the lever arm, or push button, with the diaphragm lifting plate rod on the top of the siphon unit. New hooks are readily available from plumbers' merchants in various lengths, and in an emergency you can improvise with a piece of coathanger wire.

Breakages elsewhere in the linkage are rare, but it should be obvious how the bits go together if you need to remove them. One point to check is that a lever arm hasn't come loose from the cistern; if it has, retighten the backnut.

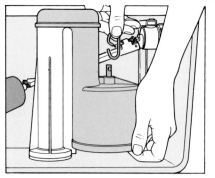

1 *If the hook has disintegrated and the rod is 'lost' inside the siphon, reach underneath the siphon unit and push up the diaphragm to reveal it.*

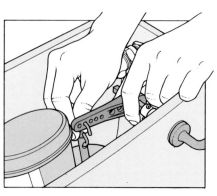

2 *On most mechanisms, the hook can be 'fiddled' straight on to the rod and lever. Sometimes, however, you need to unscrew the lever arm first.*

FLUSHING PROBLEMS 2 – SIPHON FAULTS

The most common siphon fault is a perished or torn diaphragm, but it's also possible for the siphon housing itself to have cracked.

In both cases the first step is to turn off the water supply to the cistern, then flush it to empty the contents. Bale out any remaining water or soak it up with a sponge.

Next, you must unscrew and remove the siphon unit.

On a separate cistern, you can do this without removing the cistern itself.

On a close coupled cistern, the cistern must be disconnected and unscrewed from the wall, then lifted clear of the pan so that you gain access to the siphon securing nut (see below). On a siphonic WC, it's also worth checking the seal around the 'puff pipe' which creates the vacuum between the pan traps; if this is perished or out of position, the proper flushing action will be disrupted.

Check the siphon unit body carefully for signs of cracking before reassembling the parts.

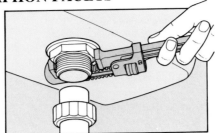

1 *On a separate cistern,* unscrew the flush pipe coupling nut, then use a large wrench or slip-joint pliers to undo the siphon nut above.

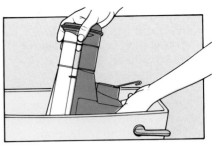

2 Lift up the siphon clear of the cistern and uncouple the hook on top of the lifting rod. You may need to remove the ballvalve float arm to clear it.

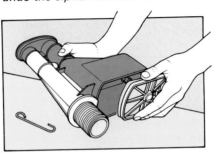

3 Slide off the lifting rod washers, noting their order, and put them to one side. Then slide the rod and plate out of the bottom of the siphon housing.

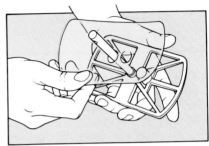

4 Remove the worn out diaphragm and draw round it to make a paper pattern. Buy a new diaphragm the same size, then reassemble in reverse order.

REMOVING CLOSE COUPLED CISTERNS

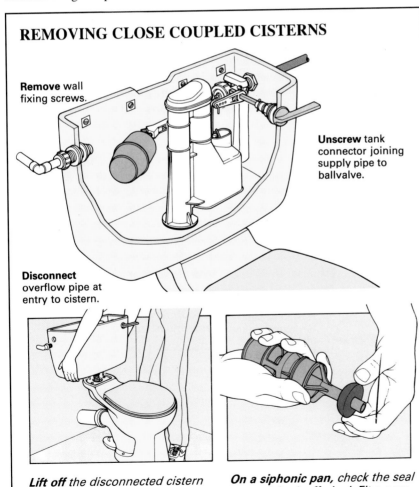

Remove wall fixing screws.

Unscrew tank connector joining supply pipe to ballvalve.

Disconnect overflow pipe at entry to cistern.

Lift off the disconnected cistern to gain access to the siphon nut and, on a siphonic pan, the seal around the 'puff pipe' passing down into the pan.

On a siphonic pan, check the seal around the 'puff pipe'. Fit a new one so that it is pushed up, as the cistern is replaced, to sit over the hole in the pan.

Trade tip

Check the flush pipe

If the diaphragm turns out to be broken, you can virtually guarantee that the rest of it is blocking the flush pipe or the flush ways in the pan. Blockages at other times are likely to be caused by foreign bodies – for example, parts of an old disinfectant dispenser.

If you can't see all the way round the flush pipe, drop a small nut on the end of a piece of string down the pipe, then use the string to drag through a small piece of rag.

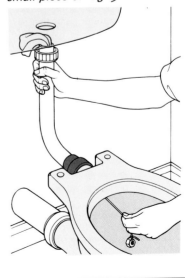

CURING LEAKS

Leaks can happen anywhere around a WC cistern, but they are most likely to occur after carrying out repair work.

Make a point of checking every washer and seal for wear as you remove it – it is false economy not to replace one which is obviously worn.

Doughnut washer – seals a close coupled cistern to the pan.

Siphon sealing washer to cistern – made of flat or stepped rubber.

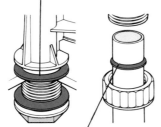

Flush pipe top washer – could be flat, or a chamfered compression type. Seal the joint with the siphon; patch temporarily with PTFE tape.

Internal flush cone – a butyl rubber or polythene push-fit fitting suitable for the new European standard WC with horizontal outlet.

Universal flush cone – a push-fit fitting which turns inside out to fit 1¼" or 1½" flush pipes. Slip a new cone on the flush pipe first.

CONVERTING A CISTERN

Converting from an obsolete high level cistern to a modern low level one may be a necessity if you can't get the parts you want. For convenience, choose a slimline plastic cistern which only requires around 150mm (6") between the wall and pan. There should also be around 600mm (24") clearance between the new cistern and the base of the pan.

Most cisterns are sold complete with siphon, lever mechanisms, ballvalve and overflow outlet. In addition you'll need a new plastic flush pipe and cone fitting, plus materials to re-route the overflow and supply pipes.

If you find later that the seat won't stay back, you can also buy cranked seat hinge fittings that bring it forward as it is raised.

Doing the conversion

Start by isolating the water supply, then disconnect and remove the old supply pipe and flush pipe; if they are badly corroded, you may have to saw through them. Afterwards, remove any screws holding the old cistern to the wall, and carefully lift it off its brackets.

The manufacturer's instructions should specify maximum/minimum heights for fitting the new cistern, so position it first, then trim the new flush pipe to suit. You'll find it easier to assemble the siphon and other parts before fitting.

Fit the flush pipe with the new cistern in place, then adapt the supply and overflow connections. The new cistern will probably offer a choice of entry positions – side or bottom – so drill out the appropriate blanking holes.

Running in the supply should be a simple matter of rerouting the pipe. To run the overflow, you'll probably have to make a new hole in the outside wall, then seal around the pipe with mastic.

WHAT'S INVOLVED

Saw through old supply, overflow and fish pipe connections which are corroded.

New cistern screws to wall. Assemble siphon, ballvalve and other parts before fitting.

New overflow – run in 19mm uPVC pipe with solvent weld joints. Use a special threaded connector at the cistern.

Check clearance behind and above pan. Slimline cisterns need around 150mm (6").

You may have a choice of side or bottom entry for the water supply and overflow connections. Bottom entry means fitting standpipes inside the cistern.

Supply pipe – reroute in copper or plastic, finishing with a tap connector for connection to the ballvalve.

New flush pipe – buy oversize then trim to fit. Fit to pan using new flush cone.

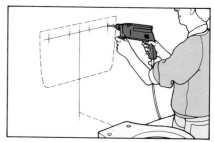

Mark a vertical line from the pan to centre the cistern, then draw a horizontal line to show where to drill and plug the wall. Screw the assembled cistern in place.

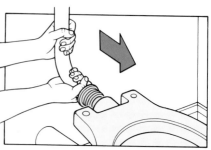

Offer up the flush pipe and trim if necessary. Fit the top to the siphon unit, then work on the flush cone and fit the lower end to the pan inlet.

REPAIRING BALLVALVES

Float-operated valves – ballvalves – are the simple devices that control the flow of water into cold storage tanks, central heating feed and expansion tanks, and WC cisterns. Like taps, they are in more or less constant use, so it's not surprising that problems sometimes occur.

Check the chart shown below for symptoms of faults and their likely causes. Leaking overflows need urgent attention, since what starts as a tell-tale drip can quickly develop into a flood – most overflows can't cope with a full-scale flow of water (strictly speaking they are only *warning* pipes). The leak may also give rise to damp problems on the wall below.

Before you start a repair, identify what sort of valve you are dealing with (see below) and make sure that the shops are open – you may have to take the valve with you to get replacement parts. Don't forget that the water will have to stay off in the meantime.

IDENTIFYING BALLVALVE FAULTS

SYMPTOM	POSSIBLE CAUSES	CURE
Valve lets water by, causing overflow	■ Washer/diaphragm worn	■ Service valve
	■ Seat cracked by frost	■ Service valve
	■ Valve mechanism jammed due to scale	■ Service valve or replace
	■ Leaking float	■ Empty float and seal or replace
	■ Valve corroded due to dezincification	■ Replace valve with dezincification-resistant type
Valve won't let water by, causing tank to empty	■ Valve jammed due to lack of use (very common on C.H. feed and expansion tanks)	■ Service valve
Tank slow to fill	■ Valve outlet blocked with grit	■ Service valve
	■ Wrong seat or valve	■ Replace seat or valve
Excessive noise from valve as tank fills	■ Wrong seat or valve	■ Replace seat or valve
	■ Worn valve	■ Service or renew valve
	■ Water hammer due to high pressure	■ Turn down pressure or fit different valve
	■ Float bouncing on surface of water	■ Fit damper to float

TYPES OF BALLVALVE

All ballvalves work on the same basic principle: an air-filled float, attached to the valve via an arm, rises and falls with the water level in the tank.

Attached to the arm inside the valve is a plunger and plastic diaphragm (diaphragm type), or a piston with rubber washer (piston type), which closes off the water supply when the level is at the right height.

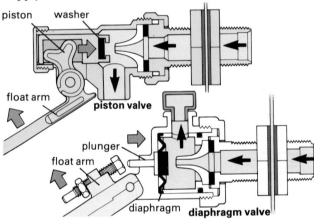

Portsmouth (piston type). For many years the standard valve on both tanks and WCs. Older all-brass versions are still common; newer models have a plastic piston and seating which is less prone to scale build-up. The Water Byelaws now ban Portsmouth valves from new installations.

Croydon (piston type) Rare, and now obsolete. Replace with a newer type if faulty.

Brass Equilibrium (piston type). Similar to the Portsmouth, but with an extra chamber that balances the force of the water pressure rather like a canal lock – resulting in quiet, smooth operation. Used in areas with abnormally high or variable water pressure.

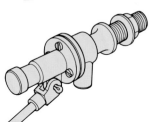

Garston (diaphragm type). Scale-resistant valve, usually plastic but sometimes brass, which has no moving parts in contact with the water. No tools needed for servicing.

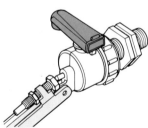

New Brass Diaphragm (diaphragm type – BS 1212 part 2). Similar in operation to the Garston, but with its water outlet mounted above the valve to eliminate the risk of back-siphonage.

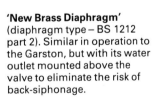

Torbeck (diaphragm type). A patented plastic valve for WC cisterns. It has a built-in damper and a collapsible underwater outlet which permits silent filling without risk of back-siphonage. ('Silent filling' tubes on ordinary valves are banned under the Water Byelaws).

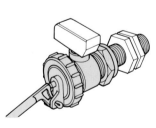
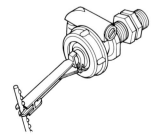
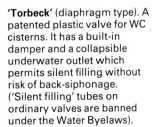

SERVICING BALLVALVES

Most ballvalves can be dismantled for cleaning and servicing, leaving the tail and supply pipe connection undisturbed. This is always preferable, especially if the supply pipe is lead, but it's not worth trying to service a very old or badly scaled-up valve – replace it instead as described overleaf.

New parts – washers, seats, floats – are widely and cheaply available from DIY stores or plumber's merchants. But as with taps, you may need to take the old parts with you.

The first step is to turn off the water supplying the valve at the nearest stopcock. Check the water has stopped flowing by pressing down on the float arm.

When unscrewing the valve body, take care not to let it turn or you'll break the seal on the tank/WC cistern and strain the supply pipe connection.

Tools and materials: Adjustable spanner, wrench, self-locking wrench, small screwdriver, pliers, PTFE tape.

SERVICING A PISTON VALVE

After removing the working part of the valve (see step below), dismantle it following the diagram.
■ Remove the split pin and unscrew the end cap, then wiggle out the float arm and slide out the piston.
■ Hold the piston with a screwdriver and unscrew the end. (Newer pistons are in one piece.)
■ Dig out the old washer; replace it

with an identical size and type.
■ Replace the seating with one of the same size and pressure rating if it looks worn or is cracked.
■ Scour off any scale, then give the piston and body a thorough clean with metal polish.
■ Before reassembling, check the condition of the union washer and replace if necessary.

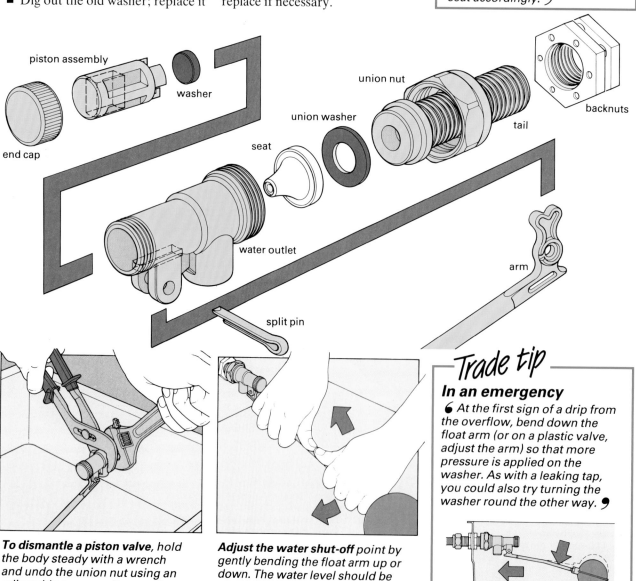

To dismantle a piston valve, hold the body steady with a wrench and undo the union nut using an adjustable spanner. Remove to a bench.

Adjust the water shut-off point by gently bending the float arm up or down. The water level should be about 25mm (1") below the overflow outlet.

SERVICING A DIAPHRAGM VALVE

■ On most diaphragm valves, the diaphragm is immediately behind the retaining nut (see diagram). But on one type the nut is in the middle of the valve (inset), and you have to slide out a cartridge to expose the diaphragm. In this case, take care not to damage the sealing washer behind the seat.

■ Dig out the diaphragm with a flat-bladed screwdriver and check that the seat is in good condition.

■ The new diaphragm only fits one way, so check the old one to see which side was marked by the seat.

■ Reassemble the valve and screw the retaining nut back on by hand. Turn on water and test immediately.

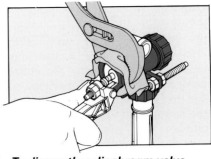

To dismantle a diaphragm valve, simply unscrew the retaining nut (if it is stiff, loosen it using an adjustable wrench with padding in the jaws).

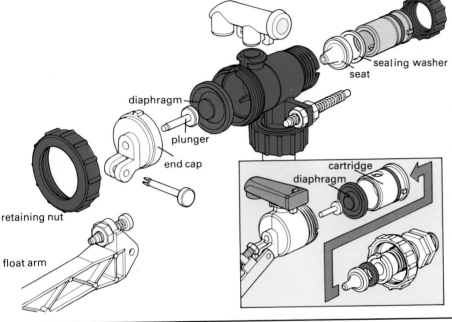

sealing washer
seat
diaphragm
plunger
end cap
retaining nut
float arm

cartridge
diaphragm

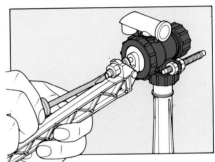

Adjust the water level by loosening the locknuts on the adjuster and screwing it in or out. Re-adjust when the washer has bedded in.

SERVICING A TORBECK VALVE

A constant drip from the front of the valve during filling is normal, but if you suspect the diaphragm needs replacing:

■ Unscrew the front of the valve body.

■ Dig out the diaphragm and clean in soapy water. It could be that this cures the problem; if not, replace the diaphragm.

■ Replace the diaphragm with the white spike pointing towards the valve. Position the bush on the outer edge of the diaphragm on the steel pin fixed to the valve body.

■ Replace the front cover, checking that the float arm engages on the plastic pins.

■ Adjust the water level by altering the position of the float on the arm.

Instead of different size seatings the Torbeck valve comes with a choice of flow restrictors for high and medium pressure. But if the valve takes more than 20 seconds to fill, it's more likely that the filter is blocked so check this first. (Early models may not have a filter.)

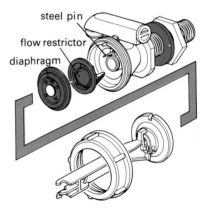

steel pin
flow restrictor
diaphragm

CURING FLOAT PROBLEMS

■ If the float develops a leak, the valve won't shut off at the correct point. Unscrew the float, empty out the water, and patch the hole with epoxy putty or tie a plastic bag over it. Replace as soon as possible.

■ Sometimes – and especially on Portsmouth valves – the float bounces on the ripples as the tank fills, causing water hammer in the supply pipe. You can cure this by fitting a purpose-made damper to the float arm. Alternatively, hang a punctured yoghurt carton in the tank, suspended from the float arm by a length of galvanized wire.

■ In a WC cistern, the float may catch on the flushing mechanism causing the valve to jam open. If necessary bend a brass arm so that the float is free to move throughout its travel; plastic arms generally have a choice of fitting positions.

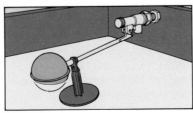

Fit a damper – proprietary or home-made – to the float arm to stop the float bouncing.

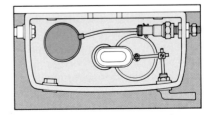

On a WC cistern, make sure the float doesn't jam – bend the arm or reposition the float to clear.

REPLACING A VALVE

New ballvalves aren't expensive, so if you can't get the parts to repair the old one (or it isn't worth repairing) then buy a matching replacement. Replacing the entire valve is likely to cause problems, so aim to 'graft' the working part of the new one on to the tail of the old one so that you don't have to disturb the supply pipe. Make sure you fit a new sealing washer where the two halves join.

If you have to replace the entire valve, or you are changing it for another type:

■ Try to ensure the new valve has the same length tail as the old one; if not, you may have to modify the supply pipe (see Problem Solver).
■ On a WC cistern, the length of the float arm may also be critical (though you can probably swap over the old one).
■ Specify whether the valve is for high pressure or low pressure application (see Tip on page 346).
■ If you live in a water area where dezincification is a problem, make sure the valve is plastic, or has a **DR** mark, indicating that it is dezincification-resistant.

Before you start, apply some penetrating oil to the connector nut and valve backnuts. Then, after turning off the water, open a tap lower down in the system to drain any water left in the supply pipe.

New valves are often supplied with self-sealing, nylon backnuts which don't need washers, but make sure the area around the nuts is clean and free of old jointing compound so that the seals are watertight. On a WC, don't over-tighten the nuts.

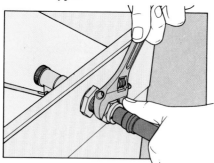

1 Taking care to support the supply pipe, undo the tap connector nut linking it to the valve tail. Pull the joint apart and gently ease the pipe away.

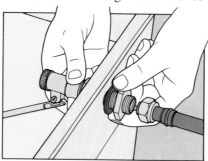

2 Using slip-joint pliers and an adjustable wrench, loosen the backnuts holding the old valve in place. Unscrew the outer backnut and lift away the old valve.

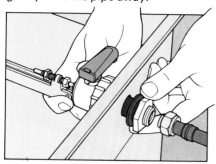

3 Fit the new valve in place, not forgetting any sealing washers, and screw on the outer backnut. Hold the valve upright as you tighten it.

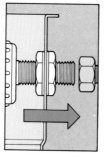 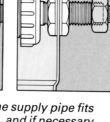

4 Check that the supply pipe fits the valve tail, and if necessary adjust the backnuts. Fit a new fibre washer and retighten the connector nut.

Trade tip

Valves with standpipes

❝ Some modern WCs require a bottom entry valve, which includes an integral standpipe. Valve operation is identical to the usual side-entry type.

If you're fitting an identical replacement, you should be able to leave the standpipe in place and simply undo the valve at the union. Otherwise, be sure to quote the length of the standpipe when ordering a new valve. ❞

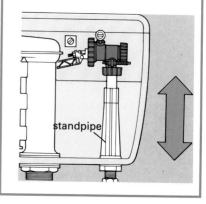

standpipe

PROBLEM SOLVER

Bridging the gap

If you can't get a new valve to match up to the existing supply pipe, don't force the pipe – it may cause the joint to leak, or weaken others along the run.

Normally, adjusting the positions of the backnuts on the valve tail gives you enough room to manoeuvre. Failing this, you may find that a screw-on *tap shank adaptor* is long enough to bridge the gap. Otherwise, you have no option but to saw off the old tap connector and fit a new one, together with a new section of pipe.

Persistent valve problems

The Keraflo valve is a patented design which uses ceramic discs instead of washers to shut off the water. It is only made to fit WC cisterns, but is claimed to be maintenance free and very reliable.

The valve comes in a basic unit to which you add a side entry connector or a separate standpipe for bottom entry. The fitting procedure is the same as for other ballvalves, but you may need an extending arm if the flushing handle restricts the float travel.

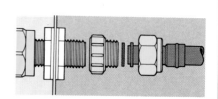

You may be able to bridge a small gap using a tap shank adaptor.

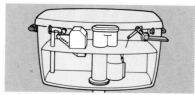

The Keraflo ceramic disc ballvalve for fitting to WCs.

REPAIRING LEAKING TAPS

Taps are usually the hardest working components in a plumbing system, so it's hardly surprising if they develop the occasional fault.

Leaking from the spout is usually due to a worn or split washer – the part that seals the tap's inlet. So long as you know where to turn off the water, fitting a new washer is a simple job requiring only basic tools. And if this doesn't cure the problem, it's usually possible to regrind the seat – the part the washer closes against. This is much easier (and cheaper) than replacing the tap – see page 352.

Leaking from the handle, or a handle that's hard to turn, are two faults to do with the tap mechanism. Since you'll be exposing this to replace the washer, it's worth servicing it as well – see page 351.

Spare parts for taps are sold by plumber's merchants and hardware stores. First identify what type and size of tap you're dealing with (see below). Then, if possible, take the old parts with you so that you can buy matching replacements. Failing this, make sure you can describe the tap and what it is fitted to.

Washers, seals and other parts are cheap, so buy a set of spares so that you don't get caught out again. Also, buy a tube of silicone gel for lubricating the mechanism.

KNOW YOUR TAPS

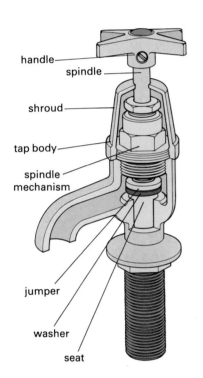

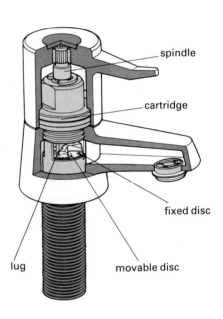

Taps come in many styles (see below), but work in one of two ways:

Washered taps (left) have a spindle mechanism, on the end of which is a backing plate (jumper) holding the washer. Turning the handle closes the washer against the inlet (seat), shutting off the water.

Washers need replacing at intervals, as do the seals around the spindle. It's also possible for the seat to wear or become damaged.

Ceramic disc taps (right) have a pair of finely ground discs which open and close the water inlet as the handle (often a simple lever) is moved through a quarter turn.

The diamond-hard discs are supposedly maintenance-free, but faults have been known to occur and most manufacturers offer free replacement cartridges for taps under five years old. The cartridges come in left (hot) and right (cold) versions and aren't interchangeable.

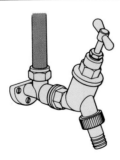

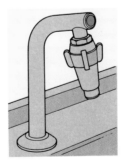

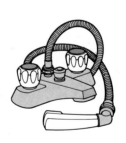

Pillar taps come in two inlet sizes – ½" for sink and basin taps, ¾" for baths.

Older styles have chromed brass capstan handles and shrouds; newer designs have clear acrylic handles. Ceramic disc versions often have levers.

Bib taps are for outside use and utility rooms, and are normally the ½" size. They work in the same way as washered pillar taps and take the same washers, but use leather washers outside for increased frost resistance.

Supataps can be rewashered without turning off the water. The special washers come ready-fitted to a brass backing plate (jumper), but vary widely between models and aren't easy to find; if you do, buy plenty of spares.

Mixer taps for the kitchen may be *two-hole* or *monobloc* (single hole), with washered or ceramic disc mechanisms.

A swivel spout may leak around its base when the seals inside wear out, but these are easily replaced.

Bath shower mixers, like sink mixers, may have washered or disc mechanisms.

Water is switched from spout to shower head by a washered *diverter mechanism.* When water comes out of both outlets, washer needs renewing.

CHANGING WASHERS

Start the job by turning off the water and opening the tap to drain down what's left in the pipe.

Next, gain access to the tap mechanism. On plastic handled taps, the handle pulls off, or is held by a screw under the coloured insert (prise this up with a screwdriver).

On brass taps, unscrewing the shroud will often leave enough room to get a spanner on the mechanism nut. If not, undo the handle – held by a small grub screw – and remove the shroud completely. (See Problem Solver for problem handles.)

Washer fittings vary widely (see Step 2), so have a small crosshead screwdriver and a pair of long nosed pliers handy. If you can't get the old washer off, or the new one is a loose fit, prise off the jumper and fit a new combined washer/jumper or a plastic insert (see overleaf).

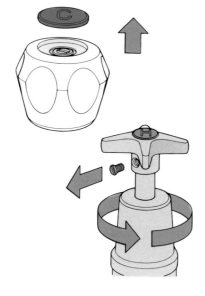

Plastic handles have a hidden screw or pull off the spindle.
Brass handles are held by a small screw. The shroud unscrews.

Trade tip
Washer wise

❝ If you're stuck without a washer, try turning the worn one the other way around, – but don't expect it to last long.

If you have a Continental tap, you may not be able to buy exact-size replacements. In this case buy the nearest Imperial size and trim the washer to fit with a Surform-type plane. ❞

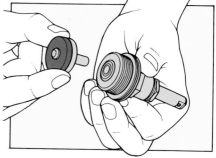

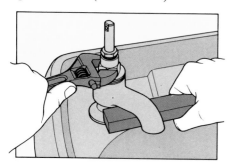

1 Remove the handle or loosen the shroud enough to get an adjustable spanner on the mechanism nut. Support the tap firmly, and unscrew.

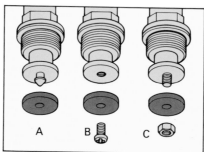

2 The washer could be a push fit (A), screwed to its jumper (B), or held by a small nut (C). Prise off or undo the old one and fit a replacement.

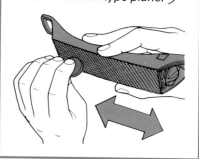

Alternatively, the washer may be combined with its jumper, which is a push-fit into the spindle. Use this type to replace a washer seized in its jumper.

REPAIRING SUPATAPS

You shouldn't need to turn the water off to rewasher a Supatap – but find out where to do it just in case. The temporary seal relies on a check valve dropping down from inside the tap when you unscrew the mechanism – so when you see the pin poke out, don't try to push it back in or you're likely to end up soaked!

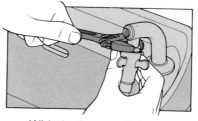

1 With the Supatap fully open, loosen the retaining nut using an adjustable spanner and unscrew the nozzle section from the body of the tap.

2 The washer is fitted to the anti-splash device inside the nozzle. Tap it out through the larger end and prise off the washer with a small screwdriver.

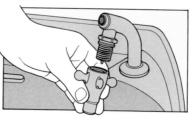

3 Fit an exact size replacement, refit the anti-splash device in the nozzle, and screw the nozzle back on the tap (water will spray as you do this).

CERAMIC DISC TAPS

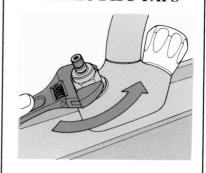

Remove the cartridge as for a washered tap. Inside the cartridge are the two ceramic discs, one of which remains fixed while the other is turned across it to open the inlet.

Sometimes, the small lugs turning the movable disc wear down, allowing it to slip very slightly and leaving the inlet partly open. The only cure is to fit a complete new cartridge.

SERVICING TAPS

While rewashering, check the tap for leaks around the handle and shroud, and for binding.

Leaks are caused by wear in the spindle seals. Older type *rising* spindles are sealed with fibre packing; new type *non-rising* spindles have rubber 'O' ring seals.

On the old type, undo the *gland* nut on top of the mechanism (which governs the tightness of the spindle). Wind a few turns of PTFE tape around the spindle and poke it down into the body of the mechanism, then apply a smear of silicone gel and replace the nut. Try the tap:

if the spindle is too tight, loosen the nut a fraction; if it still leaks, tighten half a turn.

On the new type, hook out the circlip holding the spindle and withdraw it from below. Lever off the 'O' rings, smear on some silicone gel, and slide on the replacements.

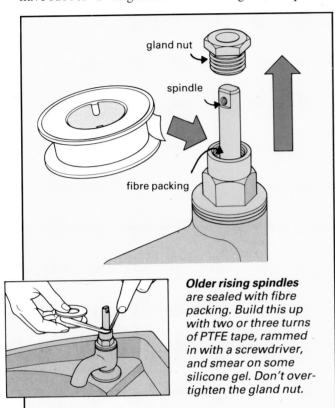

Older rising spindles are sealed with fibre packing. Build this up with two or three turns of PTFE tape, rammed in with a screwdriver, and smear on some silicone gel. Don't over-tighten the gland nut.

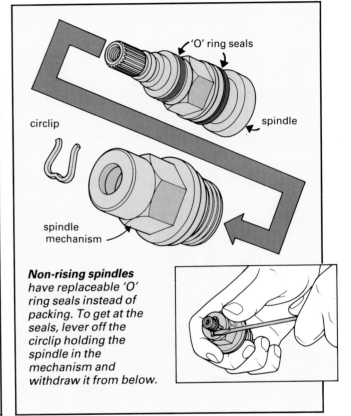

Non-rising spindles have replaceable 'O' ring seals instead of packing. To get at the seals, lever off the circlip holding the spindle in the mechanism and withdraw it from below.

MIXER TAP REPAIRS

Replacing the washers on washered mixer taps is the same as for pillar taps – they simply have two mechanisms within a single body.

Leaking swivel spout

Renewing the 'O' ring seals on a leaking swivel spout means removing the spout. It may be held by:

■ A small grub screw on the tap body which slots into a groove in the spout to lock it.

■ A screw-on shroud, underneath which is a circlip. Dig the circlip out with a small screwdriver or pliers.

■ A lug which passes through a slot in the tap body. Simply align the spout and body, then pull.

Replacing a diverter

There is no need to turn off the water to replace the diverter washer on a shower mixer.

In the most common design, the

washer is mounted on the end of the sprung-loaded diverter mechanism inside the tap body. To remove the mechanism, lift up the diverter knob or lever, get a small adjustable spanner on the flattened stem, and unscrew anti-clockwise.

The washer is attached to the mechanism like an ordinary tap washer. Remove it by undoing the retaining nut, fit a new one, then refit the diverter mechanism.

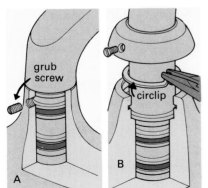
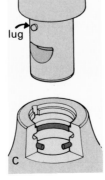

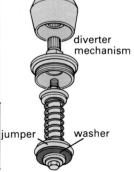

Mixer swivel spouts may be held by a grub screw (A), a circlip under a screw-on shroud (B), or a lug which you release by aligning the spout with the tap body (C).

Shower mixer diverter mechanisms screw into the body of the tap. The diverter washer is usually held in its jumper by a small nut or crosshead screw.

RESEATING A TAP

When a tap seat becomes worn, no amount of rewashering will stop it dripping. Nor is the problem only confined to old taps: new tap seats can wear prematurely if particles of grit or metal find their way into the mechanism. Either way, regrinding the seat is a lot easier and cheaper than replacing the taps. There are two ways to go about it.

Metal reseating tools can be hired with interchangeable cutters to suit ½″ and ¾″ taps.

Plastic reseating kits consist of a universal clip-together plastic tool, plus spare washers and a set of disposable abrasive grinding discs.

In both cases, check the seat first for signs of score marks. These will show up as black lines when you start grinding, but disappear as soon as the seat is properly ground-in. Make sure you don't over-grind.

Trade tip

No reseating tool?

❝ *If you can't get hold of a reseating tool, there are two other things to try:*

Fit a Holdtite washer, *which sits deeper inside the seat than an ordinary washer to compensate for any wear. The only drawback is that the tap must be turned more times to open and close it. The Holdtite washer comes with its own jumper, which has a peg that fits most tap mechanisms.*

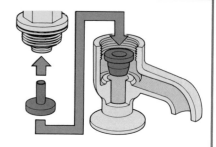

Fit a 'universal' plastic insert *which comes in a kit to suit many older tap designs.*
■ *Remove the tap mechanism as you would for rewashering.*
■ *Push the insert into the seat with the flange uppermost.*
■ *Exchange the old jumper and washer for the new ones supplied.*
■ *Reassemble the tap, then open and close the tap a few times to push the new seat fully home.* ❞

1 **To use a metal tool,** fit the correct size cutter for the tap and screw it into the tap body. Adjust until you feel the cutter touch the seat.

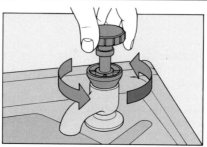

2 Turn the handle a few times, then remove the tool and check the effect. Repeat, checking frequently, until any score marks on the seat disappear.

Plastic reseating tools can be used like metal ones, but have disposable grinding discs. To grind, push into the tap body and press down while turning.

PROBLEM SOLVER

Removing stubborn handles

If a tap handle proves difficult to remove, it's a good idea to try the other tap – you may be forcing the handle against a hidden screw.

Failing this, there are several things to try before resorting to brute force.

Plastic handles which screw on may have had the screw covers stuck down – try prising them up with a small screwdriver.

If you are sure they are the pull-off type, try tapping a pair of wooden wedges underneath to lift them off.

It's also possible that the handles have broken and been glued back on. In this case you have no choice but to break or saw them off and fit new ones.

Brass handles and shrouds are easily damaged; use a pair of slip-joint pliers (rather than

Mole grips) and wrap the jaws in a rag to avoid scratching.

If a handle remains stuck after you've removed the grub screw, wrap it with a cloth and pour on boiling water followed by cold. Alternatively, apply a squirt of penetrating oil, leave for an hour, and try again.

Another trick is to use the shroud to force off the head.
■ Open the tap fully and undo the shroud.
■ Place two small pieces of wood under either side so that you force the shroud against the handle.
■ Close the tap in the normal way. As you do so, the handle should start to lift off.

If the shroud is stuck, you could try loosening it with a *chain wrench* – used by car mechanics to remove oil filters (remember to protect the chrome).

Use the shroud to force off a stubborn chromed brass handle.

Loosen a shroud with slip-joint pliers. Pad the jaws with cloth.

PLUMBING IN A WASHING MACHINE

Plumbing in a washing machine for fully automatic operation is a job where it pays to have a go yourself. Often, modern connection gadgets make it possible to do without plumbing skills altogether. And even where the installation isn't quite so easy, you can save money by doing some of the work yourself, then calling in a plumber for the tricky parts.

Siting the machine

The job falls neatly into two stages: providing a water supply, and arranging drainage.

As a rule, the nearer the washing machine is to hot and cold pipes and to a drainage outlet, the easier the installation. For many people, this means siting the machine in the kitchen, near the sink. But cloak-rooms and downstairs utility rooms shouldn't be ruled out, since they, too, often have the necessary plumbing facilities – plus the advantage of more space.

Bathrooms are more of a problem. The regulations on using electrical appliances here are so restrictive that in most cases it simply isn't practical to install a washing machine. In a very large bathroom it may just be possible, but seek expert advice before proceeding.

Making connections

When you've decided on a location, run through the connection options overleaf and see which suit it best. You should also read through the installation details supplied with the washing machine and make a note of any special recommendations.

Supply With some machines, you have a choice of connecting to both hot and cold supplies, or to cold only (so saving on hot water). The connections are the same for both.

Drainage Most machines pump out the waste water, allowing you to connect the drain hose to the nearest waste pipe via a special trap or a screw-in connector. But a few still rely on siphonage to remove the waste, and must be connected via a vertical *standpipe*.

Some makers also advise stand-pipe installation as a safeguard against blockages caused by fluff. In this case, connection by any other method may invalidate the warranty.

Where a washing machine is within easy reach of water supply pipes and a drainage outlet, it can be plumbed in simply using DIY connectors.

....Shopping List....

Washing machine plumb-in kits normally give you all the parts needed for Supply or Waste Options 1 overleaf. For other types of supply connection you may need:

Washing machine stoptaps These are sold with push-fit or compression connections for the supply pipes, and threaded connections for the machine supply hoses.

15mm supply pipe and fittings These can be plastic push-fit or copper with compression joints. Work out the length and direction of the pipe runs beforehand: you'll need tee fittings for joining to the existing pipes, plus 90° elbows for making bends. Buy pipe clips, wallplugs and screws if the runs are longer than 1m (3′).

For other types of waste connection you may need:

Washing machine trap This replaces an existing plastic sink trap and has a mixture of screw-on and adjustable push-fit parts, enabling alignment with the existing pipes. There is normally a push-on fitting for the machine outlet hose.

Standpipe These are sold in kit form, complete with trap. Buy 38mm (1½″) plastic pipe plus wall clips to make up a new waste run, or a *swept tee* fitting for connection to an existing waste pipe. Choose from push-fit or solvent-weld (glued) joints. See Problem Solver for other types of waste connection.

Tools (depending on connection method): junior hacksaw, adjustable spanner, electric drill.

Self-cutting connectors (below) for the supply and waste pipes get round the need for traditional plumbing skills.

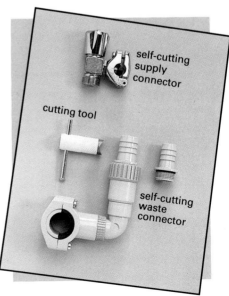

self-cutting supply connector

cutting tool

self-cutting waste connector

SUPPLY OPTIONS

1: SELF-CUTTING CONNECTORS

The simplest way of joining to the existing hot and cold pipes is to use self-cutting connectors. As long as the taps on the fittings are kept closed, you don't even have to turn off the water.

Each connector has a clamp which you fit around the supply pipe, and a stoptap which then screws into the clamp. The stoptap inlet contains a circular cutter that automatically breaks through the pipe wall, plus a washer to guarantee a watertight join.

Various makes work slightly differently, but two main types of stoptap are available. Within reach of the washing machine hoses, choose taps with threaded outlets that allow you to attach the hoses directly. For connections some way from the machine, opt for taps with compression fittings on the outlets so you can run branch pipes as in Supply Option 2, and then fit hose connectors to the pipe ends.

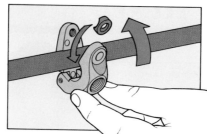

1 Decide where to site the stoptap, then offer up the clamp to the pipe. Some types fix to the wall, in which case drill and plug, then screw in place.

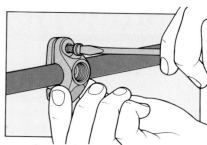

2 Screw the clamp body together over the pipe. Some are in two parts while others are hinged. The clamp body has a screw thread inside to accept the tap body.

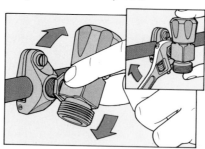

3 Screw the tap body into the clamp until it's hand-tight. Some types need an extra quarter of a turn with a spanner. Adjust the tap body so it is vertical.

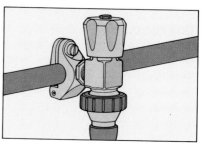

4 The tap shown is threaded for direct hose connection. With the sealing washer inside the plastic hose connector, screw it on and tighten with a spanner.

2: BRANCH PIPES WITH TEES

The conventional way of supplying a washing machine is to turn the water off and insert tee fittings in the supply pipes. From here, you run branch pipes to a point near the machine and fit compression-jointed stoptaps with threaded outlets to accept the machine hoses. See overleaf for how to make connections in copper pipes.

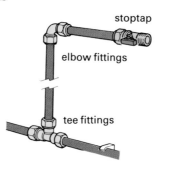

stoptap

elbow fittings

tee fittings

3: STOPTAP TEE FITTINGS

This is a variation of Option 2, used where the connections to the supply pipes can be made close to the machine, but where you aren't allowed to use self-cutting connectors.

Instead, you cut the supply and fit compression jointed tee fittings with built-in stoptaps. As with Option 1, these allow the hoses to be attached direct.

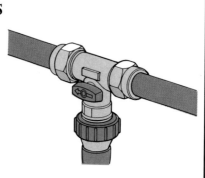

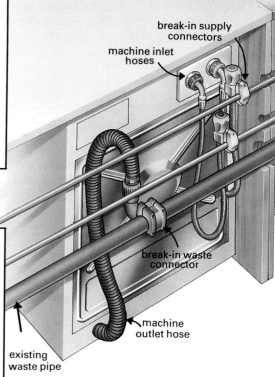

break-in supply connectors

machine inlet hoses

break-in waste connector

machine outlet hose

existing waste pipe

Above: A typical installation *near the kitchen sink, using self-cutting connectors to break into the supply and waste pipes.*

WASTE OPTIONS

1: DIRECT CONNECTION

If there is a sink waste pipe running behind or along the side of the machine (and providing the machine is suitable), connect the outlet hose directly to it using a self-cutting connector similar to the one used in Supply Option 1. Such connectors are designed to fit standard 38mm (1½″) pipe.

You don't need any special tools: the connector has its own cutting tool which is removed from the saddle clamp once the hole has been cut, ready for the hose connector assembly to be screwed to the clamp body.

1 Fit the adjustable clamp (complete with internal seal) round the waste pipe and screw in the cutter to make the hole. Remove the cutter.

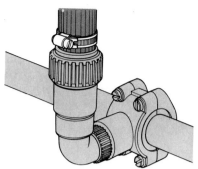

2 Attach the hose connector and non-return valve to the clamp, with or without the elbow supplied, depending on the angle. Then fit the machine outlet hose.

2: REPLACE SINK TRAP

Near the kitchen sink, it may be easier to replace the sink trap with one incorporating a washing machine hose outlet.

Unscrew the old trap, using a damp cloth to grip the locking rings. Assemble the new trap according to the instructions, then screw to the sink outlet and waste pipe, letting the trap's push-fit joints take up any adjustment. Finally, fit the drain hose to the outlet on the side of the trap.

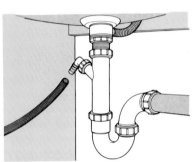

Washing machine traps have an outlet for the machine's drain hose. They are a simple replacement for the whole of an existing plastic sink trap.

3: FIT STANDPIPE

A standpipe prevents siphonage of the waste during washing by incorporating an air break.

The standpipe itself should be about 600mm (24″) high (check the machine instructions), and must have a trap fitted below it. If there is an existing waste pipe running near the machine at floor level, connect the standpipe as shown. See Problem Solver if you have to run a new waste pipe.

1 Mark the position of the swept tee fitting on the waste pipe, allowing for the amount taken up by the joints. Cut the pipe with a junior hacksaw.

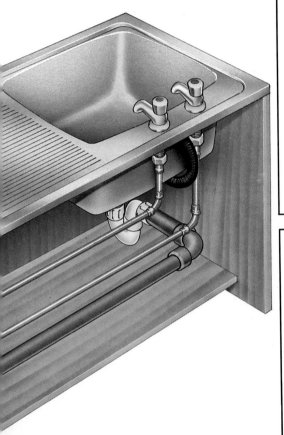

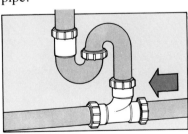

2 Fit the tee fitting with the swept part angled in the direction of the flow. Follow by adding the two parts of the trap and the standpipe.·

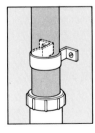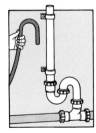

3 Secure the assembly to the wall using 38mm (1½″) pipe clips. Finally, simply slip the washing machine outlet hose into the top of the standpipe.

Local bye-laws
Some water authorities only permit certain types of connection, and others forbid taking the cold supply direct from the rising main. Phone the authority's engineer's department and check what rules apply in your area before buying any parts.

TRADITIONAL CONNECTIONS

Breaking into the hot and cold supplies (and if necessary, running branch pipes) isn't too difficult so long as you can turn off the water. The method shown uses 15mm copper pipe with compression joints. This and other methods are covered more fully in later chapters.

If you take the cold supply from the rising main, don't forget to turn off the water at the main stopcock. If the supply is fed from a storage tank, check the machine's instructions – you may need to remove the flow inhibitor fitted on the inlet hose. In all cases, open the nearest taps to drain down the pipes before cutting into them.

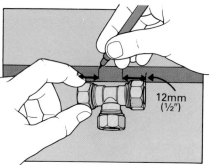 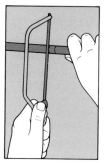

1 *To fit a tee*, offer up the fitting and mark how much needs to be cut out of the supply pipe. Subtract 12mm (½") each side to allow for the joints.

2 Cut the pipe using a junior hacksaw. Use an old knife or nailfile to smooth off the ends, then slip on the capnuts and sealing rings (olives).

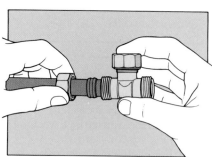 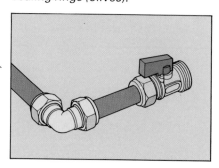

3 Slip the tee over one pipe end, then slot in the other pipe end. Slide the olives up to the tee, wrap on some PTFE tape, then tighten the capnuts.

4 Assemble branch pipes in the same way, using compression elbow fittings where you need to turn corners. Fit washing machine stoptaps at the end of the runs.

PROBLEM SOLVER

Arranging drainage

When problems do arise with washing machines, it's usually either because there is no convenient trap or waste pipe to break into, or because you need to fit a standpipe and the existing waste pipe is too high. The diagrams show two possible solutions.

One is to run a new length of waste pipe out through the house wall to a nearby gully. For this, you'll need a hammer drill and heavy duty masonry bit long enough to pierce the brickwork.

The other is to connect a new run of waste pipe to a nearby plastic soil pipe using a fitting called a *strap-on boss connector*. If you're lucky, the soil pipe will be inside the house (though it may be hidden behind vertical boxing). If the soil pipe is outside, you'll have to run the pipe through the wall. Old cast-iron soil pipes are not suitable for connection in this way.

Arrange for the new waste pipe to slope fractionally so that the water drains correctly. (The exact slope is not critical.)

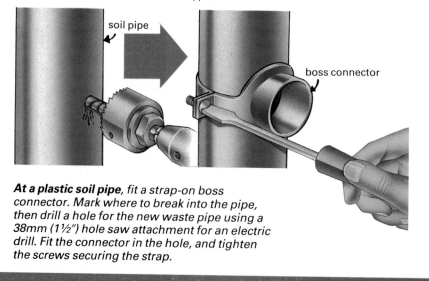

At a gully, run the pipe down below the surface of the grille (old open type), or connect into the spare inlet hole (modern closed type).

At a plastic soil pipe, fit a strap-on boss connector. Mark where to break into the pipe, then drill a hole for the new waste pipe using a 38mm (1½") hole saw attachment for an electric drill. Fit the connector in the hole, and tighten the screws securing the strap.

PLUMBING IN A DISHWASHER

Plumbing in a dishwasher is no more difficult than plumbing in a washing machine – and in many cases it's easier. Normally there are less restrictions on how and where you can make the connections. And the dishwasher's natural location – beside the kitchen sink – means that there are water and drainage supplies conveniently close to hand.

Unlike washing machines, however, most dishwasher ranges include models for building into an existing run of kitchen units. These are designed to fit a standard 600mm (2′) wide base unit, and can be fitted either with a laminate 'decor' panel or a false door front to match the kitchen system. Most also have removable plinths and adjustable feet, for easy fitting under a worktop.

If building-in is an important consideration, make sure your chosen model is designed with this in mind. Check too, that the maker of the kitchen units offers laminate panels or door fronts as accessories.

A dishwasher can be built into an existing run of kitchen units.

....Shopping List....

Before you buy any parts, read through the maker's installation instructions: these are largely the same from model to model, but there may be specific recommendations that have to be followed in order to validate the guarantee.

Water supply Most dishwashers are cold-fill only (or are recommended for such), so you can take the supply from the rising main feeding the sink cold tap.

The easiest method is to fit a washing machine *self-cutting connector* incorporating a stoptap tee and a standard ¾″ BSP thread for the dishwasher supply hose. Make sure the connector you buy carries water authority approval.

Drainage outlet Break into the sink waste pipe using a 38mm (1½″) self-cutting connector, or replace the existing sink trap with a *washing machine trap* incorporating a hose connection. (Some makers recommend installing a washing

machine standpipe, but this isn't strictly necessary if you take care how you fit the dishwasher drain hose – see overleaf. For other supply and drainage problems, see *Plumbing in a washing machine*.)

If the dishwasher is to be built in, the instructions will give details of what size laminate decor panel or door front to order. Decor panels are clipped to the door of the machine using the trim pieces supplied. False doors screw to

brackets or lugs on the front of the machine. Buy a 600mm (24″) length of new plinth panel to match the units if you can't adapt the old one to fit.

Tools checklist: Screwdriver, adjustable spanner, electric drill and bits, panel saw, tape measure.

A typical connection set-up (below), showing the inlet hose supplied via a self-cutting connector and the outlet hose linked to a washing machine trap.

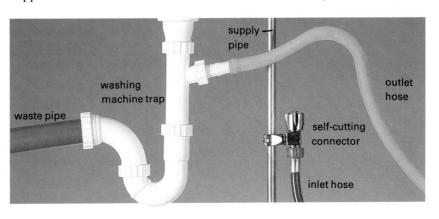

ARRANGING THE WATER SUPPLY

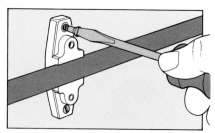 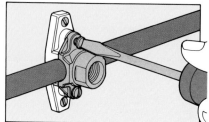 

1 *Choose an accessible site for the self-cutting connector within easy reach of the dishwasher hose. For a wall-mounted type, drill and plug holes and screw in place.*

2 *Fit the clamp over the pipe – some types are hinged, others are in two parts – not forgetting the internal seal if supplied. Screw the two parts of the connector tightly together.*

3 *Screw in the stoptap to pierce the pipe wall (some types need an extra turn with a spanner), and adjust it to sit vertically. Fit the rubber seal in the supply hose and screw to the outlet.*

ARRANGING DRAINAGE

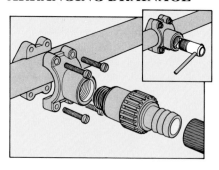 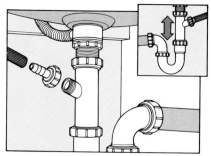

Option 1: *fit a self-cutting connector to the existing waste pipe. Screw in the cutter, then attach the hose connector and non-return valve, followed by the machine outlet hose.*

Option 2: *fit a washing machine trap in place of the sink trap. Most types have sliding seal joints and need no adjustment, otherwise trim the parts to fit with a hacksaw.*

Trade tip

Avoiding siphonage

❝ *If there isn't a non-return valve on the drainage outlet, avoid back-siphonage by curving the machine's outlet hose over the trap or waste pipe connector as shown. If necessary, fix up a bracket using a cup hook and a piece of wire.* ❞

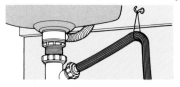

BUILDING IN

Where there is a convenient 600mm (2′) wide unit: simply remove it and slot the dishwasher into the vacant space. (In a new kitchen, you can allow for this at the planning stage.) Where the units are all 500mm (20″) or 1m (3′3″) wide, remove a metre's worth and custom-build a unit to fit the 400mm (16″) gap that's left.

To remove a unit:

■ Unclip or unscrew the plinth (you may be able to re-use it).
■ Remove any doors or drawers, plus their hinges and runners.
■ Remove the drawers in the units on either side and undo the cabinet connecting screws linking them.
■ Remove any screws joining the unit to the worktop.
■ Slacken the adjustable feet (if

fitted) and slide out the unit.

Fitting the machine

■ Prepare the machine following the instructions. This may involve unscrewing the plinth, the false worktop and the door assembly.
■ Slide the machine into position and level using the adjustable feet. This is likely to be the most convenient time to make the plumbing connections. You may have to cut slots or drill holes for the pipework in the adjacent units.
■ Screw the false door to the machine (you may need to supply fixing screws), or fit the decor panel using the trim strips supplied.
■ Refit the old plinth, or a new section. You may have to cut a piece out of the plinth to clear the door. Do this with a jig saw, drilling holes in the corners so the blade can cut the 'blind' side.

A typical built-in set-up (left): *the false door screws to spring-loaded brackets and closes with the machine door.*
Laminate decor panels (inset) *clip directly to the machine door using the trim strips supplied.*

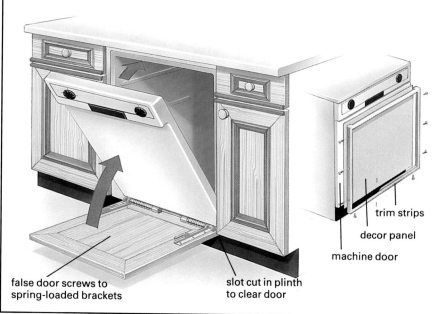

false door screws to spring-loaded brackets

slot cut in plinth to clear door

trim strips

decor panel

machine door

CLEARING BLOCKED TRAPS AND WASTES

Traps – sometimes called 'U' bends – are sections of waste pipe which remain permanently filled with water to stop smells filtering back through the drains. Every water-holding plumbing fitting has one, usually connected directly to the waste outlet, but sometimes further along the waste pipe itself.

Unfortunately, traps are also a natural place for waste particles to collect. Better design and the use of plastic have helped to make modern traps smoother – and therefore less likely to block – than the old metal type. But no amount of good design can eliminate the problem altogether. In the end, it's up to the user to be careful about what is washed down the drain – and that's easier said than done.

Even so, it pays to be aware of the kinds of things which cause trap blockages, not least because this knowledge can help you decide how to deal with the problem. The worst offenders, in order, are:
- Tea leaves and coffee grounds.
- Meat fats washed away with washing-up liquid.

The classic symptoms of a blocked trap. Clearing is messy rather than difficult.

- Food particles – rice, peelings.
- Household fillers and plaster.
- Hair (particularly in baths).

Often, it's possible to clear a trap without resorting to dismantling it (see *Shifting blockages* overleaf). But stubborn blockages and obstructions further down the waste pipe may call for more drastic action.

Trade tip

Tell tale signs

6 Blocked traps don't always occur suddenly – often there is a gradual build-up of debris which causes the water to drain away increasingly slowly. This is the time to act, before you have the added problem of getting rid of the waste water. 9

TYPES OF TRAP

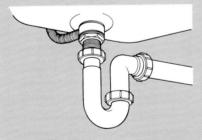

Plastic 'U' bends have an easy flow line, so are less likely to block – though if they do, they are quickly dismantled. The two sections are joined by threaded unions.

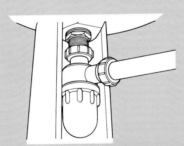

Plastic bottle traps are more compact than 'U' bends, making them the natural choice for basins. The lower half unscrews for clearing, or has a push-and-turn bayonet fitting.

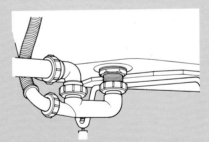

Low level bath traps are used where a deeper 'U' bend or bottle trap would be impossible to fit, and some models have an integral overflow. The horizontal section is prone to collect hair.

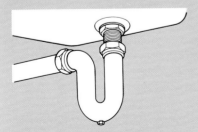

Metal 'U' bends of lead or copper are difficult to dismantle and so often have a small threaded clearing eye. Lead traps are easily damaged, and there's a risk of the eye snapping off.

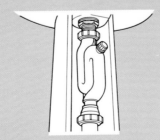

Straight-through traps are mostly found behind basin pedestals where space is limited. The tight bends are a natural place for blockages, so there is usually a clearing eye in the top.

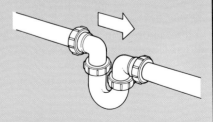

Running traps are mostly found in shower wastes where access beneath the tray is restricted. A common cause of blockages is that the trap is fitted the wrong way round.

SHIFTING BLOCKAGES

Most traps are easily dismantled, but gaining access to them is often more difficult. For this reason, it's always worth trying to clear the blockage by simpler means.

Plunging works best where there is a single appliance connected to the trap. Where there are several, such as a two-bowl kitchen sink with drainer hoses, it is less effective.

Poking with coathanger wire or a sink auger works well on 'U' bends, less so on bottle traps.

Burning with caustic soda is very effective on blockages caused by build-ups of grease – but the chemical itself is highly dangerous and must be used with care.

Caustic soda can damage old lead piping but won't harm plastic. Any water trapped in the fitting must be removed first (see Problem Solver).

CLEARING METAL TRAPS

Place a bucket or bowl under the trap to catch the contents.

■ Unscrew the clearing eye by gently tapping on one of the lugs with a hammer and bolster – or similar wide-bladed tool. If the eye is tight, arrange some means of support to avoid placing strain on the trap.

■ Hook out the obstruction with a piece of bent coathanger wire.

■ Wrap a few turns of PTFE tape around the thread of the eye before replacing it, and take care not to overtighten.

1 *Before plunging a trap*, block up the overflow with a wet rag and fill the fitting to overflow level. This helps to create a good pressure build-up.

2 *Using the largest possible plunger*, place it over the waste outlet and work it up and down vigorously to build up the force of the push-pull effect.

Trade tip

Making a plunger

❛ If you don't have a plunger, try using an old plastic ball cut in half – or at a pinch, a large saucepan lid. Simply pump up and down over the waste outlet in a rapid succession of short, sharp strokes. ❜

1 *To use a sink auger*, begin by feeding it down through the waste outlet into the trap. Turn the handle as you go to help the screw past the blockage.

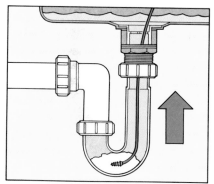

2 *When you feel the auger move easily*, withdraw it slowly turning the handle at the same time. With luck, the screw will carry the obstruction with it.

⚠ USING CHEMICALS

Caustic soda and other proprietary drain clearing products are extremely harmful to the skin, so always follow the manufacturer's instructions. Wear gloves and some form of eye protection when using caustic soda, and keep the tin out of the reach of children.

Also, never mix household cleaning products (for example, bleach and lavatory cleanser) in an attempt to clear a trap. Some combinations produce a gas which is, quite literally, lethal.

DISMANTLING PLASTIC TRAPS

Make sure the container you place under the trap is big enough to hold the contents of the sink or basin before you begin dismantling. See Problem Solver if there is no room to get a container underneath.

With the trap apart, you should be able to hook out the obstruction with coathanger wire. Take the opportunity to clear away any debris around the waste outlet.

Blockages in the waste pipe

If the blockage is further down the waste pipe, removing the trap should make it possible to reach it – either with a sink auger or coathanger wire. With upstairs fittings, check the hopper head too: this can easily become blocked with fallen leaves, resulting in the same symptoms as a blocked trap.

If all else fails, you could try using water pressure from a garden hose to shift the blockage. However, to conform with the water byelaws, this **must** have a double check valve fitted somewhere along its run to guard against back-siphonage. (You may be able to run it from an outside tap containing such a valve.) Pack the mouth of the pipe around the hose to build up pressure in the waste pipe. Few blockages will resist this method.

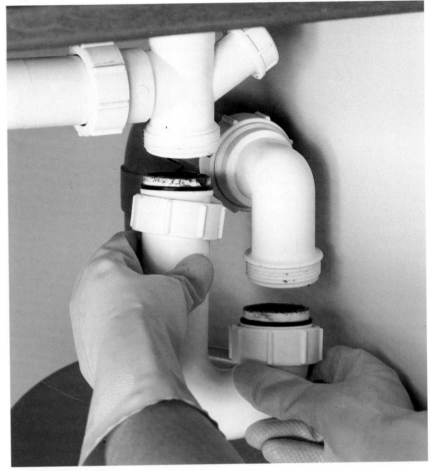

Most types of plastic trap are easily dismantled for clearing, but note which parts go where as you undo them and be sure to save the seals.

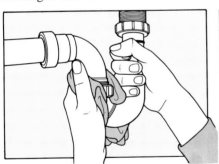

If a plastic nut is hard to undo, wrap a piece of rag around it to gain extra purchase, or wear a glove. Only use a wrench if all else fails.

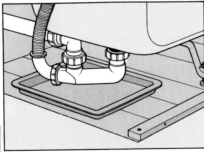

Remove the bath panel to gain access to a bath trap. Empty the bath, and place a tray or old towel under the trap to catch the remaining water.

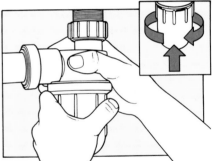

Bottle traps are the easiest to undo. Most types simply unscrew, but some newer designs have a bayonet fitting which must be pushed up and turned.

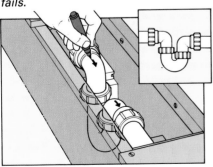

Running traps found on shower wastes may be some way from the actual tray. Mark the direction of flow on the side of the trap in pencil before dismantling.

Hopper head blockages sometimes produce the same symptoms as a blocked trap in a fitting upstairs. Hook out the debris and flush with a hose.

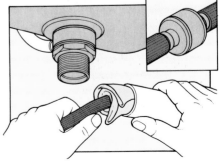

A hose used to flush a waste pipe blockage must have a double check valve fitted. Pack around the mouth of the pipe with a wet rag to build up the pressure.

REASSEMBLING THE TRAP

Take care not to damage the rubber seals or overtighten the nuts when reassembling a plastic trap. Silicone lubricant – as used to make push-fit joints on supply pipes – helps prevent damage to the seals.

If you find the trap leaks after refilling, don't tighten the nuts any further. Instead, dismantle the trap once more and check for the following faults:
■ Grit in the seal.
■ Old jointing compound – this attacks the plastic.
■ Serious misalignment between the various pipes.
■ Distortion of the waste pipe end.
■ Pinched, cracked or broken seals.

On some traps, the waste pipe simply pushes into the end of the trap. If possible, smear the ring seal with silicone lubricant to avoid damage during reassembly.

'Universal' screw-fit connections are now taking over from push-fit joints. Fit the rubber seal on the outside of the waste pipe, before inserting in the trap.

PROBLEM SOLVER

Siphoning out water

Where you're faced by a bathful of water to empty before using caustic soda or dismantling the trap, you'll find siphoning a lot quicker than baling with a bucket.
■ Connect a garden hose to a nearby tap and turn it on for a few seconds to fill the hose with water.
■ Keeping the hose filled, remove the tap end and plug it. Insert the other end in the bath and weight down near the waste outlet.
■ Run the hose out of the window (or better, to a drain) below the level of the bath. Unplug the end and the water will siphon away.

Replacing a trap

A trap which is damaged or old and difficult to unblock is best replaced with a modern 'multifit' design. There are many different patterns, but the 'Universal' type can be adjusted to fit virtually any pipe/waste outlet position. Remember to buy the 32mm (1¼") size for a basin waste, a 38mm (1½") trap for other fittings.

Check before you start that the new trap will fit. If there is a gap to be made up between the trap and the existing waste pipe, buy a multifit push-fit connector and a length of the same-size plastic waste pipe.
■ Sever the waste pipe as near to the old trap as possible using a hacksaw.
■ Unscrew the old trap with a large adjustable wrench.
■ Fit the new trap on the waste pipe and screw to the outlet.

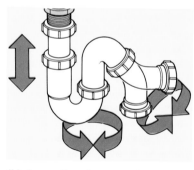

'Universal' replacement traps can be adjusted to fit almost any waste pipe/outlet layout.

Persistent blockages

If you have a complicated waste pipe run which is prone to regular blocking, it could be worth fitting an *access tee* to make clearing or auguring easier. As many waste pipes, particularly lead, are incompatible with certain fittings, it's safest to use a push-fit 'multifit' tee fitting such as the McAlpine 'VM'. The access branch can be sealed with a blank cap from the same range.

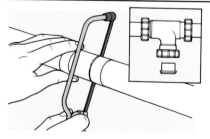

1 Position the tee so that it provides the best possible access to the problem section of waste pipe. Offer up the fitting, mark the pipe with tape, and cut with a fine toothed hacksaw.

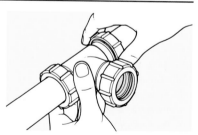

2 Sand the cut pipe ends smooth, then slip on the nuts and sealing rings and jiggle on the tee. Hand-tighten the nuts, and fit the blanking cap on the access branch.

PLUMBING

CLEARING BLOCKED DRAINS

The discovery of blocked drains is enough to send most people rushing for professional help. But providing you have a few simple pieces of equipment, clearing the blockage yourself is usually neither difficult nor particularly unpleasant. The secret is not to be daunted by the fact that drainage systems largely run underground – although you can't see them, their workings are deceptively simple.

Drains which are totally blocked and flooding over are the most unpleasant, so act promptly if you encounter any of the following:
- Abnormal gurgling sounds.
- 'Drain' smells inside the house.
- Overflowing gullies outside.
- Raised water levels in the WC.

Polypropylene drain rods provide an answer to most blockages.

....Shopping List....

Most blockages can be removed with a set of *polypropylene drain rods*, using one or other of the attachments shown below. Some sets include a selection of attachments as part of the kit; with others, you have to buy them as and when the need arises, which is less convenient.

Although you can hire them, drain rods are cheap enough to pay for themselves in a single job. They also have many other uses (see Tip). Don't, however,

be tempted to buy an old set of wooden rods as these have a tendency to break.

Other equipment for unblocking drains which is useful to have available includes:
- Gloves and a face mask.
- A garden hose.
- A WC (cooper's) plunger. (This differs from the sink type in having a longer handle and a flat rubber disc for dealing with S-shaped WC traps.)
- A crowbar or spade for lifting

manhole covers (see Problem Solver).

A sink or drain auger may also come in handy for some types of blockage, but is rarely essential.
Hiring tools should only be necessary for really stubborn blockages. You may need:
Powered augers for cutting through tree roots.
High pressure water jetting equipment for flushing drains.
Flexible drain rods on a drum for coping with very long drain runs.

Trade tip

Uses for drain rods

6 One good reason for buying a set of drain rods is that they have plenty of other uses around the house – threading cables under floors, sweeping chimneys (with a brush attachment) and clearing leaves from rainwater pipes to name but a few. 9

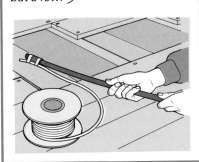

DRAIN ROD ATTACHMENTS

Rubber discs in 100mm and 150mm (4" and 6'") sizes to suit standard drain sizes. Used for plunging and clearing blocked gulleys, inaccessible runs and interceptors (see Problem Solver).

Worm screw for withdrawing roots and other fibrous blockages.

Small brush for degreasing and cleaning the inside of pipes.

Folding scraper for withdrawing silt and debris from the bottom of pipes.

Flexible wire leader for tight bends.

Wheel for overcoming tight bends and obstructions.

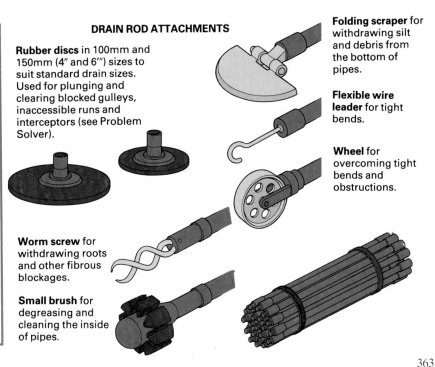

363

WHERE TO START

No matter how the drains run, there is a set procedure for dealing with blockages:

■ Establish that the problem isn't caused by a blocked appliance trap or waste pipe.

■ Lift the manhole (inspection chamber) cover nearest the house (see Problem Solver).

■ If the manhole is full of effluent, you know the blockage is downstream of this point. Start rodding here, away from the house.

If this doesn't work, move to the next manhole, If this is full too, rod the downstream end; otherwise, rod back up towards the full manhole to attack the blockage from the other side.

■ If the manhole is empty, you know the blockage is upstream. Get a helper to try various taps and appliances around the house while you watch the manhole to see which pipes are blocked. You can then rod the affected pipe.

Safe and clean

Never leave a manhole uncovered when you aren't there, and erect a makeshift barrier if you have to leave it unattended.

After clearing the blockage, flush all pipes and manholes with a hose. Wash all equipment in disinfectant and give yourself a good scrub-down.

Trade tip

Water power

6 Don't underestimate the power of hydraulics – in this case the water trapped in the drain – to shift blockages. Often you can harness this power without much difficulty using only a couple of rods and a rubber disc attachment.

Push the rod assembly into the drain at any convenient point upstream of the blockage, then pump vigorously backwards and forwards. In many cases the pressure built up by the water already in the drain will be enough to clear the blockage. Make sure, though, that you hold on tightly to the rods, otherwise the suction effect created by the pumping will draw them down into the pipe. 9

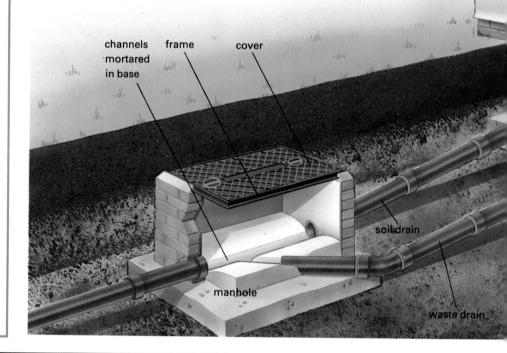

channels mortared in base   frame   cover

soil drain

manhole

waste drain

USING DRAIN RODS

If the blockage can't be cleared by pumping (see Tip), try physically shifting it using several rods screwed together. Which attachment you fit is largely a matter of trial and error, Start with a rubber disc unless you have reason to think the problem is caused by roots (in which case

fit an auger).

Keep turning the rods clockwise as you push them down into the drain, so that there's no risk of them unscrewing. When working without an attachment, count the rods down and count them back up again to double check that

none are left behind.

Full manholes

A manhole full of effluent is a daunting sight, but normally there's no need to empty it before rodding. You know that there is only one outlet hole, so just keep pushing the rods towards the downstream end.

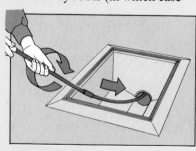

Keep turning rods in a clockwise direction all the time they are in the drain to stop them unscrewing. When you meet resistance, push and turn at the same time to dislodge the debris.

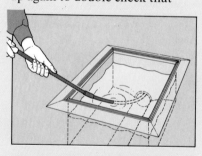

If the manhole is full, insert the rods 'blind' and push towards the downstream end. The channels mortared into the base of the manhole will guide the rods towards the outlet hole.

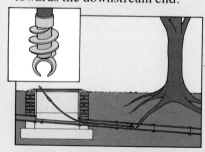

Tree roots won't respond to a rubber disc: fit a cutting attachment instead, or hire a purpose-designed root cutting auger which can be powered from an extension lead.

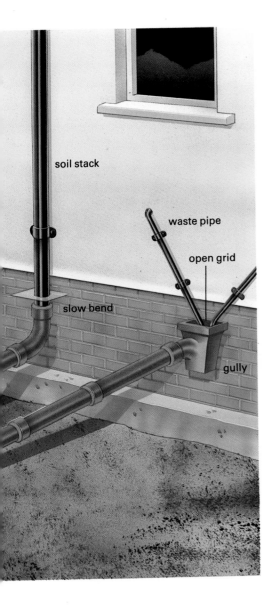

A typical drain layout, where the pipes from the external soil stack and waste gully meet at a manhole near the house. From here the drain could run to another manhole, or to the sewer.

(labels in illustration: soil stack, waste pipe, open grid, slow bend, gully)

BLOCKED GULLIES AND STACKS

Gullies are notoriously prone to blockages, particularly the older open-grid type where leaves are often the problem. You can prevent this by covering the grid with wire mesh.

Blockages further down are usually caused by a build-up of silt, or by an accumulation of grease and food particles (especially from sinks). In this case, remove the cover or grid and reach into the gully to feel for the blockage; you may have to remove quite a lot of debris before the outlet hole clears.

There are two ways to deal with more serious blockages in the gully trap:
■ By plunging from the gully end using a cooper's plunger or drain rod with rubber disc.
■ By rodding up the pipe connecting the gully with the nearest manhole. (But take care not to force the blockage further into the gully trap.)

Soil pipes and combined soil/waste stacks rarely block on the vertical section – usually the trouble lies in the bend at the foot of the stack.

In most cases the blockage can be shifted by rodding back up from the nearest manhole, though as with a gully blockage you should take care not to compress it further into the stack. Alternatively, there may be a rodding eye or access trap in the stack itself, allowing you to insert a drain auger.

Failing this, it's possible to rod down the stack from the top – but only if you have safe access to the roof. It's best to consider this a last resort.

Waste pipes generally block at the hopper head or at the open end above the gully. Blockages can often be cleared by hand; if not, treat as for other stacks.

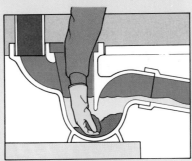

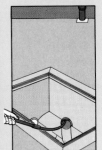

Most gully blockages occur in the base of the gully or at the mouth of the trap. They are best shifted by hand, using stiff wire to break up any hard debris.

Stacks often have screw-on access traps or rodding eyes, allowing you to insert a wire or auger. If not, rod towards the stack from the nearest manhole.

WC BLOCKAGES

Like other appliances, WCs have traps which are prone to blocking. Often the cure is to pour down some bleach and leave for a while. If this doesn't work, try pouring in several buckets of water in quick succession – preferably from a height of around 1m (3') to increase the momentum.

More stubborn blockages generally respond to plunging with a cooper's plunger – or failing this, a drain rod with rubber disc attachment. The only exceptions are syphonic WCs with double sealed traps; on these, use an auger instead.

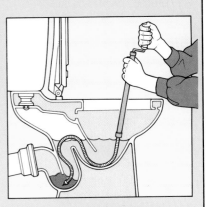

Most blockages in WC traps can be shifted using a cooper's plunger. Work it backwards and forwards vigorously in the mouth of the trap to bring hydraulic pressure to bear on the blockage.

Double sealed WC traps don't respond to plunging. If the blockage can't be shifted using bleach or by pouring in buckets of water, it must be cleared using a sink or drain auger.

Lifting manhole covers

Manhole covers are never easy to lift, but rust can make matters worse still. There are several things you can try:

■ Gently tap all the way around the edge with a heavy hammer or lump of wood.

■ Apply heat from a blowtorch around the edges to release the seal.

■ Apply penetrating oil to the edges and leave to work for several hours.

■ Use an old garden spade as a lever to lift the cover.

■ Thread ropes through the cross bars and around a stout length of timber, then lift with the aid of a helper (but check first that the bars haven't rusted through).

When replacing a cover, apply motor grease around the seal to prevent future jamming.

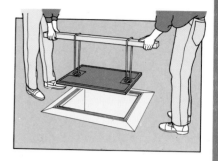

Covers with cross bar handles *can often be shifted using rope and a piece of stout timber.*

Hidden manhole covers

Manholes or smaller *clearing eyes* are supposed to be included wherever a drain branches or changes direction. Very few drains are laid without them, so if you can't find any covers the chances are they have been hidden – usually by garden outbuildings or loose-laid paving.

Larger and older properties may also have a manhole inside – often in the hallway. This should be the *double-sealed* type, with a screw-down cover.

The positions of hidden manholes can usually be fixed by taking the soil stack, gully and road as reference points: drains always run in straight lines between 'features' and you know that they must eventually converge towards a public sewer in the road. Bear in mind, though, that you may share a manhole with your neighbour – or even with several neighbours if you live on an estate served by a *private sewer*.

Another trick is to check where the manholes are in neighbouring properties – if the houses are identically built, you can assume that your own manholes are in the same place. And as a last resort, you could hire a metal detector to track down the covers.

Work out the position *of a hidden manhole cover using other drain 'features' as reference points.*

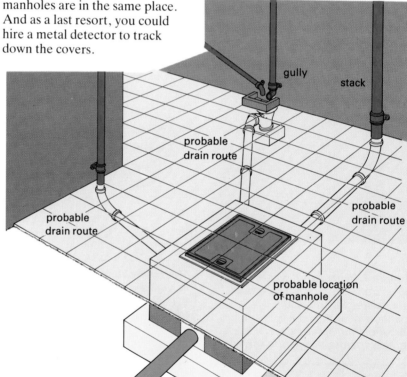

gully

stack

probable drain route

probable drain route

probable drain route

probable location of manhole

Blocked interceptors

An old fashioned method of providing a seal between the household drains and the public sewer was to place a U-shaped trap after the last manhole in the run. Known as *interceptors*, these are a common place for blockages to occur.

Usually the trap responds to rodding with a rubber disc attachment in the same way as any other manhole. If not, hook out the stopper covering the bypass pipe above the trap.

This should partially empty the manhole, allowing you to rod through both the bypass pipe and the main outlet. If this doesn't work, there are two possible causes of the problem.

■ The blockage is further down the run, possibly near the public sewer. In this case call in your local water undertaking, since the problem is likely to involve other properties connected to the same system.

■ The chain holding the stopper has rusted through, allowing the stopper to fall into the interceptor trap. In this case you should seek professional advice.

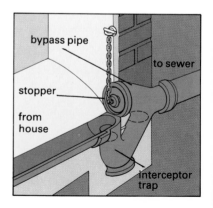

bypass pipe

to sewer

stopper

from house

interceptor trap

Interceptor traps *have a bypass pipe running above them covered by an earthenware stopper.*

ELECTRICS

UNDERSTANDING ELECTRICITY

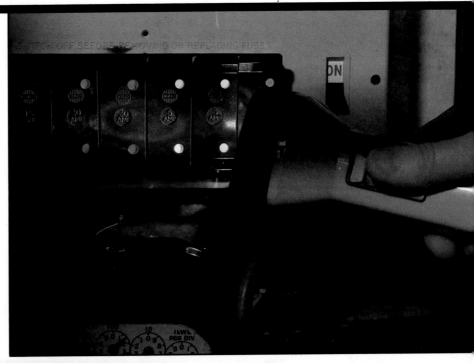

Everyone knows electricity can kill, but that's no reason to fear it; in fact, electrical work is much easier to carry out than many other do-it-yourself jobs because it requires very few special skills.

What's important is that you understand completely how your electrical system works before you attempt to touch it.

This section begins by looking at how the electricity gets to your house. Then there's a guided tour of the fusebox, showing what happens to it when it arrives, and some practical advice on how to get the best from your system.

From power station to home

The thing to remember about electricity is that it flows in circles – unlike water, which runs in at one end of the system and out at the other. However, like water, electricity needs 'pressure' – electricians call this voltage – to drive it round the system.

High voltages are used on the loops between power stations and area substations, to overcome the distances involved, and lower voltages on the shorter loops between local substations and individual homes. Transformers separate the various loops and reduce the voltage at each stage.

By the time the electricity reaches the final loop – your home's electrical system – it is down to a level of 240 volts. After flowing in from the local substation, it travels round the loops (circuits) powering your lights and appliances. Then it flows back to the substation again.

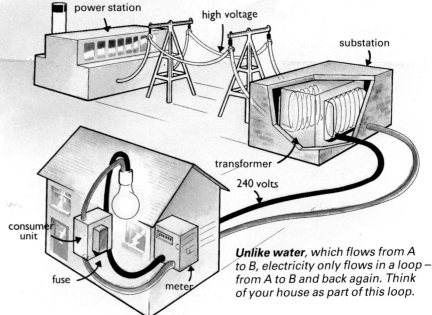

Unlike water, which flows from A to B, electricity only flows in a loop – from A to B and back again. Think of your house as part of this loop.

SOME ELECTRICAL TERMS

Amps (A) measure the amount of current flowing in a circuit.
Cable is used for all fixed circuit wiring, and consists of insulated copper conductors plus a bare earth conductor (wrapped in an outer sheath of PVC at connection points).
Conductors (cores) are metal wires through which current flows.
Earthing provides a safe escape route for the current in the event of certain electrical faults. When insulated (as they are in flex), earth conductors are green and yellow.
Flex (flexible cord) has multi-strand insulated conductors encased in a flexible sheathing. It's used to connect appliances to the mains.

Fuses are weak links fitted into circuits to prevent overloading and protect against short circuits.
Insulators are materials that don't carry electricity, and sheathe conductors so they're safe to handle.
Live describes a conductor carrying current to where it is needed. Live conductors in cable have red insulation; in flex it is brown.
Miniature circuit breakers (MCBs) are protective devices that cut off current in circuits when overloading or a short circuit takes place.
Neutral describes a conductor carrying current back to its source in a circuit. Neutral conductors in cable have black insulation; in flex the

insulation is blue.
Overloading occurs when more current is drawn from a circuit that it was designed to supply.
Residual current devices (RCDs) are safety devices found on modern installations; they protect against electrical shocks and fires.
Short circuits occur when a fault allows the current to bypass its proper route.
Units or kiloWatt hours (kWh) measure the amount of power an appliance uses in one hour.
Volts (V) measure the pressure driving current round a circuit.
Watts (W) measure the amount of power an appliance requires.

UNDER THE STAIRS

The heart of your home's electrics is the point where the main supply cable – which may arrive overhead or underground – is connected to the equipment controlling the distribution of electricity to the various circuits in the house.

The illustration shows a typical installation; the equipment is usually mounted together on a wall-mounted backing board. which is often sited under the stairs, in an alcove cupboard or even in a cellar. The various components are:

1 The meter This records your home's electricity consumption in units (see *Electrical Terms*).

2 The consumer unit (fuse box) A unit housing individual circuit fuses or MCBs, from which all the house's circuits originate.

3 The system's main on/off switch Here housed within the consumer unit but often found as a separate box on older systems.

4 Individual circuit cables

5 Meter tails These link the meter to the consumer unit and the main service fuse.

6 Consumer unit earth cable

7 Main earth terminal

8 Cross-bonding earth cable – to gas and water pipes (see below).

9 Service head This contains the electricity board's main fuse.

10 Earth clamp Found on sheath of main supply cable connected to in-ground earth rod if supply is by overhead cable).

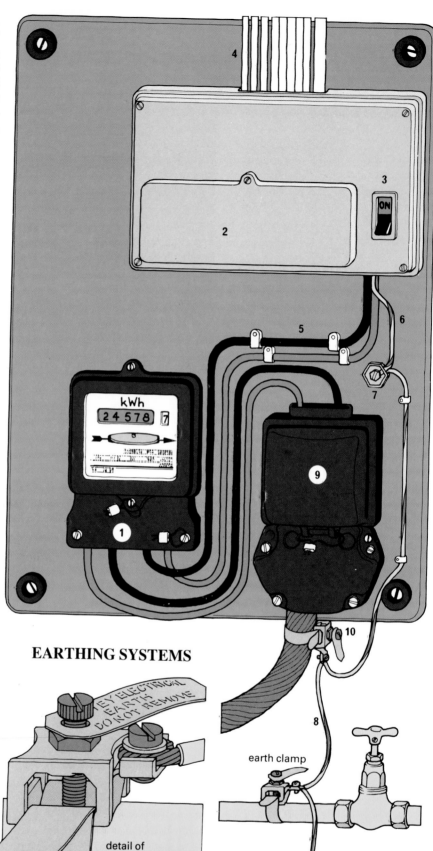

THE METER

The meter records the amount of electricity (in units – see *Electrical Terms*) that your system uses. It's the property of the electricity board (as is all the equipment between the consumer unit and the supply cable) and must never be tampered with.

Modern installations have easy-to-read digital meters.

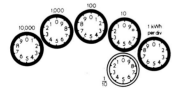

Older homes have awkward-to-read dial-type meters.

EARTHING SYSTEMS

detail of
earth clamp

earth clamp

earth clamp

cross-bonding
cables to pipes

In most town houses, the main earth terminal is connected to a clamp on the sheath of the main service cable. This provides a safe path for a fault current to pass back along the cable to the local substation, where it finally runs to earth.
In some country areas, or where the supply cable runs overhead, the earth cable may be connected to a copper earth rod driven into the ground.
Cross-bonding You may find further cables linking your gas and water pipes to the main earth clamp. These are called cross-bonding cables, and let current flow to earth if a live wire should touch a metal pipe.

MODERN CONSUMER UNIT

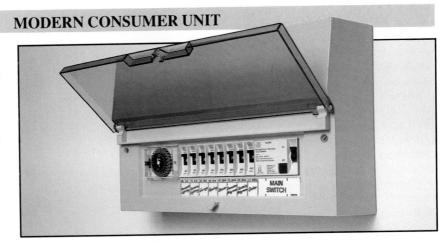

New homes should have a consumer unit containing miniature circuit breakers (MCBs) to protect and control individual circuits, plus a residual current device (RCD) acting as a protective device for the whole system and as a main isolating switch.

The advantages of such a system are:
■ Excellent electrical safety – the RCD guards against shocks and fire; MCBs react instantly to overloads.
■ Abuse-proof circuit protection – MCBs cannot be tampered with.
■ Convenience – MCBs allow circuits to be switched off easily.

OLD-TYPE CONSUMER UNIT

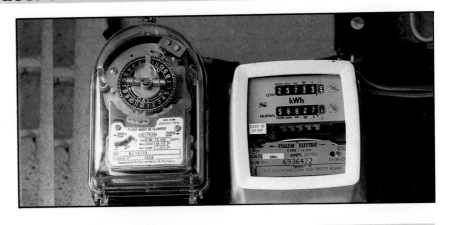

Homes with reasonably modern electrical installations (and quite a number of new homes) will have a consumer unit containing rewirable or cartridge fuses (see overleaf) instead of MCBs, and usually no RCD – if one is present, it will be in a separate box. This is adequate but not ideal:
■ Rewirable fuses take more than their rated current to blow, making it possible for overloads to occur, and they can also be rewired with improper objects – a serious safety hazard;
■ Cartridge fuses can be overloaded, but at least are more tamper-proof.

ECONOMY 7 DUAL-RATE METER

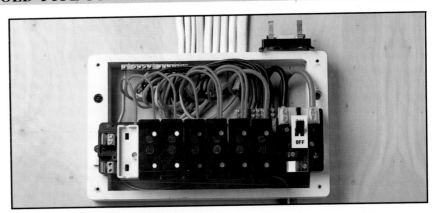

In homes wired up to take cheaper night-rate electricity for space and water heating, there will be a separate white meter to record night-rate electricity consumption and a time switch to switch the supply over when the cheap-rate period starts and finishes.

Modern systems have a two-part consumer unit, while older systems may have separate units for circuits taking full-rate and cheap-rate electricity. If you inherit such a system and don't use electric space heating, you can still use cheap-rate electricity for overnight water heating, washing and so on.

OLD MULTI-BOX SYSTEMS

Before one-piece consumer units were introduced in the 1950s, most homes had individual metal fuseboxes with isolating switches for each circuit.

Such an installation may be safe if it is wired up with PVC-sheathed cable, although the system will suffer the same drawbacks as old consumer units, and may prove difficult to extend. If you find old rubber-sheathed cable, the system is probably dangerous and should be checked over immediately by a qualified electrician. He will probably recommend a complete rewire and replacement of the boxes with a modern consumer unit.

WHICH FUSE?

Your home's wiring system consists of several separate electrical circuits. Each one starts and finishes at your consumer unit (or at its own fusebox, if you have an old-fashioned multi-box system) and is protected by its own fuse or MCB. The fuseholders or MCBs have a current rating stamped on them; fuse holders may also have a colour-coded spot (see right).

- 5-amp (white spot) = light circuit
- 15-amp (yellow) = immersion heater
- 20-amp (blue) = immersion heater or power circuit
- 30-amp (red) = power circuit or small cooker
- 45-amp (green) = large cooker

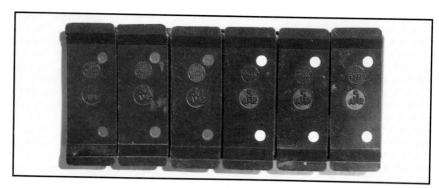

What's on each circuit

It's essential to know which fixed appliances, power points and lights are on each circuit. To do this, you need to isolate each circuit in turn. If you have MCBs, you can simply switch them off one by one, but with fuses you must turn off the main isolating switch first and then pull out the fuseholders (see right).

Go around the house, switching on lights and plugging in appliances so you can record which are on each circuit. Then number your fuses or MCBs; or stick a label inside the consumer unit describing each circuit – upstairs lights, cooker and so on.

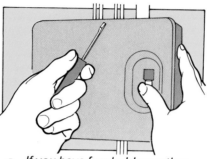

1 If you have fuseholders rather than MCBs, turn off the main isolating switch and remove the screw-on plate covering the fuses.

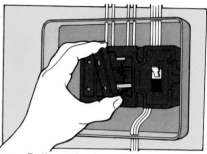

2 Pull out the fuses in turn, each time switching the power back on and checking which lights or appliances they control.

1 IMMERSION HEATER	2 UPSTAIRS POWER	3 DOWNSTAIRS POWER	4 UPSTAIRS LIGHTS	5 DOWNSTAIRS LIGHTS	6 DOOR BELL

Label your fuses with the circuits and appliances they control as shown above. If there isn't room below them, stick a label on the fusebox cover.

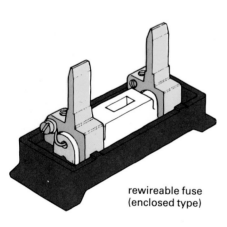

rewireable fuse (enclosed type)

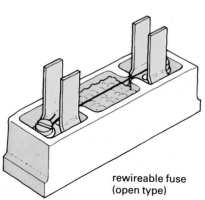

rewireable fuse (open type)

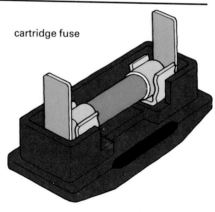

cartridge fuse

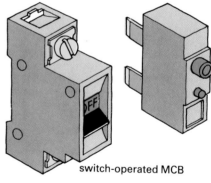

button-operated MCB

switch-operated MCB

TYPES OF FUSE

There are three types of protective device used in fuse boxes and consumer units.
Rewirable fuses are the oldest and most primitive. They have a replaceable wire link between the terminals of the plug-in holder, this wire being available in different ratings. It is vital to use the right wire in each holder – and not to use any other metallic material instead.
Cartridge fuses have a sealed cartridge containing the wire fuse

link in place of the loose wire, and each fuse (except the 15 and 20-amp sizes) is a different size, so it's impossible to fit the wrong rating. Both types are designed to melt if an overload or short circuit takes place, but neither is very sensitive.
Miniature circuit breakers (MCBs) are electro-mechanical switches which turn themselves off if they detect an overload or short circuit, and are much more sensitive than fuses. They have the added advantage of being easy to switch off if you need to work on an individual circuit. Also, if they trip they cannot be reset until the fault is mended.

TOOLS FOR ELECTRICAL WORK

Working on household electrics is much easier and safer if you have the right tools to hand. A basic kit is fairly cheap and you can easily add more specialized tools as required. A starter kit could comprise pliers with built-in wire cutters, a pair of wire strippers and small and large electrical screwdrivers (including a test screwdriver).

Buying electrical tools is one time when it really pays to buy the best you can afford – poor quality electrical tools are potentially hazardous. The plastic insulation may be thin, and not provide sufficient protection from shocks. It may also come off, leaving bare metal dangerously exposed. The metal of cheap tools is often very soft, so that pliers jaws or screwdriver plades distort easily – and loose terminal screws are dangerous.

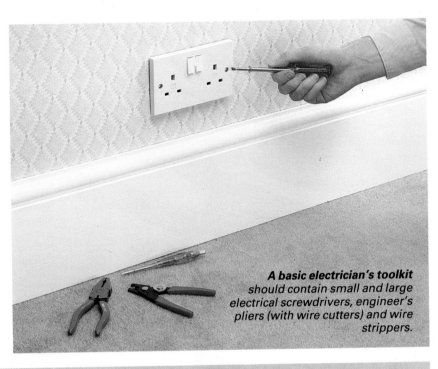

A basic electrician's toolkit should contain small and large electrical screwdrivers, engineer's pliers (with wire cutters) and wire strippers.

ELECTRICAL SCREWDRIVERS

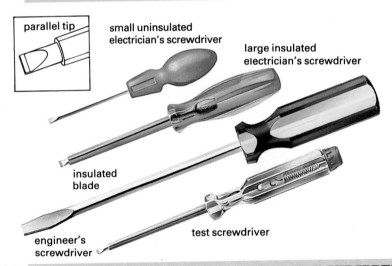

parallel tip

small uninsulated electrician's screwdriver

large insulated electrician's screwdriver

insulated blade

engineer's screwdriver

test screwdriver

An *electrician's screwdriver* has a slim blade with a parallel tip which doesn't widen out near the end, unlike a conventional *engineer's screwdriver*; this is so it can undo deeply recessed terminal screws. The handle is thickly insulated and the blade may be bare metal, or PVC insulated for all but 12mm (½″) or so at the tip.

Screwdrivers are sized by blade length and tip width. Four sizes should cover most jobs:
- 75×3mm (3×⅛″) (uninsulated blade) for ceiling rose terminals and small connector blocks.
- 100×5mm (4×³⁄₁₆″) and 150×5mm (6×³⁄₁₆″) (insulated blade) for large terminals.
- 150×6mm (6×¼″) engineer's screwdriver for securing ceiling roses, mounting boxes, etc.

An alternative to either of the first two is to buy a *mains tester screwdriver*, which can also be used to check whether a component is live.

WIRE STRIPPERS

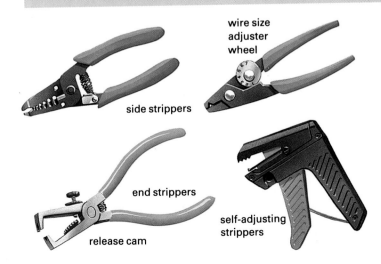

wire size adjuster wheel

side strippers

end strippers

release cam

self-adjusting strippers

Although you can strip insulation from cable or flex cores with a knife, wire strippers are quicker and there is less risk of damaging the conductors. However, they won't strip the outer insulating sheath – you still need a small sharp knife for this.
Side strippers have scissors-type blades. These have a plain section for cutting wire, and V-shaped notches for stripping it; an adjuster wheel restricts the overlap of the jaws to prevent them cutting into the core as well as the insulation).
End strippers have V notches in the end of the jaws and a screw adjuster. Good ones have a *release cam* to override the screw setting. This allows the strippers to be used for cutting wire.
Self-adjusting strippers cut and strip insulation in one go. Insert the wire into the jaws as far as required, and squeeze the trigger. *Crimping pliers* can also be used for wire-stripping (see overleaf).

PLIERS AND WIRE CUTTERS

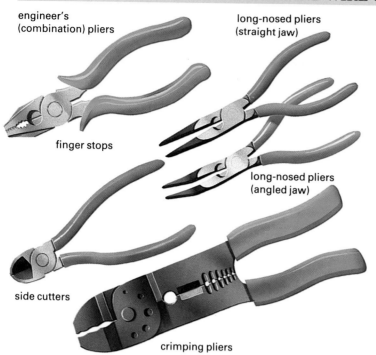

engineer's
(combination) pliers

long-nosed pliers
(straight jaw)

finger stops

long-nosed pliers
(angled jaw)

side cutters

crimping pliers

Pliers and cutters for electrical work usually have PVC sheathed handles. To be effective against shocks, the insulation must cover the handles entirely – heavy duty pliers have finger stops moulded into the insulation to prevent fingers accidentally sliding up the handles and touching bare metal. Some types are spring-loaded.

Engineer's (combination) pliers are what most people think of as pliers; sizes range from 150–200mm (6–8″). They have serrated jaws with round and flat sections for gripping, and a pair of wire cutting jaws. These cut flex and cable up to 2.5mm² with ease, but won't cope with larger sizes. Use *side cutters* or a *junior hacksaw* instead.

Long-nosed pliers (needle-nosed or radio pliers) have thin tapered jaws (straight or angled) for working in confined spaces. The jaws don't exert as much grip as engineer's pliers and have much finer serrations. Wire cutters on these are best reserved for flex. Sizes range from 130 to 200mm (5½–8″).

Side cutters have cutting edges along the entire jaw, and will cope with most wires – from cable and flex to fencing wire. Sizes are 125 to 150mm (5–6″).

Crimping pliers are intended for repair work on car wiring, but the stripping and wire cutting sections work equally well on household cable and flex.

OTHER TOOLS AND ACCESSORIES

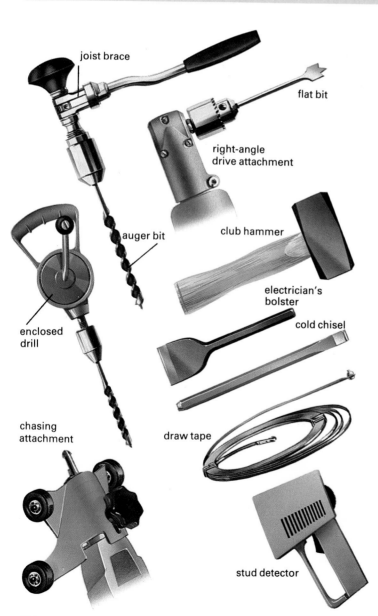

joist brace

flat bit

right-angle
drive attachment

auger bit

club hammer

enclosed
drill

electrician's
bolster

cold chisel

chasing
attachment

draw tape

stud detector

In addition to the basic tool kit there are several other items that it's worth keeping handy or which are essential for more advanced jobs. Many of these are useful for other jobs as well and most are available from hardware shops or DIY superstores. Some of the more specialized tools may only be available at a major electrical suppliers.

General purpose items

Trimming knife for cutting the outer insulating sheath on cable or flex and for trimming the core insulation if wire strippers aren't available. *Junior hacksaw* for cutting thick cables and cable conduit or trunking. *Electric drill and range of bits* for making mounting or access holes. *Insulating tape* (preferably brightly coloured) for temporary repairs. Don't use it to replace green/yellow earth sleeving on a cable earth core. *Fuses* and/or *fuse wire* in a range of current ratings (amps) to suit appliance plugs and the consumer unit.

Tools for running cable

For making cable access holes in joists use an *auger* or *flat bit* to suit the cable size. A 12mm (½″) bit will suffice for anything up to 2.5mm² cable. Where access is limited use the bit in a *right-angle drive attachment* that clamps on to the collar of an electric drill – alternatively use a stubby *enclosed hand drill* or a special brace called a *joist brace* (these may even be cheaper than the drill attachment).

For recessing cable into walls or floors, or cutting the hole for a backing box, use a *club hammer* with an *electrician's bolster* for plaster, and a ½–¾″ *cold chisel* for brick. A *chasing attachment* for a drill makes cutting chases easy, but isn't worth the cost for just one small job.

A *draw tape* is used as a guide for cable. It's flexible enough to be pushed under floorboards and up cable conduit without snagging. When it emerges at the other end the cable is attached to it and pulled through. Some wind into a storage cassette.

Detectors

Use a detector to find cables and obstructions hidden in the wall. *Metal detectors* will locate pipes or cables, while *stud detectors* locate the timbers inside a partition wall or ceiling.

REPAIRING BLOWN FUSES

Home electrical systems have a series of weak links built into them to protect the wiring from overheating in the event of an overload or short circuit.

■ Virtually every plug-in appliance has its own fuse inside the plug, and there are similar fuses inside fused connection units (FCUs) and other devices (see page 378). These protect the circuit from appliance faults and vice versa.

■ Inside the consumer unit (fuse box) are the fuses or miniature circuit breakers (MCBs) which protect the main lighting and power circuits.

Tracing fuse faults

Repairing or replacing a blown fuse is simple enough, but for safety's sake it's essential to find out what caused it to blow in the first place.

Use the chart below to help you. The fault is more likely to be in the appliance than the circuit, so check the plug fuse first (see page 378). Sometimes, however, appliance faults cause the circuit fuse to blow too.

You may need an electrician to confirm your suspicions by testing the relevant circuits. Even so, you'll save time and money if you can point them in the right direction.

Circuit fuse faults

There are two faults which can be cured simply by repairing the circuit fuse (or resetting the MCB):

Power surges occur naturally, blowing fuses that have become oversensitive with age.

Overloads mainly affect old radial circuits which were not designed with modern power-hungry appliances in mind. The maximum power rating of a radial circuit is 7200W (7.2kW), so if you suspect an overload, add up the wattages of all the appliances on the circuit (given on their rating plates) and check that the total does not exceed this figure.

Taking precautions

Fuses can blow at any time, so don't be caught unprepared:

■ Get to know your consumer unit: check what type of fuses are fitted (see overleaf), then buy spares for each rating or a card of fuse wire as appropriate. If you haven't already done so, label each fuse or MCB with the circuit it protects.

■ Buy packs of spare plug fuses.

■ Store the spares, together with a torch and a screwdriver, near the consumer unit.

TRACING FUSE FAULTS

To use the chart, answer the question on the right. Then follow the green arrow for a 'Yes' answer, or the red arrow for a 'No' answer. Continue in this way, answering questions and following the appropriate arrows, until you've traced the fault.

NB Some systems have a *residual current device* (RCD) as well as fuses or MCBs. This does not affect the chart.

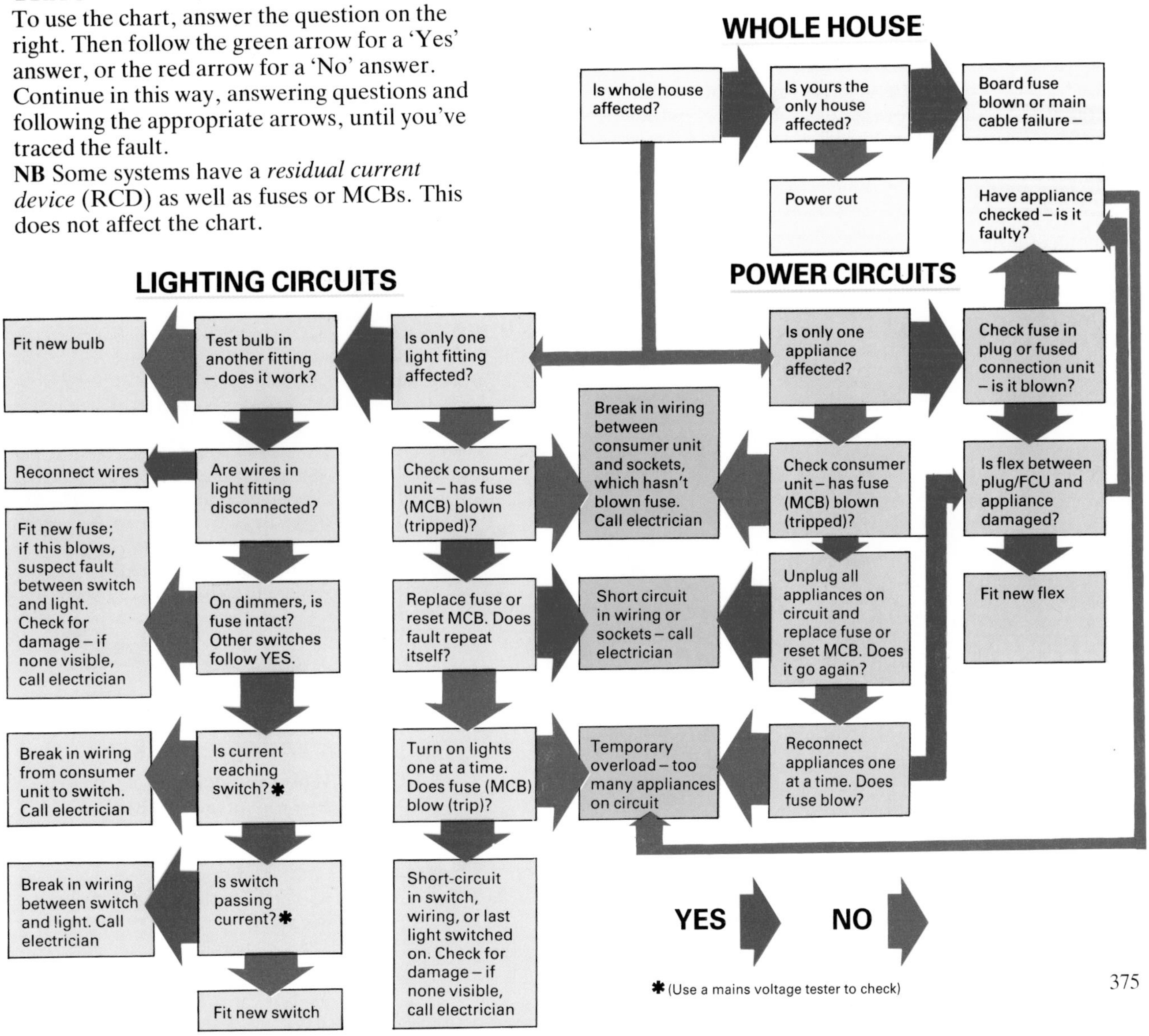

WHOLE HOUSE

- Is whole house affected?
- Is yours the only house affected?
- Board fuse blown or main cable failure –
- Power cut
- Have appliance checked – is it faulty?

LIGHTING CIRCUITS

- Fit new bulb
- Test bulb in another fitting – does it work?
- Is only one light fitting affected?
- Reconnect wires
- Are wires in light fitting disconnected?
- Check consumer unit – has fuse (MCB) blown (tripped)?
- Break in wiring between consumer unit and sockets, which hasn't blown fuse. Call electrician
- Fit new fuse; if this blows, suspect fault between switch and light. Check for damage – if none visible, call electrician
- On dimmers, is fuse intact? Other switches follow YES.
- Replace fuse or reset MCB. Does fault repeat itself?
- Short circuit in wiring or sockets – call electrician
- Break in wiring from consumer unit to switch. Call electrician
- Is current reaching switch?✱
- Turn on lights one at a time. Does fuse (MCB) blow (trip)?
- Temporary overload – too many appliances on circuit
- Break in wiring between switch and light. Call electrician
- Is switch passing current?✱
- Short-circuit in switch, wiring, or last light switched on. Check for damage – if none visible, call electrician
- Fit new switch

POWER CIRCUITS

- Is only one appliance affected?
- Check fuse in plug or fused connection unit – is it blown?
- Check consumer unit – has fuse (MCB) blown (tripped)?
- Is flex between plug/FCU and appliance damaged?
- Unplug all appliances on circuit and replace fuse or reset MCB. Does it go again?
- Fit new flex
- Reconnect appliances one at a time. Does fuse blow?

YES ▶   NO ▶

✱ (Use a mains voltage tester to check)

REPAIRING CIRCUIT FUSES

The consumer unit contains a bank of circuit fuses or MCBs mounted beneath a protective cover. On modern units the cover simply hinges out of the way, but in some older models it is held by screws.

The fuses or MCBs have different ratings, depending on whether they protect lighting circuits, power circuits, or special circuits for individual high-power appliances.

Always replace a fuse with one of the same rating (see chart on page 378). And whatever the fuse, always turn off at the main switch before removing or replacing the holder.

Fuses and circuit breakers

When there is an electrical fault in a fuse-protected circuit, it creates a surge of current which eventually causes the fuse to melt – or trip, in the case of an MCB. But this doesn't always happen immediately: it's still possible for the wiring to be damaged – or for a person to be electrocuted – before the surge grows large enough to blow the fuse.

For this reason, many newer consumer units have the added protection of a resettable *residual current device* (RCD), also called *residual current* or *earth leakage circuit breakers* (RCCBs or ELCBs). RCDs detect the leakage of current to earth when there's a fault in the circuit – at which point they trip, cutting off the power. They react much faster than fuses, and are therefore safer. RCD protection can be fitted to older systems, but this job is best left to a professional. You can buy plug-in versions for individual appliances.

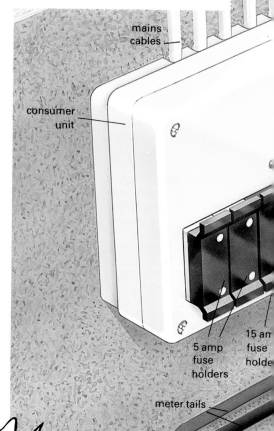

mains cables

consumer unit

5 amp fuse holders

15 am fuse holde

meter tails

electricity meter

REWIRABLE FUSES

There are three main designs of rewirable fuse, but they all work in the same way. A wire link (the *fuse wire*) bridges the two terminals of the ceramic or plastic holder, and melts if a fault occurs.

Turn off the power at the main switch and remove the consumer unit cover. Pull out the fuse holder and see whether the fuse wire has burnt – on the enclosed type there is a viewing window in the porcelain tube.

Replacing the wire

■ The fuse wire is secured by a screw at each end of the holder. Undo the screws completely (watch out for the small metal washers fitted beneath the screw heads) and pull out the burnt ends.

■ Cut a length of fuse wire of the correct rating (see chart on page 378).

■ Feed the wire between the two terminals. This is slightly fiddly on the enclosed type, since the wire needs to be fed through holes in the holder.

■ Refit the screws loosely and twist the ends of the fuse wire around them in a clockwise loop.

■ Tighten the screws just enough to hold the fuse wire and trim off any excess wire.

■ Replace the holder in the consumer unit, refit the cover, then turn on the power supply.

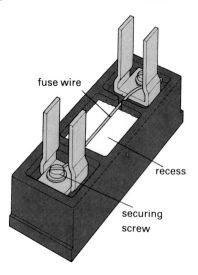

fuse wire

recess

securing screw

In exposed fuse holders, the fuse wire simply runs across a recess between the two terminals.

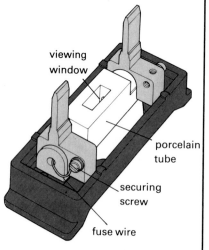

viewing window

porcelain tube

securing screw

fuse wire

In protected fuse holders, the fuse wire runs through a porcelain tube.

Trade tip

Leave some slack

6 When you fit new fuse wire to a rewirable fuse don't pull the wire too tight. On thin, 5 amp fuse wire in particular, there is a risk that it will stretch and snap as you tighten the screws. Leave a little slack. 9

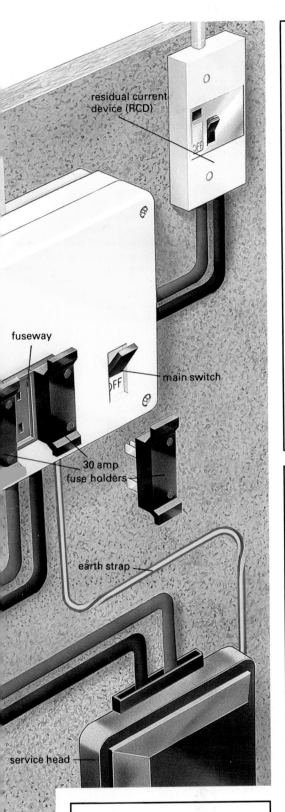

residual current device (RCD)

fuseway

main switch

30 amp fuse holders

earth strap

service head

MINIATURE CIRCUIT BREAKERS

You can see instantly if an MCB has tripped – the coloured button shoots out of the plug-in holder, or the switch clicks to the 'off' position. The button or switch cannot be set to 'on' until the fault which caused the MCB to trip in the first place has been fixed.

If an MCB trips persistently for no apparent reason, it may be faulty: simply unplug it and swap it with another of the same rating (this is marked on the body, and sometimes indicated by the colour of the button or switch). If the fault transfers to the other circuit, the MCB is definitely faulty. Buy and fit a replacement MCB of the correct rating.

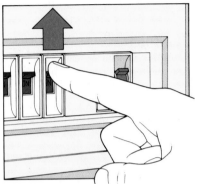

Reset a tripped MCB by pressing in the coloured button or returning the switch to 'on'.

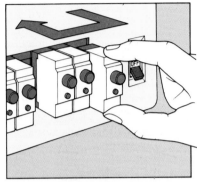

A faulty MCB may keep tripping. Swap it with another one of the same rating to test.

CARTRIDGE FUSES

Many modern consumer units have fuse holders that take a cartridge type fuse. These are generally less fiddly to repair than rewirable fuses, though some types of holder make the job trickier than it needs to be.

The fuse holders are rated differently according to the circuits they protect, and accept only the correct size replacement cartridges (except for 15 and 20 amp fuses, which are interchangeable). This makes it almost impossible to fit a replacement fuse of the wrong rating.

1 Unplug the fuse holder from the consumer unit. With most designs the fuse simply clips into the holder: prise it out with a small screwdriver.

2 Clean up the metal clips with a little wet and dry paper if they look dirty. Clip in the new fuse cartridge, refit the holder and turn on the power.

One type of fuse holder is in two parts, held together by a screw. Separate the parts, then remove the cartridge from its hooped terminal clips.

THE BOARD FUSE

The board fuse protects the mains supply from serious fire or flood damage. It is very rare for it to fail.

You are not allowed to fix the board fuse yourself. The box in which it is fitted (the *service head*) is sealed with a special wire tag to prevent tampering, so call the Electricity Board if you suspect it has blown.

CHECKING PLUG FUSES

Cartridge-type fuses are found not only in plugs, but also adaptors, extension blocks, triple sockets, shaver points and fused connection units (FCUs). Dimmer switches may have miniature cartridge fuses to protect their sensitive circuitry.

FCUs and sockets

FCUs have a fuse in a holder mounted on the faceplate.

Triple sockets (which are prone to overloading) have a similar arrangement to protect the fixed circuit wiring. So do shaver points, though in this case the fuse may be the miniature 1 or 2 amp type.

On some designs the fuse carrier is a tight push-fit in the faceplate and can be prised out with a screwdriver. The other common fitting has a small securing screw.

Adaptors and extensions

The fuses in plug adaptors are usually in a red-coloured holder alongside the plug pins: lever out the holder with a screwdriver. Extension blocks are similarly equipped, though here the holder may be held by a screw.

More rarely, the fuse is found inside the adaptor casing. Undo the screws holding the casing together and very carefully pull it apart: you'll find the fuse clipped into a small circuit board.

Built-in fuses

Dimmer switch fuses (where fitted) are either hidden in the casing or fitted in a pull-out holder.

To gain access to the body-mounted type, turn off the power at the main switch and remove the appropriate lighting circuit fuse. Undo the two fixing screws and pull the entire switch away from the wall. Make a note of where the wires go, release them and remove the switch.

On some designs the fuse is concealed under a plastic insulating cover which must first be unclipped. Double dimmer switches have two fuses, one of which may be difficult to reach since access to it is blocked by the other dimmer control – it is just possible to ease it out with a small screwdriver.

Appliance fuses are normally fitted to a screw-in holder near the flex outlet. If the internal fuse blows, the symptoms are the same as if the plug fuse blows, so check this too if the plug fuse appears to be sound.

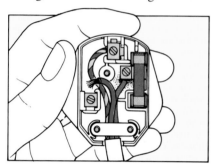

1 *Before testing a plug fuse, check that none of the wires have come adrift and watch out for chafed insulation. The flex should be tight in the grip.*

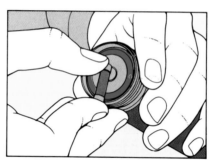

2 *Test the fuse by holding one end against the metal part of a torch casing, and the other end to the battery. The torch will light if the fuse is sound.*

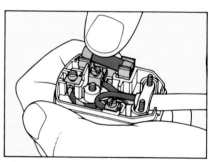

3 *Make sure you replace a fuse with one of the correct rating. Clean the terminals, then push the fuse into its clips and refit the top of the plug.*

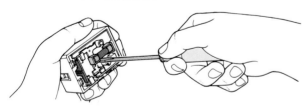

The fuse holder *in FCUs and adaptors can usually be prised out with a screwdriver.*

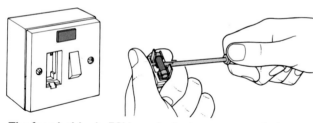

Some adaptors *have a fuse mounted on a small circuit board inside the casing.*

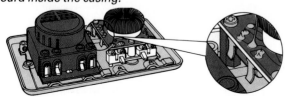

On double dimmer switches, *one of the fuses is obscured – ease it out carefully with a screwdriver.*

TYPES OF CARTRIDGE FUSE

CONSUMER UNIT CARTRIDGE FUSES (marked 'BS1361')

Rating	Colour
5 amp	White (lighting circuits)
15 amp	Blue (single appliances up to 3kW)
20 amp	Yellow (single appliances up to 4.5kW)
30 amp	Red (power and cooker circuits)
45 amp	Green (cooker circuits over 12kW)

FUSE WIRE RATINGS
Rewirable fuses have three ratings instead of five:

5 amp	(lighting circuits)
15 amp	(single appliances up to 3kW)
30 amp	(power and cooker circuits)

PLUG CARTRIDGE FUSES (marked 'BS1362')

Rating	Colour
2 amp	Black
3 amp	Red
5 amp	Black
10 amp	Black
13 amp	Brown

NB 3 amp and 13 amp are the most commonly used ratings; only fit fuses of other ratings where specified by the appliance manufacturer.

MINIATURE CARTRIDGE FUSES (marked 'BS646')

Rating	Colour
1 amp	Green
2 amp	Yellow
3 amp	Black
5 amp	Red

PLUG AND FLEX REPAIRS

Plugs and flexes get a lot of heavy use. Although they may have been fitted correctly, damage and wear can make plugs unsafe, while those on older appliances may have been wrongly fitted in the first place. The picture below shows some of the hazards which may be lurking unsuspected, all of which can be put right for very little time and money.

Most appliances are connected to the mains via a plug and three-core (earthed) flex. The exceptions are double insulated appliances which do not need an earth, and lamps which have no metal parts. Both of these may be wired with two-core flex. Lamps with metal parts should always be earthed.

If an appliance is rarely or never unplugged (eg a waste disposer or tumble drier), the alternative is to wire it directly to the mains via a fused connection unit. This is more reliable, and avoids tying up a socket permanently.

There are several kinds of flex for connecting different appliances and lights. Don't confuse them with *cable*, which is used for fixed wiring behind walls and under floors.

All flex has fine stranded wire conductors, and the insulated cores are coloured differently from cable.

Flexes and colour coding

Modern three-core flex has two cores coloured BROWN for LIVE and BLUE for NEUTRAL, plus a GREEN/YELLOW striped core which is the EARTH conductor. Two-core flex has no earth conductor. The cores are either coloured brown and blue, or left uncoloured.

Old three-core flex has a red Live core and a black Neutral core (the same as cable), plus a plain green Earth core. Flex old enough to have this colouring should be checked to make sure it has not deteriorated.

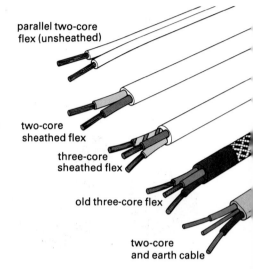

parallel two-core flex (unsheathed)

two-core sheathed flex

three-core sheathed flex

old three-core flex

two-core and earth cable

Modern flex colour codes are distinctive. Red and black insulation is used on old flexes and on modern cable. Uncoded flex is mainly used for lighting.

PLUG AND FLEX FAULTS

Wrong fuse fitted in plug: if too high-rated may not blow quickly if there is a fault. Change fuse.

Badly fitted plug: flex not gripped securely and wires are loose. Could pull out leaving live wire exposed. Rewire.

Extension cable overloaded: insulation could melt. Use extensions safely or rewire to avoid using them at all.

Cracked plug: terminals could become exposed. Replace with new one, possibly tough rubber type to withstand knocks.

Flex too long: can be accidentally pulled down by children, trailed across hob or dropped in sink. Shorten flex.

Damaged flex: insulating tape repairs are potentially dangerous. Replace flex or join with a flex connector.

FITTING PLUGS AND FUSES

Nowadays, appliances are normally connected using identical plugs with three square pins – but the fuse in the plug is changed to suit its purpose (see opposite).

Old type round-pin plugs were unfused and their presence generally indicates a wiring system which is old enough to need renewing.

In the old system there were three different sizes of plugs – 2 amp for lighting, 5 amp for low current appliances (up to 1kW) and 15 amp for high current (1-3kW) appliances.

Plastic plug: Normally the cheapest type. The pins are often plain brass and the flex grip is usually a strap tightened with two screws.

Safety-type plug: Flex grip is built in and the pins are partially insulated to prevent accidents caused by touching live parts when pulling out the plug.

Unbreakable plug: Has a durable casing made of tough rubber to resist knocks and heavy use. Particularly good for things like power tools.

Easy-fit plug: Various patterns. All wires are normally the same length. Terminals and cord grip are designed to work without needing a screwdriver or stripper.

Round-pin plugs: Unfused, made in different sizes for different ratings. Only used with old installations; probably indicates rewiring is needed soon.

WIRING A PLUG – THE RIGHT WAY

Fitting plugs safely is a matter of taking care to get the wires the right length, and using the right tools to fit them. You probably need to cut and strip the wires even when the appliance manufacturers have stripped them for you. Because plugs differ so much, it's very unlikely that the ends will be exactly the length you need to do the job properly, and in many cases you are better off cutting them short and starting again.

The correct lengths for the wires depend on your plug. On several types of plug, all the wires are trimmed to the same length. But on most plugs the earth wire is longer, and the live and neutral may also be different from each other.

There may be instructions on the packaging to tell you the correct lengths of inner and outer insulation to strip. Otherwise try the wires in place to see that they fit neatly into the flex grip and plug channels as shown below.

CORRECT PLUG WIRING

All bare wires held by terminals.

Wire stripped correctly: insulation not split, core wires undamaged and no stray strands.

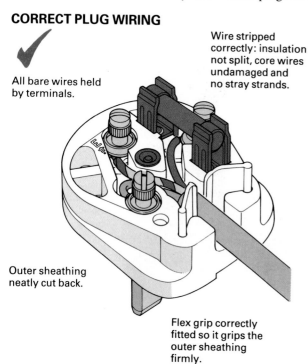

Outer sheathing neatly cut back.

Flex grip correctly fitted so it grips the outer sheathing firmly.

UNSAFE PLUG WIRING

Wire stripped badly, leaving frayed and cut strands.

Wires wrong lengths: either too long and twisted or too short and stretched.

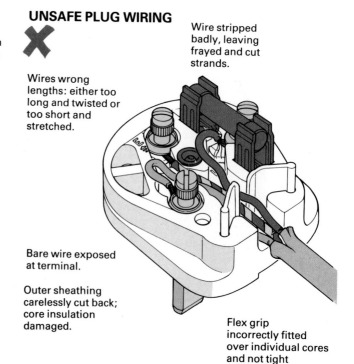

Bare wire exposed at terminal.

Outer sheathing carelessly cut back; core insulation damaged.

Flex grip incorrectly fitted over individual cores and not tight enough to grip.

USE THE RIGHT FUSE

It's important to fit a fuse with the correct rating. The fuse protects the wiring from overloading if there is a fault or short circuit. It is designed to form a 'weak link in the chain' and blow before the flex or internal wiring in the appliance itself can overheat. If you fit one designed for a higher current than is needed, there is a risk that it may not blow if there's a fault.

Plug fuses are normally rated at either 3 amps or 13 amps. 3 amp fuses are coloured red and are used for low-powered appliances drawing up to 720 Watts (720W). 13 amp fuses are coloured brown and are used for any appliances drawing from 720W to 3000W (3kW). Some examples of low and high power apparatus are shown below, but you should check the rating plate on the appliance (see right).

HOW TO READ THE RATING PLATE

Somewhere on the appliance should be a rating plate giving useful information. The most important is the power rating (measured in Watts), which governs the type of fuse (and flex) needed. It should say something like 'W 350' (350 Watts) or '2000W at 240V' (2000 Watts). Some high ratings may be in kilowatts (1kW=1000 Watts) and low power apparatus (like a radio adaptor) may give the current in mA (milliamps) instead. Fit a 3 amp fuse to anything this low powered.

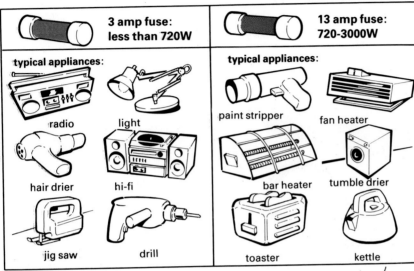

3 amp fuse: less than 720W

typical appliances:
radio, light, hair drier, hi-fi, jig saw, drill

13 amp fuse: 720-3000W

typical appliances:
paint stripper, fan heater, bar heater, tumble drier, toaster, kettle

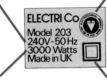

voltage and frequency requirements

approvals symbol

ELECTRI Co.
Model 203
240V–50Hz
3000 Watts
Made in UK

power or current rating in Watts or kilowatts

double insulated symbol (appliance needs no earth)

STRIPPING/CONNECTING

You need an electrical screwdriver, trimming knife, and something to strip the wires. It's possible to manage with a knife alone, but there's a risk of damaging the wires accidentally. A cheap pair of wire strippers makes the job much easier and helps to ensure all your wiring is as safe as possible.

Cut back any outer sheathing leaving the inner cores long enough to reach the terminals and make the connections. The right amount of the core insulation to strip depends on the terminals (right).

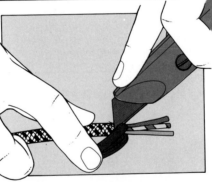

1 Use a knife to slice the insulating sheath and peel it open. If there's a woven cover pull this away. Bend the sheath back and cut away the surplus.

How you connect the wires depends on the terminals.

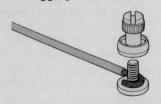

Post type: bend the bared end back on itself then push into the hole. This prevents the ends of the wire snagging on the hole.

Screw type: wind the end of the wire clockwise around the screw. Make sure the end of the flex is trapped by the clamp nut.

2 If the flex has a woven cover, wind on insulating tape to prevent fraying or roll back the inner rubber sheathing over the woven sheath for a short way.

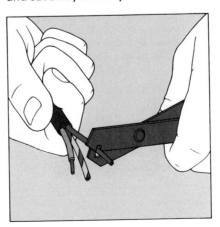

3 Cut the inner cores with wire strippers. Strip off the right amount of insulation, ensuring you don't cut the wire. Twist the strands to prevent fraying.

Clip type: push the bare end into the clip. Some patterns have a snap-on catch, others lock when the cover is replaced.

EXTENDING FLEX

Extension leads are intended for temporary use. If you need a long flex on one particular appliance for most of the time, then ideally you should have the existing flex replaced with a longer length of the same type or avoid the problem by adding a new socket. But if this isn't possible, you can extend the existing flex using a *flex connector* or an *in-line switch*.

A flex connector can also be used to join a flex which has been accidentally damaged, after first cutting out the damaged section. However, it's preferable to wire the appliance with a new flex if you can.

Flex connectors come in two types – fixed and plug-in. Both normally have three terminals, although there are two-terminal versions for double insulated appliances and lamps with no metal parts.

In-line switches are a sensible alternative for appliances such as bedside lights, since they both extend the cable and put control of the light within easy reach.

With either type of extension, make sure the new length of flex is as near identical to the old one as possible. Flex differs in its current rating and in the durability of its insulation, both of which vary to suit the application.

A coiled extension lead is useful as a temporary flex extender, but should not be used all the time – especially for appliances which take a lot of power.

A multi-socket block makes a more versatile extension, but will be overloaded if the total power drawn by the appliances plugged into it exceeds 3000 Watts (3kW).

Trade tip

Take time to unwind

❝ If you use high-powered appliances like a fan heater or kettle (1.5kW or more) on an extension lead, **make sure** you uncoil the lead completely. A coiled lead can generate enough heat to melt its own insulation and cause a short circuit. ❞

WIRING A FLEX CONNECTOR OR IN-LINE SWITCH

Check the current rating of the connector you buy is suitable for your appliance (see page 381). Fixed connectors are normally rated at 13 amps, 3000 Watts (3kW). Plug-in types may be rated at a maximum of 5 Amps, 1200 Watts (1.2kW).

Follow any labelling on the connector, or instructions stating which way round it should be connected. Terminals may be labelled L, E, and N for Live, Earth and Neutral. Plug-in types should state which side is connected to the mains. This is essential for safety.

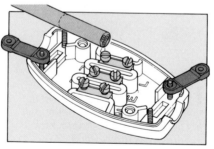

1 **To fit a fixed flex connector** unscrew the cover and loosen the screws of the two flex grips at either end. Check the length of wire you need to strip.

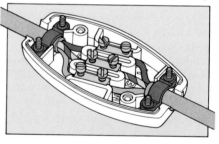

2 Strip the ends of both lengths of flex and insert them into the connector under the flex grips. Tighten these later to clamp the outer sheath.

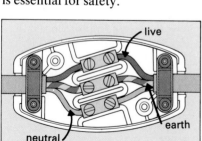

3 The terminals may not be labelled. Connect the earth wires to the centre terminals and connect brown to brown and blue to blue on the outer terminals.

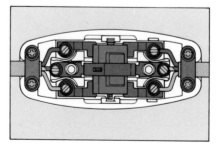

An in-line switch is fitted in almost the same way as the fixed flex connector, but the terminals are connected to the switch itself rather than to each other.

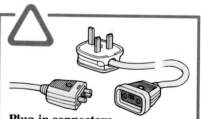

Plug-in connectors

These must be wired so that the plug part (with projecting pins) connects to the appliance. If you connect this half to the mains, the pins could become live when the connector is pulled apart.

REPLACING A SOCKET OUTLET

Socket outlets are generally reliable, and the most common reason for changing one is because the old one is damaged. Stiff or broken pin contacts make plugging in difficult and place a strain on other components, while cracks or holes in the body of the socket are highly dangerous – especially if any of the terminals are exposed. Don't use a socket in such a condition.

Swapping an old, damaged socket for a new one of the same size and type is among the easiest of all electrical jobs. But if the socket is only a single one, you might consider taking the opportunity to replace it with a double – or even triple – outlet socket. This is usually quite safe (but it's best to consult a qualified electrician), and is a lot better than relying on adaptors or extension leads.

Replacement socket *faceplates* – the part containing the contacts and terminals – come in standard sizes with a choice of single, double or triple outlets. They may be switched (safer) or unswitched, and the triple type has a built-in 13 amp fuse to guard against overloading.

Faceplates are the same, whether the socket is flush or surface mounted, and so too are the screw positions. See overleaf if you need to replace a surface mounted backing box as well.

Socket styles
Socket designs vary in detail between makes, and you may have to shop around to get an exact match. If you are replacing several sockets to blend in with a new decorative scheme, there is a choice of bright coloured plastic, brass or aluminium (the last two in 'period' styles) as well as traditional white plastic. However, metal faceplates **must** go on a metal backing box (see overleaf).

Tools and materials: Electrical screwdrivers, trimming knife, green and yellow PVC sleeving (maybe), a small length of 2.5mm² PVC sheathed cable (maybe).

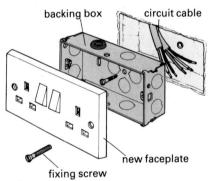

backing box   circuit cable

new faceplate

fixing screw

Trade tip

Life savers
‘If you're replacing a socket that's regularly used to supply garden appliances, think about fitting one with a built-in residual current device (RCD). They're more expensive than plug-in RCDs, but can't be mislaid or forgotten.

RCD sockets are designed to fit a standard double socket backing box, so a single socket box must be converted to suit.’

REMOVING AND REPLACING

Removing an old socket faceplate is a simple job, since it's only held by two screws and the mains wiring. The procedure is the same for both single and double sockets.

Before you start . . .

■ Switch off the power at the consumer unit and isolate the appropriate circuit fuse or MCB.

■ Plug in an appliance to check there's no power to that socket.

Checking for damage Remove the faceplate and check the cable(s) for damage and correct fitting.

■ On metal backing boxes there should be rubber grommets where the cable(s) enter to stop the PVC sheathing chafing. If there aren't any, it's advisable to remove the backing box and fit some.

■ The earth cores should all be insulated with individual lengths of green and yellow PVC sleeving. Again, if they have been left bare, fit new sleeving before you fit the socket faceplate.

■ Sockets on metal backing boxes must now have a 'flying earth' – a direct connection between the earth terminal on the faceplate and the box itself. You can make the connection using a length of earth wire cut from ordinary 2.5mm circuit

cable, but don't forget to cover it with a length of green and yellow PVC sleeving.

Fitting the new faceplate

The terminals on the new faceplate will be clearly marked: the red wires go to 'L' or 'live', the black wires to 'N' or 'neutral', and the sleeved earth wires to the terminal marked with an earth symbol (see step 4 below).

Where there is more than one cable, check that all the bared ends are pushed fully home in their terminals (see top inset, step 4) before tightening the screws.

1 Undo the faceplate mounting screws, and on a flush socket, cut around any decorations using a trimming knife. Gently ease the socket away from the backing box.

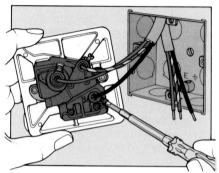

2 Use an electrical screwdriver to slacken off each of the cable terminal screws in turn. Pull the wires free and discard the old faceplate.

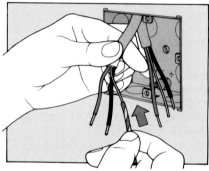

3 Check the condition of the cable(s). All earth wires should be sleeved, and a metal backing box should have rubber grommets at the entry points.

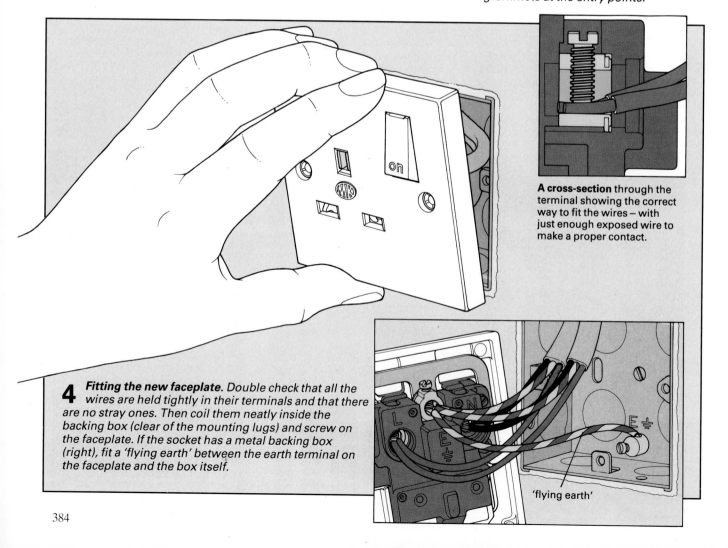

A cross-section through the terminal showing the correct way to fit the wires – with just enough exposed wire to make a proper contact.

4 *Fitting the new faceplate.* Double check that all the wires are held tightly in their terminals and that there are no stray ones. Then coil them neatly inside the backing box (clear of the mounting lugs) and screw on the faceplate. If the socket has a metal backing box (right), fit a 'flying earth' between the earth terminal on the faceplate and the box itself.

'flying earth'

FITTING DIMMER SWITCHES

Dimmer switches allow you to set the light level anywhere between off and full on, and come in styles to blend with any room. The controls vary (see below), but models with separate on/off switching can be left at a preset level, while others have to be dimmed right down to switch off.

Choosing a dimmer

Apart from looks and convenience, there are several practical points to check when choosing:

■ Dimmers can be used with all types of light fitting, but most only work with tungsten filament bulbs (fluorescent tubes need special dimmers, which are not covered here). If you want the dimmer to operate a large number of powerful bulbs, or one very low power one, check that its power rating is suitable.

If you want to fit dimmers to lights with two-way switching (such as hall lights controlled from upstairs and down), not all types are suitable. Two-way dimmers may be wired in pairs like conventional switches, but you can also get 'master' switches with special exten-

Dimmer switches are perfect for controlling harsh overhead light.

sion controls to allow switching from several points.

■ Dimmers normally fit straight into the old switch mounting box. However, if you are replacing a double (*two-gang*) switch or other multiple switch, your choice is more limited unless you replace the

mounting box. Double switches are usually the same width as single ones, but most double dimmers are designed for wider boxes.

■ If your existing switch is fitted in a shallow mounting box, this may also affect your choice unless you replace the box too.

....Shopping List....

single gang rotary dimmer

'Georgian' brass rotary dimmer

'hi-tech' rotary dimmer

rotary dimmer with rocker switch

single gang rotary dimmer

single gang rotary dimmer

Dimmers come in styles from traditional to hi-tech, with various types of control:

Rotary dimmers are most common, and lowest in price. They can have the on/off control combined as a rotary switch or there may be a separate rocker switch.

Touch switches turn on and off with a light tap on the faceplate and are controlled by holding your finger down. They often have extra extension controls.

Remote control dimmers come with a hand-held transmitter which beams a signal to the switch. They can also be operated by touch.

Multi-gang dimmers are available with rotary or touch operation and two, three or four controls. Most need wide boxes.

The only tool normally required is a small electrical screwdriver. If you change the mounting box, you may need extra tools as well as the new box itself (see overleaf).

touch dimmers

remote control dimmer

remote control unit

two-gang rotary dimmer
(120mm fitting)

two-gang rotary dimmer

two-gang touch dimmer

CHANGING A SWITCH TO A DIMMER

Check your existing switch as shown (right) and described on page 385. If it is a multi-gang or two-way switch you have much more limited choice of replacement. Also check the depth of the mounting box. If this is too shallow it must be replaced at the same time.

Surface mounting boxes can be measured without undoing anything. To check a flush mounted box, switch off the power and undo the screws, then ease off the faceplate.

To fit the new dimmer, turn off the power, unscrew the existing switch and remove the wires from their terminals after checking which one goes where and labelling them.

If the mounting box needs replacing, do this next. Then, unless otherwise instructed, connect the wires to the dimmer in the same way as the original switch.

TYPICAL OLD AND NEW CONNECTIONS

existing switch
(one way, single gang)

dimmer switch

two-way switch   multi-gang switch

multi-gang dimmer

Single-gang switches normally have two terminals and the wires can go either way round. If there are three terminals to allow two-way switching, one is usually labelled 'Common' and the others something like '1' and '2'. If this type is wired for one-way switching, the extra terminal is left empty, so one wire will go to Common and one to 1.
Two-way switches have a third wire to the spare terminal.
Multi-gang switches have groups of terminals like single switches.

Dimmer connections are often the same as an ordinary switch, but sometimes there are extra terminals for two-way switching and extension controls. There should be an instruction sheet showing which terminals correspond to the terminals in the switch you are replacing.

⚠ **Turn off the power**

Before you start, turn off the main switch at the consumer unit (fusebox). If you need power in the meantime, remove the fuse (or trip the MCB) for the circuit of which the light is a part and turn on the main switch again. Test the light switch to double-check the circuit is dead before proceeding.

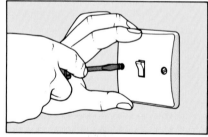

1 With the power off at the consumer unit, undo the screws holding the old switch plate and ease it away. Unscrew the terminals and remove the wires.

Trade tip

A switch in time . . .

❝ If you are replacing a switch which is connected with more than two wires, label them so you can remember which ones went where. Use a piece of masking tape and write the name of the terminal on it before you remove the wire. This makes it easy to find the corresponding connections on the dimmer. ❞

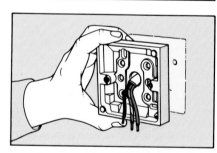

2 If you need to replace a surface mounting box, undo its fixing screws and lift it away from the wall. Ease it over the projecting cable.

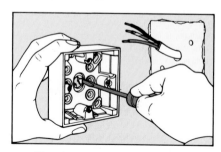

3 Knock out one of the blank holes in the new box so you can fit it over the cable. Screw it to the wall, drilling and plugging new holes if necessary.

4 To replace a flush box you need to chop out a deeper hole with a cold chisel. Thread the cable through a knock-out and screw the box to the wall.

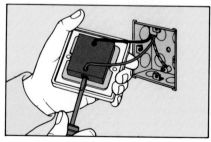

5 Slip the ends of the wires into the terminals on the new switch and tighten the screws. Then fit the faceplate to the box and secure the screws.

FITTING A NEW PENDANT LIGHT

A simple pendant bulb holder tends to cast a harsh, shadowy glare over a room, even when heavily shaded. Spots, tracks and wall lights are all good alternatives, but fitting any of these is likely to involve running new wiring.

A simpler solution is to replace the existing pendant with a modern adjustable or glare-free design such as the one shown below. You may also want to take the opportunity to move the light to a better position – centred over the table for example.

.... Shopping List ....

Replacement pendant lights are sold complete with bulb holder and flex. Many include a built-in shade, and some have a replacement ceiling rose or push-on rose cover. For more versatile lighting effects consider fitting an **adjustable pendant**, which has a separate hanging block so that it does not have to hang directly below the rose.

Other types of ceiling light require more work to fit, including replacement of the rose itself. This applies to **chain-hung chandeliers**, which require a hook fixing and may be very heavy. It also applies to the coiled-flex or counterbalanced **rise-and-fall pendants** which can be lowered to give low-level sidelamp-style illumination.

Tools and other materials:
Screwdriver, wire strippers.

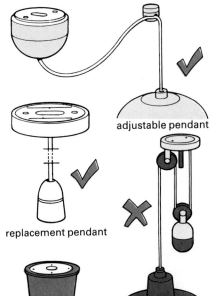

adjustable pendant

replacement pendant

counterbalanced rise-and-fall pendant

Trade tip

Check the rose fixings

❦ If the existing ceiling rose is loosely fixed – as they often are – fitting a new pendant light of any type is likely to make matters worse.

You should be able to check without removing the cover. If there's any sign of movement, make sure you have some plugging compound and hollow wall fixings before you start. ❞

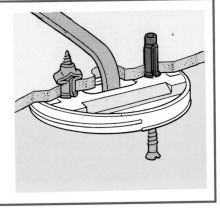

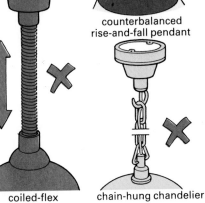

coiled-flex rise-and-fall pendant

chain-hung chandelier

FITTING THE NEW LIGHT

Turn off the power at the consumer unit and remove the appropriate lighting circuit fuse (or trip the appropriate MCB). Switch the light on and off to double check.

If, as is most likely, the new light has a plastic bulb holder and body, the flex will have two cores – brown for live, blue for neutral. But lights with metal fittings may have a three core flex incorporating a green/yellow insulated earth wire.

No matter how the rose is wired (see right), you simply connect the new flex cores in place of the old ones. But note the following:

■ If the flex cores are not coloured (two-core flex only), it doesn't matter which way round they go.

■ If the original flex is very old and has the old style colour coding, connect brown in place of red and blue in place of black.

■ If the old flex has two cores, but the new one has three, the extra green/yellow flex core should be connected to the terminal occupied by the green/yellow (or unsheathed copper) circuit cable cores ('Earth' in the diagrams).

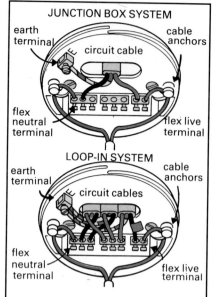

What you may find when you remove the ceiling rose cover. Older-style junction box wiring (top) leaves one circuit cable visible at the rose; new-style loop-in wiring (above) leaves two or three. The type of wiring employed does not affect how you connect the new flex.

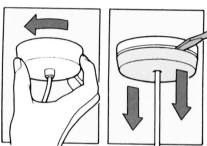

1 With the power off, remove the ceiling rose cover. Some types simply unscrew; others are a push-fit and can be prised off with a screwdriver.

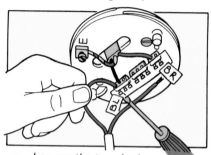

2 Loosen the terminal screws and pull out the old flex wires one at a time, marking the relevant terminals with pieces of tape as you go.

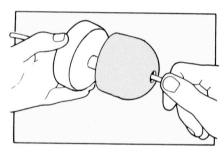

3 Cut the new flex if you need to alter the height of the light. Feed the flex through the hole in any trim cover supplied, then through the rose cover.

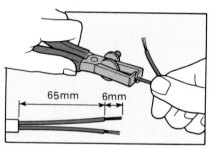

4 If the end of the new flex isn't prepared, strip back the outer sheath for about 65mm (2½"), then bare the ends of the cores about 6mm (¼").

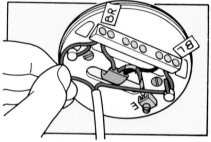

5 Connect the wires to the appropriate terminals and loop them around the anchors in the rose. Refit the rose cover, then push on the trim cover (if fitted).

▌ PROBLEM SOLVER

Loose roses

A properly fitted ceiling rose will be screwed to a piece of board nailed between the upstairs floor joists or direct to a joist. These rarely come loose.

However, it's not uncommon for the rose to be part-screwed to a joist, to the laths in an old lath and plaster ceiling, or straight through the plasterboard in a new ceiling. Any of these 'bodges' will cause the screws to come loose as soon as any weight is put on them.

The answer is to screw into something more secure. Plastic wing cavity wall fixings are particularly good for plugging holes made into plasterboard, while spring toggle cavity fixings help to spread the load in a lath and plaster ceiling. But if the screw has pulled out a chunk of plaster, patch the hole with plugging compound and screw into this.

Be sure to turn the power off before working on the rose.

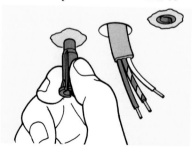

Plug loose rose fixing holes with hollow wall fixings or a similar lightweight cavity fixing.

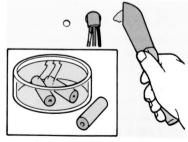

Use plugging compound if the screws have torn away some of the ceiling plaster.

FITTING SPECIALITY PENDANT LIGHTS

Some pendant lights can't simply be hung from an existing ceiling rose, either because there is no way to connect them to the rose terminals or because they are not supported by the flex alone (see right).

The solution in most cases is to remove the rose and replace it with a special fitting called a *conduit* box (sometimes called a *BESA* box). This has built-in threaded mountings to which the light can be attached, and the connections between the light flex and the mains cable can be made inside it using terminal blocks.

Fitting a conduit box

The normal way to fit a conduit box is to screw it to a mounting board running between two ceiling joists. On a top floor this shouldn't pose a problem as you can gain access to the joists from the loft. On lower floors the job becomes more involved, since you have to lift carpets and floorboards.

Where you can't get at the joists from above – for example, in a downstairs flat or single storey extension – the box must be fitted from below by cutting a hole in the ceiling (see Problem Solver). You may also prefer to use this method if the upstairs flooring is very difficult to lift.

LIGHTS NEEDING A CONDUIT BOX

Chandeliers and similar fittings are suspended on a chain from a special *chandelier hook*. The hook attaches direct to a conduit box.

Rise-and-fall pendants operated by a spring-loaded cord have a mounting plate that can be screwed direct to a conduit box.

Ceiling mounted lights with an open base must be fitted over a conduit box to satisfy the Wiring Regulations, which state that connections must be made within a non-combustible enclosure.

.... Shopping List ....

A conduit box (BESA box) has a round heat-resistant plastic casing with two holes for screwing it to the ceiling. Inside the box are two threaded brass mounts for attaching the light. The mounts are designed to take machine screws and are set at a standard spacing of 50mm (2"), which is compatible with most light fittings.

Boxes come with various cable outlets to cope with virtually any wiring installation. The most useful for light fittings are back outlet boxes, or side outlet *terminal boxes*. Double outlet boxes can hold more cable.

Conduit boxes can safely carry lights weighing up to around 3kg (6½lb), but above this they need reinforcing. Most have slots for *metal bracing clips*, although these are not commonly used.

Heat resistant terminal blocks are used to make the final connection between the mains cable and the light flex; ask for the 15 amp size. It comes in a strip from which you need to cut a 3-way block, and possibly a single block as well.

Supports can be made from offcuts of timber; useful sizes include 75×25mm, 50×25mm and 25×25mm (3×1", 2×1" and 1×1"). You also need some 20mm and 38mm (¾" and 1½") No.6 screws, nails and filler.

Tools checklist: Hammer, tape measure, screwdrivers, bolster, electric drill and bits, padsaw, jigsaw or floorboard saw (maybe), bradawl (maybe); trimming knife (maybe).

Conduit boxes

machine screws

chandelier hook

terminal blocks

mounting plate

REMOVING THE ROSE

■ Turn off the power at the consumer unit and remove the fuse or trip the MCB for the appropriate lighting circuit. Try the light switch to double check.

■ Unscrew or unclip the rose cover.

■ Disconnect the old light flex from the terminals and remove the light.

Finally, disconnect the lighting circuit cable(s) from the rose, noting where the wires go. The number of cables varies depending on the wiring system – one for a junction box system, three for a loop-in system (or two, if the rose is on the end of the circuit). This doesn't affect the job, so long as the wires end up connected to the new terminal block in the same way.

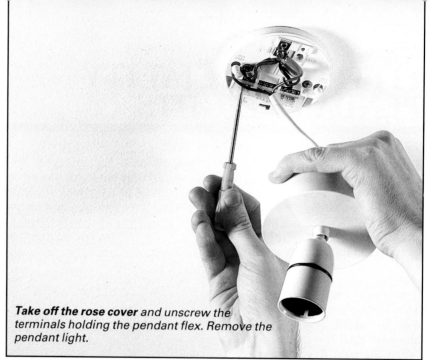

Take off the rose cover and unscrew the terminals holding the pendant flex. Remove the pendant light.

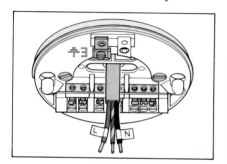

Label the wires to show how they were connected. Where there is only one cable, label the red core 'Live', and the black core 'Neutral'. There is no need to label the Earth core.

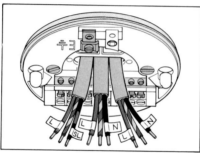

If there are three cables, label all three reds 'Loop-in' and label the two blacks sharing a terminal 'Neutral'. The other black should be flagged red and labelled 'Switched Live'.

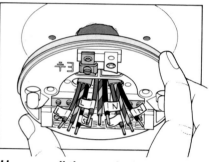

Unscrew all the terminals and remove the wires. Then undo the two fixing screws and gently ease the rose away, guiding the labelled cable wires through the holes in the back.

RAISING FLOORBOARDS

Floorboards often contain screwed-down access panels. If not, measure across the floor to find the position of the rose and lift the boards according to type:

Square edged boards are best lifted with a bolster. Knock it into the gap 50mm (2″) from one end and lever up the edge, then work in a wedge and lever from the other side. Repeat until the board springs up.

Where a board runs continuously from one skirting to the other, lever up the section you want to remove between the nearest joists. Drive in wedges to hold it above the surface, then saw through.

Tongued and grooved boards are more difficult to remove. Cut through the tongues on each side of the board, using a floorboard saw or a jigsaw. Then prise up as above.

Chipboard floors are the most difficult. If you can't remove an entire board, use a jigsaw to cut out an access panel between the joists. Refit the panel to a framework of 50×50mm (2×2″) battens nailed along and across the joists.

Prise up continuous boards with a bolster, wedge, and then saw across them close to the nails.

Separate the tongues on tongued and grooved boards by sawing through them with a jigsaw.

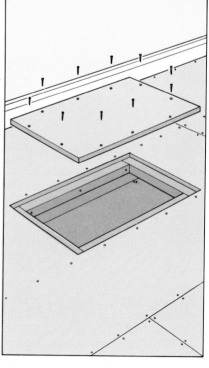

Make pocket cuts in a chipboard floor, using a jigsaw, then refit the panel to a batten framework.

FITTING THE CONDUIT BOX

First decide where to position the hole for the new box. If the rose was fitted directly to a joist, the hole should be between here and an adjoining joist at a point the cables will reach (there should be some slack); otherwise the hole can go where the rose was.

Make up the mounting board from a strip of scrap wood or board measuring about 75×25mm (3×1"), using 25mm (1") angle brackets or lengths of 25×25mm (1×1") batten for the supports. If you use battens, don't forget to drill them for the joist fixings before you screw them to the board.

Positioning the box

Ask a helper to hold the box in position flush with the ceiling while you fit the mounting board from above. If the ceiling plaster is too thick for the box to sit flush, cut a piece of plywood to the same diameter and sandwich this between the box and mounting board to make up the difference.

After screwing the box to the board and feeding through the cables, make good the area around the hole with filler and leave to dry. Make sure the cable Earth cores are fitted with lengths of green and yellow PVC sleeving.

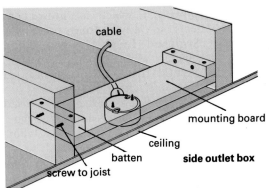

cable

mounting board

ceiling

batten

screw to joist

side outlet box

back outlet box

The conduit box screws to a mounting board *fixed between the joists on battens or angle brackets. On a back-outlet box, drill a hole in the board to accept the cable outlet. On a side outlet box, cut a slot in the ceiling and feed the cables under the board.*

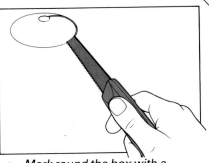

1 *Mark round the box with a pencil, then drill a starting hole and cut round the line with a padsaw. Remove the cut section, and clean up any rough edges.*

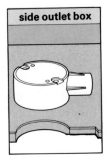

2 *Cut the mounting board to fit exactly between the joists. Screw a pair of angle brackets or pre-drilled battens to the ends ready for mounting.*

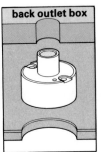

back outlet box   **side outlet box**

3 *Depending on the box, drill a hole in the board to accept the cable outlet, or chop out a slot in the ceiling for a side outlet so that the box will sit flush.*

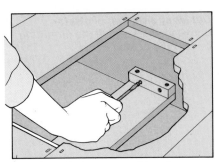

4 *Get a helper to position the box flush with the ceiling from below. Lay the mounting board on top, mark the fixing positions and screw in place.*

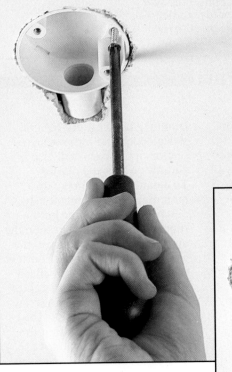

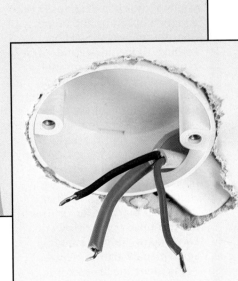

5 *Screw the box to the board from below. Feed the cables through the outlet ready for the electrical connections, and fill any large gaps round the box.*

FITTING THE NEW LIGHT

You can't fit the new light until the connections are made, so ask your helper to support the light while you wire it up. Start by linking the cable cores to the terminal block.

Connecting the cables
■ If there is only one cable, use a three-way section of terminal block to take the separate Live, Neutral and Earth cores.
■ If there are three cables, use a three-way section for the Switched Live, Neutral and Earth cores. Then wire the three red Loop-in cores to a separate single terminal.

Connect the light flex to the terminal block. Normally it will be two-core, in which case **brown** connects to 'Live' (one cable) or 'Switched Live' (two or three cables), while **blue** connects to 'Neutral'. If the cores are uncoded they can go either way round.

If the flex is three-core – used where the light has a metal casing – make sure you connect **green/yellow** (earth) to the Earth terminal.

After connection, carefully fold the wires and terminal blocks into the box and screw on the light fitting as shown on the right.

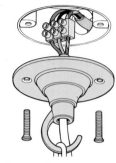

On a chain-hung light, screw the chandelier hook to the conduit box.

On a rise-and-fall pendant, fit the mounting plate and push on the cover.

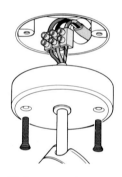

For a spotlight, screw the baseplate directly to the mountings in the box.

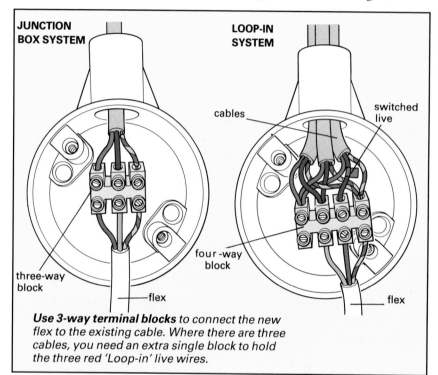

JUNCTION BOX SYSTEM

LOOP-IN SYSTEM

cables

switched live

four-way block

three-way block

flex

flex

Use 3-way terminal blocks to connect the new flex to the existing cable. Where there are three cables, you need an extra single block to hold the three red 'Loop-in' live wires.

▌PROBLEM SOLVER▐

Fitting from below

Where you can't gain access to fit a mounting board from above, you have no choice but to cut out a section of ceiling and fit the board from below. Start by turning off the power and removing the rose as normal.
To make the cut-out, drive a bradawl into the ceiling at various points near the old rose position until you find the centre of the nearest joist. Measure across from here to find the next joist – normally 400mm or 600mm (16″ or 24″) – double check with the bradawl, then draw lines marking the centres of the two joists. Link them with two lines roughly 200mm (8″) apart to mark the cut-out.

Cut along the lines with a trimming knife against a metal straightedge and remove the section of plasterboard. Use a padsaw on lath and plaster.
To mount the box, make up a mounting board as previously described, but with the batten supports or angle brackets on the underside. Screw the box to the board, then position the board so that the edge of the box is flush with the ceiling. Feed the cable through into the box, and screw the mounting board to the joists.

Afterwards, patch the hole with pieces of plasterboard or plywood supported on the joists and on skew-nailed battens. Nail on the patches, then make good with one-coat repair plaster or ready mixed skimming plaster.

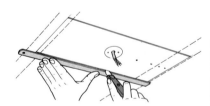

Cut away a section of plaster between joists and fit the mounting board with box attached.

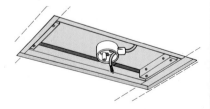

Patch the hole with plasterboard or plywood nailed to batten supports and make good.

FITTING SPOTS, TRACK AND DOWNLIGHTERS

Downlighters (left) have a fairly limited light spread and so are best fitted in groups, directly above the area to be lit.
Spotlights (above) can be angled to project light into virtually any part of the room, so the mounting position isn't critical.

Modern light fittings can transform your decorations – and with careful setting up will give either soft, glare-free background lighting, or punchy highlights as required.

There are three main alternatives to pendants and chandeliers:

Spotlights are inexpensive and come in single, double and triple configurations. If you fit a spotlight in place of the existing ceiling rose, it may be as easy to install as a pendant light. The main factor affecting this is the type of wiring connections.

Wiring Regulations insist that all connections are made inside an enclosed heatproof box. If the spotlight has an enclosed base with the terminals inside, it should meet this requirement so you can screw it directly to the ceiling and lead the cables inside. Lights without an enclosed baseplate must be mounted over a plastic conduit box (BESA box) recessed into the plaster. If a conduit box isn't already fitted it could mean a lot of extra work to install one.

The other possible complication is if you want a spotlight in a different position from the existing rose. This will mean extending the wiring (see Problem Solver).

Track lighting consists of a long conducting track into which lights can be plugged wherever you need them. This is quite expensive but easy to fit and wire.

Wiring is normally straightforward; because the track takes power where you need it you are less likely to have to extend the existing cables. Tracks can be tailored to suit small or large rooms by adding extra lengths with purpose-designed couplers.

Downlighters are often more difficult to fit; because they are intended to be positioned over the area to be lit they usually require extra wiring (see Problem Solver). Recessed types need a large hole cut in the ceiling (making them unsuitable for lath and plaster) and a fair amount of clearance above. Surface-mounted downlighters can be fitted to lath and plaster ceilings.

.... Shopping List ....

The extra fittings you need depend mainly on the system you choose:
Spotlights Buy a conduit box and terminal block if the connections are exposed.
Track lighting Track comes in 1–3m (3–10') lengths:
Track couplers in various shapes are used to join sections.
Lampholders (the individual lights) must be compatible with the track system. Pendant lights and other standard accessories can be connected using a *track adaptor*.
Downlighters normally need no extras except to extend the wiring. Check your ceiling is plasterboard before buying a recessed type.
To extend the wiring buy 1mm^2 two-core and earth cable, green/yellow earth sleeving and a junction box (3-terminal for junction box lighting, 4-terminal for loop-in).
Tools checklist: Drill and bits, screwdrivers (standard and electrical), wire strippers and possibly a padsaw.

FITTING SPOTLIGHTS

In a small room, a spotlight cluster is normally fitted in the centre of the ceiling, in place of an existing rose. This makes the connections simple, but if the light needs to go elsewhere see Problem Solver on extending the wiring. Where the light has an enclosed base, make the connections inside it – otherwise fit a conduit box recessed into the surface of the ceiling.

Lightweight spotlights can be hung from the ceiling plaster using hollow wall fixings, but heavier ones should be screwed to a joist. If the chosen position for the new light doesn't coincide with a joist, the only solution is to fit a mounting board between two joists and screw the light to it.

Fitting a conduit box to take a spotlight also involves fitting a mounting board between the joists. The light then fixes directly to the box – boxes have screw threads to take M4 (4mm) machine screws which may come with the light.

Make certain the power is off before you start. Switch off at the consumer unit and remove the fuse or trip off the MCB for the circuit you are working on. Flick the light switch to check.

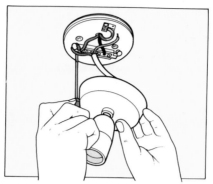

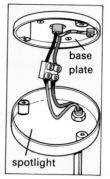

base plate / conduit box / spotlight

1 With the power switched off, remove the existing rose. If there is more than one cable present, label them to show the connections.

2 Some spotlights have a two-part base which encloses the connections. If the base is open, you must fit a conduit box and wire up inside it.

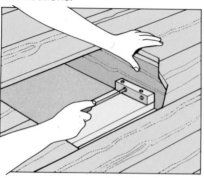

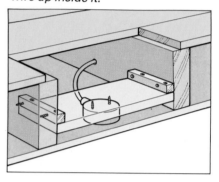

3 To fix a heavy spotlight between joists you need to fit a mounting board to take the screws. Lift floorboards to gain access from above.

4 If you need to fit a conduit box, fix a mounting board so that you can screw it in place flush with the ceiling. Lead the cables into the box.

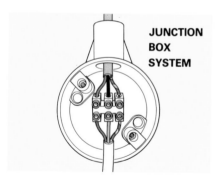

JUNCTION BOX SYSTEM

5 **Wire to a single cable** so that red goes to Live, black goes to Neutral and green/yellow goes to Earth. Use a terminal block connector if none is provided.

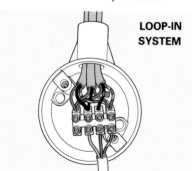

LOOP-IN SYSTEM

6 **For multiple cables** (loop-in wiring) wire up using 15 amp terminal block connectors to restore the connections in the same order as in the rose.

7 If you fitted a conduit box, attach the light to it by using machine screws. If the light has a two-part base, the machine screws are used to attach the light to the base after this has been screwed in place with woodscrews.

394

INSTALLING A TRACK SYSTEM

Track fixings must be screwed into the joists, so work out the track position before you start.

Flush fitting tracks are screwed straight to the ceiling and normally must run under a joist.

Clip fixing tracks are attached to metal clips screwed to the joists. The clips may be positioned at any point on the track, so the track can run with or across the joists.

Suspended fixings (brackets or wires) allow the track to hang away from the ceiling. Like clip fixings they run with or across the joists.

Switch off at the consumer unit before wiring into the lighting circuit. There are two options:

■ The easy option (the only one for suspended track) is to run a flex from the existing rose to the track terminals. On a loop-in rose this avoids having to fit a junction box to take all the connections.

■ The alternative for a flush fitted track is to remove the rose and wire directly to the lighting cables. On a loop-in system, or if the cable is too short, restore the connections using a junction box and add an extension cable (see Problem Solver). Patch the hole left by the rose or fit a screw-on *rose cover*.

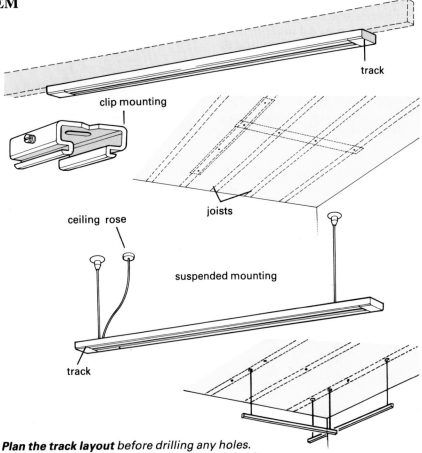

Plan the track layout before drilling any holes. Decide where to connect into the lighting circuit, and align the track so that the mountings are screwed into the joists.

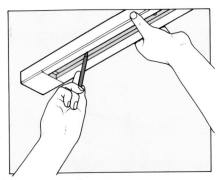

For a direct fixing system position the track with the cable entry hole over the ceiling rose position, mark the screw positions and drill the holes.

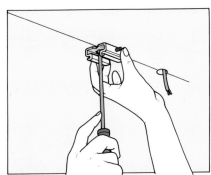

For clip fixing systems mark the track position with a pencil. Position the clips to align with the joists, make the screw holes and screw the clips in place.

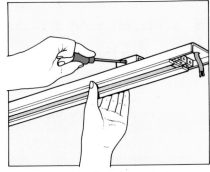

Feed the cable/flex through the entry hole. Screw the track to the ceiling, or slot it over the mounting clips, then tighten the screws to secure the track.

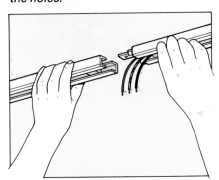

To join tracks slide in the connector and lock it in place with the screws provided. Slide in the next track section, lock it, and tighten all the fixings.

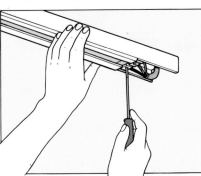

Wiring up depends on whether you wire to the cable or flex. Connect red or brown to live, black or blue to neutral, and green/yellow to earth.

Trade tip

Patching the holes

❝ When making good the hole after removing the ceiling rose, stuff a wad of paper into the hole. This gives the filler something to grip on and stops it pushing through the plaster.

For larger holes, use a scrap of expanded polystyrene.

Apply filler over the top and leave to harden thoroughly before sanding. ❞

FITTING A DOWNLIGHTER

Surface-mounted downlighters are fitted like spots. All other types go into holes cut in the ceiling, and the size of the hole is critical – if it's too loose the fixing clips won't grip. Most lights come with a template for accurate marking.

You are unlikely to want a downlighter in the same place as the old light so the wiring is likely to need extending (see Problem Solver). With most types the cable leads straight into the back and a junction box can be used to take the original rose connections. Before wiring up, make sure the power is off at the consumer unit.

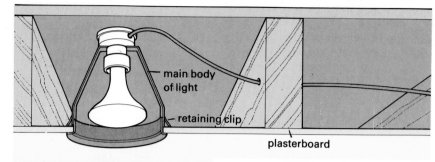

main body of light

retaining clip

plasterboard

outer flange

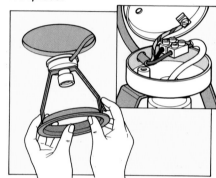

Recessed downlighters fit into a hole in the ceiling. When the light is pushed up, the legs of the clip spring outwards to lock it in place.

1 Mark the hole using a template or the light itself. Drill a hole inside the line then use a padsaw to cut out the circle. Be careful not to cut it too large.

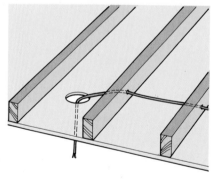

2 The downlighter should be a snug fit in the hole. If it's too tight, ease the sides gently with coarse sandpaper until it fits properly.

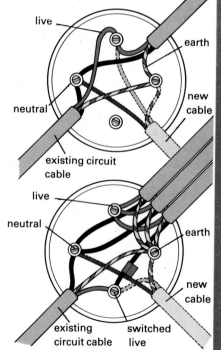

3 Connect the cable to the light. Adjust the retaining clip to suit the thickness of the ceiling then push the downlighter into place until it locks in.

PROBLEM SOLVER

Extending the wiring

To extend the lights to a new position use 1mm² cable.

If you can work from above drill a hole 50mm (2") below the top of each joist, midway between the floorboard nails, to run the cable across them.

If there is no access from above, cut small holes under each joist to pull the wiring through. Probe to find the joist positions, and cut a 100×50mm (4×2") hole in the plaster below each one. Notch each joist to take the cable using a chisel.

Make a loop in the end of the new cable and feed it towards the first hole starting from the existing wiring. Hook the cable from each hole in turn using a bent coathanger wire. Screw metal plates to each joist to hold the wire in the notches. Finally, patch the ceiling with plasterboard and filler.

Connect up with a junction box taking the place of the existing rose and joining the new cable.

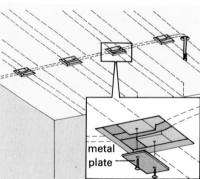

metal plate

Run cable through holes in the joists by lifting floorboards, or run it underneath the joists, using a bent coathanger to pull it through holes cut in the plaster.

live

earth

neutral

new cable

existing circuit cable

live

neutral

earth

new cable

existing circuit cable

switched live

You can connect to the existing circuit cable either with a new junction box (top) or by making use of an existing 4-terminal box (bottom).

WIRING AN EXTENSION PHONE

Since the end of 1986 you have been permitted to wire as many as three extension phones to your existing line, subject to certain limits. Most importantly, you *must* have a line with a modern, square master socket. Only British Telecom (BT) or other approved Telecomms Operator can fit these, but if you're having a phone installed for the first time, you automatically get a new-type socket. If you have an older system without one, BT will convert it for a standard charge.

new master socket
old joint box

All you then need is a suitable telephone and extension kit (see Shopping List). You're dealing with low voltages so there's no safety risk – and even if anything does go wrong, it shouldn't affect your existing phone.

APPROVED for connection to telecommunication systems specified in the instructions for use subject to the conditions set out in them.
PROHIBITED from direct or indirect connection to public telecommunication system. Action may be taken against anyone so connecting this apparatus.

By law, no phone equipment can be sold without an approvals sticker. You cannot connect a phone or extension kit to a BT line unless it carries the 'green circle' approved sticker. If equipment has a 'red triangle' sticker it is *illegal* to connect it to a BT line.

Trade tip

Don't overload
❝ The number of extensions you can have on one line is limited to four by the power available – overdo it, and one or more of them may not ring.
All phones, answering machines, etc have a power demand rating called a REN (Ring Equivalence Number). Ren=1 is the rating of a standard phone, but some are higher than this (a machine like a computer modem may be as high as Ren=3). If your **total** loading exceeds 4, you'll probably need another line. ❞

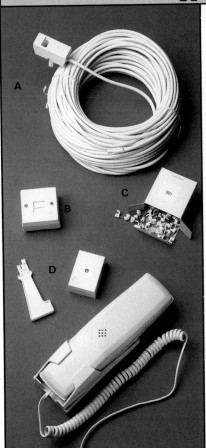

.... Shopping List ....

Extension kit Cable, sockets, and all the other parts you will need are available separately, but it is simplest to buy (from your nearest Telephone Shop) a complete, approved kit consisting of a plug-in converter and cable (A), extension socket (B), clips (C) and screws. Double extension packs and other kits are also available. The picture shows a BT kit; others vary in detail.

The cable supplied with the single kit is normally about 15m (16yd) long – if you need more you can buy extra and join it using a joint box (D). You will also need a joint box if you are going to install more than one socket branching from a single point (see overleaf).

Telephone Make sure that the telephone you buy has a green approval sticker (see left) and that it is suitable for use as an extension.

Tools for the job A small hammer, trimming knife, drill, screwdriver and a pair of pliers.

WHICH LAYOUT?

The first decision to make is how many sockets you want and where to put them. Even though you are limited to a total of four *phones* (a master and three extensions), you can have more *sockets* provided they aren't all in use at once. You shouldn't put sockets in areas where they will be exposed to damp or condensation such as in the bathroom, or near a sink, cooker, washbasin or toilet.

A single extension can be taken off the existing master socket (or an existing extension socket). Because the power is limited, the only restriction is that there must not be more than a *total* of 50m (55yd) of cable between the master socket and *any* extension.

Multiple extensions work on the same principle, but there are two alternative layouts. Each socket can be connected to the next one, in a chain or *series*, or they can all branch out from a single point. In the first case you can make all the connections inside the extension sockets themselves. In the second, you need a *joint box* to connect all the branches together.

A SINGLE EXTENSION

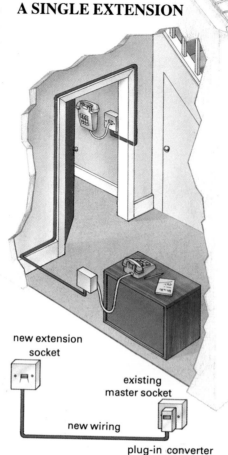

new extension socket

existing master socket

new wiring

plug-in converter

A common situation is where the master socket is in the hall and you want an extension in the kitchen or bedroom. This is normally within reach of a single 15m cable, but try to plan the neatest, least noticeable route.

RUNNING CABLE

Although few people will have the same *expertise* as a professional engineer, doing it yourself does mean that you can afford to take more *trouble* over running the wiring neatly than most professionals have the time for. Getting a neat, functional system is largely a matter of care, common sense and these simple rules:

■ Don't run within 50mm (2″) of any mains cables or sockets – they can cause interference on phone.
■ Don't run under carpets.
■ Don't run cables outdoors.

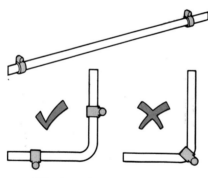

1 *Clip the cable every 300mm (12in), pulling it straight as you go. Don't clip right into corners – put a clip either side, about 40mm (1½in) away.*

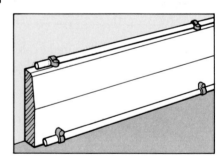

2 *Clip the cable into the angle along the top or bottom of skirtings – wherever is easiest, least noticeable, and best protected from knocks.*

Trade tip

Get it straight

❝ If the cable has been left coiled it can be hard to get it to lay straight. But I find that pulling it through a rag to protect my hand usually removes the kinks. ❞

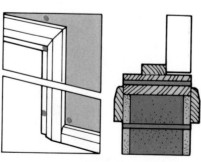

3 *Don't run cable through a doorway where it may get trapped. Drill through the frame or wall at a corner – as indicated in red.*

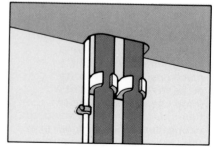

4 *Going upstairs, see if you can route the cable along a cold water pipe (not a hot pipe or mains cable). Use a bent wire coat hanger to pull it through.*

CONVERTING THE MASTER SOCKET

This is the property of the telephone company and must not be tampered with. Instead, you plug in a converter which has a socket for the original phone and a length of extension cable already attached.

Don't plug in the converter until you've finished the wiring: you could get an unpleasant (though not dangerous) jolt if someone rings up while you are handling the bare wires.

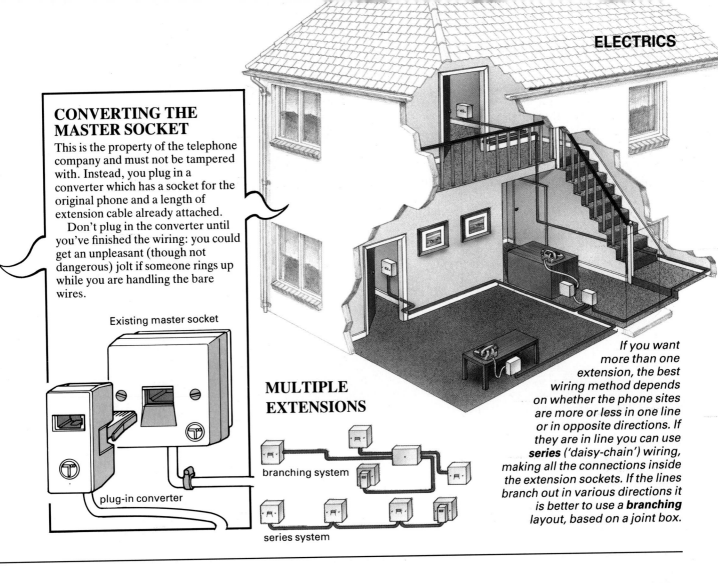

Existing master socket

plug-in converter

MULTIPLE EXTENSIONS

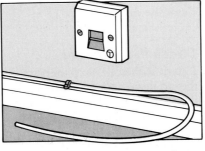

branching system

series system

If you want more than one extension, the best wiring method depends on whether the phone sites are more or less in one line or in opposite directions. If they are in line you can use **series** ('daisy-chain') wiring, making all the connections inside the extension sockets. If the lines branch out in various directions it is better to use a **branching** layout, based on a joint box.

STRIPPING AND CONNECTING

The outer sheath is simple to strip, as there is a drawstring to split it without damaging the conductors. There is no need to strip the inner wires, as the terminals in telephone sockets have a pair of sharp jaws which score the insulation and make their own contacts.

However, if you have not done it before, it is worth practising stripping some surplus cable. It is *not* a good idea to cut the cable to the exact length you need to start with, as a mistake means moving the socket or buying a new cable.

1 Screw the socket to the wall and leave plenty of surplus cable beyond it. If you trim too close, there is no margin for error and no second chance.

2 Slit the sheath lengthways beyond the point you want to stop at (cutting around the cable is likely to nick the wires). Find the drawstring and ease it out.

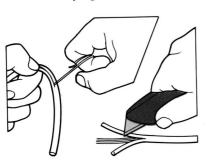

3 Take a couple of turns of the string around your finger (if you don't it can cut you) and pull it along the cable to split the sheath. Snip off the waste.

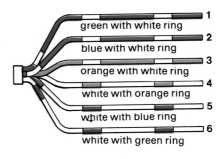

1 green with white ring
2 blue with white ring
3 orange with white ring
4 white with orange ring
5 white with blue ring
6 white with green ring

4 There are six colour-coded conductors – three white with narrow coloured rings, and three coloured with narrow rings of white. See over for connections.

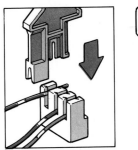

5 Kits contain a disposable tool for inserting the wires into the terminals as shown. You must push hard to make a contact, so take care not to break the tool.

399

THE RIGHT CONNECTIONS

A SINGLE EXTENSION

Trim the six wires inside the cable to leave plenty of slack and cut back the outer sheath so it will tuck neatly inside the box (use pliers to break open the notch where the cable enters the box). Connect the wires to the terminals as shown below.

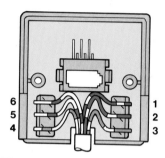

The coloured wires with white rings go to the right, the white wires with coloured rings to the left. Check that the numbers correspond to the diagram.

WIRING IN SERIES

You can use an extension socket as shown to connect two lengths of cable where you are wiring up multiple extensions in series. However, the terminals aren't big enough to take *more* than two sets of wires.

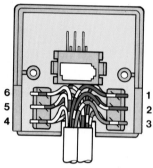

Both sets of wires are connected in the same colour order as a single extension – simply put the second set on top of the first and connect to the same terminals.

USING A JOINT BOX

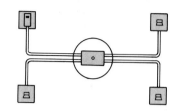

To connect more than two cables together, use a joint box. This takes one incoming and up to three outgoing cables.

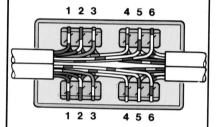

Connect the six wires in the first cable to one side of the box as shown, then connect the second set over the top. Connect the third and fourth set to the opposite side of the box in the same way.

PROBLEM SOLVER

If it won't work . . .

Most likely, the wire isn't making proper contact with a terminal in the socket or joint box and needs to be inserted again. Or, a wire may have broken internally due to being kinked too often.

Neither fault is easy to see, so check back along the run to narrow down the cause. (Ideally, check each extension as you finish wiring it.)

The phone is more likely to send and receive calls than to

ring, so ask a friend to call and check the ringer.

Check in this order . . .

1 Start with your old phone at the old master socket. Unplug the adaptor and check the phone still works. If it doesn't, the fault must lie in the line or old socket; get BT to check them.
2 Plug in the adaptor and try your old phone. If it doesn't

work now, the adaptor is at fault.
3 Plug your old phone into the *first* extension. If this doesn't work, the fault is in the cable from the adaptor, or its socket connection.
4 & 5 Work down any other extensions in sequence away from the first. If there is a fault, it must lie in the area shown shaded red in the diagram.

Finally, test your new phone in a socket you know works.

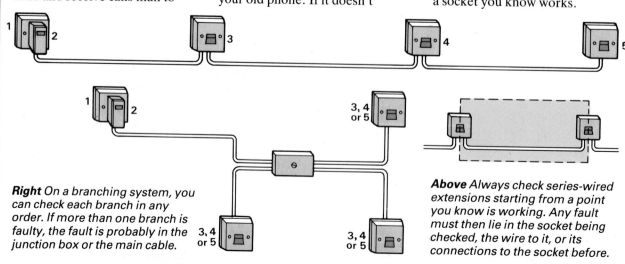

Right On a branching system, you can check each branch in any order. If more than one branch is faulty, the fault is probably in the junction box or the main cable.

Above Always check series-wired extensions starting from a point you know is working. Any fault must then lie in the socket being checked, the wire to it, or its connections to the socket before.

ADDING EXTRA TV AERIAL SOCKETS

In most reception areas, a television set gives a much better picture with a fixed roof aerial. Usually, there's only one room with an aerial connection, and to watch TV anywhere else you either need to use a portable aerial or plug in a clumsy aerial extension lead. But in fact it's neither difficult nor expensive to connect several sockets to the roof aerial. This allows you to:

■ Plug a TV into the roof aerial anywhere in the house.

■ Use another TV at the same time.

■ Connect up your video so that you can play it back through a TV set in another room.

Even if you're not keen on tackling mains electrical work, aerial wiring is one job you can do with complete confidence. There is no risk of shocks and no risk of damage to the set. The only limitations on aerial extensions are:

■ You must NOT take a mains powered TV into the bathroom – this is extremely dangerous.

■ In poor reception areas, or if the cables are very long, you may need to fit a device which boosts the signal. This is covered in detail in Problem Solver.

A second TV in the bedroom or elsewhere in the house can have just as good a picture as the main set if you install a branch cable off the roof aerial.

....Shopping List....

The main fittings for extending aerial wiring are cable, plugs, sockets and signal splitters.

Aerial cable TV aerials are wired up with 'low-loss' UHF *co-axial* cable (sometimes called 'co-ax'). This usually has brown or white outer insulation. Other types of co-ax are made for audio wiring, so be sure to use the right sort.

Plugs and sockets Co-ax cable is connected up with co-axial plugs and sockets. The aerial cable connects to the set via a 'male' co-axial plug. 'Female' plugs are used on video connections and for extending cables fitted with male plugs.

For a neater installation, you can fit wall-mounted sockets and connect the TV via a short length of cable (known as a fly lead) with a plug at each end.

Signal splitters enable you to divide the aerial signal between two or more TV sets. There are several types (see overleaf).

Signal boosters or filters may be needed to solve reception problems. These are covered in detail in Problem Solver.

Tools: Screwdrivers, electric drill and bits, trimming knife, hammer. A cheap pair of wire strippers is worth having, but you can manage with a knife.

Aerial fittings (right) are widely available from hobby electronics shops and DIY stores.

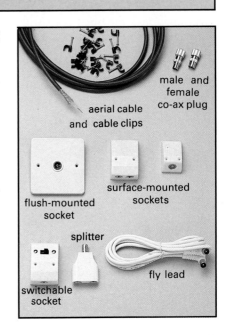

aerial cable and cable clips

male and female co-ax plug

flush-mounted socket

surface-mounted sockets

splitter

fly lead

switchable socket

EXTENDING YOUR SYSTEM

A typical roof aerial has a length of co-axial cable running down the side of the house. This usually comes in through a window frame and plugs into the back of the set. Or it may lead to a socket mounted on the skirting board or wall, with a separate length run to the TV.

Alternatively, the cable may enter the house via the loft, or the aerial itself may be installed in the roof space. This makes little practical difference, except that the conversion is simpler because all the cables are accessible from indoors.

What you need to add

To extend the system, you break into the cable coming from the aerial at a convenient point, and install a signal splitter and branch cable. Where to do this depends on:

Convenience The shorter the cables, the better. And think about the ease of running the cable from the branch point to the TV.

Accessibility There's no point in trying to branch off at a point you can't get at easily.

Cover Don't branch the cable at any point where it will be exposed to the elements. If you can't avoid this, use a weatherproof splitter.

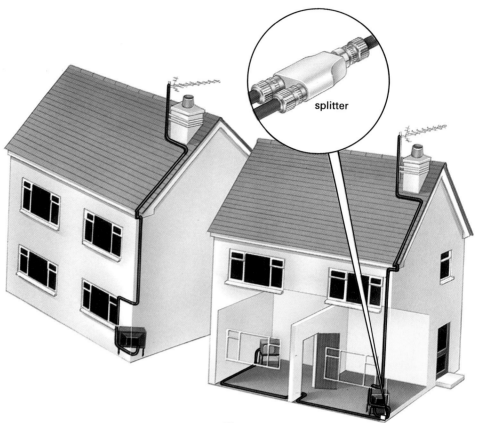

splitter

The lead from the roof aerial (above) *commonly runs down the outside of the house and enters via a hole in the living room window frame.*

One way to extend the system (above) *is to fit a signal splitter to the end of the existing cable and run a new length to the second socket.*

WORKING WITH CO-AXIAL CABLE

Co-ax cable is the heart of an aerial system. The single insulated core in the middle, which carries the signal, is surrounded by a braided sheathing of fine wire strands under the outer plastic insulation. This stops interference reaching the core.

It's worth practising stripping and connecting a spare piece of co-ax. The main thing to ensure is that none of the fine strands of the sheathing touch the inner core or its terminal. There is no risk of a 'short circuit' – it simply means that the TV signal could be interrupted.

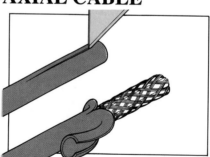

1 Strip co-ax by slitting the sheathing for 25mm (1") or so with a trimming knife. Cut off the insulation and fold back the sheathing to expose the core.

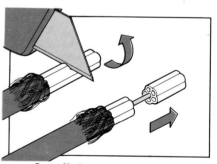

2 Cut off about 12mm (½") of the inner insulation to expose the core wire. This insulation is often cellular, and needs care to cut it cleanly.

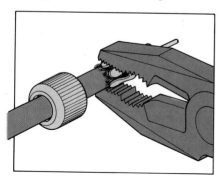

To fit a plug, *unscrew the cap. Slip this and the sheathing grip over the cable so the grip encloses the braid completely, then close the grip with pliers . . .*

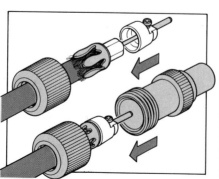

*. . . **Slip the core** wire into the centre pin, which may have a clamp screw. Cut off any surplus wire projecting from the end. Then reassemble the body.*

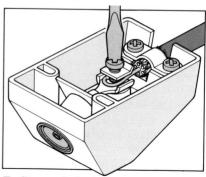

To fit a socket *wind the core wire clockwise round the inner terminal screw and tighten. Trap the sheathing in the outer clamp. Make sure no stray strands touch.*

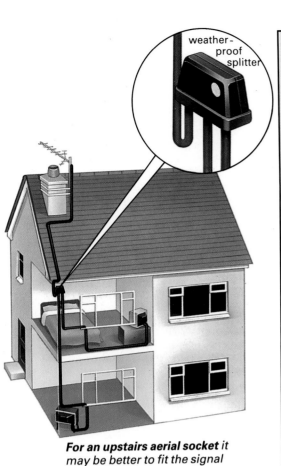

For an upstairs aerial socket it may be better to fit the signal splitter partway down the cable, nearer to the TV, to keep the leads short.

TYPES OF SIGNAL SPLITTER

Splitters divide a single aerial signal to feed two or more TVs. Some types are combined with signal boosters for use in poor reception areas (see Problem Solver).

Plug-in splitters are the simplest type. They fit into plugs attached to the ends of the aerial leads.

Surface-mounting splitters combine a socket for the first TV with a connection for the second.

Switchable sockets allow you to divert the aerial signal from one outlet to another.

Weatherproof splitters can be installed outdoors – usually on the aerial mast – with leads to feed more than one socket.

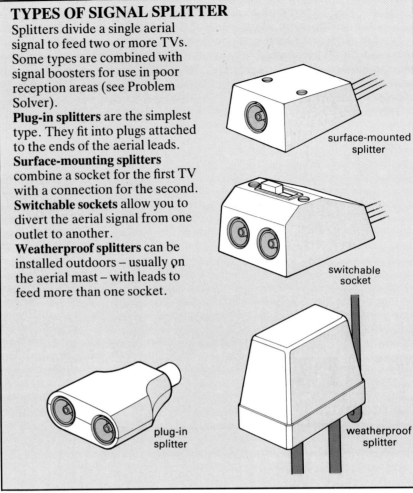

RUNNING THE CABLES

Aerial cable is bulky, and won't run round tight corners easily. For this reason, route it inconspicuously wherever possible, and don't pull it tight or force it around bends.

Run the cable under the floorboards if these are accessible and you can lift them easily. Otherwise take it along the tops of skirting boards, either clipped in place or hidden in plastic mini-trunking.

Don't be tempted to run the cable under a carpet where people can walk on it – this is likely to damage both, the cable and the carpet. Where it is exposed, decide whether white or brown sheathing is least obvious.

Sockets come in different styles and can be bought with single or double outlets or combined with splitters (see above). The main choice is between surface mounting or flush mounting fittings.

Flush mounted fittings are exactly the same size as power sockets and are designed for use with standard socket or switch backing boxes, for fitting to the wall itself.

Surface mounted fittings need no backing box and normally screw to the skirting board.

Under floorboards is one route for the cable, if you can get at the boards easily. Use a bolster, spade or crowbar to lever up a series of boards for access.

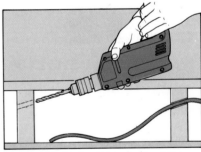

Drill holes in the joists to feed the cable through and let it hang slackly between them. Drill a hole in the floor to feed the cable up to the skirting.

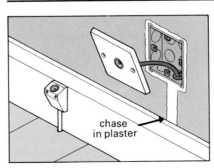

Surface mounted sockets can be screwed to the skirting. To fit a flush wall socket, you need to cut a channel in the plaster and fit a backing box to the wall.

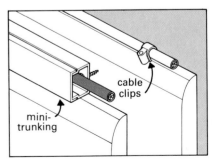

Run exposed cable along the top of the skirting board with cable clips. Alternatively route it in plastic mini-trunking, nailed or glued to the wall or skirting.

VIDEO PLAYBACK

It is possible to play back a video recorder over your aerial system so that you can view it on any TV in the house. This needn't prevent you from watching transmitted TV at the same time – the only disadvantage is that the video won't be controllable from the extension.

The cheapest option is to connect the video so that it receives a signal straight from the main aerial. Use a splitter at this point to distribute the video output to both the main TV and the extension. You can then tune either TV to a transmitted channel or select the video channel to view a playback.

This arrangement works, but it is possible that the picture quality may suffer because of the long leads and multiple connections. An alternative is to use a *distribution amplifier* designed to work with video. These are powered from the mains and cost around as much as three or four video cassettes. They have a single aerial input and two or more amplified outputs to compensate for the loss of signal strength.

You can also buy *video sender units* which plug into your video recorder and transmit signals to all the TVs in the house. However, while it is legal to sell them in the UK, it is illegal (for reasons of interference) to use them!

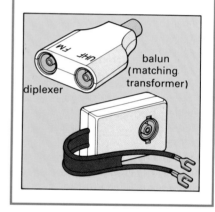

diplexer   balun (matching transformer)

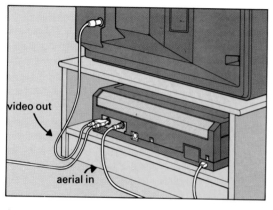

Connect your video like this as an inexpensive means of playing it back over a TV plugged into an extension socket, as well as the main TV. Select either the video or transmitted signals in the ordinary way.

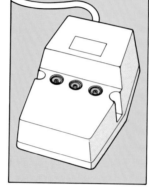

A distribution amplifier makes up for the loss in signal strength caused by splitting the signal from the video in the way shown on the left. It needs a mains power supply and may have a variety of different outputs.

PROBLEM SOLVER

Signal strength problems

It is important for the signal reaching the set to be the right strength, otherwise the picture goes fuzzy and won't hold. Colour TVs need a stronger signal than black and white, and tend to suffer more.

Extending the aerial causes a slight loss of strength, and if the picture gets worse after you have completed the job, you may need to fit a booster.

Signal boosters

Indoor signal boosters and *mast-head amplifiers* (fitted at the aerial) are mains-powered. They compensate for loss of signal strength caused by a long cable run or by multiple extensions. However, the booster may also increase the strength of any interference present – though

you can get devices called *filters* designed to remove this. Many boosters have multiple outlets for a number of different TV sets, so you can do without separate splitters.

Aerial alignment

If the picture is unsatisfactory to start with, make sure that the aerial is properly aligned. This isn't all that easy, and if the aerial is hard to reach you may prefer to call in an aerial installer.

Professional installers use special *field strength meters* to set the aerial up. But if you want to have a go yourself and can get to the aerial, do the job when the test card picture is being broadcast. Get someone to watch the set and call out whether the picture gets better or worse as you move the aerial.

An indoor booster fitted in the main cable increases the signal strength to extra outlets.

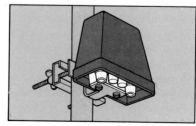

A mast-head amplifier has a weatherproof casing and may have several outlets.

FITTING A BURGLAR ALARM

There are several good reasons why you might want to fit an alarm:

■ As a back-up to conventional door and window locks.

■ Your house is particularly at risk (although an alarm relies on having someone nearby or a phone link).

■ An insurance company insists on it or offers a reduced premium (they may exclude DIY systems).

However, a burglar alarm is by no means a magic answer to worries about burglary – it's the last line of defence, to warn you that someone has *already* got in. And although the sight of an alarm box may act as a deterrent, it can also suggest there is something worth stealing. So weigh up the pros and cons.

First, ask yourself if your home really is as secure as you can make it, with stout, thief-proof locks on every door and window.

Then there's the question of false alarms, for which burglar alarms are notorious. Although installation faults are frequently to blame, the cause is all too often the owners – they simply can't adjust to the restrictions on lifestyle which living with a burglar alarm impose. Either way, constant false alarms seriously reduce a burglar alarm's effectiveness. And if you've ever ignored a bell going off in the street, it's

worth asking yourself whether neighbours will respond.

Buying alarms

If you want a warning system to wake the household if anyone breaks in at night, a simple DIY *intruder alarm* (see below) costs relatively little. Full alarm systems to alert the neighbours or police are more expensive and complicated.

Buying outright is the only option if you use a DIY kit. You can also buy from a company who install the

A burglar alarm buys peace of mind, but is not without its drawbacks.

system and offer a maintenance contract to cover repairs. The alarm can be sold on if you move (it's rarely worth taking it with you).

Renting means going to a specialist company who fit the alarm and service it regularly. You pay a monthly or quarterly charge, but repairs may cost extra. The company still owns the alarm and will take it out if you move.

DIY INTRUDER ALARMS

Intruder alarms are simple devices which sound a warning to members of the household if someone gets in at night. There is no external bell to alert anyone outside the house.

Battery-operated alarms are screwed to doors or windows and are set off if these are opened. Some types are armed by a push-button code or key; for interior doors a simple switch is adequate.

Plug-in alarms use infra-red detectors which plug into any mains socket. These work by sensing the heat of an intruder and come with a bracket for mounting in the corner of a room (the ideal position).

The control unit also plugs into any convenient socket and uses the mains wiring to pick up signals from the detectors. If an intruder tries to unplug a detector or the control unit while the system is armed, the bell goes off.

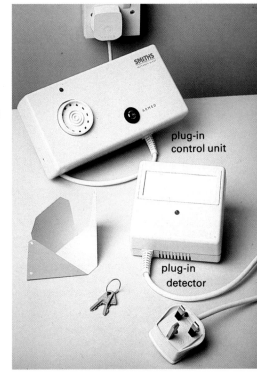

Battery alarms (above) are fitted to individual doors or windows.
Plug-in alarms (right) fit into any socket to sense an intruder.

BURGLAR ALARM SYSTEMS

A whole-house alarm system consists of a control unit, an alarm bell or siren, and a number of different types of detector. These include contacts which respond when doors and windows are opened and 'presence detectors' to sense an intruder within a room. DIY kits tend to have fewer types of detector.

Most alarm systems are linked by thin cables running around the house as shown here. Some DIY alarms, however, are linked by radio transmitters which take the place of the fixed wiring (see page 410).

Zoning

In basic systems the whole house is on the same circuit and all the detectors have either to be armed or turned off. More costly systems are designed so that parts of the house are on separate circuits called 'zones' – for example, Zone 1 could be outer doors and windows; Zone 2 the inner doors and presence detectors. This provides more flexibility: in the example given, you could turn on the outer zone at night to detect a break-in, while leaving the inner off in case you have to get up in the night.

Parts of a system

Control unit. At its simplest this is a box with a key-operated switch, a delay setting so you can enter or leave when the system is armed, and a test button and lights to warn that the system is armed or faulty. Most contain a battery in case of a power cut, and some recharge the battery continuously. More expensive models have features like zoning and push-button arming codes.

Automatic telephone diallers can be used with some control units. These plug into a phone socket and dial a pre-set number – the police,

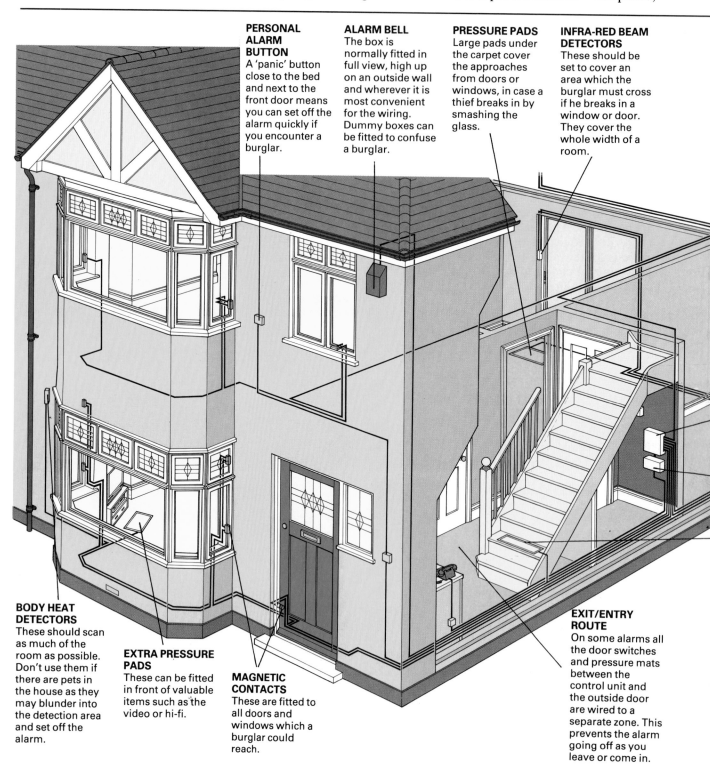

PERSONAL ALARM BUTTON
A 'panic' button close to the bed and next to the front door means you can set off the alarm quickly if you encounter a burglar.

ALARM BELL
The box is normally fitted in full view, high up on an outside wall and wherever it is most convenient for the wiring. Dummy boxes can be fitted to confuse a burglar.

PRESSURE PADS
Large pads under the carpet cover the approaches from doors or windows, in case a thief breaks in by smashing the glass.

INFRA-RED BEAM DETECTORS
These should be set to cover an area which the burglar must cross if he breaks in a window or door. They cover the whole width of a room.

BODY HEAT DETECTORS
These should scan as much of the room as possible. Don't use them if there are pets in the house as they may blunder into the detection area and set off the alarm.

EXTRA PRESSURE PADS
These can be fitted in front of valuable items such as the video or hi-fi.

MAGNETIC CONTACTS
These are fitted to all doors and windows which a burglar could reach.

EXIT/ENTRY ROUTE
On some alarms all the door switches and pressure mats between the control unit and the outside door are wired to a separate zone. This prevents the alarm going off as you leave or come in.

say – to raise the alarm. Some even allow you to ring and check that all is well. A rented system may be connected to a control station, who check whether it's a false alarm then contact the police.

Alarm bell/siren. This is encased in a weatherproof box with a switch to set the alarm off if anyone tries to remove it; some boxes have a flashing warning light too.

On most systems, the bell can also be triggered – whether or not the system is activated – by hitting a *personal alarm button* ('panic button') mounted indoors. This can only be turned off with a key.

Detectors come in four main types:
- *Magnetic contacts* are for doors and windows. A tiny *reed switch* is fitted to the frame and a small magnet goes on the opening part. When separated, the switch trips.

There are surface- and flush-mounted types. Surface mounting is simpler, but the detectors are easily tampered with. Flush-mounted detectors are virtually undetectable.
- *Pressure pads* under the carpets activate when trodden on. Large pads go in front of a door, and special narrow mats on stairs.

- *Presence detectors* are mostly infra-red devices which react to body heat or project an invisible beam to trigger the alarm if someone walks through it.

Ultrasonic and microwave types send out a regular wave pattern. When someone moving around upsets this, it triggers the alarm.
- *Glass detectors* are for windows or glazed doors. Stick-on foil strip and wires are rarely used in the home; unobtrusive vibration sensors react to the glass being broken (but these may be prone to false alarms unless correctly set up).

A typical system for a three-bedroom semi. Most DIY kits are about this size, but some of the detectors and other features shown are only likely to be available in a professionally installed alarm.

WIRING
Most systems use two-core flex or bell wire. Some systems use four-core anti-tamper flex. Two of the cores form a continuous circuit to and from the control unit: if a burglar tries to cut the cable, the alarm goes off.

CONTROL UNIT
This should be fitted out of sight, but where you can reach it within the delay time allowed for getting in and out of the house.

TELEPHONE DIALLER
This should be in reach of the phone, but concealed so that if a burglar gains entry the phone plug won't simply be pulled out of its socket.

STAIR PADS
Narrow pressure pads designed for stair treads should be laid under the carpet of the second stair.

Trade tip

Fire alarm
❛ Many alarm systems have the facility for connecting a smoke detector. If the detector senses a fire it will set off the main alarm (and any automatic phone dialling system too). ❜

GETTING A SYSTEM INSTALLED

Professional installation of a basic alarm is likely to cost at least three times as much as a DIY kit. Against this, weigh up the peace of mind that you get from the guarantee on the installation, and the option of a service contract. At a price, you can probably also add features not found in DIY systems.
- First, ask several firms for an estimate. They will only give a firm quote after carrying out a survey, but should be able to suggest a price range for a given type of house. Get their catalogues to check what the 'basic' installation includes (control unit features, the number of detectors and so on). Any extras will add to the cost.
- When you know roughly what you want, ask for a quote. Most firms send round a surveyor to work out a tailor-made system for your home and give you an accurate costing – make sure you specify any non-standard extras.

Most companies quote for surface-mounting the wiring; if you want it hidden, this costs extra.

Preparation
- Before the fitters come round, move any furniture and have fitted carpets taken up (unless this was included in the quote). The fitters may not have the special tools to take up carpets; even if they do, the job will take longer and the charges increased accordingly.
- Fitting an alarm to an average four-bedroomed house takes about 1–1½ days, depending on the number of sensors and how hard it is to run the wiring. Make sure there's someone around in case the fitters run into any problems. For example, if they are forced to drill into a wall at some visible point you may have to decide where you least mind this showing.

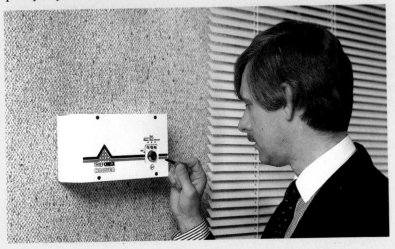

After installation the alarm company will thoroughly test the system before issuing a guarantee.

DIY ALARM KITS

A DIY system usually comes as a 'starter kit' designed to suit a normally sized house. To this you add extra detectors (and wiring) as needed. The alternative to a conventionally wired system is a radio controlled type which offers easier installation (see page 410).

All alarm equipment runs at low voltages, making it very safe to work with. The only exceptions are the control unit (and sometimes the bell), which must be plugged into the mains. There is nothing very complicated about the installation, but there is a lot of wiring to run. Careful fitting and setting up of the installation is the key to avoiding false alarms.

Take great care to get the various switches and pressure mats in the right places, and the wiring neatly and unobtrusively routed. All the wiring should be done in one go, zone by zone, to make sure nothing gets missed. The simplest order is:
■ Fit the control unit.
■ Fit the alarm bell and run its wires into the house.
■ Fit the detectors.
■ Complete wiring up and test.

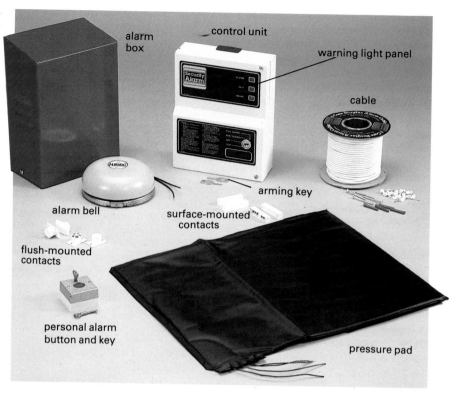

A typical DIY kit includes a control unit, alarm bell and box, an array of detectors, and a reel of cable. The standard kit should cope with an average house, but extra detectors and cable are sold separately.

FITTING THE CONTROL UNIT AND ALARM

The control unit should be screwed to the wall where the electrical connections to the mains and the rest of the alarm system are easy to run. (An understairs cupboard is often a good choice, but make sure you will be able to reach it in time to switch off the alarm.)

The unit needs a permanent mains supply. The simplest option is to plug it into a nearby socket, but this means you lose the use of that socket. A more satisfactory solution is to have a fused connection unit (FCU) wired off the downstairs power circuit and connect to this.

Don't make the final mains connection until the system is fully installed.

The alarm bell should be screwed to the outside wall as near to the eaves as possible so that the wires can be run through the roof space. Make sure you have safe access.

The bell can be powered from the control unit, or from the mains – normally by wiring into the upstairs lighting circuit.

It's usually easiest to run the cable between the soffit board and the wall, then on into loft. Where this isn't possible, feed the wiring through a hole drilled in the wall and pack around it with mastic.

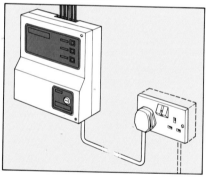

The control unit is screwed to the wall out of sight and near the main exit door. One way to power the unit is to plug it into a nearby socket . . .

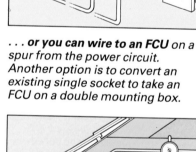

. . . or you can wire to an FCU on a spur from the power circuit. Another option is to convert an existing single socket to take an FCU on a double mounting box.

The alarm box is screwed to the outside wall, working from an extension ladder. Fit it close to the eaves to make running the cables easier.

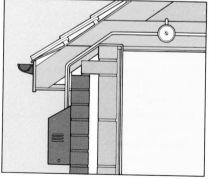

Run the cables into the roof space up under the eaves or through the wall. Mains power can often conveniently be taken off the lighting circuit.

FITTING DETECTORS AND WIRING UP

Magnetic contact and pressure pad wiring runs from the control unit to one detector, then on to the next. It makes sense to wire up as you go, but connect to the control unit last.

Magnetic contacts go on the frame, with the magnet on the opening part. Use flush-mounted switches on doors; surface-mounted on windows.

Fit the switch on or near the closing side, but with no more than 5mm (³⁄₁₆″) gap between the two parts. Connect the wire and feed it out – on flush-mounted switches, through a hole drilled behind.

Pressure pads go under carpets on routes from windows and doors. (On some systems you can't put one on your own exit/entry route.)

■ Lift the carpets and cut holes the size of the pad in any underlay.

■ Lay the pad in place. Stick it down with double-sided carpet tape – or secure to a wooden floor with tacks if locating tags are provided.

■ Connect the wires (ideally solder them for trouble-free connections).

■ Run the wiring out beneath the underlay. If there is a ridge, cut a small channel in the underlay.

Personal alarm buttons screw to the wall at the most convenient point. The wiring runs straight back to the control unit.

Running the wiring

Run the wires unobtrusively but also directly. Suitable routes include:

■ Along skirtings and around door frames; secure using cable clips.

■ Along the gap between carpet gripper strips and skirtings.

■ Under the upstairs floorboards and through holes in the ceiling.

Connections

All the wiring runs back to the control unit, where there are separate terminals for the two kinds of circuit employed.

Normally closed (NC) circuits trigger the alarm when broken. Most circuits are like this.

Normally open (NO) circuits trigger when they are completed. Pressure pads use this type.

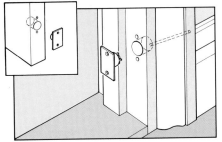
On doors, fit flush-mounted magnetic contacts on or near the opening side. They are set into pre-drilled holes with a further hole to feed the wire through.

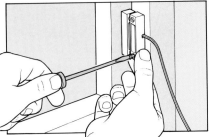
On windows, screw surface-mounted contacts to the frame on or near the opening side. The wiring can be led down the frame and on to the next contact.

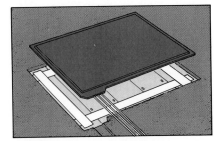
Pressure pads fit under the carpets. Cut out a section of underlay the same size to avoid leaving a lump and fix the pad to the floor.

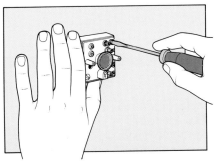
Panic buttons are screwed to the wall at a convenient height. Run the wiring straight back to the control unit using the most direct route.

Run the wires neatly along the tops of skirting boards and door architraves, along the edge of a fitted carpet, or under the floor and down through the ceiling.

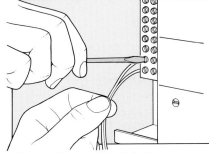
Connection terminals in the control unit should be marked to show the type of circuit. Wire the detectors according to the kit instructions.

TESTING

With the wiring complete, turn on the mains and test the system. Most alarms have a test buzzer so you can check everything works without rousing the whole street. Systems vary in detail, but the standard test and set-up procedure normally runs something like this:

■ Shut all the doors and windows and ensure that there's nothing on the pressure pads.

■ With the power switched on, check that any 'mains power' warning light is on. Turn the key or key-in the code number to arm the system – and select the outer zone if there is more than one. Check that the exit/entry buzzer sounds.

■ Wait for the buzzer to go off, then open a door or window in the zone under test – the alarm should sound. Switch off the alarm and repeat the check for all the other switches on the same circuit, including pressure pads and presence detectors.

■ Repeat the testing sequence for any other zones.

■ Finally, adjust the exit and entry timers to give you enough time to get out of and into the house, then test this by going out, shutting the door and coming back in again. As you re-enter the house, the buzzer should sound; leave it running to check that the alarm sounds.

RADIO ALARMS

Installation of a radio alarm is similar to the fixed wired type, except that there are no long cable runs. Instead, each group of detectors is wired to a transmitter or movement sensor with its own radio code signal; there is a separate signal for each 'zone'. Fitting is straightforward:

■ Fit the detectors.

■ Fit the movement sensors to scan the area you want.

■ Screw a transmitter to the wall near each detector group.

■ Run the detector wires to the nearest transmitter or movement sensor. The connections depend on the type being wired up.

■ Mount the siren on an outside wall as high up as possible. Wire this into a convenient mains supply.

■ Connect the control unit to the mains and test the alarm.

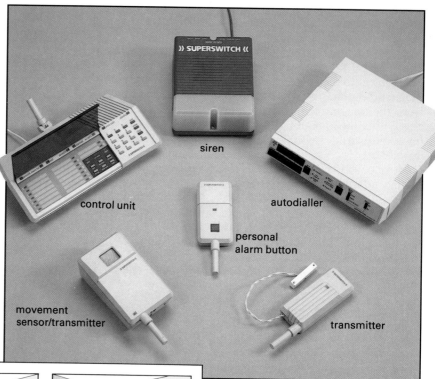

control unit

siren

autodialler

personal alarm button

movement sensor/transmitter

transmitter

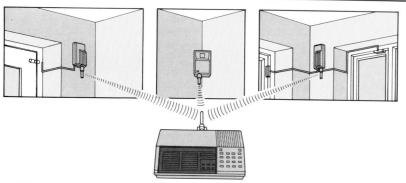

Radio alarm kits (above) have a control/receiver unit, a siren and a range of detectors. The detectors can be linked to transmitter units or to movement sensors (which have a transmitter built in).

When installed (left), each group of detectors is wired to a transmitter which then beams a coded signal to the control unit.

▌PROBLEM SOLVER▌

Troubleshooting

If a new installation is faulty, the problem is most likely the wires or connections. The warning lights on the control unit may give a clue where the fault lies.

No mains power light means no power is reaching the control unit. Test the plug or FCU fuse and all the mains connections.

Panic button light on (without button being triggered) suggests a fault in the anti-tamper switches for the control unit and bell, since these share the same circuit. Check the switches in their cases; there should be a distinct 'click' as the cover goes on. If necessary, bend the operating arm gently with pliers so that it bears harder on the casing or screw.

Alarm circuit lamp on (or alarm won't set) indicates a faulty detector – it could be a switch or pressure pad – or the wiring.

Test the wiring by disconnecting the alarm from the mains and removing the wires from the detector nearest the control unit. Connect a continuity tester between the two wires; if it lights, the wiring is sound up to this point. Reconnect the detector and test the next one.

If the bulb fails to light at any point, the circuit is broken between here and the previous detector – either this detector is

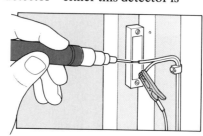

Test the wiring by disconnecting at each detector in turn and checking for continuity.

faulty or a wire is loose.

Test a detector by connecting the continuity tester across the correct terminals and then bringing a magnet close to the switch; continuity should register with the magnet in place.

Check a pressure pad by linking the tester to the correct wires and placing a weight on the pad. If the tester fails to light, or stays lit with the weight removed, the pad is probably faulty.

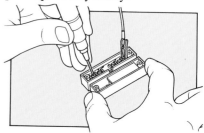

Test a magnetic switch by moving the magnet close to it and checking for continuity.

FITTING SMOKE DETECTORS

Fire protection need not cost a fortune. The priorities are:

■ Identify danger spots and take common sense precautions

■ Learn how to fight small fires and buy fire extinguishers and fire blankets to help you do so safely

■ Install smoke detectors to create a warning system, and plan an escape route so you can get to safety.

Types of smoke detector

There are two types of detector: *ionization detectors,* which measure the change in an electric current when smoke or fume particles enter a test chamber inside the unit; and *optical detectors,* which use photocells to sense when smoke interferes with a light beam.

Both are efficient, but optical detectors are generally more effective at detecting the early stages of smouldering fires and giving an early warning. On the other hand, ionization detectors may react faster to a blazing fire.

When buying a detector, look to see what features it has:

■ Domestic smoke detectors for DIY fitting are battery powered, making them self-contained and easy to fit.

■ Audio alarms are standard, and there may be a built-in emergency light (very useful if the fire has fused the main lights) which comes on automatically when the alarm is triggered. Some types have a flashing warning light; this operates for up to 30 minutes and is powered by a separate battery.

■ For added security, some detectors are designed to be linked to others around the house using bell wire so that if one detects a fire they all sound the alarm.

■ Most detectors have a battery check warning. When the detector senses that the battery is running down, the alarm sounds at intervals or a warning light flashes until you fit a new one.

Installing a detector

Fitting a single smoke detector in the hall or at the bottom of the stairwell gives reasonable protection to any two-storey house (though more units will increase the chances of early detection). Check, though, that you can hear the alarm in the bedrooms with the doors shut and a radio on. If not, fit a second detector near the bedrooms and link it to the downstairs unit so that both sound together. This isn't as easy as it sounds – running the wires may involve making holes in the ceiling or lifting floorboards.

Houses with over two storeys or bedrooms at the ends of passages also need more than one detector. In a bungalow, fit the detector in the hall between living areas and bedrooms, as close to the living areas as possible.

When deciding exactly where to position a detector, make sure you can reach it easily to test or replace the batteries. In addition, think about how the wiring is going to run between linked detectors.

Position ceiling mounted detectors at least 300mm (12″) from walls and lights, and wall mounted types 150-300mm (6-12″) below the ceiling.

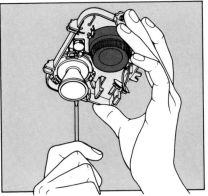

To fit a detector, *remove the cover, hold the unit in position and mark the fixing holes. Drill and plug the ceiling or wall and screw in place.*

Fit the battery, *making sure it is held firmly in its clips. Replace the cover and push the test button to check that the unit is working properly.*

Smoke detectors *ensure that any fire which does start will be detected early to make escape easier and safer. They come in various shapes and sizes.*

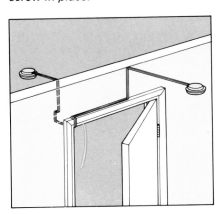

To link detectors, *run two-core bell wire between the units. Clip or staple the wire along skirtings and architraves or between the wall and ceiling.*

Connect the bell wire *to the same terminals of each unit or it won't work correctly. Check that all the detectors sound when any one of them is activated.*

PROTECTING YOUR HOME

It's important to plan exactly what equipment you need and where to fit it. Smoke detectors will give a much more reliable warning if they're sensibly positioned, and fire-fighting equipment such as blankets or extinguishers must be instantly accessible in an emergency.

A typical two-storey house should be well protected by installing the equipment shown below. Check the manufacturer's leaflets for fitting instructions, and make sure you know how to use extinguishers and blankets *before* you have to use them.

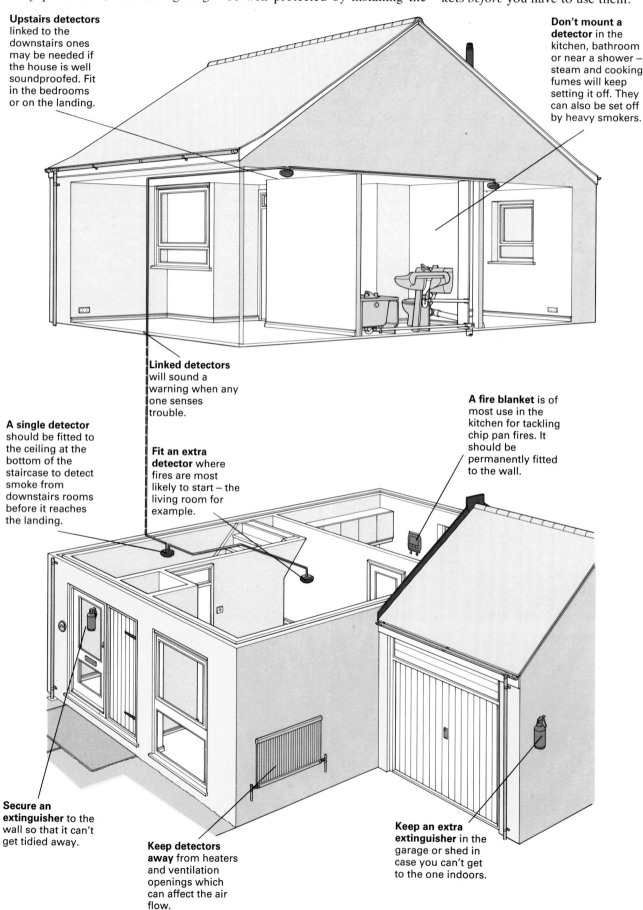

Upstairs detectors linked to the downstairs ones may be needed if the house is well soundproofed. Fit in the bedrooms or on the landing.

Don't mount a detector in the kitchen, bathroom or near a shower – steam and cooking fumes will keep setting it off. They can also be set off by heavy smokers.

Linked detectors will sound a warning when any one senses trouble.

A fire blanket is of most use in the kitchen for tackling chip pan fires. It should be permanently fitted to the wall.

A single detector should be fitted to the ceiling at the bottom of the staircase to detect smoke from downstairs rooms before it reaches the landing.

Fit an extra detector where fires are most likely to start – the living room for example.

Secure an extinguisher to the wall so that it can't get tidied away.

Keep detectors away from heaters and ventilation openings which can affect the air flow.

Keep an extra extinguisher in the garage or shed in case you can't get to the one indoors.

412

INDEX